THE
COLONIAL WARS
SOURCE BOOK

*'The Gentleman in Khaki':
inspired by Kipling's poem,
Richard Caton Woodville's
1899 portrayal of a defiant
British soldier perhaps exemplifies the later Victorian
image of 'Tommy'. It was an
immensely popular illustration
and was reproduced on items
as diverse as ladies' fans to
sculpted versions as table cen-
trepieces.*

THE COLONIAL WARS SOURCE BOOK

PHILIP J. HAYTHORNTHWAITE

Oh, it ain't so much the strategy that make an army win,
As sitting back and holding tight like mad through thick and thin.
The general in his cocked hat thinks out the thing to do,
But once the guns go buzzing he's no more than me or you.

— F. Norreys Connell

BCA

LONDON   NEW YORK   SYDNEY   TORONTO

CONTENTS

This edition published 1995 by BCA
by arrangement with
Arms and Armour Press
An Imprint of the Cassell Group
Wellington House, 125 Strand,
London WC2R 0BB

CN 1431

Designed and edited by DAG Publications
Ltd. Designed by David Gibbons; layout
by Anthony A. Evans; edited by Michael
Boxall; printed and bound in Great
Britain.

Acknowledgements
The author wishes to extend especial
thanks to: Thomas E. and Gayle DeVoe;
Sir Archibald Dunbar, Bt.; and to Sid
Horton.

The quotation on the title-page
is from F. Norreys Connell's 'The
Strength of Armies', in *Navy and Army
Illustrated,* vol. VI, 1898, and exemplifies
the characteristics required of troops in
many colonial campaigns.

INTRODUCTION

'Few men read observations and notes ... for the small merit they contain is like a bad gold mine, and will not, I fear, repay the trouble of working. After this honest confession, I consider that all accounts of conscience between myself and the reader are clear.'[1] Despite this opinion by Sir Charles James Napier, some introductory comments to this book are necessary.

The process of compilation of this work, as has been noted in previous *Source Books*, is akin to that described by Gowing: 'My object has been to compress the largest amount of information into the smallest possible space, and to insert in one volume some of the most surprising and interesting events that have ever taken place.'[2] The result, perhaps, is what Surgeon-General William Munro described as 'a Bundle of Fagots';[3] or, as described by a review of Captain Basil Hall's *Patchwork* (which was criticised in best 19th-century style for 'an unaccountable backsliding from orthodox John Bullism in extolling Buonaparte'!), an 'omnium gatherum'.[4]

The term 'colonial wars' requires definition, for in the widest sense it refers to all European colonisation of other regions of the world; but to English-speakers at least, the term is probably applied most commonly to British colonisation during the Victorian period. To keep the subject in compass, the latter definition is most appropriate to the present work, except that for reasons of continuity the concentration is upon the whole of the 19th century, with some details of earlier campaigns, and extending to the conclusion of the South African War in 1902. Campaigns in India are included, even though the subcontinent was never a 'colony' in the strictest sense of the term.

The text is divided geographically, with separate sections on the Indian subcontinent, Africa and the Mediterranean, the East, the Americas and the Atlantic, and Australasia and the Pacific, with countries or regions covered separately within each section. Each includes concise accounts of the military operations, and brief details of the forces involved, though limitations of space preclude detailed orders-of-battle for either the British or opposing

forces. Other sections include a survey of the British Army and Navy, which formed the nucleus of the forces that conducted most of the campaigns, with notes on weapons and tactics; brief biographies of some of the leading military figures; comments on written and pictorial sources; and a glossary.

The width of coverage has made it impossible to provide minute details of uniforms and equipment; such information can be found by consulting works named in the lists of references which follow each section. Such lists are in no way comprehensive, but represent merely a cross-section of the huge amount of published material available for further study, although they do include some of the most significant and most accessible sources. Although many earlier works have been reprinted, in most cases the details given are those of the original publication. Few regimental histories have been listed (for which bibliographies are mentioned in the section on sources), and similarly only a few of the huge number of published 'eye-witness' or autobiographical accounts. Footnotes are used primarily only to identify the source of quotations. In addition, anecdotal material is distributed throughout the text, to provide examples of contemporary writing and to enliven what might otherwise be no more than a collection of facts.

The subject of colonial warfare can arouse sentiments not applicable to some other periods of military history, notably concerning the entire philosophy behind the very concept of colonisation. The purpose of the present work is merely to record in a factual manner, and not to present any opinion or commentary upon the divergent viewpoints which did, and still do exist, ranging from unqualified support to the condemnation of the whole process as imperialist exploitation. Nevertheless, it is necessary to remark that although most modern works tend to treat both sides of a colonial conflict with equanimity, and are more sensitive than before to the culture and independence of the peoples with whom the colonising powers came into contact, this was not always the case in earlier histories. This factor should hardly be surprising, espe-

cially in accounts of those who had been engaged personally in colonial warfare, against enemies often regarded as
'savages' who respected none of the traditions of 'civilised'
European warfare. Typical expressions might be quoted:

'It pleases the Almighty, for His own inscrutable purposes, that English power should become "paramount"
throughout the vast territory of the Indian peninsula, and,
in furtherance of His will, that, by the overthrow of the
Sikhs in a war of short duration, its sway should now be
undisputed.'[5] 'Some people in England raise an insane cry
about not taking the Kafirs' country from them. Is England to swarm with an overgrown population to her own
destruction, while this enormous tract of country is left as
a hunting-ground – a scene of rapine, murder, and witch-
craft – for the infidel? Why were the Portuguese permitted
by Providence to discover it?'[6] Some contemporary statements now appear extraordinary: '... never did I see so
happy a race as the slaves. Their life appeared one continued laugh, and I can safely assert that, in the six years I
served in the West Indian Islands, I never saw or knew one
instance of cruelty towards them ... the Emancipation Act
ruined them all ... I much doubt whether it tended to the
amelioration of the slave, or improved their morality in
any way ... the once prosperous West India Islands have
become a splendid ruin ...'[7]

It should be remarked, however, that even at the time
of the most widespread colonisation, such views were not
universal; indeed, a not inconsiderable body of public
opinion questioned the entire process and motivation,
even if British colonising methods were regarded as generally less objectionable than those of some other nations.
As representative of the views of those opposed to a
process which the writer claimed necessarily involved 'Violence and Injustice', this account of 1847 remarks in
ironic fashion on the difference between British and foreign colonisation:

'There are differences in the manner in which conquered countries are brought efficiently into the condition of led-farms. The Spaniards ... gave their preaching
first, and did their killing afterwards. The English reverse
the practice. Not that they ever want to kill; it is only people's own blame if they won't be quiet, and so get knocked
on the head. True, it is all the same in the end; but it is satisfactory to go by regular rules ... [8] (As might be expected,
a military criticism of foreign colonial practices dating
from approximately the same period refers not to the
effect upon those colonised, but upon the unmanly developments attributed to most foreigners!: 'The first thing a
Frenchman thinks of after fighting is the theatre; they
have one in Algiers, also billiard-tables, coffee-houses,
guinguettes, etc., milliners, *marchandes de modes, perruquiers*,
and dancing-masters. This they call colonising!'[9]

However, not all those involved in a military capacity in
colonial campaigns were sympathetic to the process of
colonisation. A vehement comment by a distinguished

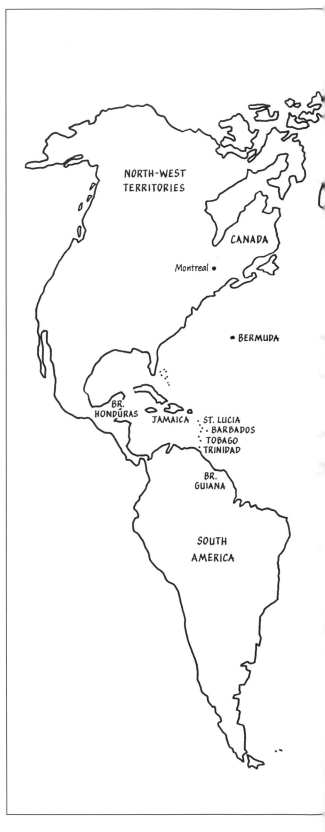

ALTAR
Tangiers
MALTA
CYPRUS
PERSIA
EGYPT
Suez Canal
Bushire
AFGHAN-ISTAN
NEPAL
Peking
CHINA
JAPAN
Shanghai
ARABIA
SUDAN
Suakin
Delhi
Calcutta
BURMA
HONG KONG
ABIA
Khartoum
Aden
Bombay
INDIA
Madras
Rangoon
INDO-CHINA
GOLD COAST
NIGERIA
Lagos
Magdala
ABYSSINIA
SOMALILAND
CEYLON
MALAYA
SARAWAK
RA
NE
UGANDA
Singapore
ST. HELENA
Zanzibar
JAVA
RHODESIA
MAURITIUS
FIJI
BECHUANALAND
MADAGASCAR
NORTHERN TERRITORY
QUEENSLAND
TRANSVAAL
ORANGE FREE STATE
NATAL/ZULULAND
CAPE COLONY
Cape Town
WESTERN AUSTRALIA
NEW SOUTH WALES
VICTORIA
Melbourne
NEW ZEALAND
TASMANIA
North Island
South Island

commander – albeit one with very individual political views – was that made by Lieutenant-General Sir Charles James Napier in his editorial remarks on the English translation of *Lights and Shades of Military Life*, a French account of Napoleonic campaigns, in which Napier compares the results of Napoleon's campaigns with those arising from British colonisation:

'All the horrors committed by the French and Spanish soldiers upon each other, and upon women and children, are hateful, as are all the cruelties of a similar nature perpetrated in the East Indies and in the colonies ... It is vain that sophistry and national prejudice endeavour to throw off from the shoulders of an English government the responsibility for crimes committed in an unjust war. Napoleon was the author of the Spanish aggressions. The English were the aggressors in India ... to enrich a parcel of shopkeepers; the "shopocracy of England", as it has been well termed; and a more base and cruel tyranny never wielded the power of a great nation. Our object of all our cruelties, was *money – lucre*: a thousand millions sterling are said to have been squeezed out of India in the last sixty years. Every shilling of this has been picked out of blood, wiped, and put into the murderers' pockets; but, wipe and wash money as you will, the "damned spot" will not "out". There it sticks for ever, and we shall yet suffer for the crime as sure as there is a God in heaven, where the "commercial interests of the nation" find no place, or heaven is not what we hope and believe it to be! ... I may be singular, but, in truth, I prefer the despotic Napoleon to the despots of the East India Company. The man ambitious of universal power generally rules to do good to subdued nations. But the men ambitious of universal peculation rule only to make themselves rich, to the destruction of happiness among a hundred millions of people. The one may be a fallen angel; the other is a hell-born devil!'[10]

Napier, of course, was the conqueror of Sind, one of the most criticised of all colonial wars.

Napier was not alone in his doubts concerning the benefits of colonisation; for example, adverting to a belief that cholera was only introduced into India after the arrival of the Europeans, J. W. Sherer remarked that when assessing the benefits of colonisation upon those colonised, 'an argumentative Bengalee might perhaps pen an essay on the inquiry, whether Shakespeare and patent leather boots were real benefits, when accompanied by brandy and cholera-morbus.'[11] However, even those who shared Napier's views would probably mostly have agreed with the sentiments expressed by one military writer in 1846: 'I fully believe that the great majority of our wars with savages ought never to have been waged at all. I have much greater trust in the gallantry and physical powers of British soldiers than in the moderation (not to say integrity) of British traders. From their cupidity, a greater number of our conflicts with barbarians (if not those with civilised nations also) have directly or indirectly sprung ... but how-ever unwilling to see injustice backed by force, I cannot brook the spectacle of disgrace inflicted on the British arms, or the needless loss of British soldiers sacrificed for the vices of others.'[12] A similar opinion was given by Sir William Butler, who served in South Africa and perhaps had the Zulu War in mind: 'Five-sixths of our African wars have their beginnings in wrongs done in the first instance by white men upon natives.'[13]

Conversely, many looked askance at 'the cambrick-handkerchief philanthropists' who pronounced on matters of which they were unacquainted personally, 'in the approved whine adopted at the last West African-Flannel-Waistcoat-and Propriety Tract Society. I should like to put such philanthropists on what we call a "Commando" here ... Hang one Chief publicly ... and there will be a sudden pause in cattle-stealing,' as an officer's wife remarked from South Africa in 1844![14]

A factor which permeates much contemporary writing by British authors on colonial campaigns is a tendency to regard the indigenous peoples whom they encountered (and fought) in a disparaging light, reflecting opinions widespread throughout society. Some regarded their foes with understanding, even compassion ('I object to no man, "haply, because his complexion is black", having lived too long in tropical countries to cavil about colour. Worth makes the man of all shades, the want of it the fellow ...';[15] but others were quite uncompromising: 'No more barbarous or bloodthirsty race has existed upon the face of the earth than the Ashantee ... war was of necessity declared, and after some vicissitudes the brutal savages were completely defeated ... Their capital was a charnel-house; their religion, a combination of cruelty and treachery; their policy, the natural outcome of their religion.'[16]

Many British officers developed a very genuine affection for their 'colonial' troops, as remarked upon by Francis Cornish, who had transferred from the Somerset Light Infantry to the 17th Bengal Lancers: 'There *is* something rather fine in commanding these grim Pathans who ride "with the Koran strapped to their saddle-bow", or six-foot Sikhs with their curled beards ... I thank God that I shall only have to command Orientals, who have real ideas of the dignity of discipline and who are bred and born with a martial spirit in them. Orientals go on service with a soldier spirit in them. Tommies I think only get it by regiments and after long campaigning ...'[17] Nevertheless, contemporary writings often reflect the disdain felt by many British soldiers for the indigenous inhabitants of the various colonies; elements of racial antipathy were widespread among the British, as described in Frank Richards' *Old Soldier Sahib* (London, 1936), one of the most remarkable accounts by an 'other rank' even though it just post-dates the Victorian period. Although such attitudes are quite rightly unacceptable by modern standards, they were not regarded as reprehensible at the time; and while it is easy to sympathise with the exclusion of such senti-

A stalwart veteran: General Sir John Alexander Ewart, uniformed as colonel of the Argyll & Sutherland Highlanders. Commissioned in 1838, he served with the 93rd in the Crimea, captured a Colour at the Secunderabagh and lost his left arm to a cannon-ball at Cawnpore. He was awarded the KCB in 1887, and the Légion d'honneur and the Turkish Order of the Medjidie for service in the Crimea; he was colonel of the Wiltshire Regiment 1883–4, Gordon Highlanders 1884–95, and of the Argyll & Sutherland Highlanders 1895–1904.

ments from modern works, to do so would conceal an important facet of contemporary opinion which influenced much of what was written on the colonial wars.

The attitude of British superiority, which was ingrained deeply and doubtless affected the conduct of British policy and even field operations, is exemplified by a dispatch dating from as late as 1908, when Lieutenant H. L. Homan of the 1st Southern Nigeria Regiment praised the courage and composure of Company Sergeant-Major Bakari Ibadan in an action on 11 December 1908 in the Sonkwala valley: 'I do not think I can give him greater praise than state that he was quite as good as a white man.'[18] (This heroic NCO received the West African Frontier Force Distinguished Conduct Medal for this action). It should be noted, how-

ever, that the attitude of British 'superiority' evident in many British writings was not restricted to the indigenous inhabitants of colonial territories; whether arising from national pride or regimental *esprit de corps*, the British soldier tended to regard *all* foreigners in the same light, and some of those who served in both Europe and colonial campaigns reserved their greatest criticism for Europeans. Gowing of the Royal Fusiliers, for example, describing an altercation between one of his comrades and a group of drunken Frenchmen in the Crimea, remarked with disdain that 'Foreigners have no more idea than a child how to use their hands; they will scratch and kick, but if you give them a good go-along, they will not face up again.'[19] Such attitudes were not even restricted to foreigners; another campaigner who had had wide experience of both East and West Indies declared that the most uncivilised and savage people he ever encountered were the inhabitants of Lancashire, especially those of Burnley, 'a most atrocious place, celebrated for cockpits, up-and-down fighting, and the immense quantity of liquor imbibed ... the lower orders [are] far, very far, greater savages than the poor Irish, who are so abused ... whoever has been at Todmorden ... will, I am sure, never forget that misfortune. I would sooner have been stationed at Timbuctoo ...'[20]

Contemporary accounts contain other opinions equally unacceptable to modern standards, such as the following, which would now be regarded as offensive to both Indians and women: 'The scarcity of European women is the reason why half-castes are increasing so rapidly in India ... the Anglo-Indian empire will yet be subverted by them ... Government ought, therefore, attentively to consider the matter: and if they would prevent the threatened danger, should send annual cargoes of women, suitable to be the wives of soldiers, to India ...'[21] However objectionable such sentiments appear to modern eyes, 19th-century standards should be taken into account, and understanding be given to the fact that such opinions were regarded as not unreasonable at the time. Similar sentiments were by no means a uniquely European characteristic; national jealousies and hatreds were equally prevalent among nations encountered by the British, and the caste system provided a further complication. Harry Lumsden received a lesson in 1847 when he required a bugler for a hazardous task: 'When I asked the Seikh [*sic*] officer commanding the force to call for a volunteer bugler he replied, "No, you would then get a really good man; let me pick you out a haramzada [worthless or base-born man], and it will not matter if he is killed."'[22] Indeed, even at the time some took into account the different standards held by other cultures, such as this explanation of, and lack of condemnation for, Dervish atrocities at Metemma: '... those who loudly condemn the forcible methods by which the Khalifa put down the rebellion of the Jaalin tribe have forgotten the methods employed under somewhat similar circumstances even in good old England! Different nations have different standards of thought, and what in Europe would be classed as an outrageous massacre, in the Sudan would seem a mere excess of zeal.'[23]

It should also be noted that the belief in the superiority of British arms served as an important bolster to morale, to forces frequently outnumbered and campaigning in difficult terrain, in an alien environment and often bereft not only of reinforcement but even of supplies and water. For example, after considering some of the British successes in India, William Hodson remarked that 'a nation which could do this is destined indeed to rule the world ... This is a proud feeling, and nerves one's arm in many a time of difficulty and danger, as much almost as the conviction that we must conquer, or worse than death awaits us.'[24] The confidence arising from such morale was often necessary for simple self-preservation, and martial prowess or the threat of force could also be used to avoid conflict by discouraging a potential aggressor, as in this case of a voyage up the Niger:

'The commander himself, the Sàliki-n Yaïki, or king of battle, came alongside in his canoe ... We had thus an opportunity of examining their *matériel* and munitions of war; of which the most formidable, at least in appearance, was a small rusty cannon lashed in the bow ... As the Sàliki-n Yaïki appeared to have displayed his warlike paraphernalia to the best advantage, we thought it might be edifying to him to know what manner of reception we could give him; and as the most convincing argument we could adduce of our capability of making it a warm one, the carronade on the forecastle was suddenly revealed to his astonished eyes, and slued rapidly round in every direction, which excited the greatest surprise; but when the horrid muzzle yawned upon him, he, with most of his mighty men of valour, dropped involuntarily into the bottom of the canoe. We then politely handed him a shot, even a 9-pounder, requesting him to feel the weight of it. He passed it round among his "merry men all" who eyed it askance, and did not deem themselves safe until it was removed from their vicinity.'[25]

In reality, however, colonial warfare could be waged with much greater bitterness than experienced in 'civilised' European campaigns, and service abroad, often for many years without even a though of home leave, caused a curious feeling of isolation. This was expressed eloquently by William Hodson, writing home in 1849 after receiving news of the death of a young relative: '... the prevailing impression on my mind for days was simple unbelief of the reality of that sweet child's actual death. I have been so long *alone* – home has been for so long a time more a pleasant dream than reality – I have been for many a weary day, as it were, dead to you all, and the sense of separation has grown so completely into one's being, that I find it difficult to separate that which is possible to see again from that which is impossible. Thus is seems to me incredible that any greater barrier can sever me from this darling child than that ever-present one which divides me

The relief of Lucknow: the besieged welcome the arrival of the 78th Highlanders in a somewhat melodramatic rendition of the event. The 78th served in this part of the Mutiny wearing their red dress tunics (which were actually double-breasted), kilt and hose, and forage caps with white covers. (Engraving after H. M. Paget)

from all of you. Can you understand this? I know it to be a delusion, and yet I cannot shake it off ...'[26] Yet such isolation could also intensify national feeling; as Hodson had written some three years earlier, 'If I have one feeling stronger than another, it is contempt for a "regular Indian", a man who thinks it fine to adopt a totally different set of habits and morals and fashions, until, in forgetting that he is an Englishman, he usually forgets also that he is a Christian and a gentleman.'[27]

Another important characteristic of colonial warfare, which pervades many memoirs, was the ever-present threat of fatal disease, often far more destructive than the enemy's shot. Sickness was a fact of military life; indeed, in 1858 it was noted that the mortality of troops in barracks was greater than that of the civilian population, attributed by one medical opinion to want of physical labour, and overcrowding, 'whereby the men breathe over and again air fouler than a horse-pond',[28] compounded by the fact that most soldiers 'had absolutely no idea of looking after their own health, and had to be treated almost like children'.[29] In the climates in which most colonial campaigns took place, however, it was local conditions that were so destructive. When stationed at Peshawar in 1862, Surgeon William Munro of the 93rd recorded a typical year's sickness among his regiment, which including women and children numbered 1,214 souls: cholera, 267 cases; fever, 1,451 cases, 801 of them severe; other illnesses, 939. Of these 2,657 cases, 93 of the cholera victims died, and although Munro kept no record of mortality among the non-cholera cases, he noted that as a result many were incapacitated from further service, or were long in recovering. In purely statistical terms, this is equivalent to every member of the regiment falling ill more than twice in the year. Munro himself escaped any pestilence, but the stress and over-work of attending to so many patients produced a heart murmur which took years to overcome.[30]

Such sickness was extremely destructive to morale: 'To the solider, nothing is more terrible ... he sees his comrades dying hourly around him, until the horrible feeling at length fastens upon his mind, that his own end is rapidly approaching, and that he, too, must die like them. A thousand times sooner would he fall on the battle-field, when his blood is warm and his mind excited, and the shout of victory or defiance on his lips. There is a charm in a death of this sort, unlike death from sickness, when the spirit is bowed down and broken by bodily anguish, and the faculties of the mind benumbed with pain, as the destroyer presses his icy hand slowly and heavily upon the heart, and draws aside the veil from another world';[31] 'The cholera lasted fourteen days with us, and in that time we lost 149 men, 11 women, and 27 children, out of a total strength of about 340 ... it is almost impossible to keep the men's spirits up ... Some said they would sooner face the foe, twenty to one; they might have a chance to sell their lives dearly or to die hard. But here there was an unseen enemy, with no chance to combat it ...'[32]

However, the effects of the ill-health which was so much a part of colonial service can perhaps best be appreciated when considering individual cases, as in this letter from a hardened campaigner, in garrison in India in 1869:

'This is a world of troubles and sorrows; my heart is almost too full to say much ... I told you in my last that cholera, in its worst type, had broken out among us ... the heavy blow that I have received is enough to give one a stroke of apoplexy. My poor heart is near bursting with grief. The stroke has been so sudden that I can hardly realise it ... Six of my dear children have been called away to the bright realms above, all in a few hours. On the morning of the 15th inst., they were all well. Eight dear little ones, wife and self sat down to breakfast, all hearty and well ... Before four o'clock, six of my fine boys and girls had passed away into the arms of Him who does all things well. We shall never hear their sweet prattling tongues any more: all is silent as the tomb. Before six o'clock p.m. on the 15th, they were all laid in one common grave, wrapped in sheets, without coffins ... my poor dear wife was pronounced dead by one of the doctors, and carried to the dead-house, or mortuary, about 2.30 p.m. on that fatal 15th. Thank God, however, life was found in her: she was carried back to hospital ... I am thankful to say that she is rapidly improving. But I sometimes feel that I cannot live: all, all are gone that we loved so well ... My officers, from the Colonel downwards, are very kind to me. The Colonel and his lady called this morning to sympathise with me in my sore trials. I cannot say more at present ...'[33]

Spellings

An especial difficulty arising from the study of colonial warfare is the range of spellings which can be encountered, arising mainly from those cases where the original language did not use the Roman alphabet, and thus relied on phonetic renderings to approximate to local pronunciation. This problem was recognised by early writers: for example, the official history of the Zulu War gave its readers four different versions of the name of the Zulu King on its first page (Ketchwayo, Cetewayo, Cetywayo, Cetshwayo);[34] but some early chroniclers advocated a less confusing course, the omission of foreign names apparently on the premise that they were of limited important because they *were* foreign. For example, a review of William Siborne's *History of the Waterloo Campaign* stated that 'very few readers have a memory capable of retaining so many names; nor can their wish be very great to remember numerous names of men whom they never heard of before – names, too (many of them), of excessive length, and so rugged as to defy pronunciation by English lips ... our heads turn dizzy with endeavouring to remember them. Some pages ... completely bristle with them ... We hope that Captain Siborne is preparing an abridgement [in which] nine out of ten of these hard names will, no doubt, be omitted ...'[35] Words taken from languages which used a different script presented even more difficulty; so that, for example, when writing of the Sikhs, the editor of *Colburn's United Service Magazine* noted that 'We do not know what effect the enumeration of the strange names has had on the powers of our readers' recollection; but we confess, for our own part, that the constant repetition of the word "Singh", has with us the effect of confusing our memory', so he omitted it.[36] Even as late as 1898 a reputable publication could state that 'It is not proposed to give long strings of heathen names, which are spelt differently in every atlas, except where they are altogether omitted.'[37]

Such sentiments must have inhibited any attempt to establish a 'correct' spelling of even proper names. An example is Isandlwana, scene of the great Zulu victory of 1879. This spelling, or 'Isandhlwana' is now the generally accepted version; but in contemporary documents it may be found with such diverse spellings as Sandhlwana, Insalwana, Isandula, Insandusana, and a number of other variations.[38] Similarly, personal names may be found with many variations, for example 'Tipu Sahib' or 'Tippoo Sultaun' (or variations); 'Hyder Ali' or 'Haidar Ali', or even more complicated, the name of the originator of the T'ai-p'ing (or 'Taiping') Rebellion, Hung Siu-ts'üan, Hung Hsiu-ch'uan, Hung-Tsue-Schuen or Hung Hsiu-ch'wan; that his original name was Huo-hsin, and the title he adopted was T'ien Wang, serves only to confuse the issue further. Even the simplest words may be found with a variety of spellings, according to the preference of the writer; the Indian Army rank of *naik*, for example, may be encountered as widely divergent as '*naicque*' or '*naigue*', and even *dak* (post) is varied as *dâk* or *dawk*. Place-names are often recorded in contemporary sources by an approximate phonetic rendition irrespective of any recognised common practice ('Deyra Dhoon' for Dehra Dun, for example) and some anglicisation of foreign words are quite bizarre. Another complication concerns words with more than one meaning; Lord Roberts remarked upon the Pushtu word *tarbur* which officially signified a cousin (of any description) but was used colloquially for 'enemy' (perhaps a reflection upon family relationships in the region in which it was used). This even occurred with words that were taken into common English usage; for example, it is possible to find the contraction '*tat*' used to describe either an Indian pony (or *tattoo*) or a room-cooling panel or mat (or *tatty*); the fact that both words also had English meanings as well (tattoo, a military ceremony;

the other a contraction of 'tattered') could have caused even greater confusion. Fortunately, however, the meaning of words spelled eccentrically in contemporary sources is usually evident, for example 'Seikh' for 'Sikh', 'Baluchi', 'Beluchi' or 'Beloochee', or 'Zooloo' for 'Zulu'.

A further complication is the fact that modern usage has changed some spellings which were previously largely universal; Bharatpur for Bhurtpore was an early change, but more extensive modern changes are exemplified by Kanpur in place of Cawnpore, Beijing for Peking, and Thukela for Tugela. This applies more widely than to place-names; for example, the two sections of the Xhosa people, generally named as 'Galeka' and 'Gaika' in earlier works, may now be found with the more correct spellings 'Gcaleka' and 'Ngqika'. In the face of irreconcilable differences between contemporary and modern spellings, and considering the necessity to assist the process of further reading in older works, in most cases in this book the more familiar versions have been used, even if these are philologically not the most correct in modern usage; but alternative versions are also noted in parentheses. Despite the general use of modern spellings of such names as Sind, Maratha, Gurkha, etc., for the use of regimental titles the correct contemporary spelling is retained, e.g., Scinde Horse, Mahratta Light Infantry, Goorkhas, etc.

Notes

1. Editorial comments by Lieutenant-General C. J. Napier to the translation of *Lights and Shades of Military Life*, 2nd edn., London 1850, p. viii.
2. Gowing, T. *A Soldier's Experience; or, a Voice from the Ranks*, Nottingham, 1907.
3. Munro, Surgeon-General W. *Reminiscences of Military Service with the 93rd Sutherland Highlanders*, London, 1883, p. 4.
4. *United Service Journal*, 1841, vol. I, pp. 406–7.
5. Anon. 'Our Tribute to the Army of the Sutledj', in *Colburn's United Service Magazine*, 1846, vol. II, p. 1.
6. 'The Alarm: A Frontier Story from South Africa', by 'H. W.', in ibid., vol. II, p. 385.
7. Stuart, Colonel W. K. *Reminiscences of a Soldier*, London, 1874, vol. I, pp. 126–7.
8. 'Conquests', by 'W. C.', in *Chambers' Edinburgh Journal*, 23 January 1847.
9. Wilkie, Lieutenant-Colonel, 'The British Colonies Considered as Military Posts', in *United Service Journal*, 1840, vol. III, p. 187.
10. *Lights and Shades of Military*

Life, ed. Sir Charles Napier, 2nd edn., London, 1850, pp. 297–8. The recent reprint, including Napier's editorial remarks, is titled *Life in Napoleon's Army: The Memoirs of Capt. Elzéar Blaze*, London, 1995.
11. Sherer, J. W. *Havelock's March on Cawnpore, 1857*, London, n.d., p. 290.
12. 'Combats with Savages', by 'TT', in *Colburn's United Service Magazine*, 1846, vol. I, pp. 122–3.
13. Butler, Sir William. *Far Out: Rovings Retold*, London, 1881, p. ix.
14. 'Notices from Kafirland, Written on the Spot', in *Colburn's United Service Magazine*, 1844, vol. III, p. 183.
15. O'Connor, Major L. S. 'Leaves from the Tropics', in ibid., 1849, vol. II, p. 527.
16. Holmes, R. R. *Naval and Military Trophies and Personal Relics of British Heroes*, London, 1896, text to plate II (unpaginated); the final sentence is an extract from Wolseley's dispatch on the capture of Kumasi.
17. Letters of 2 September 1895 and 20 January 1898, in *Let-*

ters and Sketches of Francis T. Warre Cornish, Eton, 1902, pp. 186–7, 281–2.
18. Dispatch, 12 December 1908; *London Gazette*, 21 December 1909.
19. Gowing, *op. cit.*, p. 264.
20. Stuart, *op. cit.*, vol. II, pp. 56, 76, 77.
21. *Camp and Barrack-Room; or, The British Army as it is, by a Late Staff Sergeant of the 13th Light Infantry*, London, 1846, p. 165.
22. Quoted in Lumsden, General Sir Peter, and Elsmie, G. R. *Lumsden of the Guides*, London, 1899, p. 33.
23. Anon., 'A Short Account of the Work of the Egyptian Cavalry during the Atbara and Omdurman Campaigns', in *Cavalry Journal*, April, 1910, vol. V, p. 165.
24. *Twelve Years of a Soldier's Life in India, being Extracts from the Letters of the Late Major W. S. R. Hodson*, ed. Revd. G. H. Hodson, London, 1859, p. 247.
25. Allen, Commander W. 'Records of an Expedition up the Quorra with Lander', in *United Service Journal*, 1839, vol. II, p. 445.
26. Hodson, *op. cit.*, pp. 94–5.

27. Ibid., p. 30.
28. 'On the Sanitary Condition of the British Army', a lecture by Dr. Guy, quoted in *Chambers' Journal*, 26 June 1858, p. 415.
29. Baden-Powell, Lieutenant-General Sir Robert. *Indian Memories*, London, 1915, p. 100.
30. These statistics from Munro, *op. cit.*, pp. 283–4.
31. *Camp and Barrack-Room, op. cit.*, pp. 102–3.
32. Gowing, *op. cit.*, p. 397.
33. Ibid., pp. 395–6.
34. *Narrative of the Field Operations connected with the Zulu War of 1879*, London, 1881, p. 1.
35. Anon., 'On Some Recent Writers of Military History', in *Colburn's United Service Magazine*, 1845, vol. III, pp. 17–18.
36. 'Editor's Portfolio', ibid., 1844, vol. I, p. 149.
37. *Navy and Army Illustrated*, 26 March 1898, vol. VI, p. 21.
38. An exposition on this particular name can be found in 'What's in a Name', by Ian Knight, *Soldiers of the Queen* 65, Victorian Military Society, 1991.

I
GREAT BRITAIN

GREAT BRITAIN

THE BRITISH ARMY

Of the many organisations that contributed to the creation and maintenance of the British Empire, none was more important than the regular army. In time of war it formed the most reliable part of forces that often contained a large proportion of locally-raised or allied troops, and in general the British elements were regarded as the only men who were completely trustworthy and disciplined, even though the local forces might be more suited to their own environment. In time of peace the army was scattered in garrisons throughout the world, wherever British administration maintained the *Pax Britannica*. Such garrisons varied in size from brigade strength to the smallest possible detachment, like that which garrisoned Tristan da Cunha; in 1841 it was reported to consist of a single bombardier: 'From his representing in his own person the Governor, the Chief of Staff, and the entire garrison, together with his position in mid ocean, he has every right to be a *swell* ... This modern Crusoe is consoled with the company and conversation of his wife; which, no doubt, he finds more entertaining than that of man Friday or the parrot.'[1]

The duties undertaken by the army underpinned the entire structure of the empire; in addition to conventional military duties, its members acted as peace-keepers, police, construction-workers, road-builders, surveyors, and by the secondment of its members helped run the civil administrations. The army had to be prepared to mount operations virtually anywhere in the world (although between the Battle of Waterloo and the outbreak of the First World War, the only major campaign fought outside the colonial sphere was that in the Crimea), and to guarantee the security and internal tranquillity of the homeland. (It is noteworthy that the first officer killed in action during the reign of Queen Victoria fell not along Kipling's 'far-flung battle-line'[2] but at Bossenden in Kent: Lieutenant Henry Bennett of the 45th was killed by the maniac 'Sir William Courtenay' (alias 'Mad Tom', real name John Tom) during the latter's attempted insurrection in May 1838.) This sad case was quoted as proof of the general superiority of British arms: '... victorious often against vast odds of numbers and of arms, and even with incapable leaders ... nor do I believe there has ever been an instance in which a savage race, when they could get at them hand to hand, have not been beaten by our men, unless when absolutely overwhelmed by numbers, as in the case of Sir Charles Macarthy's disaster, in 1824. The Kentish ploughmen who followed the impostor Tom, opposing their sticks to the muskets and bayonets of a more numerous body of soldiers, exhibited a much greater instance of courage than has ever been evinced by any foreign race. True, they were fanatics; but amongst what other fanatics, however besotted, can we discover such a manifestation of unflinching daring and nerve?'[3]

The extent to which units were deployed overseas depended upon the requirements of the day, troops being switched from one garrison to another according to need, but some idea of the typical deployment may be gauged from the following locations of regiments on 1 April 1842; of especial note is the large Canadian garrison, in the wake of the late disturbances:

Home stations: *Ballincollig*, 7th Dragoon Guards; *Belfast*, 54th; *Birmingham*, 6th Dragoons; *Bolton*, 1/60th; *Brighton*, 2nd Dragoons; *Cahir*, 5th Dragoon Guards; *Canterbury*, part 6th; *Cork*, 8th; *Devonport*, 24th; *Dublin*, 10th Hussars, 12th Lancers, 45th, 58th; *Dundalk*, 4th Dragoon Guards; *Edinburgh*, 17th Lancers, 53rd; *Gosport*, 73rd; *Hounslow*, 11th Hussars; *Ipswich*, 13th Light Dragoons; *Leeds*, 1st Dragoons; *London*, 1st and 2nd Life Guards, 1/ and 3/ Grenadier Guards, 1/Coldstream Guards, Scots Fusilier Guards; *Manchester*, 8th Hussars, 66th; *Newbridge*, 6th Dragoon Guards; *Newcastle-on-Tyne*, 61st; *Newport*, 11th; *Nottingham*, 3rd Dragoon Guards; *Plymouth*, 65th; *Portsmouth*, 32nd, 34th; *Sheffield*, 2nd Dragoon Guards; *Templemore*, 37th; *Winchester*, 16th; *Windsor*, Royal Horse Guards, 72nd; *Woolwich*, 15th.

A scene repeated in countless garrisons throughout the Empire: morning parade. (Print after Richard Simkin)

Royal Sussex Regiment in white foreign service helmets; a print after Richard Simkin, published 1893. A version of white helmet was also introduced experimentally for troops serving at home, but did not become general issue.

Overseas: *Antigua*, 81st; *Barbados*, 52nd, 92nd; *Bengal*, 3rd Dragoons, 16th Lancers, 3rd, 9th, 13th, 21st, 31st, 44th, 50th, 66th; *Bermuda*, 20th, 2/Rifle Brigade; *Bombay*, 4th Dragoons, 14th Light Dragoons, 2nd, part 6th, 17th, 22nd, 40th, 41st, 94th; *Canada*, 1st Dragoon Guards, 7th Hussars, 2/Grenadier Guards, 2/Coldstream Guards, 2/1st, 14th, 23rd, 30th, 36th, 43rd, 56th, 64th, 67th–71st, 74th, 76th, 83rd, 85th, 89th, 93rd, Royal Canadian Rifle Regiment; *Cape of Good Hope*, 27th, 75th, part 91st, Cape Mounted Rifles; *Cephalonia*, 5th, 42nd; *Ceylon*, 90th, 95th, Ceylon Rifle Regiment; *China*, 18th, 26th, 49th, 55th, 98th; *Corfu*, 38th, 77th; *Demerara*, 47th, 1st West India Regiment; *Gibraltar*, 1/1st, 7th, 46th, 48th, 79th; *Jamaica*, 2/60th, 82nd, 2nd West India Regiment; *Madras*, 15th Hussars, 4th, 39th, 57th, 63rd; *Malta*, 19th, 88th, 1/Rifle Brigade, Royal Malta Fencibles; *Mauritius*, 12th, 35th, 87th; *Newfoundland*, Royal Newfoundland Companies; *New South Wales*, 28th, 51st, 80th, 96th, and 99th *en route* to NSW; *St. Helena*, part 91st; *St. Vincent*, 33rd; *Sierra Leone*, 3rd West India Regiment; *Trinidad*, 59th; *Zante*, 97th; *en route* to India, 9th Lancers, 10th, 25th, 29th, 78th, 84th, 86th.

After reductions following the Napoleonic Wars, by 1821 the regular army numbered 101,031 men under arms, of whom 31,572 were stationed in the colonies and 19,267 in India; by the beginning of 1854 the total had risen to 140,043, including 39,754 in the colonies and 29,208 in India. The army was never very large given the multiplicity of tasks it was expected to undertake, which was one reason for the employment of local forces, often of inferior training and reliability. The pressure upon resources was eased considerably from the early 1870s by the policy of allowing local forces to take over the principal duties of defence of self-governing colonies, leaving British regular troops at only the most important strategic points.

Infantry

The most numerous and arguably most significant part of the army, the infantry was organised into regiments of one or more battalions, the battalion being the principal (and independent) tactical element. In the reductions which followed the end of the Napoleonic Wars, almost all regiments became single-battalion corps; new 2nd battalions were formed subsequently, but only in the 25 senior line regiments; the rifle corps always maintained more battalions, rising to four each. The combatant strength of a battalion varied considerably according to circumstance; in 1898, for example, battalions serving at home had an authorised strength of 24 officers, 41 NCOs and 816 other ranks; in the colonies, 28 officers, 48 NCOs and 936 other ranks; and in India 29 officers, 47 NCOs and 956 other ranks, these excluding the one sergeant-piper and five pipers in each Highland battalion. In the same way that augmentations of strength were carried out by the addition of new battalions to existing regiments, instead of creating new regiments, so augmentations of strength within a battalion were achieved by increasing the number of men per company, battalions maintaining eight companies each throughout the period. (In addition to the field battalions, to take as an example the date of the statistics quoted above, each regiment's home depot comprised five officers, ten NCOs and 53 or 54 other ranks, unless both battalions of a regiment were serving abroad, when the depot was increased to fourteen officers, 29 NCOs and 608 or 609 other ranks.)

Infantry regiments were numbered in sequence from the most senior (1st or Royal Regiment), the number rising as high as 135 in the late 1790s, but at the conclusion of the Napoleonic Wars the highest number was 104. The 95th Rifles was taken out of the line and given a separate identity as the Rifle Brigade, and higher-numbered regiments were re-numbered accordingly; in 1817–19 the numbers from 95 upwards were disbanded, only for the 95th–99th to be re-formed in 1823–24. A new 100th Regiment (Prince of Wales's Royal Canadians) was created in 1858 in Canada as a response by that colony to the Indian

Mutiny, and in 1861–2 regiments with succeeding numbers were incorporated into the British Army from the East India Company's old European regiments: the 101st–103rd being the old 1st Bengal, 1st Madras and 1st Bombay Fusiliers respectively, the 104th from the 2nd Bengal Fusiliers, the 105th–107th from the 2nd Madras, 2nd Bombay and 3rd Bengal Light Infantry respectively, and the 108th and 109th from the 3rd Madras and 3rd Bombay regiments respectively.

Among modernisations from 1870 (sometimes styled the 'Cardwell Reforms' from the Secretary of State for War) was the creation in 1872 of 'brigade sub-districts', which had the effect of linking battalions in pairs, each with a fixed recruiting-district and depot. There were at that time 25 two-battalion regiments (nos. 1–25) and 83 single-battalion; 66 sub-districts were formed, the two four-battalion rifle corps being recruited nation-wide and having a common depot at Winchester. Associated with the sub-districts were the two home-service forces, militia and volunteers. The militia was the traditional home-defence force of county infantry battalions, recruited by a system of 'quota', each area being set a number of men to be enrolled, raised by the 'conscription' of a ballot among the eligible male population if insufficient volunteers were forthcoming, which was almost always the case. Embodied for full-time home-defence duties only in wartime, the militia had slipped into abeyance from 1816, but was re-constituted in 1852, again using the system of 'universal military obligation' to remedy shortages of volunteers. The Volunteer Force itself was a purely part-time 'home guard', which had existed during the Napoleonic Wars, but had been largely replaced by the Local Militia in 1808, with surviving units disbanded in 1814. In 1859, under the

'Rifle' uniform was worn by a number of corps: this print after Richard Simkin, published 1895, shows the King's Royal Rifle Corps wearing 'rifle green' (very dark green) uniform with red facings, and the busby re-adopted from 1890. The 'Oliver' pattern of canteen, introduced in 1875, is worn by the bugler (left) and rifleman (right).

fear of French invasion, an immense new formation, largely of rifle volunteers, was created, as before consisting of part-time amateurs enrolled initially for local defence. (A few volunteers were enrolled before this date: the Glasgow Sharpshooters existed 1820–4 during a period of radical agitation, and the Exeter and South Devon Rifles were authorised in January 1853, but for all practical purposes the second volunteer movement may be said to have originated in 1859.)

Under the 'brigade sub-district' system, it was intended that one regular battalion of each pair should be at home and the other abroad, the home battalion training the other's recruits, and a militia battalion acting as a source of reinforcements if both regular battalions should be abroad. The system was not entirely satisfactory and in 1877 a committee named after Colonel Stanley proposed a new organisation, involving two-battalion regiments, integrating the militia, and with a common depot for all battalions of a regiment. This involved the amalgamation of all single-battalion corps, the creation of 'territorial' titles, and the disappearance of the old numbers. ('Territorial' titles were not new, almost all regiments having borne a county name from 1782, although this was not necessarily an accurate reflection of the area from which recruits were drawn.) Accordingly, in 1881 the Ellice Committee on the Formation of Territorial Regiments formulated a plan of combining all the single-battalion regiments and replacing numbers with titles; some of the proposed amalgamations and many of the original titles were amended, so that, for example, the planned unification of the 42nd and 79th into the Black Watch and Cameron Royal Highland (Queen's Own) Regiment, and that of the 73rd and 90th into the Clydesdale Regiment, never occurred. As now, the army's *esprit de corps* was dependent to a considerable extent upon the regimental system and the loyalty it engendered; thus the amalgamations and loss of the old numbers were resented at first. (As William Forbes-Mitchell stated of his own battalion, 'I don't ask them ever to pray for the men who took away the numbers from our regiments; may their beards be defiled, is the only feeling I have for them.')[4] In some cases, regiments continued to use their old numbers unofficially, to distinguish between their new 1st and 2nd battalions.

The regiments created by the 1881 amalgamations are listed below, showing their component parts; the regular battalions are the old numbered regiments, with titles borne at the date of amalgamation, and subsequent battalions (generally 3rd and 4th) are given with their old militia identity. The process of integration of the volunteer forces was of longer duration, and the following lists those ultimately affiliated to each regular regiment, although in some cases this affiliation was delayed by some years. At this period volunteer battalions were not numbered consecutively after the militia, but until 1908 were titled as the 1st, 2nd, etc., Volunteer Battalion of the regu-

> Bureaucracy in colonial administrations sometimes copied the worst aspects of War Office practice, for example in the Indian case in which a clerk, 'who had grasped the fact that every soldier has a name as well as a number, wrote to a Battery of Artillery that had lost a horse, number 43,587, asking "What was the deceased horse's name?" The Major in command was fortunately a wag himself, and it is recorded that he wrote back to say that "The deceased horse's name was Tommy Rot," with which the Babu was perfectly satisfied.'
> ('The Red Tape Demon' by 'Spex', in *Navy and Army Illustrated*, vol. III, p. 275, 16 April 1897)

lar regiment. The titles of the new regiments are those adopted in 1881; in some cases the more familiar titles were adopted subsequently, for example the King's Light Infantry (Shropshire Regiment) became the King's (Shropshire Light Infantry) in 1882; the King's Own Borderers became the King's Own Scottish Borderers in 1887; and the King's Own Light Infantry (South Yorkshire Regiment) became the King's Own (Yorkshire Light Infantry) in 1887.

The Royal Scots (Lothian Regiment)
Regulars: 1st (Royal Scots)
3rd Bn: Edinburgh (Queen's Regiment) Light Infantry Militia
Volunteers: 1st and 2nd Edinburgh, 1st and 2nd Midlothian, 1st Berwick, 1st Haddington, 1st Linlithgow; 1st Berwick transferred to King's Own Borderers 1887.

Queen's Royal West Surrey Regiment
Regulars: 2nd (Queen's Royal) Regiment
3rd Bn: 2nd Royal Surrey militia
Volunteers: 2nd, 4th, 6th, 8th Surrey.

The Buffs (East Kent Regiment)
Regulars: 3rd (East Kent) Regiment (Buffs)
3rd Bn: East Kent Militia
Volunteers: 2nd and 5th Kent.

King's Own (Royal Lancaster Regiment)
Regulars: 4th (King's Own) Regiment
3rd and 4th Bns: 1st Royal Lancashire Militia (Duke of Lancaster's Own)
Volunteers: 10th Lancashire.

Northumberland Fusiliers
Regulars: 5th (Northumberland Fusiliers)
3rd Bn: Northumberland Light Infantry Militia
Volunteers: 1st and 2nd Northumberland, 1st Newcastle.

Royal Warwickshire Regiment
Regulars: 6th (Royal 1st Warwickshire) Regiment
3rd Bn: 1st Warwickshire Militia
4th Bn: 2nd Warwickshire Militia
Volunteers: 1st and 2nd Warwickshire.

Royal Fusiliers (City of London Regiment)
Regulars: 7th Royal Fusiliers
3rd Bn: Royal Westminster Light Infantry Militia

4th Bn: Royal London Militia
5th Bn: Royal South Middlesex Militia
Volunteers: 5th, 9th–11th, 22nd, 23rd Middlesex, 1st Tower Hamlets.

King's (Liverpool Regiment)
Regulars: 8th (King's) Regiment
3rd and 4th Bns: 2nd Royal Lancashire Militia (Duke of Lancaster's Own Rifles)
Volunteers: 1st, 5th, 13th, 15th, 18th, 19th Lancashire, 1st Isle of Man.

Norfolk Regiment
Regulars: 9th (East Norfolk) Regiment
3rd Bn: 1st (West) Norfolk Militia
4th Bn: 2nd (East) Norfolk Militia
Volunteers: 1st–4th Norfolk.

Lincolnshire Regiment
Regulars: 10th (North Lincoln) Regiment
3rd Bn: Royal North Lincolnshire Militia
4th Bn: Royal South Lincolnshire Militia
Volunteers: 1st and 2nd Lincolnshire.

Devonshire Regiment
Regulars: 11th (North Devon) Regiment
3rd Bn: 2nd South Devon Militia
4th Bn: 1st East Devon Militia
Volunteers: 1st–5th Devonshire.

Suffolk Regiment
Regulars: 12th (East Suffolk) Regiment
3rd Bn: West Suffolk Militia
4th Bn: Cambridgeshire Militia
Volunteers: 1st and 6th Suffolk, 1st and 2nd Cambridgeshire.

Prince Albert's (Somerset Light Infantry)
Regulars: 13th (1st Somersetshire) (Prince Albert's Light Infantry)
3rd Bn: 1st Somersetshire Light Infantry Militia
4th Bn: 2nd Somersetshire Light Infantry Militia
Volunteers: 1st–3rd Somerset.

Prince of Wales's Own (West Yorkshire Regiment)
Regulars: 14th (Buckinghamshire or Prince of Wales's Own) Regiment
3rd Bn: 2nd West York Light Infantry Militia
4th Bn: 4th West York Militia
Volunteers: 1st, 3rd, 7th West York.

East Yorkshire Regiment
Regulars: 15th (York East Riding) Regiment
3rd Bn: East York Militia
Volunteers: 1st and 2nd East York.

Bedfordshire Regiment
Regulars: 16th (Bedfordshire) Regiment
3rd Bn: Bedfordshire Light Infantry Militia
4th Bn: Hertfordshire Militia
Volunteers: 1st Bedford, 1st and 2nd Hertfordshire.

Leicestershire Regiment
Regulars: 17th (Leicestershire) Regiment
3rd Bn: Leicestershire Militia

Volunteers: 1st Leicestershire.

Royal Irish Regiment
Regulars: 18th (Royal Irish) Regiment
3rd Bn: Wexford Militia
4th Bn: 2nd or North Tipperary Light Infantry Militia
5th Bn: Kilkenny Fusiliers Militia
(Irish regiments had no volunteers affiliated).

Princess of Wales's Own (Yorkshire Regiment)
Regulars: 19th (1st York North Riding) Princess of Wales's Own Regiment
3rd Bn: 5th West York Militia
4th Bn: North York Rifles Militia
Volunteers: 1st and 2nd North Yorks.

Lancashire Fusiliers
Regulars: 20th (East Devonshire) Regiment
3rd Bn: 7th Lancashire Rifle Militia
Volunteers: 8th, 12th, 17th Lancashire.

Royal Scots Fusiliers
Regulars: 21st (Royal Scots Fusiliers)
3rd Bn: Scottish Borderers Militia (Dumfries, Roxburgh, Kirkcudbright and Selkirk)
4th Bn: Royal Ayrshire and Wigton Rifles Militia (Prince Regent's)
Volunteers: 1st and 2nd Ayrshire, 1st Dumfries, Galloway, 1st Roxburgh and Selkirk (all except Ayrshire corps transferred to King's Own Borderers 1887).

Cheshire Regiment
Regulars: 22nd (Cheshire) Regiment
3rd Bn: 1st Royal Cheshire Light Infantry Militia
4th Bn: 2nd Royal Cheshire Militia
Volunteers: 1st–5th Cheshire.

Royal Welsh Fusiliers
Regulars: 23rd (Royal Welch Fusiliers)
3rd Bn: Royal Denbigh and Merioneth Rifle Militia
4th Bn: Royal Caernarvon Rifles Militia
Volunteers: 1st Denbigh, 1st Flint and Caernarvon.

South Wales Borderers
Regulars: 24th (2nd Warwickshire) Regiment
3rd Bn: Royal South Wales Borderers (Royal Radnor and Brecknock Rifles) Militia
4th Bn: Royal Montgomery Rifles Militia
Volunteers: 1st Brecknock, 1st–3rd Monmouth.

King's Own Borderers
Regulars: 25th (King's Own Borderers)
3rd Bn: 3/Royal Scots Fusiliers transferred 1886 as 3/KOB
Volunteers: 1st Berwick, 1st Dumfries, Galloway, 1st Roxburgh and Selkirk.

Cameronians (Scottish Rifles)
1st Bn: 26th (Cameronians) Regiment
2nd Bn: 90th (Perthshire Volunteers) Light Infantry
3rd Bn: 1st Bn 2nd Royal Lanark Militia
4th Bn: 2nd Bn 2nd Royal Lanark Militia
Volunteers: 1st–4th and 7th Lanark.

Royal Inniskilling Fusiliers
1st Bn: 27th (Inniskilling) Regiment

2nd Bn: 108th (Madras Infantry)
3rd Bn: Fermanagh Light Infantry Militia
4th Bn: Royal Tyrone Fusiliers Militia
5th Bn: Prince of Wales's Own Donegal Militia.

Gloucestershire Regiment
1st Bn: 28th (North Gloucestershire) Regiment
2nd Bn: 61st (South Gloucestershire) Regiment
3rd Bn: Royal South Gloucestershire Light Infantry Militia
4th Bn: Royal North Gloucestershire Militia
Volunteers: 1st and 2nd Gloucestershire.

Worcestershire Regiment
1st Bn: 29th (Worcestershire) Regiment
2nd Bn: 36th (Herefordshire) Regiment
3rd Bn: 1st Bn Worcestershire Militia
4th Bn: 2nd Bn Worcestershire Militia
Volunteers: 1st and 2nd Worcestershire.

East Lancashire Regiment
1st Bn: 30th (Cambridgeshire) Regiment
2nd Bn: 59th (2nd Nottinghamshire) Regiment
3rd Bn: 5th Royal Lancashire Militia
Volunteers: 2nd and 3rd Lancashire.

East Surrey Regiment
1st Bn: 31st (Huntingdonshire) Regiment
2nd Bn: 70th (Surrey) Regiment
3rd Bn: 1st Royal Surrey Militia
4th Bn: 3rd Royal Surrey Militia
Volunteers: 1st, 3rd, 5th, 7th Surrey.

Duke of Cornwall's Light Infantry
1st Bn: 32nd (Cornwall) Light Infantry
2nd Bn: 46th (South Devonshire) Regiment
3rd Bn: Duke of Cornwall's Own Royal Cornwall Rangers (Rifles) Militia
Volunteers: 1st and 2nd Cornwall.

Duke of Wellington's (West Riding Regiment)
1st Bn: 33rd (Duke of Wellington's) Regiment
2nd Bn: 76th Regiment
3rd and 4th Bns: 6th West York Militia
Volunteers: 4th, 6th, 9th West York.

Border Regiment
1st Bn: 34th (Cumberland) Regiment
2nd Bn: 55th (Westmorland) Regiment
3rd Bn: Royal Cumberland Militia
4th Bn: Royal Westmorland Light Infantry Militia
Volunteers: 1st Cumberland, 1st Westmorland.

Royal Sussex Regiment
1st Bn: 35th (Royal Sussex) Regiment
2nd Bn: 107th (Bengal Infantry)
3rd Bn: Royal Sussex Light Infantry Militia
Volunteers: 1st and 2nd Sussex, 1st Cinque Ports.

Hampshire Regiment
1st Bn: 37th (North Hampshire) Regiment
2nd Bn: 67th (South Hampshire) Regiment
3rd Bn: Hampshire Militia
Volunteers: 1st–4th Hampshire, 1st Isle of Wight.

South Staffordshire Regiment
1st Bn: 38th (1st Staffordshire) Regiment
2nd Bn: 80th (Staffordshire Volunteers)
3rd and 4th Bns: King's Own 1st Staffordshire Militia
Volunteers: 1st, 3rd, 4th Staffordshire.

Dorsetshire Regiment
1st Bn: 39th (Dorsetshire) Regiment
2nd Bn: 54th (West Norfolk) Regiment
3rd Bn: Dorsetshire Militia
Volunteers: 1st Dorsetshire.

Prince of Wales's Volunteers (South Lancashire Regiment)
1st Bn: 40th (2nd Somersetshire) Regiment
2nd Bn: 82nd (Prince of Wales's Volunteers)
3rd Bn: 4th Royal Lancashire (Duke of Lancaster's Own) Light Infantry Militia
Volunteers: 9th, 21st Lancashire.

Welsh Regiment
1st Bn: 41st (Welsh) Regiment
2nd Bn: 69th (South Lincolnshire) Regiment
3rd Bn: Royal Glamorganshire Light Infantry Militia
Volunteers: 1st–3rd Glamorgan, 1st Pembroke.

Black Watch (Royal Highlanders)
1st Bn: 42nd Royal Highland (Black Watch) Regiment
2nd Bn: 73rd (Perthshire) Regiment
3rd Bn: Royal Perth Rifles Militia
Volunteers: 1st Fife, 1st–3rd Forfar, 1st, 2nd Perth.

Highland soldiers were especially popular in the later 19th century; this print depicting the Black Watch, published in 1894, is typical of Richard Simkin's style. The private and officer (centre) are both wearing the Egypt Medal and the Khedive's Egypt Star; the piper is wearing the Royal Stewart tartan traditionally used by pipers of the regiment.

Oxfordshire Light Infantry

1st Bn: 43rd (Monmouthshire Light Infantry)

2nd Bn: 52nd (Oxfordshire Light Infantry)

3rd Bn: King's Own Royal Bucks Militia

4th Bn: Oxfordshire Militia

Volunteers: 1st, 2nd Bucks, 1st, 2nd Oxford.

Essex Regiment

1st Bn: 44th (East Essex) Regiment

2nd Bn: 56th (West Essex) Regiment

3rd Bn: Essex Rifles Militia

4th Bn: 1st West Essex Militia

Volunteers: 1st–4th Essex.

Sherwood Foresters (Derbyshire) Regiment

1st Bn: 45th (Nottinghamshire Sherwood Foresters) Regiment

2nd Bn: 95th (Derbyshire) Regiment

3rd Bn: 2nd Derbyshire Militia (Chatsworth Rifles)

4th Bn: Royal Sherwood Foresters (Nottinghamshire) Militia

5th Bn: 1st Derbyshire Militia

Volunteers: 1st, 2nd Derbyshire, 1st, 2nd Nottinghamshire.

Loyal North Lancashire Regiment

1st Bn: 47th (Lancashire) Regiment

2nd Bn: 81st (Loyal Lincoln Volunteers) Regiment

3rd and 4th Bns: Duke of Lancaster's Own Regiment of Lancashire Militia

Volunteers: 11th, 14th Lancashire.

Northamptonshire Regiment

1st Bn: 48th (Northamptonshire) Regiment

2nd Bn: 58th (Rutlandshire) Regiment

3rd Bn: Northamptonshire and Rutlandshire Militia

Volunteers: 1st Northamptonshire.

Princess Charlotte of Wales's (Berkshire) Regiment

1st Bn: 49th (Princess Charlotte of Wales's Hertfordshire) Regiment

2nd Bn: 66th (Berkshire) Regiment

3rd Bn: Royal Berkshire Militia

Volunteers: 1st Berkshire.

Queen's Own (Royal West Kent) Regiment

1st Bn: 50th (Queen's Own) Regiment

2nd Bn: 97th (Earl of Ulster's) Regiment

3rd Bn: West Kent Light Infantry Militia

Volunteers: 1st, 3rd, 4th Kent.

King's Own Light Infantry (South Yorkshire Regiment)

1st Bn: 51st (2nd Yorkshire West Riding or King's Own) Light Infantry

2nd Bn: 105th (Madras Light Infantry)

3rd Bn: 1st West York Rifles Militia

Volunteers: 5th West York.

King's Light Infantry (Shropshire Regiment)

1st Bn: 53rd (Shropshire) Regiment

2nd Bn: 85th (King's Light Infantry) Regiment

3rd Bn: Shropshire Militia

4th Bn: Royal Herefordshire Militia (initially in 1881 the Royal Montgomery Rifles Militia formed the 4th Bn, but in the same year was transferred to become the 4/South Wales Borderers)

Volunteers: 1st Hereford, 1st, 2nd Shropshire.

Duke of Cambridge's Own (Middlesex Regiment)

1st Bn: 57th (West Middlesex) Regiment

2nd Bn: 77th (East Middlesex or Duke of Cambridge's Own) Regiment

3rd Bn: 5th Middlesex (Royal Elthorne) Light Infantry Militia

4th Bn: Royal East Middlesex Militia

Volunteers: 3rd, 8th, 11th, 17th Middlesex.

King's Royal Rifle Corps

Regulars: 60th King's Royal Rifle Corps

5th Bn: Huntingdonshire Militia

6th Bn: Royal Flint Rifles Militia

7th Bn: 2nd Middlesex (Edmonton) Royal Rifle Regiment (Militia)

8th Bn: Carlow Rifles Militia

9th Bn: North Cork Rifles Militia

Volunteers: 1st, 2nd, 4th–6th, 9th–13th, 21st, 22nd, 25th–27th Middlesex, 1st–4th London.

Duke of Edinburgh's (Wiltshire Regiment)

1st Bn: 62nd (Wiltshire) Regiment

2nd Bn: 99th (Duke of Edinburgh's) Regiment

3rd Bn: Royal Wiltshire Militia

Volunteers: 1st, 2nd Wiltshire.

Manchester Regiment

1st Bn: 63rd (West Suffolk) Regiment

2nd Bn: 96th Regiment

3rd and 4th Bns: 6th Royal Lancashire Militia

Volunteers: 4th, 6th, 7th, 16th, 17th, 20th, 22nd Lancashire.

Prince of Wales's (North Staffordshire Regiment)

1st Bn: 64th (2nd Staffordshire) Regiment

2nd Bn: 98th (Prince of Wales's) Regiment

3rd Bn: King's Own 2nd Staffordshire Light Infantry Militia

4th Bn: 3rd King's Own Staffordshire Rifle Militia

Volunteers: 2nd, 5th Staffordshire.

York and Lancaster Regiment

1st Bn: 65th (2nd Yorkshire North Riding) Regiment

2nd Bn: 84th York and Lancaster Regiment

3rd Bn: 3rd West York Light Infantry Militia

Volunteers: 2nd, 8th West York.

Durham Light Infantry

1st Bn: 68th (Durham Light Infantry) Regiment

2nd Bn: 106th Bombay Light Infantry Regiment

3rd Bn: 1st South Durham Fusiliers Militia

4th Bn: 2nd North Durham Militia

Volunteers: 1st–5th Durham.

Highland Light Infantry

1st Bn: 71st (Highland Light Infantry)

2nd Bn: 74th Highlanders

3rd Bn: 1st Royal Lanark Militia

Uniforms and equipment were adapted for overseas service from an early date. In the Eighth Cape Frontier War the 74th Highlanders wore canvas smock-frocks, as worn by troops aboard ship, dyed brownish-buff; tartan trews; an undress bonnet fitted with a peak as an eyeshade; and replaced the knapsack with a folded blanket-bundle suspended from the knapsack-straps, forming a comfortable and serviceable fighting kit.

Volunteers: 5th, 6th, 8th–10th Lanark.

Seaforth Highlanders (Ross-shire Buffs, Duke of Albany's)

1st Bn: 72nd (Duke of Albany's Own Highlanders)

2nd Bn: 78th Highland Regiment (Ross-shire Buffs)

3rd Bn: Highland Rifle Militia (Ross, Caithness, Sutherland and Cromarty)

Volunteers: 1st Inverness (transferred to Queen's Own Cameron Highlanders 1883), 1st Elgin, 1st Ross, 1st Sutherland.

Gordon Highlanders

1st Bn: 75th (Stirlingshire) Regiment

2nd Bn: 92nd (Gordon Highlanders)

3rd Bn: Royal Aberdeenshire Highlanders Militia

Volunteers: 1st–4th Aberdeen, 1st Banff, 1st Kincardine and Aberdeen.

Queen's Own Cameron Highlanders

1st Bn: 79th (Queen's Own Cameron Highlanders) (a second regular battalion was authorised in 1897)

2nd Bn: Inverness, Banff, Moray and Nairn (Highland Light Infantry) Militia

Volunteers: 1st Inverness.

Royal Irish Rifles

1st Bn: 83rd (County of Dublin) Regiment

2nd Bn: 86th (Royal County Down) Regiment

3rd Bn: Royal North Downshire Militia (Rifles)

4th Bn: Antrim Militia (Queen's Royal Rifles)

5th Bn: Royal South Down Light Infantry Militia

6th Bn: Louth Rifles Militia.

Princess Victoria's (Royal Irish Fusiliers)

1st Bn: 87th (Royal Irish Fusiliers)

2nd Bn: 89th (Princess Victoria's) Regiment

3rd Bn: Armagh Light Infantry Militia

4th Bn: Cavan Militia

5th Bn: Monaghan Militia.

Connaught Rangers

1st Bn: 88th (Connaught Rangers)

2nd Bn: 94th Regiment

3rd Bn: South Mayo Rifles Militia

4th Bn: Galway Militia

5th Bn: Roscommon Militia

6th Bn: North Mayo Fusiliers Militia.

Princess Louise's (Sutherland and Argyll Highlanders) ('Argyll and Sutherland' from 1882)

1st Bn: 91st (Princess Louise's Argyllshire) Highlanders

2nd Bn: 93rd Sutherland Highlanders

3rd Bn: Highland Borderers Light Infantry Militia (Stirling, Dumbarton, Clackmannan and Kinross)

4th Bn: Renfrew Militia (Prince of Wales's Royal Regiment)

Volunteers: 1st Argyll, 1st Clackmannan, 1st Dumbarton, 1st–3rd Renfrew, 1st Stirling.

Prince of Wales's Leinster Regiment (Royal Canadians)

1st Bn: 100th (Prince of Wales's Royal Canadian) Regiment

2nd Bn: 109th (Bombay Infantry) Regiment

3rd Bn: King's County Rifles Militia

4th Bn: Royal Queen's County Rifles Militia

5th Bn: Royal Meath Militia.

Royal Munster Fusiliers

1st Bn: 101st (Royal Bengal Fusiliers)

2nd Bn: 104th (Bengal Fusiliers)

3rd Bn: South Cork Light Infantry Militia

4th Bn: Kerry Militia

5th Bn: Royal Limerick County Militia (Fusiliers).

Royal Dublin Fusiliers

1st Bn: 102nd (Royal Madras Fusiliers)

2nd Bn: 103rd (Royal Bombay Fusiliers)

3rd Bn: Kildare Rifles Militia

4th Bn: Royal Dublin City Militia (Queen's Own Royal Regiment)

5th Bn: Dublin County Light Infantry Militia.

Rifle Brigade (Prince Consort's Own)

Regulars: Prince Consort's Own (Rifle Brigade)

5th Bn: 2nd Queen's Own Royal Tower Hamlets Light Infantry Militia

6th Bn: Prince of Wales's Royal Longford Rifles Militia

7th Bn: 1st King's Own Royal Tower Hamlets Light Infantry Militia

8th Bn: Leitrim Rifles Militia

9th Bn: Westmeath Rifles Militia

Volunteers: 7th, 14th–16th, 18th–21st, 24th, 26th Middlesex.

The Militia occasionally served in overseas garrisons to release regulars for active service, for example during the Crimean War and notably during the South African War of 1899–1902, when the 3rd Battalions of eight regiments served in the Mediterranean, their duties including the guarding of Boer prisoners; others were employed on line-of-communication duties in South Africa. Despite their status as home-defence forces, the volunteers contributed 'volunteer service companies' to reinforce their regular battalions in South Africa, as well as supplying personnel to specially created units like the City Imperial Volunteers. The first employment of volunteers on active service was in 1882, when members of the 24th Middlesex Rifle Volunteers (formed at the General Post Office in London in 1868) were sent to Egypt to run the Army Post Office Corps, using their civilian skills.

In addition to the line regiments, there were the three regiments of Foot Guards: 1st or Grenadier Guards, 2nd or Coldstream, and 3rd or Scots Guards (titled 'Scots Fusilier Guards' 1831–77). As the senior infantry regiments in the army, they enjoyed many privileges and were usually stronger than the equivalent line regiments: throughout the period under review, all maintained two battalions (the Grenadiers three), and eventually three battalions each. As the monarch's household troops, some battalions were always stationed in London, and rarely employed outside Europe, notably in Canada (2/Grenadiers and 2/Coldstream 1838–42, 1/Grenadiers and 2/Scots 1861–4), Egypt and the Sudan. From 1897 one battalion of each regiment was stationed for a year's duty in the Mediterranean. For a comparison with the 1898 establishment of line regiments noted above, for home service a Foot Guards battalion comprised 28 or 29 officers, 42 warrant officers or sergeants, and 800 or 940 other ranks; for Mediterranean service the same but for 29 officers and 936 other ranks (plus a sergeant-piper and five pipers per Scots Guards battalion). The three regiments shared a common depot with a total establishment of nine officers, 26 warrant officers and sergeants, and 243 other ranks.

Cavalry

The old distinction between regiments of heavy and light cavalry diminished progressively, so that by the end of the Peninsular War the 'heavy' regiments were capable of performing the outpost duty normally associated with the lighter regiments, and the distinction became even more blurred towards the end of the 19th century. The line cavalry consisted of the 1st–7th Dragoon Guards, and a separately numbered list of dragoons (heavy and light), beginning with the 1st Dragoons. The 'light' regiments

Lieutenant-Colonel C. W. Gore, officers and drum-major, 2nd Battalion, Duke of Wellington's Regiment, pictured at Pietermaritzburg, c.1894. Most are wearing dress uniform, including the white helmet, although the officer at the extreme right is wearing the scarlet service frock, cord riding-breeches (presumably indicating the mounted infantry company) and the blue home service helmet. Note that two stands of Colours are carried, the ordinary ones plus a second set awarded to the 76th Foot (the precursor of the 2nd Battalion) by the East India Company in 1807.

The Royal Irish Regiment in Egypt, 1882, wearing the white foreign service helmet and red 'serge frock'. (Print after Richard Simkin)

The khaki drill uniform approved for all foreign service in 1896; the subject is believed to be Private Jew of the 2nd Battalion, Worcestershire Regiment, photographed at Malta in 1897. The unique regimental valise-star is prominently displayed.

titled and uniformed as hussars and lancers originally retained their designation as light dragoons, although by 1861 all the light regiments had become either hussars or lancers, and from that date the title 'light dragoons' ceased to be used, until resurrected in 1992 for the amalgamation of the 13th/18th and 15th/19th Hussars. In the 1790s the number of light dragoon regiments rose to 33, but by the end of the Napoleonic Wars the number of dragoon regiments had been reduced to five (numbered 1–6, the fifth place being vacant following the disbandment of the 5th Dragoons in 1799 after the infiltration into its ranks of Irish rebels, who plotted mutiny), with nineteen light dragoon regiments (numbered 7–25), of which the 7th, 10th, 15th and 18th had been converted to hussars from 1806. In 1816 the 9th, 12th, 16th and 23rd Light Dragoons were converted to lancers, and in the reductions following the end of the Napoleonic Wars the regiments numbered 18 and above were disbanded. New 5th and 18th regiments were created in 1858, and in 1860–1 new 19th–21st from the European light cavalry regiments of the East India Company, upon the integration of these into the British Army.

The cavalry regiments bore the following titles:

1st (King's) Dragoon Guards
2nd (Queen's) Dragoon Guards; 1872, 2nd Dragoon Guards (Queen's Bays)
3rd (Prince of Wales's) Dragoon Guards
4th (Royal Irish) Dragoon Guards
5th (Princess Charlotte of Wales's) Dragoon Guards
6th Dragoon Guards (Carabiniers)
7th (Princess Royal's) Dragoon Guards
1st (Royal) Dragoons
2nd (Royal North British) Dragoons (Scots Greys); 1877, 2nd Dragoons (Royal Scots Greys)
3rd (King's Own) Light Dragoons; 1861, 3rd (King's Own) Hussars
4th (Queen's Own) Light Dragoons; 1861, 4th (Queen's Own) Hussars
5th (Royal Irish) Lancers (formed 1858)
6th (Inniskilling) Dragoons
7th (Queen's Own) Hussars
8th (King's Royal Irish) Hussars (converted from light dragoons 1822)
9th (Queen's Royal) Lancers
10th (Prince of Wales's Own Royal) Hussars
11th Light Dragoons; 1840, 11th (Prince Albert's Own) Hussars
12th (Prince of Wales's Royal) Lancers
13th Light Dragoons; 1861, 13th Hussars
14th (Duchess of York's Own) Light Dragoons; 1830, 14th (The King's) Light Dragoons; 1861, 14th (King's) Hussars
15th (King's) Hussars
16th (Queen's) Lancers
17th Lancers; 1876, 17th (Duke of Cambridge's Own) Lancers

18th Light Dragoons (Hussars) raised 1858; 1861, 18th Hussars
19th Light Dragoons (formed 1861 principally from 1st Bengal European Cavalry); 1861, 19th Hussars; 1885 19th (Princess of Wales's Own) Hussars
20th Light Dragoons (formed 1861 from 2nd Bengal European Cavalry); 1861, 20th Hussars
21st Light Dragoons (formed 1861 from 3rd Bengal European Cavalry); 1861, 21st Hussars; 1897 21st Lancers; 1898 21st (Empress of India's) Lancers

Unlike the infantry, cavalry regiments had no 'county' recruiting grounds, but were recruited from the whole country (although the 2nd Dragoons recruited principally in Scotland). Regimental establishments fluctuated according to circumstances, and taking 1898 as an example for comparison with the infantry statistics quoted above, a regiment serving in India had 29 officers, 56 warrant officers and sergeants and 539 other ranks; in the colonies 24, 49 and 520 respectively; in Egypt 21, 43 and 424 respectively. Two establishments existed for regiments serving at home, 'higher' and 'lower', those returning from overseas having the lower establishment and subsequently moving up to the higher: 23, 47 and 508, and 26, 53 and 617 respectively. The number of troop-horses on the establishment was invariably lower than the number of 'other ranks', and it became the practice that regiments did not take their horses to India, but on arrival in that country took over the horses of the regiment which they had replaced in the Indian garrison.

During this period regiments were divided into one reserve and three active squadrons; those serving in Egypt or the colonies maintained a depot of two officers, four sergeants and 111 other ranks at a common location, Canterbury, the depot being formed from the reserve squadron.

There were also the three Household Cavalry regiments, 1st and 2nd Life Guards and Royal Horse Guards, which as the sovereign's bodyguard were stationed permanently in London and Windsor; elements were always retained at home to perform ceremonial duties, so that regiments never took the field complete, and the Householders saw no foreign service whatever from Waterloo until the dispatch of squadrons to Egypt in 1882. For comparison with the above statistics, the 1898 regimental establishment comprised 24 officers, 55 warrant officers and sergeants, and 351 other ranks.

The cavalry had no reserve equivalent to the militia, and the yeomanry (the mounted equivalent of the infantry volunteers) was not affiliated to the regular regiments. In addition to fulfilling a valuable role in home security, the yeomanry provided the basis for the active service companies of Imperial Yeomanry created during the South African War of 1899–1902, which formed a valuable addition to the army's mobile capability. Not all Imperial Yeomanry companies were drawn directly from existing yeo-manry corps, and individual companies were numbered and organised in battalions. Some battalions maintained a 'local' composition (for example, the companies in the 6th Battalion were all Scottish, 9th all Welsh, 3rd Yorkshire and Nottinghamshire), but others had divergent origins; for example, the 1st Battalion comprised companies numbered 1, 2 and 63 (all Wiltshire), 3 (Gloucestershire) and 4 (Glamorganshire); 2nd Battalion comprised companies numbered 5 and 103 (both Warwickshire), 21 and 22 (both Cheshire), 32 (Lancashire) and 110 (Northumberland).

Artillery

Until 1855 the army's artillery and engineer services were administered by the Board of Ordnance, with their own command, establishment and system of promotion; but from that date both the Royal Artillery and Royal Engineers came under the command of the War Office and the Commander-in-Chief. Within the Royal Regiment of Artillery there had been a separate branch from 1793, the Royal Horse Artillery, organised in cavalry-style troops instead of the infantry-style companies and battalions of the 'foot' artillery. The separation of field and garrison batteries (into the Royal Field and Royal Garrison Artillery) occurred only in 1899, and lasted until 1924. Horse and field batteries generally consisted of six guns and attendant vehicles, but exceptions existed; for example, in the 1890s the batteries equipped with 9pdr RML and 12pdr BL guns had six pieces each, but those equipped with 13pdr RMLs had but four guns per battery. Originally batteries were identified by the name of their commander, but later by letters and numbers; there were up to seven changes of designation within a 60-year period, but in 1889 the system was simplified, horse troops being identified by a letter and the much more numerous field batteries by a number. The East India Company artillery was integrated into the Royal Artillery, without the formation of a special department (although some units have since borne subsidiary titles recalling their Indian origin), but the mountain batteries of the Royal Artillery were not included in the numbered list of field batteries, but maintained their own numbering. In 1898 the artillery establishment comprised 21 horse batteries (designated A–U), 103 planned field batteries (numbered 1–103, although ten of these had not yet been formed), and ten mountain batteries (numbered 1–10), with depots for both horse and field artillery. Ammunition-columns and parks existed in cadre, for mobilisation in wartime. Establishments fluctuated according to circumstances, but for comparison with the previous statistics, in India in 1898 a horse or field battery comprised five officers, nine NCOs and 148 other ranks, and a mountain battery five, nine and 97 respectively, not including Indian drivers.

Garrison artillery was organised into Eastern, Southern and Western divisions (according to location in Britain), each comprising a number of companies; as originally planned, 40 companies were to be stationed in British garrisons, 37 in the colonies and 27 in India. Militia artillery, formed at the time of the Crimean War, ultimately consisted of 32 battalions of between four and eight companies each, divided between the three garrison artillery divisions. The artillery portion of the volunteer force ultimately numbered 65 units (from one to seventeen companies strong), existing for home service only and with some trained as garrison artillery.

Supporting services

Throughout the empire, the duties of the Corps of Royal Engineers ranged from the construction of fieldworks to bridging, road-building, surveying, barrack-construction, water supply, the building and maintenance of railways,

The development of railways had a profound effect on the conveyance of troops and the logistics of campaign; this appropriately named locomotive is seen with its crew of Royal Engineers.

and latterly even the manning of observation-balloons. The officers were frequently employed upon detached services, and often in a civil capacity to assist the administration of colonial territories; and all members were trained to fight as infantry when required. Under the aegis of the Board of Ordnance until 1855, the engineers originally comprised two branches: the Royal Engineers, a corps exclusively of officers, and the Royal Sappers and Miners, comprising the rank and file of the engineer service; the two were merged as the Corps of Royal Engineers in 1856. Upon the assimilation of the East India Company's European forces into the British Army after the Indian Mutiny, their engineers were merged into the corps; and subsequently the Royal Engineers were responsible for the provision of officers and NCOs for the Indian engineer units. The principal tactical element was the field company, which in 1898 comprised three officers, 22 NCOs and 160 other ranks, increasing to six, 34 and 171 respectively for war service. By this date the corps included eighteen fortress, twelve submarine mining, four survey and two railway companies, bridging and telegraph battalions, depot units, balloon section, field parks and a mounted field detachment. Field, fortress, railway, survey and submarine mining companies were numbered in a single list; of the first ten, for example, nos. 1–3, 5–6 and 9 were fortress companies, 4 submarine mining, 7 field and 8 and 10 railway. The value of the corps may be exemplified by the fact that the conduct of the final stage of the South African War was due entirely to their efforts in the construction of some 8,000 blockhouses and almost 4,000 miles of barbed wire fencing.

Units to administer the army's supply and transport usually occupied a high profile only in wartime. After the disbanding of the Royal Waggon Train in 1833, the army was without any such organisation until the formation of the Land Transport Corps in January 1855 for Crimean service. It was disbanded at the end of the war and replaced in 1856 by the Military Train which lasted until 1869. Subsequently, commissariat and transport was the responsibility of two corps, both formed in 1869: the Army Service Corps ('other ranks' only), and the Control Department (officers). In December 1875 the latter was re-titled as the Commissariat and Transport Department, and in August 1881 the ASC was re-named the Commissariat and Transport Corps. In December 1888 the title 'Army Service Corps' was resurrected for the entire organisation, officers and men henceforth belonging to the same unit. The basic tactical element was the company, the strength of which and the number of vehicles it maintained varying according to the formation to which it was attached (e.g., infantry brigade or division, cavalry brigade, or for 'corps troops' not deployed at brigade or divisional level). Companies usually operated independently, and detachments could be deployed at less than company strength; for example, in the Desert Column of the Khartoum Relief

British Army rations, 1878:
Peacetime ration per day: ¾ pounds meat, 1 pound bread per man; 37 pounds coal per twelve men; 2 ³⁄₁₆th gills of oil per eighteen men; plus whatever groceries and vegetables the soldier chose to buy.
Wartime ration per day: 1½ pounds bread or 1 pound biscuit; 16 ounces fresh meat if procurable, if not, salted; 2 ounces rice; 2 ounces sugar; 1 ounce coffee or ¼ ounce tea; ½ ounce. salt; 1 gill spirits; fresh vegetables when available, or preserved potatoes and compressed vegetables.
Daily ration in India: 1 pound bread, 1 pound meat, 4 ounces rice, 2½ ounces sugar, ⁵⁄₇th ounce tea or coffee; ⅔ ounce salt; 1 pound vegetables; 3 pounds firewood.

Expedition, the Commissariat and Transport Corps detachment comprised three officers, 27 other ranks, 153 natives and 601 camels. An associated organisation was the Ordnance Store Corps, formed in 1881 from the Ordnance Store Companies of the ASC; in 1896 the unit was amalgamated with the Ordnance Store Branch (formed 1877) to form the Army Ordnance Corps.

Medical officers formed part of the staff of each regiment until 1873, when they were transferred to the Army Medical Staff. The 'other ranks' of the medical service were the Army Hospital Corps (formed 1855), supplemented in 1884 by the Medical Staff Corps; in 1898 officers and other ranks were united into one Royal Army Medical Corps. Latterly, in addition to the medical officers attached to every infantry battalion and cavalry regiment (plus two other ranks, and two stretcher-bearers per company), bearer companies were attached at brigade level, to transport casualties to the field hospital maintained by every division.

The Officer Corps

Throughout the period, the 'officer class' of the army was drawn largely from the upper echelon of society, although it was by no means impossible for a brave and capable man to rise from the ranks; perhaps the most notable of these was the tragic 'Fighting Mac', Sir Hector Macdonald, who enlisted as a private in the 92nd Highlanders in 1870 and by his own merits rose to the rank of major-general. (After being appointed to command the troops in Ceylon, he left in mysterious circumstances in 1903 and committed suicide in Paris, apparently to avoid a scandal involving alleged homosexuality.) The concept of the officer corps as an aristocratic institution is, however, incorrect, for comparatively few members of the peerage or their offspring served in the army. For example, the 1857 *Army List* reveals that of those serving as regimental officers (i.e., of the rank of lieutenant-colonel and below), including the Royal Artillery and Royal Engineers, there were ten peers, 22 who bore the title 'Lord', and 113 other sons of peers;

17 baronets, one knight, two Knights of Hanover, one holder of a Portuguese knighthood, one German prince and one Italian count. No less than 44 per cent of these 'titled' officers (74 individuals) were concentrated in the Household Cavalry and Foot Guards. The majority of the other officers, in addition to the comparatively few who had risen from the ranks, and a larger number from what would at the time have been considered 'humble' backgrounds, were drawn from the gentry and professional middle class, including a large number from families with a long tradition of military service.

There is ample evidence that such officers were preferred by the rank and file to those who had risen from the ranks or from the mercantile middle class. For example, Colonel. W. K. Stuart remarked that 'The men themselves prefer the gentleman born ... the British soldier is proud of, and likes to be commanded by, the blue blood. I recollect once in India my Colour-Sergeant, Hutchinson, coming to me on the eve of my departure for England. "Oh, Sir," he said, "what will the company do now you are going to leave us?" I said, "You have got a smart officer, Mr. B...., to look after you all." "Yes, Sir," he replied, "but he is not a gentleman."'[5] Mortimer Menpes discovered the same during the South African War: 'For the last two or three hundred years the English soldier has been led by the English gentleman – the ploughboy at the calf's tail gladly following his master's son to do battle for their common country. Tommy knows an English gentleman (to use an expressive vulgarism) "down to the ground", and he never makes a mistake. He will be led only by a gentleman, and in the ordinary way there is between the two a quiet understanding, and (I may say) a silent friendship, which is none the less real because, for reasons of discipline, it is unexpressed.'[6]

The purchase of officers' commissions was permitted until November 1871; the last officer to have purchased his first commission continued to serve until January 1910. The sums involved were considerable; in 1844, for example, the prices of commissions were:

Unit	Lt-Col	Maj	Capt	Lt	Cornet/Ensign
Life Guards	£7,250	£5,350	£3,500	£1,785	£1,260
Royal Horse Guards	£7,250	£5,350	£3,500	£1,600	£1,200
Cavalry	£6,175	£4,575	£3,225	£1,190	£840
Foot Guards	£9,000	£8,300	£4,800	£2,050	£1,200
Infantry	£4,540	£3,200	£1,800	£700	£450*

*(£500 for fusiliers and other corps having 2nd lieutenants instead of ensigns).

This practice and its consequences can be over-emphasised, however; the worst aspects of the system had been eliminated by the Duke of York's reforms in the early 19th century, and in addition to the previous testimonial of character required of prospective ensigns, latterly educational qualifications were demanded, and the accelerated promotion which had once been possible was prevented; in 1844, for example, no officer could become a captain until he had served two years as a subaltern, and no one could become a major without having been six years in the service. Promotion without purchase was still possible, to vacancies caused by the death of the previous incumbent. Also abolished in 1871 was the archaic system by which Foot Guards officers held 'double rank', their regimental rank and a substantive rank one higher, so that (for example) Guards lieutenants ranked as captains in the line. After the elimination of purchase, cavalry and infantry officers were appointed from cadet establishments where they had received training, as had artillery and engineer officers all along (there being no 'purchase' for these branches); and militia subalterns could still be granted regular commissions.

The decline of 'purchase' resulted in a higher level of military education for officers than had been usual before, although the course of the Royal Military College, Sandhurst (from which officers graduated) was initially perhaps not the most demanding of trials, and it took some considerable time for the benefits of the Staff College (founded 1858) to be recognised fully. Indeed there was some prejudice against perceived 'intellectuals' and as late as 1897 the Commander-in-Chief (Wolseley) wrote that he hoped that the British officer would never degenerate into a bookworm, but would continue to prefer outdoor sports! Certainly it was advantageous for officers to be active and possessed of what was termed 'pluck', but too many who commanded in colonial campaigns exhibited military ineptitude. Bravery was no guarantee of tactical ability or intelligence, and the annals of colonial warfare are punctuated with the blunders of inept commanders like Brigadier Walpole, who ordered a frontal attack on the fort at Ruiya during the Indian Mutiny, instead of simply striding over the scarcely existing rear wall, at the cost of considerable slaughter; so disgusted was his command that it was said officers broke their swords and refused to serve under him, and the rank and file seriously considered setting fire to his tent! Fortunately, in the majority of cases the very experience of colonial warfare had the effect of increasing the professionalism of the officer corps, and reducing or eliminating any social divisions between the minority of aristocrats and those drawn from the professional middle class. Henceforth, such divisions as existed were probably more between the officers of regiments which served abroad and those which generally stayed at home, Guards and heavy cavalry (which to a degree remained the preserve of the aristocracy).

The rank and file

Unlike many European armies, there was no system of conscription in the British Army, enlistment being voluntary, with service originally for life (i.e., until a man's ser-

This portrait apparently preceded the khaki cotton drill approved for all overseas service in 1896, as the tunic is being worn with dark blue home-service trousers. The badge on the right upper arm (crown and gun above three chevrons) indicated the rank of sergeant-major in the Royal Artillery from 1881; like the skill-at-arms badge on the left forearm, it is attached only loosely, such badges generally being removable to facilitate the frequent laundering of the khaki uniform.

reserve, later amended to seven and five respectively; changes were made to the periods of service for the other arms, but the principle remained.

At the beginning of the 19th century, soldiering was perhaps the least respectable of all occupations; its conditions appealed only to the lowest elements in society, the desperate or the fugitive, hence Wellington's oft-misunderstood remark concerning 'the scum of the earth'. Despite great improvements in living conditions and welfare of the rank and file, and despite the popularity of the army during times of successful campaigns, the civilian view of the individual redcoat (as different from that of the army) remained predominantly one of suspicion. A typical view was described by an Irish 'gentleman-ranker' who enlisted in the 1840s out of penury, and bemoaned his inability to mix with his friends once he had put on a red coat:

'... I could no longer have intercourse with them on terms of equality as hitherto ... I had sunk from their level in society; betaken me to what is considered the last resource of the unfortunate and the profligate; and an insuperable bar was placed between our future associating, according to the conventional usages of the world ... although there was much order and regularity, in a military point of view, among the old soldiers, their conduct in other respects was frequently abominable, and their language of so foul a character, as almost to make my blood curdle and my flesh creep when I recall it. In many instances, the lips of sergeant and private teemed alike with pollution, and their horrible oaths and execrations coupled with expressions of obscenity pained my ears tenfold more than the shrill screaming of the troops of jackalls [*sic*] that came nightly from the graves and tombs to prey upon the offal of the camp ... The British army, as is well known, is the *dernier resort* of the idle, the depraved, and the destitute, the larger part of whom make good soldiers, and therefore become useful, if not even valuable, servants of the state.'[7]

The latter point was taken up by the defenders of the soldier, who knew him better than those who knew only his public reputation. Surgeon-General William Munro, perhaps influenced by his long association with the 93rd, one of the best regiments of the service, wrote:

'It was not uncommon ... to hear people speak, perhaps in ignorance, but sometimes in contempt, of the "common soldier". He was, in their view, a creature to be shunned by the good and virtuous of society, to be excluded from certain places of public amusement, an outcast not to be thought of or considered until his services were required to fight his country's battles ... I have been associated with the soldier for nearly forty years, under every circumstance of service, and my experience has taught me that, as a rule, he is truthful, generous, and chivalrous, grateful for any kindness, and repays those who think of and care for him with gratitude and affection ...'[8]

vices were no longer required or until he was physically unable to perform his duties). To attract recruits of a better standard, a system of 'limited service' had been introduced during the Napoleonic Wars, by which an infantry recruit enrolled for seven years' service, cavalry ten and artillery twelve; but in 1829 lifetime service again became universal. In 1867 a law provided for a reserve of men who had served in the regular army, and a second reserve of militiamen who in exchange for a bounty agreed to join the regulars in case of mobilisation; but the major reformation of recruiting was the 1870 Enlistment Act. It was realised that for a rapid enlargement of the army in time of war, it was necessary to maintain a reserve of trained soldiers eligible for recall to the Colours; thus the 1870 Act established a 12-year enlistment, part of which would be spent on the reserve. Initially the term of service for the infantry was six years with the Colours and six on the

Henry Marshall, Deputy Inspector of Army Hospitals, went even further: 'Nowhere have I met with more honourable or more excellent men, than I have found in the ranks of the Army. The manual labour class of society are endowed with similar capabilities of observation with the class above them, and with similar faculties for the acquisition of knowledge, and the exercise of the moral virtues.'[9] Nevertheless, the predominant view remained that expressed in Kipling's *Tommy*:

'It's Tommy this, an' Tommy that, an' "Chuck him out, the brute!" But it's "Saviour of 'is country" when the guns begin to shoot.'

Dudley Kidd of the South Africa General Mission found such public disdain echoed in conversations with soldiers in the South African War and earlier:

'In 1892 a soldier said, "People appear to be frightened of us, even in the churches; the ladies squeeze up into the corner of the pew for fear that the red paint might come off our coats, and gentlemen look down on us as a bad lot. Who cares?" ... We have found that the vast majority of people looked askance at the soldiers' work. Some mothers did not wish their daughters to come near us because red coats could be seen in our meetings. Others thought the work very vulgar, and taunted us with having "scarlet fever". Judge our surprise when there was a sudden upheaval of all this feeling at the declaration of war. People became almost hysterical in their devotion to the long-forgotten Tommy. I remarked to one of the men how glad I was to see the general interest shown in the welfare of the soldiers. His answer set me thinking: "You should just hear what we fellows say in the barracks. Now it's all 'Tommy this and Tommy that', but just you wait till the war is over and then it will be, 'Get out of the way with you, you dirty fellow'. We have seen this sort of thing before, and we know how long the interest will last."'[10]

Such attitudes tended to exacerbate the friction which sometimes existed between military and civilians; although rivalries and feuds existed between regiments, soldiers usually stood together against the rest, sometimes with unfortunate consequences. For example, in April 1897 Charles Tavener, an ex-Royal Artilleryman living in Battersea, interfered in a quarrel between a soldier and a civilian, declaring, 'If you hit a soldier you hit me'; this typical expression of military comradeship cost Tavener his life, for he was killed in the fight which followed.[11]

Much of the military's bad reputation was ascribed to over-indulgence in alcohol, partly the consequence of men having no other way to spend their off-duty hours, and especially marked among Europeans serving in the colonies; as one old officer remarked, pointing to a mountain, 'Do you see that peak? Place a Bengal artilleryman alone on top of that peak in the morning, and he'll be drunk before night, wherever it may come from! Upon my soul, I think they could get liquor out of the rock itself!'[12]

An example of the attempt to improve soldiers' social conditions: a medal of the Soldiers' Total Abstinence Association, India, in silver with sky-blue ribbon, awarded for one year's abstinence; a clasp inscribed 'Fidelity' was issued to mark a second year's abstinence.

Attempts were made to combat excessive drinking, including the establishment of canteens where wholesome beer could be purchased instead of lethal local brews, libraries and sports facilities; and education was so encouraged that additional pay was granted to holders of certificates. Also of significance were temperance movements which sought to reduce the consumption of alcohol, if not outlaw it completely. A founder of one of these organisations was Henry Havelock, whose conversion to the Baptist faith led him to espouse the cause of temperance, and he came to be regarded as the model 'Christian hero'. Initially temperance associations were formed by individual regiments, many of which awarded medals to those who remained sober; most of these existed in India, presumably because in that country the effect of the local drink was especially lethal. The first was formed by Havelock in his 13th Light Infantry, and his followers were nicknamed 'Havelock's Saints'. A more universal movement was the Soldiers' Total Abstinence Association, formed at Agra in 1858 by a Baptist missionary, the Revd. John Gregson, to which regimental branches were affiliated. Gregson's organisation made considerable progress (unlike some of his calling, he actually experienced active service as chaplain to the 72nd in Afghanistan in 1879), and received support from many in authority, notably Lord Roberts, who in 1887 amalgamated the STAA with another, less influential movement, the Outram Institutes (founded by Sir James Outram in 1860 to provide facilities for the useful employment of soldiers' off-duty hours). The result was the Army Temperance Association (Roberts believing that temperance would have wider appeal than total abstinence), which was extended from India to Britain in 1893. Its membership (almost 36,000 by 1896 when both Indian and 'Home Organisation' are included) was sufficiently extensive to cause a marked decline in drunkenness, crime and punishment, and members were awarded medals which at ATA functions could actually be worn in uniform (upon the right breast).[13]

It is perhaps worthy of note that, as the army abstinence associations reflected those which existed in the civilian world, and despite the unpopularity of the military in some quarters, so the civilian temperance movement in some cases adopted military terminology to increase its impact. For example, holidaymakers at Whitby on Good Friday 1878 must have been alarmed by a banner which announced 'War is declared. Recruits are wanted'; but not, as might then have been expected, war against Russia, but by the 'Hallelujah Army' against the work of the Devil! Similarly, popular military or patriotic tunes were given new words by the temperance movement, for example *Heart of Oak*:

'Come, cheer up my lads, there's a bright day in store,
We'll stand by the flag till the battle is o'er ...
The reign of the foe it is passing away!
The hosts of the drink how they fill with dismay!'

Even the most popular tune of the Crimean War, the emigrant song *Cheer, Boys Cheer*, written by Charles MacKay and Henry Russell, was given new words. Its original version, played on campaign as late as the Abyssinian expedition of

1868, contained such sentiments as

'Cheer, boys, cheer! For country, mother country.
Cheer, boys, cheer! The willing strong right hand ...'[14]

whereas the temperance version ran,

'Cheer, boys, cheer! For truth shall be victorious,
Firm to the pledge, let us labour evermore.'[15]

Despite the progress of the temperance and educational institutions, and the provision of facilities to enable the soldier to pass his off-duty time harmlessly, Kipling's assertion that 'single men in barracks don't grow into plaster saints'[16] remained accurate, and a huge burden continued to be placed upon the army medical establishment by the incidence of venereal diseases. This was a sensitive subject among Victorian society, and measures to combat it were not satisfactory. The Contagious Diseases Prevention Act of 1864, extended in 1866, authorised the military medical authorities in named garrison towns to examine prostitutes compulsorily and detain the infected; but this process was condemned in parliament and the act was repealed in 1886. A similar system applied in Indian cantonments from 1865 until 1888, and not until 1897 was a new order instituted to remove brothels and enforce the treatment of the infected. Lest this be thought a minor problem, it was estimated that before the Act, about one-third of all admissions to army hospitals were caused by venereal disease; by 1867 this had dropped to one-fifth. British preventive measures seem to have been less effective than those in other European armies; for example, from 1876 to 1892 German Army venereal disease cases varied between 2.6 and 4.1 per cent of annual admissions to hospital; French between 4.4 and 6.5 per cent; and Austrian between 6.2 and 8.1. In the British Army at home the figure varied between 14.6 and 27.5 per cent, and in India between 20.3 and 50.3 per cent. For the period 1890–2, the average percentage of hospital admissions was 43.8 in India and 20.3 at home; excepting the Dutch troops in the East Indies (45.6 per cent), the British figure greatly exceeded those of the other major powers, the next highest being the 7.7 per cent of admissions of the US Army. In 1894 only 37 per cent of troops in India had never been treated for venereal disease, and 28 per cent had been treated for syphilis; in that year, from an average strength of 70,983 men, 36,325 were admitted to hospital, a rate of 51.2 per cent. In 1897 the Royal College of Surgeons expressed their concern over the matter, not so much for the effect upon the army but on the 'grave danger to the health of the nation at large ... the risks to which the civil population in this country are exposed when these men return home'.[17]

Equipment

There is insufficient space here for even a brief account of the changes in uniform which occurred during the 19th century, although it is noteworthy that alterations in the regulation uniform, to take account of colonial climates, occurred from the earliest times. In the 18th century it was

A disheartening comment was recorded by a young soldier preparing to embark for India:
'... all were ready for starting; and the order, right form four deep, quick march, being given, our little column, as it defiled in front of the several squads now at drill, commenced cheering loudly. "Ah!" remarked an old soldier, as we passed through the gate, "You shouldn't cheer till ye were comin' back: there won't be so many of you then, I warrant, and they'll not be in a cheering humour."'
(*Camp and Barrack-Room; or, the British Army as it is, by a Late Staff-Sergeant of the 13th Light Infantry*, London 1846, pp. 28–9)

common for uniforms for colonial service to be made of unlined or lighter material, or for more suitable patterns of coat, legwear and head-dress to be substituted for those worn in Europe; and the most fundamental changes in uniform and equipment were a direct result of the experiences of colonial service. The general unsuitability of 'European' uniform was described in 1841:

'Take the most active *light bob* that ever trod on neat's leather; buckle him up in a tight red jacket, when the thermometer is about 80°; place across his breast two buff-leather belts, about a quarter of an inch in thickness, and each what the milliners call a nail in breadth; hang to one of them a cartouche-box containing sixty rounds of ball cartridges, each of these above an ounce in weight; strap across his shoulders a square well-packed wallet, containing four shirts, with or without frills, and other *notions*; plant a cap on his head which in point of weight is equal to an iron pot; then place over his shoulder a musket and bayonet weighing a stone; with three days' provisions in his haversack, and a couple of quarts of liquid in a canteen: start this man against a savage, in the lightest marching order (stark naked), with no other weight to carry than ten or twelve asseghai spears, weighing a dozen pounds, and we shall soon see who will win the race.'[18]

Probably the most notable casualty of the experience of colonial warfare was the infantry's traditional red coat. Examples of its replacement on campaign occur from the early 19th century; for example, it was remarked in 1805 that some Indian units wore their red uniforms only for parade, not combat, and by the time of the Sikh Wars there were cases of British infantry wearing their white undress jackets in hot weather on campaign. Amendments were made regimentally; for example, in South Africa in 1851 the 74th Highlanders adopted dark brown or buff canvas blouses, the 'smocks' issued for sea voyages dyed locally and with cuffs and shoulders reinforced with leather, worn with lightened equipment, local footwear (*feldt-schoen*), and with peaks added to their forage caps.

Khaki uniforms first appeared in India, when Harry Lumsden of the Corps of Guides dressed his men in mud-coloured cloth, the colour most suitable for frontier warfare; it was apparently first worn in action in December 1849 at Sangao in the Yusufzai country, which led a gunner to call out, 'Lord! sir; them is our mudlarks!'[19] The colour was copied subsequently by many regiments, which initially dyed or stained their white Indian summer uniforms, producing a wide range of 'mud' colours; eventually the term 'khaki' became universal (from Urdu *khak*, dust). Other expedients adopted during the Indian Mutiny included that by the Bengal Europeans who fought in shirt-sleeves, with shirts and trousers dyed greyish-khaki (1st) or brownish-khaki (2nd), hence their nickname 'Dirty-Shirts'; others used the brown holland 'boat-coats' intended for use in China, and the 79th Highlanders used ships' smocks dyed light blue.

At regimental level unofficial modifications continued to be made (for example, the staining of white helmets and belts with earth or tea, as employed during the Zulu War), but in addition to the adoption of sun-helmets (common from the time of the Indian Mutiny), the first uniform specifically designed for colonial service was devised for the Ashanti expedition, including a light, cork and canvas helmet and a uniform of grey-brown tweed, loose-fitting and designed for utility rather than appearance. Undress uniform was commonly used on active service from the 1870s, a simplified version of the dress tunic styled a 'serge frock', red for infantry and heavy cavalry (to which some regiments added facings and braid) and blue for others (rifle-green or black for rifle corps). Although the red remained in use (in Egypt in 1882, for example), other expedients became common; grey uniforms were worn by troops sent from Egypt to the Sudan in 1884–5, khaki by those sent from India, and the latter was found preferable to the grey in desert conditions. Following the widespread use of khaki in Afghanistan from 1879, khaki drill service dress was introduced universally

'Tommy Atkins': the infantry home service uniform, including the 1878 helmet and 1882 valise equipment, worn by a private of the Queen's (Royal West Surrey) Regiment. The rifle is a Martini-Henry.

in India from 1885, with khaki covers for the white helmets until khaki helmets were produced. In 1896 Indian-style khaki was approved for all foreign service outside Europe, and in 1902 khaki was introduced for home service also, finally relegating the traditional red coat to a ceremonial role.

It is perhaps surprising that the red coat endured so long, for even when faded to the colour of brick-dust, and accompanied by helmet and accoutrements stained with tea or mud, it was not an ideal colour. It could be too conspicuous: for example, at Narnaul in the Indian Mutiny it was said that Lieutenant-Colonel John Gerrand of the 1st Bengal Europeans was singled out as a target and killed because he was one of only two men in the entire force still wearing red. The red could have advantages on campaign, however; for example, Gordon urged that a few red-coated soldiers be present in the vanguard of the Khartoum relief force, to over-awe the Mahdists (for which the Guards lent some serge frocks to the 1/Royal Sussex); and when the Cape Infantry was formed in 1882 they wore red in response to requests that as the red coats represented regular troops, the sight of such would be more welcome in up-country areas than that of volunteers or irregular forces. The idea that red coats shook enemy morale led to the 1/Black Watch and 1/South Staffords exchanging grey frocks for red prior to the action at Kirkeban, and at Ginnis in the Sudan (30 December 1885) the 1/Green Howards, 1/Royal Berkshire and 1/Royal West Kent were ordered to discard their khaki and change into red coats and blue trousers, and 1/Camerons red coats and kilts, so as to appear more formidable to the dervishes. Ginnis was the last major action in which the red coat was worn, but it was worn on campaign by the regular infantry engaged in the suppression of the Zulu rebellion in 1888 (by the 1/Royal Scots with helmets and equipment stained with red clay, although their mounted infantry wore another campaign expedient which was not uncommon, blue jerseys as worn by the mountain battery which accompanied them). Regimental Colours were last carried in action as late as 1881, by the 58th at Laing's Nek.

WEAPONS

Small-arms

The weaponry of the British Army improved in efficiency throughout the 19th century, but a factor that should not be overlooked is the delay which often occurred between the authorisation of a new pattern and its universal issue. In some cases outdated weapons continued in use for many years, and were often re-issued to second-line or irregular forces; and as late as the early 20th century, regular troops in India used the old Snider rifle (obsolete by 1880) to be carried by sentries at night, to fire buckshot and thus have a better chance of hitting a thief in the dark-

ness! It was also common for native troops to retain old weapons longer than British units; not always the result of making the best use of available resources, but for some considerable time after the Indian Mutiny as a consequence of less than complete trust in the loyalty of the Indian soldiers, to ensure that there would not be equality of weapons with the British in the event of a second mutiny.

In the early 19th century the army was still using the flintlock musket, technologically little changed from the later 17th century. Known by the generic name 'Brown Bess' (a term of endearment probably deriving from the German *buchse*, gun, and the 'brown' from darkened barrels or simply as an alliterative addition to 'Bess'), it existed in a number of patterns, the most common at the end of the Napoleonic Wars being the 'India Pattern', based upon those purchased by the government from the East India Company. There was never a universal firearm carried by all arms of service; many variations included shorter muskets or carbines for cavalry, artillery and engineers, lighter muskets for sergeants and light infantry, and rifled muskets for rifle corps.

The smoothbored flintlock musket had only limited range (fire was normally reserved until the enemy was within about 100 yards), was prone to misfire, slow to use (two or three shots per minute in combat was probably the

Equipment was often adapted as a result of the experience of campaign. Captain P. C. Newbigging, Royal Artillery, writes on the uselessness of revolvers on active service:
'... it is a well-known maxim ... that in the event of being rushed by a native, it is utterly useless to keep popping at him with a revolver. The custom is to dismount, and, resting on one knee, if necessary, to give him a rifle bullet at 10 or 15 yards. This will effectually stop him, otherwise, even if hit by a revolver, he will manage to assegai you. So well is this understood, that a man who lost his life through neglecting to do it, would be considered to have deserved his fate. To give our drivers revolvers is absurd. They are most delicate weapons, and want constant cleaning and fine handling, as well as considerable skill in their use. Far better give them a plain strong double-barrelled pistol, carrying a large bullet, and with some simple breech-action, such as is used in our sporting guns. Such pistols are easily loaded, easily cleaned, and stand much knocking about. When a driver comes to want to fire more than two shots at a time, he and his team must be in a baddish way, and had better make tracks as speedily as possible'.
('Revolvers for Drivers', *Minutes of Proceedings of the Royal Artillery Institution*, vol. XIV, p. 320, Woolwich 1886)

average) and wildly inaccurate (although by the tactics of the period, it was necessary only to register a hit anywhere upon a compact body of enemy troops). Contemporary test-statistics of effectiveness are varied, according to the conditions under which they were carried out, but Richard Henegan, head of the Field Train Department during the Peninsular War, calculated that if all the French casualties at Vittoria had been caused by musketry, only one shot in every 459 took effect, an estimate of efficiency which becomes even worse when casualties by artillery fire are considered. Nevertheless, the process of finding a better firearm was delayed after the end of the Napoleonic Wars, partly for economic reasons and partly, no doubt, because the flintlock had done all that had been required of it. The development of tactics accompanied improvements in weapons-technology, as the latter made possible the increased use of 'skirmish' tactics and the deliberate aiming at individual enemy soldiers, instead of merely pointing the gun-barrel in the general direction of a solid mass of troops.

The first major advance was the adoption of the percussion system of ignition; a percussion lock had been patented by the Revd. Alexander Forsyth in April 1807, but although used in sporting weapons it was not adopted for military use until the late 1830s. Trials with old muskets fitted with percussion locks having proved satisfactory, percussion weapons were introduced as the patterns of 1838 and 1839, revised in 1842; some were conversions

This view of an infantry battalion in line gives a good idea of the frontage occupied by such a unit in the period during which linear tactics prevailed. The illustration shows the 3rd Battalion, Seaforth Highlanders in Cairo in 1900, the first militia battalion (the old Highland Rifle Militia, Ross, Caithness, Sutherland and Cromarty) to serve in that country. The band and pipes and drums are in column at the rear; on the right flank is either the battalion's pack-transport or their mounted infantry company.

and some new, and they included carbines and even a rifled version for sergeants of Foot Guards. Their issue took some time to become universal, however, and old flintlocks were still being used by regular units in the later 1840s; but the improvement was marked. For example, writing of an action in Sind, an officer contrasted the arms of the 3rd and 50th Foot: '... we received the order to "fire", then "advance firing"; that advance firing was beautiful: I never saw anything equal to it, it was one regular roar. We had the percussion caps; and the Buffs, who were looking at us, say it was the most beautiful sight they ever saw: they knew the value of the percussion-cap, their men kept flinging their firelocks on the ground, swearing at the flint-lock, which required knocking every two or three moments, to make it go off.'[20]

Despite the improved system of ignition, accuracy remained poor and effective range no more than about

150 yards until the introduction of the rifled barrel. Rifled muskets had been used by rifle corps from the beginning of the century; the Baker rifle carried during the Napoleonic Wars was a splendid weapon, the Brunswick rifle of 1837 much less suitable, but the concept of issuing rifles to all infantry was new. In 1851 the Belgian Minié rifle was adopted, and 100 were issued to the most expert shots of each regiment; its effective range was 800 yards, but a target could be hit at twice that distance. It was used on a similar scale in the Crimea, although by then another weapon had been approved, the 1853-pattern Enfield rifle, lighter and of a smaller calibre (.577in against the .702in of the Minié). Although not carried by all British forces in the Indian Mutiny, its superiority over the older weapons was such that it might be regarded as one of the causes of British success (and acknowledged as such in Havelock's dispatch of his victory at Fatehpur). As a rough calculation of the accuracy of the new rifles, it has been estimated that in the Crimean War one shot in sixteen took effect, a most marked difference from the calculations concerning the 'Brown Bess' quoted above.

All these weapons were muzzle-loaders, so the next development was to increase the rate of fire by a breech-loading mechanism. Breech-loaders were known in the 17th century, and issued to British troops as early as 1777 when the Ferguson rifle was used briefly in America, but not until the late 1860s was a practicable weapon issued universally. After a number of breech-loading carbines had been tested and issued to some regiments, including the American Sharps, the Birmingham-made Calisher & Terry, and the Westley Richards 'monkey tail' (named from the shape of the lever which opened the breech), the same principle was applied to the infantry rifle. Experiments with the Lancaster and Whitworth patterns were unsuccessful, but a conversion of the 1853 Enfield with the Snider patent breech was approved in 1866, using a brass cartridge devised by Colonel Edward Boxer, Superintendent of the Royal Laboratory at Woolwich, and bearing his name, making the Snider an efficient and fast-firing weapon. This raised the usual rate of fire from 2–3 rounds per minute with the Enfield to about ten rpm.

Experiments took place with smaller-calibre weapons, and the .450in Westley Richards carbine was chosen for service in 1866, but quickly superseded by the .577in Snider. In March 1871 a superior breech-loading rifle of .450 calibre was approved, the Martini-Henry, sighted to 1,450 yards and with a rate of fire of twelve rpm; the carbine version was adopted in 1877. Further reductions in the size of bullet could only be contemplated if an increase in muzzle-velocity were possible, so as not to reduce the projectile's stopping-power, yet lead bullets were too soft to be propelled through the rifle-barrel at greater speed. The solution was found by a Swiss artilleryman, Colonel Rubin, who discovered that a lead bullet encased in harder metal would stand greater velocity, thus permitting a reduction in calibre. This gave the advantages of flatter trajectory (thus potentially greater accuracy), longer range and lighter weight, the latter permitting the soldier to carry more ammunition than before, an important consideration with weapons capable of increased rates of fire. Consequently, in 1888 .303in calibre was adopted for British rifles, which also featured another major development, the box magazine and bolt action designed by James Lee. The action of the bolt ejected the spent cartridge and the spring in the magazine automatically forced another round into the breech; the first magazines held eight rounds of black-powder ammunition. The next great development was the invention of a smokeless propellant, cordite, used in all service small-arms ammunition from 1892; the new ammunition increased muzzle-velocity from 1,800 to 2,000fps and the capacity of the Lee magazine was increased to ten rounds. The bolt-action rifle was officially styled Lee-Metford in April 1891, and in 1895 the modification of the barrel produced the Lee-Enfield, which in numerous Marks and variations remained the standard arm of the British Army until the adoption of the L1A1 self-loading rifle in 1957. A bolt-action carbine was not produced until the Lee-Enfield model of 1896, but artillery and colonial troops continued to employ the single-shot Martini action, which when fitted with a new barrel became the Martini-Enfield.

Despite the capabilities of the Lee magazine, the new rifles were often used as single-shooters, reloaded by hand after every shot, the magazine being held in reserve; volley-firing was still used. Nevertheless the efficacy of the new rifles was demonstrated at Omdurman: the British opened fire at 2,000 yards' range and stopped the Dervishes at 800 yards, whereas the Martinis of the Egyptians opened at 1,000 yards and stopped them at 500. Speedy re-loading of the magazine was possible from 1892 when Lee invented his 'charger' by which five rounds could be loaded simultaneously, but this was not adopted until after the South African War.

Artillery

During the first half of the 19th century the British Army's artillery consisted of muzzle-loading, smoothbore cannon, firing solid roundshot or 'canister' (musket-balls or large grapeshot in a container which ruptured as it left the gun, spraying the charge like a giant shotgun; also styled 'case-shot', and used only at close range); and howitzers capable of indirect fire (i.e., over obstacles or the heads of friendly troops), using exploding 'common shell' or 'spherical case' (the latter also known as shrapnel; shells filled with musket-balls which burst in the air over the enemy's head). The principal field artillery of the mid-19th century were the 6pdr and 9pdr cannon, and 12pdr and 24pdr howitzers, classifications (or 'natures') which described the weight of projectile. Heavier guns, initially intended for siege work but sometimes used in the field, were the 18pdr 'position' guns and 8in howitzers, as used against the Sikhs, and even heavier guns such as the six 24pdrs from HMS *Shannon*, mounted upon land carriages and manned by the naval brigade during the Indian Mutiny. Mortars – high-trajectory weapons firing explosive 'bombs' and mounted upon a flat bed instead of upon a wheeled artillery carriage – were intended exclusively for siege work.

Ranges of ordnance depended upon both elevation and type of projectile, given a standard propellant charge. The following ranges in yards are according to statistics of 1843, with the most common pieces of brass ordnance:

Nature	Project-ile	Point-blank	Elevation				
			1°	2°	3°	4°	5°
Medium 12 & 9pdr, long 6pdr	solid	300	700	1000	1200	1400	–
Light 12 & 6pdr	solid	200	600	800	1000	1200	–
12 & 9pdr	case	150	250	350	–	–	–
6pdr	case	100	200	300	–	–	–
12pdr how	shell	–	400	600	800	1000	1100
12pdr how	case	100	200	300	–	–	–
24pdr how	shell	250	450	650	850	1025	–
24pdr how	case	150	250	350	–	–	–

The heavier guns, all iron after the Napoleonic Wars, had the following ranges:

12pdr, 9ft long	solid	360	720	1075	1337	1540	1700
12pdr, 7 ft 6in long	solid	340	710	1040	1307	1500	1650
18pdr, 8ft long	solid	340	710	1075	1347	1560	1730
18pdr, 9ft long	solid	360	730	1080	1377	1600	1780
24pdr, 9ft long	solid	360	755	1125	1417	1670	1850
32pdr, 9 ft 7in long	solid	380	760	1130	1455	1730	1950

(One of the advantages of smoothbore guns was that, *in extremis*, virtually anything could be used as a projectile: the defenders of Arrah during the Indian Mutiny must have been surprised when a brass piano-castor was fired at them by the mutineers!)

The Indian Mutiny was the last major conflict fought with smoothbore weapons of the old type. In the quest for increased range and reduced weight (and thus enhanced mobility), the first development was the Armstrong gun, ordered in January 1859 and first employed in China in 1860. Its rifled barrel was breech-loading and was strengthened by shrinking wrought-iron layers on to the tube. It fired a shell which could be fuzed to air-burst as shrapnel, explode on impact, after penetrating a wall, or shortly

after leaving the muzzle, producing a case-shot effect. It was considerably lighter (a 12pdr Armstrong needed only a six-horse team, instead of eight required for an old 9pdr), and the range and accuracy of the early rifled breech-loaders (RBL) were of standards scarcely imagined before: the Armstrong could fire more accurately at two miles than a smoothbore at one quarter of the distance, and the 12pdr Whitworth (a British-made RBL used in the American Civil War) could project a shell almost six miles. The batteries sent to China were equipped with 12pdr Armstrongs, and these and 6pdrs were used in New Zealand; but many batteries continued to use smoothbores. A giant 110pdr Armstrong was landed and crewed by the Royal Navy in New Zealand; it was part of the ordnance which bombarded the Gate Pa, and included in the battering-train were also two 40pdr Armstrongs, two 24pdr howitzers, three 6pdr Armstrongs and six Coehorn and two 8in mortars. The Armstrongs had been much more effective against Maori fortifications than smoothbores, but in this case the 110pdr (probably the heaviest gun employed in colonial warfare) had limited effect, firing all 100 rounds which had been brought ashore in one day, but mis-targeted at a flagpole believed to be the centre of the Pa, but which was actually planted on a hill 50 yards behind the defences.

Despite the advantages of the Armstrong, it was decided that breech-loading was unnecessary, so on grounds of simplicity and cost, after trials in the later 1860s, there was a reversion to muzzle-loaders, albeit with rifled barrels. Breech-loaders were not discarded immediately (12pdrs were deployed in the Ambela and Abyssinian expeditions), but from 1871 the 16- and 9pdr rifled muzzle-loader (RML) became the standard weapon for field and horse batteries respectively, with a range up to 4,000 yards. Although the brass 9pdr RML was approved for Indian service in 1869 (brass guns being lighter and easier to manufacture), brass guns were withdrawn from service in favour of iron in 1874. The Armstrongs were the last to have wooden carriages; the 1871 RMLs had wrought-iron carriages, soon replaced by steel. Other varieties of ordnance remained in use, however, including 'siege' or 'position' guns; for example, in Afghanistan 40pdrs were used, sometimes dragged by teams of elephants. The new guns were not an unqualified success, the 9- and 16pdr RMLs being superseded by a 13pdr RML with a range of 4,800 yards; this was used in Egypt by the horse and some field batteries (others had 16pdrs, and one from India 9pdrs), but the necessity for modernisation was realised, and breech-loading was again adopted. From 1885 a 12pdr RBL was issued to both horse and field batteries, a lighter version for horse batteries from 1892 and that for field batteries converted to accept a 15pdr shell. These remained the standard artillery weapon for the remainder of the century, firing shrapnel shell and case-shot ('common shell' was no longer used); for the 15pdr the steel shrapnel shell contained 200 bullets for air-burst, 314 for case-shot, both using a propellant of 1lb of cordite. The limited anticipated use of case-shot was reflected in the ammunition carried with the gun: on each side of the carriage two shrapnel shells and one case, and in the limber 38 shrapnel and two case; maximum range for the 15pdr was 6,000 yards, or 3,400 yards with time-fuze. For the horse artillery's 12pdr the shrapnel shell contained 156 bullets, case-shot 314, both using a 12oz cordite charge; the limber contained 46 shrapnel and two case-shot, and maximum range was 5,500 yards, or 3,700 yards with time-fuze.

Siege artillery was divided into heavy, middle and light sections; a heavy section comprised four 40pdrs and ten 8in howitzers, a middle section six 40pdrs and ten 6.6in howitzers, and a light section eight 25pdrs and eight 6.3in howitzers; all were muzzle-loaders, although in the late 1890s breech-loading 4in and 5in guns and 6in howitzers were introduced. Even heavier guns were used for garrison fortifications, up to the 16.25in gun which fired a 16cwt. shell up to 12,000 yards. As field guns were not especially effective against buildings and entrenchments, the howitzer was re-introduced into the field artillery in 1896, not mixed into each battery as before, but in six-gun howitzer batteries; they were first used in the bombardment of Omdurman. The first pattern was a 5in breech-loader which fired a steel shell almost 50lb in weight, filled with 372 shrapnel-bullets and a bursting-charge of the new explosive, Lyddite (named from the place of manufacture, Lydd, Kent). Other heavy guns included improvisations used during the South African War, 4.7in naval guns (or 45pdrs) and eighteen 5in naval breech-loaders being mounted on land carriages. Attempts to control recoil were not successful until after the South African War, when a mechanism for the absorption of recoil led to the 'quick-firer', a field-gun which did not have to be re-aligned between shots.

Light, portable guns had been used from the 18th century, notably the 'galloper guns' attached to some cavalry regiments in India, but the use of mountain batteries dated from the mid-19th century. Mule-borne 3pdrs were used in Afghanistan in 1842, but these were not the only animals employed to carry light artillery, elephants and camels also being used, and even Indian bearers. (Over difficult terrain, elephants were used to transport large field guns as well; oxen were used in South Africa to drag the heavier artillery, but the experiment of using traction engines was not a great success). The mule-borne guns were broken down into their component parts and carried on pack-animals. Originally the Indian batteries were equipped with four 3pdr SBs and two 4⅖in SB howitzers, but the Royal Artillery mountain batteries employed 6pdr RBLs or 7pdr RMLs; two mule-batteries equipped with the latter served in Abyssinia. A much improved design, used in the later stages of the Second Afghan War and adopted as the standard weapon for mountain batteries from 1880 was the 'screw-gun', a 7pdr RML of 2.5in calibre, both longer and heavier than before (thus increasing range and striking-power; the range was about twice that of the previous 7pdr). This was accomplished by making the barrel in two pieces, which screwed together to produce a length of 69 inches; hence 'screw-gun'. Two mules carried the halves of the barrel, and one each the carriage, axle and wheels, with five extra mules to relieve the others; each gun had six mules to carry ammunition, normally 24 shell, 60 shrapnel, sixteen case and three star-shell per gun. The range was 4,000 yards, 3,400 with time-fuzed shrapnel. These remarkable weapons provided the most important fire-support for many actions, and were able to go virtually anywhere an infantryman could; they formed the primary artillery weapon on the North-West Frontier of India, and were also used in Egypt, Burma and Southern Africa. The refrain of Kipling's poem was truly accu-

The primary weapon for field artillery in the late 19th century, a 15pdr rifled breech-loader, with crew in khaki and foreign service helmets.

rate: 'You can go where you please, you can skid up the trees, but you don't get away from the guns!'[21]

Machine-Guns

The concept of multi-barrelled or repeating firearms was known in the 16th century, but not until the mid-19th century was a true machine-gun adopted for military use. After some service in the American Civil War, the machine-gun designed by Richard Jordan Gatling (1818–1903) was tested by the British Army at Shoeburyness in August–September 1870; three calibres (.42, .65 and 1in) were compared against the French Montigny *mitrailleuse*, artillery, and companies of riflemen. Having proved its worth, the Gatling was recommended for adoption by the British forces. It consisted of a group of breech-loading, rifled barrels, rotated by a hand-operated crank-handle, each barrel firing in rotation; cartridges dropped by gravity from a magazine into the breeches of the barrels. The Model 1871 Gatling usually had ten barrels, but could be supplied with five or six; the first used by the British Army were the six-barrelled 1874 Model, of .45in calibre, mounted on a wheeled carriage like that of a field gun. Rate of fire depended upon the speed at which the handle was cranked, but in an American test of 1873, 4,000 rounds were fired in 10 minutes 48 seconds, and between 64,000 and 65,000 rounds without the gun being cleaned. In the 1870 Shoeburyness test, the Gatling scored over 19 per cent of hits at 1,400 yards.

The Royal Navy appreciated the potential of the machine-gun at an early date, whether Gatlings or the rival Gardner. The first use of Gatlings ashore was in the Ashanti campaign, when on 3 January 1874 one of two Gatlings taken on campaign was fired at Prahsu, in a demonstration to impress Ashanti envoys. Apparently this had such an effect that one of the envoys (named 'Quamina Owoosoo' by Captain Henry Brackenbury) shot him-self on the following day! The Gardner gun was invented in 1874 by William Gardner of Toledo, Ohio, and was manufactured by Pratt & Whitney of Hartford, Connecticut; the type adopted by the Royal Navy had five barrels arranged horizontally, with cartridges in clips fed vertically into breeches; it was hand-operated and of .45in calibre. The principal failing of both Gardner and Gatling was the propensity to jam at a critical moment, which necessitated the use of specially trained crews. The Royal Artillery manned the two Gatlings employed in the Jowaki expedition in 1877, and the two in the Second Afghan War, but they were not successful in the latter. At Charasia, the two guns fired only 150 rounds; as Lord Roberts remarked, 'At the tenth round one of the Gatlings jammed, and had to be taken to pieces ... being found unsatisfactory, [they] were made but little use of.'[22]

Naval Gatlings were used in the early stages of the Zulu War, and four RA Gatlings in the later stages, two of which were quite effective (despite jamming) at Ulundi. In the following campaigns most machine-guns were manned by the Royal Navy, including six Gatlings in Egypt in 1882, and Gardners in the Nile expedition and Suakin campaign; their jamming had serious consequences at Tamai and Abu Klea. A pack-battery of four Gardners was crewed by the Royal Artillery in Burma in 1885, but these were on loan from the navy. Another gun adopted by the Royal Navy was the Nordenfelt, invented by the Swedish engineer Heldge Palmcrantz, and named after the financier of the project, Thorsten Nordenfelt. It had horizontally fixed multiple barrels (one, two, four, five or ten), hand-cranked and with automatic loading by a hopper above the breeches, into which bullets fell by action of gravity, each barrel having its own channel. An average rate of fire of 400–600rpm was recorded in trials with a .45in calibre five-barrelled gun, and 80–100rpm with a four-barrelled 1in gun. The Nordenfelt was used by the Royal Navy as a

Gatling machine-gun on a field carriage, crewed by members of the 3rd London Rifle Volunteers (affiliated as a volunteer battalion of the King's Royal Rifle Corps from 1881).

shipboard weapon; in 1912 1in guns with two and four barrels, five-barrelled .45 and three-barrelled .303 guns were still in use. The rifle-calibre guns saw limited land service; some accompanied Hicks' force in the Sudan, and in British military service two five-barrelled guns mounted upon land carriages were used by the 22nd Middlesex Rifle Volunteers (Central London Rifle Rangers), for example.

The next development was the gun invented by the American Hiram Maxim, which employed the force generated by each shot to load, fire and eject spent cartridge-cases as long as the trigger was depressed, producing a truly automatic machine-gun. (Sir Henry Bessemer patented a similar idea in 1854, but Maxim's was the first workable application). Belt-fed, the single-barrelled Maxim fired up to 600rpm, and the barrel was encased in a water-filled jacket to prevent over-heating. Maxim's first patent was taken out in 1884, and after extensive trials the resulting gun was taken into British Army service in 1891; initially it had wheeled carriages (for cavalry a 'galloping carriage' drawn by two horses, for infantry drawn by a mule), and the first tripod mount was approved in December 1897. From its introduction, the Maxim was allocated to each infantry battalion or cavalry regiment, and crewed by members of the unit, no longer being the preserve of the Royal Artillery. Initially the Maxim was of .45 calibre and used a black-powder propellant; later it used the new rifle calibre (.303) and smokeless powder, although in some cases the old calibre and powder were retained for some time: the Northern Rhodesia Police used theirs at the beginning of the First World War, until it was realised that the smoke produced by black-powder cartridges provided too obvious a target. Maxims were sighted to 2,500 yards and carried ammunition in belts of 250 rounds, each belt in a box, of which fourteen were stowed on a cavalry carriage and sixteen on an infantry carriage.

The first use of Maxims was by colonial forces; in 1889 the Gold Coast Constabulary had one, and Maxims on 'galloping carriages' accompanied the Pioneer Column into Rhodesia, later taken over by the Chartered Company forces. In 1891 Lugard's forces in Uganda included a Maxim which had been given by the inventor to H. M. Stanley; in Uganda it was operated by a detachment under Captain W. H. Williams, RA. The Bechuanaland Border Police had four Maxims on 'galloping carriages', and these were used in the 1893 Matabele revolt, with conspicuous success. The first use by regular troops on campaign was on the North-West Frontier in 1892 (by 2/KOYLI, although not used in action), and by the Chitral campaign the first .303 guns, using cordite ammunition, had arrived in India. The greatest concentration of Maxims was that deployed at Omdurman, where twenty were positioned behind the British *zareba* (four crewed by 1/Royal Irish Fusiliers, six by British and ten by Egyptian artillery), with 24 more in the naval gunboats. Their most successful

deployment was in such static positions; a lack of manoeuvrability perhaps accounts for their comparative lack of success in the South African War, although enterprising commanders who carried Maxims and tripods on horseback (for example Thorneycroft of the Mounted Infantry which bore his name) found them useful, albeit in a largely defensive role.

In 1888 the Maxim and Nordenfelt companies amalgamated, and in 1897 the concern was bought by Vickers; the new company, Vickers, Son & Maxim, continued production at both the old Maxim and Nordenfelt factories in Kent. Maxim also designed a machine-gun of 1.46in calibre, which fired a 1pdr explosive shell; known as a 'pom-pom' from the noise it made, it was used with considerable effect by the Boers against the British in the South African War, but this was not a case of a British company having 'traded with the enemy', the guns having been sold to France and subsequently sold-on. The other important machine-gun of the period, the Hotchkiss, was not used by British forces; but the single-barrelled Colt Automatic Gun, which operated on a similar principle, was used by the Imperial Yeomanry in South Africa.

Rockets

The explosive rocket designed by, and named after, Sir William Congreve, was used with some effect during the later Napoleonic Wars; it existed in a number of sizes for field and bombardment work, and although wildly inaccurate (and liable to double back upon the firers), was of considerable use in undermining enemy morale. Having seen the British rocket troop use them at Leipzig in 1813, the Russian General Wittgenstein remarked that 'They look as if they were made in hell, and surely they are the devil's own artillery,'[23] which is an apt description.

The Bengal Horse Artillery formed a rocket troop in 1816, and Congreve rockets were employed in a number of colonial campaigns, perhaps in greatest numbers in Burma in 1824-5. The 12pdr Congreve was recommended for battlefield use, although the heaviest 'field' rocket was the 32pdr, which was also the lightest for bombardment work; the Congreve used a long stick for stabilisation and was fired from a portable tube set upon tripod or bipod mounts. The rocket head of the Congreve carried explosive shell, incendiary or case-shot charge, and it was used up to, and including, the Crimean War. The succeeding Hale pattern also had a casing of light iron, and carried either explosive or incendiary material, but used the gases of the burning propellant (a mixture of charcoal, nitre and sulphur) to rotate metal vanes in the exhaust vent at the rear of the projectile, to impart a spin which theoretically kept the missile on course. It existed in 9pdr (field) and 24pdr (bombardment) varieties, and was fired from a 'trough' upon a tripod. Despite the improvements, the Hale was very inaccurate (at maximum range of about 1,500 yards, the average deviation was 40 yards), but its psychological effect was considerable, especially against foes who had not previously encountered them, as it travelled with a shrieking noise and sparking smoke-trail. Often crewed by Royal Navy personnel, the most prominent use of the Hale rocket was probably in Abyssinia, the 1874 Ashanti campaign, in South Africa (notably at Isandlwana and Ulundi), and in the 1881 Transvaal campaign. The rocket was largely redundant by the mid-1880s, having been retained by Britain longer than by other European powers (presumably because of its psychological impact upon 'savage' enemies), but was occasionally used thereafter. Major F. R. Burnham recorded that in Rhodesia in 1893 scouts were sent out to fire rockets to create a diversion, setting them off having first tied them to trees; and they were of such little effect in the Tirah campaign of 1897 that the Afridis against whom they were fired retaliated by slapping their backsides in contempt!

ROYAL NAVY

Although sometimes not immediately associated with colonial campaigns, the service of the Royal Navy was of crucial significance during the 19th century. As during the Napoleonic Wars, the Royal Navy was responsible for keeping open the sea-lanes for commerce and the transportation of troops to the colonies; and its presence and strength helped to deter potential aggressors.

The nineteenth century witnessed a revolution in warship design, the Royal Navy progressing from a wooden, sail-driven fleet to the most modern of navies employing armoured, steam-powered vessels with strength and armament unimagined by the generation of seamen who had fought in the Napoleonic Wars. The advances in warship design, however, had only limited relevance to colonial campaigning, in the increase of speed which reduced the time to transport men and equipment to the various out-

posts of empire; for during the period from the Battle of Navarino in 1827 (the one-sided destruction of a Turko-Egyptian fleet by British, French and Russian warships, the last major sea-battle under sail) until the outbreak of the First World War, the Royal Navy was not engaged in a 'fleet action'. Instead, almost all the maritime services required were those of patrolling, the maintenance of the *Pax Britannica*, and engagements against a variety of poorly armed enemies, from Bornean pirates to slave-runners.

The Royal Navy was reduced in size drastically after the Napoleonic Wars, a process gradually reversed as the century progressed. The adoption of new technology was at first slow; although a transatlantic crossing was made by a ship (*Savannah*) which combined steam and sail-power in 1819, the first steam vessel built for the Royal Navy was not on the navy list until 1831 (the three-gun paddle-vessel *Comet*, built at Deptford in 1822), and not until 1835 was a naval Inspector of Machinery appointed, and two years later a Comptroller of Steam Machinery. Against some opposition from reactionary elements, not until 1846 were steam vessels in excess of 1,000 tons built (one paddle-wheeler and two propeller-driven frigates, used only as troopships); and only after the experience of the Crimean War did the Admiralty acknowledge that steam-powered, armoured vessels represented the future. HMS *Warrior* of 1860, a 9,210-ton steam frigate armed with eleven 110pdrs, twenty-six 68pdr MLs and four 70pdr BLs, was the first warship with an iron hull, 4½in armour backed with teak; yet she and the steamships which followed still carried masts and sails, and not until the 1880s did the dual reliance on steam and sail give way to steam alone.

The first warships with armaments mounted in traversible turrets were the 1857 screw-driven 1st-rater *Royal Sovereign* (converted 1862–4), the 1864 iron turret-ship *Prince Albert* and the 1868 turret-ship *Monarch*. The latter had an armoured belt 9ft 9in wide and 7 inches thick, two revolving turrets of 10in armour, carrying two 12in guns,

Cruisers performed most of the navy's routine patrolling. This is the 1891 2nd class cruiser HMS Retribution, *for some time flagship of the South-East Coast of America station; armament included two 6in., six 4.7in., eight 6pdr and one 3pdr guns.*

Nothing so exemplifies the Royal Navy's ability to fight on land as this illustration of 1878, showing seamen aboard ship practising forming square, the drill for 'prepare to receive cavalry'. The Martini-Henry rifles have a sword-bayonet which could also be used as a cutlass. (Print after W. H. Overend)

and two 9in and one 7in deck guns. The navy's turret-ship expert, Captain Cowper Coles, designed a ship with a lower freeboard, HMS *Captain* of 1869; the failings of such low-standing vessels were demonstrated when she capsized on her maiden voyage, in the Bay of Biscay in September 1870, drowning Coles and most of the others aboard. The improved designs which followed involved both increased offensive power and protection, in the form of stronger armour. The 1876 battleship *Inflexible* and her class represented the concentration of main armament into an armoured 'citadel' amidships, in this case four 16in guns. HMS *Collingwood*, begun in 1880, was the first of the *Admiral* class in which main armament (four 12in guns) was mounted in barbettes (protected gun-positions), one at each end of the ship, with secondary armament (in this case six 6in guns and others) broadside-mounted between the barbettes; her armour was up to 18 inches thick, 11½ inches on the barbettes. This distribution of armament became standard. Another major development was the adoption of the steam turbine, invented by Sir Charles Parsons and demonstrated at the 1897 Spithead review in his yacht *Turbina*, which achieved the amazing speed of 34.5 knots. Even faster was the destroyer *Viper*, launched in 1899 and the first warship to be fitted with four turbines. Perhaps equally significant, in the context of colonial warfare, was the emergence of what has been termed 'gunboat diplomacy', minor naval operations virtually in a police role, patrolling the coasts of the empire, quelling insurrections or preventing unrest by the mere presence of a symbol of British authority, with the ability to arrive quickly wherever trouble threatened.

The essential characteristics of the gunboat included shallow draught for coastal and river navigation, small size (many were about 100–120 feet long) but with armament as heavy as possible, and the dual power of engine and sails. There were many variations of design; representative of those mounting the heaviest gun possible was the *Staunch* of 1867, 75 feet long and 180 tons displacement, but mounting a 9in gun which was raised and lowered hydraulically into a well; in effect, a floating gun-platform. The twin-screw class named after the *Medina* of 1876 were 110 feet long, with additional bow-rudders to enhance manoeuvrability, and carried three 64pdrs and three machine-guns. Larger vessels were the single-screw seagoing cruisers named after the *Cockchafer* of 1881 (125ft, two 64pdr RML, two 20pdr RBL, two machine-guns) and *Thrush* of 1889 (165ft, six 4in BL, two 3pdrs). The latest 19th-century design was the class named after the twin-screw *Bramble* of 1898, 180 feet long, designed for river service and thus with a draught of only 8 feet, with sails reduced to a light fore-and-aft rig, and carrying two 4in guns, four 12pdrs and ten machine-guns.

Royal Navy sloops performed much the same duties as gunboats. The class named after *Wild Swan* of 1876 were single-screw, 170ft steel vessels with two 7in and four 64pdr guns, or two 6in and six 5in guns. The twin-screw, 195ft class named after *Beagle* of 1889 carried eight 5in guns and eight machine-guns; the single-screw *Torch* and *Alert* of 1894 were 180ft steel vessels armed with six 4in and four 3pdr guns and two machine-guns, and the six vessels of the *Condor* class (1898–1901) were similar but with enhanced speed. In addition to their steam engines all were fully-rigged, *Beagle* schooner-rigged and the others barque-rigged.

Gunboats were built for empire naval forces, notably the *Paluma* and *Gayundah* for Queensland (115 feet long, twin-screw, one 8in, one 6in and one 3pdr gun), and *Protector* for South Australia (188ft, one 8in, five 6in and five Gatling guns); all these were built in 1884. Other gunboats were built specifically for river-navigation, including the

Gunboats were among the more useful of the Royal Navy's armed vessels: here, HMSs Dee *and* Don *of 1877 are shown on passage to Egypt in 1882 to protect the Suez Canal; both of 363 tons, they were armed with three 64pdr guns.*

stern-wheel paddle-steamers *Mosquito* and *Herald* of 1890, prefabricated vessels to be transported overland, for service on the Zambezi and armed with six 3pdrs and machine-guns. The class of river gunboats named after *Sandpiper* of 1897 was similar, armed with two 6pdrs, as were the larger *Woodcock* and *Woodlark* (also 1897), built for Chinese river service; similar vessels for Chinese service were produced in the early 20th century. Perhaps the best-known river gunboats were those which operated on the Nile; the *Sultan* class, for example, were 143 feet long and had a displacement of 140 tons, but had a draught of only two feet; armament comprised a 12pdr, a howitzer and four machine-guns. (This vessel should not be confused with the 1870 battleship HMS *Sultan*, which also served in this theatre, in the 1882 Egyptian campaign.) Kitchener's flotilla of gunboats and armed steamers prepared for the 1898 campaign included three prefabricated vessels built in Britain to his specifications and shipped out in sections (*Fateh*, *Naser* and *Zafir*), to supplement those of 1885 vintage, later reinforced by more modern vessels with screw-propulsion instead of a stern-wheel (*Melik*, *Sheik* and *Sudan*). The supporting fire of gunboats contributed to the victory of Omdurman, notably *Melik* and *Abu Klea*.

Although not part of a war, it is interesting to note the first combat in which British ships engaged an ironclad vessel. In May 1877 the Peruvian rebel Nicholas de Pierola and his followers seized and embarked upon the Birkenhead-built Peruvian turret-ram *Huáscar*, and, following alleged interference with British mail-steamers and the theft of coal from a British barque, the commander of the British Pacific squadron, Rear-Admiral de Horsey, was sent to apprehend the rebel. Horsey's unarmoured, wooden corvettes *Shah* and *Amethyst* engaged *Huáscar* on 29 May 1877 when the Peruvian refused to surrender. *Huáscar* had 5½in turret armour and 4½in belt armour, and was armed with two turret-mounted 300pdrs, two 40pdrs and

one 12pdr, all Armstrong RMLs. The efficacy of the armour was proven: only one shot out of an estimated seventy to eighty hits actually penetrated the armour-plating, and the Peruvian escaped under cover of darkness, having more than held her own, despite her deck-guns having to be abandoned when fired on by Gatling guns mounted in the British fighting-tops. (The British pursued, only to find that Pierola had surrendered to the Peruvian authorities.) The same vessel took on virtually the entire Chilean navy in October 1879, and was captured only after a shot entered the turret.

An equally important use of Royal Naval crews was as soldiers on land; all were trained in the use of small arms and

A feature of some colonial warfare was the often uncompromising nature of the conflict, as exemplified by an action involving a British 38-gun frigate on a cruise in the Java region:

'The *Sir Francis Drake*, Capt. HARRIS, lately ... fell in with eight Malay prows. Captain HARRIS sent a boat to examine them: if they were armed, it was his orders to capture or destroy them; if they were employed only in the peaceful pursuits of commerce, they were not to be molested. The Malays made no resistance to the examination, but, on the contrary, enticed four of the men below, whom they instantly murdered, *cut them in quarters*, and hung their mangled remains up in the shrouds! Capt. HARRIS, highly exasperated at this treacherous and cruel murder of four of his brave crew, stood the *Sir Francis Drake* closer to the shore, and fired at them, till not a vestige of them was to be seen. The whole of the crews, consisting of not less than 400 of these barbarians, who were not killed by the shot, found a grave in the sea.'
(*The Courier*, 22 April 1811)

light artillery, to enable them to serve in landing-parties. 'Gunboat diplomacy' demanded considerable ability from lower-ranking officers often acting away from immediate supervision, and similar capabilities were required of officers who commanded landing-parties, which could be supplied from virtually any naval vessel. In times of crisis it was often more convenient to employ naval personnel in this way, than to await the arrival of soldiers, for the navy was always on hand for immediate service in coastal areas. The Royal Navy also maintained its own troops, who served alongside the seamen in naval vessels: the Corps of Royal Marines, which from 1855 to 1923 was divided into the Royal Marine Light Infantry and Royal Marine Artillery, the latter trained to man ships' guns and the field-guns which could be employed by landing-parties.

In addition, naval brigades were employed to considerable effect in a number of campaigns, especially in managing the naval artillery used on land, notably during the Indian Mutiny. Although seamen from three Royal Naval ships served in this campaign (plus many from the East India Company's navy), it was the naval brigade of HMS *Shannon* which saw the hardest service. This frigate was commanded by Captain William Peel, who was the son of the statesman Sir Robert, and had won the VC in the Crimea when serving ashore with the naval brigade. *Shannon* was one of three ships sent from China when the Mutiny began, Peel forming a naval brigade at Calcutta composed of some 450 seamen and marines, later reinforced by men from merchant ships at the port; the navy also landed six 68pdr and eight 24pdr guns, two 8in howitzers and eight rocket tubes, which proved of great value in the subsequent campaigning. Peel's brigade served their eight heavy guns with the greatest effect in the operations to Lucknow (four Victoria Crosses were won on 16 November at the assault of the Shah Najaf (or 'Nujeef') mosque), and equally at Cawnpore. Peel was severely wounded in the thigh at Lucknow; he was created a KCB

in January 1858, but while recuperating from his injury was fatally stricken by smallpox; he was aged only 33.

Among other campaigns where naval personnel fulfilled a similar role were those in New Zealand, China and South Africa. In the Zulu War a naval brigade, ultimately more than 800 strong, was drawn from the iron screw corvettes *Active* and *Boadicea*, the armoured frigate *Shah*, the wooden screw corvette *Tenedos* and the gunboat *Forester* (and from the troopships *Euphrates*, *Himalaya*, *Orontes* and *Tamar*). Naval brigades served in Egypt and the Sudan, including at Tel-el-Kebir, El Teb, Tamai, in the Nile expedition, Abu Klea, Tofrek and Suakin. In the South African War, heavy guns manned by the naval brigade formed a vital resource; among the ships with the largest number of men on campaign were the 1st class cruisers *Powerful* and *Terrible*, and 2nd class cruisers *Doris* and *Forte*; almost all returned to their ships in 1901. Naval and marine personnel also served most valuably in China during the Boxer Rebellion; the Legation Guard was composed of Royal Marines, and naval detachments from a large number of ships served in the operations to secure the Taku Forts and relieve the legations. Among the ships which contributed the largest contingents to the naval brigade for the relief of Peking were the battleships *Barfleur*, *Centurion* and *Goliath*, 1st class cruisers *Endymion* and *Terrible*, armoured cruisers *Aurora* and *Orlando*, and the destroyer *Whiting*. In this campaign the Royal Navy was supplemented by the Royal Indian Marine and by the naval contingents of New South Wales, South Australia and Victoria. The ability of the Royal Navy to operate both on land and sea, and its wide dispersal which ensured that elements were always at hand near to any potential crisis, led to the British seaman's nickname, 'The Handy Man', as in E. H. Begbie's rhyme:

'Handy afloat, handy ashore, handier still in a hole,
    Ready to swarm up a mountain-side, or walk on a greasy pole.'[24]

The 1898 1st-class gunboat HMS Dwarf, *one of a class of vessels designed specifically for river service in tropical climates, with a draught of only 8 feet; 710 tons, 180 feet long, the class was armed with two 4in, four 12pdrs and ten machine-guns. Serving until 1926,* Dwarf *had been one of the longest-serving vessels in the class.*

In the context of the navy's participation in so many and varied colonial campaigns, it was surely an accurate description.

Notes

1. Lieutenant-Colonel Wilkie, 'The British Colonies Considered as Military Posts', in *United Service Journal*, 1841, vol. I, p. 318.
2. *Recessional*.
3. 'Combats with Savages', by 'TT', in *Colburn's United Service Magazine*, 1846, vol. I, p. 123.
4. Forbes-Mitchell, W, *Reminiscences of the Great Mutiny 1857–59*, London, 1897, p. 52.
5. Stuart, Colonel W. K. *Reminiscences of a Soldier*, London, 1874, vol. II, p. 276.
6. Menpes, M. *War Impressions*, London, 1901, p. 183.
7. *Camp and Barrack-Room; or, the British Army as it is*, by 'A Late Staff Sergeant of the 13th Light Infantry' (Staff-Sergeant Percival), London, 1846, pp. 8, 128–9, 269.
8. Munro, Surgeon-General William, *Reminiscences of Military Service with the 93rd Sutherland Highlanders*, London, 1883, pp. 140–1.
9. Marshall, H. 'Historical Details Relative to the Military Force of Great Britain, from the Earliest Periods to the Present Time', in *United Service Magazine*, 1842, vol. I, p. 181.
10. Kidd, D. *Echoes from the Battlefields of South Africa*, London, 1900, pp. 166–7.
11. *The Times*, 19 April 1897.
12. Bancroft, N. W. *From Recruit to Staff Sergeant*, Simla, 1900, pp. 37–8.
13. For more comprehensive accounts of this significant movement, see articles by S. C. Wood, 'Temperance and its Rewards in the British Army', National Army Museum *Annual Report 1976–7*, pp. 9–16; a chapter with the same title in *The Victorian Soldier: Studies in the History of the British Army 1816–1914*, ed. M. Harding, London, 1993; and 'The Other Half: Further Developments in Recording the History of British Military Temperance Movements', in *Army Museum '86* (NAM annual report 1986), pp. 27–33.
14. The full version is in Winstock, L. *Songs and Music of the Redcoats*, London, 1970, pp. 165–7.
15. Both temperance songs from *Hoyle's Hymns and Songs for Temperance Societies and Bands of Hope*, London and Manchester, nd., pp. 155, 178.
16. *Tommy*.
17. *The Times*, 3 April 1897.
18. Wilkie, *op. cit.*, *United Service Journal*, 1841, vol. I, p. 235.
19. Lumsden, General Sir Peter, and Elsmie, G. R. *Lumsden of the Guides*, London, 1899, p. 80.
20. *Colburn's United Service Magazine*, 1844, vol. I, p. 613.
21. *Screw-Guns*.
22. Field Marshal Lord Roberts of Kandahar. *Forty-One Years in India*, London, 1900, p. 406.
23. *Edinburgh Evening Courant*, 20 January 1814.
24. *Navy and Army Illustrated*, vol. IX, 6 January 1900, p. 409.

BRITISH MINISTRIES AND COMMANDERS

British Ministries in the 19th century

Titles of prime minister in parentheses if better-known by their ordinary surname; dates of birth and death given on their first entry in the list.

July 1794	William Pitt (the younger) (1759–1806) (Tory)
March 1801	Henry Addington (Viscount Sidmouth) (1757–1844) (Tory)
May 1804	William Pitt (the younger) (Tory)
Feb 1806	William Windham (Baron Grenville) (1759–1834) (Whig)
March 1807	William Cavendish-Bentinck, Duke of Portland (1738–1809) (Tory)
Oct 1809	Spencer Perceval (1762–1812) (Tory)
June 1812	Robert Jenkinson, Earl of Liverpool (1770–1828) (Tory)
April 1827	George Canning (1770–1827) (Tory)
Sept 1827	Frederick Robinson, Viscount Goderich (Earl of Ripon) (1782–859) (Tory)
Jan 1828	Arthur Wellesley, Duke of Wellington (1769–1852) (Tory)
Nov 1830	Charles, Earl Grey (1764–1845) (Whig)
July 1834	William Lamb, Viscount Melbourne (1778–1848) (Whig)
Nov 1834	Arthur Wellesley, Duke of Wellington (Tory)
Dec 1834	Sir Robert Peel (1788–1850) (Tory)
April 1835	William Lamb, Viscount Melbourne (Whig)
Sept 1841	Sir Robert Peel (Tory)
July 1846	John, Earl Russell (1792–1878) (Whig)
Feb 1852	Edward Stanley, Earl of Derby (1799–1869) (Tory)
Dec 1852	George Gordon, Earl of Aberdeen (1784–1860) (Peelite-Whig coalition)
Feb 1855	Henry Temple, Viscount Palmerston (1784–1865) (Whig)
Feb 1858	Edward Stanley, Earl of Derby (Conservative)
June 1859	Henry Temple, Viscount Palmerston (Whig)
Nov 1865	John, Earl Russell (Whig)
July 1866	Edward Stanley, Earl of Derby (Conservative)
Feb 1868	Benjamin Disraeli (Earl of Beaconsfield) (1804–81) (Conservative)
Dec 1868	William Gladstone (1809–98) (Liberal)
Feb 1874	Benjamin Disraeli (Earl of Beaconsfield) (Conservative)
April 1880	William Gladstone (Liberal)
June 1885	Robert Cecil, Marquess of Salisbury (1830–1903) (Conservative)
Feb 1886	William Gladstone (Liberal)
Aug 1886	Robert Cecil, Marquess of Salisbury (Conservative)
Aug 1892	William Gladstone (Liberal)
March 1894	Archibald Primrose, Earl of Roseberry (1847–1929) (Liberal)
July 1895	Robert Cecil, Marquess of Salisbury (Conservative)
July 1902	Arthur Balfour (Earl Balfour) (1848–1930) (Conservative)

British Army: Commanders-in-Chief during the 19th Century

1795–1809	Frederick, Duke of York
1809–11	Sir David Dundas, Bt.

1811–27	Frederick, Duke of York
1827–8	Arthur, 1st Duke of Wellington
1828–42	Rowland, 1st Viscount Hill
1842–52	Arthur, 1st Duke of Wellington
1852–6	Henry, 1st Viscount Hardinge
1856–95	George, Duke of Cambridge
1895–1900	Garnet, 1st Viscount Wolseley
1900–4	Frederick, 1st Earl Roberts

Adjutants-General

1799–1820	Lieutenant-General Sir Harry Calvert, Bt.
1820–8	Major-General Sir Henry Torrens
1828-30	Lieutenant-General Sir Herbert Taylor
1830–50	Lieutenant-General Sir John Macdonald
1850–3	Lieutenant-General Sir George Brown
1853-4	Major-General Hon. Sir George Cathcart
1854-60	Lieutenant-General Sir George Wetherall
1860–5	Lieutenant-General Hon. Sir James Scarlett
1865–70	Lieutenant-General Lord William Paulet
1870–6	Lieutenant-General Sir Richard Airey
1876–82	Lieutenant-General Sir Charles Ellice
1882	Lieutenant-General Garnet Wolseley
1882	Lieutenant-General Sir Richard Taylor
1882–5	Lieutenant-General Garnet, 1st Lord Wolseley
1885	Lieutenant-General Sir Archibald Alison, Bt.
1885–90	General Garnet, 1st Viscount Wolseley
1890–7	General Sir Redvers Buller
1897–1901	General Sir Henry Evelyn Wood

Quartermasters-General

1796–1803	General David Dundas
1803–11	Lieutenant-General Robert Brownrigg
1811–51	General Sir James Willoughby Gordon, Bt.
1851–5	Major-General James Freeth
1855–65	Lieutenant-General Sir Richard Airey
1865–70	Lieutenant-General Sir James Hope Grant
1870–1	Major-General Frederick Haines
1871–6	Major-General Charles Ellice
1876–80	Major-General Daniel Lysons
1880–2	Lieutenant-General Sir Garnet Wolseley
1882–7	Lieutenant-General Arthur Herbert
1887	Major-General Sir Robert Biddulph
1887–90	Major-General Sir Redvers Buller
1890–3	Lieutenant-General Sir Thomas Baker
1893–7	Lieutenant-General Sir Henry Evelyn Wood
1897–8	General Sir Richard Harrison
1898	Major-General Sir Charles Burnett
1898–9	Lieutenant-General Sir George White
1899–1903	Lieutenant-General Sir Charles Clarke, Bt.

Masters-General of the Ordnance

1795–1801	Charles, 1st Marquess of Cornwallis
1801–6	John, 2nd Earl of Chatham
1806–7	Francis, 2nd Earl of Moira
1807–10	John, 2nd Earl of Chatham
1810–18	Henry, 1st Earl of Mulgrave
1819–27	Arthur, 1st Duke of Wellington
1827–8	Henry, 1st Marquess of Anglesey
1828–30	William, 1st Viscount Beresford
1830–4	Sir John Kempt
1834–5	Sir George Murray
1835–41	Sir Richard Vivian, Bt.
1841–6	Sir George Murray
1846–52	Henry, 1st Marquess of Anglesey
1852	Henry, 1st Viscount Hardinge
1852–5	Fitzroy, 1st Lord Raglan

References

Anglesey, Marquess of. *A History of the British Cavalry 1816-1919*, London, 1973–86.

Anon. *Camp and Barrack-Room; or, the British Army as it is*, 'by a Late Staff-Sergeant of the 13th Light Infantry' (Staff-Sergeant Percival), London, 1846.

Barthorp, M. *The British Army on Campaign 1816-1902*, London 1987–8 (four-part work covering campaigns, uniforms, equipment and tactics; those of colonial interest are Parts I (1816–53), III (1856–81) and IV (1882–1902).

– *British Cavalry Uniforms since 1660*, Poole, 1984.

– *British Infantry Uniforms since 1660*, Poole, 1982.

Duncan, J., and Walton, J. *Heroes for Victoria*, Tunbridge Wells, 1991 (survey of a number of colonial campaigns and the forces involved).

Fabb, J., and Carman, W. Y. *The Victorian and Edwardian Army from Old Photographs*, London, 1975.

Fabb, J., and McGowan, A. C. *The Victorian and Edwardian Navy from Old Photographs*, London, 1976.

Farwell, B. *For Queen and Country*, London, 1981 (social history of the Victorian and Edwardian army).

Featherstone, D. *Weapons and Equipment of the Victorian Soldier*, Poole, 1978.

Fortescue, Hon. Sir John. *A History of the British Army*, London, 1899–1930 ('dated' and somewhat partisan but still of much interest).

Goldsmith, D. *The Devil's Paintbrush: Sir Hiram Maxim's Gun*, London, 1989.

Grierson, Lieutenant-Colonel J. M. (later Lieutenant-General Sir James). *The British Army*, London, 1899, published under pseudonym 'A Lieutenant-Colonel in the British Army'; orig. pub. in German 1897; repr. as *Scarlet into Khaki: the British Army on the Eve of the Boer War*, intro. Colonel. P. S. Walton, London, 1988.

Harding, M. (ed.). *The Victorian Soldier: Studies in the History of the British Army 1816-1914*, London, 1993.

Harries-Jenkins, G. *The Army in Victorian Society*, London, 1977.

Henderson, D. M. *Highland Soldier: A Social Study of the Highland Regiments 1820-1920*, Edinburgh, 1989.

Hughes, Major-General B. P. *British Smooth-Bore Artillery*, Harrisburg, Pennsylvania, 1969.

Jeans, J. T. (ed.). *The Naval Brigades in the South African War 1899–1900*, London, 1901.

Markham, G. *Guns of the Empire: Firearms of the British Soldier 1837–1987*, London, 1990.

Maxwell, L. *The Ashanti Ring: Sir Garnet Wolseley's Campaigns 1870–1882*, London, 1985.

Mollo, B. *The British Army from Old Photographs*, London, 1975 (very good assembly of images from the National Army Museum collection).

Padfield, P. *Rule Britannia: the Victorian and Edwardian Navy*, London, 1981.

Richards, W. *Her Majesty's Army*, London, nd. (c.1890).

– *Her Majesty's Army: Indian and Colonial Forces*, London, nd. (c. 1890)

Skelley, A. R. *The Victorian Army at Home*, London and Montreal, 1977.

Spiers, E. M. *The Army and Society 1815-1914*, London, 1980.

– *The Late Victorian Army 1868-1902*, Manchester, 1992.

Strachan, H. *From Waterloo to Balaclava: Tactics, Technology and the British Army 1815-1854*, Cambridge, 1985.

– *Wellington's Legacy: the Reform of the British Army 1830-1854*, Manchester, 1984.

Wahl, P., and Toppel, D. *The Gatling Gun*, London, 1966.

Walter, J. (ed.). *Arms and Equipment of the British Army, 1866: Victorian Military Equipment from the Enfield to the Snider*, London, 1986 (reprint of parts of manuals *Equipment of Infantry*, 1865, and rifle exercises from *Field Exercises and Evolutions of Infantry*, 1867).

Walton, Lieutenant-Colonel P. S. *Simkin's Soldiers: the British Army in 1890*, vol. I, Dorking, 1981, vol. II, Chippenham, 1986.

Winton, J. *Hurrah for the Life of a Sailor: Life on the lower-deck of the Victorian Navy*, London, 1977.

Wolseley, Viscount. *The Soldier's Pocket Book*, London, 1886.

TACTICS

It is difficult to identify a system of tactics that was peculiar to colonial warfare, as this embraced everything from 'set-piece' battles against an enemy operating on a similar tactical system, to guerrilla actions against warriors armed with virtually medieval weapons. Indeed, it was partially in matters of weaponry by which colonial wars were characterised. Charles Callwell, whose book *Small Wars: Their Principle and Practice* (1896) was in effect a textbook on the conduct of a colonial campaign, described them by a term already in use before his book was published: that a 'Small War' 'may be said to include all campaigns other than those where both the opposing sides consist of regular troops. It comprises the expeditions against savages and semi-civilised races by disciplined soldiers, it comprises campaigns undertaken to suppress rebellions and guerrilla warfare in all parts of the world where organised armies are struggling against opponents who will not meet them in the open field ...'[1] By such criteria, not all 'colonial' wars could be styled 'small wars': if India is considered as a 'colony' (which in the strictest sense it was not), then the Sikh army and the organised enemy in the early stages of the Mutiny do not fit into this definition. The very term 'small war' suggests a downgrading of the nature of the operation, yet in no sense should 'small' refer to numbers or suggest a denigration of the enemy: few would under-estimate the formidable nature of the Zulu army, for example, or would overlook the immense numbers of British troops that had to be deployed during the South African War of 1899–1902, yet by the accepted criteria both of these would rate as 'small wars'.

The tactics employed in colonial campaigns were based upon those that had evolved from European warfare. It is sometimes believed that the heavy losses incurred during the Crimean War resulted from a lack of progress which afflicted the British Army in the period following the Napoleonic Wars; but in fact there was considerable evolution in military theory, practice and technology during the period 1815 to 1854. A significant factor was the number of colonial wars that occurred at the time of the 'long peace' in Europe, which ensured that there were always some officers and troops with experience of actual warfare; although there was a tendency to denigrate 'sepoy generals' as representing a lower grade than those whose careers had been spent in Europe. Perhaps understandable in the early 19th century, such discrimination persisted so long that Robert Baden-Powell had cause to remark that 'Critics love to disparage our "Sepoy Generals"; but though their tactics may not be suitable to European warfare, they have at any rate learnt to handle men in difficult circumstances. They have had to adapt their common sense to the situation; they have been faced with intricate problems of organisation and supply, and above all they have learnt to know themselves under the ordeal of war, which cannot be imitated even in the best manoeuvres.'[2]

Adverse opinions of 'sepoy warfare' could lead to a hazardous under-estimation of the capability of those encountered beyond the boundaries of Europe, when compared with the foes faced in the Napoleonic Wars: 'The young know nothing of arms but from history ... The trade of soldiering has no longer any necessary connection with fighting. Its duties are merely the drill and parade, and the wearing of gay clothes. And although the officers, in their different grades, are hardly so well paid as merchants' clerks, still there is always a sufficient number found for so easy and amiable a service. It is true they have a chance of being drafted, at some time or other, to the farther East, several thousand miles away; but they know very well that in India they will meet with no such equal enemies as were formerly grappled with in Europe, while in China, it is a mere amusement to bring down the baldheaded Celestials ...'[3]

A significant factor which perhaps tended to reinforce this opinion was the comparatively small number of troops involved in colonial warfare. For example, whereas in the later stages of the American Civil War, Ulysses Grant was in overall command of in excess of half a million men, the largest 'colonial' command, until the South African War of 1899, was the approximately 35,000 men deployed in Egypt in 1882. These relatively small numbers permitted a commanding general to supervise in person a considerable part of an army's operations, and thus perhaps inhibited the development of more sophisticated staff systems, which were required as numbers increased. Nevertheless, with the exception of the Crimean War, it was only in colonial campaigns that practical experience could be acquired, and it was from such campaigns that the most effective commanders and reformers arose, such as Wolseley.

The evolution of tactics was linked inseparably with the development of military technology, and nowhere was this more marked than in colonial campaigns; whereas at the beginning of the 19th century the British Army was equipped with firearms not much different from those of their opponents, by the end of the century it was possible for weaponry of almost 20th-century sophistication to be

Below: Even in the days of long-range, rapid-fire rifles, old tactics were still practised: this Simkin illustration of c.1893 depicts members of the East Yorkshire Regiment forming square, the old defence against a cavalry charge.

deployed against swords and spears. Such was not always the case, however, for their opponents' skill with 'modern' weapons was also a cause for changes in British tactical practice.

Changes in tactics according to improvements in weaponry was not always immediate, sometimes as a consequence of the deployment of troops in situations where enhanced weapon-performance was not significant (the storming at bayonet-point of defended positions during the Indian Mutiny, for example, was little different from similar operations during the Napoleonic Wars). On other occasions, technological superiority exerted less influence because of the fact that issues of new arms were not made simultaneously to all elements of the British forces. Colonial corps usually retained their old weapons longer than those of the British Army, so that, for example, while the British used the greatly-superior Enfield rifle during the Indian Mutiny, most of the British–Indian corps carried exactly the same old-fashioned muskets with which their enemies were armed. The consequence of this was sometimes marked; in Abyssinia, for example, Napier made specific reference to the inferiority of the old muskets carried by the 23rd Pioneers at Arogee, resulting in this unit being the only one seriously jeopardised by the enemy being able to press home their attack against inferior musketry.

That European tactics were unsuitable for some colonial campaigns was a fact which became obvious. In the aftermath of the tribulations of the First Afghan War, the editor of the *United Service Magazine* indicated the way forward:

'... we have adhered too much to the cumbrous tactics of Europe, and the still more lumbering modes of India ... In making war against barbarians and warlike tribes, while we retain the great advantage of discipline, we should assimilate our tactics and modes of living to those of the enemy we have to deal with. We do not learn from the his-

torians of Alexander that he found any material difficulty in twice traversing this same country; nor does it appear that his officers had either camp equipage, brass beds, canteens, or slipper baths. However, we have a case nearer home and more directly to the point – the French army in Algiers. When the French first took the field against the Arabs, they marched out with all the forms they had been used to in Europe: they gained possession of certain towns and fortresses, and placed strong garrisons in them, which, the moment the troops returned to Algiers, became insulated, and surrounded with enemies ... The system continued for a course of years; but seeing at last its inefficiency, they changed their plans: their men were clothed and armed as lightly as possible, and, accompanied by Arab cavalry, that they had bought over, scoured the country in movable columns: when they obtained sight of their enemy [they] rushed to the attack ... Since this mode was adopted ... the French have advanced more in their conquest in one year than they did in the preceding eleven ...'[4]

In a paper 'On Bush-Fighting' published in the same year, Captain Sir James Alexander of the 14th Foot proposed a similar theory, which included training all men as light infantry, reducing equipment to a minimum, placing emphasis on marksmanship and woodcraft, and changing the whole system of operation. His ideas have a remarkably modern complexion: 'Cautiously creeping on the enemy, taking advantage of cover, and rushing on him, and striking with lead or steel, when he is caught at advantage, are the principles of bush-fighting'; and he quoted an example of how the rigidity of contemporary theory could hinder the emulation of the successful tactics employed by the enemy. 'During a protracted struggle in the bush of Cafferland [sic], it was proposed that chosen bands, composed of men of tried courage, should creep on the Caffers seated round their fires, and should pour on them, unprepared, a destructive volley, and then immediately retire. The enemy, thus harassed, it was supposed would soon have sued for peace. But this mode of bringing matters to a conclusion was thought un-English and cowardly, and it was never adopted ...'[5]

Imperfections in the British Army's mode of operation were recognised; as one critic remarked in 1842, 'Britain's honour has as yet *never* been tarnished ... and so long as our antagonists are confined to opium-eating Chinese – degraded Fellah Egyptians – indolent Spaniards, or rustic Boers ... we may continue with impunity our present system; but the recent disasters in Afghanistan ought to be a lesson ...'[6]

The quotation above which criticised the quantity of officers' camp-equipment highlights a factor peculiar to many colonial campaigns: the immense trains of baggage and camp-followers which often outnumbered the combatant part of an army. Some of these 'followers' were a necessity: terrain which precluded the use of wheeled vehicles compelled the use of baggage-animals and their handlers, and expeditions often had to carry not only all the provender required by men and animals, but even huge quantities of water in arid regions. Nevertheless, much of an army's 'tail' was an unnecessary encumbrance, and in later campaigns efforts were made to reduce to a minimum the quantity of portable goods, even to the extent of forbidding officers to carry their customarily permitted portable baggage. In the Hunza and Nagar operations of 1891, for example, baggage was reduced to the very minimum, with no more than one 'coolie' being permitted to carry the equipment of each officer, not even tents being permitted; yet even under such circumstances, E. F. Knight, who commanded a company of the irregular unit 'Spedding's Pathans', contrived to find room for his golf clubs; which, it was said, might well have been the first time that such had been taken on campaign on the North-West Frontier. Presumably it represents Knight's personal scale of priorities, which would probably have been appreciated by most other British officers!

It is interesting to compare contemporary opinions of the various types of 'follower'; in 1803 John Pester wrote that 'Under the heavens there is not a more inhuman, barbarous set of brutes than that blood-thirsty crew who are called camp followers of an Indian Army. They accompany it solely with the intention of plunder ... hell-hounds [who] put every helpless wretch to death who attempts to remonstrate with them.'[7] Conversely, the esteem with which a regiment's servants might be held is demonstrated nowhere more clearly than when the rank and file of the 9th Lancers were asked to recommend a member of the regiment for the Victoria Cross as a reward for the regiment's service in the Indian Mutiny; they voted unanimously for the head *bhistie* (water-carrier) as being the most deserving for devotion to duty!

The climate in which colonial campaigns might be conducted caused variations in the customary tactical practice, not least in the common use of nocturnal marches to avoid the heat of the day:

'A European soldier might smile, but let him try the sun – the Indian sun. It is really wonderful what an hour's difference makes: those who are marching cheerfully and strongly along will, in one hour's time, be completely done men, not having scarcely the strength of children. For these reasons we have commenced marching at twelve o'clock at midnight, so that our sleep has been but short, and it will be some little time ere we regain our former strength ... When I speak of the sun with reference to the men, I meant to bring to notice their dress, which is (egregious folly) the same as in Europe, the throat covered with the leathern stock, which is in itself enough to overpower the strongest men. Put our dress on a native, and he would be sooner enfeebled than the Europeans ...'[8] Much the same point was made more colourfully by an officer who remarked of an Indian post, 'There is only a sheet of brown paper between this and h—l.'[9]

Another factor characteristic of much colonial warfare was the great disparity in numbers between small British forces and huge hordes of opponents which often occurred. To compensate, a tactic commonly applied from the earliest times, and persisting at least until the British achieved a marked superiority in weapons-technology, was to rush upon the enemy at the earliest opportunity, to redress their huge numerical superiority by attacking and throwing them off-balance before their ill-disciplined masses could respond. Arthur Wellesley (the future Duke of Wellington) expressed this point in 1803: 'The best thing you can do is ... dash at the first party that comes into your neighbourhood ... If you ... succeed in cutting up, or in driving to a distance, one good party, the campaign will be our own. A long defensive war will ruin us, and will answer to no purpose whatever.'[10] He may have been writing more in strategic terms, but the practice was equally valid in the realm of 'minor tactics', when a combination of discipline and boldness was the best counter to disparity of numbers. William Hodson remarked during the Indian Mutiny that 'in Indian warfare I have always found "toujours l'audace" not a bad motto',[11] or as Harry Lumsden expressed rather more prosaically when describing how audacity had compensated for lack of numbers on one occasion in 1847, 'Swagger did the trick.'[12] Against a disciplined enemy, a policy of immediate frontal attack could be costly, as Gough discovered against the Sikhs; yet the same policy was recommended by Robert Baden-Powell at the end of the 19th century: to get the enemy on the run, and keep them on the run, for 'our only chance of bringing the war to an end is to go for them whenever we get the chance, and hit as hard as ever we can; any hesitation or softness is construed by them as a sign of weakness, and at once restores their confidence and courage'. (He took this tactical point one stage further by adding, 'they must, as a people, be ruled with a hand of iron in a velvet glove; and if they writhe under it, and don't understand the force of it, it is of no use to add more padding – you must take off the glove for a moment and show them the hand. They will then understand and obey ...')[13]

Although the distinction between the various 'arms' was sometimes blurred, it is possible to consider the tactics of infantry, cavalry and artillery separately.

Infantry

In the early 19th century, infantry tactics employed in colonial warfare were largely the same as those used in Europe during the Napoleonic Wars, relying upon close-order formations of the line for firing and charging, columns for manoeuvre, and the battalion square as a defence against cavalry; the European system was also applied to the mechanics of siege warfare against defended positions. In broken country, forest or bush, in mountainous terrain or against an enemy using guerrilla or 'ambush' tactics, close-order formations were unsuitable, so that each company had to learn how to skirmish and act independently. This was no new skill, having been perfected by the light infantry and rifle corps during the Peninsular War, and by the light company of each line battalion; but the instruction of an entire battalion in such tactics was largely a new departure, sometimes initiated by progressive commanders and sometimes learned through costly experience. Nevertheless, the tactical manuals of the mid-19th century were still only refinements of those in use at the end of the 18th, despite the major technological developments of the percussion cap and the more widespread use of rifled muskets, with the resulting enhancement of weapons-effectiveness.

The experiences of the Crimean War did not form a total watershed in tactical method, for the 1857 infantry manual continued to advocate the use of column and line,

protected by a screen of skirmishers, with volley- or file-firing from a standing position being advocated for all except skirmishers, who were advised to use cover, and kneeling and prone firing. Despite the enhanced powers of the soldier's firearm, some of the tactics employed in the Indian Mutiny were virtually of 'Peninsular' style. Although the superiority of the Enfield rifle was recognised (as in Havelock's dispatch concerning Fatehpur, which attributed success to a combination of British spirit, artillery, divine favour and the Enfield), in a number of actions the determining factor was the bayonet and the will to press home with it. Bayonet-charges were largely a matter of morale, delivered against an enemy who was already shaken or in disorder, and who usually broke before contact was made, the terrifying sight of a disciplined charge with levelled bayonets being sufficient to shake the morale of all but the most determined; yet it could be equally frightening to those delivering the charge, as an officer of the 50th recalled in Sind: 'This was the first time I had been in a charge of infantry with British troops, and under so heavy a fire of grape and cannister (sic), that when I heard the whiz of the grape, I could not help making a face like a chap who is going to take a dose of salts.'[14]

Despite the advice of official manuals, tactics were often adapted according to circumstances, and contrary to old-fashioned wisdom. This was demonstrated by an incident involving the 93rd when under artillery fire during the Indian Mutiny, when 'old Colonel Leith-Hay was calling out, "Keep steady, men; close up the ranks, and don't waver in face of a battery manned by cowardly Asiatics." ... MacBean, the adjutant, was behind the line telling the men in an undertone, "Don't mind the colonel; open out and let them [the roundshot] through, keep plenty of room and watch the shot."'[15] (William MacBean won the Victoria Cross at Lucknow; Alexander Leith Hay had entered the army in 1835 when tactical practice was virtually Napoleonic.)

The 1859 infantry manual retained the eight-company establishment of an infantry battalion (changed only in 1913), but following the abolition of 'flank companies' in 1858 the existing practice was formalised, that all companies should be capable of acting as light infantry in skirmish order. The pace of manoeuvre was increased from 108 to 110 paces per minute, and greater use was made of 'double time' (150 paces per minute) which had hitherto been authorised only for skirmishers. Although close-order drill persisted, manoeuvres were performed over greater distances to take account of enhanced range of improved firearms (about 900 yards' effective range with the Enfield, as against 100–150 yards with the 'Brown Bess'). In skirmishing, for example, the first line of skirmishers in open order would precede their support (a body of equal strength) by 200 yards, where terrain permitted; 300 yards behind them would be the reserve (no

Maxim machine-gun on wheeled carriage, crewed by seamen from HMS Excellent at Whale Island, c.1895.

less than one-third of the deployed strength), itself 500 yards in advance of the main body, giving a distance of 1,000 yards between skirmish-line and main body. The ability to engage at longer range was especially useful when confronted by an enemy whose favoured tactic was to rush in to hand-to-hand combat, and it permitted smaller, mobile forces to engage such an enemy without incurring great risk, providing the terrain were suitable. As George Cruikshank remarked,

"*Long range*" that fires and runs away,
Will live to fire another day;
But "short shot", that's in the battle slain,
Will never rise to fire again.'[16]

Against an enemy in heavy bush, or one using 'ambush' tactics, the increase of effective range was of limited significance; but in such circumstances the enhanced rate of fire, from 2–3 rounds per minute to as much as 10rpm with breech-loaders, could be decisive.

Operations under such conditions, with skirmishers operating at a considerable distance from the main body, necessitated a greater ability among company officers and even NCOs, who had to be capable of making decisions as required by the circumstances of the moment, without the opportunity of reference to higher authority.

From the later 1870s at least, the practice of attack and defence in depth became more flexible to allow for variations in circumstances and terrain. The original principles remained: that a force should be divided into three 'layers' one behind the other, and a considerable distance apart, with the first or 'firing line' itself divided into three, including immediate supports and reserve (the latter to be fed into the front line as necessary), to lay down such a fusillade that the second line could charge with the bayonet and rout an enemy thus unsteadied by musketry.

The second line's attack might be made partly on the frontage occupied by the first line, or more effectively against a flank. For an eight-company battalion it was advised that the firing-line should be composed of two companies, the second line of two companies about 180 yards behind, and the remaining four in reserve, about 300 yards further back. Ordinary pace was increased to 120 paces per minute, and 'double time' to 165. In defence, the first line would attempt to hold the enemy advance, and the second be used as a reinforcement, or to cover the flanks. In attack, the third line was to exploit the victory, or cover the retreat of the first and second lines in the event of a reverse; and in defence to deliver a counter-attack should the enemy break through the forward lines. The application of this theory varied according to circumstance, terrain, and nature of the enemy; it was remarked, for example, that there was less reason for employing a dispersed formation if the enemy were unable to reply with an equal volume of musketry. With an enemy intent upon close-quarter action, a conventional firing-line might not be able to lay down a sufficient fusillade to hold them, and might be overpowered by a determined rush; in such circumstances, an old-fashioned, close-order formation capable of delivering the maximum volume of fire would be more effective than deployment in depth. In attacks with the bayonet, it was similarly important to field the maximum force to so overawe the enemy that they would give way before actual contact. In mountainous terrain it might be necessary to deploy companies individually to hold dominating heights; yet in a more general attack it was recommended that supports and reserve be deployed only a short distance from the firing-line, so that when the high ground was taken, the entire force could be assembled quickly into a single line to lay down the maximum fire upon the retreating enemy.

The technique of advancing in dispersed order also varied with circumstance, but it was emphasised that maximum advantage should be taken of cover, provided that it did not interfere with order or cohesion. For tactical purposes each company was divided into two half-companies (commanded by subalterns), and each half-company into two sections (commanded by sergeants). As an advance approached the enemy, uniform forward movement would be replaced by 'rushes' of 30–50-yard bursts made by half-companies or sections, which would be covered during their advance by the fire of the remainder; who would then rush forward in their turn. Although in larger formations it was possible to use an entire brigade as a reserve, latterly it was usual for units to deploy in depth, rather than have a unit or sub-unit employed exclusively in a lateral fashion. For example, if an eight-company battalion mounted an attack, six companies might be deployed in line, each company with three sections in the firing-line and its supports, with the fourth section held back as the immediate reserve. The general reserve would comprise the remaining two companies. Thus, the supports fed into the firing-line would be members of the same company as originally in the line, knowing their own officers and NCOs, instead of having members of several companies mixed up throughout the line. As the general reserve would normally act independently, to exploit a breakthrough or make a counter-attack, its strength would not have been reduced by feeding men into the first two lines. In such operations, fire would often be delivered kneeling or prone, or standing only to fire, to maximise cover and reduce the size of the target. It was also important that troops capturing the crest of high ground should immediately throw themselves down, so as not to present a silhouetted target to the enemy. Against enemies not possessed of efficient firearms, the old shoulder-to-shoulder deployment was still effective, as demonstrated at Omdurman, where close-order formations using breech-loading rifles opened fire at 2,000 yards, so that few Dervishes approached nearer than about 800 yards before they were shot. In this case, battalions were deployed with all men in the firing-line, providing the maximum volume of musketry, less two companies per battalion held in reserve for use in the event of an enemy breakthrough.

In most circumstances, the effectiveness of firearms was crucial. To some extent this was dependent upon the technology of the weapon, not just the skill with which it was used, volume of fire sometimes being more important than the accuracy of the individual weapon. This was demonstrated at Omdurman where British magazine rifles stopped the enemy at 800 yards, whereas the Egyptians with single-shot Martinis stopped their opponents at 500 yards, such was the difference in fire which could be laid upon a charging enemy. Marksmanship was taught and

encouraged, but normally firing continued to be delivered in volleys, generally by section, except at close range when the order for independent firing might be given. Maintenance of fire-discipline was paramount (one reason for the use of volley-fire on command), and a tendency to fire too quickly in action was noted, a slower, deliberate and better-aimed fire being more effective; so, as Emilius De Cosson remarked, the officers' main employment was to prevent the too rapid expenditure of ammunition (in the hottest action he lit and smoked his pipe, presumably to exude an appearance of calm). It was also regarded as important to avoid premature firing, to reserve fire until an attacking enemy was within closer range, so that more of them would be hit before they decided to withdraw.

An important factor in the effectiveness of musketry was the correct estimation of distance. A bullet did not fly upon a level trajectory, but was affected by gravity during its flight, and the arcing trajectory which had to be used varied according to rifle, projectile and range. To hit a target at 700 yards, for example, firing over even ground, a Martini-Henry bullet had to describe an arc of which the highest point was more than twenty feet above ground level; the same for a Lee-Enfield was ten feet. When sweeping an area with volley-fire, the bullets would fly in an imaginary cone-shaped trajectory, the 'cone of dispersion', the ground upon which the bullets fell being termed the 'beaten zone', which decreased in size as the target became more distant. Between the edge of the 'beaten zone' and the marksman was the 'dangerous space', the area in which the lowest bullet of a volley would strike a man as it dropped, between head-height and the ground. This varied with the height of the target: at 1,000 yards, for example, the 'dangerous space' for a mounted man would be 105 yards, but for a prone man only thirteen yards. So accurate gauging of distance was paramount; although rifle-sights were calibrated, the whole process relied upon correct instructions being given to enable the sights to be set correctly. The difficulty of making such assessments resulted in the use of 'combined sights', in which different groups fired at the same target with rifles variously sighted, to ensure that *some* shots hit the target; this also permitted a greater extent of terrain to be swept, even though a proportion of shots would inevitably miss. A sustained fire of perhaps five shots per minute was advocated, with bursts of rapid fire interspersed, sometimes directed upon a particular target; with short breaks to allow the fire-controller to assess the effect and perhaps switch to another target.

Such tactics were suitable for the open field, but had to be varied according to circumstance. In hill warfare, for example, it was found that volley-firing was largely useless, and that it was more effective for men to fire independently, selecting their own targets; this was especially true in regions like the North-West Frontier, where the target was either an individual or a small party, usually at least partially concealed. Independent fire had another advantage before the advent of smokeless powder: it was noted that those targeted were able to duck behind cover upon seeing the smoke of a volley – although it was thought that volley-firing kept a unit steadier than firing at will. Even after the advent of rifles capable of great accuracy, standards of marksmanship and training were criticised; in 1885 it was remarked that against a moving target, and with men having to gauge range for themselves, 'you will not find ten men in a hundred who will hit a haystack'.[17]

The bayonet was still recommended as a vital weapon at close quarters: 'Apart from fanatics and from exceptionally brave savages like the Zulus, irregular warriors, be they Pathan hill-men or Somalis or Boxers or Boers, have no stomach for the infantryman's cold steel.'[18] As before, a bayonet-charge was used as the final incentive to the enemy to run away, having already been mauled by musketry; indeed, a charge should not have been delivered until the enemy were believed to have been on the point of breaking. In defence, a rapid bayonet-charge was regarded as the quickest method of repelling an enemy break-through; and it still played an important role in combat in confined spaces and in the storming of fortifications.

An action conducted on ideal lines, and embodying many of the features noted above, was described by Lieutenant Charles Grant, VC, who in March 1891, with 50 men of the 2nd Burmah Battalion and 30 of the 43rd Gurkhas, attacked more than 800 troops of the Manipuri army, many armed with better weapons than the Sniders of the 2nd Burmah (only the Gurkhas carried the superior Martini):

'My men were in fighting formation. Ten my men 2nd Burmah Battalion of Punjaub Infantry (new name), and ten Ghoorkas in firing line at six paces interval between each man, and twenty my men in support 100 yards rear of flanks in single rank, and twenty my men and twenty Ghoorkas reserve, baggage guard 300 yards in rear with elephants, and thirty followers of the Ghoorkas (Khasias, from Shillong Hills). We opened volleys by sections (ten men) and then advanced, one section firing a volley while the other rushed forward thirty paces, threw themselves down on ground, and fired a volley, on which the other section did likewise. Thus we reached 100 yards from the enemy, where we lay for about five minutes, firing at the only thing we could see, puffs of smoke from the enemy's loop-holes, and covered with the dust of their bullets. I had seen one man clean killed at my side, and had felt a sharp flick under arm, and began to think we were in for about as much as we could manage; but the men were behaving splendidly, firing carefully and well directed. I signalled the supports to come up wide on each flank; they came with a splendid rush and never stopped on joining the firing line, but went clean on to the bank of the river, within sixty yards of the enemy, lying down and firing at their heads, which could now be seen as they raised them to fire; then the for-

mer firing line jumped up and we rushed into the water. I was first in, but not first out, as I got in up to my neck and had to be helped out and got across nearer to the bridge, the men fixing bayonets in the water. The enemy now gave way and ran away all along, but we bayoneted eight in the trenches on the right, found six shot through the head behind the compound wall. At the second line of walls they tried to rally, but our men on the right soon changed their minds, and on they went and never stopped till they got behind the hills on top of the map; our advance and their retreat was just as if you rolled one ruler after another up the page on which the map is.'[19]

A feature of a number of colonial campaigns was the use of the square. At the beginning of the 19th century the square was usually small, generally battalion-sized, formed in close order to present a hedge of bayonets on all four sides, the infantry's principal defence against cavalry attack. The concept of the 'fighting square' or square for movement, as used later in the century, was the most effective way of forming a defensible perimeter, to shelter the more vulnerable parts of an army; whereas the battalion square could have a frontage as small as the space occupied by fifty men, standing shoulder-to-shoulder, the later type could be enormous. The square formed by the force advancing on Tamai in the Suakin campaign (2 April 1885), for example, occupied in excess of twenty acres. Its front face of some 200 yards was composed of three companies of Coldstream Guards, and its rear face was formed by the 15th Sikhs. The flanks were some 500 yards in length, the right flank composed of the Scots Guards, the East Surrey Regiment and the 28th Bombay Native Infantry, and the left of five Coldstream companies, a detachment of Royal Marines, and the King's Shropshire Light Infantry. This enormous oblong was filled almost to bursting with artillery (324 men), mountain guns, rocket troop, four Gardner guns, two field hospitals, eight ambulance wagons, regimental water-carts, animal transport including 1,639 camels and 930 mules, dhoolie bearers, 1,773 'followers' attending the transport, some 200 commissariat and transport personnel, two companies of Royal Engineers and some 40 staff officers. Four companies of the New South Wales Contingent were originally inside the square, but subsequently were brought into the line to make the square even larger. Only the cavalry was not contained within it, being deployed as scouts and skirmishers outside the front and flanks. A square of this nature could be termed 'elastic', as opposed to the 'rigid' close-order battalion square.

An extension of the concept of the square was the *zareba*, a defensive perimeter constructed from thorn or other bushes, forming a breastwork to prevent an enemy charge reaching hand-to-hand range unchecked. A *zareba* did not necessarily require every foot of it to be defended, especially if it had to be made sufficiently large to accommodate pack-animals and transport within it; but for additional security, smaller fortified posts might be constructed within or beside a larger *zareba*, or provide a refuge if the main 'wall' were breached. For example, the *zareba* which was so fiercely assaulted at Tofrek (22 March 1885) before it had been completed, was intended to measure some 120 yards square (thus enclosing almost three acres), but had smaller squares constructed at opposite corners, some 75 and 65 yards square, which were used as strong points, with fields of fire covering both outside and inside the larger *zareba*.

As in earlier campaigns, the square was only of use against an enemy determined to engage in hand-to-hand combat, for it was most vulnerable against an enemy able to concentrate fire against such a tightly-packed target. Against an enemy armed primarily with edged weapons, however, the square of all sizes was of great value. For example, reverting to the action at Tofrek: a half-battalion of the Berkshire Regiment was caught outside the *zareba* when the attack began; they formed a 'rallying square', a closely-packed formation with all-round defence, and firing slowly and with effect, drove off every attack. More than 200 enemy were later found dead around the square; the Berkshires suffered only one man wounded, by a spear flung by an assailant who had run within range before being shot. As the attack receded, the half-battalion retired into the *zareba*, hoisting helmets on rifle-muzzles to indicate through the smoke to the defenders of the *zareba* that they were not enemies.

Laagered wagons could be used in a similar manner to a *zareba*, in defining a defensive perimeter, or for use as a mobile fort from which troops could operate in the open field, a secure base into which they could withdraw if necessary. Laagers could be arranged in a number of styles, sometimes more than one being formed to provide mutually supporting fire; in addition to a simple barricade of wagons, sometimes chained together, refinements could include shelter-trenches, *zarebas* or fences of thorn-bushes, and gun-positions at the angles. Draught-animals were normally secured within the perimeter.

The advent of long-range fire resulted in wide dispersion of forces when both sides were equipped with modern firearms; indeed, the concept of 'the empty battlefield' was established by the time of the South African War of 1899–1902. Mortimer Menpes, attempting to sketch battle-scenes at first hand, observed hardly anything: 'I saw no fight – that was all miles away – yet I was in the thick of a battle ... And so it has been all through this modern warfare: you can't honestly paint a battle-scene nowadays. You see very little of the fighting. You see the effects of a battle, men mangled and villages destroyed; but as to seeing the enemy, that is an absolute impossibility, even through a telescope. The saying is quite true that a modern battle reduced itself to one man and a puff of smoke – or rather one man and no smoke, the powder being smokeless.'[20]

Cavalry

The role of the cavalry in colonial warfare was considerably limited, both by the small size of the available force, and by the lack of opportunity to employ it in the European manner. In few campaigns was the cavalry able to perform its traditional 'shock' action, in the execution of a decisive charge, which under favourable circumstances could be devastating; but the capability remained, and one of the most famous cavalry charges was executed at the very end of the 19th century, by the 21st Lancers at Omdurman, in which Winston Churchill rode. This was, however, an exception to the cavalry's usual employment. By the post-Napoleonic period, the tactical difference between supposedly 'heavy' and 'light' regiments was negligible; all were expected to be capable of offensive action in the charge, as well as reconnaissance and skirmishing and in furnishing the flank-, rear- and vanguards of an army. Although regimental-sized operations remained possible, units could operate effectively as semi-independent sub-units, in squadrons or troops. The traditional offensive role was presumably why Sir Baker Russell (who commanded the 13th Hussars 1880–5 and from whom the regiment took its nickname 'Baker's Dozen'!) remarked that the duty of cavalry was to look smart in peacetime and get killed in wartime. For 'shock' action the principal weapon remained the sabre, which was improved progressively from the unwieldy patterns used during the Napoleonic Wars to a weapon capable of executing both cut and thrust; although it was not until 1908 that an ideal weapon was issued, suitable for thrusting only, the most lethal blow, by which date the cavalry sabre was redundant. The lance was carried by regiments designated as lancers, and from 1892 by the front rank of all regiments (it was discontinued as a combat weapon in 1903, only to be re-introduced universally in 1909), and while of use in attacking squares (the 16th Lancers were spectacularly successful at Aliwal) and broken infantry who could be pursued and speared, the lance could be an

John R. Harvey, who enlisted in the 16th Lancers in 1882 as a 'gentleman-ranker' before he was granted a commission, recalled receiving instruction on how a British soldier should comport himself:
'I was informed that I could now safely be trusted outside without danger of getting entangled with my own legs, or tripping myself or others up with my spurs; in fact I was supposed to "know how to walk". The drill instructor dismissed me with the following injunction – "Now, from this time you will be allowed out of barracks, and don't let me see you go slinking along with a hump on your back, but 'throw a chest' and swagger down the street as if you had five pounds in your pocket, and didn't care a damn for anyone – even if you haven't a penny to your name."'

encumbrance in a mêlée; it is interesting to note that in the pursuit of the Zulus after Ulundi, the 17th Lancers used their lances only in the initial contact, most continuing the fight with the sabre instead. Cavalry firearms were initially of negligible value, but the introduction of breech-loading carbines enabled the cavalry to adopt a more effective role in skirmishing.

The 1869 cavalry regulations continued to concentrate on 'shock' action, and to recommend the pattern of attack defined by the Duke of Wellington in 1815: a first line of about one-third of the whole; a second body some 400 yards in the rear, in line or column, to act as a support for the first; and a reserve (never less than one-third of the whole) a further 400 yards back, in column, to exploit a victory or cover the retreat of the forward lines. Discipline and the essential necessity of rallying immediately after a charge was vital. The 1874 cavalry regulations paid greater attention to skirmishing, not as chiefly done originally from horseback, but with greater emphasis upon dismounted action. Even so, dismounted service and reconnaissance were not popular with some senior cavalry commanders, and the ability of regiments to perform these duties was patchy. As the opportunity for 'traditional' cavalry actions declined, so those which did occur (like the 'moonlight charge' at Kassassin or the 21st's at Omdurman) were publicised out of proportion to the frequency of such services.

Only after their carbines had been replaced by rifles was dismounted cavalry fully effective, and on occasion only experience led to changes of practice, sometimes adopted on campaign and without official sanction. Lord Roberts, for example, wrote of the difficulties of dismounted service in Afghanistan in 1879, when the cavalry was '... much impeded by their long boots and their swords dangling between their legs; the sight, indeed, of [unhorsed] Cavalry soldiers trying to defend themselves on foot without a firearm confirmed the opinion I had formed during the Mutiny, as to the desirability of the carbine being slung on the man's back when going into action ... during the remainder of the campaign the men of the 9th Lancers placed their carbines on their backs whenever the enemy were reported to be in sight. At the same time I authorised the adoption of an arrangement ... by which the sword was fastened to the saddle instead of round the man's body ... in 1891 an order was issued sanctioning its adoption by all mounted troops.'[21]

The comparative paucity of numbers of regular cavalry led to the employment of local forces or *ad hoc* formations. The Indian Army provided the necessary mounted troops in that country, but alternatives were needed elsewhere; in New Zealand, for example, members of the Military Train and Royal Artillery were employed in a cavalry role, and locally raised forces were used in South Africa, where units like the Cape Mounted Rifles were not so much a poor substitute for regular cavalry but actually of more use,

being used to the country and its conditions. Such units helped initiate the formation of mounted infantry.

The concept of mounted infantry was not new: troops trained to act as infantry but using horses to give them the mobility of cavalry were like the dragoons of the 17th century, but the idea was re-developed in the later 19th century. As early as 1796–1802 the 91st had a mounted company at the Cape, for example, but one of the first serious mounted infantry organisations was created in South Africa in 1875 by Lieutenant Carrington of the 1/24th, who formed a small mounted infantry company with horses he purchased himself. Detachments from this battalion and the 88th were employed in the Frontier War of 1877–8, and in the latter year Carrington created the Imperial Mounted Infantry, two 150-strong squadrons formed from four line battalions, with a number of Basutos attached as scouts. The practice spread from South Africa to Egypt and Burma, and included the employment of camel-borne infantry in the Desert Column of the Gordon Relief Expedition. From 1888 training schools for mounted infantry were established at Aldershot and the Currah; by 1896 150 officers and 4,000 men had been trained at the former. After training, the men returned to their units, enabling battalions on foreign service to maintain a mounted infantry company capable of acting independently or combining with others to form a battalion. In 1898 a manual was issued and the establishment of a battalion was regulated, and it was ordered that two MI companies be attached to each cavalry brigade.

Such formations were found to be so valuable that during the later stages of the South African War, mounted infantry became a dominant force in the army: there were eventually 28 battalions, usually of four companies each, drawn from the infantry, and the same role was adopted by local forces (the entire battalion of Kaffrarian Rifles, for example, was converted to mounted infantry in 1900), Imperial Yeomanry and the colonial contingents. Some of the latter, for example the Australians, were composed of backwoodsmen for whom mounted infantry service was merely an extension of their everyday life, and thus were ideally suited for such duty.

Although the best mounted infantry became extremely proficient in anti-guerrilla operations in South Africa, they were often at a disadvantage when compared to the Boer commandos: in some cases their marksmanship and horsemanship were inferior to that of the Boers, and they were at a numerical disadvantage by having to employ one-quarter of their men as horse-holders in action, whereas the Boer horses were trained to stand unattended. The innovative nature of mounted infantry service did not always find a commander appreciative of their merits: for example, it was said that at Magersfontein an Australian officer offered to take his two squadrons around to the Boer rear to dislodge their riflemen, to which Methuen replied that 'That is not fair war,' (!) and that such tactics might tempt the Boers to do likewise and cut his communications.[22] Despite the success of mounted infantry in the South African War, supporters of the cavalry argued that while the cavalry could perform mounted infantry duty, the latter could not charge effectively, having neither sword nor lance; an example was provided by the pursuit of the Zulus after Kambula, when the mounted riflemen picked up assegais to use as lances. Even though the smaller and often hardier ponies used by mounted infantry were generally easier to keep fit than the larger cavalry horses, the mounted infantry concept was regarded as less useful in Europe than in colonial warfare, and by 1914 they were virtually extinct.

Artillery

Employment of artillery was originally like that in European conflicts, and although the Company's artillery in India was generally adequate in quantity, elsewhere artillery was often in short supply, leading to its supplement by naval landing-parties and ordnance brought ashore from ships. Guns were of limited use in guerrilla-style operations, but were invaluable when faced by fortifications, for example the New Zealand *pa*s.

In the early 19th century artillery tactics drew away from the piecemeal deployment of guns and towards the use of larger concentration of fire, which was believed to have greater effect than the sum of its parts; although the often limited amount of ordnance available to British commanders generally precluded the assembly of 'massed batteries' employed by some European armies. Usually artillery fire was directed against enemy troops, counter-battery fire (against the enemy artillery) generally being regarded as a waste of ammunition.

Tactics adopted against the Sikhs adumbrated the later style of heavy bombardment as the prelude to an advance. So powerful was the Sikh artillery that latterly it was found necessary to mount a bombardment before and during the infantry attack, and sufficient ordnance was available: at Gujerat, where the offensive power of artillery was demonstrated, some 86 guns were employed. Significantly, these included a strong force of heavy ordnance (ten 18pdrs and ten 8in howitzers) positioned centrally, with the lighter guns on the flanks and advancing with the army as part of a concerted effort. The bombardment was deliberate and prolonged over three hours; average ammunition-expenditure ranged from about 26 rounds per hour from the 6- and 18pdrs to 9rph from the 8in howitzers, considerably below the theoretical maximum rate of fire. For all the protection of fieldworks and the proficiency of their own gunners, the Sikh army was so shattered that when the British advanced only a quarter of the battalions present had to fire a shot. Gough remarked that 'The cannonade now opened upon the enemy was the most magnificent I ever witnessed, and as terrible in its effects ... To Brigadier-General Tennant, commanding that splendid arm, the artillery, to whose irresistible power I am mainly indebted for the glorious victory of Goojerat, I am indeed most grateful ... never was its superiority over that of the enemy, its irresistible and annihilating power, more truthfully shown than in this battle. The heavy batteries manoeuvred with the celerity of light guns; and the rapid advance, with scientific and judicious selection of points of attack ... merit my warmest praise.'[23]

Battery organisation remained reasonably standard, each company or horse artillery troop operating six pieces of ordnance, with one gun, limber, ammunition-wagon and crew forming a 'subdivision', which usually operated in pairs; the incorporation of howitzers in each battery ended with the advent of rifled guns. The greatly enhanced range of these weapons allowed effective fire to be executed at greater distances, but in many colonial campaigns the artillery was sufficiently limited in quantity that most

Screw-guns': a battery of mountain artillery in India.

had to be used to provide immediate fire-support for the infantry, rather than as a decisive force in its own right. The development of mountain guns enabled such support to be provided in terrain which would otherwise have precluded the employment of artillery, although their range and striking-power was often restricted. The increased capabilities of ordnance resulted in changes in tactics; for example, the 1875 artillery manual gave battery-commanders the freedom to determine their own actions, rather than being tied to the infantry or cavalry which they were supporting; and the fitting of seats on the guns greatly enhanced manoeuvrability, with gunners all riding on the battery vehicles, so that field artillery was no longer restricted to the speed of a marching man. Nevertheless, despite the innovations, for some colonial campaigns the earlier style of employment had to be retained: against an enemy with a penchant for mass attack and hand-to-hand combat, the security of artillery required the close co-operation of infantry for protection. This was exemplified at Maiwand, where E/B battery RHA was left to face the Afghans alone, and was almost overrun before it limbered-up and withdrew, leaving one section in Afghan hands. In some circumstances, excluding the very mobile type of artillery such as that carried on mule-back, guns could limit an army's freedom of movement over difficult terrain; Gordon remarked especially on this, and even attributed Hicks' defeat partly to his being burdened with artillery.

Improvements in ordnance towards the end of the 19th century caused a further revision in tactics, towards the assembly of larger concentrations of artillery, piecemeal infantry support being replaced by co-ordinated fire; a 'brigade' of three batteries was allocated to each infantry division and was intended to fire *en masse*, providing a bombardment of considerable power. In Afghanistan the field-gun had been found largely ineffective against buildings and entrenchments, so the howitzer was re-introduced, not integrated as before but in separate batteries. The deployment of guns in concentration during the South African War was not always as effective as intended: targeting was made difficult by the often dispersed deployment adopted by the Boers, and the absence of protective shields on gun-carriages left crews and teams vulnerable to the extended range of Boer musketry.

The revised tactics made infantry support depend upon the lighter artillery and machine-guns. The former were the mountain batteries, carried on mule-back and thus able to accompany infantry over virtually any terrain; although batteries consisted of six guns, it was common for them to operate in two-gun sections, which could be managed better in mountainous terrain, cover and suitable firing positions often being more easily found for two guns than for a whole battery. The early machine-guns, manned by naval or artillery crews, were used initially as a form of light artillery; but from 1891 Maxim guns were introduced into the cavalry and infantry, manned by

members of the unit, initially on a scale of one per battalion or cavalry regiment. Perhaps because of the unreliability of the early machine-guns, they were regarded as support weapons rather than as a primary force as they became in the First World War, hence the low allocation to each unit (although Mounted Infantry formations had two-gun sections). That their potential was not always appreciated would seem to be confirmed by a remark of 1899, that while useful they were actually an auxiliary which should not become 'a burden or a hindrance',[24] and that no special protection should be accorded them. Machine-guns were often combined in two-gun sections under the direction of the brigade or divisional commander, and to maximise enemy casualties concentrated enfilade fire upon the point of attack was recommended, although in general it was believed that they were more use in defence, for securing a flank or important position, than in attack. Cavalry guns, however, were intended to gallop forward and rake the target of a cavalry attack, continuing to fire until masked by their own advance; it was believed their major importance was in the provision of sufficient fire-support that cavalry need not dismount part of their strength for rifle-firing. It was also recommended that no more than two guns be employed together, to minimise vulnerability to artillery-fire.

In colonial operations, it was believed that restrictions applied to the employment of machine-guns: that in mountainous terrain they had little chance of hitting individual marksmen, and although light artillery could be used to some effect in bush-fighting, the close range at which such combat took place made the machine-gunners too easy a target. Again emphasis was placed upon the defensive use of machine-guns, in strategic places in laagers, sangars or *zarebas*, and for repelling mass attacks, which might unsteady infantry but against which machine-guns would maintain their fire automatically. However, the early guns were so unreliable, delicate and easily-damaged (and even Maxims over-heated at Omdurman), that Charles Callwell articulated what was probably a common view, that unreliable machine-guns were worse than none at all, for if undue confidence were placed upon a 'broken reed' which failed at a critical moment, 'its presence with the force may have done incalculable harm'.[25] Nevertheless, even the unreliable earlier guns could play an important psychological role, in stiffening the resolution of those who possessed them, and in undermining the morale of the enemy.

Higher Tactics

Colonial campaigns included features and hazards not applicable in more conventional warfare, some simply the consequence of the terrain over which campaigns were conducted. In addition to the ammunition and rations which had to be transported in both European and colonial campaigns, in the latter additional provision often had to be made for the carriage of animal-fodder and drinking-water, involving considerable logistic effort. The maintenance of lines of communication was of crucial significance to all but the smallest expeditions, not only for the security of supply-routes but for the evacuation of casualties, for unlike European conflict the injured could rarely be left to the mercy of the enemy to treat. Their preservation from deliberate butchery was not only a matter of humanity, but their abandonment would have had an adverse effect upon morale. The need to protect the wounded and lines of communication was expensive in resources, but the detachment of troops for such duty was an absolute necessity.

Another feature of colonial campaigns concerned the nature of forces employed. Usually only limited numbers of British troops were available, so that most forces were formed of local troops around a British nucleus; and although some local corps were so experienced as to be more efficient than an equivalent number of British troops (for example the Cape Mounted Rifles in South Africa, or elements of the Indian Army used to the conditions of the Frontier), in many cases they were regarded as less reliable than the British, often with good reason. For example, even though grossly outnumbered and outgunned, had all Burrows' force at Maiwand been as steadfast as his one British battalion, the outcome might well have been different. From the earliest period in India, it was the practice that a European battalion should be in the centre of the line-of-battle between two sepoy battalions, so that the Europeans should provide the maximum steadying influence; and especially after the Mutiny it was common for British units to be integrated, generally at brigade level, to raise the calibre of the whole. (This practice was not restricted to colonial warfare: it was demonstrated perhaps most clearly by the incorporation of Portuguese brigades into Wellington's Peninsula divisions, and the same general's disposition of his 'infamous army' with its small British nucleus in 1815.) For example, the infantry of the Kabul–Kandahar Field Force was organised in this manner:

1st Brigade: 92nd Highlanders, 23rd Pioneers, 24th Punjab Native Infantry, 2nd Gurkhas.
2nd Brigade: 72nd Highlanders, 2nd and 3rd Sikh Infantry, 5th Gurkhas.
3rd Brigade: 2/60th Rifles, 15th Sikhs, 25th Punjab Native Infantry, 4th Gurkhas.

Some tactical considerations were dictated by the nature of the enemy. Never experienced in European warfare, but encountered in colonial actions, was the suicidal bravery of religious fanaticism. William Forbes-Mitchell recounted a furious charge by green-clad Ghazis during the Indian Mutiny, who were recognised as such, Sir Colin Campbell calling to the 93rd and 42nd, 'Ghazis! Ghazis! Close up the ranks! Bayonet them as they come on!' So determined was this attack that no prisoners could be taken, and in a few moments 133 lay dead in front of the 42nd's Colours, after a fight in which the 42nd lost only about twenty men wounded, so wildly had the Ghazis thrown themselves upon the Highlanders' bayonets.[26] The British emphasis upon rapid attack has already been noted, and continued throughout the period of colonial warfare. An allied factor which also influenced the conduct of warfare was the reluctance even to appear to be withdrawing; because, as Wolseley remarked, 'every retrograde step is regarded by uncivilised races as a sign of weakness and fear'.[27]

In many cases of British reverse or costly victory, it is perhaps less accurate to blame the prevailing military system

A vital means of communication in many colonial campaigns: the heliograph. Sergeant-Major W. Beard instructs signallers in the use of the 12in heliograph at India's Central School of Army Signalling at Kasauli. A smaller (5in) heliograph is seen at the right; the seated men are watching for the reply, using telescopes.

than those who interpreted it; for some were the result of failures in command. For example, it was obvious to many at the time that Gough's frontal attacks on strong Sikh positions would cause severe casualties, just as it was obvious to regimental officers that Colley's tactics at Laing's Nek were doomed to failure; his actions at Majuba almost defy explanation, yet he was one of the militarily best-educated commanders in the army. The scattered deployment adopted at Isandlwana was perhaps the only formation which could have allowed the Zulus to win; a laagered position, as used by Evelyn Wood later in the campaign, and an adequate supply of ammunition would probably have held them in check. The Highland Brigade suffered so severely at Magersfontein by advancing in closely packed formation, to help retain order in a nocturnal march, and was caught before it could deploy into open order for attack; and the fate of the 5th (Irish) Brigade at Colenso was the result of a similar formation, when Major-General Arthur Hart deployed his leading battalion (2/Royal Dublin Fusiliers) in line of companies in fours, with the remaining three battalions in quarter- columns behind, a formation suicidally compact when facing well-positioned Boer marksmen. The resulting carnage was

compounded by the supporting artillery, which drew up in line within rifle-range, and only two guns out of twelve could be extricated.

The main principle of tactics in colonial campaigns was probably the necessity to adapt to the nature of the terrain and the enemy, which was not always achieved. The prescribed 'system' was frequently inappropriate; for example, infantry formation in three 'waves' was often unnecessary, as few 'tribal' enemies retained their own reserves, partially obviating the necessity of a British third line, only a reserve to block any breakthrough of the firing-line. Sometimes the enemy could be dispersed by no more than the first line of skirmishers; at other times a unit's entire firepower was required to stop a determined charge. In terrain most suitable for guerrilla actions, the problem was less one of defeating the enemy than bringing them to battle; in such cases the priority was to outmanoeuvre the enemy and cut their line of retreat, so that British superior firepower could destroy them. Given the arduous and varied conditions in which campaigns were waged, it is perhaps less surprising that the British suffered some reverses than the fact that, despite the failings of some commanders, the army proved to be as adaptable as it did.

Notes

1. Callwell, C. E. *Small Wars: Their Principle and Practice*, London, 1906, p. 21.
2. Baden-Powell, Lieutenant-General Sir Robert. *Indian Memories*, London, 1915, pp. 205–6.
3. *Chambers Edinburgh Journal*, 23 October 1847.
4. *United Service Magazine*, 1842, vol. III, p. 289.
5. Alexander, Sir James. 'On Bush-Fighting', in *United Service Magazine*, 1842, vol. III, p. 355.
6. 'A Few Hints on the Education of Candidates for the British Army', by 'Once a Cadet and Student of the Senior Department of the Military College', in *United Service Magazine*, 1842, vol. III, p. 590.
7. Pester, J. *War and Sport in India 1802-1806: An Officer's Diary*, ed. J. Devenish, London, nd, p. 174.
8. *United Service Journal*, 1839, vol. III, p. 421.
9. 'Campaigning in India', by 'a late non-commissioned officer of the 13th Light Dragoons', in *Colburn's United Service Magazine*, 1844, vol. I, p. 530.
10. To Colonel Stevenson, 17 August 1803; *Dispatches of Field Marshal the Duke of Wellington*, ed. J. Gurwood, London, 1834–8, vol. II, p. 210.
11. Hodson, W. S. R. *Twelve Years of a Soldier's Life in India*, ed. Revd. G. H. Hodson, London, 1859, p. 245.
12. Lumsden, General Sir Peter, and Elsmie, G. R. *Lumsden of the Guides*, London, 1899, p. 39.
13. Baden-Powell, Lieutenant-General Sir Robert. *The Matabele Campaign 1896*, London, 1900, pp. 23–4.
14. *Colburn's United Service Magazine*, 1844, vol. I, p. 617.
15. Forbes-Mitchell, W. *Reminiscences of the Great Mutiny 1857–59*, London, 1897, p. 40.
16. *A Pop-Gun fired off by George Cruikshank in Defence of the British Volunteers of 1803, against the Uncivil Attack upon that Body by General W. Napier*, London, nd, p. 27.
17. De Cosson, Major E. A. *Days and Nights of Service with Sir Gerald Graham's Field Force at Suakin*, London, 1886, p. 23.
18. Callwell, *op. cit.*, p. 399.
19. Grimwood, E. St. C. *My Three Years in Manipur*, London, 1891, pp. 291–3.
20. Menpes, M. *War Impressions*, London, 1901, p. 78.
21. Field Marshal Lord Roberts of Kandahar. *Forty-One Years in India*, London, 1900, p. 437.
22. Quoted in 'The Battle of Magersfontein, 1899', in *Journal of the Society for Army Historical Research*, 1941, vol. XX, p. 200.
23. Gough's dispatch, 26 February 1849, *London Gazette*, 19 April 1849.
24. Grierson, J. M. *The British Army*, 'by a Lieutenant-Colonel', London, 1899, p. 147.
25. Callwell, C. *op. cit.*, p. 440.
26. Forbes-Mitchell, *op. cit.*, pp. 255–6.
27. Wolseley's dispatch, 1 March 1885.

References (see also 'Great Britain')

Alexander, Major-General Sir James. *Bush Fighting: Illustrated by Remarkable Actions and Incidents of the Maori War in New Zealand*, London, 1873.
Barthorp, M. *The British Army on Campaign 1816-1902*, London, 1987–8 (four-part work covering campaigns, uniform and equipment, but also a good guide to tactical developments; Part I 1816-53, Part II the Crimea 1854–6, Part III 1856–81, Part IV 1882–1902).
Callwell, Colonel C. E. (later Major-General Sir Charles). *Small Wars: Their Principles and Practice*, London, 1896; the 1906 revised edn. was reprinted as *Small Wars: A Tactical Textbook for Imperial Soldiers*, intro. by Colonel P. S. Walton, London, 1990 (very significant study on colonial warfare).
Hughes, Major-General B. P. *Firepower: Weapons Effectiveness on the Battlefield 1630-1850*, London, 1974 (includes the Sikh Wars).
Strachan, H. *From Waterloo to Balaclava: Tactics, Technology and the British Army 1815-1854*, Cambridge, 1985 (very significant study with comprehensive bibliography).
Younghusband, Captain G. J. *Indian Frontier Warfare*, London, 1898 (as much tactical as historical, comparing aspects of frontier warfare with those in Europe; for example, likening the Charasia operation to the tactics of Frederick the Great, and the pacification of Burma to the methods used by Hoche to suppress revolt in the Vendée).

II
INDIA AND
ASSOCIATED REGIONS

INDIA AND ASSOCIATED REGIONS

INDIA: THE EARLY CAMPAIGNS

The first European contacts with India were motivated by reasons of trade rather than territorial acquisition, and during the first century of European contact oriental trade was monopolised by Portugal. Goa was seized by Portugal early in the 16th century, and became the capital of Portuguese India from 1530; but their influence declined in the early 17th century, under pressure from Dutch and English interests, the latter led by the 'Company of Merchants of London trading into the East Indies', which was granted a royal charter on 31 December 1600. For the next two and a half centuries, British presence in India was founded upon this mercantile concern, which became the East India Company and ultimately assumed the rights and privileges of virtually a sovereign state.

The first conflicts involving Europeans in India were not against the powerful and well-established Indian states, but were contested between the Europeans, notably the defeat of Portuguese fleets by English forces at Swally in 1612 and 1615. British settlement on mainland India can be dated from December 1612, but the most famous of the early settlements was Fort St. George, established at Madras in 1640. From the earliest period, European settlement was dependent upon the friendship of local states; the early mercantile concessions, for example, were granted by the Mogul Empire which controlled much of the subcontinent. From the early 17th century the Europeans became involved in some of the internal warfare of the Indian states (conflict between the indigenous states or dynasties being endemic before the Europeans arrived), and until the mid-18th century the various European powers opposed one another, either for reasons of rivalry within the subcontinent, or arising from hostilities being conducted in Europe.

The first British trade-concession in Bengal was granted in 1651, and as part of the Portuguese marriage settlement Charles II received Bombay from that nation. The first British troops (as opposed to Company employees) sent to India accompanied the governor of Bombay in 1662; after some wanderings around the coast they finally arrived in Bombay in 1665, by which time tropical illnesses had reduced their number to scarcely one-quarter of the 400 who had set out.

In 1668 Bombay was made over to the East India Company at a rent of £10 per annum, and permission was granted for the Company to enrol its own military forces, initially British and including a militia of soldiers granted half-pay to settle there; thus the close co-operation between the Company's soldiers and those of the king was established from this early period. Bombay was fortified and the first of the Company's Indian units were enrolled in 1683–4, and from 1687 Bombay became the principal British post in India. The Company's first 'campaign', if it can be thus described, arose in 1686 on the opposite coast,

over disagreements concerning tariffs with the Mogul viceroy of Bengal, and the Company was forced from its settlements until peace was restored in February 1690. The main event in these skirmishes was the establishment of a fortified post to which the Company withdrew its personnel, the foundation of Calcutta. It also marked a change in the relationship between the British and the Indian powers: previously British aims had been mercantile, without territorial aspirations beyond those required for successful trade; but as the Mogul empire decayed, the Company took on the role of an independent state, which eventually supplanted the Moguls as the dominant power in the subcontinent. Although a change from the original commercial emphasis, it was not a usurpation of British government authority, for by the charter granted the Company following the restoration of Charles II, it was legally empowered to send ships and troops for the defence of its 'factories' (trading-settlements), and to make peace with or declare war upon any non-Christian peoples it encountered.

The first serious hostilities involving the British in India were occasioned by renewed European colonisation. As the influence of the Portuguese and Dutch declined to virtual irrelevance, France became Britain's principal rival. Although the French East India Company was established in 1609, not until 1668 was their first Indian factory established, and in 1674 their principal base was founded at Pondicherry. The increasing importance of the British and French settlements coincided with the accelerating decline of the Mogul empire, with the rise of numerous states which threw off imperial control, even though some maintained a formal allegiance to the old regime. One of the most significant of the new powers was that which became known as the 'Maratha Confederacy' (the earlier spelling was usually 'Mahratta'), which expanded north from the Maratha states including Baroda, Gwalior and Indore; at times supportive of the emperor, they were at other times hostile, and indeed defeated the emperor Mohammed Shah in battle outside Delhi in 1737. The decline of imperial power was accelerated further by an invasion of north-west India by the Persian monarch Nadir Shah, who in 1739 defeated Mohammed Shah at the battle of Karnal and occupied Delhi; he left Mohammed on his throne but returned home with a vast treasure and annexed the Mogul territories north and west of the Indus.

Anglo-French hostility during the War of the Austrian Succession spread to India in what is sometimes termed the First Carnatic War (named from that region of India). Learning of the approach of a British fleet, the French governor-general, Joseph, Marquis de Dupleix, appealed for help to the French admiral La Bourdonnais at Mauritius, and the two collaborated in the capture of the British base at Madras (September 1746). They defended their position against the Nawab of the Carnatic, Anwar-ud-Din

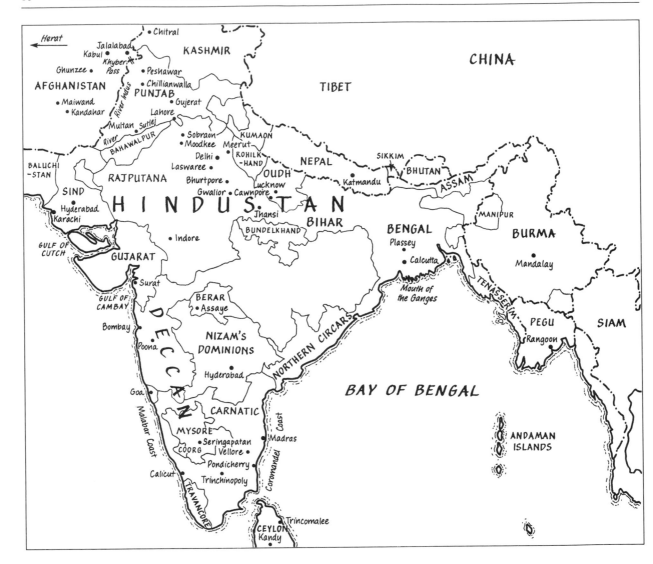

(or 'Anwarudeen'), who attempted to enforce Dupleix's promise to deliver Madras to him, rather than keep it for France. A decisive action took place near St. Thomé, a short distance south of Madras, on 4 November 1746, when an immense Indian army attempted to intercept a small French detachment. The Nawab's forces, commanded by his son Maphuze Khan, numbered some 10,000 men and artillery, strongly positioned on the bank of a river. On the other side was a French force comprising some 230 Europeans and 700 French sepoys, commanded by Louis Paradis, a Swiss officer. Paradis adopted a tactic which would have been familiar to every later British commander on the subcontinent: an immediate attack to redress the disparity in numbers by throwing the Indian force into confusion, and exploiting its lack of European-style discipline. Paradis' headlong charge over the river caused the massive Indian force to break and flee in disorder. It has been stated that this action caused a total change in the relationship between the Europeans and the indigenous powers, for no longer were Indian armies regarded with the awe hitherto inspired by their huge numbers; Sir John Fortescue even remarked that 'The memory of Paradis should be honoured in England since he taught us the secret of the conquest of India.'[1]

Operations for the remainder of the war were inconclusive. The British government, having determined to assist the Company with ships and men, sent a fleet under Admiral Edward Boscawen; but as the French were unsuccessful in their siege of the British post of Fort St. David, some twelve miles south of Pondicherry, so Boscawen was unable to take Pondicherry, and soon after the siege was lifted in October 1748, news was received of the Treaty of Aix-la-Chapelle which ended Anglo-French hostilities in Europe, and which restored Madras to the British. Although officially at peace from then until the outbreak of the Seven Years War, hostilities between Britain and

France continued in India from their involvement in the internal politics of the region.

From 1713 the Deccan had been ruled by the Mogul emperor's viceroy, Nizam-ul-Mulk, whose death in 1748 was followed by the usual contest for succession, between his grandson Muzaffar Jang, who had the emperor's support to succeed as the Nizam of Hyderabad, and Nizam-ul-Mulk's second son, Nasir Jang. A further quarrel ensued for the nawabship of the Carnatic between Anwar-ud-Din, the incumbent, and Chanda Sahib, the son-in-law of his predecessor. Dupleix and the French supported Muzaffar Jang and Chanda Sahib; the British, their opponents. In 1749 Chanda, Muzaffar and a French force under Charles, Marquis de Bussy, advanced upon Arcot, the capital of the Carnatic; Anwar opposed them but was defeated and killed at Amoor (3 August 1749). The defeat and assassination of Nasir Jang (16 December 1750) made Dupleix the effective power in the region, via virtual client-states of the French, with Chanda as Nawab of the Carnatic and Muzaffar Jang as the Nizam. Upon the death of the latter in January 1751 Dupleix installed Salabat Jang, a younger brother of Nasir Jang, as puppet-ruler.

Anglo-French hostilities re-commenced in 1751, but as these nations were officially at peace the conflict was conducted by their respective Indian 'clients', the British supporting Mohammed Ali, Anwar-ud-Din's successor, who held Trinchinopoly. Chanda Sahib invested that place in July 1751, besieging in it most of the British troops in India. Its salvation was Robert Clive, a Company clerk turned military officer, who launched a daring diversionary expedition to relieve the pressure on Trinchinopoly. Gathering all the disposable British forces (200 Europeans and 300 sepoys), he advanced from Madras, captured the fort of Arcot (which was but lightly defended, Chanda's army being occupied at Trinchinopoly), and held it against some 10,000 of Chanda's forces which returned to re-possess the capital. After a siege of fifty days and an unsuccessful assault, the besiegers departed, leaving Clive in possession. From this point, French fortunes declined as the British recruited more allies, notably the Marathas; Dupleix was recalled to France, and in January 1755 his successor and his British counterpart concluded a treaty for the suspension of hostilities.

The 1755 truce was but a brief interruption in hostilities, the focus of which switched to Bengal and the British base of Calcutta. The Nawab of Bengal, who nominally governed in the name of the Mogul emperor, had become virtually an independent prince; the Nawab who succeeded in 1756, Suraj-ud-Daula, objected to the defences being raised by the British against possible French aggression. In June 1756 he captured Calcutta and incarcerated in the infamous 'Black Hole' those Europeans who had not been evacuated by sea; few escaped alive. An expedition was mounted from Madras under Robert Clive and the commander of the British naval forces at Madras,

Admiral Charles Watson; Clive's army comprised only some 1,500 sepoys and 900 Europeans, including part of the 39th Foot, the first British regiment to be sent in support of the Company to India, where they had arrived in 1754; hence the motto 'Primus in Indis' of the Dorsetshire Regiment. Calcutta was re-occupied in January 1757, and a treaty was negotiated with Suraj-ud-Daula.

Anglo-French hostilities having been renewed in Europe, Clive captured the French base of Chandernagore on 23 March 1757, which forced the Nawab to take the part of the French. A treaty was concluded with one of the Nawab's chief supporters, Mir Jafar; so that although Clive's forces were outnumbered hugely, the possibility of treason in the Nawab's camp made Clive's advance less of a gamble. On 23 June 1757 he confronted Suraj-ud-Daula at Plassey; opposing Clive's 800 Europeans, 2,100 sepoys and ten guns, the Nawab mustered some 53,000 men and 50 guns, including a small party of French. Without treachery in the ranks of the Nawab's advisers, it is unlikely that Clive would even have offered battle; but after the Nawab was persuaded to depart, Mir Jafar encouraged Clive to attack, holding aloof his own forces. Despite sterling resistance from the French, the Nawab's forces were routed, Clive losing only 23 killed and 49 wounded; Suraj-ud-Daula was assassinated soon after and Mir Jafar installed in his place, virtually a client of the

Robert Clive, 1st Baron (1725–74), most famous of the British soldiers and administrators in 18th-century India. (Engraving by G. Stodart after N. Dance)

Company. The date of the Battle of Plassey was later sometimes regarded as marking the beginning of the British Empire in India.

Despite the increasing influence of the Company, and the enriching of it and its employees, both at the expense of the fragmenting Mogul empire and those semi-independent rulers whose allegiance to it was fragile, the French still exercised much influence in the south. In April 1758 they received reinforcements and a new commander, Thomas Arthur, comte de Lally, an Irish Jacobite, who on 2 June 1758 captured Fort St. David, but besieged Madras unsuccessfully. Lally was not the most inspired of commanders, and on 22 January 1760 perhaps the most decisive blow against the French in India was struck when he was defeated by Sir Eyre Coote's British force at Wandewash. Lally retired to Pondicherry, where he was besieged, and this principal French base surrendered on 15 January 1761; for all his efforts, Lally was arrested upon his return to France and most unjustly executed for treason in May 1766. Pondicherry was restored to France by the Treaty of Paris, but French interests in India had received a fatal blow, and no longer did they provide any serious rivalry to the British in India. (Pondicherry, an enclave of some 115 square miles, remained French, except for its occupation by the British during periods of Anglo-French hostility, 1778–83, 1793–1802, 1803–16; but it had no military significance.)

A further elimination of European rivalry to the British occurred in 1759, when the jealousy of the Dutch over British successes in Bengal caused them to initiate hostilities in the area of the Hugli (or Hooghly) river, where their post of Chinsura was situated. Their small force was routed and their fleet captured (24–5 November 1759); the Dutch action was repudiated by their authorities in Europe, who were officially allied to Britain, and this served to end any military threat to British India from that quarter. Henceforth, military operations involving British forces would be conducted against Indian rulers, and the only Europeans they encountered in battle in India from then on were those acting in a private capacity.

From 1760 desultory conflicts occurred in Bengal, involving small Company forces. Among the most significant operations were those conducted against Mir Kasim, who had supplanted his father-in-law Mir Jafar as Nawab, initially upon Company instigation, until he endeavoured to assert his independence. The British commander in Bengal, Major Thomas Adams, with a small force of British and the Company's sepoy troops (and including a French unit which had taken service with the British after the fall of Pondicherry), defeated forces of the Nawab at Cutwa (19 July 1763) and Gheria (2 August 1763); Adams died of the hardships of campaign in December 1763. The last phase of the conflict in Bengal was fought between Company forces commanded by Major Hector Munro, and the combined forces of the emperor Shah Alam and Shujah-

ud-Daula, Nawab of Oudh. In September 1764 Munro had to suppress a mutiny among his own sepoys, a protest against a tightening of discipline; suppression involved the execution of 24 sepoys by the appalling practice of 'blowing from guns', in which the victim was tied with back or breast to the muzzle of a cannon, and literally blown into fragments when the gun was fired. With some 1,000 Europeans, 5,300 sepoys and 900 allied native horse, Munro met Shujah-ud-Daula on 23 October at Buxar; the Nawab had between 40,000 and 50,000 men, including units disciplined in the European manner, and artillery with European crews. Despite the disparity in numbers, the discipline and firepower of the British and their sepoys overthrew Shujah-ud-Daula's army; thousands were slain as they broke and trampled upon one another when attempting to flee across a marshy water-course. It was said that a 300-yard causeway was formed from the bodies of these unfortunates. No less than 167 guns fell into the hands of the victors, whose casualties totalled almost 850. Buxar was a crushing blow; the emperor Shah Alam sent Munro his congratulations and placed himself under British protection; and although Shujah-ud-Daula remained intransigent, he declined to meet the British again in the open field.

Military Forces to 1800

Indian armies. The 'traditional' Indian mode of warfare in some respects resembled that of medieval Europe, perhaps most notably in the comparative importance of cavalry and infantry. Armies were formed on semi-feudal lines, and unlike the popular opinion of the military in some European states, the status of warrior was regarded highly. Under the Moguls, mounted troops formed the most numerous and prestigious part of an army; the traditional comparative importance of the two 'arms' may be exemplified by the army of Shir Shah in the 16th century, whose 'standing army' comprised some 150,000 cavalry and 25,000 infantry. The consequences of the prestige of the mounted warrior were that little attempt could be made towards the imposition of discipline; and the infantry came to be regarded almost as camp-followers or servants, armed with unreliable matchlock muskets. Artillery pieces were regarded as status symbols as much as weapons, so that many were large, unwieldy and slow to operate, with a rate of fire sometimes as low as four shots per hour. In these aspects, in a form of warfare dependent upon hand-to-hand combat between mounted warriors with only limited ability for cohesive movement, and confirmed by the occasional use of elephants in battle, traditional Indian warfare was very outdated in comparison with the disciplined European style.

An important change was introduced into Indian warfare as a result of European involvement in the region. Just as the Europeans formed their own 'native' regiments, principally infantry which was armed, drilled and fought in European fashion, so the Indian rulers followed. The employment of mercenaries was already common in India, and a number of states hired Europeans to instruct their armies in European-style discipline and methods of fighting. Among the first to adopt such a policy was Mir Kasim, who by 1762 had no less than 25,000 infantry trained in European style, an artillery regiment almost entirely European in composition, and a foundry capable of producing cannon equal to anything manufactured in Europe. Three of the mercenaries he employed to organise his army were Armenians (Markar, Aratoon and Gurghis Khan), but the most influential was the German Walter Reinhard, who was known by the nickname 'Sombre', changed to 'Somroo' or 'Sumroo' by the Indians. In the event it benefited Mir Kasim little, for Sumroo, Markar and their brigades were bribed to defect to Shujah-ud-Daula; Sumroo commanded at Buxar but in the following year took his followers to new masters, leaving Shujah-ud-Daula in the same position as he had left Mir Kasim. Not all the European military adventurers were so duplicitous, however. Perhaps the best-known was Claude (or Claud) Martin (1735–1800), who went to India to serve under Dupleix, but took service with the British East India Company after the fall of Pondicherry in 1761. Commissioned in the Bengal Army in 1763, he rose to the rank of major-general, and was permitted to become superintendent of the arsenal at Lucknow in the service of the Nawab of Oudh, retaining his Company rank but ultimately going on half-pay. He became fabulously rich, maintained a *zenana*, and on his death left bequests to establish charitable institutions in India and in his native Lyons, including the famous Martinière at Lucknow.

The Marathas. The Marathas (or 'Mahrattas') were one of the most powerful forces in India in the second half of the 18th century. The origin of their name is uncertain, being neither tribal, social nor religious, but in the widest sense could be applied to all those resident in the Maharashtra region (Sanskrit 'the great kingdom'), or who spoke the Mahratti language. The Marathas came to prominence in the 17th century with the revolt of Sivaji, the greatest Maratha hero, who rebelled for reasons of nationality and religion against the Mogul regime (whose emperor was Muslim, the Marathas Hindu). A hardy race living in west-central Deccan, east and south-east of Bombay, from the time of their expansion under Sivaji the Marathas were transformed from mountain-dwelling foot-soldiers into the best light cavalry in the subcontinent. Sivaji first rebelled against the Muslim king of Bijapur in the Deccan in 1657, then took on the Mogul emperor Aurangzeb, creating and expanding a Maratha kingdom which continued after Sivaji's death in 1680. The excellence of the Maratha light horse was his creation, for Sivaji imposed discipline and organisation quite different from the more 'chivalric' form of warfare experienced elsewhere. His cavalry was organised into units with its own command-structure: a

panch hazari commanded a corps of 5,000 men, formed of 1,000-man units each commanded by an *ek hazari*, themselves subdivided into 50-man units under a *jumladar*, each of two 25-man platoons commanded by a *havildar*.

After Sivaji's death the Maratha state fragmented into several dynasties, sometimes styled the Maratha Confederacy. The king, as Sivaji's descendant, was still venerated, but actual power resided in the hands of the dynasty of the minister or Peshwa, an office which became hereditary; although the princes of Maratha states were in many respects autonomous rulers, making peace or war as they chose, all owed allegiance to the Peshwa at Poona, who continued to obtain the sanction of his nominal sovereign before any major policies were implemented. Ultimately the Marathas controlled all of western and much of central India, but were not unchallenged: the growing power of the Sikhs prevented the Marathas from making permanent progress in the Punjab, the Nizam of the Deccan was established in Hyderabad, and the Mysore state in the south. The Marathas suffered a severe defeat at Panipat (near Delhi) on 14 January 1761, at the hands of Ahmed Shah Abdali whose Afghan forces had been raiding northern and central India; the unstable conditions which followed facilitated consolidation of the British position.

The Marathas were among the most important Indian forces to form European-style units under European officers. Probably the best of these was the Savoyard Benoît de Boigne, who from 1784–5 created a European-style army for the Maratha prince Sindhia, who admired the British troops and recognised the imperfections in his undisciplined Maratha forces. De Boigne, who had served in the French and Russian armies and in the Company's Madras Army, created battalions of British-style infantry (Sindhia even purchased red cloth for their uniforms!); established a regular rate of pay, thus attracting suitable recruits and avoiding a reliance upon Marathas who were not ideal for infantry service; and created an arms-manufactory under a Scottish mercenary and artisan, George Sangster. The officers selected for the most important commands included Britons, Frenchmen, Germans, Italians and even an American (J. P. Boyd, late of the US Army), some of shady character but many who knew their business. De Boigne's creation was very European in character: eleven infantry battalions in red coats, blue turban and black leather equipment, cavalry in green with red turban, and a European artillery corps serving heavy ordnance drawn by bullocks and light field-pieces with two-horse teams; with all the necessary supporting services. He later enlarged the force into two brigades of ten battalions each, each battalion of 600 men in eight companies; the first brigade was commanded by Colonel Frémont, a French royalist who had resigned his French commission upon the revolution in France; and the second by Pierre Perron, who ultimately succeeded de Boigne in overall command. Perron, whose real name was Pierre Cuillier

(1755–1834), was a French seaman who had deserted on the Malabar coast, enlisted under Sangster and joined de Boigne in 1790; after some treachery to his employer, he was superseded in command upon the outbreak of war between Sindhia and the British in 1803, and fled to British protection. The rank and file of such units also often reflected the diverse origin of the officers: de Boigne's infantry were mostly from Oudh and Rohilkhand, the cavalry mostly Pathans. The number of European officers remained small: a battalion might have no more than two white or mixed-race officers, and Perron is said to have managed 40 battalions and an artillery-park of 380 guns with no more than 300 European personnel, including those who supervised the armament-works. Administration, discipline, organisation and training were in completely European style.

Against other Indian forces, such European-style armies were most effective; but when compared to Europeans or Company forces including European elements, they were regarded as adequate on the defensive but inferior in manoeuvring in the open. In offence, the more traditional irregular light horse operating in a semi-guerrilla manner were probably more effective.

Not all European-style units were organised similarly; in some cases, French influence may have resulted in fewer companies per battalion than in British-style units, and the number of light field pieces attached to each battalion was often greater, five instead of the two of Company regiments. The brigade organisations were styled *compoo*s, and in addition to 'battalion guns', heavier artillery was deployed at *compoo* level.

A number of Indian rulers formed such 'European' armies; for example, the Nabob Omdat ul Omrah of the Carnatic dressed his bodyguard in the uniform of the British 10th Light Dragoons, in emulation of the Prince of Wales, whose regiment it was. Occasionally such forces came into conflict: for example, the Nizam of Hyderabad employed the French mercenary Colonel (or 'Monsieur') Raymond to organise an army, which performed reasonably in the Nizam's defeat by the Marathas at Kardla in 1795; another example was the battle of Poona (25 October 1802), in which Holkar of Indore defeated Sindhia and the Peshwa, with British officers commanding units on both sides. At other times more than one European-style army might collaborate: Sindhia's forces at Assaye, for example, were not all his own. In addition to the usual horde of light horse, three *compoo*s of 'regular' infantry were deployed, under the command of an ex-sergeant of the Hanoverian army, Pohlmann. Pohlmann's own *compoo* (formerly commanded by a British colonel, Sutherland), of eight battalions of 800 men and five guns each, belonged to Sindhia, as did the four-battalion *compoo* of Baptiste Filoze, a half-Neapolitan, half-Indian who had inherited his *compoo* from his father and brother. (He was not present at Assaye, his troops being commanded by a Dutch officer, John Dupont). The third *compoo*, however, of five battalions and 25 guns, was owned by the Begum Sumroo, Reinhard's widow, who was a feudal vassal of Sindhia.

Mysore. The state of Mysore presented a brief but formidable challenge to the British, following the usurpation of its throne by Hyder (or Haidar) Ali (c.1722–82). A Muslim soldier-adventurer, Hyder Naik was supposedly the first to form an Indian unit in European style, armed with muskets and bayonets, and to enrol Europeans in a corps of artillery. At first a commander in the Mysore forces, he rose to be ruler of the kingdom and in 1763 changed his name to Hyder Ali Khan Bahadur. It was his son, Tipu Sultan (or 'Tippoo Sahib'), who succeeded on Hyder Ali's death in 1782, who became most notorious among the British, and against whom the principal campaigns of the Mysore Wars were fought.

At the time of Hyder Ali's death the Mysore army was estimated to be 88,000 strong; by the beginning of the Third Mysore War Tipu is said to have commanded some 123,000 infantry and 8,000 cavalry (the latter figure probably too low), of which some 48,000 infantry and 3,000 cavalry were 'regulars' of European style. Originally battalions were styled *risala*s, commanded by a *risaldar*, and composed of companies or *juq*s, led by a *juqdar*, several battalions comprised a brigade or *cushoon*, commanded by a *sipahdar*. Before the Third Mysore War, Tipu reorganised his 'regulars' into four brigades of infantry and four of

Hyder Ali of Mysore (c.1722–82), portrayed in 1770. (Engraving by I. Maidstone after J. Leister)

cavalry, styled *cutcheries*, commanded by a *bakshi*; each infantry brigade comprised six regiments, now styled *cushoons*, commanded by a *sipahdar*, and each cavalry brigade comprised five regiments or *mokums*, commanded by a *mokumdar*. Each *cushoon* had five 'battalion guns' attached; rockets were included with the artillery park. The remainder of the army was irregular infantry and light horse, possessing little discipline; but the cavalry was exceptionally skilled in guerrilla-style operations and in concealing the movements of the army with a skirmish-screen; in the wars against the British they were a continual threat to isolated detachments and greatly disrupted communications and the line-of-march. (An excellent account of the career and military forces of Tipu, and an extensive bibliography, can be found in D. Forrest's *The Tiger of Mysore*, London, 1970.)

First Mysore War

Following Hyder Ali's assumption of power in Mysore, he came into conflict with the British-supported Nabob of the Carnatic, Mohammed Ali, and Nizam Ali, Nawab of the Deccan, who were themselves mutually antagonistic. The Madras government somewhat unwisely attempted to treat with all parties, an unsuccessful negotiation which resulted in a union of Hyder Ali and Nizam Ali, against whose forces the Madras commander-in-chief, Colonel Joseph Smith, fought with some distinction. Despite Smith's victories against heavy odds at Changama (3 September 1767) and Trincomalee (26–7 September 1767), no decisive action occurred, and when Hyder Ali, himself a skilled general, brought an army almost to the gates of Madras, the Madras government accepted his peace terms (April 1769), which provided for the restitution of captured territory and a mutual defensive alliance.

In 1771 the Peshwa Madoo Rao attacked Hyder Ali and forced from him territorial concessions; Hyder appealed for British assistance, due under the terms of the 1769 treaty, but the Madras government declined (indeed, they were under pressure from Mohammed Ali to support Madoo Rao *against* Hyder). The death of the Peshwa in November 1772 gave opportunities to both Hyder and Mohammed Ali; the latter persuaded the Madras government to besiege and capture Tanjore for him (August 1773), and in the following year Hyder recovered the territory recently lost to the Marathas. Hyder Ali endeavoured to renew the 1769 treaty, but as negotiations depended upon the approval of the new supreme government at Calcutta, the discussions were so protracted that Hyder withdrew, abandoning all hope of collaboration with the British.

First Rohilla War

A minor campaign occurred in 1774, styled the First Rohilla War, in which a brigade of the Bengal army assisted Shujah-ud-Daula against the Rohillas, in pursuance of his attempt to gain possession of Rohilcund. Colonel Champion's Bengal brigade defeated the Rohillas at Kutra (23 April 1774), whereupon Shujah-ud-Daula's troops devastated the captured territory; Champion remarked with a bitterness felt by his entire force, that they had the honour of the campaign but Shujah's 'banditti' had the profit!

First Maratha War

The First Maratha War arose from the attempt of the Bombay government to increase its influence by supporting its own nominee for the Peshwa's throne at Poona, Raghunath Rao (also known as Ragobah). This brought the Bombay government into conflict from 1775 with Raghunath's opponents, the Maratha leaders Sindhia and Holkar. The ill-led Bombay forces were humiliated by the Marathas, who fought an indecisive action at Worgaum (12–13 January 1779), and having cut off the retreat of the Bombay force, extracted from them a treaty on terms dictated by the Marathas. The balance was redressed by the governor-general, Warren Hastings, who sent a force from Bengal under General Goddard to confront the Marathas; he conquered the province of Gujerat without encountering much opposition, and captured by escalade the hitherto impregnable fortress of Gwalior, which was taken on 3 August 1780 by a few Europeans and 1,200 sepoys led by Captain William Popham. After some skirmishing but no decisive action, Hastings negotiated a peace, to leave himself free to face the greater threat from Mysore. A treaty with the Marathas was concluded at Salbye (or Salbai) on 17 May 1782, by which virtually all the territory acquired by the British in the recent operations were restored, and Raghunath was set aside as Peshwa.

Second Mysore War

This (sometimes referred to as the First by disregarding the earlier hostilities) was again waged against Hyder Ali. When news of the declaration of war against France was received in India in 1778, the British moved to capture the French bases of Pondicherry (18 October 1778) and Mahé (on the Malabar coast) early in the following year. Still annoyed by British failure to support him against the Marathas, Hyder Ali sided with the French and sent troops to assist in the defence of Mahé. British attempts at conciliation failed, and in June 1780 Hyder Ali marched against the British with some 90,000 men, including a powerful force of infantry trained in European fashion, and a small French contingent. The Madras government forces were scattered and heavily outnumbered, but two forces prepared to confront Hyder: the main contingent under the commander-in-chief of Madras, Sir Hector Munro (the victor of Buxar), and a smaller division under Colonel William Baillie. Expecting that Munro would reinforce him, Baillie engaged the Mysore army at Parambakum (10 September 1780). After a severe trial,

Baillie's hugely outnumbered force was heartened by the sight of approaching red-clad columns, with drums beating the British *Grenadiers' March*; but they were dismayed to find that instead of Munro's reinforcements, they were Hyder Ali's regulars, an example of the confusion which could arise when both sides included troops drilled and organised upon European lines. Completely surrounded, and having suffered severely, Baillie's command surrendered upon the guarantee that the lives of the survivors would be spared; but as soon as they laid down their arms, Hyder's troops began to slaughter them, and the fight was renewed as the British snatched up their weapons. Responding to the entreaties of his few French officers, Hyder Ali regained control of his troops, and Baillie's survivors were carried into an appalling captivity. The troops involved in this, the most severe disaster ever to have befallen British arms in the subcontinent, consisted of 81 members of the Royal Artillery, 113 Madras Europeans, 301 men of a flank battalion formed of the 1/71st flank companies and Madras European grenadiers, and 3,358 Native Infantry, including 46 European officers. Despite the difficulties of the task he had been set, part of the blame must rest with Munro.

Upon news of the disaster at Parambakum, Sir Eyre Coote was sent by sea to Madras with as much of the Bengal Army as could be spared, to be followed by others marching down the coast. For a period Coote was doubly threatened by Hyder Ali's army on land and a French fleet cutting off his supplies, but the latter's commander failed to appreciate the situation and sailed away (February 1781), depriving Hyder of assistance and perhaps even saving the British hold on India, which could have been weakened had Coote's force been starved into surrender.

Coote confronted Hyder Ali at Porto Novo on 1 July 1781. Coote's army numbered about 7,500, including only three European battalions (71st Highlanders, Bengal and Madras Europeans), with nine sepoy battalions, a tenth formed from detached companies, 48 guns and some 500 Native cavalry; Hyder had about 80,000 men, at least one-third of whom were disciplined 'regulars'. Coote advanced, assailed a flank, and maintained such a disciplined fire that the Mysorean counter-attacks were repelled, and Hyder withdrew, having sustained perhaps 9,000 casualties; Coote's casualties were a little more than 300. Lacking sufficient cavalry for a determined chase, Coote seconded his victory slowly; Hyder Ali was beaten again (with huge losses) at Pollilore (27 August 1781), and on 27 September 1781 he engaged Coote at Sholinghur. Again there was a vast disparity in numbers (Coote had about 11,000, Hyder about 70,000), but Hyder's attacks foundered upon British discipline, and his army was beaten away.

Coote had been so deprived of transport and the means to further the campaign, by the incompetence of the Madras government and the parsimony of supposed Indian allies (particularly Mohammed Ali), that his achievements were considerable against so formidable an opponent; but, much affected by the strain of the campaign, Coote died in April 1782. Hyder Ali received little help from his French allies, even though the French capture of Trincomalee (25 August 1782) gave them a convenient base, and operations were comparatively minor until Hyder died in December 1782. He was succeeded by his son, Tipu Sultan, who had been a subordinate commander of the Mysore army in the recent campaigns. He continued the war, but peace between Britain and France in 1783 left him bereft of allies, and after some minor campaigning he made peace (11 March 1784) by a treaty which agreed mutual restitution of captured territory. Those of Hyder Ali's prisoners who had not died of neglect (including Baillie) or been murdered by Tipu were released from their terrible captivity; among them was David Baird, who was to play a significant role in Tipu's ultimate demise.

Third Mysore War

In 1786 Charles, Marquess of Cornwallis (the same whose army had surrendered at Yorktown) was appointed to the joint posts of governor-general and commander-in-chief in India. His rule in India is perhaps most marked for his refining of the system of civil administration founded by Warren Hastings, and for his settlement of permanent land revenue in Bengal, later extended to Madras and Bombay; but in a military sense, his tenure was marked by the renewal of war against Tipu.

Tipu Sultan (1753–99) possessed military talents inferior to those of his father, and was renowned for great cruelty; but he was a formidable opponent by virtue of the army he inherited from Hyder Ali. Remaining determinedly hostile to the British, Tipu aroused British animosity by ravaging the territory of a British ally, the Rajah of Travancore, in late 1789; Cornwallis responded by forming an alliance with Nizam Ali and the Marathas, by which each agreed to furnish 10,000 light horse to cooperate with British forces. Tipu's attempt to enlist French assistance, at a time when that country was in the throes of revolution, was unsuccessful.

Cornwallis organised an advance against Tipu from mid-1790; initially there were inconclusive minor actions, although on 10 December a small British force routed a much larger Mysore detachment at Calicut. Cornwallis took personal command of his forces at Madras in January 1791, and attacked Bangalore in early March. Despite the threatening presence of Tipu's main army in the vicinity, Cornwallis captured the town on 7 March and successfully stormed Bangalore fort on 21 March. Having established a base of operations, Cornwallis and his Indian allies pushed Tipu into the region of his capital, Seringapatam, and began to reduce other fortified posts. The mighty fortress of Nundydroog was stormed on 19 October 1791

Foreign climates provided a convenient excuse for malingerers. An officer recalled how an army surgeon in India discovered 64 cases of delirium tremens in a detachment of 240 men, who were also adept at feigning illness:

'A party of them came to the hospital to get some medicine, to escape parade altogether. One came forward; "What is the matter with you?" "Oh, I am very bad in my inside, Sur." "Go into the surgery, and you'll get some medicine. Serjeant, give this man some of the black bottle on the upper shelf." A horrid mixture, composed of salts, senna, tobacco-water, assafoetida, &c. Pat tasted it, and not liking it, slyly emptied the glass into his cap. The Doctor watched him, and calling him to him, told him to put on his cap. "I'll do that outside, Sur." "No, put it on now; you know a soldier should never take his cap off." It was done cautiously. "How long have you been sick?" "It's been coming on for some time, Sur." "What's that running over your eyes?" The patient putting up his hand, "Oh! 'tis nothing but the sweat, Sur." "How comes it black? Serjeant, bring him another dose of the same." Pat swallowed this with a terrible grimace and shudder; whilst the others, watching outside, cried to Pat, "By the powers but he's done for ye," and forthwith disappeared.'
(Sir James Alexander, 'A Sleigh Drive in Canada West', in *Colburn's United Service Magazine*, 1843, vol. II, pp. 260–1)

with such determination that this hitherto near-impregnable position was taken with very few casualties (the storming-party of the flank companies of the 36th and 71st Foot lost only two killed). The even more formidable fortress of Savandroog (called 'the Rock of Death' from its defences and pestilential climate) was stormed on 21 December 1791, the storming-party of the flank companies of the 52nd and 76th Foot, and the grenadiers of two sepoy battalions, being played into action by the band of the 52nd with *Britons, Strike Home!*; but the defenders of the 'impregnable' fortress bolted and the place was captured at the cost of one man wounded. The effect of such successes was startling: when on 24 December 1791 the British stormed the nearby fort of Ootradroog, up a path so steep that the attackers had to climb up with the help of ropes and unravelled turbans, the defenders again fled, the British having only two men wounded plus about thirty bruised when attacked by a herd of wild cattle.

In early 1792 Cornwallis advanced against Seringapatam with some 22,000 men, plus some 18,000 Indian light horse of the Nizam's, and a small Maratha contingent (most of the latter having left on a plundering raid). On 6–7 February the outlying fortifications were attacked, and as determinedly counter-attacked by Tipu's army from within; but after much hard fighting Tipu held only

Seringapatam fort. As the siege of this progressed, Tipu sued for peace, and a treaty was concluded on 19 March 1792, by which the Marathas and the Nizam recovered most of the territory taken by Hyder Ali, and the British received more, notably Malabar and Coorg.

Fourth Mysore War

In 1798 a new governor-general arrived in India: Richard, 2nd Earl of Mornington, elder brother of the future Duke of Wellington. His policy was directed towards the increase of British power, not primarily by conquest but by alliances with existing Indian states. The scheme was to give a defensive guarantee to what were to be almost client-states, with the Company stationing troops within the territory of the Indian state, paid for by that state, a form of 'protection' which had the effect of transferring the state's external or 'foreign' policy into the hands of the Company. At the time of Mornington's arrival the major Indian powers included the Maratha Confederacy, nominally still owing allegiance to the Peshwa in Poona, although the more important chieftains like Doulut Rao Sindhia and Holkar were virtually independent rulers; Mysore, still controlled by Tipu, smarting under the terms imposed upon him after the Third Mysore War; the Nizam Ali of Hyderabad, traditionally the premier Muslim ruler in India, but weakened by his defeat by Sindhia in March 1795; and other states, primarily Oudh and in the Carnatic, largely dependent upon Company support.

Another of Mornington's concerns was a threat of French intervention: the French had at that time an expedition in Egypt, and Tipu was corresponding with the French government. De Boigne had left Sindhia's service, with the advice not to oppose the British; but his successor, Perron, encouraged the influx of French officers into Sindhia's 'regular' army. Even more threatening were the 23 battalions of the Nizam, commanded by a Frenchman, Michel Joachim Marie Raymond, who was so openly antagonistic to the British that his units carried the colours of the French republic and bore the 'bonnet of liberty' on their buttons; and he was in communication with Tipu. (In common with other European commanders in Indian service, Raymond was granted honorific titles; at the Nizam's court he was styled Mutahvarul-Mulk Azharud Daulah Azhdar Jung Bahadur: 'Furious against enemies of the realm, Dragon of State, Brave like a Dragon in Battle'!)

Mornington applied pressure on Hyderabad to dismiss that state's French troops (now commanded by another Frenchman, Piron), and to increase the British element in the Nizam's army from two to six battalions; the French-led units were disarmed in October 1798, and the Marathas judged it expedient to remain neutral in the approaching conflict between the British and Tipu.

After unsuccessful attempts to negotiate with Tipu, who was still leaning towards France, Mornington ordered two armies to advance into Mysore territory. The principal force assembled at Vellore under General George Harris, almost 21,000 strong, including two British cavalry regiments (19th and 25th Light Dragoons), two British brigades (one comprising the 12th, 74th and Scotch Brigade, commanded by Major-General David Baird, one of Hyder Ali's ex-captives, the other of the 33rd, 73rd and de Meuron's Swiss regiment), with Madras Native Cavalry and Infantry and a brigade of Bengal Native Infantry. They were joined by 16,000 men from Hyderabad, including the six 'Hyderabad Contingent' battalions of Bengal and Madras Native Infantry, 6,000 of the Nizam's cavalry, and 3,600 of the Nizam's old French contingent. The latter force was put under the command of the governor-general's brother, Colonel Arthur Wellesley of the 33rd, who added his own regiment to it; much to the unhappiness of Baird, who believed himself more deserving of the command. A separate force of 6,400 of the Bombay Army, commanded by Lieutenant-General James Stuart, invaded Mysore by a separate route. The invasion began in February 1799.

Tipu's response was somewhat timid, and his army's half-hearted stand at Mallavelly (27 March 1799) was defeated. An isolated success for the Mysore army was Arthur Wellesley's failure to capture a grove of trees, the Sultanpettah Tope (5 April), perhaps the only military failure in that officer's immortal career; but by the middle of April Tipu was besieged in Seringapatam. As he was running short of supplies, Harris stormed the city as soon as a practicable breach had been opened, Baird leading the assault of 4,800 men on 4 May 1799. The Mysoreans made a stout defence, led by Tipu; but the British, many unwilling to give quarter in view of Tipu's reported brutalities, burst in and quelled resistance within two hours. British casualties in the storming were 81 dead, 280 wounded and six missing, and in the whole operation 322, 1,087 and 122 respectively, the greater proportion of casualties being sustained by the European units; as many as 10,000 Mysoreans were killed in the assault, among them Tipu, whose body was dragged from beneath a pile of dead by the city's northern gate.

The fall of Seringapatam earned Mornington the title of Marquess Wellesley, raised the prestige of British arms in the subcontinent, and removed forever the threat from Mysore. The central portion of Tipu's territory, the old Mysore lands, Wellesley restored to the descendant of the dynasty dethroned by Hyder Ali; the remainder was divided between the Nizam and the British. Harris was recommended for a peerage, but as a consequence of the hostility of the East India Company he received nothing until 1815, and in the interim was legally pursued by them over the question of the Seringapatam prize-money, until it was confirmed for him by the Privy Council some six years later.

Minor operations followed the fall of Mysore, notably against Doondia Wao, a bandit warlord who had once been in Hyder Ali's service, had been imprisoned by Tipu, and had escaped on the day of the fall of Seringapatam. He gathered a band of Tipu's followers and began to plunder, proclaiming himself sovereign of the province of Bednore. He was pursued by two British flying columns and his forces harried out of existence (July–August 1799), and the Marathas completed his destruction. Minor operations quelled resistance from other chieftains, but in early 1800 Doondia re-appeared with a new force of bandits, and in May overthrew some 5,000 Marathas who had been sent against him. The governor-general then appointed his brother, Arthur Wellesley, to lead an expedition to annihilate the troublesome bandit, whose followers were said to number as many as 40,000. In a mobile operation which taught Wellesley the importance of husbanding his resources and the significance of supplies – of great value to his later career – he pursued Doondia with a column of European and the Company's native troops and Maratha cavalry, overturning several detachments until he cornered Doondia at Conagul (10 September 1800). Wellesley led his four cavalry regiments in a charge which routed the 5,000 bandits and killed Doondia in the process. The remainder were extirpated by other British forces and the Maratha and Hyderabad cavalry.

Military Forces to 1800

British. Until after the Indian Mutiny there were two 'British' armies in India: a small number of 'King's' regiments ('Queen's' after 1837), and a much larger number of East India Company regiments. Each retained a quite separate identity, establishment and officer corps, but on campaign were integrated under a unified command. The disparity in numbers was marked; for example, on 25 May 1809 there were 19,843 members of the British Army in India, plus 5,115 in Ceylon; whereas the Company troops numbered 4,051 Europeans and 128,418 'natives', which means that about 87 per cent of the 'British' troops in India were members of the Company's private army.

The first British regiment sent to India was the 39th, in 1754; the next was the 84th, raised in England in 1758 with Eyre Coote as its lieutenant-colonel commandant. It arrived in India in 1759 and after much hard service was ordered home for disbandment in 1763, but remained in India for some time and upon its eventual extinction most of its personnel entered Company service, an early example of how officers in particular might on their own initiative transfer from one service to the other, although there was no institutionalised process to facilitate this. The first British cavalry regiment to serve in India was the 19th Light Dragoons, raised for service there in 1781, then numbered the 23rd, which arrived in India in October 1782 and was the only British cavalry unit in the subcontinent for some sixteen years. Although the need for a nucleus of 'King's' regiments in India was obvious, the cost of maintaining a garrison was not inconsiderable. An alarm over possible renewed French involvement in India in 1787 led to the raising of four infantry regiments specifically for service in India (74th–77th in the British line: two Highland, two English), and while the threat existed the East India Company was content to underwrite the costs, but when the danger passed attempted to repudiate the arrangement. Consequently William Pitt introduced the East India Declaratory Bill, to compel the Company to guarantee that 'the expense of raising, transporting and maintaining such troops as may be deemed necessary for the security of the British possessions and territories in the East Indies, shall be defrayed out of the revenues accruing from such possessions and territories'; which assured that an adequate garrison of 'King's' troops would remain in India.

During the rule of the Company, their organisation was divided into three areas, later styled 'presidencies': Madras, Bengal and Bombay, each of which maintained its own independent military force. The charter granted by Elizabeth I had established control of the Company in the hands of a governor and 24-strong committee, but from the mid-18th century it was felt necessary to impose some control by the British government over the increasing territory in which the Company ruled or exercised influence. Lord North's Regulating Act of 1773 appointed Warren Hastings, then governor of Bengal, as the first governor-general of India, and established that successive holders of this office, although nominated by the Company's 'court of directors', should be subject to the approval of the British government. The governor-general, assisted by a four-man council, was entrusted with the power of peace and war; they held legislative power, but an independent judiciary was established, with judges appointed by the crown. Pitt's 1784 India Bill extended the transfer of power from Company to the British government by the creation of a board of control as a government department, to superintend British affairs in India. The board was given authority over the Company's mercantile policy in 1813 and removed its monopoly of the India trade, and in 1833 its monopoly of the China trade; from this period the Company became an administrator of its Indian possessions more than a trading concern, although not until 1858 were its responsibilities transferred entirely to the crown. The increasing role of the government applied equally to military affairs, and although Company officers were entirely separate from those of the British Army, the integration of forces necessitated a unified structure of higher command: it became the practice of the Company to appoint the British commander-in-chief as theirs as well. At various times there was some friction at lower levels, some Company officers suspecting that King's officers were treated with more favour, but rarely did this become serious.

Although the Company had enrolled units for the protection of its factories from the earliest period, only from the mid-18th century did a Company army truly exist. The forces of each of the three presidencies are treated separately below.

Bengal Army. The senior and most reliable elements of the Company forces were those formed from European troops. The Bengal European Regiment was organised in December 1756 from British detachments from Madras and Bombay who volunteered to remain in Bengal, and by 1763 had three battalions of nine companies each. In 1779 the number doubled, fell briefly to four, but by 1786 there were again six battalions, organised into three regiments of two battalions each in May 1796; the 3rd Regiment was disbanded in 1798 and the 2nd in 1803.

The first 'native' corps formed in Bengal was the 'Lal Paltan' ('Red Regiment': throughout the history of the Company armies, uniform and equipment was of British style, including the traditional red infantry coat), a battalion raised in Calcutta in January 1757. They fought well at Plassey, and two more battalions were formed in August 1757 (2nd) and February 1758 (3rd). The numbered battalions rose to 21 but of these the 2nd, 3rd and 5th were destroyed by Mir Kasim's forces under Sumroo at Patna in June 1763, and in 1764 the eighteen surviving battalions were re-numbered according to the seniority of their commanding officer. In 1765 these were organised in three brigades; in 1767 the number was increased to thirty, but in 1775 reduced to 21 battalions, re-numbered and organised in three brigades (1st Brigade, 1st–7th battalions; 2nd, 8th–14th; 3rd, 15th–21st). The infantry was increased when the Nawab of Oudh agreed to maintain nine battalions, and by 1781 there were 42; one of these was disbanded and the 1st, 2nd and 4th–7th, serving in Bombay, were removed from the Bengal list; they returned in 1784, whereupon six of the other battalions were disbanded. By 1785 there were 36 battalions in six brigades, and in 1796 a complete re-organisation produced twelve regiments of two battalions each.

Bengal's regular cavalry originated in September 1762 with the formation of three European troops, disbanded in 1764; a bodyguard troop for the governor existed from 1763 to 1772. In 1773 an Indian bodyguard was formed, the Governor's Troop of Moguls, styled the Governor-General's Bodyguard from 1781; an infantry and artillery detachment also existed. Native cavalry regiments were established in 1776 when two regiments were formed by the Nawab of Oudh, and a third in the following year; the first two were disbanded in May 1783 and the third reduced to a troop in 1786, but it was expanded to regimental strength as the 1st Bengal Native Cavalry in December 1787. The 2nd Regiment was formed in 1787 from the Kandahar Horse, a Pathan corps raised by the Nawab of Oudh in 1778; 3rd and 4th Regiments were formed in October 1796 and March 1797 respectively, and the 5th and 6th in June 1800. Irregular troops of 'Mogul Horse' existed in 1765–72, and in 1796 de Boigne's bodyguard of 600 Persians and four light field-pieces entered Company service from that of Sindhia.

Company artillery was primarily European in composition, the first artillery company in Bengal being created in June 1748, a second in September 1758, a third in September 1763 and a fourth in August 1765; by 1779 there were two battalions of seven companies each, plus three invalid companies, and from 1796 three battalions. Indian gun-crew performed the more menial tasks and manned the infantry's 'battalion guns' under the direction of European gunners, and in August 1777 a corps of Golundauze or Native Artillery was formed, taking over the 'battalion guns' in 1778; but as the authorities were fearful of Indians possessing artillery, they were disbanded in November 1779. Lascars were recruited to perform the heavy work, and a Golundauze corps was re-formed in 1781, but this was a short-lived experiment, as was a mixed European and Indian company of 1798–1802. An 'Experimental Brigade' of horse artillery was formed in 1800. A corps of engineer officers was apparently first established in Bengal in 1764 (although engineer officers had been present before: throughout the period of British rule, military and civil engineering duties frequently overlapped); four artificer companies were raised in 1776, and an ephemeral pioneer company existed in 1764.

Madras Army. European companies existed at Madras from the earliest period; there were three in 1742 and seven in 1748 when they were formed into a regiment, expanded to three in 1766. A fourth regiment was formed in 1774, and in the same year they were re-organised into two regiments of two battalions each. The expansion of the Native Infantry into six brigades in 1777 led to the formation of two more European battalions, enabling one to be present in each brigade, but in 1796 the number was reduced to two, and in 1799 to a single battalion, styled the Madras European Regiment.

The Madras government maintained some 3,000 Indian infantry, commanded by Indian officers, but as they were neither disciplined nor reliable in December 1748 the first regular sepoy battalions were formed, with European officers. These 1st and 2nd Battalions of Coast Sepoys were followed by the 3rd–6th (1759), 7th–9th (1761), 10th (1762), 11th–13th (1765), 14th (1766) and 15th–19th (1767); in June 1769 the units in the south were re-titled as the 1st–13th Carnatic Battalions, those in the north as the 1st–5th Circar Battalions (and one of the previous battalions was disbanded). By 1782 there were 27 Carnatic and eight Circar battalions, but in October 1784 all were re-numbered as the 1st–35th Madras, reduced to 21 in August 1785 and increased to 28 in the following year. Until 1788 numbering was dependent upon the seniority of the commanding officer. In 1796 they were re-organised into thirteen regiments of Madras Native Infantry of two battalions each, plus four 'extra battalions' taken into the line in 1799 to bring the total to fifteen regiments.

The Madras Governor's Body Guard was a small European escort formed in October 1778, and enlarged by a native troop in 1781; the European element was disbanded in 1784. This was the senior unit of Madras cavalry, but the first was a European troop raised in January 1748 and disbanded in 1752; another was created in 1758. In July 1767 the Nawab of Arcot placed 2,000 of his cavalry under European command, but some defected to Hyder Ali and only four regiments were retained. In 1784 it was decided that these should be taken over by the Company as a force of regular cavalry, but three regiments revolted at the prospect, leaving only the 3rd Regiment, which was re-numbered as the 1st, and a new 2nd was formed from the loyal members of the other three. Two more regiments were raised in 1785 and another in 1787, but as numbering depended upon the seniority of the commandant, the lineage is confused until fixed numbering was introduced in 1788. The 5th Regiment was disbanded in July 1796, but new 5th and 6th Regiments were created in September 1799.

A small European artillery corps was formed at Madras in 1748, increasing to a battalion of five companies by 1768; by 1786 there were two five-company battalions. Gun-lascars were organised to assist the Europeans in 1779, and a battalion of Native Artillery was formed in November 1784. The Madras establishment included engineer officers from the mid-18th century; there was also a corps of Indian pioneers, originating in 1759 but soon disbanded; another was formed in September 1780, the original two companies increasing to fourteen.

Bombay Army. The Bombay European regiment developed from independent companies formed in 1662, and was styled the Bombay Regiment as early as 1668. The strength rose to three battalions, then reduced to one, increased to two in 1778, but again reduced to one in August 1796.

Indian infantry existed in Bombay from an early period, some being attached to the European companies in 1668, and others serving under Indian officers, but they were not even uniformed until 1756. Two regular battalions were created in August 1768, followed by the 3rd (1769), 4th (1770), 5th and 6th (1775) and a Marine Battalion (to serve on Company ships) in 1777. There were fifteen battalions by 1780, reduced to six and the Marine Battalion by 1784, increased to two brigades of six battalions each by 1788; in 1796 they were re-organised into five regiments of two battalions each, increasing to eight regiments by 1800. Ephemeral troops of cavalry were formed at Bombay in 1672–8 and c.1720–7, but no further mounted force existed in the 18th century, reliance being placed upon the light horse of allied Indian states. A European artillery contingent was created as early as 1748, but it only became separate from the European infantry in 1759; six companies existed by 1797. Until 1777 Bombay's engineer officers were part of the artillery; in the same year a pioneer corps was formed, expanded to four companies in 1797.

Company Forces. In all East India Company forces, organisation, equipment and tactics were based on those of the British Army. Infantry battalions generally consisted of ten companies, of which latterly two were 'flank' companies; but unlike British units, in which one flank company was composed of grenadiers and one of light infantry, Indian regiments tended to have two grenadier companies, as it was thought that sepoys were less reliable in skirmishing than in disciplined, close-order formations. For example, Arthur Wellesley noted in 1803 that 'The sepoys must not be employed upon these light troop services; they are entirely unfit for them,' and advised that such duties should be performed by irregulars (and presumably by the forces of allied Indian states); for 'If they are beaten, it is of no consequence. If the sepoys are beaten, although in such small bodies, we lose the opinion in our favour, which is our principal hold in this country.'[2] This articulated a belief common throughout British service in India: that a crucial consideration was the intimidating aspect of a reputation for invincibility.

The 'native' units were uniformed and equipped in European manner, including the infantry's red coat, with facings varied according to the regiment, equipment and musket; although concessions to Indian styles were the head-dress (caps or hats based upon native turbans) and legwear, which sometimes included European-style long trousers but more often Indian *jangirs* (shorts which left the lower leg uncovered), and sandals or bare feet. British officers of 'native' corps, and the Company's European infantry, wore complete British infantry uniform, generally with the concessions to the climate as used by the British regiments, such as coats of lighter make, trousers instead of breeches and gaiters, and sometimes modified head-dress, including the use of 'round hats' in the later 18th century. Artillery generally wore a uniform like that of the British Royal Artillery (dark blue with red facings), and regular cavalry wore British light dragoon style, except for head-dress in the form of caps or turbans, which were usually a more ornate or formalised version of the indigenous Indian styles.

INDIA 1800–1825

Second Maratha War

Although the defeat of Tipu left the Marathas as the chief rivals to Britain, the Second Maratha War arose initially from internal conflict within the Maratha Confederacy. The Peshwa, Baji Rao II, was still the official head of the Marathas, but the most powerful were Doulut Rao Sindhia of Gwalior, and Jaswant Rao Holkar of Indore; lesser powers were the Gaekwar of Baroda and Ragogee Bhonsla, Raja of Berar. Marquess Wellesley's attempts to bring these states into his 'subsidiary' system were unsuccessful, and civil war among the Marathas resulted in the utter defeat

Richard, Earl of Mornington and Marquess Wellesley (1760–1842). (Engraving by T. Hunt after Sir Thomas Lawrence)

of the Peshwa's forces by Holkar at the battle of Poona (25 October 1802). Baji Rao II fled to British protection, and by the Treaty of Bassein formed an alliance with the British, ceding territory for the maintenance of a subsidiary force, and agreeing to treat with no other power. This considerably extended British influence in western India, but Wellesley was still concerned over possible French interference, given the French influence in the Maratha forces, notably from Perron.

Marquess Wellesley determined to support the Peshwa, and Arthur Wellesley led a force which re-installed Baji Rao in Poona, without opposition, on 13 May 1803. By early August, negotiations with Sindhia having failed, the governor-general moved against the two principal Maratha forces: a combined army of Sindhia and the Raja of Berar in the Deccan, about 50,000 strong, including 10,500 regular infantry; and further north, Sindhia's main army, about 35,000 strong, commanded by Perron. Marquess Wellesley formed two armies, the northern under General Gerard Lake, and the southern under Arthur Wellesley. Collaborating with the latter was the Hyderabad Contingent, some 9,400 strong, and in addition to Wellesley's own army, more than 11,000 strong, were some 5,000 allied Mysore and Maratha light horse.

On 6 August 1803 Arthur Wellesley received news of the failure of negotiations, and marched immediately upon the fortification of Ahmednuggur. On 8 August he stormed and took the city, laid siege to Ahmednuggur fort, and accepted its surrender on 12 August. This success had a profound effect upon the Maratha chieftain Goklah, one of the Peshwa's supporters whose forces were present with Wellesley; he wrote that 'These English are a strange people and their General a wonderful man. They came here in the morning, looked at the pettah-wall, walked over it, killed all the garrison, and returned to breakfast.'[3]

Wellesley encountered the army of Sindhia and Ragogee Bhonsla at Assaye on 23 September. The latter numbered between 40,000 and 50,000 men, including three brigades of regular infantry, the largest under the command of the ex-Hanoverian sergeant, Pohlmann. Despite the numbers, Wellesley determined to attack; as Colonel Stevenson's Hyderabad force was not within range of support, Wellesley had only some 7,000 men, of whom perhaps 500 had to guard his baggage, and of the remainder, he had only three European regiments (19th Light Dragoons, 74th and 78th). The Mysore and Maratha light horse, some believed to be of dubious loyalty, could not be used in the main action. Despite sustaining heavy casualties in their frontal attack, the small British and Company force won a considerable victory; it was Wellesley's first major success, and one which he always held in the highest estimation, even when compared to his later triumphant career. His losses, however, were severe, numbering nearly 650 Europeans and more than 900 Indian troops; from a strength of about 500 rank and file, the 74th lost ten officers and one volunteer killed and seven

wounded, and 124 other ranks killed and 270 wounded, a casualty-rate of about three-quarters of those engaged.[4] Having sustained such casualties (which exemplified the savage combat which could occur, European troops fighting with added determination because of the dire consequences of defeat against an enemy who did not always observe the conventions of so-called 'civilised' war), and having fought the battle after a 24-mile march, Wellesley was unable immediately to pursue his defeated enemy, who had left 98 guns on the field, which they had bravely attempted to defend.

Wellesley pressed on in due course, until the Raja of Berar's army, with large numbers of Sindhia's cavalry, made a stand at Argaum on 29 November 1803. They numbered probably between 30,000 and 40,000, Wellesley's army about 10–11,000, the European part being only the remains of those who had fought at Assaye, plus the 94th Scotch Brigade from Stevenson's force. The European infantry outpaced the rest as Wellesley ordered a frontal attack; the Marathas broke, abandoning 38 guns, and Wellesley's cavalry did severe execution in the pursuit. Wellesley suffered barely 360 casualties in all. On 15 December 1803 a ferocious British assault captured the fortress of Gawilghur; the Raja of Berar sued for peace next day, and on 17 December ceded the province of Cuttack to the Company, and other territory to its allies.

In the northern sphere of the War, Lake's plan of campaign in Hindustan was directed toward the destruction of Perron's field army, given that officer's importance not only as the leader of a large, trained force, but also as one exerting considerable influence over the puppet emperor,

Maratha Light Horse.
(Engraving by 'TSS')

Shah Alum. Lake advanced and on 4 September took the fort of Aligarh by storm; three days later he received a letter from Perron announcing his resignation from Sindhia's service. He was succeeded in command of the 'regulars' by another Frenchman, Louis Bourquain, who with 19,000 men (including sixteen regular battalions and some 6,000 light horse) marched to attack Lake near Delhi on 10 September; Lake's 4,500 men drove them from the field, capturing 68 guns, which as usual with the Marathas had been well-served and had caused some havoc among Lake's force. Four days later Bourquain gave himself up, and on 16 September Shah Alum welcomed Lake into the capital of the Mogul empire. In the wake of Lake's success, the Raja of Bhurtpore, a powerful Jat chief, concluded an alliance with the British, and on 17 October Lake accepted the surrender of Agra from its English commanders, two of Sindhia's 'foreign' officers. Regarded as the key to Hindustan, the fall of this great fortress was a decisive blow; yet in the field there still remained about 9,000 of Sindhia's regular infantry, and 4–5,000 light horse, under the Maratha general Abaji. Lake engaged them on 1 November 1803 at Laswaree. His initial cavalry attack was beaten off by the Maratha artillery (72 guns, chained together by their axle-trees), and awaited the arrival of his infantry, half-exhausted after a forced march of 25 miles under a fierce sun. They rushed forward to escape the Maratha artillery bombardment and swept away Abaji's force, taking all its artillery and virtually destroying the splendid regular troops, originally de Boigne's and hitherto known as the Deccan Invincibles. Lake's casualties numbered 824, the largest proportion being among his European cavalry (8th, 27th and 29th Light Dragoons) and the 76th Foot, the latter being especially distinguished. So fierce had been the fight that Lake had two horses shot from under him, his coat burned by the ignition of a matchlock musket, and his son desperately wounded at his side. Sindhia sued for peace and a treaty was concluded on 30 December 1803, by which he yielded much territory.

Having failed to support Sindhia and the Raja of Berar, it might have been expected that Jaswant Rao Holkar of Indore would not have challenged the British on his own; but he did, and won a considerable victory by almost annihilating a force of some five battalions under Colonel William Monson in a running fight as Monson retired to Agra (24–31 August 1804). This defeat caused Britain's allies to waver (the Raja of Bhurtpore had already been corresponding with Holkar); so it was determined to mount a full expedition against Holkar, and no longer to rely upon the operations of smaller detachments to bring him to heel. Delhi had been besieged; Lake effected its relief on 15 October 1804, and after marching 350 miles in two weeks in his pursuit of Holkar, Lake's surprise attack at Furruckabad (17 November) routed the Marathas, who lost some 3,000 dead, mostly in the pursuit

The Revd. Thomas Jones applies (successfully) to the Directors of the East India Company for an appointment for his son, a document which perhaps describes the type of individual of use to the Company:
'... I have a parcel of fine boys, and not much cash to provide for them. My eldest son I intended for a pillar of the Church: with this in view I gave him a suitable education at school, and afterwards entered him at Cambridge, where he has resided the usual time, and last Christmas took his degree with some reputation to himself; but I must at the same time add, that he is more likely to kick a church down, than to support one. He is of a very eccentric genius – he had no notion of restraint to chapel, gates, lectures, &c.; and when rebuked by his master, tutor &c. for want of obedience to their rules, he treated them in the contemptible light of not being gentlemen, and seemed to intimate, that he should call them to account, as an affair of honour, &c. This soon disconcerted all my plans for him ... [but] if he will suit your service, and you can help me, do. He is now about 20, near 6 feet high, well made, stout, and very active, and is as bold and intrepid as a lion. He is of a Welsh extraction for many generations: and, I think, as my first-born, he is not degenerated. If you like to look at him, you shall see him, and judge for yourselves ...
P.S. If you like him, I will equip him.'
(*Gentleman's Magazine*, 1813, vol. I, pp. 612–13).

after they had broken, against a British loss of 28 casualties. On 13 November another part of Holkar's army was defeated before Deig, an action in which the British commander, General Fraser, was killed; thirteen of the 87 guns captured on this occasion had previously been taken from Monson, who now re-possessed them, he being one of Fraser's brigade-commanders. Deig belonged to the Raja of Bhurtpore, and as he had openly supported Holkar, it was determined that the fortress of Deig should be taken; Lake stormed the outer defences on 23 December, and on Christmas morning the town and citadel surrendered. From there Lake moved to the mighty fortress of Bhurtpore, opening his bombardment on 7 January 1805. Unsuccessful assaults were made on 9 and 21 January, 20 and 21 February, and then Lake abandoned the siege; but the Raja of Bhurtpore concluded a peace with the British, advantageous to the latter, on 10 April 1805.

Before the war ended, Marquess Wellesley's period of governor-generalship had ended; his successor, again Cornwallis, landed at Calcutta on 30 July 1805. He determined to bring the war to a rapid conclusion by offering generous terms to Holkar and Sindhia (the latter again on the verge of open hostility); but Cornwallis died on 5 October. Holkar had marched into the Punjab in the hope of attracting support from the Sikhs, and Lake followed;

but when it became obvious that the Sikhs were better disposed towards Lake than towards himself, Holkar sued for peace, which was concluded by treaty on 24 December 1805. Under the terms initiated by Cornwallis and continued by his successor (Sir George Barlow, senior member of the governor-general's council), the Marathas received more concessions than they might have expected (Holkar, for example, had his lands restored intact), and those princes who had provided vital assistance to the British were deprived of the promised support, and virtually abandoned to the mercies of Sindhia and Holkar. It could be argued that the result of all this costly campaigning against the Marathas was simply to provide a platform for future conflict.

Vellore

During the next decade serious military operations in India were few, as potential friction between the growing power of the Sikhs and the British was averted by the Treaty of Amritsar (15 April 1809), which defined the River Sutlej as the boundary between the two. In 1806, however, there occurred one of the most serious outbreaks of mutiny among the Company forces, from which the native regiments had never been immune. Their discipline was not always immaculate; for example, in July 1802 the escort for the Persian ambassador (provided by the Bengal Volunteers, recently returned from Egypt) got into a row with his retinue, and in the ensuing fight killed the dignitary they were supposed to be protecting. Also significant was the consequence of under-estimating the religious and cultural sensitivities of the sepoys, not always understood by British officers but ignored at their peril.

In November 1805 the commander-in-chief of the Madras Army, Sir John Cradock, ordered a change in head-dress from turban to 'round hat', and the removal of beards, face-painting and 'joys' (jewellery). Caste-marks, ornaments and beards often had religious significance, and 'round hats' were regarded as synonymous with Christians in the eyes of the sepoys; thus the new regulations were seen as an attack upon the troops' religion. These objections, and rumours circulated by fakirs that the government was mixing pigs' blood into the salt sold in public, as a deliberate attempt to defile the religious, were used as excuses by the sons and retainers of Tipu, who lived in their palace at Vellore on East India Company pensions, to raise a revolt.

These factors conspired to cause a mutiny at Vellore, which was garrisoned by three Madras battalions (1st/1st, 2nd/1st and 2nd/23rd), and four companies of the 69th Foot. The Indian regiments rose on the night of 10 July 1806, massacred the 69th's sick in their hospital, murdered officers and fired into the European barracks. By delaying to pillage the fort, they allowed the surviving British to congregate on the ramparts; and an officer who was outside the fort when the rising began went for help to the nearest

military post, Arcot, the station of the 19th Light Dragoons and some Madras Native Cavalry, who were unaffected by the unrest. Providentially the 19th was commanded by Sir Rollo Gillespie, one of the most capable and energetic officers in India, and he set out with a relief-force within a quarter of an hour of the alarm being raised.

Gillespie dashed ahead with about twenty men, and arriving at Vellore found the surviving Europeans, about sixty men of the 69th, commanded by NCOs and two assistant-surgeons, still clinging to the ramparts but out of ammunition. Unable to gain entry through the defended gate, Gillespie climbed the wall with the aid of a rope and a sergeant's sash which was lowered to him; and to gain time led the 69th in a bayonet-charge along the ramparts. When the rest of the 19th arrived, Gillespie had them blow in the gates with their galloper guns, and made a second charge with the 69th to clear a space inside the gate to permit the cavalry to deploy. The 19th and Madras Cavalry then charged and slaughtered any sepoy who stood in their way. The massacre of the helpless European sick so aroused the British that no mercy was shown; about 100 sepoys who had sought refuge in the palace were dragged out, placed against a wall and blasted with canister shot until all were dead. John Blakiston, the engineer who had blown in the gates, recalled that although such punishment was revolting to all civilised beliefs, 'this appalling sight I could look upon, I may almost say, with composure. It was an act of summary justice, and in every respect a most proper one.'[5] Such was the nature of combat in India where the 'civilised' conventions of European warfare did not apply. This snuffed out the unrest at a stroke, and provided the history of the British in India with one of its true epics; for as Gillespie admitted, with a delay of even five minutes, all would have been lost.

Nepal (or Gurkha) War

In the next campaign in which the British were engaged, they encountered one of their most formidable enemies. The Gurkhas claim descent from the Hindu Rajputs of Chitor in Rajputana, who were driven from their own country by Muslim invasion in the 14th century. They took refuge in the hill country around Kumaon, and pushed eastwards into Nepal; the name 'Gurkha' originated from the village of Gorkha, captured in 1559 and itself named after the saint Gorakhnath, who once lived there in a cave. Nepal was conquered by 1768, by Prithwi Narayan, a commander of considerable talent who had become chieftain of Gorkha in 1742. He overthrew the existing kingdom and recruited allies from those tribes already resident in the area; thus the peoples described as Gurkhas (or to use the 19th-century spelling 'Goorkhas') were a mixture of races, including the Aryan and Rajput clans which invaded, and the Mongolian races whom they conquered. The principal of these were the Magar and Gurung of central Nepal (of which there were many clans), and the Limbu and Rai of eastern Nepal; those of Rajput ancestry were known by the general name of 'Khas' Gurkhas, including the Khas tribes and the Thakurs. Often regarded as the founder of the nation, Prithwi Narayan brought organisation to the Gurkha forces, although their bravery and martial reputation were already evident, especially skill with their fearsome sword-knife, the kukri.

Nepal had maintained contacts with the British from the mid-18th century, and in 1765 Jaya Prakasha, raja of Katmandu, had asked for British assistance when attacked by Prithwi Narayan. A small force was sent by the Company under Captain Kinloch which temporarily checked the Gurkhas, although Katmandu fell shortly after. By the time of his death Prithwi Narayan had been proclaimed king of Nepal, although in succeeding years feuding within the ruling classes resulted in the subjugation of the authority of the king to that of the maharaja or prime minister. Gurkha territory expanded by conquest, until by 1790 their lands extended from Bhutan in the east to the Sutlej in the west, and from the borders of Tibet in the north to the states under British protection in the south. An invasion of Tibet in 1790 brought a retaliatory counter-invasion by China and some loss of Gurkha territory, and with westward expansion blocked by the Sikhs, it was towards the south that the Gurkhas looked for further progress. The Gurkha state entered into a commercial treaty with the British in 1791, and appealed for assistance at the time of the Chinese invasion (the British sent only a mediator, who arrived after the conclusion of peace); another treaty was signed in October 1801 and a British Resident sent to the court at Katmandu, but was withdrawn after less than a year as he was being ignored. From this time the Gurkhas infiltrated and raided over the frontier into the Terai, a strip of territory forming Nepal's southern border, which had been ceded to the East India Company by the

Nawab of Oudh in 1801. Negotiation having proved unsuccessful, the Governor-General, Lord Moira, declared war in November 1814 and launched an expedition to end these outrages.

Having under-estimated the martial qualities of their opponents and the difficulties of the mountainous terrain, British success was mixed. Four columns were sent into Nepal, two advancing on Katmandu (Major-General Marley from Dinapore, Major-General Wood from Benares), and two into the Gurkha holdings in the west, Major-General Sir Rollo Gillespie into Garhwal from Meerut, and Major-General Sir David Ochterlony in the extreme west, along the Sutlej from Ludhiana. The columns advancing on Katmandu achieved nothing, and the heaviest fighting occurred in the west, where the Gurkha forces were commanded by their best general, Amarsing Thapa. Gillespie was killed (31 October) assaulting the fort at Kalunga, north of Dehra Dun, which was held by Balbahadur (whose name was recorded by the British as 'Bulbudder Sing'), Amarsing Thapa's nephew. Gillespie was succeeded in command by Colonel Sebright Mawby of the 53rd, whose attack on 27 November also failed; but on 30 November the remnant of the garrison evacuated the fort. The scenes inside the fort, piled with Gurkha dead and those too seriously wounded to escape, women and children included, appalled the victors; even Mawby reported that the sight 'presented so much misery that, the most obdurate Heart must have bled'.[6] The surviving wounded, and some tiny children whose parents had been killed in the defence of the fort, were taken into care by the British, who were immensely impressed by the courage displayed by the Gurkhas. The attack on 31 October had cost the British 32 dead and 229 injured; between 25 and 30 November, 48 and 441 respectively. It was perhaps this action which brought home to the British what formidable soldiers the Gurkhas were.

Mawby was succeeded in command by Major-General Martindell, and having captured Jaitak, a stronghold defended stoutly by Ranjur Singh, Amarsing Thapa's son, the column was ordered to join Ochterlony. This force made steady progress, and when Malaun was besieged Amarsing Thapa negotiated an end to hostilities, upon terms dictated by Ochterlony, including the evacuation by the Gurkhas of all territory between the rivers Sutlej and Kali, including Garhwal and Kumaon, and their holdings in Sikkim (on the eastern boundary of Nepal). The Gurkha prime minister Bhim Sen Thapa declined to ratify the treaty, so in January 1816 the campaign was renewed, Ochterlony advancing upon Katmandu by the route which had defeated Marley; he outflanked the Gurkha defences and captured their position, commanded by Ranjur Sing, at Makwanpur (or 'Muckwampore') on 28 February, only for the Gurkhas to launch a most violent counter-attack, which was beaten off with heavy casualties. With the enemy thus virtually at the gates, the Gurkhas sued for

> The martial qualities of the Gurkhas became clear to the British during their defence of Kalunga in 1814. Colonel Sebright Mawbey of the 53rd, who temporarily succeeded to the command of the British force after the death of Rollo Gillespie, recounted an anecdote exemplifying the unbreakable spirit of the Gurkhas: 'To show the determined conduct of these people, the orderly Jemadar to Bulbudder Sing, in attempting to escape with his Chief, was wounded and taken Prisoner – finding that the wound would not put him to death, he abused both Officers and Men in the grossest terms in hopes that, they would by that means shoot him – but finding that this would have no effect on their feelings – he beat his head against the Stones in the hope of putting an end to his existence – which all failing, he requested fire to warm himself, and when left by the Sepoys, he took an opportunity of throwing the whole of it on his breast – which was no sooner discovered than it was removed – he has, however, since died.'

peace, confirmed by the Treaty of Segauli (March 1816) by which they relinquished much of their captured territory, and agreed to the installation of a British Resident in Katmandu.

The conclusion of the war ended hostilities between the British and the Gurkhas, although there was dynastic strife within Nepal, leading to the emergence of Jung (or Jang) Bahadur, a leading military commander who became prime minister following the 'Kot massacre' (15 September 1846, the Kot being the assembly of the royal court) in which many of Jung Bahadur's enemies were eliminated. This marked a significant change in relations between Nepal and the British, for Jung Bahadur was a staunch Anglophile, and was greatly impressed by the reception he received upon his state visit to Britain in 1850, when he met the Queen and the Duke of Wellington. Consequently, in addition to the Gurkhas who had been enlisted in the Company forces from 1815, during the Indian Mutiny Jung Bahadur placed his entire military forces at the disposal of the British; the Nepalese army performed much valuable service in the war, and Jung Bahadur, who had taken the field in person, was awarded the KCB for his support. Relations between Nepal and the British continued to be most cordial. Jung Bahadur died in 1877 and was succeeded by his brother, Sir Ranadip Singh Bahadur, who was murdered in 1885 and succeeded by his nephew, Sir Shamsher Jung, who upon his death was succeeded in 1901 by his brother, Deb Shamsher; in the same year he was deposed in favour of another brother, Chandra Shamsher Jung. Despite the occasional internal plots, Anglo-Nepali relations were unaffected: Chandra Shamsher Jung aided the British during the 1904 Tibet war, was awarded the GCSI and even appointed as a major-general in the British Army. The Gurkha troops enrolled in British service have given loyal and courageous service in countless campaigns, and from 1947 have formed an integral part of the British Army.

Third Maratha (or Maratha and Pindari) War

Of uncertain origin, the term 'Pindari' described a type of irregular light horse-cum-bandit which flourished in central India in the late 18th and early 19th centuries, originating with the break-up of the Mogul armies. Of no one race, tribe or religion, they included any to whom the prospect of lawlessness appealed, including Marathas, Afghans and Jats; generally organised in loose bands led by chieftains, they sometimes served the Maratha states, receiving no wage but even paying for the prospect of loot and plunder. They congregated in Malwa, with the tacit approval of Sindhia and Holkar, from where they set out, usually in November, to plunder throughout Hindustan, into British territory and even to the Coromandel coast. The most powerful chieftain, Amir Khan, had regularly organised regiments, estimated at 12,000 light horse, 10,000 infantry and an estimated artillery train of between

John Blakiston, perhaps best known for his service with the Portuguese Army during the Peninsular War, was an engineer officer at the time of the mutiny at Vellore, and tells the story of a sentry who performed his duty to the end:
'In the course of this business a singular instance of courage, sense of duty, and determination, was evinced by a soldier of the 69th, who stood sentry over the magazine. In the midst of the work of slaughter, an officer, who was running for his life, passed him at this post, and, seeing him walking up and down with the utmost composure, hastily asked if he knew that the sepoys were murdering all the Europeans. "I thought as much," he replied. "Why don't you fly for your life then?" exclaimed the officer. "I was posted here," he said, "and it is my duty to remain. I've six rounds in my pouch, and I'll sell my life dearly." The noble fellow was afterwards found dead on his post ...'
(Blakiston, J. *Twelve Years' Military Adventures in Three-Quarters of the Globe*, London, 1829, vol. I, pp. 310–11)

80 and 200 guns; to which other Pindari bands added a further 15,000 cavalry, 1,500 infantry and 20 guns.

By 1817 the ravages of these bandits had become intolerable, so the Governor-General (and Commander-in-Chief), the Earl of Moira (later Marquess Hastings) determined to crush them; but the renewed hostility of the Maratha powers turned what began as a drive against freebooters into a war against the peshwa, Indore, and the Bhonsla raja of Nagpore. (Jaswant Rao Holkar of Indore had died in 1811, and in the minority of his successor, his favourite mistress became regent; she was murdered by the Indore military commanders in 1817, who committed their forces to the peshwa when hostilities began). To combat this menace, the Governor-General formed two armies, taking personal command of the Grand Army which assembled at Cawnpore in four divisions, each of two infantry and a cavalry brigade; and General Sir Thomas Hislop's Army of the Deccan, seven divisions strong. Troops from all three presidencies were involved.

Two of the possible foes provided little opposition; Sindhia was pressured into neutrality, and by signing the Treaty of Gwalior agreed to take action against the Pindaris, whom he had been protecting; and the Pindaris themselves did not pose the predicted threat. Amir Khan accepted conditions imposed by the British and disbanded his forces, in return for a territorial settlement which became the state of Tonk in Rajputana; the remaining Pindari forces were attacked and dispersed, one of their principal leaders, Karim, surrendering, and another, Chitu, fled to the jungles where he was killed by a tiger.

More serious was the reaction of the other Marathas, whose simmering discontent turned into open war in November 1817. As Peshwa Baji Rao II assembled his forces, the commander of the British units at Poona, Colonel C. B. Burr, withdrew from the cantonments with the Resident, and concentrated on a ridge at Kirkee. The residency at Poona was burned, and on 5 November 1817 the Peshwa's army moved to attack the position at Kirkee; their strength was estimated as up to 18,000 cavalry, 8,000 infantry and fourteen guns, against which Burr had five Bombay sepoy battalions and an auxiliary battalion, about 2,000 strong, and 800 Europeans (Bombay Europeans and a detachment of 65th Foot). Burr attacked immediately and the Marathas bolted, the Peshwa's entire force being routed for the loss of nineteen dead and 67 wounded, only two of these casualties falling upon Burr's European troops. General Lionel Smith arrived to reinforce Burr on the 13th, and on 17 November another action was fought at Poona which completed the defeat of the Peshwa's army.

At Nagpore the Bhonsla mustered his forces, ostensibly for a drive against the Pindaris, but turned against the British when news was received of the Peshwa's revolt. The British force at Nagpore was only about 1,300 strong, comprising three troops of 6th Bengal Cavalry, the 1/20th and 1/24th Madras Native Infantry, and some auxiliaries, commanded by Lieutenant-Colonel H. S. Scott. Like Burr, Scott withdrew from the cantonments to a defensible position; at Seetabuldee on 26 November he was attacked by 18,000 men of the Nagpore army, including some 3,000 Arabs employed by the Bhonsla. After a fight of some eighteen hours the Nagpore army withdrew, Scott's force having sustained 367 casualties, testimony to the determination with which sepoy units could fight, even without European support. On 12 December relief arrived in the form of Brigadier-General J. Doveton's 2nd Division of the Army of the Deccan, which assaulted Nagpore on 16 December. After several hours' fighting the 21,000-strong Nagpore army was routed, some thousands withdrawing into the city, where they capitulated on 24 December after several days of bombardment.

Despite the defeat at Poona, the Peshwa's army was still in being, and, about 28,000 strong, on New Year's Day 1818 fell upon a British detachment at Corygaum. Commanded by Captain Staunton of the 2/1st Bombay Native Infantry, this comprised only about 600 of his own battalion, two Madras Artillery 6pdrs and 300 auxiliary horse. Staunton occupied that part of Corygaum village not held by the enemy, and a house-to-house fight raged from noon until 9 p.m. This remarkable defence, in which only Staunton and two other officers remained unscathed, resisted all efforts of the Peshwa's army, which retired and broke up upon news of the approach of General Lionel Smith. Concerning the exertions of the British officers (even two assistant-surgeons, one of whom was killed, had led bayonet-charges throughout the day), Smith described their efforts as 'almost unparalleled ... in such a struggle the presence of a single European was of the utmost con-

sequence, and seemed to inspire the native soldiers with the usual confidence of success';[7] but this action, coming at the end of a 28-mile march, reflected equal credit upon the sepoys as upon their leaders.

After vainly attempting to negotiate to prevent the state becoming hostile, Sir Thomas Hislop engaged the army of Indore at Mahidpore on 23 December 1817. The Indore forces mustered some 30,000 light horse, 5,000 infantry and 100 guns; Hislop's 5,500-strong 1st and 3rd Divisions of the Army of the Deccan included few Europeans, only the flank companies of the 1st Foot and Madras Europeans. Because of the disparity in numbers, Hislop attacked immediately; the Maratha horse fled, but the infantry and gunners (trained in European style) made a gallant stand until they were overthrown. Hislop lost 174 killed, 614 wounded and three missing. Mahidpore virtually ended the war, as peace was concluded with Indore shortly after. Following a chase, Baji Rao II surrendered to Sir John Malcolm in May 1818, and was sent as a state pensioner to Bithur, near Cawnpore, devoid of power or influence; his heir, Nana Sahib, would become infamous forty years later. An infant was recognised as raja of Nagpore, under British guardianship, and when the Bhonsla died without direct heirs in 1853, his territory was annexed. The war finally ended the power of the Maratha states, although Gwalior was still not completely negated as an opponent.

Nowah

Minor operations continued against recalcitrant tribes or chieftains, none of which involved major battles; but an example in which serious fighting did occur was the reduction of the fort of Nowah in January 1819. This position was held in opposition to the Nizam of Hyderabad, in whose territory it lay, on the frontier of Berar, by a garrison of about 500, principally Arabs. The British Resident in Hyderabad (R. Russell) dispatched part of the Hyderabad Contingent under Major Pitman to bring the chief to heel; the fort was taken by assault on 30 January 1819 and most of the garrison were killed (439 bodies were buried and 100 men were captured, 80 of them wounded). Losses of the Contingent in the last two weeks of January amounted to 38 dead and 180 wounded.

Military Forces 1800–25

British and Company Forces were enlarged during this period, a notable feature from this time being the formation of 'irregular' or auxiliary units, commanded by European officers, to impose greater discipline and training upon the allied forces that had operated with the British in earlier campaigns. The 1796 re-organisations of the Company forces had tended to increase the influence of British officers at the expense of that of the Indians, which made it even more important that British officers be sensitive to the features peculiar to Indian regiments. This point was articulated in a report produced by the Company which argued (successfully) for the independence of their own forces, and to keep their establishment separate from that of the King's army:

'The Indian army is the main instrument by which the Company have acquired and retained the territorial possessions they have added to the British empire. The people of those countries submitted more easily to an authority exercised by means of a body formed from among themselves. We fought battles, and governed provinces as the native powers did, and our new subjects, undisgusted with the sight of a foreign conquering army, supposed the government to continue substantially the same ... The constitution and character which this Indian army has acquired have been the subject of just admiration. These have been owing, essentially, to the happy mixture of bravery and generosity, of firmness and kindness, exercised towards the sepoys by their European officers. The superior lights and energy of the European character have directed the powers, and conciliated the prejudices, of the native troops, but it was because the officers knew the people and their prejudices well. These officers have been trained up among them from an early age; the nature, the usages, and the language of the natives, were become familiar to them; and the natives, remarkably the creatures of habit, in return, from being accustomed, became attached to them. Without such knowledge, however, on the part of the officers, they might every day have revolted the minds of so peculiar a race, and have alienated them from our service and Government.'[8]

The necessity of close connection and mutual understanding between officers and sepoys was to be ignored at peril.

Bengal Army. The single European Regiment which existed from 1803 was expanded to two in 1822, which were amalgamated again in 1829. The number of Native Infantry regiments was increased, rising from 27 to 30 in 1815, with two more formed in 1818 and the 33rd and 34th in 1823. In 1824 each battalion took a separate number, 1st–68th; and in 1825 the 1st–6th Extra Battalions were formed. 'Local' infantry had existed in the Bengal presidency in the 18th century, but the practice was increased after 1815, when the existing corps (Calcutta Native Militia, Ramgarh Local Battalion, Bhagalpur Hill Rangers, Dinajpur Local Battalion) were joined by others, numbered as the 1st–15th Local Battalions in 1823. The corps listed above were the 1st–4th respectively; in numerical order the others were the Champaran Light Infantry, 1st and 2nd Nasiri, Sirmoor, and Kumaon Battalions, Rangpur and Gorakhpur Light Infantry, 1st and 2nd Rampura, Mharawa and Bencoolen Battalions; the 16th Sylhet Light Infantry was raised in 1824. Most notable were the two Nasiri ('Friendly'), Sirmoor and Kumaon battalions, the first Gurkha corps in British service, enrolled during the Nepal War; except for periods when organised as line

The origin of one of the most famous names in the Indian Army: Lieutenant-Colonel James Skinner (1778–1841), son of Lieutenant-Colonel Hercules Skinner and a Rajput lady. He served under de Boigne and Perron but entered British service before the Second Maratha War; a great leader of light horse, he gave his name to perhaps the most famous of all Indian Army units, Skinner's Horse.

units, the Gurkha units were rifle corps, exploiting their indigenous skills practised in mountain warfare in their homeland. In 1826 the number of Local Battalions was reduced to eleven, of which the Gurkha units were numbered 4th–7th.

Two more Native Cavalry regiments were formed in Bengal in 1806 (7th and 8th); the cavalry changed its title to Bengal Light Cavalry in 1819, and two extra regiments were formed in 1824, being numbered 9th and 10th in 1826. In 1803 Captain James Skinner brought his regiment into Company service, having served in Sindhia's army, the origin of the famous Skinner's Horse. Others followed: Gardner's Horse in 1809, 1st–3rd Rohilla Cavalry in 1815, two more regiments of Skinner's Horse in 1814, and Gough's Horse in 1823. The 2nd and 3rd Rohilla and 2nd Skinner's were disbanded in 1819, and in 1823 the survivors were numbered as the 1st–5th Bengal Local Horse, respectively 1st Skinner's, Gardner's, 1st Rohilla, 2nd Skinner's (known as Baddeley's Frontier Horse) and Gough's. European officers of these units wore British-style uniform but the rank and file a dress

Left: Light company havildar (left) and sepoy of a battalion company, Madras Native Infantry; print by I. C. Stadler after Charles Hamilton Smith, published 1 March 1815. The uniform is typical of the East India Company's 'native' troops, uniting British and Indian styles of dress, the latter including a stylised 'turban' and janghirs (shorts).

Joseph Budworth, an officer of the 72nd Royal Manchester Volunteers at the great siege of Gibraltar, and best-known as the author of *A Fortnight's Ramble to the Lakes in Westmoreland, Lancashire, and Cumberland* (3rd edn., 1810), writes in that work of the fellowship common among Europeans in a foreign and often hostile land; upon joining the Bengal Artillery, Budworth encountered Colonel Patrick Duff, then commanding, who:

'told me, that a Gibraltar soldier should ever be treated in the Bengal Artillery as if he had commenced his career amongst them – "Here you dine to-day, and here shall be a plate for you whenever you please; but at present mix with your brother officers: they will be as happy to hail you as a comrade as I am"... Similar instances are not unusual in India: the heart expands in proportion to the distance from their native country, and the frequent warfare they are engaged in; and war ever brings home the soldier's feelings to the noblest effects. A systematic cold-blooded Indian is almost a phenomenon in their armies ...'
(Patrick Duff was known universally as 'Tiger Duff', for his having killed with a bayonet a tiger which had leaped upon him)

based upon Indian costume, including medieval-style helmets with sliding nasal bars; the famous yellow coat of Skinner's Horse originated from this period. Arms were originally of Indian style, including lances, and most irregular cavalry was formed upon the 'silladar system', by which each man provided his own horse, accoutrements and subsistence in return for a higher rate of pay.

The Bengal Artillery increased in strength; the horse artillery was made a separate unit and expanded to three troops in 1809, and native troops were added when the cavalry's light artillery was withdrawn in 1817. A Golundauze corps was re-formed in 1806, rising to a strength of two battalions of eight companies by 1827. In 1808 the pioneer corps (raised 1803) was increased to eight companies, and a unit of miners was formed; they merged to produce the Bengal Pioneers and Sappers, and a further corps of Sappers and Miners was created in 1819.

Madras Army. A second battalion of Madras Europeans existed from 1824 to 1830, and the Native Infantry was increased to 25 numbered corps; 1st–6th Extra Battalions existed in 1804–5 and from 1819 to 1821, and four numbered battalions of Hill Rangers in 1818–19. In 1824 each regiment's two battalions each became a regiment, producing fifty numbered regiments, including four of light infantry (3rd, 23rd, 31st, 34th), their predecessor battalions having been designated as such in 1811. The battalions which mutinied at Vellore were disbanded after the rising. The 7th and 8th Native Cavalry were formed in 1800 and 1804 respectively, and in 1819 the mounted units changed their title to Madras Light Cavalry. The Native Artillery battalion was disbanded in 1802, but one Indian company was added to each European battalion in 1805. In 1819 the Indian element formed the 3rd Battalion of Madras Foot Artillery, which became the 4th when a 3rd European Battalion was raised in 1819. The Madras Horse Artillery was created in 1805, six troops strong by 1819 (two of Europeans, one armed with rockets, and three Indian). In 1803 the pioneer corps was increased to two battalions, totalling sixteen companies. From 1818 to 1821 there also existed a corps of Sappers and Miners, one company European and one Indian.

Bombay Army. The Bombay European Regiment maintained two battalions between 1824 and 1829. The Native Infantry increased to nine regiments in 1803 and more were added, with two Extra Battalions formed in 1820 and the Marine Battalion numbered as the 1st/11th in 1818.

Governors-General of India
with dates of appointment

1774	Warren Hastings (having been governor of Bengal from 1772)
1786	General Charles, Earl Cornwallis
1793	Sir John Shore
1798	Richard, Lord Mornington (Marquess Wellesley)
1804	General Charles, Marquess Cornwallis
1805	Sir George Barlow
1807	Gilbert, Earl of Minto
1813	General Francis, Earl of Moira
1823	William, Lord Amherst
1828	General Lord William Bentinck
1836	George, Baron Auckland
1842	Edward, Earl of Ellenborough
1844	Rt. Hon. Sir Henry Hardinge
1848	James, Earl of Dalhousie
1856	Charles, Viscount Canning
1862	James, 8th Earl of Elgin and 12th of Kincardine
1864	Rt. Hon. Sir John Lawrence, Bt.
1869	Richard, Earl of Mayo
1872	Thomas, Earl of Northbrook
1876	Edward, Baron Lytton
1880	George, Marquess of Ripon
1884	Frederick, Earl of Dufferin
1888	Henry, Marquess of Lansdowne
1894	Victor, 9th Earl of Elgin and 13th of Kincardine
1899	George, Baron Curzon of Kedleston
1905	Gilbert, Earl of Minto

Each battalion formed a new regiment in 1824, numbered 1–24, with the 1st and 2nd Extra Battalions forming the 25th and 26th. A troop of Bombay Cavalry was created in 1804 and a second in 1816, expanded in 1817 to create the 1st and 2nd Bombay Light Cavalry, with the 3rd formed in 1820. An irregular corps, the Poona Auxiliary Horse, was raised in 1817. An extra Foot Artillery company was formed in 1802 and three in 1820, when the corps was re-organised into two battalions of five companies each, of four companies each from 1824. Troops of horse artillery were raised in 1811 and 1820, and two more in 1824; a company of Sappers and Miners was formed in 1820.

Hyderabad Contingent. With the extinction of French influence in the 'regular' forces of the Nizam of Hyderabad, the Hyderabad Contingent became the most significant of the auxiliary forces. It was financed by the Nizam, but unlike his personal forces was under British control, and initially might even have been regarded as a way of keep-

ing the Nizam in order. The cavalry was re-organised into three regiments in 1816, and in 1813 the British Resident, Henry Russell, formed the two regular battalions which became known as 'Russell's Brigade'.

Service Outside India. The first Indian troops to serve outside the subcontinent were the force sent to the Egyptian campaign of 1801 under Sir David Baird, to support the British Army engaged against the French. Involving 'volunteer battalions' of sepoys assembled for the purpose, the Indian contingent saw no action despite making a most arduous march across the desert. Indian units were also engaged in the First Burma War (1824–6), covered in the section concerning that country.

INDIA 1825–1857

Bhurtpore

Bhurtpore (or 'Bharatpur'), the fortress which had defied a British siege in 1804–5, was the focus of the next Indian campaign. The raja who had held the fortress against Lake, Ranjit Singh, died in 1805, and his successor, Baldeo Singh, in 1824. He was succeeded by his infant son, Balwant Singh, but his throne was usurped by a cousin, Durjan Sal, who proclaimed himself regent. Sir David Ochterlony, the British Resident in Delhi, having acknowledged the succession of the child, prepared a force to evict the regent, only to have his expedition prohibited by the governor-general, Lord Amherst. (Ochterlony resigned over this lack of support, which was said to have accelerated his death, at Meerut in July 1825.) However, eventually it was realised that action had to be taken against the usurper, and an expedition of the Bengal Army was formed under the Commander-in-Chief in India, Lord Combermere (hitherto best-known as Wellington's best cavalry commander in the Peninsular War). With one cavalry and two infantry divisions he invested the city in early December 1825; an immense siege-train was assembled (40 guns, twelve howitzers and 58 mortars) and opened a bombardment at the end of the month. On 18 January 1826 two columns, led by the 14th and 59th Foot, fought their way through the resulting breach and captured the fortress. Combermere's dispatch announced starkly that 'the entire military power of the Bhurtpoor [*sic*] State has been annihilated',[9] involving the death of some 4,000 of the defenders; the remainder surrendered, were disarmed and set at liberty. Durjan Sal, his family and 160 cavalry attempted to break out but were apprehended by Combermere's cavalry screen which cut off the retreat of the defenders; Durjan Sal was deported to Benares, and the infant was restored to his throne. Given the outcome of the previous siege, the capture of this mighty fortress was a considerable achievement. (On two subsequent occasions the state came under British control: in 1853, during the minority of its ruler, and in 1900 when the then maharajah, Ram Singh, was deposed following the murder of one of his attendants; during the minority of the son who succeeded him, the government was run by a state minister and council, under the superintendence of the British political agent.)

Coorg

The state of Coorg lay on the plateau of the Western Ghats, an isolated region next to Mysore. Hyder Ali became involved in the state's dynastic disputes, and from 1780 until 1788 Coorg was under Mysore control, until the head of the ruling family, Vira Raja, escaped from captivity, raised a rebellion and drove the Mysoreans from the state. During the British conflict with Tipu, Coorg provided help to Britain. A second Vira Raja (nephew of the one who had fought Tipu, who had died in 1809) assumed power in Coorg in 1820, but his cruelty towards perceived opponents (including members of his own family) forced Britain to intervene, and on 11 April 1834 he was deposed by Colonel Fraser, political agent of the force sent in by the British; on 7 May the territory was annexed by the East India Company. (Vira Raja was deported to Vellore; he later visited Britain, where Queen Victoria acted as sponsor at his daughter's baptism.) In April-May 1837 the 'Coorg rebellion' occurred, arising from taxation and involving one Virappa who claimed to be raja; but the rebellion had little support and failed. It is probably best remembered for the issue of one of the earliest medals commemorating service in India, following those for the Deccan (1778–84), Mysore (1790–92) and Seringapatam (1799). The Coorg Medal, in gold and silver, was given to Coorg soldiers who remained loyal, 'For Distinguished Conduct and Loyalty to the British Government'; it portrayed a Coorg warrior brandishing the distinctive, curved 'Coorg knife', a weapon akin to the Gurkha kukri.

First Afghan War

Details of the Afghan War of 1839–42 are given in the section concerning that country.

Baluchistan

Baluchistan lies to the north-west of India, between the Indus valley and Afghanistan. A mountainous territory, it was named from the principal inhabitants, although the term 'Baluchi' covered peoples of Arab extraction, who were found throughout Baluchistan, as well as those of Persian and Dravidian origin. The rulers of Baluchistan had once acknowledged the suzerainty of the kings of Afghanistan, but by the time of the conflict in Baluchistan in 1839 had long been virtually independent; the dominant ruler was the khan of Kalat, who in 1839 was Mehrab Khan.

Britain's support of Shah Shujah, which led to the First Afghan War, involved the negotiation of a treaty with Mehrab Khan, who in return for an annual subsidy was to acknowledge the supremacy of Shujah, and to protect and

'A Chief of the Jekranee Beloochees'; a typical costume of the Baluchis against whom Sir Charles Napier campaigned. (Engraving after Captain Postans)

assist the passage of British forces through Baluchistan *en route* to Afghanistan. The khan was not enthusiastic, but the conflict which arose resulted from the duplicity of his wazir (chief minister), Muhammed Hasan, in revenge for the khan having murdered his (Hasan's) father; he told the British that Mehrab Khan was hostile, and vice versa, and encouraged the Baluchi tribesmen to plunder the British as they passed. Following the installation of Shujah in Kabul, a brigade of the Bombay Army under Major-General Sir Thomas Willshire was sent to repay Mehrab Khan for what was believed to be his treachery. Willshire reached Kalat on 13 November 1839, drove the khan's followers into the city, stormed and captured it; the unfortunate Mehrab Khan was killed in the fighting. Although Muhammed Hasan's duplicity became evident, it was not Mehrab's heir who was appointed to the throne of Kalat, but a rival claimant, Shah Nawaz Khan. He lacked the necessary support of the local chieftains, however, and abdicated when Mehrab Khan's son, Nasir Khan, returned to claim his inheritance in August 1840; the British political officer and his small garrison were overwhelmed. Upon this, a new British expedition was sent, under Major-General William Nott, which reoccupied Kalat at the end of the year. Skirmishing occurred until October 1841, when a compromise was reached which confirmed Nasir Khan on his throne.

The sensation of being under fire for the first time produced reactions which participants found difficult to
explain; an officer of the Bengal Europeans wrote of
this at the assault of Ghanzi in July 1839:

'They fought so well, and the rush was tremendous,
that the Queen's who were leading, were twice driven
back upon us, and it was not till the third charge of
their bayonets, backed by a heavy fire from our
grenadiers, that we made good our footing. Then a
scene of rout and slaughter ensued, that I have often
read of, but never before witnessed. The dead and
dying, both Europeans and natives, were lying in heaps
amidst the smoking ruins of the gateway, which we
passed through. I never thought I could have passed
such a scene with such carelessness and total want of
feeling. The cheering, shouting, and rattling of musketry on all sides was tremendous; and as we charged
through into the body of the place, drowned every
thought but the proud one of our success ... Not more
than two or three of us were ever under fire before;
and we can scarcely believe that it is not all a dream ...
The effect of the artillery, the flashes from which, rendered every object for the moment visible; the blue-
lights, which threw just such a gleam as they would
have done in such a scene upon the stage, were perfectly theatrical. If it had not been for the whistling of
shot over my head, the anything but agreeable hissing
of matchlock balls about my ears, and the men falling
around me, I could have fancied myself a spectator at
some show in Vauxhall Gardens ... we marched quietly
back to breakfast, which, I assure you, I enjoyed more
than any I had ever sat down to in my life.'
('Assault of Ghunzee', by 'S', in *United Service Journal,*
1840, vol. I, pp. 146-8)

There were other minor actions in the region: at
Kahan, the principal town of the Marri tribe, a small
British garrison (principally 300 men of the 5th Bombay
Infantry) was attacked in April 1840, and an attempted
relief-force was beaten off (31 August). After a five-month
siege of Kahan fort the Marri chief, Dodah Khan, agreed
to the garrison's safe passage from his territory in return
for the surrender of the fort.

There were no further important British military operations in Baluchistan, although relations were at times
strained. Following dynastic conflict and the ensuing anarchy, relations between Britain and the Kalat state were sev-
ered in 1874; a new treaty was negotiated in 1876, by which
British troops were stationed in the state, and in November
1887 British Baluchistan was incorporated into British India.

Sind

As the Baluchis spread from Persia into north-west India,
they also settled in Sind ('Scinde' in 19th-century

spelling), a region in the Indus valley, south and east of
Baluchistan. Originally independent, it was incorporated
into the empire at the time of the emperor Akbar (himself
born in Sind in 1542), but local powers arose again with
the collapse of the Mogul empire, the amirs of Baluchi origin ruling from the capital of Hyderabad (which should
not be confused with the city and state of the same name
in central India). The Baluchi rulers of Sind presided over
a nation of Baluchis, native Sindians and Hindus, and, it
was said, considerably oppressed their subjects. The Sind
campaign arose primarily not to relieve this oppression,
however, but because of the geographical and strategic
position of the region, which formed a buffer between
British India and the threat of Russian-inspired hostilities
from either Afghanistan or Persia.

Initially, with their own territory threatened by the
Sikhs in the Punjab, the amirs accepted British terms for
an alliance in a treaty of April 1838, by which a British Resident was appointed to Sind, and an agreement extracted
that future territorial disputes would be decided by the
mediation of the Government of India, in effect handing
Sindian foreign policy to the British. During the First
Afghan War, British forces used Sind as a conduit to
Afghanistan (in addition to trading concessions already
extracted), and the amirs undertook to finance a force to
protect the lines of communication. They had been naturally resentful in accepting British terms, and British
reverses in Afghanistan, and troubles in Baluchistan such
as the expulsion of the garrison of Kahan, led relations to
deteriorate as Baluchi marauders made attacks on British
troops. To restore the position it was decided that Sind
should be annexed; and however beneficial it might have
been to the native Sindians to have Baluchi rule replaced
by British, there was little justification for the move, as
many British commentators remarked at the time, the
Sind campaign being condemned widely.

Sir Charles Napier was sent to Hyderabad in 1842 to present a more stringent treaty to the amirs, which they could
not accept. On 15 February 1843 they retaliated by attacking the Residency at Hyderabad; its defenders, the light
company of the 22nd Foot under Major (later General Sir
James) Outram, escaped via the Indian Marine vessels
Planet and *Satellite* which were lying in the Indus. Using this
as the cause for war, Napier resolved to attack the amirs
immediately before their estimated strength of 22,000
could be reinforced. Napier had only some 2,800 men,
comprising the 22nd Foot (less two dead and four
wounded in the residency fight), the 1st, 12th and 25th
Bombay Native Infantry, the 9th Bengal Light Cavalry,
Scinde Irregular Horse and a detail of the Poona Irregular
Horse, and twelve guns. The armies met on 17 February at
Miani ('Meeanee'); the Baluchis attacked as Napier
described: 'The brave Beloochees, first discharging their
matchlocks and pistols, dashed with desperate resolution,
but down went these bold and skilful swordsmen under the

The Battle of Miana ('Meea-nee'). (Engraving by C. H. Jeens after E. Armitage)

superior power of the musket and bayonet,' and the fight lasted about three hours, 'with great fury, man to man'.[10] Finally the Baluchis broke when their flank was turned by a charge of the 9th Bengal and Scinde Horse; Napier estimated their losses at 5;000 (others much fewer), and the British sustained 256 casualties. On the following day many of the chief amirs surrendered (including Rustum Khan, and Nasir, Shadad and Husein Khan of Hyderabad), and Hyderabad was occupied on 20 February.

The Amir Shere Mahomed was among those who remained undaunted, and after fruitless negotiation Napier's reinforced army, 5,000 strong, attacked Shere Mahomed's 20,000 men in an entrenched position at Dubba, a short distance from Hyderabad, on 24 March 1843. Napier carried the position for a loss of 267 casualties, reporting that 500 enemy were left dead on the field, and that the surrounding villages were filled with dead and wounded. Significantly, Napier's one European regiment (22nd Foot) incurred the heaviest casualties (23 dead, 124 wounded) and captured fourteen of the nineteen Baluchi standards taken in battle, exemplifying the comportment expected of the small European elements within British–Indian armies throughout the period.

This action (which although fought at Dubba is called the battle of Hyderabad) was the last major conflict of the Sind campaign; as Napier reported, 'Shere Mahomed has fled into the desert ... Three Beloochee Chiefs fell in the action; one of them was the great promoter of the war, Hoche Mahomed Seedee; and, I have every reason to believe, that not another shot will be fired in Sinde.'[11] The annexation of Sind is perhaps most famous for Napier's one-word dispatch announcing its capture, '*Peccavi*' ('I have sinned'); but although a good story, it is apparently not authentic.

Baluchi bandits continued to raid from their mountain dwellings, necessitating minor campaigns such as Napier's three-month Cutchi Hills expedition of 1847, in pursuit of one of the leading troublemakers, Beja Khan, who eventually surrendered. As governor of Sind, Napier was so relentless in his pursuit of malcontents and bandits that he was named 'the Devil's Brother' by the tribesmen! Although the later operations were more skirmishes than general actions, they included the remarkable epic at Truckee. In one of his drives against robbers in the Baluchistan hill-country, Napier appropriated a draft of men from the 13th Foot who had volunteered to stay in India when their regiment was ordered home, and had been posted to the 39th. Mounted on camels, they were sent against the Baluchi bandits, and on 8 March 1845 a party of sixteen men and a native camel-driver, under Sergeant John Power, mistook an officer's signal to withdraw for an encouragement to go on, and so ascended a cliff at Truckee where some seventy bandits were concealed. Eleven soldiers reached the summit, where six were killed and the others wounded; having killed seventeen bandits, the survivors retired. The desperate nature of the combat was exemplified by the injury sustained by Private John Maloney, who survived and saved two of his comrades; he was seriously wounded by his own bayonet, having driven it through a Baluchi who unfixed it, pulled it from his own body and then stabbed Maloney! A

Baluchi practice was to tie a red or green cord around the wrist of a warrior who had proved himself a hero in battle, the red being the most honourable distinction they could award. When the bodies of the six British soldiers were recovered, they were all found to have a red cord tied around *both* wrists, an unprecedented salute from their enemies which inspired Sir Francis Doyle's poem *The Red Thread of Honour.*

Gwalior

Doulut Rao Sindhia of Gwalior died without issue in 1827, and a distantly related child was adopted as heir by Sindhia's widow; on his death in 1843 another child-heir was adopted by his widow, under the name of Jayaji Rao Sindhia. Unsettled by years of turbulence and intrigue, the military force of Gwalior posed a threat to British possessions, especially in view of tension in the Punjab and Sind; and when the Gwalior council of regency refused to discuss the situation with the governor-general, Lord Ellenborough, conflict resulted in 1843. That the Marathas should make this final attempt to assert their independence was not surprising, as the reduction of their forces as required by the British would have jeopardised the livelihood of those Marathas who followed their ancestral calling as warriors.

To suppress the Gwalior forces, armies were formed at Agra, under the commander-in-chief, Sir Hugh Gough, and at Jhansi, under Major-General John Grey. Opposing them was an army which included European-trained 'regulars' and a formidable force of artillery. On 29 December 1843 Gough's two cavalry and three infantry brigades encountered about 17,000 Marathas in a strong position at Maharajpore. Gough attacked without hesitation (in his typical style, which received criticism for his apparent carelessness of casualties), and despite sterling resistance in a series of entrenched positions, the Maratha force was routed and 56 guns captured. Gough suffered 797 casualties and admitted that he had under-estimated the martial qualities of his opponents: 'I regret to say, that our loss has been very severe, infinitely beyond what I calculated on; indeed I did not do justice to the gallantry of my opponents. Their force ... so greatly exceeded ours, particularly in artillery ... so well served, and determinedly defended, both by their gunners and their infantry ... that it could not be otherwise.'[12]

Advancing in conjunction with Gough, on the same day Grey's column encountered a second Maratha force, some 12,000 strong, at Punniar, about twenty miles away from Gough's position. Again the British attacked, with the same result: the Marathas were routed and their artillery captured, for a British loss of 35 killed and 182 wounded, 113 of these casualties falling upon the 3rd and 50th Foot. Under these twin blows, the Gwalior regency capitulated and on 31 December a treaty was signed which reduced the strength of the Gwalior army, and assigned territory and revenue sufficient to support a contingent under

A subaltern of the 2nd Queen's Regiment records his emotions at the storming of Kalat in 1839, beginning with the anxious moments before being sent into action:

'This is always the most trying time to the nerves, just before the commencement of a bloody deed; but no symptom of flinching might be observed nor a pale cheek seen. The men girded their loins, and the officers with one accord threw away their scabbards, that they might not encumber them in the charge. All's ready now; and ... I had progressed with my company some two hundred yards on the road to glory, when – oh horror! – an order came for Lieutenants —— [the author] and Addison to fall out, and take charge of the colours. Ungrateful wretches! How did we blaspheme! – though that order was, in all probability, the saving of our lives ... As soon as the advance got in, the reserve was moved up, and placed under cover near the gate. While waiting here for orders, Addison and myself had an agreeable episode of six shots passing in succession between our heads, for we were too proud to stoop, nor could we perceive from whence they were directed, till an Engineer Officer stepped forward with a fowling-piece, and discharged both barrels into a loop-hole not twenty yards in our rear. Presently a drummer came up with one of my swords, a Sohlingen blade which I had lent to a brother officer before the fight. "What, then, has become of Mr. Gravatt?" I inquired. "Shot dead, sir," was the reply, "right through the heart." Then followed a doolee, with poor Holdsworth in it, apparently dying. There was no standing this any longer; and, in defiance of orders, off I cut with the colour, followed by Addison, a lad not twenty years of age, but true as steel ...'

('The Campaign in Affghanistan, in a Series of Letters, by an Officer of the Queen's', in *United Service Journal*, 1840, vol. II, pp. 333–4. Both colour-bearers survived their unauthorised charge: Thomas Addison continued to serve in the regiment, and was severely wounded in South Africa in 1851, in the frontier war for which he received his brevet-majority. Lieutenant T. Gravatt was the only British officer killed at Kalat; Lieutenant Thomas Holdsworth was returned as 'severely wounded' but survived to serve in South Africa and as deputy quartermaster-general in Nova Scotia, going on half-pay as a lieutenant-colonel in 1854)

British control to be stationed in the capital; and a council of regency was formed during the minority of the maharajah, to act under the guidance of the British Resident. Although the war was of such brief duration, the Marathas upheld the martial traditions of their ancestors; as Gough admitted in his Maharajpore dispatch, 'I may safely assert, that I never witnessed guns better served, nor a body of infantry apparently more devoted to the protection of their regimental guns.'[13] (The Gwalior contingent revolted during the Indian Mutiny, but the maharajah remained loyal, and fled from his state until restored by the British; and Gwalior fort was occupied by British troops until 1886.)

First Sikh War

The principal independent power remaining in India was the Sikh state of Punjab, one of the most formidable military forces against which the British had to contend. The Sikhs were not originally a nation, but the followers of the reformist religion propounded by Guru Nanak (1469–1539), who was born near Lahore in the Punjab, on the border between Islam and Hinduism. It was in this area that Sikhism grew, on the premise that both the aforementioned faiths confused the truth of a single divine creator; the reformer Jaidev made similar criticisms as early as the 12th century, but it is Nanak who is regarded as the founder of Sikhism, even though some of his precursors' work is incorporated in the religion's holy book, the *Granth*. The name 'Sikh', given by Nanak to his followers, simply means 'disciple' or 'learner'. Instead of the new faith promoting harmony between Islam and Hinduism, however, it provoked hostility, and the fifth of Nanak's successors as guru or head priest, Har Govind, became the first of the religion's military leaders. The tenth guru, Govind Singh, introduced the political element into the religion; he succeeded as guru in 1675, preached the Khalsa (the 'pure') by which his followers were known, and it is to his teachings that the Sikh religion owes its martial character. He introduced the word 'Singh' ('lion') to the names of all the adherents of the religion, and the visible signs of faith in the 'five Kakkas' or 'five Ks': *kes*, the uncut hair, which when wrapped around the head provided a protection against swordcuts; *kachh*, short drawers, more convenient when fighting than conventional legwear; *kara*, an iron bangle, resembling the Sikh throwing-weapon, the sharpened steel ring known as a *chakram* or *charka*; *khanda*, a dagger; and *khanga*, a comb (the fifth 'k' is sometimes stated to be a *kirpan*, or sword). The last of the gurus was Govind Singh who declared that henceforth the religion was in the hands of God, not in those of a succeeding guru. He was assassinated in 1708.

A basic tenet of Sikhism was a lack of caste or class-distinction, which gave a wide appeal; although within the Sikhs were several groups, including the Jat Sikhs (perhaps descendants of a Scythian race, mainly peasant-farmers, although the term 'Jat' is perhaps more familiarly applied to the Hindu Jats of Hindustan), the Khatris (an 'upper class'), and the Mazbi (or Mazhabi) Sikhs, a term meaning 'faithful', applied to the sweepers or outcasts who brought back the body of Teg Bahadur, the ninth guru, Govind Singh's father, after his murder by emperor

Aurangzeb for his refusal to embrace Islam in 1675. Some aspects of Sikhism were familiar and easily comprehended by Europeans, so that one contemporary opinion declared that instead of fighting them, the progress of the Sikhs 'ought to be advanced, not hindered, by the British. Sikhism is the intermediate step to Christianity, without which, to all human appearance, Christianity has but little chance in India ... here is nothing extravagant in the idea that, by a series of judicious measures, the Sikhs might be led back to their original standard – "Peace on earth, and good-will towards men."'[14] Such considerations, and the bold and martial spirit of the Sikhs, produced a mutual respect between Sikh and Briton, even in time of conflict. Curiously, MacMunn identified another similarity; claiming that the Jat Sikhs, who made the best soldiers, were 'proverbially thick in the uptake'. 'As a fighting man, his slow wit and dogged courage gave him many of the characteristics of the British soldier at his best!'[15]

The Punjab is named from the 'five rivers', tributaries of the Indus, which run through it: Jhelum, Sutlej, Chenab, Beas and Ravi. Here, as the Mogul empire collapsed, the Sikhs rose as a political power. After long internal struggles, Ranjit Singh, 'the Lion of the Punjab', emerged as the dominant chieftain; born in 1780, he established his capital at Lahore in 1799, and united the Sikhs to control most of the Punjab. The treaty of Amritsar in 1809 defined the Sutlej as the boundary between British and Sikh territory; in 1818 Ranjit Singh took Multan, and in the following year annexed Kashmir, followed by the Peshawar valley. His army, including a large 'regular' contingent drilled and organised in European style, was the most formidable 'native' army in the subcontinent. The cordial Anglo-Sikh relations ended after Ranjit Singh's death in 1839, which was followed by a period of internal unrest, in which the army and its leaders became the most important factor. The British annexation of Sind raised fears that the Punjab would be their next target, and with British reputation still suffering from the reverses in Afghanistan, the Sikh army could not be restrained from making a pre-emptive strike into British India. On 11 December 1845 the Sikh army (*Khalsa*) under Lal and Tej Singh crossed the Sutlej into British territory. Internal politics were such that several leading political and military figures remained in contact with the British, and were even prepared to countenance the defeat of their own forces for political advantage; this, and the erosion of discipline in the Sikh army which had occurred since the death of Ranjit Singh, contributed significantly to the Sikh defeat.

Sir Hugh Gough, the Commander-in-Chief in India, marched to intercept the Sikh invasion. Although brave and bold, Gough's military abilities were not marked by any great subtlety, his favoured tactic being an immediate frontal attack against any odds. On the afternoon of 18 December 1845, insufficient reconnaissance caused his force of about 12,000 when 'in a state of great exhaustion, principally from want of water'[16] after a day's march, to be surprised at Moodkee by a Sikh army which Gough estimated to consist of 15–20,000 infantry and the same number of cavalry, but was perhaps actually about half that number. As his cavalry drove back the Sikh irregulars on the flanks, Gough advanced with his weary troops despite heavy fire from the well-served Sikh artillery, and only after a most severe fight were the Sikhs pushed back. Nightfall brought the action to a close, leaving Gough in possession of the field and fifteen Sikh guns (with four more destroyed), but having lost 215 dead and 657 wounded.

Gough pushed on and on 21 December encountered Lal Singh with a force of infantry and artillery estimated at between 35,000 and 50,000 strong, in an entrenched position at Ferozeshah. Singularly, the governor-general, Sir Henry Hardinge (an experienced soldier who had lost a hand at Ligny in 1815), offered to serve as Gough's second in command, an arrangement fraught with difficulty. Reinforced to about 18,000 strong by the arrival of a fourth division, Gough attacked the Sikh entrenchments, which were defended desperately; by nightfall, only a portion had been taken. A renewed assault on the following day finally evicted the Sikhs, but at fearful cost; and then a new Sikh army arrived under Tej Singh. Gough withdrew his shattered units into the entrenchments to await the attack, but after some firing the Sikhs marched away. Tej Singh has been accused of deliberate treachery; his own explanation was that he thought it unlikely that he could drive the British from their position, and he could not know that Gough's army was exhausted and almost out of ammunition. Whatever the case, it was a fortuitous escape. Gough captured 72 Sikh guns, but his loss was 696 dead and 1,729 wounded.

Gough now decided to await reinforcements from Sind, which were being organised under Sir Charles Napier; but he detached two cavalry and four infantry brigades under Sir Harry Smith to counter the threat to his communications and to the British garrison of Ludhiana, posed by a subsidiary Sikh force under Runjoor Singh which had crossed the Sutlej. On 28 January 1846 Smith's force of about 10,000 men encountered the Sikhs (some 20,000 in number, with 67 guns), strongly entrenched at Aliwal. Smith attacked, the 16th Lancers making a famous charge on the Sikh right flank; with the Sutlej at their backs, the Sikhs were unable to retire in order and were routed, losing all their ordnance (52 guns captured, two spiked, and thirteen sunk in the river). Smith lost 151 killed, 413 wounded and 25 missing.

This left only one major Sikh concentration east of the Sutlej, at Sobraon, upon which Gough advanced in early February 1846, having been reinforced and re-united with Smith. The Sikh bridgehead over the Sutlej was protected by a formidable entrenchment, 35,000 men and 67 guns,

with more artillery on the Sikh side of the river. On 10 February Gough attacked in his usual frontal manner, his forces suffering severely as they approached the entrenchments, but after a furious fight the Sikhs were thrown back across the Sutlej, losing all their artillery and 8–10,000 dead, wounded and drowned; Gough lost 320 killed and 2,063 wounded. This ended the First Sikh War; Gough advanced and entered Lahore on 20 February. On 11 March a treaty was concluded, by which the Sikhs paid reparations in money and territory (the Jullundur Doab, a tract between the rivers Sutlej and Ravi, was annexed by Britain), re-formed their army in much-reduced numbers, and the Punjab, though not annexed, had a British Resident and local assistants appointed to supervise the council of regency which ruled during the minority of the young maharaja, Duleep Singh. Henry Lawrence, as Resident in Lahore, was conspicuously successful in his work of administration.

Second Sikh War (or Punjab Campaign)

Peace in the Punjab was disturbed by minor frontier troubles, suppressed by the unusual combination of Sikh troops accompanied by their recent enemies, the British. Such was the case in the 1846 Kashmir campaign. A Sikh possession from 1819, Kashmir was awarded to Maharaja Gulab Singh of Jammu by the treaty which ended the First Sikh War, and its independence was confirmed by a separate treaty with Britain which included a mutual military alliance. The Sikh governor in Kashmir, Imam-ud-din, declined to surrender his authority, whereupon the British and Sikhs mounted a military expedition to evict him. The British forces remained in reserve, and the expedition was

A rare account of a hand-to-hand fight in a skirmish at Gumrolah, during the Second Sikh War, is provided by William Hodson:

'...a party of Akhalees (Fanatics) on foot stopped and fought us, in some instances very fiercely. One ... beat off four sowars one after another, and kept them all at bay. I then went at him myself, fearing that he would kill one of them. He instantly rushed to meet me like a tiger, closed with me, yelling "Wah Gooroo ji", and accompanying each shout with a terrific blow of his tulwar. I guarded the three or four first, but he pressed so closely to my horse's rein that I could not get a fair cut in return. At length I pressed in my turn upon him so sharply that he missed his blow, and I caught his tulwar backhanded with my bridle hand, wrenched it from him, and cut him down with the right, having received no further injury than a severe cut across the fingers; I never beheld such desperation and fury in my life. It was not *human* scarcely ...'
(*Twelve Years of a Soldier's Life in India*, ed. Revd. G. H. Hodson, London, 1859, pp. 81–2)

composed of Sikh forces under generals Shere Singh and others, with the British agent and other British officers accompanying them. Imam-ud-Din capitulated without resistance, and Gulab Singh entered Kashmir city on 9 November 1846.[17]

In April 1848 the governor of Multan, Mulraj (a Hindu, not a Sikh) was dissatisfied with the new regime. His resignation was accepted, but when a new Sikh governor arrived, Mulraj's supporters revolted and murdered the two British officers who had accompanied him, prompting Mulraj into open rebellion. Some checks were inflicted upon the rebels by a force of Sikhs and Pathans under Lieutenant Herbert Edwardes, and it was thought best that the revolt be suppressed by Sikh troops; but after some minor actions around Multan, it was decided to dispatch a force from Lahore under Major-General H. S. Whish to capture the city. Whish took the outlying works around Multan (10 and 12 September 1848) but the Sikh forces who were supposed to be assisting had no stomach for the fight, and their general, Shere Singh, declared for the rebels after his father, Chuttur Singh, had raised the flag of revolt in north-west Punjab. Faced with such odds, Whish lifted the siege of Multan and withdrew to await reinforcement.

Shere Singh left Multan on 9 October, joining other rebels and concentrating at Ramnuggar, on the east bank of the river Chenab. Gough marched against him with one cavalry and three infantry divisions; minor actions took place at Ramnuggar (22 November, chiefly memorable for the death of the British cavalry commander, Brigadier-General C. R. Cureton, a sad loss to the army) and Sadullapur (14 December), after which Shere Singh withdrew and Gough was able to cross the Chenab. Meanwhile Whish had recommenced the siege of Multan, captured

Harry Lumsden recounts the misfortune which befell him at Sobraon:

'I had just got the boys in line, and was looking out to prevent them throwing away their fire by taking long shots, when I was shot through the foot by some desperate rascal but I was so excited at the time that I scarcely knew that I was hit, and sat on my charger, who was also shot through the leg about the same time, until the Cavalry were driven into the river, after which I felt very sick, and would have fallen off my horse had not an officer of the 10th Foot, seeing that I was wounded, given me a glass of brandy, which refreshed me very much, and enabled me to do my duty until the action was over. My foot was so swollen that I was obliged to get one of the men to cut the boot and stocking off, and found that a musket ball had entered on the top of the little toe, and come out half way down the foot. When I got home I was obliged to have the wound opened from end to end, and all sorts of queer-looking little bones taken out. This, I was told, was the only chance of saving the foot, so I was obliged to submit, like a good boy, though, I must confess, it was anything but agreeable at the time. However, our M. D. tells me that the wound is wonderfully well, and will not make me the least lame; on the contrary, I shall now be able to put on a much more fashionable boot. If you hear of an old boy wishing a cure for corns, just recommend him to have a musket shot sent through them.'
(Letter of 26 February 1846; quoted in *Lumsden of the Guides*, General Sir Peter S. Lumsden, and G. R. Elsmie, London, 1899, pp. 16–17)

This view of a regiment of Native Infantry on the march in India, 1848, gives a good idea of the enormous amount of baggage and, therefore, 'followers' that customarily accompanied troops in India. The column is preceded by the regimental band (right, in peaked caps); at the left are servants, one carrying officers' possessions in a pettarah (boxes suspended from a pole), and another with a dining-chair on his head. (Unsigned engraving, 1848)

The storming of Multan: the 1st Bombay Europeans carry the Kooni Boorj breach on the afternoon of 2 January 1849, from a sketch by an officer of the 32nd. Artillery officers at the breaching-batteries cheer on the assault.

the city on 3 January 1849 and extinguished the revolt in that region when the citadel capitulated on 22 January. Mulraj was tried for complicity in the murders of the British envoys and sentenced to imprisonment for life.

With about 12,000 men, Gough advanced to confront Shere Singh's army (30–40,000 men and 62 guns) at Chillianwalla on 13 January 1849. Despite the jungle and broken terrain which separated the armies, Gough made his usual frontal attack, incurring appalling casualties (602 killed, 1,651 wounded, 104 missing); although the Sikhs were pushed back, with about 8,000 casualties, it was not as comprehensive a victory as Gough reported, 'complete as to the total overthrow of the enemy; and his sense of utter discomfiture and defeat will, I trust, soon be made apparent'.[18] The Sikhs even reclaimed many of their cap-

tured guns when Gough retired a short distance. So severe were the British losses that it was decided to replace Gough by Sir Charles Napier; but before this could be done Gough had won the war.

Shere Singh and Chuttur Singh took up a position at Gujerat, their forces supplemented by Afghan cavalry sent to their assistance by Dost Muhammed, a combined strength of about 60,000. Reinforced by Whish and others to a total of about 24,000, Gough's army followed and advanced on the Sikh position at Gujerat on 21 February. After a heavy bombardment which almost silenced the Sikh artillery, and with the Sikh cavalry repelled from the flanks, Gough's infantry attack broke the Sikh centre after determined resistance, and the Sikhs withdrew, having sustained heavy casualties and lost 53 guns. For once, Gough's casual-

Typical Indian campaign uniform of the British Army is shown in this engraving from a sketch by an officer of the 32nd, depicting troops in Multan after its capture in early January 1849. The infantrymen are wearing their ordinary jackets with white trousers, and forage caps with white covers.

The martial qualities of the Sikhs were admired by the British, like this officer who wrote an account of Ramnuggar:

'Nothing could exceed the accuracy of the enemy's fire; their range was beautifully taken for certain points, showing that they must have discovered them previous to our advance; and our artillery officers say they never saw anything finer than the way their Horse Artillery were brought up to the edge of the river, and formed up. No nation could exceed them in the rapidity of their fire ... No men could act more bravely than the Sikhs. They faced us the moment we came on them, firing all the time, and, when we did come on them, some opened out and immediately after closed round us, while others threw themselves on their faces or turned their backs, protected by a shield from the stroke of the Dragoon sabre, and the moment that was given, turned round, hamstrung the horse, and shot the rider, while their individual acts of bravery were the admiration of all. Many stood before a charging squadron, and singled out a man, after killing or wounding whom they themselves were cut down immediately; while many, before their blows could take effect, received the point of a sabre, and fell in the act of making a cut.'
(Anon., 'Camp, Ramnuggar, 25 November 1848' in *Illustrated London News*, 27 January 1849)

Punjab Campaign Medal; the obverse bears a portrait of Queen Victoria, the reverse a scene of Major-General Sir Walter Gilbert accepting the surrender of the Sikhs. Three clasps were issued: 'Mooltan' and 'Goojerat' as illustrated, and 'Chilianwala'. The designer was William Wyon.

ties were not excessive: 96 dead and 706 wounded. Major-General Sir Walter Gilbert was given the task of pursuing the Sikhs, but the revolt was crushed. The Afghans returned to their own country, and on 14 March at Rawalpindi Shere Singh and his army surrendered to Gilbert.

Punjab was annexed as a British province on 2 April 1849, with a three-man administrative board, replaced by a chief commissioner in 1853. Duleep Singh was given a pension of £50,000 p.a. and permission to live anywhere except in the Punjab; he settled in Britain. British and Company troops were stationed in the Punjab, and a new corps was formed, the Punjab Frontier Force, under the orders of the chief commissioner. From this period Sikhs provided some of the finest recruits to the Indian Army, and during the Mutiny the chief commissioner, Sir John Lawrence, was not only able to maintain the security of his province but sent troops to assist the British elsewhere. The enlargement of the province in 1858 led to the elevation of its administrator to the rank of lieutenant-governor.

Military Operations 1849–57

The major campaigns involving Indian forces during this period were the Second Burma War and the expedition to Persia (covered in the sections on those countries), but there were also operations on the North-West Frontier, the border between British India and Afghanistan created by the annexation of the Punjab. The tribes living in these mountainous and inhospitable areas were a constant problem, raids and other hostile acts against the British or their allies often necessitating punitive expeditions to maintain the security of the border, some of small size and short duration, and incurring limited casualties. They included the following between the annexation of the Punjab and the Mutiny:

Baizai expedition: led by Lieutenant-Colonel J. Bradshaw to collect revenue from the Baizais, a tribe resident between the Swat River and British territory, 3–11 December 1849. The principal villages were destroyed but no serious conflict occurred.

Kohat expedition: a punitive expedition in response to a raid by Kohat Pass Afridis on a party working on the road near Kohat; commanded by Brigadier-General Sir Colin Campbell but accompanied by the Commander-in-Chief, Sir Charles Napier, 9–15 February 1850. Some villages were destroyed but the Afridis remained hostile, some weeks later forcing the abandonment of a police post on the Kohat Kotal. Peace was negotiated in November 1850 by adjusting the subsidy paid to the Afridis to ensure the maintenance of order.

Mohmand expedition: hostilities by this tribe resulted in a brief expedition led by Campbell in April 1852 to expel raiding-parties from British territory; no serious action occurred.

Ranizai and Utman Khel expeditions: two brief expeditions led by Campbell, March–May 1852, against raiders from the Ranizai clan and Utman Khel tribe, residents in the Swat River region.

Waziri expedition: a raid to destroy Sapari and Garang villages in response to Waziri hostilities, led by Major John Nicholson, 20–22 December 1852. This was the first of the operations described in which no British troops were present, Nicholson's force comprising elements of the 1st, 2nd and 4th Punjab Infantry, 2nd Punjab Cavalry, and Punjab police.

Black Mountain expedition: a punitive expedition led by Lieutenant-Colonel F. Mackeson, the commissioner of Peshawar, 19 December 1852 to 2 January 1853, to avenge the murder of two British customs officers by the Hassanzai clan of the Yusufzais, in the Black Mountain region at the northern end of the Punjab frontier. The expedition comprised three columns and a reserve, one column commanded by the future Lord Napier of Magdala, then a lieutenant-colonel in the Royal Engineers; the only regulars involved were artillery, sappers, a Corps of Guides detachment and the 1st Sikh and 3rd Bengal Native Infantry, the remainder being irregulars, police and local levies. The expedition destroyed some villages. On 6 January 1853 Mackeson's troops fought a brief skirmish against the so-called 'Hindustani fanatics', followers of the mullah Ahmad Shah, who had been killed in fighting against Ranjit Singh's Sikhs in 1829. Having sided with the Hassanzais, the fanatics seized a small fort at Kotla, which belonged to the Khan of Amb, an ally of the British. They fled as Mackeson's Sikhs approached and the fort was repossessed by the Khan's troops.

Shirani and Kasrani expeditions: a march by Brigadier J. S. Hodgson, commander of the Punjab Irregular Force, using his own troops and police, through Shirani territory, to discourage the plundering of the Shirani and Kasrani tribes; this was accomplished without conflict, 30 March–12 April 1853.

Bori valley expedition: commanded by Colonel S. B. Boileau, 29 November 1853, to discourage raiding by the Jowaki Afridis, one of the Kohat Pass clans; the destruction of villages in the Bori valley led to the surrender of the Jowakis in the following February.

Rahim Dad expedition: a raid under Colonel S. J. Cotton, 31 August 1854, to destroy villages and seize cattle belonging to the Mohmand chief Rahim Dad, who refused to pay the tribute due from him.

Aka Khel operations: a blockade and retaliatory raids upon the territory of the Aka Khel Afridis to punish their plundering; the principal action was an expedition of 27 March 1855 under Lieutenant-Colonel J. H. Craigie.

Miranzai expedition: an expedition from Kohat led by Brigadier-General Neville Chamberlain, 4 April–21 May 1855, to disperse bandits in the Miranzai valley. This was not the first expedition to this area, Waziri bandits having been pursued by a small force under Captain J. Coke in October–November 1851, and Chamberlain had to take the field again in October–November 1856 for the same purpose.

Orakzai expedition: the Orakzai tribe of Pathans residing north-west of Kohat began minor hostilities during the Miranzai expedition, and in September 1855 Chamberlain destroyed some of their villages.

Bozdar expedition: an expedition led by Chamberlain against the Bozdar tribe, resident near Dera Ghazi Khan, at the southern end of the frontier; some operations had been mounted by Hodgson in 1853, and in March 1857 Chamberlain led another, which fought its way into Bozdar territory on 7 March, and withdrew after inflicting some punitive destruction on property.

The Santal Rebellion

The twelve tribes of Santals had emigrated into northern Bengal from the late 18th century, settling in the Bhagalpur district some 200 miles north-west of Calcutta. Peaceful agriculturalists, their settlement was encouraged by the British who employed them in railway-construction; but the malign influence of moneylenders and corrupt railway officials caused grievances which the Santals were unable to remedy by legal means. Exploitation caused them to take up arms and from mid-1855 some 30,000 primitively armed Santals were in open insurrection (probably only with reluctance against the Company, and probably only because it was regarded as protecting those responsible for the exploitation). The rebellion, with no single leader but a number of chiefs, including the brothers Sidhu and Khanu, involved attacks on neighbouring areas and massacre of both Europeans and Indians. The authorities were surprised initially, given the normally pacific demeanour of the Santals, but after some reverses forces were deployed to secure the area, to garrison Bhagalpur and to prevent the Santals ranging into other areas; the rebels were hunted down, their villages destroyed and peace restored by August 1856. A form of administration more acceptable to the Santals was established, and a more equable form of land-settlement instituted.

Military Forces 1825–57

Baluchis. The Baluchis had no regular forces, but were tribal groups led by local chieftains, expert guerrilla fighters and raiders but at a great disadvantage when fighting a disciplined opponent in the open field. Like the Afghans, they were armed with matchlock *jezails* and preferred

The costume of the East India Company's forces at the outbreak of the Mutiny is illustrated in this engraving of the grenadier company of the 21st Madras Native Infantry, 1857. Left to right: regimental lascar (hired labourer); water-carrier or 'puck-ally' (from the puckals, leather water-bags, carried by the bullock); 'pension boy' (son of a deceased soldier, supported by the regiment until he enlisted or attained the age of 18 years); sepoy in marching order (with covered turban); havildar, full dress; drummer, full dress. Ordinary troops wore wickerwork, lacquered turbans; peaked head-dress, like the 'Albert' shako worn by the drummer, were restricted to Indian or Eurasian Christians.

hand-to-hand combat with sword and shield; despite their skill with these weapons, they could hardly have expected to prevail against disciplined troops, as Napier remarked in his Miani dispatch: 'Then ... was seen the superiority of the musket and bayonet over the sword and shield and matchlock'.[19] Nevertheless they were a formidable foe, not least for their bravery in the attack; and it was noted that even when retiring under fire they would not break into a run but would maintain their customary loping stride, having slung their shields on their backs for protection.

Sikhs. As organised by Ranjit Singh, the Sikh army was the most formidable opponent faced by the British at this period, combining indigenous methods of combat with a nucleus of regulars, organised and trained in European style. From the early 19th century Ranjit Singh had attracted soldiers from other armies, including some (like Marathas) who had been defeated by the British or had deserted from other 'regular' forces. The value of European discipline soon became evident in various conflicts, and from 1809 European or Eurasian mercenaries were employed to train the Sikh army. Some were British, but the main influence was French: Jean François Allard trained the cavalry, Jean Baptiste Ventura the infantry (although he was apparently Italian by birth), and their drill-manual, translated from French, produced a regular army which fought in the style of Napoleonic France, responded to orders given in French, and manoeuvred to drum- and bugle-calls in the best European fashion. Another Frenchman, Henri Court, supervised the artillery, and among the principal administrators was an Italian, Paolo de Avitabile. Although most left after Ranjit Singh's death, as late as the eve of the First Sikh War there were some 39 European officers in Sikh employ, principally French and British or Anglo-Indian but even including three Americans.

The Sikh army or *Khalsa* comprised the regular army (*Fauj-i-Ain*), irregular units, and a feudal levy (*Jagdir-i-Fauj*) which could be mobilised on the instructions of local chieftains. The 'regulars' were divided into what might be termed brigade groups or 'mini-divisions', of three or four infantry battalions, a cavalry regiment and one or two artillery batteries; these formations were styled *derah*s or 'camps', a term both organisational and geographical, as it also applied to the camps in which they were stationed in peacetime. In 1845 the *Khalsa* was estimated to be up to 150,000 strong, with apparently about 54,000 regular infantry, 6,000 regular cavalry and 11,000 gunners, the balance being irregulars, of whom the number was estimated variously. There were twelve *derah*s with an average strength of more than 4,000 each, although there were considerable variations.

Infantry regiments comprised two battalions each, although each battalion was an independent tactical entity. Each battalion was about 8–900 strong, in eight companies (styled *pelotons* in the French manner); two *pelotons* comprised a *region*, and two *regions* a *demi-bataillon*. Of 62 infantry battalions, 52 were Sikh, the remainder Muslim, Hindu and even Gurkha units (although the latter were mostly Kashmiris, rather than genuine Nepalese Gurkhas). The regular infantry wore uniforms copied from the British: red jackets with white lace across the breast and with regimental facing-colours, white or blue turban and trousers (the blue trousers with a broad red stripe), with a summer dress of white jacket and trousers with turban perhaps coloured according to the regiment; equipment and weapons of British style. The Gurkha battalions were dressed in British 'rifle' style, like those of the Company: green with red facings and black caps. The regular cavalry contained about the same proportion of Sikhs as the infantry; they wore crimson jacket and turban and dark blue trousers with a red stripe, and were armed in European fashion with sabre and carbine. So eager were the Sikhs to emulate European styles that it was reported some of their drums bore legends copied from the British, obviously irrelevant to the Sikhs but perhaps thought to have some mystic significance, such as 'Waterloo' or 'Pinsular' (*sic*).

The Sikh artillery was among the best elements of the army, the guns being regarded as objects of veneration and often superbly decorated. The personnel included the smallest proportion of Sikhs of any part of the army, over half the gunners being Muslim, and their skill was unsurpassed; Harry Lumsden wrote in amazement of the Sikh gunners he witnessed in 1847: 'I never saw such rifle shooting as the Seikh [*sic*] artillery made with their six-pounders ... They literally prevented the enemy from raising their heads.'[20] By using 'prepared ammunition' (projectile and propellant in one), the Sikh gunners were able to fire faster even than the Company artillery. There were three varieties of artillery: *Aspi* batteries, the lightest guns (4- and 6pdrs), generally organised in batteries of 8–10 guns, of which 32 existed in 1845, drawn by horses; the heavier and less-mobile *Jinsi* batteries, drawn by bullocks or even elephants; and *Zamburak*s, 1pdr or lighter swivel-guns often mounted on camel-back, of which there were batteries in 1845, with up to 40 guns each. The horse batteries were deployed among the *derahs*, but the others were six independent. An estimate of the strength of Sikh ordnance in 1845 was 381 field-pieces and 104 howitzers, garrison-guns and mortars. Sikh guns were notably heavier than their Company counterparts, and there was much less standardisation, which must have complicated ammunition-supply; for example, the guns captured by the British at Ferozeshah comprised no less than twelve different 'natures' of cannon, ranging from 3- to 32pdrs; one 42pdr and one 24pdr howitzer, and a 10in mortar. The most numerous included nineteen 9pdrs, thirteen 8pdrs, eight 18pdrs and seven 3pdrs. Artillery uniform was of British style, a black or dark blue jacket with red facings and yellow lace, blue trousers with red stripe, and a curious head-dress which appears to have been a black, red-corded bearskin cap.

The largest element of the irregular forces were the cavalry, styled *Ghorchurras*, socially the élite of the army and equipped accordingly, including traditional clothing, Persian-style helmets and body-armour, mail shirts, shields, matchlock muskets, lances and swords. They were organised in *derahs*, each of which comprised a number of *misl*s or 'troops' varying in size from fifteen to seventy men. The irregular infantry, conversely, was drawn from the lowest strata of society, wearing ordinary civilian clothing and armed with matchlocks, swords and shields; although their organisation was like that of the regular infantry, training and discipline were very inferior, and they were often employed only in garrison duty. Among the irregular forces were the Akalis, wild and fanatical religious zealots who in peacetime were regarded with suspicion or as bandits. Although many preferred to fight half-naked, normally they wore blue shirts and turbans (that colour signifying a zealot), the turban sometimes conical to accommodate several *chakram*s, the sharpened throwing-quoit; they were also heavily armed with swords, daggers and matchlocks. In combining such intrepid individuals with disciplined and steady units, the *Khalsa* was a most fearsome and intimidating foe.

British and Company Forces. British Army regiments continued to provide the nucleus of the British forces in India, although smaller operations might be undertaken by Company forces alone. During the period further use was made of Indian troops outside the subcontinent, for example in the First China War, and in Aden in 1839.

Bengal Army. A 2nd Bengal European Regiment was raised in 1839, the 1st being designated as light infantry; both became Fusiliers in 1850 and 1846 respectively, in recognition of services in the Punjab, and in 1854 a 3rd Regiment was formed, as light infantry. The 68 regiments of Bengal Native Infantry were increased to 69, but the 47th was disbanded for refusing to participate in the Arakan expedition, and the 69th was re-numbered to take their place; in 1829 the numbers 69–74 were allocated to the 1st–6th Extra Battalions. In 1842–3 the 26th, 35th, 42nd and 43rd became light infantry, and the 16th a grenadier corps in 1845. The 34th was disbanded after difficulties in the Sind campaign, and in 1846 a new 34th was created from the infantry of the Bundlecund Legion, an irregular corps raised in 1838. Unrest over the withdrawal of the allowance for 'foreign' service for units serving in the Punjab caused the 66th to mutiny in 1850; it was disbanded and its place taken by the Nasiri Battalion, henceforth titled 66th or Gurkha Regiment of Bengal Native Infantry. Local battalions continued to be formed, for example the Oudh Local Force, formed in 1836 from an auxiliary contingent under British command, initially including two infantry regiments; in early 1856 it was expanded into the Oudh Irregular Force of three artillery batteries, three cavalry and ten infantry regiments, but it mutinied and was disbanded in 1857. Others were more permanent: the Shekhawati Contingent, for example, raised in 1835 and consisting of cavalry, artillery and infantry, was taken over from the state of Jaipur in 1843, the infantry battalion remaining loyal during the Mutiny and passing into the regular Indian Army.

The 2nd Bengal Light Cavalry was disbanded in 1841 for misconduct in Afghanistan; in 1848 its number was taken by the 11th, which had been formed in 1842. The Bengal Local Horse was re-named Bengal Irregular Cavalry in 1840, the 6th from the Oudh Irregular Cavalry formed in 1838, the 7th in 1841, the 8th in 1842, the 9th in 1844 from the 1st Christie's Horse of Shah Shujah's service, the 10th from the Bundlecund Legion in 1847, and the 11th–18th raised in 1846 as the 10th–17th, and renumbered in 1847. By 1842 the native gunners of the Bengal Artillery had been formed into two battalions of ten companies each, and three battalions of six each in 1845; these were numbered the 7th–9th Battalions, the others being European. In 1833 the Bengal Pioneers were merged into the Sappers and Miners.

Punjab Regiments. With the extension of British influence into the Punjab, units were raised there after the First Sikh War. The first was the Corps of Guides, infantry and cavalry, formed in December 1846 under Harry Lumsden; it was the first unit to adopt dust-coloured or khaki uniforms, most seviceable for the terrain in which they operated. More conventional uniform was worn by the 1st–5th Regiments of Punjab Cavalry, raised in 1849. In 1846–7 the 1st–4th Sikh regiments were formed, as the 'Infantry of the Frontier Brigade', styled 'Sikh Local Infantry' from 1847. The 1st–5th Regiments of Punjab Infantry were formed in 1849 (most wearing 'drab' or khaki uniform), and a 6th was converted from the Scinde Camel Corps, which had been created in 1843. In 1851 the 'Frontier Brigade' became the Punjab Irregular Force, to which the Corps of Guides was added; it was from the initials of this formation that the nickname 'Piffers' originated, which was retained when it was re-titled the Punjab Frontier Force in September 1865. The force included mountain artillery, No. 1 Horse Light Field Battery, created in 1849, No. 2 in 1851, No. 3 converted in the same year from an existing field battery raised at Lahore in 1849, No. 4 (garrison company) in 1851, and the Peshawar Mountain Train in 1853.

Madras Army. A 2nd Battalion of Madras Europeans was formed in 1839, becoming light infantry in 1842; in 1843 the 1st Battalion became the Madras European Fusiliers, and a 3rd Battalion was formed in late 1853. In 1826 the Native Infantry was increased by the formation of the 1st–4th Extra Battalions, of which the 1st and 2nd became the 51st and 52nd Madras Native Infantry, and the remaining two were disbanded in 1830. The Madras Rifle Corps, which had existed from 1810, was dispersed among eight infantry regiments in 1830, providing rifle companies for these units and retaining their original green clothing. In 1831 the Madras Horse Artillery was reduced to four European and two Native troops; a fourth European Foot Artillery battalion was created in 1845. In 1831 the 1st Battalion Pioneers became the Madras Sappers and Miners, joined by the 2nd some three years later.

Bombay Army. In 1839 a 2nd Bombay European Battalion was created; in 1844 the 1st became the Bombay Fusiliers and the 2nd light infantry, and in 1853 a 3rd Battalion was formed. In 1846 27th–29th Regiments of Native Infantry were formed, and the acquisition of Sind resulted in the creation of the 1st and 2nd Baluch Battalions in 1844 and 1846 respectively. In 1842 the 1st Bombay Light Cavalry became the 1st Bombay Lancers. The Poona Auxiliary Horse became Irregular Horse in 1847, and additional units of Irregular Horse were formed in 1839 (Gujerat and 1st Scinde Regiments), 1846 (2nd Scinde) and 1850 (South Mahratta). In 1830 the engineer and pioneer units were amalgamated, named Bombay Sappers and Miners in 1840.

A number of local corps were formed for the Bombay Army, most importantly the 'Bheel Corps'. Bhils (or 'Bheels') were a Dravidian people of central India, the name originating from *bil*, a bow (hence Bhils = 'bowmen'), who rebelled against the Marathas and became nomadic outlaws. To control them the British formed a Bhil Agency in 1825, and a corps of Bhils to police the remainder, as little else had curbed their bandit tendencies. The first unit was the Candeish Bheel Corps, formed in the Khandish area in 1825 under Lieutenant James Outram (later Sir James), trained partly as light infantry and partly as a local auxiliary police. The scheme was successful and further Bhil corps were raised subsequently.

Hyderabad Contingent. In 1826 the cavalry of the Hyderabad Contingent was re-organised into five regiments, the 1st–3rd being the Nizam's three regiments, the 4th newly formed and the 5th being the ex-Ellichpur Horse, a corps tracing its origin to 1803. The 5th was disbanded in 1853, and in 1854 the 1st–4th Nizam's Cavalry were re-titled as the 1st–4th Cavalry, Hyderabad Contingent. The 1st and 2nd Battalions Russell Brigade, 1st–4th Berar Battalions, and 1st and 2nd Battalions Ellichpur Brigade became the 1st–8th Regiments of Nizam's Infantry respectively; in 1853 the 5th and 6th were disbanded, their numbers being taken by the 7th and 8th, and in the following year the units were re-titled as the 1st–6th Infantry, Hyderabad Contingent.

General James Michael tells a story concerning the Madras Sappers and Miners:

'In the Sappers and Miners, especially, English is very much spoken by officers and men; in fact, they pride themselves on being very English indeed. When the Indian contingent came to London after the early part of the Egyptian campaign, I took the Madras subadar and naique to see some of the sights of London, among others, to Madame Tussaud's, where we saw an effigy of Arabi Pacha. I had been explaining things to them and conversing with them in Tamil, when to my astonishment and amusement of the bystanders, the little naique stepped forward, shook his fist in Arabi's face, and broke out in excellent English, with: "Ah, you rascal! What a lot of trouble you have given."'

(Richards, W. *Her Majesty's Army: Indian and Colonial Forces*, London, n.d., p. 139)

THE INDIAN MUTINY, 1857–1858

The 'Great Mutiny' which began in 1857 had the most profound consequences of any event in the history of the British presence in the subcontinent. Its causes were complex and varied, of which only a brief summary can be made here.

The Earl of Dalhousie, who became governor-general in 1848, proceeded with a policy of annexing any Indian state whose ruler died without leaving a natural heir. Even if done for the highest of motives, this produced a feeling of insecurity among the Indian princes, and caused offence by the forcible elimination of hereditary rule in cases where the ruling family had been guilty of nothing save the inability to produce a direct heir. Most notable of the territories annexed in this manner were Nagpur and Jhansi; even more inflammatory was the deposition of Wajid Ali, King of Oudh, in 1856, on the grounds that he was unfit to rule (he refused to recognise the legitimacy of the British assumption of power, but settled near Calcutta on a handsome government pension). Such annexations caused disquiet among the population, fearing a policy of replacing indigenous rule and customs with those of a foreign culture; and the fact that much of the Bengal Army was recruited from Oudh, and the high caste of many which led them to fear an upset in the social order, caused the greatest discontent among that part of society most necessary for the preservation of order, the army. Such fears were exploited by those Indian princes unhappy with their lot, for example Nana Sahib, the heir of the dispossessed peshwa, Baji Rao II, whose state pension had ceased with his death despite Nana Sahib's attempts to have it extended to him. The troubles which followed did not extend beyond the Bengal Army, the sepoys of Madras and Bombay remaining loyal. The situation of Oudh, home of much of the Bengal Army, is one explanation for the limited nature of the outbreak; another may be the poor financial rewards received by Bengal sepoys in comparison with the more generous treatment of their counterparts in the armies of the other two presidencies, whose rates of pay and allowances were significantly greater.[21] Financial aspects were complicated by the fact that as a result of the 'silladar system', many cavalrymen were heavily in debt, and this might have favoured a change of rule in order to absolve them of their financial responsibilities.

Mutinies in Indian forces were not unknown, perhaps most notably the violent outbreak at Vellore in 1806, and were even regarded as a fact of life by some officers: for example, long before the 'Great Mutiny' an officer told J. W. Sherer that 'though John Sepoy seems such a quiet fellow in the lines, on such matters as his caste, his religion, or his women, if he gets off his head, there is no violence or cruelty he would not commit.'[22] It was essential that officers appreciate and be sympathetic to the religion and culture of their troops; yet in the years before the Mutiny there was a tendency for officers to become more removed from their men, less sensitive to their concerns and to the validity, in their own eyes at least, of their complaints. The system of promotion of Company officers, by seniority, was another factor, resulting in commanders insufficiently active to play a useful role. In 1850 William Hodson wrote:

'At the age at which officers become colonels and majors, not one in fifty is able to stand the wear and tear of Indian service. They become still more worn in mind than in body. All elasticity is gone; all energy and enterprise worn out; they become, after a fortnight's campaign, a burden to themselves, an annoyance to those under them, and a terror to every one but the enemy! The officer who commanded the cavalry brigade which so disgraced the service at Chillianwalla, was not able to mount

At least in the early stages of the Indian Mutiny, the British forces had the unusual experience of fighting an enemy dressed, equipped and trained in the same style as themselves. This unsigned engraving depicts John Nicholson's defeat of the mutineers from Sialkot, who were marching on Delhi, near Gurdaspur.

a horse without the assistance of two men. A brigadier of infantry, under whom I served during the three most critical days of the war, could not see his regiment when I led his horse by the bridle until its nose touched the bayonets; and even then he said faintly, "Pray which way are the men facing, Mr. Hodson?" This is no exaggeration, I assure you. Can you wonder that our troops have to recover by desperate fighting, and with heavy loss, the advantages thrown away by the want of heads and eyes to lead them?'[23]

The Mutiny should not have been unexpected; indeed, Charles Napier and others had forecast problems, and even Dalhousie had warned against the reduction of European troops. In 1856 there were about 45,000 British and 233,000 Indian troops; and when the Mutiny began the percentage of British had declined from approximately 16 per cent of the forces in India to about 12¼ per cent. Given the time taken for reinforcements to arrive from Britain, this was dangerous in the event of discontent among the sepoys; but although the Bengal Army was virtually destroyed by the Mutiny, other Indian troops were instrumental in its suppression. As acknowledged at the time, no more loyal servants of the British could have been found than those, including Sikhs and Gurkhas, who resolutely opposed the mutineers and their allies.

Although not the result of any centralised planning by a single leadership, the Mutiny of 1857 was not entirely spontaneous, and had been predicted for some time in certain quarters. There was also the mysterious circulation of *chuppatties* (Indian cakes or biscuits) throughout north-

---

The difference between the forces of the three Indian presidency armies was marked. During the Mutiny, J. W. Sherer met a Madras Artillery soldier who was apparently relishing bombarding the Bengal mutineers and their supporters:

'He was a little chap, but wiry and strong enough. He spoke English well, and was, I suppose, a Roman Catholic. He said: "You have never seen, I dare say, a native soldier like me. We are much nearer the English than the fellows up here. There is very little difference; we can eat any meat we choose, and drink wine." "And fight, I suppose?", I said; "the English are thought to be very fond of fighting." "Oh, fight", he cried. "I should think so. We are just English over again, only a different colour."'

(Sherer, J. W. *Havelock's March on Cawnpore, 1857*, London, n.d., pp. 267–8)

---

western India, a kind of edible chain-letter of which no one knew the significance, but a chain Indians were loath to break in case it was a portent of some great event. The most famous cause of the outbreak, however, was the issue of new cartridges which it was rumoured were greased with cow and pig fat, thus abhorrent to both Hindus and Muslims, worse in that the cartridges had to be put into the mouth for the end to be bitten off, and worse still considering the high caste of many sepoys, who would have regarded themselves defiled even to touch such fat. It is perhaps typical of the lack of sympathy with, and understanding of, such deeply held beliefs, that the authorities took no stringent measures to ensure that no such fat was used in cartridge-manufacture, and that the rumours circulated by many agitators were not scotched immediately. It was this matter, so trivial in European eyes unaccustomed to Indian culture, which served as the fuze to explode the incipient unrest present in the army.

Early in 1857 the 19th and 34th Bengal Native Infantry were disbanded for refusing to accept the new cartridges, and in the latter case for not apprehending a sepoy, Mangal Pande, who when under the influence of *bhang* (Indian hemp) had attempted to shoot the regimental adjutant. He was executed for his crime on 8 April 1857 (and was the origin of a British nickname applied to all mutineers, or Indians in general: 'pandies'). Unrest simmered throughout the Bengal presidency, and at Meerut on 24 April, 85 men of the 3rd Bengal Cavalry refused to accept the new cartridges. They were condemned to ten years' hard labour; but on 10 May the Meerut garrison rose, released the prisoners and began to murder Europeans, including their own officers, while the unruly elements of the civilian population began to plunder and burn British property. Even at this stage an active and determined commander might have been able to act decisively and suppress the unrest; but no such leader was pre-

---

William Forbes-Mitchell gives a unique glimpse of the trauma arising from a day's terrible carnage:

'The horrible scenes through which the men had passed during the day had told with terrible effect on their nervous systems, and the struggles – eye to eye, foot to foot, and steel to steel – with death in the Secunderabagh, were fought over again by most of the men in their sleep, oaths and shouts of defiance often curiously intermingled with prayers. One man would be calmly lying sleeping and commence muttering something inaudible, and then break out into a fierce battle-cry of "Cawnpore, you bloody murderer!"; another would shout, "Charge! Give them the bayonet!"; and a third, "Keep together, boys, don't fire; forward, forward; if we are to die, let us die like men!" Then I would hear one muttering, "Oh, mother, forgive me, and I'll never leave you again!"; while his comrade would half rise up, wave his hand, and call, "There they are! Fire low, give them the bayonet! Remember Cawnpore!" And so it was throughout that memorable night inside the Shah Nujeef ...'

(Forbes-Mitchell, W. *Reminiscences of the Great Mutiny 1857-59*, London 1897, pp. 91–2)

With characteristic modesty, Lord Roberts describes how he won the Victoria Cross as a lieutenant of the Bengal Artillery at Khudaganj, 2 January 1858, when he joined a cavalry charge:
'As we galloped along, Younghusband drew my attention with great pride to the admirable manner in which his men kept their dressing. On the line thundered, overtaking groups of the enemy, who every now and then turned and fired into us before they could be cut down, or knelt to receive us on their bayonets before discharging their muskets. The chase continued for nearly five miles, until daylight began to fail and we appeared to have got to the end of the fugitives, when the order was given to wheel to the right and form up on the road. Before, however, this movement could be carried out, we overtook a batch of mutineers, who faced about and fired into the squadron at close quarters. I saw Younghusband fall, but I could not go to his assistance, as at that moment one of his *sowars* was in dire peril from a sepoy who was attacking him with his fixed bayonet, and had I not helped the man and disposed of his opponent, he must have been killed. The next moment I descried in the distance two sepoys making off with a standard, which I determined must be captured, so I rode after the rebels and overtook them, and while wrenching the staff out of the hands of one of them, whom I cut down, the other put his musket close to my body and fired; fortunately for me it missed fire, and I carried off the standard. For these two acts I was awarded the Victoria Cross.'
(Lord Roberts of Kandahar, *Forty-One Years in India*, London, 1900, pp. 214–15)

sent, and the mutiny spread throughout the Bengal Army.

The mutineers left Meerut and marched on Delhi, where they were joined by the troops there (11 May 1857) who, with some of the civilian population, massacred all Europeans they could find. Many small dramas were played out as small parties of European officers, civilians and their families defended themselves or escaped as best they could; typical was the defence of the Delhi magazine, where Lieutenant George Willoughby, Commissary of Ordnance, and eight companions held the place until the last moment and then blew it up to prevent the munitions falling into the hands of the mutineers. The rebels declared the aged King of Delhi, Bahadur Shah II, as their leader, heir to the Moguls and 'Sovereign of the World'; his complicity in the events leading to the Mutiny is unclear, but as a frail and probably unwilling 82-year-old he was no more than a titular figurehead.

Although some have described the subsequent events as a 'war of independence', the 'Great Mutiny' was never a national rebellion or an attempt to throw off the yoke of a colonial power. The spirit of mutiny hardly touched the

Bombay Army, the Madras Army not at all, and only a minority of Indian states or rulers supported the rebellion. In some cases, the latter had no inclination to take up arms; in a few others, insurrection was prevented by the swift and decisive action which might have suppressed the first outbreak, as expressed somewhat bluntly by Sir Herbert Edwardes, when ordering loyal troops into the field 'to move down the Punjab and punch the head of any station that says knife!'[24] However, although comparatively limited, the war which followed the first mutinies was marked by revolting barbarity on both sides; European civilians, women and children were massacred without mercy and the British and their Indian supporters responded with a fury which gave no quarter. William Forbes-Mitchell of the 93rd noted that the treachery and barbarity of the Mutiny turned the campaigns 'into a *guerre à la mort* – a war of the most cruel and exterminating form, in which no quarter was given on either side ... Asiatic campaigns have always been conducted in a more remorseless spirit than those between European nations, but the war of the Mutiny ... was far worse than the usual type of even Asiatic fighting. It was something horrible and downright brutalising for an English army to be engaged in such a struggle, in which no quarter was ever given or asked. It was a war of downright butchery ...'[25] In fairness, the behaviour of some of the British and their allies, which all too often involved the killing of innocent Indians and executions without proper trial, was not entirely a matter of retribution but also of self-preservation, for in many areas affected by rebellion, the plight of the Europeans seemed desperate in the extreme. This was expressed eloquently by Sir George Tucker, who remarked when interrupting military preparations to attend church at Mirzapore, 'devotion was pretty well the only stand-by left',[26] everything else appearing hopeless.

Although the following concentrates upon the major campaigns, there were countless minor but often desperate combats fought throughout the area affected by rebellion. An example was the defence of Arrah, near Dinapore, where six European and nine Indian or Eurasian officials and their servants, three railway engineers, and fifty loyal Sikhs, fortified a billiard-hall and stood off repeated attacks until they were relieved, suffering only one fatality and two injuries.

British reaction to the events at Meerut and Delhi was slow, as the Company's European and 'Queen's' regiments were scattered, and it was clearly unwise to rely upon Indian corps whose loyalty might be suspect. The Commander-in-Chief, General the Hon. George Anson, gathered a force at Umballa to march upon Delhi, but died of cholera on 27 May 1857; he was succeeded in command of the Delhi Field Force by Sir Henry Barnard, who led some 3,000 British troops. The governor-general, Lord Canning, appealed for assistance and was fortunate to be able to divert British troops *en route* to China; and the redoubtable Sir Colin Campbell was sent from Britain to take command of the army in India. Sir John Lawrence, the efficient chief commissioner of the Punjab, instead of merely securing his own province from the threat of the spread of mutiny, sent every available man to Delhi, including many of the recently hostile Sikhs, whose loyalty and courage was of great assistance to the British.

Identifying Delhi as the seat of the rebellion, the Delhi Field Force marched to lay siege to the mutineers and civilian rebels who lay within the city. Approaching Delhi, the army defeated a rebel force at Badli-ki-Serai, five miles north-west of the city (8 June), and established itself on 'The Ridge', overlooking Delhi. The army's command changed: Barnard died of cholera on 5 July, and his successor, General Reed, was an invalid who resigned his command after twelve days; he was succeeded by Sir Archdale Wilson. It was a strange siege: the besieging British were greatly outnumbered by their enemies in the city, so that it was difficult to ascertain who were the besieged and who the besiegers. Calls for an immediate assault were rejected by the somewhat unenthusiastic commander, and the force on 'The Ridge' held its position to await reinforcement.

Two important British garrisons were besieged, Lucknow and Cawnpore. Lucknow, capital of Oudh (and thus in the centre of the rebellion) was held by Sir Henry Lawrence, who fortified the residency and its outlying works in perhaps the greatest epic of the Victorian period, which moved one experienced campaigner to echo Henry V's speech before Agincourt, 'Children yet unborn will exclaim with pride, "My grandfather fought and defended the Residency at Lucknow", or "was one of those who cut their way through a host to deliver them".'[27]

Cawnpore became famous (or rather infamous) for another reason. Nana Sahib, heir of the peshwa, accepted the leadership of the rebels in that area, and thus was held responsible for the crime which followed. The Indian regiments in the Cawnpore garrison rebelled on 4 June 1857, and from 6 to 27 June the handful of Europeans, led by General Sir Hugh Wheeler, held out inside a weak entrenchment. Without hope of relief, Wheeler surrendered upon promises from Nana Sahib of safe conduct to Allahabad; but as the British embarked upon the boats which were to carry them to safety, almost all the men were murdered, including Wheeler; those women and children who survived were carried back to captivity in Cawnpore.

At Lucknow, Sir Henry Lawrence determined to hold the Residency and adjoining posts until relieved; the defenders numbered some 1,720 men, of whom 712 were Indian troops and 153 civilian volunteers, plus some 1,280 non-combatants. Almost at the start of the siege, Lawrence was wounded by a shell, and died on 4 July; command devolved upon Lieutenant-Colonel John Inglis.

A relief-force for Cawnpore was assembled under Sir Henry Havelock, which on 7 July left Allahabad (where a

mutiny had been suppressed by Colonel James Neill of the 1st Madras Fusiliers). They fought their way through Nana Sahib's rebels at Fatehpur (12 July), Aong (15 July) and Cawnpore (16 July), after which the rebels dispersed and Nana Sahib fled. This 126-mile march, in appalling heat and fighting three battles *en route*, was a triumph of endurance, but of no avail: when the British re-entered Cawnpore they found the captive women and children butchered and thrown down a well. Regarded at the time as the most atrocious crime in the annals of British India, this provoked the British into abandoning any attitude of chivalry which they might have possessed for their opponents, and turned the war into a campaign of virtual extermination of those who opposed the British, involving the hanging and shooting of many only suspected of

The defender of Lucknow: Major-General Sir John Eardley Wilmot Inglis, who as lieutenant-colonel of the 32nd Foot assumed command of the Lucknow garrison after Lawrence's death. An experienced officer, he had been first commissioned in 1833 and had served in the 1837 rebellion in Canada, and in the Punjab campaign. (Engraving by C. Holl)

The blowing of the Kashmir Gate at Delhi was one of the epics of the Mutiny, as portrayed somewhat inaccurately in this unsigned engraving, in which Lieutenant Philip Salkeld of the Bengal Engineers, mortally wounded, hands the portfire to light the explosive charge to Lieutenant Duncan Home of the same corps; bugler Robert Hawthorne of the 52nd (inaccurately portrayed in full dress, including the 1844 'Albert' shako) stands nearby. All three received the Victoria Cross for this incident, as did Sergeant John Smith of the Bengal Sappers and Miners; Salkeld's was the first to be awarded posthumously.

complicity in the rebellion. Leaving Neill (now a general) at Cawnpore, Havelock pushed on with about 1,500 men towards Lucknow, but twice fell back in the face of opposition, on the second occasion defeating a rebel force at Bithur on 16 August. He was joined by Major-General Sir James Outram, who by rights should have assumed command; but Outram placed himself under Havelock's orders and accompanied the force in his civil capacity as chief commissioner of Oudh, although the co-operation between the two was not without minor difficulties.

Meanwhile, the force on 'The Ridge' at Delhi had been reinforced from the Punjab, the last arriving on 7 August with Brigadier-General John Nicholson. This near-legendary character put heart into Wilson (according to Sir John Lawrence, it was only Nicholson's presence that resulted in the capture of Delhi), and after a bombardment to open breaches, and the blowing-in of the Kashmir Gate by a party of engineers, the city was stormed on 14 September. (The blowing of the Kashmir Gate was a noted exploit: led by Lieutenants Duncan Home and Philip Salkeld of the Bengal Engineers, the party consisted of three European NCOs, three Sikhs and a bugler; both officers, Sergeant John Smith and Bugler Robert Hawthorne of the 52nd received the Victoria Cross for the exploit. Salkeld was mortally wounded and was the first recipient of the decoration, whose VC was gazetted and presented (to his father) after the winner's death. Severe casualties were incurred in the storm of Delhi – Nicholson was among

The storming of Delhi: furious combat as the British 52nd bursts into the city after the blowing of the Kashmir Gate. (Unsigned engraving)

Commanders-in-Chief, India, to 1902

The following list differs from the version sometimes given, the early appointments on occasion being ill-defined; one list appears to include an individual who never existed, 'Alexander Champman', supposed C-in-C in 1774, his name apparently a contraction of those two commanders in Bengal, Charles Chapman and Alexander Champion. The early succession of commanders-in-chief stated below follows Sir Patrick Cadell's 'Commanders-in-Chief of the Indian Army', in *Journal of the Society for Army Historical Research*, vol. XXII, 1944, pp. 220–1; dates are those of their respective appointments:

Admiral Hon. Edward Boscawen	29 July 1748 (to October 1749)
Stringer Lawrence (rank rising from major to major-general)	14 March 1752 (to September 1754; November 1757–April 1759, March 1761–April 1766)
Major-General Eyre Coote	2 July 1770 (to mid-1771)
Lieutenant-General Sir John Clavering	2 November 1774 (to August 1777)
Lieutenant-General Sir Eyre Coote	28 December 1778 (to April 1783)
Lieutenant-General Robert Sloper	21 July 1785
Lieutenant-General Charles, Earl Cornwallis	12 September 1786
Major-General Sir Robert Abercromby	28 October 1793
Lieutenant-General Sir Alured Clarke	16 March 1797
Lieutenant-General Gerard Lake	13 March 1801
General Charles, Marquess Cornwallis	30 July 1805
General Gerard, Lord Lake	5 October 1805
Lieutenant-General George Hewitt	17 October 1807
Lieutenant-General Sir George Nugent	14 January 1812
General Francis, Earl of Moira	4 October 1813
Lieutenant-General the Hon. Sir Edward Paget	13 January 1823
General Stapleton, Lord Combermere	7 October 1825
Lieutenant-General George, Earl of Dalhousie	1 January 1830
Lieutenant-General Sir Edward Barnes	10 January 1832
General Lord William Bentinck	16 May 1833
Lieutenant-General the Hon. Sir Henry Fane	5 September 1835
Major-General Sir Jasper Nicolls	7 December 1839
General Sir Hugh Gough, Bt.	11 August 1843
General Sir Charles Napier	7 May 1849
General Sir William Maynard Gomm	6 December 1850
General the Hon. George Anson	23 January 1856
Lieutenant-General Sir Patrick Grant (officiating)	17 June 1857
Lieutenant-General Sir Colin Campbell	13 August 1857
General Sir Hugh Rose	4 June 1860
General Sir William Mansfield	23 March 1865
General Lord Napier of Magdala	9 April 1870
General Sir Frederick Haines	10 April 1876
General Sir Donald Stewart	8 April 1881
General Sir Frederick Roberts	28 November 1885
General Sir George White	8 April 1893
Lieutenant-General Sir Charles Nairne (provisional)	20 March 1898
General Sir William Lockhart	4 November 1898
General Sir Arthur Palmer	19 March 1900
General Viscount Kitchener of Khartoum	28 November 1902

those killed – but after six days' heavy fighting the rebels were defeated, the city secured, Bahadur Shah captured and his sons shot (after capture) by William Hodson. The fall of Delhi was the turning-point of the campaign.

On 21 September Havelock set out again for Lucknow, fighting a minor action at Mangalwar, and on 23 September captured the Alambagh, a walled group of buildings two miles from Lucknow. Havelock chose a route into Luc-know which Outram believed to be the most hazardous, and the 2,500-strong force lost some 535 men in fighting their way through, including Neill, who was killed; but on 26 September they broke through to the Residency. The relief-force was sufficient only to reinforce the garrison, with Outram taking command, and the siege closed in again. The Alambagh was also garrisoned, but cut off from the main defences.

Capture of Derby the 1st 30th March 1858
The 95th Derbyshire Regiment

Left: In the attack on the rebel-held city of Kotah, 30 March 1858, Lieutenant-Colonel Julius Raines of the 95th Foot had one of his men rescue a tethered black ram, for use as a regimental mascot; christened 'Derby', this was the origin of a succession of rams of the same name kept by the regiment and its successors, the Sherwood Foresters. The original 'Derby I' was given a scarlet coat upon which was displayed his Indian Mutiny Medal, which was also worn by his successors; Derby XIV and XV (which served 1925–37) were both presented to the regiment by the Maharaja of Kotah, birthplace of Derby I. At this time the 95th wore shell jackets and dungaree trousers, but later in 1858 adopted ships' smocks instead. (Print after Harry Payne)

The fall of Delhi released troops for operations in Oudh, and a 2,700-strong column left Delhi on 24 September under Colonel Edward Greathed, which reached Agra on 10 October; failing to reconnoitre or to post adequate sentries, Greathed was attacked surprisedly, but his British and Sikhs responded magnificently and routed the rebels. The column pushed on to Cawnpore under command of Colonel James Hope Grant, where news was received of the Commander-in-Chief, Sir Colin Campbell, who was on his way. Assuming command of the forces in India on 17 August, he had taken time to re-organise administration and transport, and did not reach Cawnpore until 3 November. He advanced on Lucknow with about 4,500 men, reaching the Alambagh on 12 November, and on 16 November stormed the fortified Sikander Bagh, his troops giving no quarter in vengeance for Cawnpore. On the following day Campbell broke through to Outram and Havelock in the Residency, but believing that a continued defence would be wasteful of resources, evacuated the garrison and its dependants (19–23 November). Havelock died from dysentery on 24 November.

Leaving Outram to hold the Alambagh, Campbell returned to Cawnpore, where the force he had left there was being attacked by a large rebel force under Tantia Topi, the most talented of the Indian rebel commanders; it included the Gwalior Contingent, that state's British-officered force which had mutinied despite the loyalty to the British of its maharajah. The Cawnpore force, under Major-General Charles Windham, had been defeated in front of the city, but on 6 December Campbell won a decisive victory over the rebels. He pursued the next stage of his campaign with care, and more slowly than some wished, securing communications with Delhi and the Punjab before advancing again upon Lucknow, operations delayed further by awaiting the arrival of Jang Bahadur's Nepalese troops, whose offer of service had been accepted some months before. Thus the British siege of Lucknow did not begin until 2 March 1858, Outram's small garrison having been holding the Alambagh throughout. The strategic positions in Lucknow were taken progressively: the Martinière was captured on 9 March; two days later the Begum Kothi (a noted strong-point) was stormed (during which William Hodson was killed), and on 16 March the residency was again in British hands. It was a measure of the symbolic importance of the defence of the Residency that, just as a Union Flag had flown throughout the siege, so one flew perpetually (except for renewal) over the ruins until 13 August 1947, when India became two separate dominions. Following the re-capture of Lucknow, Canning ordered Campbell to continue operations against the scattered rebel forces; but although columns were sent against them, in general they were too slow to intercept the guerrilla-style bands, and it was Sir Hugh Rose's campaign in central India which ended the war.

In central India the troops of some states had risen in rebellion, and were joined by the Rani of Jhansi, one of the most capable of the rebel leaders (see her entry in Section VIII). In January 1858 Major-General Sir Hugh Rose was ordered to act in concert with Campbell and direct 'flying columns' against the rebels. In contrast to Campbell's somewhat ponderous progress (though in fairness his task had been more difficult, and begun at a more critical time), after a slow beginning Rose displayed a more audacious attitude, attacking the enemy wherever encountered. Advancing from Bombay, he relieved Saugor on 3 February 1858, after a siege of seven months; where, without the stiffening of European troops, the 31st Bengal Native Infantry had remained steadfastly loyal throughout, and acting under their own Indian officers had even chased the mutinous 42nd Bengal, defeated them, and captured their Colours and 400 stand of arms. Jhansi was besieged, and Rose defeated Tantia Topi's attempted relief-force on 1 April; the city fell to an assault on 3 April. Rose pursued the rebels, defeating Tantia Topi at Kunch (1 May); and another victory was won at Kalpi on 22 May. Tantia Topi, the Rani of Jhansi and the Rao Sahib (Nana Sahib's nephew) took their forces into Gwalior, where the maharajah attempted to resist them with his personal army (the Gwalior Contingent having joined the rebellion earlier); but after a brief skirmish at Morar the Gwalior army also joined the rebels, the maharajah and his bodyguard taking flight. Leaving Kalpi on 6 June 1858, Rose made a forced march against Gwalior, defeated the rebels on 17 June at Kotah-ki-Serai (where the Rani was killed), and Gwalior was captured on 20 June. Although minor

Private James Davis (whose real name was Kelly) of the 42nd Highlanders recounts his astonishingly cool behaviour at Fort Ruhiya, 15 April 1858, for which he was awarded the Victoria Cross. Reconnoitring the enemy position, he was accompanied by Lieutenant Alfred Bramley; his company captain was John MacLeod. Lying in a ditch with Davis, Bramley looked up to see the enemy approaching:
'Before poor Bramley got down he was shot in the temple, but not dead. He died during the night. The captain said, "We can't leave him. Who will take him out?" I said, "I will." The fort was firing hard all the time. I said, "Eadie, give me a hand. Put him on my back." As he was doing so he was shot in the back of the head, his blood running down my back. A man crawled over and pulled Eadie off. At this time I thought I was shot, the warm blood running down my back. The captain said, "We can't lose any more lives. Are you wounded?" I said, "I don't think I am." He said, "Will you still take him out?" I said "Yes." He was such a brave young fellow that the company all loved him. I got him on my back again, and told him to take me tight round the neck. I ran across the open space. During the time his watch fell out; I did not like to leave it, so I sat down and picked it up, all the time under a heavy fire. There was a man of the name of Dods, who came back and took him off my back. I went back again through the same fire, and helped to take up the man Eadie. Then I returned for my rifle, and firing a volley we all left. It was a badly managed affair altogether.'
(*Strand Magazine*, March 1891, pp. 290–1)

Below: Indian Mutiny Medal. The obverse bears a portrait of Queen Victoria; the reverse, designed by L. C. Wyon, a figure of Britannia holding a wreath, and a lion. Five clasps were issued: 'Lucknow' as illustrated, 'Delhi', 'Defence of Lucknow', 'Relief of Lucknow', and 'Central India'.

operations continued into 1859 (Tanti Topi was apprehended only on 7 April 1859, and hanged eleven days later), this was the final major action of the 'Great Mutiny', and the sternest test presented to the British during their rule in India was ended.

The Mutiny had not been a national rising, but one restricted to a number of disaffected princes and elements within the Bengal Army; and some of the trouble had been caused by the opportunity it afforded for banditry on the part of lawless elements hitherto held in check, known as *badmashes* (bad characters) or *gujars* ('goojurs', a Hindu group of proverbially predatory disposition). By contrast, even in the affected areas, most of the country people remained neutral, awaiting the outcome with patience and often showing great hospitality to fugitive Europeans; and the inhabitants of the Punjab had remained notably steadfast in their loyalty to the British.

'Marching toward the sound of gunfire' is one of the oldest of military clichés, and an officer recalled the effect it had upon the 86th Foot at the conclusion of an exhausting and protracted forced march during the Indian Mutiny:

'As we marched, we distinctly heard the report of the guns attacking Chandaree. The sound had a most magical effect upon our men; some, who were almost beaten down by this terrific march, seeming to derive new life and energy from it; and as the artillery reverberated through the morning air, I think the last seven miles of our march were the quickest on record. I know my horse was obliged to break into a regular amble to keep up with the light-hearted soldiers.'

(Stuart, Colonel W. K. *Reminiscences of a Soldier*, London 1874, vol. II, p. 156)

The punishment for mutiny: the hanging of twelve deserters, and the blowing from guns of forty of the 55th Bengal Native Infantry at Peshawar, 10 June 1857. The latter had mutinied at Mardan but had been apprehended by an expedition to re-possess Mardan fort. Of the appalling punishment of 'blowing from guns', it was noted that 'it is known by those well acquainted with the Asiatic character to be quite necessary in a crisis like the present ... Horrible this punishment certainly is; but let us not forget the horror of the occasions that have made it a duty to administer it ...' (Illustrated London News, 28 November 1857). In the foreground are teams of the Bengal Horse Artillery, in which, unlike the British artillery, every horse had a rider, 'owing to the horses used in the batteries being very vicious' (ibid., 27 January 1849). (Engraving after Lieutenant G. R. Brown, Bengal Horse Artillery)

Nevertheless, the consequences of the Mutiny were immense, the government of the East India Company ending as a direct result. The 1858 Act for the Better Government of India transferred the entire administration from the Company to the Crown, so that henceforth India was governed by Britain through a secretary of state and council, with the governor-general henceforth styled viceroy. On 2 August 1858 the Queen gave royal assent to the transfer of government to the Crown, and on 1 November Canning announced the change by a proclamation, and offered amnesty to all rebels not directly concerned in the murder of British subjects, or who were not leaders of the revolt. This measure was criticised at the time (earning him the nickname 'Clemency Canning'!), but its wisdom became evident in succeeding years. Peace was proclaimed officially in India on 8 July 1859.

Military Forces during and after the Mutiny

The Rebel Forces 1857–8. The rebel armies comprised two distinct groups: the mutineers of the Bengal Army, and the remainder. The mutinous regiments initially retained their discipline, fighting in the way taught to them by the British, and retaining so much of their old regimental structure that not only did they wear their red uniforms (although the unpopular, European-style trousers were generally replaced by the indigenous *dhoti*), but even fought under their regimental Colours, kept their muster-rolls up-to-date and wore the medals awarded by the British for earlier campaigns. In an incident which seems to exemplify the sad end of the old order, Havelock's troops at Cawnpore encountered a rebel unit with its band playing their men into action against their erstwhile comrades to the tune of *Auld Lang Syne*. Surely nothing could

be more appropriate as a lament for the old Bengal Army.

The remainder of the rebel forces were equipped and fought in the traditional manner, and as the war progressed the old regimental structure deteriorated, uniforms were abandoned, and regiments were replaced by mixed bands of mutineers and civilian insurgents. A great handicap to the rebel forces was the lack of a unified command and competent leadership, for only a small number of commanders were at all proficient, which made it easier for the British to continue the practice of winning victories even when massively outnumbered; yet with adequate leadership the rebel forces were a formidable opponent, as Windham discovered at Cawnpore. It is stated sometimes that the rebels' weaponry was greatly inferior to that of the British, and undoubtedly the Enfield rifle was superior to that carried by the sepoys; yet it was carried only by British units, not by their Indian allies, and only comparatively late in the campaign was its superiority fully appreciated by the British. Havelock might attribute the victory of Fatehpur to a combination of British spirit, artillery, the Enfield and divine favour, but in many operations the bayonet rather than firepower was the decisive weapon used by the British.

British Forces 1857–65. In addition to the British Army (which was reinforced as soon as practicable), the forces deployed by the British during the Mutiny included the loyal remnant of the Bengal Army, but the majority of the Indian units were newly formed corps of irregular cavalry and Punjab infantry, with a large proportion of Sikh personnel; and Gurkha units also played a significant role. Also formed at this period were auxiliary units of Europeans and Anglo-Indians, for example the Bengal Yeomanry, Calcutta Volunteer Guards, Lahore Light Horse, Madras Volunteer Guards and Meerut Volunteer Horse (alias the 'Khakee Ressalah' from their uniform-colour). Although the Madras Volunteer Guards remained in existence, to become the most senior of the Auxiliary Force units, the majority of corps were disbanded once the crisis was past.

The effects of the Mutiny were felt far wider than in the sphere of the Bengal Army; from this period increasing emphasis was placed upon the importance of the so-called 'martial races' of the north and less upon the traditional recruiting-grounds of south and central India, reflecting the esteem felt for the military qualities of the Sikhs and the fact that units raised in the Punjab had remained loyal at a time when the traditional source of recruits had produced mutiny.

The transfer of responsibility from the Company to the Crown led to the extinction of the former's European regiments. The European artillery became batteries of the Royal Artillery, and the European infantry became British line regiments: the 1st–3rd Bengal were transformed into the 101st Royal Bengal Fusiliers, 104th Bengal Fusiliers, and 107th Bengal Infantry respectively; the 1st–3rd

William Forbes-Mitchell of the 93rd writes memorably of the assault of the Secunderabagh, when his regiment was seething with desire to avenge atrocities committed on European women and children during the Indian Mutiny:

'The Punjabis dashed over the mud wall shouting their war-cry of the Sikhs, "Jai Khalsa Jee!" led by their two European officers, who were both shot down before they had gone a few yards. As soon as Sir Colin [Campbell] saw them waver, he turned to Colonel Ewart ... and said, "Colonel Ewart, bring on the tartan – let my own lads at them." Before the command could be repeated or the buglers had time to sound the advance, the whole seven companies, like one man, leaped over the wall, with such a yell of pent-up rage as I had never heard before or since. It was not a cheer, but a concentrated yell of rage and ferocity that made the echoes ring again; and it must have struck terror into the defenders, for they actually ceased firing, and we could see them through the breach rushing from the outside wall ... Pipe-Major John M'Leod, who with seven pipers ... struck up the Highland Charge, called by some *The Haughs of Cromdell*, and by others *On wi the Tartan* – the famous charge of the great Montrose when he led his Highlanders so often to victory. When all was over, and Sir Colin complimented the pipe-major on the way he had played, John said, "I thought the boys would fecht better wi' the national music to cheer them."'

(It was in this action that the enigmatic 'gentleman-ranker' 'Quaker' Wallace personally killed twenty of the enemy, chanting the 116th Psalm (Scots version in metre) between every shot and every bayonet-thrust:

'I'll of salvation take the cup,
On God's name will I call;
I'll pay my vows now to the Lord
Before His people all.')

(Forbes-Mitchell, W. *Reminiscences of the Great Mutiny 1857-59*, London, 1897 pp. 47–8, 56)

Madras into the 102nd Royal Madras Fusiliers, 105th Madras Light Infantry and 108th Madras Infantry respectively; and the 1st–3rd Bombay into the 103rd Royal Bombay Fusiliers, 106th Bombay Light Infantry and 109th Bombay Infantry respectively. In 1858 four regiments of Bengal European cavalry were recruited in Britain, with officers from the mutinied or disarmed regiments of Bengal Light Cavalry; a 5th Regiment was formed at Peshawar from volunteers who had comprised an *ad hoc* cavalry corps during the Mutiny. In April 1861 these regiments were disbanded and their personnel encouraged to volunteer for three new British cavalry regiments, the 19th–21st Light Dragoons. The Indian engineer corps were retained, but European personnel transferred to the

Royal Engineers. (The transfer of European from Company to 'Queen's' service was not without difficulty: protests were characterised by the term 'White Mutiny'.)

Although the Indian regiments passed from Company control into that of the British administration, there was still no unified command, the presidency divisions being maintained (Bengal, Madras and Bombay), plus the Punjab Irregular Force, Hyderabad Contingent and smaller formations; not until 1860 were the Punjab units transferred from the control of the government of the Punjab to that of the commander-in-chief of the Bengal Army, and others from the same region were under direct control of the Government of India.

Bengal Army. The 1861 re-organisation of the Bengal Cavalry reduced the number of irregular units, the number having risen to 29 under the C-in-C Bengal, and seventeen under the Government of India. The former were reduced to nineteen, creating the new regular Bengal Cavalry, none of the previous corps having survived the Mutiny. Eight of the previous irregular regiments remained loyal, and occupied the first eight positions in the new list: 1st (Skinner's Horse), 2nd (Gardner's Horse), 3rd (ex-4th; the previous 3rd had partially mutinied and was disbanded in 1861), 4th–8th (ex-6th–8th, 17th and 18th respectively). The remaining numbers were occupied by regiments raised during or after the Mutiny: 9th and 10th (ex-1st and 2nd Hodson's Horse, formed 1857–8), 11th (ex-Wale's Horse or 1st Sikh Irregular Cavalry), 12th and 13th (ex-2nd and 4th Sikh Irregular respectively), 14th (ex-Murray's Jat Horse, raised 1857 as the Jat Horse Yeomanry), 15th (ex-Cureton's Multanis), 16th (ex-Rohilcund Horse), 17th (ex-Robart's Horse, raised 1857 as the Muttra Horse, a police unit), 18th (ex-2nd Mahratta Horse) and 19th (ex-Fane's Horse, raised 1860 from Hodson's Horse).

Only fifteen regiments of Bengal Native Infantry survived the Mutiny; the 4th, 58th and 73rd were disbanded, and the remaining twelve were re-numbered 1–12 in the re-organisations of May 1861 (the old 21st, 31st–33rd, 42nd, 43rd, 47th, 59th, 63rd, 65th, 66th and 70th respectively). Numbers 13 to 18 in the new list were occupied by irregular regiments which existed before the Mutiny, the Kelat-i-Ghilzie, Shekhawatee, Ferozepore, Ludhiana, Sirmoor and Kumaon. Numbers 18–22 were occupied by units raised during the Mutiny (1st Extra Gurkha Battalion, Lucknow, Loyal Purbiah and Alipore Regiments), and numbers 23–36 by the 7th–24th Punjab Infantry. Numbers 37 to 44 were occupied by the Allahabad, Fatehgarh, Mynpoorie, Bareilly, Meerut, Agra, Aligarh and Shahjehanpur Levies; 45 by the 1st Gwalior Infantry, 46 and 47 by the 1st and 2nd Assam Light Infantry, and 48 by the Sylhet Light Infantry. In October 1861 the 11th and 17th–19th were re-titled as the 1st–4th Gurkhas and extracted from the list, and the others re-numbered accordingly (so that the 20th became the 16th, and so on), reducing the numbered regiments to 44; a 45th was added in 1864, being originally the Bengal Police Battalion. A 5th Gurkha Regiment was transferred from the Punjab Irregular Force.

Madras Army. The Madras Army was largely unaffected by the events of the Mutiny; to release regulars for service outside the presidency, a few units were formed for local security, but these were disbanded by 1860. The 8th Light Cavalry was disbanded in 1857 (having refused to go to Bengal), and the 5th–7th in December 1860.

Bombay Army. The Bombay Army lost two infantry battalions to the Mutiny, the 21st and 27th; the number 21 was filled by the old Marine Battalion, and in 1858 the number 27 by the 1st Belooch Battalion; and the number of battalions was increased to 31, the 30th and 31st being formed from the loyal elements of the old 21st and 27th. Some irregular cavalry and infantry units were formed, but most were disbanded when the army was re-organised in 1861, when the 29th–31st were disbanded, the numbers 29 and 30 being filled again by the 2nd Belooch Battalion and the 1st Jacob's Rifles, irregulars formed during the Mutiny. Of the irregular cavalry which survived the post-Mutiny re-organisations, the Poona Irregular Horse formed a 2nd Regiment, which was disbanded in 1862; the Gujarat Silladar Horse survived until 1865; there were four regiments of Scinde Horse, reduced to three in 1862; the three regiments of South Mahratta Horse were reduced to one in 1862, and that was disbanded in 1865. The native artillery was disbanded, save two mountain batteries.

Other Forces. In 1865 the Punjab Irregular Force was re-titled the Punjab Frontier Force; it continued to consist of

Ingham Britcliffe of the Bengal European Fusiliers writes home of the fall of Delhi in 1857, reporting equally upon his actions and his loot:
'We lost the best part of our regiment in this protracted struggle – we were 900 strong on the 13th of May last when we marched towards Delhi; we now number but 200 able men. The enemy was estimated at 60,000 strong, while we, until the arrival of reinforcements, did not number more than 5,000 ... yet in every engagement with them we beat them back, and took their guns; as you say in your letter, we made them fly "like chaff before the wind"... I assure you that I put a fix on a great many of them the day we entered the city; I caught three, each slightly wounded in the leg, and "sent" them in part expiation of the cruelties committed on my countrywomen ... I saw seventeen of the rascals strung up to the bough of a tree and shot ... I have some nice purses and several beautiful stones; I have a gold ring with diamonds in the setting, which I wear regularly myself, and a cashmere shawl, worth five pounds, which I should like to give to mother, a double-barrelled fowling piece worth quite as much, some handsome silks, and about two hundred rupees ...'

Lord Roberts recalls the bravery of Subadar Ruttun Singh at the storming of Delhi:

'He was a Patiala Sikh, and had been invalided from the service. As the 1st Punjab Infantry neared Delhi, Major Coke saw the old man standing in the road with two swords on. He begged to be taken back into the service, and when Coke demurred he said: "What! my old corps going to fight at Delhi without me! I hope you will let me lead my old Sikh company into action again. I will break these two swords in your cause." Coke acceded to the old man's wish, and throughout the siege of Delhi he displayed the most splendid courage. At the great attack on the "Sammy House"... Ruttun Sing, amidst a shower of bullets, jumped on to the parapet and shouted to the enemy, who were storming the picquet, "If any man wants to fight, let him come here, and not stand firing like a coward! I am Ruttun Sing, of Patiala." He then sprang down among the enemy, and drove them off with heavy loss. On the morning of the assault the regiment ... falling in again, were doing so "right in front". Ruttun Sing came up to Lieutenant Charles Nicholson, who was commanding the regiment, and said: "We ought to fall in 'left in front'", thereby making his own company the leading one in the assault. In a few minutes more Ruttun Sing was mortally wounded ...'
(*Forty-One Years in India*, London, 1900 pp. 139–40)

the Corps of Guides, five cavalry regiments, and the artillery, infantry and Sikh regiments described previously. Like these, the other forces which came under the authority of the Government of India included the Hyderabad Contingent; and the Central India Horse, which originated with the Gwalior, Bhopal and Malwa Contingents, re-organised into two (briefly three) regiments of Central India Horse in 1860.

INDIA 1858–1900

Operations after the Mutiny

For the remainder of the 19th century, the Indian Army's operations were in the frontier districts or outside the borders of India; within there was comparative tranquillity. Indian forces served in China, Burma, Abyssinia, Egypt and the Sudan, and in the Second Afghan War (all covered here in their respective sections); and the 4th, 16th, 24th and 27th Bombay Regiments served in East Africa. Administration continued without radical alteration, although on 1 January 1877 the Queen was proclaimed as Empress of India (significantly, the durbar commemorating the occasion was held upon 'The Ridge' overlooking Delhi, a reminder, if one were needed, of the efforts made to maintain the British hold on India). Actual administration was conducted by the viceroy (governor-general), a post not without hazard: Canning left India in March 1862 but died within a month of his return to Britain; his successor, James, 8th Earl of Elgin, died of heart disease exacerbated by exhaustion at Dharmsala while touring the frontier in 1863; and the next viceroy but one, Richard, 6th Earl of Mayo, was murdered by a convict when visiting the penal settlement at Port Blair in the Andaman Islands in February 1872.

North-West Frontier operations involved Afghanistan in some measure, and while the smaller operations are noted below, the campaigning in Afghanistan is covered in the separate section on that country. The majority of the smaller operations were punitive expeditions, counter-raids in response to tribal incursions, or to ensure the comparative tranquillity of the frontier.

Sittana Field Force (North-West Frontier)

The only frontier troubles at the time of the Mutiny were again caused by the 'Hindustani Fanatics', reinforced by remnants of the 55th Bengal Native Infantry which had

A camp in the field: Colonel Robinson (centre, wearing forage cap) and officers of the 1st Madras Pioneers, Bolan Pass, 1883. Note the fur-covered arm-chair, and the early use of a slouch hat on active service.

been dispersed after mutinying at Mardan on 25 May 1857. Three minor expeditions were undertaken to suppress disturbances: to Shekh Jana (2 July 1857) and Narinji (21 July and 3 August), by Major J. L. Vaughan of the 5th Punjab Infantry (the latter also involving some 150 British troops from the 27th, 70th and 87th). A much larger undertaking was necessary in the following year, four columns under the command of Major-General Sir Sydney Cotton; from 25 April to 5 May 1858 a number of hostile villages were destroyed, culminating with that at Sittana on 4 May. This was the first occasion on which the Enfield rifle was used (to considerable effect) in frontier warfare.

Kabul Khel Waziris (North-West Frontier)
In December 1859 Brigadier-General Sir Neville Chamberlain made a foray against the Kabul Khel Waziris, a clan implicated in the murder of a British official in the previous month. The expedition (Punjab Infantry, Guides, supports and local levies) left Kohat on 15 December, stormed the Waziri position on 21 December and, peace having been negotiated, returned to Kohat on 14 January 1860.

Mahsud Waziris (North-West Frontier)
The second main Waziri group, Mahsuds, attempted to sack the town of Tank, defended only by a troop of 5th Punjab Cavalry under Risaldar Saadat Khan, an intrepid officer who on 13 March 1860 fought a brilliant action which killed an estimated 300 Mahsuds for the loss of one man dead and thirteen wounded. As a reprisal for the raid, from 17 April to 20 May 1860 Chamberlain led an expedition through Mahsud territory, fighting a couple of sharp actions, including an attack on the British camp at Palosin on 23 April, which was repelled at bayonet-point.

Ambela Campaign (North-West Frontier)
The Ambela campaign (or 'Umbeyla', the spelling used for the clasp on the India General Service Medal) was the most serious of the operations mounted against the 'Hindustani Fanatics'. In October 1863 Chamberlain led two brigades (together some 5,000 strong) in an intended circuitous march via the Ambela Pass to prevent the fanatics from escaping north into the hills; in so doing the British aroused the hostility of the Bunerwal tribe and, confronted by clans massing against him, Chamberlain decided to hold the Pass and await reinforcement. Much heavy fighting ensued, in broken and mountainous terrain, as the tribesmen endeavoured to capture fortified British posts in the Pass, notably 'the Eagle's Nest' and 'the Crag Picquet', which were lost and re-taken in bitter conflict. The re-capture of the latter on 20 November 1863 was regarded as so vital that Chamberlain accompanied the storming-party, and was severely wounded; he was suc-

Surgeon William Munro of the 93rd Highlanders recounts a new experience during the Indian Mutiny: 'The regiment was advancing in line, under a smart fire from the guns of the enemy. I followed immediately behind the centre, and, as usual, was accompanied by my old orderly, Private William D———. We were both old soldiers, familiar with the hiss of round shot, the rush of shell, the crack of shrapnel, and the ping of the bullet, but I had never heard the whistling flight of grape. Suddenly, as we advanced on that occasion, it seemed to me that I heard the sound of birds in rapid flight above and around me, and at the strange sound I swayed my body round, so as to present my side to it. Immediately the old orderly touched me on the arm, saying at the same time, "A'm ashamed for ye, doctor; haud yer front tae't, man, it's only grape ye're hearing." The good fellow was not ashamed of me, but for me, and explained his meaning thus: "I ken weel eneugh, but I wad think ill suld ithers suppose or say that 'the doctor' was feared for a grape shot."'
(Munro, Surgeon-General W. *Reminiscences of Military Service with the 93rd Sutherland Highlanders*, London, 1883, pp. 206–7)

ceeded in command by Major-General J. Garvock who arrived with reinforcements on 30 November. Using his augmented strength, Garvock took the offensive and, having suffered severe losses, the Bunerwals agreed to cease hostilities and to destroy the base of the 'Hindustani Fanatics' at Malka, which they accomplished on 22 December. The campaign had turned into a much more costly and protracted affair than had been intended (British losses were 238 dead and 670 wounded), but the 'Fanatics' were finally destroyed; losses among the hill tribes were estimated at more than three times those suffered by the British.

Shabkadr (North-West Frontier)
From early December 1863 to January 1864 some skirmishing occurred between the Mohmands and the garrison of Shabkadr, commanded by Colonel A. F. Macdonell of the Rifle Brigade, whose 3rd Battalion formed the principal part of the garrison. More than 5,000 Mahsuds advanced on the fort on 2 January 1864, and were routed when the British came out to meet them, the 7th Hussars executing what was stated to be the only proper cavalry charge made by British troops in the entire frontier campaigning.

Bhutan
Bhutan (or 'Bhootan', the spelling used on the clasp of the India General Service Medal) was a kingdom in the eastern Himalayas, whose boundaries with British India were disputed. After continual Bhutia raids on British ter-

ritory, and an unsuccessful diplomatic mission in 1863 (in which the British envoy, Sir Ashley Eden, was insulted and forced to sign a treaty ceding the disputed territory to Bhutan), the area was annexed in November 1864. At first there appeared to be little opposition, but in January 1865 the British were expelled from their post at Dewangiri with the loss of two mountain guns. An expedition was dispatched under Brigadier-General Sir Henry Tombs, who recaptured Dewangiri on 2 April 1865, and peace was concluded in November (although operations continued until February 1866). The Bhutias ceded all the disputed eighteen Dwars of Bengal and Assam, and released all kidnapped British subjects; but as much of Bhutan's revenue came from these regions, they received an annual subsidy in return for their good behaviour.

Black Mountain Expedition, 1868 (North-West Frontier)

On 30 July 1868 the Black Mountain tribes attacked a police post at Aghi, which had been established to curb the lawless behaviour around it. It was reinforced by Lieutenant-Colonel O. E. Rothney and the 5th Gurkhas, but despite the co-operation of local men under the Khan of Amb, it was decided that additional troops were needed to carry out the required punitive raid. So as not to denude the frontier garrisons, troops were called from the interior (two companies of Sappers and Miners arrived after marching almost 600 miles in 29 days), and two brigades were formed under Brigadier-General A. T. Wilde. From 3 to 22 October this force traversed the Black Mountain area, involving some skirmishing and destruction of villages.

Bizoti Orakzais (North-West Frontier)

Depredations by the Bizoti clan of Orakzais resident near Kohat prompted a small counter-raid by Major L. B. Jones of the 3rd Punjab Cavalry, which on 11 March 1868 was very severely handled. After an attack on a police post on 13 February 1869, a punitive expedition was mounted on 25 February under Lieutenant-Colonel C. P. Keyes; it destroyed a deserted village and was harassed in its withdrawal but, somewhat overawed by a second force from Peshawar which demonstrated to the north of the Kohat Pass at the same time, the Bizotis made peace on 4 April 1869.

Tochi Valley (North-West Frontier)

After some hostile acts by the Dawari Waziri tribe of the Tochi valley, and their refusal to pay a fine (the usual mode of reparation for minor depredations), C. P. Keyes (now Brigadier-General and commander of the Punjab Frontier Force) led an expedition to the valley on 6–7 March 1872; after some minor skirmishing in which the 1st Punjab and 1st and 4th Sikh Infantry were especially distinguished, and after some buildings had been destroyed, the Dawaris sued for peace.

Lushai

Lushai (or 'Looshai', the spelling used on the clasp of the India General Service Medal) is a mountainous district of eastern Bengal and Assam, on the Assam–Burma border. From their first attack on British territory in November 1849 the inhabitants had been troublesome, and in December 1871 two columns were formed for punitive action following a raid on the Winchester tea plantation, during which the planter's daughter was kidnapped. Brigadier-Generals G. Bourchier and C. W. Brownlow led the Cachar and Chittagong columns respectively, took some villages, retrieved the captive and dictated peace terms; operations concluded in February 1872.

Jowaki Expedition (North-West Frontier)

In 1877 the Jowaki Afridis began to raid the road between Kohat and India. Three small columns under Colonel D. Mocatta of the 3rd Sikh Infantry traversed their territory on 30 August 1877, with very little skirmishing, but as this failed to stop the raiding, two larger columns were assembled under Brigadier-Generals C. P. Keyes (from Kohat) and C. C. G. Ross (from Peshawar), which detached forces for smaller expeditions. From 9 November 1877 until the end of January 1878 they remained in Jowaki territory, with little opposition, and the Jowakis made peace shortly after.

Utman Khel (North-West Frontier)

The Utman Khel raided a camp of the constructors of the Swat Canal on 9 December 1876, but because of impending operations in Afghanistan it was more than a year before a punitive expedition could be mounted: on 14–15 February 1878 Captain Wigram Battye with 280 Guides raided the village of the chief responsible, Mian Khan, killed him and withdrew successfully; whereupon the Utman Khel paid the fines imposed upon them.

Second Afghan War: Subsidiary Operations (North-West Frontier)

A number of minor operations were conducted at the time of the Second Afghan War, against tribes that had harassed the advancing British columns. Two columns under Brigadier-General F. F. Maude traversed the territory of the Zakha Khel Afridis in mid-December 1878, and five columns in January 1879; in 1881 this tribe received a subsidy for ceasing their raiding. Minor operations were mounted against the Mohmands in April 1879 and January 1880; the larger of the two expeditions, conducted by two columns near Kam Dakka, inflicted the necessary reverse on 15 January 1880. On 8–15 December 1879 Brigadier J. A. Tytler marched a column through the territory of the Zaimukhts, involving some skirmishing; from 17 October to 6 November 1880 Brigadier C. M. MacGregor led a column through the territory of the Marri Baluchis, who surrendered without resistance; and from

A typical frontier outpost: a blockhouse on the Khyber road between Hari Singh Burj and Jamrud, c.1897, when it was garrisoned by the Khyber Rifles, a corps formed in 1878 from local Afridis.

18 April to 22 May 1881 Brigadier-Generals T. G. Kennedy and J. J. H. Gordon led columns from Tank and Bannu respectively through Mahsud territory, although the Mahsuds only accepted terms after a blockade which lasted until September 1881.

Naga Expeditions

The Naga Hills was a district in the Eastern Bengal/Assam region; its name means 'naked' and was applied by the Assamese to the hill tribes, who were remarkably turbulent and resisted repeated punitive expeditions. The most notable included a small expedition of 1875, to punish an attack upon a surveying party in January of that year; and a larger force under Brigadier-General J. L. Nation (December 1879–January 1880), after the Nagas had murdered a British commissioner on 14 October 1879 and besieged the Kohima garrison. A column was sent to relieve Kohima, and Nation marched to capture the Naga stronghold of Konoma; the Nagas finally surrendered in March 1880.

Takht-i-Suliman (North-West Frontier)

A minor expedition was mounted in November–December 1883 to protect a surveying party at the Takht-i-Suliman mountain; commanded by Brigadier-General T. G. Kennedy and composed entirely of Frontier Force units, it was involved in some minor skirmishing with the Shiranis.

Sikkim

The eastern Himalayan state of Sikkim had been at war with Nepal in the late 18th century, and was only restored to independence by the British in 1816, after the Nepal War. After some problems, Britain had to impose a treaty by force on the Raja of Sikkim in 1861; but his successor, Tho-tub Namgyé, neglected to conform to its terms and permitted the Tibetans to construct a fort at Lingtu, in contravention of the treaty, to threaten the road through the state. Diplomacy having failed, Colonel T. Graham, RA, led a small expedition to capture and destroy the fort (20–21 March 1888); but the effort had to be renewed in July, and an action was necessary in the Jelep (or Jalapa) Pass on 25 September 1888 finally to expel the Tibetans. In 1890 a convention was concluded with China to formalise Sikkim as a British protectorate, and from a supplemental treaty in 1893 the Maharaja's government was guided by a British Resident.

Black Mountain Expedition, 1888 (North-West Frontier)

Intermittent raiding by the Black Mountain tribes came to a head on 18 June 1888 when a British patrol was ambushed and two officers killed (Major L. Battye, 5th Gurkhas, and Captain H. B. Urmston, 6th Punjab Infantry). Five columns of the Hazara Field Force were assembled under Major-General J. W. McQueen, and set out on 4 October; the Akazais and Hassanzais were forced into submission, and on 13 October the settlement of the 'Hindustani Fanatics' at Maidan was destroyed. The expedition then moved on to deal with the remaining hostile tribes, and was concluded by 14 November. Notably valuable service was given by the Kashmir forces accompanying the British; and the clasp authorised for the India

General Service Medal for this expedition was 'Hazara 1888'.

Chin-Lushai Expeditions
Although the Chin Hills were not declared a province of Burma until 1895, the operations of 1889–90 are covered in the section on Burma.

Zhob Expeditions (North-West Frontier)
Minor operations were made in the Zhob Valley to curb the depredations of the inhabitants: the first, under Brigadier-General Sir O. V. Tanner, was a brief affair (1880); another, the Zhob Field Force under Major-General Sir George White, was necessary in October–November 1890 to subdue the Khiddarzai clan of the Shirani tribe, and to disperse a gang of bandits which had congregated at Thanishpa.

Black Mountain Expedition, 1891 (North-West Frontier)
Another expedition was necessary against the Hassanzais and Akazais in 1891, to enforce compliance with the terms agreed in 1888; the Hazara Field Force of three brigades under Major-General W. K. Elles was deployed from 12 March to 16 May, and began its withdrawal on 11 June. (As before, the clasp for the India General Service Medal for this operation bore the name 'Hazara', and the date 1891). A final expedition into the Black Mountain district was mounted under Major-General Sir William Lockhart, 2–11 October 1892, which destroyed some villages but met no resistance.

Miranzai Field Force (North-West Frontier)
To curb the hostilities of the Orakzais, the Miranzai Field Force was organised under Sir William Lockhart; villages were destroyed and peace imposed (January–February 1891). In April, however, the Orakzais attacked British positions along the Samana Ridge, and the Miranzai Field Force was re-formed in three columns under Lockhart, which drove the hostiles from the Samana Ridge and forced their surrender by 9 May. The clasp for the India General Service Medal bears the name 'Samana'.

Manipur Expedition
The state of Manipur on the Assam–Burma border possessed its own army, but had relied on British assistance against Burmese incursions, notably in 1762 and 1824. The death of the raja in 1886 caused a dispute over the succession, and in early 1891 the chief commissioner of Assam, James Quinton, accompanied by Lieutenant-Colonel Charles Skene and a small force of 43rd Gurkhas, went to Manipur to remove, by force if necessary, Takendrajit Singh, the *Senaputti* (commander of the Manipur army), who had engineered the deposition of one of his brothers and the installation of another. Skene attempted to apprehend the *Senaputti* by attacking the city; but the

Manipuris counter-attacked and the British were besieged in the Residency, outside the city walls. A party of British officials, including Quinton, Skene and the Resident, Frank Grimwood, went out to negotiate, but were murdered by the Manipuris. The British force, now almost leaderless, managed to escape with the Resident's young wife, Ethel Grimwood, who had been active throughout the siege and now helped guide them to safety. Three columns were then dispatched (from Kohima, Cachar and Tamu), which converged on Manipur on 26 April, to find the main protagonists had fled. The *Senaputti* was captured in May, tried and executed; two other princes, including the interloping raja, were exiled. A child of the ruling family was elevated to the throne, and during his minority Manipur was placed under British supervision. The intrepid Mrs. Grimwood was decorated with the medal of the Royal Red Cross and received a pension for life, had a subscription opened for her by the Princess of Wales, and wrote an account of her exploits. The clasp for the India General Service Medal for this episode was entitled 'North-East Frontier 1891'.

Ethel Clair Grimwood, heroine of the Manipur rebellion, shown here wearing the decoration of the Royal Red Cross, awarded for her conduct during the siege of, and evacuation from, the Manipur Residency.

Lieutenant Charles Grant, commanding a small party of the 2nd Burmah Battalion and 43rd Gurkhas, describes part of the action for which he was awarded the Victoria Cross (March/April 1891), defending an improvised fort against the Manipuri army by sallying out of the defences:

'At eight a.m. a good lot had collected behind the wall 200 yards from my left. I crept out with ten or twelve Ghoorkas, who held my rear and right under the hedge, and drove them with loss by an attack on their right flank, and we bolted back to the fort without loss. Then at eleven a.m. there was firing from behind the hedges in our front with a weapon that rang out louder than their rifles. I crept out with a havildar and six Ghoorkas close in the ditch under the hedge, out to our front from our right, up to within ten yards of the nearest of them. They opened a wild fire, and bolted as we attacked their left flank; but then we found ourselves in a bit of a hole, for thirty or forty were in a corner behind a wall, six feet high, over which they were firing at us. I had my D.B. sixteen-bore shot-gun, and six buckshot and six ball cartridges, and as they showed their heads over the wall they got buckshot in their faces at twenty yards. When my twelve rounds were fired, and the Ghoorkas also doing considerable damage, we rushed the wall, and I dropped one through the head with my revolver, and hit some more as they bolted. When we cleared them out we returned to the fort along the ditch, having had the hottest three minutes on record, and only got the Ghoorka havildar shot through the hand and some of our clothes shot through; we had killed at least ten. Next day I visited the corner, and found blood, thirty Snider and fifteen Martini cartridges, and one four-inch long Express cartridge, .500, which accounted for the unaccountable sounds I had heard. Next day I heard I had killed the "Bhudda" (old) Senaputti, or the commander-in-chief of the old Maharaj, father of the present lot of scoundrels, and also two generals ...'

(in *My Twelve Years in Manipur*, E. St. C. Grimwood, London 1891, pp. 3013)

Hunza-Nagar Expedition (North-West Frontier)

The states of Hunza and Nagar at the extreme north-west tip of Kashmir paid a nominal tribute to Kashmir, but were effectively independent (the tribute of Naga, for example, was some gold-dust and two baskets of apricots annually!). The inaccessibility of the states encouraged their rulers (both styled 'the Thum') to believe themselves invulnerable, and consequently were somewhat lawless. With a view to securing the border in the face of Russian expansionism, Britain established the Gilgit Agency in this region in 1889, and the agent, Colonel A G. A. Durand, secured an agreement by which Hunza and Nagar would cease raid-

Most Frontier actions were conducted at long range; on occasions the only visible sign of the enemy being the smoke from their rifles. Here are seen the garrison of the Manipur Residency engaging hostile forces during their withdrawal to Silchar. (Engraving after R. Caton Woodville, based on a sketch by Lieutenant H. W. G. Cole)

ing in return for a subsidy paid by the governments of Britain and Kashmir. However, viewing improved communications as a threat to their independence, the Hunza and Nagar tribes reneged on the agreement and harassed road-making parties. Consequently, Durand led an expedition (for the most part Kashmiri troops) beginning 1 December 1891, which captured the fort of Nilt on the following day; operations continued until both states had been pacified by the end of the month. Zafar Khan, the Thum of Naga, was permitted to retain his throne; the Thum of Hunza, Safdar Ali Khan, fled to China, and his half-brother Nazim Khan was made chief in his stead. The clasp of the India General Service Medal for this operation is entitled simply 'Hunza 1891'.

Lushai

Renewed operations, on a minor scale, pacified northern Lushai in 1890, and eastern Lushai in 1892; five small expeditions were mounted in January–May 1889, Septem-

The difficult and hostile terrain of the Indian frontiers was not insurmountable: during the Chitral relief expedition Major (later Lieutenant-General Sir) Fenton Aylmer, VC constructed this wooden suspension bridge over the Pang Kora River, a typically essential task performed by engineers in colonial campaigns.

ber–December 1890, and February–March 1891, and two against the eastern Lushais in March–June 1892.

Waziristan (North-West Frontier)

To settle the question of responsibility for keeping order along the North-West Frontier, in November 1893 an agreement was reached with the Amir of Afghanistan to delineate the Indian–Afghan border, by marking the 'Durand Line' named after Sir Mortimer Durand, who had negotiated with the Amir. This demarcation-line was not especially well considered and in effect produced two borders, the old administrative border basically inherited from the Sikhs, and a new political border, tribal territory over which the British exercised influence through a series of political agencies. The work of delineation produced some hostility among the frontier tribes: on the night of 2/3 November 1894 the survey camp at Wana was attacked by a large body of Mahsuds, who were driven off with heavy losses. An expedition was organised by way of reprisal; three columns (Wana, Jandola and Bannu) under Lieutenant-General Sir William Lockhart, which operated from 18 December 1894 to 17 March 1895, subduing the Mahsuds and surveying, without serious opposition.

Chitral (North-West Frontier)

The frontier state of Chitral officially became British territory by the establishment of the Durand Line, and following the death of its ruler or Mehtar in 1892, dynastic disputes led to virtual anarchy, with two succeeding Mehtars being murdered by, or at the instigation of, the old Mehtar's brother, Sher Afzal, who sought the throne for himself. The British agent at Gilgit, Surgeon-Major George Robertson, installed instead a child brother of the recently murdered Mehtar early in 1895, and from 3 March was besieged in Chitral fort by Sher Afzal's Chitrali followers and those of an allied Pathan chief, Umra Khan. The fort's garrison consisted of only Robertson, his assistant Lieutenant Bertrand Gurdon, Lieutenant Henry Harley with 99 men of the 14th Sikhs, Surgeon-Captain Harry Whitchurch of the Indian Medical Service, 301 Kashmir Infantry, the child Mehtar and his household and some 100 Chitrali non-combatants, and the commander of the military forces at Chitral, Captain Charles Townshend of the Central India Horse (the same Townshend who was to command in a less creditable siege during the First World War, at Kut-al-Amara). The Inspecting Officer of the Kashmir Imperial Service Troops, Captain Colin Campbell of the Central India Horse, was also present but incapacitated by a wound received on 3 March.

The siege of Chitral was one of the great epics of the later Victorian period. Short of ammunition and supplies, the garrison held on until the commander of the forces in the Gilgit district, Colonel James Kelly, with a party of 32nd Pioneers and Kashmiri troops, relieved first the small besieged post of Mastuj (9 April), and then Chitral (20 April 1895). Meanwhile, a full relief-force was organised at Peshawar under Major-General Sir Robert Low, which advanced, overthrew Umra Khan and reached Chitral on 15–16 May. Sher Afzul was apprehended shortly after, and Chitral was restored to the child Mehtar, Shujah-ul-Mulk.

Tochi Field Force (North-West Frontier)

In 1897 the British were faced with the most serious and widespread rising to occur on the frontier, sometimes styled the 'Pathan revolt'. It was caused by fears of the demarcation of the Durand Line, encouraged by various agitators who took the opportunity to ferment unrest (including perhaps the Amir of Afghanistan, who probably regretted the influence accorded to Britain by the Durand Line, though he did not actually assist the risings), and by mullahs who called for a *jehad* and who were known by such colourful sobriquets as Sadullah, the 'Mad Fakir' of Swat. The first outbreak was the ambush on 10 June 1897 of a small party escorting the political agent of Tochi, Mr. H. A. Gee, at Maizar in the Tochi valley, in which the commander, Lieutenant-Colonel A. C. Bunny of the 1st Sikhs, was killed. The Tochi Field Force was assembled immediately under Major-General G. Corrie Bird, which traversed and occupied the Tochi valley, almost without resistance, until January 1898.

Malakand Field Force (North-West Frontier)

The next outbreak of hostility was an attack upon the posts of Malakand and Chakdara in the Swat valley on 26 July 1897, action continuing until 30 July and 2 August respectively, during which many casualties were inflicted on the attackers. At Chakdara, 60 men of the 11th Bengal Lancers and 180 of the 45th Sikhs were estimated to have killed 2,000 of the tribesmen, for the loss of five dead and ten wounded; although it was notoriously difficult to estimate enemy casualties, it was said that the attackers themselves admitted to having lost 3,700 dead in the assaults on this post and Malakand. A punitive expedition was organised immediately; three brigades under Brigadier-General Sir Bindon Blood remained in the field until late October, punishing the guilty tribes and engaged in considerable fighting. Having dealt with this outbreak, Blood organised the Buner Field Force (involving many of the same units) to subdue the Bunerwals, an operation lasting from 2 to 17 January 1898.

Mohmand Field Force (North-West Frontier)

On 7 August 1897 the Mohmands attacked Shabkadr Fort, whose police garrison held out until relieved by the Peshawar Movable Column. The Mohmand Field Force was then organised under Brigadier-General E. R. Elles, which operated from 15 September until the beginning of October, imposing peace and fines upon the insurgents.

Samana (North-West Frontier)

A small force under Brigadier-General A. G. Yeatman-Biggs was deployed in August 1897 to counter hostilities by the Afridis and Orakzais in the Kohat district; despite Afridi attacks on a number of posts, some of the tribes remained unaffected by unrest, and the Turis of the Kurram valley actually sent a force to support the British. A minor epic occurred at Saragarhi, one of the posts attacked on the Samana Ridge on 12 September, when its garrison of 21 men of the 36th Sikhs was killed to a man

rather than surrender or attempt to escape, one Sikh defending the guard-room killing twenty of the attackers before it was burned around him. Repetitions of this heroic exploit were avoided when Forts Gulistan and Lockhart, held by the same regiment, were relieved after holding out for a day.

Tirah Field Force (North-West Frontier)

Although the Malakand Field Force was still operating, it was decided to punish the Afridis and Orakzais by an invasion of their lands in the Tirah; but as the two tribes could field some 50,000 combatants, it required the largest expedition ever deployed on the frontier. Commanded by Lieutenant-General Sir William Lockhart, the Tirah Field Force comprised two divisions (the 2nd led by Yeatman-Biggs, recently engaged on the Samana Ridge) of two brigades each, with another brigade on lines of communication duty and the Rawalpindi Brigade in reserve, with flanking-movements performed by the Peshawar and Kurram Movable Columns. In all, the force numbered almost 35,000 combatants and 20,000 followers. It advanced in early October, capturing the precipitous position of the Dargai Heights on 18 October 1897; the troops were then withdrawn, the position re-possessed by the Afridis, and on 20 October had to be taken anew, against much more determined resistance. The storming of the heights by the 1st Battalion Gordon Highlanders and 1/2nd Goorkhas was one of the most famous exploits in Victorian military history, and produced a popular hero in Piper George Findlater of the Gordons, who won the Victoria Cross for continuing to play his pipes though shot through both ankles. The Tirah Field Force continued to range throughout the area, involving considerable skirmishing, until the beginning of December; and although the Orakzais submitted, some of the Afridis remained determinedly hostile. A further foray into the Bazar valley, the territory of the Zakha Khel Afridis, was made in January 1898, involving a sharp action at the Shin Kamar Pass on 29 January. The Tirah expedition was costly (British casualties from 12 October were 287 dead, 853 wounded and ten missing) and had not quelled permanently the warlike propensities of the rebellious tribes; but it ended the 'Pathan revolt' of 1897.

The Indian Army to 1900

From the re-organisations of the 1860s the basic structure of the Indian Army remained unchanged, the Bengal, Madras and Bombay Armies remaining independent until 1895. Although it would have been possible to amalgamate the various forces under one command, independent control no longer being necessary because of improvements in communications with the spread of the railway network, such was the loyalty towards the old presidencies that changes were resisted, and each army continued to maintain its own commander-in-chief. The

The India Medal, 1895–1902. Awarded for a number of Frontier actions (seven clasps were issued), the obverse bore a portrait of Queen Victoria by T. Brock; the reverse, a British infantryman and an Indian sowar.

C-in-C Bengal was also C-in-C India, had a seat upon the governor-general's council, and commanded all troops in the subcontinent (British and Indian), save the Punjab Frontier Force. Administrative functions were pooled, however, and in 1886 the Punjab Frontier Force was transferred from control of the Government of India (and direct command of the lieutenant-governor of the Punjab) to that of the C-in-C, India. The term 'Native', which might be regarded as somewhat pejorative, was dropped from regimental titles in 1885; and in 1895 the presidency armies were finally abolished, although the units retained their own names and numbers (1st Bengal, etc.) until 1903, when a unified system of numbering was introduced and the old presidency identities discontinued. To replace the presidency armies, the army in India was divided into four commands: Bengal; Bombay (including Sind, Quetta and Aden); Madras (including Burma); and Punjab (including North-West Frontier). A few auxiliary or irreg-

ular units, the Hyderabad Contingent and the Central India Horse remained under control of the Government of India.

A further change after the Mutiny concerned the policy of recruitment. To increase *esprit de corps* greater importance was placed upon 'class' or 'tribal nationality', and their was much debate as to whether there should be 'class regiments' composed of only one race or tribe, or 'class companies', by which different 'nationalities' would be kept in separate companies within a regiment. The latter theory prevailed: Gurkha and Sikh unit maintained a 'class' identity, but most others had companies composed upon tribal or racial lines. This system worked reasonably well, but could produce difficulties, as highlighted in a story recounted by Lord Roberts concerning Afghanistan in 1878, when on one occasion only the Sikh members of the 29th Punjab Infantry were willing to fight, the Pathan members hanging back, being unwilling to engage their Muslim co-religionists.

The increasing preference given to recruiting from the 'martial races' of the north was explained by Lord Roberts when examining the Madras Army: 'I tried hard to discover in them those fighting qualities which had distinguished their forefathers ... But long years of peace, and the security and prosperity attending it, had evidently had upon them, as they always seem to have on Asiatics, a softening and deteriorating effect; and I was forced to the conclusion that the ancient military spirit had died in them, as it had died in the ordinary Hindustani of Bengal and the Mahratta of Bombay, and that they could no longer with safety be pitted against warlike races, or employed outside the limits of southern India.' Roberts encountered opposition to his ideas for recruiting more from the 'martial races', 'because of the theory which prevailed that it was necessary to maintain an equilibrium between the armies of the three presidencies, and because of the ignorance that was only too universal with respect to the characteristics of the different races, which encouraged the erroneous belief that one Native was as good as another for purposes of war ... no comparison can be made between the martial value of a regiment recruited amongst the Gurkhas of Nepal or the warlike races of northern India, and one recruited from the effeminate peoples of the south.'[28]

Consequently, a number of Madras and Bombay corps were recruited with Punjabis, Pathans and Baluchis, such units of the Madras Army being sent to serve in Burma; the Pathan and Baluchi units in Sind and Baluchistan, where service might be expected to be the most arduous. More Gurkhas and the similar Garhwalis were recruited for the Bengal Army, and the Madras Army endeavoured to recruit more warlike men from the Moplahs (adherents of Islam resident on the Malabar coast) and in Coorg; but the three regiments thus formed (11th Madras, composed of Coorg men in 1901, and two battalions of Moplah Rifles formed 1902) proved unsatisfactory, and they were disbanded in 1904 and 1907 respectively.

There were frequently more than two 'classes' in a 'class-company' regiment; for example, in 1884 the eight companies of the 5th Bengal Infantry included three of Brahmins and Rajputs, two of Jats, two of Hindustani Mohammedans and one of lower-caste Hindus. The concept of 'class' units, while encouraging *esprit de corps*, did tend to emphasise old rivalries; as late as the First World War, it was remarked that should a Brahmin and a Pathan regiment be left together unsupervised, there would not have been a man of the weaker regiment left alive after a day![29] An example was recounted by Robert Baden-Powell, concerning manoeuvres during which an Afridi unit 'defending' a position began to throw rocks at Gurkhas 'attacking' it; mayhem was only prevented when one of the

Afridi officers ordered the Gurkhas to halt, and hurled a boulder at his company's own tom-tom drummer, whose shrieks and drumming were inflaming the Afridis! A further advantage of recruiting from the frontier was that the units in question could oppose hostiles on their own terms; frequently they were kinsmen of the Indian Army troops opposing them, so the traditional skills of hill warfare were found on both sides. Whereas it was said that British and Sikh troops were better for more conventional actions such as the storming of a position at bayonet-point, for skirmishing in hill-country the Gurkha and Pathan troops were unequalled.

The number of British officers in Indian units was reduced drastically; instead of a full complement as before, from 1863 there were normally only seven per battalion or cavalry regiment, including the commanding officer, second in command, adjutant and four others; companies and troops were usually commanded by Indian officers. British officers were all officially members of the Indian Staff Corps, and were posted directly to regiments or to other duties, so that no longer were regiments denuded of officers serving on detached duty, as in the past. The standard of officer was also much more rigorously enforced, so that the inefficiencies of some of the Company officers were not duplicated. Officers of Indian mountain artillery were selected specially from the Royal Artillery, those of the Sap-

A typical group of North-West Frontier warriors: the Turi Levy, a local militia corps formed in the Kurram Valley in 1892. Commanded by two British officers, and receiving higher pay than the regular sepoy, this corps was one of those formed in the frontier districts to undertake the defence of their own area, an effective means of keeping the peace on the frontier. The men dressed in civilian clothes and armed with jezails are typical of the tribesmen against whom many of the frontier campaigns were fought.

Above: Risaldar-Major Sher Singh, 13th Bengal Lancers. The senior Indian officer of his regiment, he wears the Sudan Medal and Khedive's Star, awarded for service with his previous regiment, the 9th Bengal Lancers. The uniform illustrated was dark blue with silver lace, and blue and gold pagri.

Right: Daffadar of the 1st Bengal Cavalry, c.1895. Skinner's Horse, one of the most famous regiments of the army, wore a distinctive uniform of yellow with black facings.

pers and Miners from the Royal Engineers, and British NCOs no longer served with Indian units, save the Sappers.

Although these changes raised the standard of British officers, and increased the significance of the Indian officers, the reduction in the numbers of British officers was criticised by Roberts: 'Indian soldiers, like soldiers of every nationality, required to be led; and history and experience teach us that eastern races (fortunately for us), however brave and accustomed to war, do not possess the qualities that go to make leaders of men ... we cannot expect them to do with less leading than our own soldiers require, and it is, I maintain, trying them too highly to send them into action with the present establishment of British officers.'[30] This opinion would seem to be confirmed by difficulties following heavy casualties among British officers in the opening stages of the First World War.

Bengal Army. In the Bengal cavalry, the 16th and 17th regiments were disbanded in 1882 but re-formed in 1885, and

from 1864 to 1900 most regiments were converted to lancers. In the infantry, the 34th–37th and 41st were disbanded in 1882, and titles were changed to reflect alterations in recruiting: the title 'Punjab' was adopted by the 19th–32nd (1864); 'Rajput' by the 7th (1893), 2nd, 4th, 8th, 11th and 16th (1897); 'Jat' by the 6th and 10th (1897); 'Sikhs' by the 45th (1864), 14th and 15th (1885); 'Punjabis' by the 33rd (1890); 'Garhwalis' by the 39th (1890); 'Gurkha' by the 42nd–44th (1886) and 9th (1894); the 40th was titled 'Baluch' in 1890 and 'Pathan' in 1892; and the 38th 'Dogra' in 1890. The disbanded regiments were re-formed as the 34th Punjab, 35th and 36th Sikhs and 37th Dogras in 1887, and the 41st Dogras in 1900. The 23rd and 32nd were pioneer regiments (but still trained as infantry), and the 34th became pioneers in 1887. The 46th Punjab, 47th Sikhs and 48th Pioneers were formed in 1900–1.

Madras Army. The 1st and 2nd Light Cavalry became lancers in 1886 and the 3rd in 1891; the 4th was disbanded

Some incidents made an indelible impression upon witnesses; an infantry subaltern recalls his first experience of war:

'... when as a boy not long joined I stood in the lines of Sherpur, our fortified cantonment at Kabul, and saw a sorely tried squadron of that best of regiments, the 9th Lancers, ride into barracks after their gallant charge with the 14th Bengal Lancers against practically the whole Afghan Army in the Chardeh plain. Long before they came we knew that things had gone badly, riderless horses galloping home, a desperately wounded trooper just managing to reach the gate before he fell from his horse, and anon, a small sad procession of poor Cleland, the Colonel, wounded to the death, and brought off the field by a gallant non-commissioned officer ... Next morning I saw laid out in a large marquee the 9th Lancers' dead, all mutilated beyond belief, in accordance with the custom of our savage enemy. How many glorious incidents crowd on one's memory of those never to be forgotten days in December, 1879 ... I can see now as if it was yesterday Tim Butson on December 13 riding out at the head of the 9th Lancers, for all his seniors were *hors de combat*, and less than three hours after carried back through the same gate wrapped in a soldier's blanket, shot through the heart; and there, following him, rides Jabber Chisholm, grievously wounded, clinging to his saddle with both hands, *but* bringing in the regiment. Twenty years more of life were allotted to him, and then he too was to fall in the moment of victory at Elandslaagte. And here come the Native Cavalry, chanting a wild war song, elated with success, and waving their lances, which in many cases were covered in blood for many inches down the shaft ...'

('Reminiscences of Cavalry in War and Peace', by 'An Infantry Officer', in *Cavalry Journal*, vol. I, pp. 452–3, October 1906. The 9th's commanding officer, mentioned above, was Robert Stewart Cleland)

in 1891. Four infantry regiments were disbanded in 1864, the 18th (for misconduct) and 42nd–44th; the 1882 reductions led to the disbanding of the 34th–41st. The 1st and 4th were converted to pioneers in 1883, and the 21st in 1891. For peacekeeping in Burma, police battalions were formed of Sikhs and Gurkhas, and it was decided to incorporate these into the Madras Army, seven Burma Infantry units taking the place of numbered Madras regiments: the 1st–4th Burma took the place of the 10th, 12th, 33rd and 32nd Madras respectively in 1891; the 5th and 6th Burma the places of the 30th and 31st Madras in 1892, and the 7th Burma that of the 29th Madras in 1893. Their numbers as Burma Battalions were carried in parentheses behind their new Madras identities until the great reorganisation of 1903 when only the old 33rd Madras (3rd

Burma) retained the 'Burma' title, the remainder becoming Punjabis.

Bombay Army. Following the Mutiny, the 1st Bombay Cavalry reverted from lancers to ordinary cavalry, but became lancers again in 1880, as did the 2nd in 1883. In 1882 the 3rd Scinde Horse was disbanded, and in 1885 the 1st Poona and 1st and 2nd Scinde Horse were re-titled as the 4th–6th Bombay Cavalry; at the same date a 7th was formed (known as Jacob-ka-Risallah), re-titled as Baluch Horse in 1886 and converted to lancers in 1890. In 1882 the 6th, 11th, 15th and 18th Bombay Infantry were disbanded; the 4th was a rifle regiment from 1861, and in 1889–90 the 23rd and 25th were converted similarly. Three regiments (27th, 29th, 30th) were Baluchis, and in 1891–2 the 24th and 26th also became Baluchis, involving not only a change in the type of recruit but also uniform, the line regiments wearing red but the Baluchis green, like the rifles (24th and 26th drab). The 1st and 2nd were designated as Grenadiers, the 3rd, 10th and 27th as Light Infantry from 1871, and the 7th as Pioneers from 1900.

Other Forces. The Punjab Frontier Force continued to consist of the Corps of Guides, titled 'Queen's Own' from 1874, the 1st–5th Punjab Cavalry (4th disbanded 1882), 1st–6th Punjab Infantry (3rd disbanded 1882), and 1st–4th Sikh Infantry. The 7th Punjab Infantry (Hazara Gurkha Battalion) became the 5th Gurkha Regiment in 1861; this was not the only Gurkha corps not originally part of the Bengal Army: the re-constituted 10th Madras (1st Burma) was also Gurkha in composition.

In 1890 the 1st–4th Cavalry of the Hyderabad Contingent became lancers; the six infantry regiments of the Contingent remained unchanged, as did the two regiments of Central India Horse.

Although the ordinary artillery was out of Indian hands after the Mutiny, Indians did man mountain batteries, the light and portable guns ideally suited for service in the hilly terrain of the frontier regions. These were numbered in sequence from 1876: Nos. 1 (Kohat) and 2 (Derajat) Mountain Batteries, originally Nos. 2 and 3 Light Field Batteries; Nos. 3 (Peshawar) and 4 (Hazara) Mountain Batteries, originally the Peshawar and Hazara Mountain Trains; and the un-numbered Punjab Garrison Battery (thus named 1889; from 1901, Frontier Garrison Artillery); all these were part of the Punjab Frontier Force. Mountain batteries Nos. 5 and 6 were originally the 1st and 2nd Bombay Mountain Batteries, numbered 5 and 6 in 1889 and known as the Quetta and Jullundar Batteries respectively. Nos. 7 and 8, thus numbered in 1889, were raised in 1886 as the 1st and 2nd Bengal Mountain Batteries; in 1901 they were known as the Gujerat and Lahore Mountain Batteries respectively. Nos. 9 and 10 were raised at Abbottabad in 1898–1900, being designated Murree and Abbottabad respectively in 1901. The Hyderabad Contingent also retained its artillery.

Colour-party of the 45th Rattray's Sikhs, one of the most distinguished units of the Bengal Infantry. This depicts the scarlet uniform with the white facings (including the vertical front panel on the tunic) adopted in 1885; trousers were blue with red stripes and the turbans composed of a red kullah around which was wrapped a blue-and-white pagri or lungi. Note the steel quoit worn on the front of the pagri, a distinctive symbol representing the Sikh weapon, the chakram (throwing-quoit).

Other forces at the disposal of the Government of India included police units, which in the frontier areas especially were quasi-military formations, as exemplified by the Upper Burma Military Police which was the genesis of the Burma battalions of the Madras Army. In imitation of the British volunteer force, a similar organisation was established in India from the time of the Mutiny, eventually numbering more than 30,000 part-time volunteers available for internal security duty; composed of British and Anglo-Indian personnel, they included light horse, mounted rifles, artillery and rifle corps. Some of the latter were designated as railway battalions, the railway system being paramount for communications and transportation of troops throughout the subcontinent. The organisation and titles of these units varied considerably; for example, the Assam Valley Mounted Rifles, formed in November 1891, amalgamated the following five corps (with dates of formation): Darrang (1887), Lakhimpur (1882), Nowgong (1888) and Sibsagar (1884) Mounted Rifles, and the Gauhati Rifles (1885). Among the senior corps of each category were the Calcutta Light Horse (formed 1881), Bihar Mounted Rifles (formed 1862), the Madras Volunteer Guards (formed 1857) and the Nagpur Rifles (formed 1860). Volunteer artillery corps included Madras (1879), Rangoon (1879), Cossipore (1884), Bombay (1887), Calcutta Naval Artillery Volunteers (1883) and Karchi (1892). Railway volunteers included the Assam–Bengal (1900), Bengal Nagpur (1888), Bengal and North-Western (1892), Bombay, Baroda and Central India (1877), Rangoon and Irrawaddy (1879), Eastern (1873) and Northern Bengal (1879), East Indian (1869), Great Indian Peninsula (1875), Madras and Southern Mahratta (1885), North-Western (1886), South Indian (1884) and South Mahratta (1886). The complex lineage of some corps is exemplified by the origins of the Bengal and North-Western Railway Volunteers, formed in June 1892 by the amalgamation of the Tirhoot State Railway Volunteer Rifles with the Ghazipur Volunteer Rifles (both formed 1879).

The pipe band of an unidentified Indian Army regiment; the quoit symbol emblazoned on the base drum would suggest a Sikh corps, as many of the musicians appear to be (note the quoits encircling their turbans). The European child is presumably the son of one of the unit's officers.

Indian State Forces. Many independent states retained their own forces, many of which were ill-trained, poorly equipped and useful only for ceremonial duty. For example the army of the Nizam of Hyderabad was formed for the internal defence of the state after the loss to the Nizam of the British-commanded Hyderabad Contingent at the time of the Mutiny. In 1857 a 'Field Force' was created for the protection of the state, based on the private army of Raja Rameshwar Rao of Wanparthy (80 miles south of Hyderabad), a subject of the Nizam; to the Raja's 50-strong African bodyguard, cavalry troop and two elephant-guns, the Nizam added his own lancer squadron raised in Hyderabad. Enlargement of the force caused some local unrest in December 1859, which was suppressed by newly raised troops, and from 1864 the Nizam's regular forces were commanded by Henry Rocke of the 79th Highlanders, who had been the force's inspector-general from 1862. The army grew to include six infantry regiments, two artillery batteries (briefly four), two lancer regiments and the African Cavalry Guards, the Nizam's household unit. Another cavalry unit was formed from irregulars in 1875, and new regiments were created to form the Golconda Brigade (1884, a lancer squadron and two infantry units); in 1871 a regiment of Arabs and Afghans was created, wearing zouave dress, and in 1890 an extra unit of African lancers, which in 1896 became the bodyguard of the heir-apparent. The original two lancer regiments were disbanded in 1893 and re-formed as Imperial Service lancers (see below), and in 1897 the two brigades were amalgamated to form 'the Nizam's Regular Force', 7,760 strong, composed of two Imperial Service lancer regiments and two others, the two African bodyguards, five infantry regiments,

artillery, and the Arab–Afghan unit, the Jamiat Nizam Mahbub.

Not all state forces found the approval of the government, for they were a drain upon state finances and sometimes a danger in the event of disturbances, given their often unsatisfactory state of discipline. Following the threat of war with Russia over the 'Pendjeh incident' in 1885, when some Indian rulers had offered large sums to support the defence of India, it was suggested that part of the troops of some states should be trained to the standard of the Indian Army, to act as a reinforcement for the government forces. This suggestion was accepted with alacrity, and under British supervision the 'Imperial Service Troops' were constituted. They performed useful service in a number of frontier campaigns, notably at Chitral where the Kashmir troops were especially distinguished (Kashmir, with its unique geographical position, was alone in possessing Imperial Service artillery, two mountain batteries maintained for the defence of the Gilgit frontier). Among the Imperial Service troops were those from the following states:

Alwar: lancer corps and infantry unit, the 'Fateh Paltan' which had supported the British during the Mutiny and served in China 1900–1.

Bhavanagar: lancer unit formed 1892.

Bahawalpur: camel transport unit; state troops supported the British during the Mutiny and Second Afghan War.

Bhopal: lancer unit.

Bharatpur: infantry battalion and transport unit.

Bikaner: camel corps (the Bikaner Ganga Risala) formed 1884, and infantry unit, both serving in China 1900–1 and Somaliland 1901–4.

Presumably influenced by the French Zouaves encountered in the Crimea, a vaguely zouave-style uniform was introduced into the Indian infantry from the mid-1860s, usually featuring a collar-less jacket with a panel (often of the facing colour) placed vertically on the breast, and slashed cuffs. It was also worn by the 3rd Gurkhas (authorised 1869, but perhaps worn earlier), with black gaiters, 'pyjama' trousers and a black 'Kilmarnock' cap. (Print after H. Bunnett)

NCO, officer and private, 5th Gurkhas, c.1897, showing their rifle-green uniform with black braid. The traditional kukri is visible at the right rear of the NCO's belt.

Faridkot: two infantry companies which became Sappers and Miners in 1900.

Gwalior: three lancer regiments, two infantry battalions, and the Gwalior Imperial Service Transport Corps which served in the Chitral and Tirah campaigns.

Hyderabad: 1st and 2nd (Nizam's Own) Imperial Service Lancers, organised 1893.

Jipur: transport corps formed 1889; served in Chitral and Tirah campaigns.

Jammu and Kashmir: six infantry battalions, two squadrons and two mountain batteries; their duties were unique among Imperial Service Troops in guarding the frontier.

Jind: infantry battalion; as in other cases, this unit was not newly formed for Imperial Service but was re-organised in 1889 from the Jind Infantry, formed 1837, which had served in Afghanistan 1878–9; also served in Tirah campaign.

Jodhpur: Jodhpur Lancers, the 'Sardar Risala', formed 1888 and from the character of its personnel, supposedly the most aristocratic unit in India; served in China 1900.

Junagarh: lancer unit raised 1891.

Kapurthala: infantry unit organised as Imperial Service Troops in 1890, but had previously aided the British during the Mutiny; served on the frontier 1897–8.

Malerkotla: units of sappers and miners formed 1894 from existing pioneer corps; aided the British during the Mutiny and Second Afghan War.

Mysore: lancer regiment re-organised for Imperial Service 1892, and transport unit.

Nabha: infantry battalion re-organised for Imperial service 1889, having served in the Mutiny and Second Afghan War; served in Tirah campaign.

Rampur: lancer unit formed 1840, re-organised as Imperial Service Troops 1888.

Sirmoor: Sappers and Miners organised as Imperial Service Troops 1890; served in Tirah campaign.

An additional benefit of the Imperial Service system was said to be the fact that 'it has brought the best class of *sirdar* into touch with the best class of British officer'[31] to the improvement of Anglo-Indian relations. In addition to the Imperial Service units, state forces were maintained (often at a lower level than before, given the higher maintenance costs of Imperial Service troops), and indeed some of the state units claimed ancestry more ancient than that of even the oldest regiments of the British Army: the Bikaner Lancers, for example, were said to have originated in 1455, and the Jaipur Guard unit's battle-honours began with one dated 1621.

North-West Frontier from 1900

Lord Curzon, the viceroy from 1899 to 1905, introduced many reforms during his term of office, the most significant militarily being the creation (operative from November 1901) of a new North-West Frontier Province,

separated from the Punjab and incorporating the territory up to the Durand Line, including the agencies of Khyber, Kurram, Malakand, Tochi and Wana, all supervised by a Chief Commissioner directly responsible to the Government of India. The previous military system of isolated, advanced garrisons had been expensive and wasteful of resources, and because of the difficulties of the terrain the garrisons had not always been capable of mutual support. Under the new military organisation, the regular troops were pulled back into wholly British territory, leaving the tribal areas of the extreme frontier to be protected and policed by tribal forces under British command. Some of these, for example the Khyber Rifles, had existed for some time; others, often styled militia or scouts, were newly formed. They carried out normal patrolling, and in case of more serious action could call upon movable columns of regulars based at locations such as Peshawar and Kohat; and a Border Military Police operated in the 'settled' areas. It was this new military organisation that fought the actions on the Frontier that continued in larger or lesser extent until the outbreak of the Second World War. As for the previous several decades, most subsequent military action was on the North-West Frontier (but not exclusively; for example, the Moplah Rebellion in Malabar in 1921–2), and it is perhaps mildly ironic that after so much effort had been expended securing the North-West Frontier from the threat of invasion by Russia or Afghanistan, the most serious threat to the security of India would ultimately be presented by Japanese incursions from the north-east during the Second World War.

Military Forces: The Frontiers

Although the frontier opponents of the British varied widely, including some on the North-East Frontier who were armed primarily with bows and spears, the principal 'hostiles' were the hillmen of the North-West Frontier, often styled Pathans. This name did not describe a race or nation, but apparently was derived from the Afghan name for the language Pushtu (or Pukhtu), and was generally

> The terrain encountered in many colonial operations was often as difficult and intimidating as the enemy themselves:
>
> '... on one occasion of the march of the troops, under General Showers, a halt was made for lunch, and the General, observing some of the rebels executing a war dance on a hill beyond rifle range, apparently in derision of the Sepoys, turned to his aide-de-camp, whom he always addressed by his Christian name, and jokingly said, "Longueville, just take half-a-dozen files and fetch me down those rebels." "General," replied the astonished aide-de-camp, "do you think I am a fly?"
> (Lieutenant-General B. W. D. Morton, *Some Indian Experiences*, Cheltenham 1913 p. 60)

> The normal way of life on the North-West Frontier was as uncompromising as the territory. Francis Cornish of the 17th Bengal Lancers, having lately escaped from an ambush laid by a green-clad Afridi, reported the reaction of one of his NCOs:
>
> 'The "Barki affair" has been an excuse for most of the furlo' men coming to the camp to talk to my orderly about it. There is a very fine Duffadar called Munir Khan, of whom I am very fond, who lives in a village eight miles from here. He knows everything about the country around and all the Afridi villages within 50 miles ... and says he has had dealings with the "man in the green waistcoat", and when he comes on furlo' again when the frontier is quiet *will easily be able to shoot him!*
>
> (*Letters and Sketches of Francis T. Warre Cornish*, Eton, 1902, p. 265)

applied to tribes of Afghan origin resident in the mountainous country along the Punjab frontier. (Its pronunciation was generally 'P'than', but in British Army argot 'Paythan' was common). The Pathans were divided into tribes, the tribes into clans, and the clans into sections, so that nomenclature was often complicated and confusing, often involving the terms *zai* (e.g., Orakzai), meaning 'son of', and *khel*, meaning company or association. Clans might be styled by their own name, or with this name as a qualification of a wider association; for example, the Darwesh Khel might be referred to by that name, or as Waziris (their tribal origin), or as 'Darwesh Khel Waziris', or by the name of a sub-clan such as Madda Khel or Kabul Khel. Among the most significant of the frontier peoples were:

Afridis. The most powerful and formidable of the frontier tribes, beset by internal feuding but capable of uniting against an external threat. Their territory was bounded by the Khyber Pass, the Mastura valley and Afghanistan, although they were nomadic and moved from summer to winter homes. The eight Afridi clans, in approximate order of military strength, were the Adam Khel, including Jowakis (resident around the Kohat Pass, the Adam Khel were more settled and the least migratory), Zakha Khel, Kuki Khel, Kambar Khel, Malikdin Khel, Aka Khel, Sipah, and Kamrai Khel; although all were of lawless disposition, the Zakha Khel were acknowledged by their neighbours to be the most intractable and predatory, and were the most significant, their territory in the Maidan, Bara and Bazar valleys giving them control of the route between the winter residences of the lowlands contiguous with the Peshawar district, and the summer upland residences in the Tirah.

Bunerwals. The British regarded the Bunerwals as the most honourable and worthy of the Pathans. Named from their residence in the Buner valley, they comprised the Iliaszai and Malizai clans of the Yusufzais, and were the least rapacious of the frontier tribes, stock-raising agriculturists who only rarely resorted to war, as during the Ambela expedition and in the Malakand attack in 1897. The Buner Field Force of 1898 subdued their territory without much difficulty, but their military qualities were considerable, as was proved in 1863.

Isazais. A branch of the Yusufzais, the Isazais were the 'Black Mountain' tribes, including the Hassanzais, Akazais and Mada Khel. In numbers and reputation they were less formidable than the Afridis or Waziris.

Mohmands. Mohmand territory extended from the Peshawar district, through the tribal territory and into Afghanistan. Afghan by descent, the Mohmands comprised nine principal clans, including the Baizais (the most martial), Burhan Khel, Dawezais, Halimzais, Isa Khel, Tarakzais and Utmanzais. Their territory was especially inhospitable, including areas largely waterless and extremely hot in summer, which was stated to account for their possessing in general an inferior physique to the Afridis, as they did not migrate in summer to more healthy uplands as did the Afridis. The Safis to the north and Shilmanis to the south were subsidiary clans.

Orakzais. Neighbours and perhaps related to the Afridis, the name of the Orakzais was derived from 'lost tribes', suggesting that originally they may have been composed of refugee clans from the surrounding area; the Ali Khel branch, for example, apparently originated in Swat. Their territory was north-west of the Kohat district, which they cultivated, but retired to the Mastura valley in the southern Tirah uplands in summer. Regarded as less predatory and warlike than the Afridis, they comprised seven clans, including the Bizotis, Chamkannis, Massuzai and Rubia Khel, the latter resident on the Samana Ridge.

Swatis. The Swat valley was noted as an unhealthy region, prone to malaria, which was regarded as a reason for the inferior physique of the Swatis, compared to that of other frontier tribes. Branches of the Yusufzais, the Bazais and Ranizais were resident on the left bank of the Swat river, the Khwazazais, Abazais and Khadakzais on the right. Described as the most religiously bigoted of the frontier people, for some thirty years prior to his death in 1877 they were ruled by Abdul Ghafur, the Akhund of Swat, who after the experience of the Ambela campaign advocated peace with the British. Militarily, the Swatis were not rated as very formidable, but fought with desperate bravery in 1895–7.

Turis. Inhabiting the Kurram valley, the Turis were regarded as Pathans by virtue of speaking Pushtu, but were originally a Turki tribe. Following the Miranzai expeditions of the 1850s they exhibited few hostile tendencies, assisted the British in the Second Afghan War, and latterly were useful members of the tribal militia in the Kurram valley region.

Utman Khel. Occupying the area around the lower part of the Swat river, the Utman Khel claimed descent from Baba Utman, who accompanied Mahmud of Ghanzi in the expedition to India in 997. Their livelihood was principally agriculture (despite the mountainous aspect of their territory, which they cultivated in terraces), and they were known as a people of impressive physique.

Waziris. Waziristan is the territory between the Tochi and Gomal rivers, inhabited by the largest of the frontier tribes, regarded by their neighbours as the most lawless and predatory on the frontier. Their homeland was so barren that in addition to animal-rearing and some cultivation, robbery was something of a necessity for existence, hence their reputation. The principal clans were the Darwesh Khel and Mahsuds, and Dawaris and Bhittanis the smaller clans; the Dawaris were the least militant, and the nomadically inclined Darwesh Khel the most united. The Mahsuds, who occupied the most inaccessible part of Waziristan, were the worst bandits on the frontier, disliked by all and even regarded with hostility by the other Waziris; their depredations spread far and wide outside their own territory.

Yusufzais. One of the largest groups of Pathan tribes, they were supposedly descended from one Mandai, from whose sons Umar and Yusuf originated parts of the same people. Those descended from Umar were not warlike; but the larger Yusufzai (or Yusafzai) tribe included the Isazais of the Black Mountain region, the Malizais, Chagarzais and Swatis.

The frontier tribes possessed no formal military organisation, but virtually every adult male could be regarded as a combatant. Estimates of the strength of force which could be fielded by each group varied considerably, being notoriously difficult to calculate with accuracy, and sometimes considerably over-stated. At about the turn of the century, for example, it was estimated that the Afridis could field about 30,000 men (the Adam Khel 6,500, the Zakha Khel, Kambar Khel and Kuki Khel 5,000 each, down to the 700 of the Kamrai Khel); the Bunerwals 8,000; the Isazais perhaps 5,300 (Akazais 1,500, Hassanzais 2,200, Mada Khel 1,600); the Mohmands between 16,000 and 25,000; the Orakzais 25–30,000; the Swatis perhaps 40,000; the Turis 7,000; the Utman Khel 8–10,000; the Waziris 56,000 (Darwesh Khel 29,000, Mahsuds 14,000, Bhittanis and Dawaris 6,500 each); and the Yusufzais perhaps 65,000.

Even if accurate, such statistics did not necessarily represent the numbers that would be fielded even for major actions. Direction was normally given by tribal councils, who in the event of major hostilities would allocate a quota of combatants from each area; each man brought his own food and ammunition, and when provisions ran out the parties would either be fed by neighbouring villages or would disperse to replenish their stocks, although the latter sometimes resulted in the forces not being re-formed.

In addition to the large operations, small raids and fighting arising from feuds were constant along the frontier.

The frontier tribesmen excelled in guerrilla-style operations, using the terrain to a degree rarely matched by their opponents (which made the Afridis and others who entered British service so valuable, in their ability to meet their opposing kinsmen on equal terms). Their marksmanship was of a high degree, even with their native *jezail* muskets, whose long barrels gave greater accuracy than the weapons with which the British were armed in the early conflicts. Later, the tribesmen came into possession of percussion rifles, then breech-loading and magazine rifles, either captured, bought from Afghan or Russian traders, or home-produced; there were many ingenious craftsmen on the North-West Frontier capable of manufacturing high-quality firearms (the Adam Khel, for example, were noted as skilled armourers). Shortages of ammunition gave extra significance to the ability to shoot accurately, but the tribesmen were not just long-range marksmen: in many cases they were recklessly brave and careless of casualties, and would charge with suicidal determination to engage the enemy with their swords and large daggers (some, for example the Chagarzais, also used spears). The tendency for hand-to-hand combat declined somewhat with the acquisition of longer-range rifles, in favour of shooting from a distance and then retiring as the enemy approached. Improved rate-of-fire was of greater significance to the British, being of most use in repelling (and discouraging) charges; enhanced range and accuracy were the improvements most useful to the tribesmen, and caused their enemies hazard in more than one respect: enhanced range necessitated the posting of picquets a greater distance from their encampments and main bodies, thus making the picquets more vulnerable and slower to reinforce when attacked. Against artillery the tribes had little answer, and thus the British mountain guns were extremely effective and much disliked by those on whom they fired. The lack of organisation and discipline, however, did not prevent concerted and effective action by the tribesmen: in the campaigning of 1919 it was noted that the Mahsuds could lay down such a fusillade of aimed fire that their swordsmen could approach within charging-distance of the British without opposition. The tribes had no 'uniform' but wore their civilian clothing to fight; although some had distinctive styles, and while white was the commonest colour for clothing, dark blue or black was favoured by the Bunerwals and Turis, dark turbans by the Waziris, and so on.

Operations on the frontier were marked by innumerable small actions and desultory sniping even in time of peace, and most minor raiding and theft was the result of criminal tendencies rather than political action; the 'police' nature of many operations was exemplified by the imposition of fines and reprisals by means of destruction, rather than by annexation of territory, which would have been impracticable. Combat on the frontier could be marked by revolting barbarity on the part of the tribesmen, although the British propensity to treat the injuries of, and subsequently release, their prisoners tended to inspire admiration among the tribesmen. Those who won their trust, a small number of recalcitrant individuals apart, found them not only brave but loyal, and quite different from the characteristics of treachery and savagery which were often accorded to them.

INDIA FROM 1900

To complete the story of the evolution of the Indian Army during the period before the First World War, it is necessary to mention the organisational changes introduced by Lord Kitchener upon becoming Commander-in-Chief, India, in 1902. Most important was the final unification into one, consecutively numbered list of regiments, ending the remnant of the old system of presidency armies, references to previous presidential affiliations being removed from unit-titles. British officers ceased to be members of the Indian Staff Corps and were henceforth appointed directly to individual regiments; and the policy of replacing Madras regiments with Punjabis was accelerated. The regiments according to the 1903 re-organisations were:

Cavalry: Nos. 1–19 from the 1st–19th Bengal Cavalry: 1st Duke of York's Own Lancers (Skinner's Horse), 2nd Lancers (Gardner's Horse), 3rd Skinner's Horse, 4th Lancers, 5th Cavalry, 6th Prince of Wales's Cavalry, 7th Hariana Lancers, 8th Lancers, 9th Hodson's Horse, 10th Duke of Cambridge's Own Lancers (Hodson's Horse), 11th Prince of Wales's Own Lancers (Probyn's Horse), 12th Cavalry, 13th Duke of Connaught's Lancers (Watson's Horse), 14th Murray's Jat Lancers, 15th Lancers (Cureton's Multanis), 16th and 17th Cavalry, 18th Tiwana Lancers, 19th Lancers (Fane's Horse). From the 1st–3rd Hyderabad: 20th Deccan Horse, 29th Lancers (Deccan Horse), 30th Lancers (Gordon's Horse). From the Punjab Frontier Force: Queen's Own Corps of Guides (remaining un-numbered), 21st Prince Albert Victor's Own Cavalry, 22nd, 23rd and 25th Cavalry (Frontier Force). From the 1st–3rd Madras Cavalry: 26th–28th Light Cavalry. From the 1st–7th Bombay Cavalry: 31st Duke of Connaught's Lancers, 32nd Lancers, 33rd Queen's Own Light Cavalry, 34th Prince Albert Victor's Own Poona Horse, 35th Scinde Horse, 36th Jacob's Horse, 37th Lancers (Baluch Horse). From the 1st and 2nd Central India Horse: 38th and 39th Central India Horse.

Infantry: the new list of numbered regiments came from the old regiments of Bengal Infantry according to their numbered order of precedence (new numbers 1–8, 10–41, 45–48); from the Punjab Frontier Force, Sikh and

A photograph probably dating from the early 20th century, depicting an Afridi private of an unidentified unit, showing the distinctive style of head-dress. The medal-ribbons appear to include those of the India General Service Medal 1854–95 and the India Medal 1895–1902.

Punjab regiments in order (new nos. 51–59); from the numbered regiments of Madras Infantry in their order of precedence, less the numbers 8, 10 and 18, and with the old 25th Madras taking the precedence-place of no. 18 (new nos. 61–93); from the Hyderabad Infantry in their order of precedence (new nos. 94–99); from the Bombay Infantry in their order of precedence, less nos. 6, 11, 15 and 18 (new nos. 101–130; as it worked out, the 1903 numbering of the old Bombay Infantry consisted simply of adding '1' before the old number, so that, for example, the old 12th Bombay became the 112th in the new list). The new numbers 9, 42, 43 and 44 were occupied by the old Bhopal Levy, Deoli and Erinpura Irregular Forces, and the Mharwara Battalion respectively. The 1903 regimental titles were: 1st and 3rd Brahmans; 2nd Queen's Own Rajput Light Infantry; 4th Prince Albert Victor's Rajputs; 5th Light Infantry; 6th Jat Light Infantry; 7th Duke of Connaught's Own Rajputs; 8th and 11th Rajputs; 9th

The drab or khaki uniform was most suitable for active service, and was even the dress uniform for some corps. This illustration of the 24th Punjabis (previously 24th Bengal) shows a typical service dress of the later 19th and early 20th centuries. (Print after Major A. C. Lovett)

Bhopal Infantry; 10th Jats; 12th Pioneers (Kelat-i-Ghilzai Regiment); 13th Rajputs (Shekhawati Regiment); 14th Ferozepore Sikhs; 15th Ludhiana Sikhs; 16th Rajputs (Lucknow Regiment); 17th Loyal Regiment; 18th, 98th, 108th, 109th, 112th, 113th Infantry; 19th, 21st, 22nd, 24th–31st, 33rd, 46th, 62nd, 66th, 67th, 72nd, 74th, 76th, 82nd, 84th, 87th, 89th, 90th, and 92nd Punjabis; 20th Duke of Cambridge's Own Infantry (Brownlow's Punjabis); 23rd, 32nd and 34th Sikh Pioneers; 35th, 36th and 47th Sikhs; 37th, 38th and 47th Dogras; 39th Garhwal Rifles; 40th Pathans; 42nd Deoli Regiment; 43rd Erinpura Infantry; 44th Mharwara Regiment; 45th Rattray's Sikhs; 48th, 61st, 64th, 81st, 107th, 121st and 128th Pioneers; Queen's Own Corps of Guides (un-numbered but occupying 50th place in the list); 51st–54th Sikhs (Frontier Force); 55th Coke's Rifles, 56th Infantry, 57th Wilde's Rifles, 58th Vaughan's Rifles, 59th Scinde Rifles, all bearing 'Frontier Force' after the title; 63rd Palamcottah Light Infantry; 65th, 73rd, 75th, 79th, 80th, 86th, 88th Carnatic Infantry; 71st Coorg Rifles; 77th and 78th Moplah Rifles; 83rd Wallajahbad Light Infantry; 91st Punjabis (Light Infantry); 93rd Burma Infantry; 94th and 95th Russell's

Trumpet-banner of the 1st, or Leslie's, Troop of the Bombay Horse Artillery. The eagle device was authorised to be used by the troop for its exceptionally distinguished service at Hyderabad in 1843, and later 'The Eagle Troop' became an honour-title for the succeeding Royal Artillery battery. Crimson silk with blue velvet scrolls, gold embroidery and a silver wreath on the eagle's breast.

Infantry; 96th Berar Infantry; 97th and 99th Deccan Infantry; 101st Grenadiers; 102nd Prince of Wales's Own Grenadiers; 103rd, 105th and 110th Mahratta Light Infantry; 104th Wellesley's Rifles; 114th, 116th and 117th Mahrattas; 119th Infantry (Mooltan Regiment); 120th and 122nd Rajputana Infantry; 123rd Outram's Rifles; 124th Duchess of Connaught's Own Baluchistan Infantry; 125th Napier's Rifles; 126th Baluchistan Regiment; 127th Baluch Light Infantry; 129th Duke of Connaught's Own Baluchis; 130th Baluchis.

Gurkhas: the Gurkha regiments remained outside the numbered sequence of infantry regiments: 1st Gurkha Rifles (Malaun Regiment); 2nd Prince of Wales's Own Gurkha Regiment (Sirmoor rifles); 3rd, 4th, 6th–10th Gurkha Rifles; 5th Gurkha Rifles (Frontier Force).

Of the cavalry, three were 'class corps' (1st, Mohammedans of Hindustan and southern Punjab, 14th Jats, 15th Multanis); the remainder were 'class-squadron' corps, each squadron consisting of the members of one 'class', such as Sikhs, Dogras, Punjabis, Rajputs or Pathans. The infantry was a mixture of 'class corps' (e.g., those composed exclusively of Sikhs, Dogras, Jats, etc.) and 'class company' corps, such as the Punjabi regiments, which might include Sikhs, Mohammedans, Pathans or Dogras, in their own companies. The 'classes' were usually identified by the method of tying the turban, so that a regiment's companies might be considerably different from one another in the appearance of their head-dress.

The Indian mountain batteries (now numbered 21–30) were included in the same list as the British batteries, which occupied lower numbers. There were also three engineer units: the 1st Prince of Wales's Own Sappers and Miners (ex-Bengal, consisting primarily of Sikhs, Pathans and Punjabi Mohammedans); 2nd Queen's Own Sappers and Miners (ex-Madras, composed of Madrassis, plus one company of Burmese based in that country); and the 3rd

Kipling's poem on the 'commissariat oont' (camel) was a typical reaction by those who had dealings with this form of pack-transport:
'... "the commissariat camu-el" goes about one mile an hour, eating the trees and ... with horrible bubblings and gurglings, and if overloaded by last straws in the shape of a cooking pot or two, either refuses to get up or *rolls.* The "oont-wallahs" in the scrimmage of packing feign stupidity or are numbed with cold and become useless; and this is the sort of scene that went on every morning by moonlight. ("Mind 'e dont bite yer Sir – sh-sh-sh-sh – lie down you brute." "Mind 'e dont kick yer." "Sh-sh-sh" the oont-wallah sits on his haunches and doesn't even say "sh-sh"). You have to say "sh-sh" to the orphan child and pull at its nose to make it lie down (by no means a pleasant operation when it is snarling and roaring at you). I believe if you sit on his hump he can turn round and bite you ...'
(*Letters and Sketches of Francis T. Warre Cornish, late Captain 17th Bengal Lancers*, Eton, 1902 pp. 137–8. The references to 'commissariat camu-el' and 'orphan child' are actually quotations from Kipling's poem 'Oonts')

The forces of the Indian states, and their 'Imperial Service Troops' wore uniforms based on the styles prevalent in the British Indian army; as with the officer illustrated, Risaldar Abdul Majid Khan of Bahawalpore, c.1897.

Sappers and Miners (ex-Bombay, principally Sikhs, Marathas and Rajputs).

Kitchener's re-organisation was a consequence of the principles which he identified: that the Indian Army's chief task was to defend the frontier from Russian and Afghan incursions, with internal security as a secondary role; that all units should therefore be trained to fight on the frontier, with a rotation of units; and that organisation, training and deployment should be the same for both peace and war. At the same time, the leavening of British units was still necessary, maintaining a very considerable deployment of the British Army in India.

Notes

1. Fortescue, the Hon. Sir John. *History of the British Army*, London, 1899, vol. II, p. 184.
2. To Captain Graham, 2 October 1803; *Dispatches of Field-Marshal the Duke of Wellington*, ed. Lieutenant-Colonel J. Gurwood, London, 1834–8, vol. II, p. 363.
3. Quoted in Fortescue, *op. cit.*, London, 1910, vol. V, p. 17.
4. These figures vary slightly in various sources; those quoted are taken from Wellesley's dispatch of 25 September 1803; *London Gazette*, 31 March 1804.
5. Blakiston, J. *Twelve Years' Military Adventures in Three-Quarters of the Globe*, London, 1829, vol. I, p. 295.
6. Sebright Mawbey, 30 November 1814; MS, author's possession.
7. Dispatch, 7 January 1818; *London Gazette*, 6 June 1818.
8. Report by the Chairman and Deputy-Chairman of the Company; quoted, for example, in *Edinburgh Evening Courant*, 13 April 1812.
9. To Amherst, 19 January 1826; *London Gazette*, 10 June 1826.
10. Napier's dispatch, 18 February 1843; *London Gazette*, 9 May 1843.
11. Dispatch, 24 March 1843; *London Gazette*, 6 June 1843.
12. Gough's dispatch, 4 January 1844; *London Gazette*, 8 March 1844.
13. Ibid.
14. 'A Glance at the Sikhs', in *Chambers' Edinburgh Journal*, 5 May 1849, p. 283.
15. MacMunn, Major G. F. *The Armies of India*, London, 1911, pp. 139–40.
16. Gough's dispatch, 19 December 1845; *London Gazette*, 23 February 1846.
17. This episode is covered excellently in Sethi, R. R. 'The Revolt in Kashmir, 1846', in *Journal of the Society for Army Historical Research*, vol. XI, 1932, pp. 158–67.
18. Gough's dispatch, 16 January 1849; *London Gazette*, 3 March 1849.
19. As note 10 above.
20. Lumsden, General Sir Peter, and Elsmie, G. R. *Lumsden of the Guides*, London, 1899, p. 31.
21. An interesting exposition of this point is Majumdar, Lieutenant-Colonel B. N., 'Was there any other real cause of the Sepoy Mutiny of 1857?', in *Bulletin of the Military Historical Society*, vol. XXVI, 1976.
22. Sherer, J. W. *Havelock's March on Cawnpore, 1857*, London, nd, p. 18.
23. Hodson W. *Twelve Years of a Soldier's Life in India*, ed. Revd. G. H. Hodson, London, 1859, pp. 100–1.
24. Letter to Lumsden, 16 May 1857; Lumsden, *op. cit.*, p. 178.
25. Forbes-Mitchell, W. *Reminiscences of the Great Mutiny 1857–59*, London, 1897, pp. 31, 177.
26. Sherer, *op. cit.*, p. 103.
27. Gowing, T. *A Soldier's Experience, or, A Voice from the Ranks*, Nottingham, 1907, p. 462.
28. Field Marshal Lord Roberts of Kandahar. *Forty-One Years in India*, London, 1900, pp. 499, 532.
29. *The Times' History of the War 1914*, p. 158.
30. Roberts, op. cit., pp. 533–4.
31. MacMunn, op. cit., p. 197.

References

India: 'General' Works

Anon. *The Army in India 1850–1914: A Photographic Record*, London, 1968.
Bayly, C. A. (ed.). *The Raj: India and the British 1600–1947*, London, 1990 (National Portrait Gallery catalogue).
Beaumont, R. *Sword of the Raj: The British Army in India 1747–1947*, New York, 1977.
Bhatia, H. S. (ed.). *Military History of British India 1607–1947*, New Delhi, 1977.
Bolt, D. *Gurkhas*, London, 1967.
Desmond, R. *Victorian India in Focus*, London, 1982 (early photography in India).
Featherstone, D. *Victoria's Enemies: An A–Z of British Colonial Warfare*, London, 1989.
Gardner, B. *The East India Company*, London, 1971.
Keay, J. *The Honourable Company: A History of the English East India Company*, London, 1991.
Knight, I. *Queen Victoria's Enemies (3): India*, London, 1990.
MacMunn, Lieutenant-General Sir George. *The Martial Races*

of India, London, 1932.

Malleson, Colonel G. B. *The Decisive Battles of India from 1746 to 1849 Inclusive*, London, 1883.

Nolan, E. H. *The History of the British Empire in India and the East*, London, nd (*c.*1855).

Sita Ram (trans. Lieutenant-Colonel J. T. Norgate). *From Sepoy to Subedar*, 1873; latest edn. ed. J. Lunt, London, 1970. (The most famous account by an Indian 'other rank' of the mid-19th century.)

Woodruff, P. *The Men who Ruled India*, London, 1954 (Indian civil service).

Worsick, C., and Embree, A. *The Last Empire: Photography in British India 1855–1911*, London, 1976.

India: Early Period

Beatson, Lieutenant-Colonel A. *View of the Origin and Conduct of the War with Tippoo Sultaun*, London, 1800.

Bidwell, S. *Swords for Hire: European Mercenaries in Eighteenth-Century India*, London, 1971.

Bowring, L. B. *Haidar Ali and Tipu Sultan*, Oxford, 1893.

Compton, H. *A Particular Account of the European Military Adventurers of Hindustan from 1784 to 1803*, London, 1892.

Duff, J. G. *A History of the Mahrattas*, London, 1826.

Edwardes, M. *Clive: the Heaven-born General*, London, 1977.

– *The Battle of Plassey and the Conquest of Bengal*, London, 1963.

Featherstone, D. *Victorian Colonial Warfare: India, from the Conquest of Sind to the Indian Mutiny*, London, 1992 (includes Gwalior 1843).

Forrest, D. *Tiger of Mysore: The Life and Death of Tipu Sultan*, London, 1970.

Forrest, G. W. *Life of Lord Clive*, London, 1918.

Hill, S. C. *The Life of Claud Martin*, Calcutta, 1901.

Kincaid, C. A. *A History of the Maratha People*, Oxford, 1918–25.

Lambrick, H. T. *Sir Charles Napier and Sind*, Oxford, 1952.

Malcolm, Sir John. *Life of Robert, Lord Clive*, London, 1836.

Malleson, Colonel G. B. *A History of the French in India*, London, 1868.

– *Clive*, Oxford, 1893.

– *Dupleix*, Oxford, 1890.

– *The Decisive Battles of India from 1746 to 1849 Inclusive*, London, 1883.

Marshman, J. C. *A History of India*, London, 1867.

Misra, B. B. *The Central Administration of the East India Company 1773–1834*, Manchester, 1959.

Napier, P. *I Have Sind: Charles Napier in India 1841–1844*, London, 1990.

– *Raven Castle: Charles Napier in India 1844–1851*, London, 1991.

Napier, Major-General W. F. P. *The Conquest of Scinde*, London, 1845.

Orme, R. *Military Transactions of the British Nation in Indostan*, Madras, 1861–2.

Philips, C. H. *The East India Company 1784–1834*, Manchester, 1968.

Sen, S. *The Military System of the Marathas*, Calcutta, 1928.

Smith, Major L. F. *A Sketch of the Rise, Progress and Termination of the Regular Corps formed and commanded by Europeans in the service of the Native Princes of India ...*, Calcutta, 1804.

Thornton, E. *History of the British Empire in India*, London, 1843.

Weller, J. *Wellington in India*, London, 1972.

Young, D. *Fountain of the Elephants*, London, 1959 (biography of Benoît de Boigne).

India: Sikh Wars

Bond, B. (ed.). *Victorian Military Campaigns*, London, 1967 (includes 'The Sikh Wars 1845–9', E. R. Crawford).

Bruce, G. *Six Battles for India: the Anglo-Sikh Wars 1845–6, 1848–9*, London, 1969.

Burton, Lieutenant-Colonel R. G. *The First and Second Sikh Wars*, Simla, 1911.

Coley, J. *Journal of the Sutlej Campaign of 1845–46*, London, 1856.

Cook, Colonel H. C. B. *The Sikh Wars: The British Army in the Punjab 1845–1849*, London, 1975.

Cunningham, Captain J. D. *A History of the Sikhs, from the Origin of the Nation to the Battles of the Sutlej*, London,

1849.

Edwardes, Sir Herbert. *The Punjab Frontier in 1848–1849*, London, 1851.

Fauja Singh Bajwa. *The Military System of the Sikhs during the period 1799–1849*, Delhi, 1964.

Featherstone, D. *All for a Shilling a Day*, London, 1966 (the 16th Lancers in the 1st Sikh War).

– *At them with the Bayonet!: The First Sikh War*, London, 1968.

– *Victorian Colonial Warfare: India, from the conquest of Sind to the Indian Mutiny*, London, 1992.

Gough, Sir Charles, and Innes, J. J. *The Sikhs and the Sikh Wars: The Rise, Conquest and Annexation of the Punjab State*, London, 1897.

Hardinge, Viscount, *et al.* *The War in India: Despatches of the Rt. Hon. Lt. Gen. Vist. Hardinge ... Gen. Lord Gough ... Maj. Gen. Sir Harry Smith ... comprising the Engagements of Moodkee, Ferozeshah, Aliwal, and Sobraon ...*, London, 1846.

Knight, I. *Queen Victoria's Enemies (3): India*, London, 1990.

Kushwant Singh. *A History of the Sikhs 1469–1839*, Oxford, 1965.

– *Ranjit Singh, The Maharajah of the Punjab 1780–1839*, London, 1962.

Lawrence-Archer, Captain J. H. *Commentaries on the Punjab Campaign 1848–49*, London, 1878.

McGregor, W. G. *History of the Sikhs*, London, 1846.

Majumdar, Lieutenant-Colonel B. N. *The Military System of the Sikhs*, New Delhi, 1965.

Thackwell, E. J. *Narrative of the Second Sikh War 1848–49*, London, 1851.

India: The Mutiny

Barthorp, M. J. *British Troops in the Indian Mutiny 1857–59*, London, 1994 (includes East India Company forces).

Bonham, Colonel J. *Oude in 1857: some Memoirs of the Indian Mutiny*, London, 1928.

Cave-Browne, J. *The Punjab and Delhi in 1857*, Edinburgh, 1861.

Collier, R. *The Sound of Fury: An Account of the Indian Mutiny*,

London, 1963.

Dangerfield, G. *Bengal Mutiny: the Story of the Sepoy Rebellion*, London, 1933.

Edwardes, M. *A Season in Hell*, London, 1973 (defence of the Residency, Lucknow).

– *Battles of the Indian Mutiny*, London, 1963.

– *Red Year: The Indian Rebellion of 1857*, London, 1973.

Featherstone, D. *Victorian Colonial Warfare: India, from the Conquest of Sind to the Indian Mutiny*, London, 1992.

Forbes-Mitchell, W. *Reminiscences of the Great Mutiny 1857–59*, London, 1895.

Forrest, G. *History of the Indian Mutiny*, Edinburgh, 1904.

Grant, General J. Hope, and Knollys, H. *Incidents in the Sepoy War 1857–58*, Edinburgh, 1873.

Griffiths, C. *Narrative of the Siege of Delhi, with an Account of the Mutiny at Ferozepore in 1857*, London, 1910.

Gubbins, M. R. *An Account of the Mutiny in Oudh and of the Siege of the Lucknow Residency*, London, 1858.

Gupta, P. C. *Nana Sahib and the Rising at Cawnpore*, Oxford, 1963.

Harris. J. *The Indian Mutiny*, London, 1973.

Hibbert, C. *The Great Mutiny: India 1857*, London, 1978 (excellent modern study).

Hilton, Major-General R. *The Indian Mutiny: A Centenary History*, London, 1957.

Holmes, T. R. *History of the Indian Mutiny*, London, 1913.

Innes, M. *Lucknow and Oude in the Mutiny*, London, 1896.

Kaye, Sir John W. *History of the Sepoy War in India 1857–58*, London, 1864–7.

Kaye, Sir John W., and Malleson, Colonel G. B. *History of the Indian Mutiny of 1857–58*, London, 1897 (completion of Kaye's *History of the Sepoy War*).

Leasor, J. *The Red Fort: An Account of the Siege of Delhi in 1857*, London, 1956.

Llewellyn, A. The *Siege of Delhi*, London, 1977.

Lowe, T. *Central India during the Rebellion of 1857 and 1858*, London, 1860.

MacMunn, Lieutenant-General Sir George. *The Indian*

Mutiny in Perspective, London, 1931.

Maunsell, F. R. *The Siege of Delhi*, London, 1912.

Palmer, J. A. B. *The Mutiny Outbreak at Meerut in 1857*, Cambridge, 1966.

Perkins, R. *The Kashmir Gate: Lieutenant Home and the Delhi VCs*, Chippenham, 1983.

Rowbotham, W. *The Naval Brigades in the Indian Mutiny 1857–58*, London, 1947.

Russell, W. H. *My Indian Mutiny Diary* (ed. and intr. M. Edwardes), London, 1957 (*The Times* correspondent).

Sen, S. N. *Eighteen Fifty-Seven*, Delhi, 1957 (important history).

Stuart, V. *Battle for Lucknow*, London, 1975.

Trevelyan, Sir George. *Cawnpore*, London, 1865.

Verney, Major-General G. *The Devil's Wind: the Story of the Naval Brigade at Lucknow*, London, 1956.

Wood, Sir Evelyn. *The Revolt in Hindustan 1857–59*, London, 1908.

India: Frontier Operations

Barthorp, M. *The North-West Frontier: British India and Afghanistan, a Pictorial History 1839–1947*, Poole, 1982.

Callwell, C. E. *Campaigns and their Lessons: Tirah 1897*, London, 1911.

Caroe, Sir Olaf. *The Pathans, 550 BC–AD 1957*, London, 1958.

Churchill, W. L. S. (later Sir Winston). *The Story of the Malakand Field Force*, London, 1898.

Davies, C. C. *The Indian Frontier 1858–1918* (vol. V of the *Cambridge History of British India*), Cambridge, 1932.

Elliott, Major-General J. G. *The Frontier 1839–1947*, London, 1968.

Fincastle, Viscount, and Elliott-Lockhart, P. C. *A Frontier Campaign: a Narrative of the Malakand and Buner Field Forces on the North West Frontier of India 1897–98*, London, 1898.

Grimwood E. St. C. *My Three Years in Manipur*, London, 1891 (account of the Manipur revolt by the heroine of the affair).

Harris, J. *Much Sounding of*

Bugles: The Siege of Chitral, 1895, London, 1975.

Hobday, Major E. A. P. *Sketches on Service during the Indian Frontier Campaign of 1897*, London, 1898.

Hutchinson, Colonel H. D. *The Campaign in Tirah*, London, 1898.

Mills, H. W. *The Pathan Revolt in North-West India*, Lahore 1897.

Nevill, Captain H. L. *North-West Frontier*, London, 1912 (important work, giving complete orders-of-battle for most expeditions. Repr. London, 1992).

Paget, Lieutenant-Colonel W. H. (Rev. Lieutenant A. H. Mason). *A Record of the Expeditions against the North-West Frontier*, London, 1884.

Robertson, Sir George. *Chitral: The Story of a Minor Siege*, London, 1898.

Singer, A. *Lords of the Khyber: the Story of the North-West Frontier*, London, 1984.

Swinson, A. *The North-West Frontier: People and Events 1839–1947*, London, 1967.

Thomson, H. C. *The Chitral Campaign: A Narrative of Events in Chitral, Swat and Bajaur*, London, 1895.

Trench, C. C. *The Frontier Scouts*, London, 1985 (largely post-1904 but an excellent account of the nature of the frontier and its inhabitants).

Younghusband, Captain G. J. *Indian Frontier Warfare*, London, 1898.

Younghusband, Capt. G. J., and Younghusband, Colonel Sir Francis E. *The Relief of Chitral*, London, 1896.

The Indian Army

Barat, A. *The Bengal Native Infantry: its Organization and Discipline 1796–1852*, Calcutta, 1962.

Barthorp, M. *Indian Infantry Regiments 1860–1914*, London, 1979.

Bowling, A. H. *Indian Cavalry Regiments 1880–1914*, London, 1971.

Broome, Captain A. *History of the Rise and Progress of the Bengal Army*, London, 1850.

Cadell, Sir Patrick. *History of the Bombay Army*, London, 1938.

Cambridge, Marquess of. 'Notes

on the Army of India', in *Journal of the Society for Army Historical Research*, vols. XLVII, XLVIII, 1969–70 (detailed lineages).

Cardew, Lieutenant F. G. *A Sketch of the Services of the Bengal Army*, Calcutta, 1903.

Carman, W. Y. *Indian Army Uniforms: Cavalry*, London, 1961.

– *Indian Army Uniforms: Infantry*, London, 1969.

Farwell, B. *Armies of the Raj: From the Mutiny to Independence 1858–1947*, London, 1990.

Gaylor, J. *Sons of John Company: The Indian and Pakistan Armies 1903–91*, Tunbridge Wells, 1992 (despite the dates given in the title, earlier material is also included).

Glover, M., and Chater, C. P. *An Assemblage of Indian Army Soldiers and Uniforms*, London, 1973 (uniform-plates by Chater, but it should be noted that these were taken from secondary, usually published, sources).

Harfield, Major A. *British and Indian Armies in the East Indies 1685–1935*, Chippenham, 1984.

– *British and Indian Armies on the China Coast 1785–1985*, Farnham, 1990.

– *The Indian Army of the Empress 1861–1903*, Tunbridge Wells, 1990.

Harris, R. G. *Bengal Cavalry Regiments 1857–1914*, London, 1979.

Heathcote, T. A. *The Indian Army: the Garrison of British Imperial India 1822–1922*, Newton Abbott, 1974.

Hervey, Captain A. *A Soldier of the Company: Life of an Indian Ensign 1833–43*, ed. C. Allen, London, 1988 (although personal accounts are not otherwise included in this list, an exception is made in this case because of the exceptional quality of contemporary illustrations, from the National Army Museum collection).

Hughes, Major-General B. P. *The Bengal Horse Artillery 1800–1861*, London, 1971 (although regimental histories are not otherwise included in this list, an exception is made in this

case because of its wider co⸗ erage, for example regardir⸗ the tactical employment of artillery).

Irving, M. *A List of Inscriptions ⸗ Christian Tombs or Monumen⸗ in the Punjab, North-West Fro⸗ tier Province, Kashmir and Afghanistan*, Lahore, 1910–1 (contains much biographic⸗ information; the modern reprint is listed below unde⸗ Rhé-Philipe).

Jackson, Major D. *India's Army*, London, nd (1940) (brief regimental histories).

Jaipur, Maharaja of. *A History o⸗ the Indian State Forces*, New Delhi, 1967.

MacMunn, Major G. F. (later Lieutenant-General Sir George). *The Armies of Indi⸗* London, 1911.

Mason, P. *A Matter of Honour: ⸗ Account of the Indian Army, i⸗ Officers and Men*, London, 1974.

Mollo, B. *The Indian Army*, Poole, 1981 (excellent illus⸗ trated survey).

Rhé-Philipe, G. W. de, and Irving, M. *Soldiers of the Raj*, London, 1989 (modern re⸗ of Irving, listed above; the biographical notices were the work of de Rhé-Philipe⸗

Saxena, K. M. L. *The Military S⸗ tem of India 1850–1900*, Ne⸗ Delhi, 1974.

Singh, M. *The Indian Army und⸗ the East India Company*, Ne⸗ Delhi, 1976.

Williams, Captain J. *Bengal Native Infantry: an Historica⸗ Account ... 1757–1796*, Lon⸗ don, 1817.

Wilson, Lieutenant-Colonel W *History of the Madras Army from 1746 to 1826*, Madras, 1888.

Younghusband, Colonel G. J. *The Story of the Guides*, London, 1908.

Government of India. *Frontier⸗ and Overseas Expeditions fron⸗ India*, Calcutta and Simla, 1907–11 (official publication).

AFGHANISTAN

From its geographical position on the border of British India, Afghanistan exerted considerable influence on the policy of the British administration, both in itself and as a highroad for Russian incursions. Afghanistan's impact on the history of India, however, was considerably more ancient, although its earlier history was more concerned with that of Persia. Following the invasion of the Persian ruler Nadir Shah in 1737–8, many Afghans enrolled in Nadir's army; and following Nadir's assassination in 1747, his Afghan General Ahmad Khan was chosen by the Afghan chiefs at Kandahar to be their leader, assuming virtual kingship over the eastern part of Nadir's empire. Ahmad was styled *Dur-i-Duran*, 'Pearl of the Age', which bestowed the name 'Durani' upon his clan, the Abdalis or Sadozais. Ahmad Khan led ten invasions of India as the Mogul empire collapsed, capturing Delhi in 1757 and winning a huge victory over the Marathas at Panipat in January 1761; at his death in 1773 his Afghan empire extended over eastern Persia, Baluchistan, Kashmir, the Punjab and Sind. The empire began to disintegrate under his son, Timur Shah (who transferred the capital from Kandahar to Kabul), and warfare between some of Timur's 23 sons and their kinsmen greatly weakened Afghan power. The fifth of Timur's sons, Zaman Shah, attained the throne by threatening his brothers; but one of them, Mahmud Shah, escaped his brother's grasp and established himself at Herat. In one of the purges in the Afghan court, Painda Khan, head of the second main Durani clan, the Barakzais, was killed, whereupon his son, Fateh Khan, joined Mahmud at Herat. With Barakzai help, Mahmud deposed, blinded and imprisoned Zaman Shah in 1799, and assumed the throne; but was himself deposed by his brother Shujah ul Mulk in 1803. Mahmud and Fateh Khan remained hostile, and Mahmud resumed the throne after deposing Shujah in 1809; but after Fateh Khan was murdered by Mahmud for fear of his growing authority, Fateh's Barakzai kinsmen rose in revolt and drove Mahmud into Herat (1818), where his son, Kamran, set up an independent state. During this period of near-anarchy, and subsequent feuds among Fateh Khan's 21 brothers, Afghan power diminished steadily: Zaman Shah had ceded Lahore to Ranjit Singh, Sikh power increased and they captured Kashmir in 1819, and Sind threw off the Afghan allegiance in 1808.

In 1826 Fateh Khan's brother Dost Muhammed came to power, but declined to style himself 'Khan' because of the decline in his realm, which was largely restricted to Kabul and Ghanzi; one of his brothers ruled independently over Kandahar, and another held Peshawar. Shah Shujah, not accepting the triumph of the Barakzais, made a number of attempts to regain his throne; after a defeated attempt in 1834 Dost Muhammed awarded himself the title 'Amir'. Taking advantage of this conflict, Ranjit Singh annexed Peshawar, and Britain became involved from their anxiety to block possible encroachments by Persia or Russia. Encouraged by Russia, Mohammed Shah of Persia invaded Herat province, but that city defied the Persian army (spearheaded by a corps of Russian mercenaries under a Polish commander), and its defence was assisted greatly by Lieutenant Eldred Pottinger of the Bombay Artillery. After a siege of ten months, Mohammed Shah withdrew (9 September 1838).

As British involvement increased, Alexander Burnes was sent as British Resident to the court at Kabul. In effect, the British were forced to choose between supporting Dost Muhammed or Ranjit Singh over possession of the Peshawar region, and lack of co-operation by Dost Muhammed, and the Russian threat, resulted in a decision to support Shah Shujah's claim to the Afghan throne. With British approval, on 25 June 1838 the Treaty of Simla was concluded between Shujah and Ranjit Singh, confirming the latter in possession of the Peshawar district; Shujah agreed to accept British control of his foreign policy, would not attack his nephew Kamran in Herat, and would relinquish his claim to Sind in return for financial compensation. It was intended that Ranjit Singh should support Shujah's own followers, with only token British backing; but Ranjit was disinclined to become involved militarily, and objected to the traversing of his territory, so it was decided that Shujah should be installed by a British expedition. So determined on this course of action was the governor-general, Lord Auckland, that he was undiscouraged even by the news of the retreat of the Persians from Herat which, with a Russian re-consideration of their policy under diplomatic pressure from Britain, served at least temporarily to remove the danger from that quarter.

First Afghan War

To invade Afghanistan and place Shujah on the throne, the Army of the Indus was formed, two divisions of British and Company troops under the command of Lieutenant-General Sir John Keane, commander-in-chief of the Bombay Army; there was also a force of Shujah's own troops, organised along British lines on his behalf. Permission to cross Sikh territory having been denied, the army had to enter Afghanistan via Sind, rather than by the more obvious route through the Punjab and the Khyber Pass; one division, of the Bombay Army, went by sea to Sind, and the other, from Bengal, marched through Sind, the chiefs of which were threatened to prevent objections. The army was accompanied by a train of camp-followers immense even by the standards of Indian warfare; they suffered some harassment from local tribesmen, notably in the Bolan Pass, but little resistance was encountered from the supporters of Dost Muhammed. The British forces concentrated at Kandahar, which Shah Shujah entered on 25 April 1839, and was crowned formally on 3 May; the Afghan forces, having concentrated to meet the presumed

Kipling's *Gunga Din* commemorates the sterling service of the *bhistis* (water-carriers), providers of a commodity even more valuable in hot climates than in European warfare. This is exemplified in an account of the doomed garrison of Charikar by one of the few survivors, Havildar Mootee Ram Haid of Shah Shujah's 4th (Gurkha) Light Infantry, which he dictated to Major T. McSherry of the 30th Bengal Native Infantry in 1842. After the besieging Afghans cut off the fort's water:

'The sick and wounded, now increased to a frightful amount, were continually screaming for water in piercing accents. Our muskets were so foul from incessant use, that the balls were forced down with difficulty, although separated from the paper of the cartridge which usually wraps them round. The lips of the men became swollen and bloody, and their tongues clove to their palates ... For two days there was not a single drop of water within the walls of the fort. The men were mad with thirst, and demanded to be led against any perils to procure water. Accordingly, at midnight, Lieut. Rose conducted a party of 100 men, taking with them all the lotahs and canteens they could carry, all the Bheesties

and non-combatants, to ...where the water from the new cut had overflowed its banks ... Having luxuriated a short time in the delicious element, and filled our vessels with it, Lieut. Rose took us to a field of radishes ... Here we crammed as many as we could in our mouths, and stuck our belts full of more for our comrades in the fort ...'

As they returned they came upon an Afghan camp: 'Lieut. Rose said to us, "Give them one volley, then the steel you know how to use so well." The non-combatants carrying the water, were placed out of harm's way behind a wall. We fired together by word of command from Lieut. Rose, on the slumbering crowd of foes, within fifty yards of them. Then we charged, shouting "Goruck nath ke jai," and set the bayonet and cookery [*kukri*] to work with a will ... Those who had cookeries did most execution: there is no weapon like the cookery for a hand-to-hand fight ... We were as happy as could be that night in Chareekah ... our officers were proud of us, and we were proud of ourselves and of each other ...' ('Personal Narrative of Mootee Ram', in *United Service Magazine*, 1842, vol. II, pp. 409–10. Eventually, with water and ammunition exhausted, the beleaguered garrison attempted to break out and was virtually annihilated)

threat from the Sikhs, were unprepared for the direction from which the British came.

To extend Shujah's rule to the rest of Afghanistan, Keane marched towards Ghanzi and Kabul. The former, one of the most famous fortresses in the region, was stormed by Keane in the early hours of 23 July 1839, by blowing in the Kabul gate with a charge of powder (rather than delay to await the arrival of the siege-train). It had fallen by daylight, with about 600 of its defenders killed and 1,600 captured; British losses were 'wonderfully small considering the occasion':[1] seventeen men killed, one missing, and eighteen officers and 147 other ranks wounded. Dost Muhammed endeavoured to gather an army around Kabul, but the fall of Ghanzi undermined his support, and when his offer of peace terms was rejected, he fled to the Hindu Kush. On 7 August Shah Shujah entered Kabul; as he was unwilling to have British troops quartered in the city's great fortress, the Bala Hissar, they established cantonments outside the city. Most of the British expedition returned to India, the Bombay division pausing to deal with Kalat *en route* (as described here in the section on India).

Although Shujah was on his throne, his subjects would not accept him, and hostility increased. The British treated their Kabul garrison like a peacetime posting in India, some officers sending for their families; British diplomacy was represented at Kabul by the governor-general's envoy, Sir William Macnaghten, with Alexander Burnes as his deputy. There was some unrest, and a brief foray by Dost Muhammed ended when he surrendered to

Macnaghten on 3 November 1840; he was permitted to live in comfort in British India. Generally, however, peace was maintained initially, partly by British subsidies paid to potentially hostile chiefs, but as an economy measure these were reduced, and in late 1841 the brigade of Sir Robert 'Fighting Bob' Sale was sent back to India; but it encountered such hostility from the Ghilzai tribesmen of the Khoord–Kabul Pass, whose subsidies had been cut, that the force had to seek refuge in the fort at Jalalabad.

From this point the situation deteriorated markedly, beginning with the murder of Burnes at Kabul on 2 November 1841, his house being attacked and burned by a mob (said to have been enraged by his romantic exploits among the Afghan ladies of Kabul). Decisive military leadership was required, but after the departure of Sir Willoughby Cotton (who had commanded the British forces in Afghanistan after Keane's return to India), command was in the elderly and indecisive hands of Major-General William Elphinstone, who had seen no action since commanding the 33rd Foot at Waterloo. His troops became demoralised by lack of leadership and continuing attacks, and all Macnaghten could do was to negotiate with Dost Muhammed's son, Akbar Khan (leader of the anti-Shujah faction) for a withdrawal upon terms of safe conduct; but Macnaghten was murdered during a conference with Akbar on 23 November. Elphinstone finally agreed to evacuate the country and on 6 January 1842 began his march towards Jalalabad, with some 4,500 troops (only 700 Europeans) and 12,000 camp-followers, short of supplies and demoralised by the ineptitude of their leadership. They were harassed all the way and within a week the entire force had been destroyed; Elphinstone was taken prisoner during a peace-conference (and died in captivity), the European wives and families were captured but well-treated, but the soldiers and camp-followers were mostly killed or died of cold. The last stand of the European troops, some Bengal Horse Artillery and the remnant of the 44th Foot, was made at Gandamak in the Jagdalak Pass on 13 January. There were hardly any survivors, and the only member of the force to reach Jalalabad was Dr. William Brydon. It was a shattering defeat:

'Cabool! Cabool! thy name shall be
Synonymous with treachery.'[2]

Nevertheless there still remained the fortified posts of Ghanzi, Kandahar, Jalalabad and Khelat-i-Ghilzai (a fort between Kabul and Kandahar, about 80 miles north-east of the latter). Ghanzi, garrisoned by the 27th Bengal Native Infantry, was starved into submission on 6 March 1842, but the others held out. Major-General Sir William Nott at Kandahar conducted an energetic defence and was able to relieve Kelat-i-Ghilzai, where Captain John Craigie of the 20th Bengal, commanding the Shah's 3rd Infantry, held on for four months with a few Europeans of the Bengal Artillery, three companies of the 43rd Bengal Native Infantry and Shah Shujah's 3rd Infantry, until Nott's arrival on 26 May 1842. At Jalalabad, Sale's garrison was composed principally of his own 13th Foot, the 35th Bengal Native Infantry, supports and one squadron each of the 5th Bengal Light Cavalry and Shah Shujah's Horse; he withstood a siege from mid-November 1841 until April 1842 when the besieging Afghans retired partly as a result of Sale's own efforts and partly upon the approach of a relief-force.

The organisation of this latter had been the first act of the new governor-general, Lord Ellenborough, who arrived to replace Auckland in February 1842. A strong force was assembled at Peshawar under Major-General Sir George Pollock, who forced the Khyber Pass on 5 April 1842; an experienced officer, he deployed his forces in skirmish-order to oust the Afghans from their positions on the heights, using their own tactics against them. He reached Jalalabad on 16 April, to find that the siege had been lifted on 7 April. Ellenborough wished his two forces (Pollock and Nott) to withdraw, but both commanders believed that British prestige should be restored first; so Ellenborough permitted Pollock to advance on Kabul, while Nott was told to evacuate Kandahar and return to India via Kabul, if he wished. In the interim, Pollock had detached a column under Brigadier-General Monteath to suppress the raiding of the Shinwarie tribe, whom he defeated at Mazenia on 26 July (with the 31st Foot and 32nd and 54th Bengal Native Infantry).

Nott advanced on Kabul from 10 August 1842, defeating Afghan forces at Karabagh (30 August); dispersing Afghans on the surrounding heights, he entered Ghanzi

on 6 September and released from captivity the men of the 27th Bengal, the original garrison. Pollock marched from Jalalabad on 20 August, using his tactics of seizing the high ground to drive away Afghans who blocked his route, notably at Tezin on 13 September. The march was especially trying as it was the route that had been taken by Elphinstone's force, 'rendered horrid to us by the spectacle of the mouldering remains of our slaughtered fellow-soldiers, with which it is thickly strewn. Skeleton upon skeleton they lie in frequent heaps; the parchment-like skin still stretched over the bones, and in every variety of posture, the result of violent and painful death. Our blood boiled as we gazed on these ghastly sights ... conjuring up the frightful reality of the scenes enacted when these victims fell, if indeed imagination be equal to the task of picturing them! my pen shrinks terrified from the attempt ...'[3] Pollock entered Kabul on 15 September, and was joined by Nott two days later. The captives from Elphinstone's force were released (Sale had the joy of personally receiving into British hands his wife and daughter, when freed from their captivity), and after suitable punishments had been made (the bazaar was blown up) the British quit Kabul on 12 October 1842. They regrouped at Jalalabad and marched through the Khyber Pass to India, where Ellenborough met them with the 'Army of Reserve', a force assembled to ensure that the retiring troops would not be molested by the Sikhs. Nott's rearguard had been harassed in the retreat, but no serious opposition was encountered, and the arrival of the army at Ferozepore on 23 December effectively ended the British action in Afghanistan.

Because of Pollock's actions, the war was announced as having had a successful outcome, but was in reality a reverse; the diminution of the Russian threat had not been the result of military action but of diplomatic activity in London and St. Petersburg, and the defeat of Elphinstone had dispelled the air of invulnerability which had surrounded British arms in the subcontinent, which was to have a considerable effect. As for Afghanistan, Shah Shujah was not party to the events of the later stages of the war: ever unpopular, he had been assassinated in March 1842. His son Shahpur took his place, but after he was disposed of by Akbar, Dost Muhammed returned as Amir. Akbar, who became *wazir* (chief minister), was not long a rival to his father (with whom he was frequently at odds), for he died in 1847, leaving Dost Muhammed in the position he occupied before the war.

(Contemporary accounts of the First Afghan War contain spellings of proper names markedly different from those now generally accepted; British campaign-medals, for example, use the spellings 'Ghunzee', 'Cabul' and 'Candahar', and contemporary accounts use such versions as 'Cabool' and, for the name of the Shah, variations like 'Shoojah-ool-Moolk', 'Shuja', 'Soojah', 'Sujah' and 'Soujah'. The battle-honour which, together with the 'mural crown', was awarded to the 13th Foot and borne upon its badges as the Somerset Light Infantry, was spelled 'Jellalabad', as on the campaign-medal.)

Military Forces: Afghanistan

At the time of the First Afghan War there was no organised Afghan 'army' in the European sense of the term. Afghan society was based on tribal allegiance, the population including both ethnic Afghans and others, perhaps most notably the Qizilbashes resident around Kabul, descendants of the Persian garrison established there by Nadir Shah. (They were also different in religion, being members of the Shi'a branch of Islam, the remainder of the inhabitants being members of the Sunni branch). Administration of the country was based partly upon the tribal structure and partly upon the *jagirdari* system, a form of feudal land tenure. Tribal chiefs or *sirdar*s, although necessarily members of the tribal nobility, were elected by tribal elders so that sirdarship was not necessarily dependent upon direct succession, and the control exercised by a *sirdar* over his followers often depended upon his ability to distribute largesse. The necessary revenue was often obtained by the grant of a *jagir* by the government or ruler, a land grant from which the *jagirdar* drew revenue, in return for an obligation to field a certain number of troops when required. *Jagirdar*s were not necessarily tribal or clan *sirdar*s, but their influence was greater when they were, and such were their powers that the *jagirdar* became in effect the government of the area. With warriors' allegiance being primarily to *sirdar* or *jagirdar*, internal conflict was made more likely than had the troops' allegiance been directed towards the head of the nation; and when first mobilised, the initial responsibility for maintaining forces in the field fell upon the *jagirdar*, only reverting to central government after a period of service, which tended to limit the time an Afghan army could remain in the field.

The employment of 'regular' soldiers (foreign mercenaries) was possible, but expensive, although military capability was an important factor in achieving or maintaining power; Dost Muhammed, for example, was helped to power by the support of the Qizilbash palace guard, his mother having been a member of one of the noble Qizilbash families. With no 'regular' army, the Afghan method of combat was without much discipline, but most proficient at skirmish tactics, using their long *jezail*s to good effect from behind natural cover, and harassing an enemy's flanks. The most prosperous served as cavalry, some wearing Indo-Persian helmets and armour; the remainder wore their civilian clothing, including turban or skull-cap, loose tunic and trousers, cummerbund, and in winter a heavy *poshteen*, a sheepskin coat with the fleece on the inside. *Jezail*s, swords, round shields (*dhal*s) and long-bladed knives were the usual arms. However, Captain James Airey wrote of seeing Afghans drilling in European fashion at Kabul, and noted his amusement '... at the extraordinary dresses of the men, viz., over an Afghan's flowing robes you would see an officer's coatee; or under them, a pair of tight regimental trousers. I gave my cocked hat and plume to the non-commissioned officer of our guard, who was very proud of it at first, and asked if it made him a *General*. He soon brought it back, however, saying that his comrades laughed at it so much that he begged to return to his turban. What galled us most was, to see the colours of some Native Infantry regiment carried at the head of one of these ragamuffin corps.'[4]

A quite different Afghan army was 'Shah Shujah's Force', formed prior to the campaign, of British-style regiments, raised in British territory, commanded by Britons and paid by the Company; Shujah himself had little to do with its formation. Initially two regiments of cavalry, five of infantry (the 4th composed of Gurkhas) and a troop of horse artillery was formed, commanded by Major-General E. H. Simpson (19th Bengal Native Infantry). After Shujah was installed on the throne a second troop of horse artillery was formed, a mountain battery, a sixth infantry regiment, the cadre of a unit entitled 'the Shah's Own Artillery', and a corps of sappers and miners comprising 300 Hindustanis, 200 Gurkhas, and 100 Afghans and Hazaras. The force served with some distinction during the First Afghan War, but suffered severely. The 4th (Gurkha) Infantry was destroyed in November 1841 at Charikar (from which massacre only one officer escaped with one Gurkha and the intrepid Eldred Pottinger, political officer, though one *havildar* and one or two men escaped independently); the 2nd Cavalry, 6th Infantry, half the sappers and mountain train, and the force commander, Brigadier J. T. Anquetil, went to their deaths with Elphinstone. The 1st, 5th and half the 2nd Infantry formed part of the Kandahar garrison, the 3rd part of that at Kelat-i-Ghilzai, others served with Nott, and elements of the 1st Cavalry, mountain train and half the sappers were at Jalalabad with Sale. The survivors returned to India, where three units were incorporated in the Company forces: the 3rd Infantry, in recognition of their conduct there, became the Kelat-i-Ghilzie Regiment (ultimately the 12th Bengal, keeping their distinctive title as pioneers in the 1903 reorganisation); the horse artillery was absorbed into the Bengal Horse Artillery, and the sappers into the Bengal Sappers and Miners.[5] As a token of appreciation, Shah Shujah awarded to British officers the Order of the Durani Empire, a decoration not always well-received: 'That a nation professing the slightest regard for the honour of the military profession should allow its officers to wear the badge of so worthless a scoundrel as Shah Soojah, is one of the wonders of the times ... That officers might have this Dooranee Order inflicted on them they could not help; but that they should ask permission of their own Sovereign to wear in public the marks and tokens of such a stupid savage, is beyond all credibility.

They were not worthy to be hung on the neck of a New-foundland dog.'[6]

Second Afghan War

Following the First Afghan War, the British remained suspicious of the possible expansion of Russia and its influence upon the region. Dost Muhammed sent forces to assist the Sikhs in the Second Sikh War, but in 1855 agreed a treaty of perpetual peace and co-operation with the British, and remained neutral during the period of the Mutiny, when the British were at their most vulnerable. He extended his rule to Kandahar and Herat, which he captured in May 1863, but died in the following month, and was succeeded by his son Sher Ali. He was deposed in 1866 in favour of his brother Mohammed Afzal, who was himself replaced by another brother, Muhammed Azam, in 1867; but in 1869 Sher Ali regained the throne. He tried to avoid involvement in Anglo-Russian rivalry, which again came to a crisis in the mid-1870s, with a forceful policy by the governor-general, Lord Lytton, to ensure that Afghanistan favoured Britain, and with the chance of Anglo-Russian hostilities in the near east arising from the Russo-Turkish War of 1877. Sher Ali declined closer relations with Britain, only for a Russian mission to arrive uninvited. Lytton demanded that Britain be represented similarly; but when that representation was denied access, and even turned back at the frontier, even though the Russian mission had been ordered to withdraw by the Russian government, Lytton obtained British governmental approval for the strongest possible action. An ultimatum was issued to Sher Ali, who appealed to the Russian governor of Turkestan for assistance; but none was forthcoming, and when no reply was received from Sher Ali by the date demanded, 20 November 1878, British troops invaded Afghanistan.

Three British columns were employed. Lieutenant-General Sir Donald Stewart's Kandahar Field Force marched from the south, from Quetta to Kandahar, where they arrived unopposed in January 1879. In the centre, Major-General Frederick Roberts' Kurram Field Force marched from Kohat over the Peiwar Kotal; and Lieutenant- General Sir Sam Browne's Peshawar Valley Field Force in the north marched into the Khyber Pass towards Jalalabad. The two latter columns encountered opposition from Afghan forces and from the tribes whose territory they traversed; Roberts found his way blocked at the Peiwar Kotal, so outflanked the Afghan defenders and cleared the way in a sharp action on 2 December 1878. Browne encountered the fort of Ali Masjid ('Ali Musjid' on the clasp of the Afghanistan Medal) and tried without success to capture it (21 November 1878), but the garrison evacuated the position during the night on learning that Browne was endeavouring to outflank them, and most were captured when they retired into the brigade which blocked their escape.

Dost Muhammed. (Unsigned engraving)

Although hostilities by local tribesmen continued against the Kurram and Peshawar forces, Sher Ali fled north, and died at Mazar-i-Sharif in February 1879. With three British columns established in his country, his successor, his son Yakub Khan, decided to negotiate. On 26 May a treaty was concluded at Gandamak, between Yakub and Lytton's representative, Louis Cavagnari, by which the Kurram valley and Khyber Pass were assigned to the British, who gained control of Afghan foreign policy with a mission at Kabul; in return Yakub was recognised as Amir, and both British protection for Afghanistan and an annual subsidy were guaranteed. Lytton was not enthusiastic about Yakub Khan remaining as Amir, but the treaty was welcome in view of some unpopularity at home of the Afghanistan adventure, and of the outbreak of cholera among the British forces. The Peshawar Valley Field Force was withdrawn, with the Kandahar to follow, but Roberts was to remain in the Kurram. Cavagnari, now Sir Louis, went to Kabul as British agent, with a small escort from the Corps of Guides.

Cavagnari entered Kabul on 24 July, but in late August there arrived regiments from Herat, which had been unengaged in the late campaign, were resentful of a foreign presence and were expecting three months' back-pay.

3rd Goorkhas on the march in Afghanistan, 1878; used traditionally by armies in the subcontinent, elephants were used by the British to haul artillery and transport and, as here, occasionally for the conveyance of troops. At this stage of the war the Gurkhas wore their dark green zouave-style uniform with black facings, but later adopted khaki, which was apparently of a slate-blue shade.

When on 3 September they received only one month's pay, they attacked the British Residency. The Amir tried to suppress the unrest (though with how much enthusiasm is unclear), and the attack continued until all four Britons in the mission, and the bulk of the 75 Guides, were dead. The Afghans called upon the few survivors, led by Jemadar Jewand Singh, to surrender and save their lives; but true to their duty, the Guides declined and charged out to their deaths. No more heroic action can ever have taken place than that performed by this small contingent of Guides. (Seven only survived, four who were on duty elsewhere when the attack began, and three sent with unavailing appeals for assistance to Yakub Khan, and who were taken prisoner.)

British reaction was immediate: the order to withdraw from Kandahar was cancelled, and Roberts was ordered to advance on Kabul with a new Kabul Field Force. As he began, Yakub Khan arrived, pleading friendship, and for a period it was maintained that the British were acting on his behalf to suppress rebellion. A strong force of such 'rebels', led by the *sirdar* Nek Muhammed, blocked Roberts' path at Charasia on 6 October; again Roberts dispersed them by executing a flanking manoeuvre. On 8 October Roberts entered Kabul, but Yakub Khan was not restored to his throne; on 12 October he abdicated, claiming that recent experiences had caused him to lose sympathy with his own people. Roberts installed his force in the Sherpur cantonment, a mile from Kabul,

The Khyber Pass and the fort of Ali Masjid (top right); a view published in the Illustrated London News (9 November 1878), based on drawings by none other than Sir Louis Cavagnari (British agent at Kabul, killed in the Afghan attack on the Residency in September 1879) and by Major C. W. Wilson.

Infantry in open order were not supposed to be able to stand fast against cavalry, especially lancers, but the following account of an action in March 1879 at Deh Surruck during the Second Afghan War exemplifies the resistance which could be put up by determined men: '... almost before our leading companies could deploy, the Shinwarries (the pluckiest of all the Afghan tribes) advanced to the left of their village on our right towards us over the broken ground, two companies of the 5th ("H" and "I") and two of the 17th Foot were then extended to the right and ordered to advance, opening fire at six or seven hundred yards on the enemy ... under cover of the smoke from our rifles, and after we had driven the Afghans perhaps a mile or so behind their village, a squadron of native cavalry (13th Bengal Lancers) were posted behind some buildings ... the "Retire" was sounded on the bugles, and the fighting line of Infantry fell back in good order ... on came the Afghans with savage yells, but they had been caught in a trap, the Cavalry ... came charging down on their flank; no sooner did the enemy see the Cavalry bearing down on them than they turned their attention to them, and when barely 200 yards, they poured a ragged volley into the ranks of the advancing horsemen, and several saddles were emptied; having delivered their fire, the Shinwarries formed up in small groups, mostly of four men back to back, and faced their foes like men; the first shock of the Charge over, the Cavalry reformed, and wheeling round, charged once more; after this the scene was for some time a confused mass of riderless horses, dead Afghans and troopers, and here and there individual combats and hand-to-hand fights, this went on for some ten or fifteen minutes, the Cavalry then reformed and retired towards the village, the Infantry now advanced, and ... covered the retreat ... nearly all the way back to Bassoule the column was fired on, and our Flank and Rear Guards had their work cut out for them ...'
('Some Afghan Days' by 'M. J', in *St. George's Gazette* (regimental journal of the 5th Fusiliers), vol. IX, Dover, 1891, pp. 180–1. In this action 'H' company of the 5th alone expended 3,260 rounds, more than 65 rounds per man)

The next major action was fought in April 1880, when Sir Donald Stewart (having left the defence of Kandahar to Major- General J. M. Primrose) marched towards Kabul; he encountered a force of tribesmen near Ghanzi, and defeated them in a rather desperate fight at Ahmad Khel on 19 April.

Yakub Khan had two possible successors: his brother Ayub Khan, governing Herat, and Abdur Rahman, a nephew of Sher Ali. Anxious to leave Afghanistan, and needing to find a practicable choice as Amir, the new viceroy, Lord Ripon, overcame his doubts and on 22 July 1880 Abdur Rahman was proclaimed Amir, on condition that he follow British advice in regard to foreign policy; in return he was to receive British protection from external aggression. The province of Kandahar was removed from

General Sir Samuel James Browne, VC (1824–1901) one of the great heroes of the Indian Army, after whom the 'Sam Browne' belt was named. Commissioned as ensign in December 1840, he served at Chillianwalla and Gujerat, and lost his left arm when capturing a cannon during the Indian Mutiny, at Seerporah, 31 August 1858, for which he was awarded his VC. As a lieutenant-general he commanded the Peshawar Field Force at Ali Masjid in the Second Afghan War. The breast-stars seen in this portrait are those of the Orders of the Bath (GCB) and Star of India (KCSI).

which though fortified was so large that its defence was difficult with the 7,000 troops at Roberts' disposal. In December, Afghan forces gathered in opposition to the occupation of their capital, and after some actions in which Roberts sought to disperse them in detail, by 14 December he was virtually besieged in Sherpur. On 23 December a mighty assault, involving up to 100,000 Afghans, was beaten off by Roberts who lost only three dead, and his pursuit of the retiring Afghans completed their discomfiture.

Attacks on outlying detachments were commonplace on the Indian frontiers, so that even strong concentrations of troops could never feel entirely secure. Typical everyday occurrences were recorded by Captain Arbuthnott Dunbar of the 92nd Highlanders when serving with the Kurrum Valley Field Force in the Second Afghan War in 1879:

'Thull, 31st March. Last night 5 grass cutters of the 14th Bengal Lancers were cut to bits. We now have picquets and sentries round the camp and their rifles are loaded. The Kurrum River is just below us. Thull is only a mud village but now of course surrounded with tents, Commissariat and Warlike Stores ...

'10th April. Peiwar. Arrived here this morning. We are just at the foot of the Peiwar Kotal and right up at the top of the Kurrum Valley which we look down upon... The first place we saw was a new little cemetery in which were 6 graves of men killed: one was poor Captain Goad (Hyderabad Contingent). A neat wooden cross with his name, etc. was at the head. We next went to the forts of which there are two – one our company is in – it is simply a courtyard surrounded by a mud wall ... There were 7 prisoners brought into the fort yesterday for having cut up five grass cutters. Villainous looking rascals, they had sentries with loaded rifles over them! When Napier put his hand round his throat and rolled his eyes playfully to imitate that they would probably be hung, they grinned!

'12th April. Peiwar. Yesterday between this and the Kotal an unfortunate Syce was fired at 5 times, 2 hit him and three brutes then hacked him about with swords. Fortunately three of the 8th were there and shot some of the scoundrels. The prisoners we saw in Kurrum have been shot ...'

('Napier' was Lieutenant the Hon. John Scott Napier, second son of 10th Baron Napier, who rose to command the 2nd Battalion Gordon Highlanders 1895–7. The author is grateful to Sir Archibald Dunbar, Bt. for permission to quote these letters)

the control of Kabul, and Sher Ali Khan, a member of the Barakzai family, was installed as its ruler as Wali of Kandahar. Ayub Khan, however, was anxious to extend his power by seizing Kandahar, and to oppose his forces the Wali requested British support. This Primrose provided in the form of a brigade under Brigadier-General G. S. Burrows (66th Foot, 1st and 30th Bombay Infantry, and supports); but the Wali's troops fled, leaving Burrows' 2,600 men exposed and greatly outnumbered by Ayub Khan. On 26 July Burrows' brigade was overwhelmed and virtually annihilated at Maiwand, the 66th making a gallant and famous 'last stand'. The survivors reached Kandahar, which was besieged almost immediately.

Upon receiving news of this catastrophe, Roberts marched out of Kabul with a mobile force of some 10,000 men, a minimum of baggage and only mountain artillery carried on mule-back; for three weeks they marched over mountains and desert burning by day and freezing by night, devoid of support and communication. Averaging some fifteen miles per day, Kandahar, some 300 miles away, was reached on 31 August; the exploit not only confirmed Roberts' reputation as the leading Indian commander of his day, but so arduous was the march and so remarkable the achievement that a campaign medal was struck in commemoration, the 'Kabul to Kandahar Star', one of the few awards for a manoeuvre rather than for an

A wide variety of campaign uniform-styles, worn by officers of the 4th Battalion, Rifle Brigade in Afghanistan, 1879. The commanding officer, Lieutenant-Colonel (later Lieutenant-General Sir) Henry Richard Legge Newdigate, is seated third from left, wearing a fur poshteen; standing second from right is 2nd Lieutenant (later Lieutenant-General Sir) Henry Fuller Maitland Wilson, who commanded the British 4th Division in France and Flanders 1914–15, and XII Corps in Macedonia 1915–17.

The death of Major Wigram Battye of the Corps of Guides at Fatehabad, Afghanistan, 2 April 1879. Battye was one of the most famous names in the Indian Army, especially in the Guides. Four sons of George Wynyard Battye of the Bengal Civil Service won considerable fame in India: Wigram; Lieutenant Quintin Battye of The Guides, killed at Delhi in 1857; Major Legh Battye, 5th Gurkhas, killed by Black Mountain tribesmen in 1888; and Lieutenant-Colonel Frederick Battye, Commandant of the Guides, killed in the Chitral campaign in 1895. Legh's son, Lieutenant Richmond Battye of the 6th Bengal Cavalry, was killed in the Tirah campaign in 1897. (Engraving after Richard Caton Woodville)

actual combat. On 1 September Roberts defeated Ayub Khan in an action outside Kandahar, which effectively brought to an end the Second Afghan War.

The policy of dividing Afghanistan was abandoned, and British forces were withdrawn as Abdur Rahman extended his rule over the entire country, Sher Ali Khan abandoning Kandahar when it became obvious that he would no longer have British military support. The merits of the British involvement in the country were debatable; although it involved much gallantry, made some reputations and destroyed others (neither Burrows nor Primrose ever received further employment, for example), and did establish on the throne of Afghanistan a ruler with whom

the British could co-operate, the cost was severe. Despite the British victories, some of the most abiding memories of their involvement in Afghanistan were of the disasters suffered by Elphinstone and at Maiwand, two of the most severe defeats suffered during the entire period of 'colonial' warfare.

Military Forces: Second Afghan War

The Afghan forces which fought the British in 1878–80 were considerably different from those encountered in the First Afghan War, as a consequence of Sher Ali's construction of a regular army. British intelligence reports before the war estimated that it comprised 62 infantry reg-

The arrival of Yakub Khan at Gandamak, prior to the conclusion of the treaty at that place, May 1879. Yakub Khan leads the cavalcade, flanked by General Sir Sam Browne (on his right) and Louis Cavagnari (on his left). Immediately behind Browne, and wearing a European topee, is the Afghan commander-in-chief, Daud Shah. (Engraving after William Simpson)

Above: Typical warriors of the North-West Frontier and Afghanistan, armed with the characteristically curved stock jezail. (Unsigned engraving)

Above right: Afghan cavalrymen, 1879: Byram from Herat and Futteh Mohammed from Kelat-i-Ghilzai, sketched by William Simpson who remarked on their 'large black sheepskin caps, the

long hair of which came down over the eyes and face, giving a wild look to the wearers. They said this was the Turcoman style of head-dress, and that it was common with the troops at Herat and along the northern border of Afghanistan' (Illustrated London News, 27 September 1879). (Engraving by F. Dadd after William Simpson)

iments (nominally of 690 men each, although there was probably considerable variation, the total infantry force being estimated at 37,200 men), sixteen cavalry regiments of 600 men, and 49 6-gun artillery batteries, 22 of horse artillery, eighteen mountain-gun mule batteries, seven drawn by bullocks and two by elephants. Although equipped with a mix of old and new ordnance, the artillery was adjudged to be the most proficient element of the army and performed creditably during the war; and although only a minority of pieces were breech-loading, rifled guns, the same was true of the British artillery. The infantry carried a wide variety of firearms, including Sniders, Enfields, rifled carbines and even old Brunswick and 'Brown Bess' muskets. A considerable amount of the regular army's weaponry was originally supplied by Britain: the heavy artillery battery, for example (four 18pdrs and two 8in howitzers), 5,000 Sniders and 29,000

muzzle-loading firearms, had been presented to the Amir by Britain. The army's uniforms were similarly mixed, and may even have included old British clothing, perhaps the red tunics worn by some cavalry (with blue trousers and black felt or fur caps); other cavalry wore blue, with brass helmets. The infantry generally wore brown with red facings, and black caps, but the most bizarre unit was the Amir's 'Highland Guard', which dressed in an imitation of British Highland uniform, with red Scottish-style doublet, red-and-white checked 'kilt' over red trousers, and British-style white sun-helmets; they were armed with Sniders. For the regular army at least, there were few problems with regard to the supply of munitions: ammunition and Afghan copies of Snider and Enfield firearms could be manufactured without difficulty at Kabul.

The regular army was dispersed in garrisons around the country, from which locations come the terms of

Lord Roberts recounts a story demonstrating the characteristic devotion of his two Sikh and two Gurkha orderlies, under fire in Afghanistan in 1878:
'My orderlies during this little episode displayed such touching devotion that it is with feelings of the most profound admiration and gratitude I call to mind their self-sacrificing courage. On this (as on many other occasions) they kept close round me, determined that no shot should reach me if they could prevent it; and on my being hit in the hand by a spent bullet, and turning to look round in the direction it came from, I beheld one of the Sikhs standing with his arms stretched out trying to screen me from the enemy, which he could easily do, for he was a grand specimen of a man, a head and shoulders taller than myself.'
(*Forty-One Years in India*, London, 1900, p. 361)

Kabul, Kandahar or Herat regiments, etc., and although there was some jealousy between regiments and garrisons, discipline was not so affected as to preclude regiments from one garrison from collaborating with those from others; at Maiwand, for example, there were five regiments from Kabul, three from Herat and one from Kandahar. Central control was not sufficiently strong, however, to prevent parts of the army from following a local leader, as in the case of those regiments which formed part of Ayub Khan's army. Some turbulence was evident within the ranks, especially when they nursed a grievance, exemplified by the attack by the Heratis on the British Residency at Kabul.

In addition to the regular army, there was a considerable force of irregulars which could be mobilised by the Amir or by individual *sirdars*; the Amir paid some *sirdars* for the maintenance of some 24,000 irregulars in peacetime, and many more could be mobilised for war. They were armed, equipped and fought in much the same manner as during the First Afghan War and as the tribes of the North-West Frontier. It was perhaps in reference to these irregulars that Lord Roberts remarked that long-range fire was not usual: 'Afghans seldom play at long bowls, it being necessary for them to husband their ammunition, and when ... they outnumber their adversary by forty to one, they universally try to come to close quarters and use their knives.'[7]

Afghanistan after 1880

Abdur Rahman remained as Amir until the end of the century, although not without opposition: once the British had left, Ayub Khan took possession of Kandahar in July 1881, but was defeated outside that city by Abdur Rahman on 22 September 1881, and as his base of Herat had been taken by one of the Amir's generals, he sought refuge in Persia. Ayub Khan made another attempt from Persia, and the Amir's cousin, Ishak Khan, rebelled in Afghan

Turkestan, but both were unsuccessful, and Abdur Rahman enforced his control over the country more completely than had been achieved by his predecessors. During discussions to fix the northern boundary of Afghanistan, disputed with Russia, there occurred a potential cause of war in the 'Pendjeh (or Pandjeh) incident', when that place, in the disputed territory, was attacked by Russian troops and its Afghan defenders driven out (30 March 1885). Abdur Rahman was at that time in conference at Rawalpindi with the viceroy, Lord Dufferin, and given the British assurance to protect Afghanistan from external threat, the potential existed of Anglo-Russian conflict; but the crisis was overcome by diplomacy, and Russia agreed to resume negotiations regarding the frontier. These were completed by an Anglo-Russian Boundary Commission, and the frontier was agreed in 1887; but the 'Pendjeh incident' and the continuing Russian expansionism caused alarm in India, leading to reforms in the Indian Army and the improvement of communications with the frontier, so that troops could be conveyed there by rail or road with greater ease than before, to facilitate resistance to any Russian threat. The boundary between Afghanistan and British India was fixed by the 'Durand Line' in 1893.

For the first time in Afghanistan's history, Abdur Rahman established a centralised administration to unify and hold in check any dissident elements within his territory; he maintained friendly relations with, and received assistance from, British India, but maintained a strict policy of permitting no foreign interference in internal affairs. He confirmed his control by the maintenance of a regular army which avoided the complications of the *jagir* system. The standing army was distributed in the major garrisons and along the borders, and in 1896 a system of semi-conscription was introduced, by which one man in every eight aged between 16 and 70 took a turn at military training, by which it was calculated that this 'reserve' force would produce an army a million strong, trained and armed with modern weapons, had transport and finance been sufficient to permit their mobilisation. Such was the strength of Abdur Rahman's administration that his death (1 October 1901) was not followed by civil war or a disputed succession, for the first time in generations. His son, Habibulla, was accepted as Amir and reigned until his assassination in 1919, which was followed by the Third Afghan War. Ironically, Yakub Khan outlived not only Abdur Rahman but also his son; he died in 1923, having reigned in Afghanistan for less than a year and having lived as a pensioner of the British for the next forty-four.

Notes
1. Keane's dispatch, 24 July 1839, *London Gazette*, 30 October 1839.
2. 'Cabool' by Colonel Blacker, in *Colburn's United Service Magazine*, 1843, vol. II, p. 173.
3. 'Journal of the Last Three Months' Operations in Afghanistan', by 'An Officer of Her Majesty's Service', in *Colburn's United Service Magazine*, 1843, vol. I, p. 335.

4. 'The Cabool Captives', by Captain J. Airey, in *Colburn's United Service Magazine*, 1846, vol. I, p. 266.

5. For a history of this formation, see 'Shah Shujah's Force', by Brigadier-General H. Biddulph, in *Journal of the Society for Army Historical Research*, vol. XX, 1941.

6. 'On the Errors and Faults in our Military System', by Colonel Firebrace, in *Colburn's United Service Magazine*, 1843, vol. I, pp. 55–6.

7. Lord Roberts of Kandahar, *Forty-One Years in India*, London, 1900, p. 434.

References

Barthorp, M. *The North-West Frontier: British India and Afghanistan, a Pictorial History*, Poole, 1982.

Bruce, G. *Retreat from Kabul*, London, 1969.

Diver, M. *Kabul to Kandahar*, London, 1935.

Edwardes, M. *Playing the Great Game: A Victorian Cold War. British and Russian involvement in Afghanistan*, London, 1975.

Eyre, Lieutenant V. *The Military Operations at Cabul*, London, 1843.

Featherstone, D. *Victoria's Enemies: An A–Z of British Colonial Warfare*, London, 1989.

Forbes, A. *The Afghan Wars 1839–42, 1878–80*, London, 1892.

Gleig, Revd. G. R. *Sale's Brigade in Afghanistan, with an Account of the Seizure and Defence of Jellalabad*, London, 1846.

Greenwood, Lieutenant. H. M. *Narrative of the Late Victorious Campaign in Affghanistan [sic] under General Pollock; with Recollections of Seven Years' Service in India*, London, 1844.

Hanna, Colonel. H. B. *The Second Afghan War 1878–79–80*, London, 1899–1910.

Heathcote, T. A. *The Afghan Wars 1839–1919*, London, 1980.

Hensman, H., *The Afghan War 1879–80*, London, 1881.

Hough, Major. V. *A Narrative of the March and Operations of the Bengal Column of the Army of Indus in the expedition to Afghanistan in the years 1838–1839*, London, 1841.

Kaye, J. *History of the War in Afghanistan*, London, 1857.

Knight, I. *Queen Victoria's Enemies (3): India*, London, 1990.

Macrory, P. *Signal Catastrophe: The Story of the Disastrous Retreat from Kabul 1842*, London, 1966.

MacMunn, Lieutenant-General Sir George, *Afghanistan, from Darius to Amanullah*, London, 1929.

Maxwell, L. *My God! – Maiwand: Operations of the South Afghanistan Field Force 1878–80*, London, 1979.

Norris, J. A. *The First Afghan War 1838–1842*, Cambridge, 1967.

Richards, D. S. *The Savage Frontier: A History of the Anglo-Afghan Wars*, London, 1990.

Robson, B. *The Road to Kabul: The Second Afghan War, 1878–1881*, London, 1986 (outstanding modern study: includes a comprehensive bibliography).

Sale, Lady. *A Journal of the Disasters in Affghanistan [sic] 1841–2*, London, 1843; r/p as *Lady Sale: The First Afghan War*, ed. P. Macrory, London, 1969.

Shadbolt, S. H. *The Afghan Campaigns of 1878–80*, London, 1882.

ARABIA

British naval and military operations in the Arabian peninsula were usually undertaken in support of an ally or in the protection of trade, rather than as a policy of colonisation. One of Britain's principal allies in the region was the ruler of Oman, the state on the eastern littoral of the Arabian peninsula, commanding the Gulf of Oman, which leads via the Straits of Hormuz into the Persian Gulf. The coast of Oman was occupied by the Portuguese until 1650, when Persia occupied the region. Persian domination ended in 1759 when Ahmad Ibn Säid expelled them and established the Ghafari dynasty; in 1798 his son made a treaty with the East India Company, designed to exclude the French from Oman. During the early part of the 19th century, Oman was at war with the Wahhabi empire, named after the puritanical Islamic movement which originated in Nejd, founded by Ibn 'Abd ul-Wahhab, who was said to have died in 1791, and to which empire Oman was for a time a tributary. Ahmad Ibn Säid's grandson, Sayyid (Sultan) Säid, who reigned from 1804 to 1856, finally achieved the independence of Oman after the overthrow of the Wahhabi empire by Egypt in 1817–18, but a number of British expeditions to the region were necessary. The first of these was organised in 1809, to discourage the piracy of the Jāwasimi (or 'Qawasim') Arabs, Wahhabites who preyed upon shipping in the Gulf region. Mounted from Bombay, the force was commanded by Lieutenant-Colonel Lionel Smith of the 65th Foot and comprised his regiment, the flank companies of the 47th, the 2nd Bombay Native Infantry, and artillery, with the 36-gun frigates *Caroline* and *La Chiffonne*. Leaving Bombay in September 1809, the expedition attacked and reduced the pirate stronghold of Ras al-Khaima on the so-called 'Pirate Coast' of the south-eastern littoral of the Persian Gulf, and dismantled the old Portuguese fort there. On 27 December the expedition arrived off Linga (Bander Lingah, on the Persian side of the Straits of Hormuz) and destroyed another nest of piracy.

In 1817 the Jāwasimi pirates again became troublesome, and as naval forces were found to be insufficient to suppress them, a second expedition was organised from Bombay in 1819, under Major-General Sir William Grant Keir; again the 65th and flank companies of the 47th were employed, with the 1/2nd, 11th, and flank companies of the 1/3rd Bombay Native Infantry, conveyed by East India ships and the 50-gun 4th rater HMS *Liverpool*. Attempts were made to negotiate with the Jāwasimi pirates, via the Sultan of Oman, but these proving fruitless, Keir disembarked at Ras al-Khaima on 3 December. A bombardment by 24pdr guns landed from *Liverpool* breached the defences, but when stormed on 10 December the garrison was found to have escaped. The British units were sent to a reported concentration of Arabs at the hill fort of Zaya, but by 18 December Keir reported that all pirate strongholds had been destroyed and that their chiefs had submitted. For these operations, and those of 1809, the 65th received the unique battle-honour 'Arabia'.

A third expedition was necessary in 1821, occasioned by the piracy and hostility of the Beni Bu Ali tribe, resident at that fortified place ('Beni Boo Alli' in contemporary spelling), about 50 miles south of the port of Soor (south of Muscat: not to be confused with Sohar, to the north). In 1820 the Sultan's troops, with six companies of Native

Infantry under a Captain Thomson, were sent against them, but were routed; only a remnant regained Soor, from where they had advanced. Consequently, a punitive expedition was organised under Lionel Smith, now a Major-General, comprising the 65th Foot, 2nd Bombay Europeans, 2/1st and 1/7th Bombay Native Infantry, a battalion formed from the flank companies of the 2/2nd, 1/3rd, 1/4th, 2/9th and 1/11th Bombay Native Infantry, and detachments of Bombay Horse and Foot Artillery. The expedition landed at Soor on 28 January 1821, and on 10 February their camp near Soor was attacked by an Arab force which penetrated the lines of the Bombay Europeans, but was driven off. Leaving a garrison at Soor, Smith advanced and on 2 March completely defeated the Arabs in a fierce combat outside Beni Boo Alli, culminating in the surrender of the fort. All the guns captured by the Arabs in the earlier action were recovered. The destruction of their fort and ships (in separate operations) again brought the pirates to submission. (The British naval forces involved again included HMS *Liverpool*, with the frigates *Eden* and *Topaze*, and the brig-sloop *Curlew*.)

Sultan Sāid expanded his possessions during his long rule, his capital at Muscat becoming an especially prosperous port, and established his rule in Zanzibar. On his death in 1856 a younger son took possession of the latter, and several dynastic disputes occurred in subsequent years over the throne of Oman; the British and French governments guaranteed the independence of the Sultan in 1862, and latterly he was paid a subsidy from British-Indian revenue, in return for a guarantee not to cede any territory without British approval. Minor British operations took place in the region during subsequent years: in 1883 Muscat was besieged by the rebellious chief of the Rchbayin, who was responsible for holding the Wadi Kahza, the pass into the interior, in the name of the Sultan; this threat to Muscat was dispersed by the presence of the British gunboat HMS *Philomel*. In 1895, with Turkish encouragement, Sheikh Jasim ben Thani of Qatar attacked Sheikh Isa of Bahrein, but his fleet was destroyed by the Royal Navy, and Bahrein was subsequently detached from Oman and taken directly under British protection.

Britain's only colony in Arabia was established at Aden, an important post at the entrance to the Red Sea, and of consequent significance to the 'overland' route to India. (The island of Perim, at the entrance to the Red Sea, had been occupied by an expedition from Bombay as early as 1798, and a garrison was maintained there during the 1801 Egyptian expedition; abandoned after the French war, it was not occupied again by Britain until 1857). In 1835 an agreement was made with the local Sultan for the use of Aden as a British coaling station, but following the maltreatment of the crew of a wrecked British ship in 1837, the Sultan agreed with the Bombay government to make restitution and to sell his port to the British. Captain Stafford Haines of the Indian (i.e., East India Company's) Navy was sent to complete the negotiation, but the objection of the Sultan's son and local chiefs resulted in the dispatch of a small expedition to take possession in 1839: elements of the 1st Bombay Europeans, 24th Bombay Native Infantry, Bombay Artillery and Marine Battalion, under Major T. M. Bailie of the 24th Bombay, together with East India Company ships and the Royal Navy vessels *Volage* (frigate) and *Cruizer* (brig-sloop). Their landing (19 January 1839) was opposed, but a bombardment covered the disembarkation and the local Arabs surrendered. Aden was annexed to British India, and after some skirmishing in November 1839 and May 1840, no further threats were made against British possession. British territory was some 80 square miles in extent (including Perim), but the hinterland of the Aden Protectorate, whose chieftains were under British political control, extended to some 9,000 square miles; administration was conducted by a political Resident, who was also the military commander. Politically, Aden was part of British India, under the government and, later, governorship of Bombay. The garrison maintained there was under the control of the Bombay Army, and there was later an Aden Brigade under Indian Army control.

The territory's own military force originated in 1855 with the formation of the Aden Troop, from members of the Scinde Horse, reconstituted in October 1867 under Lieutenant C. B. Myers, with volunteers from the 1st and 2nd Scinde and Poona Horse, and including an Arab Levy to act as guides. In 1890 the latter unit was reduced to just six men, and the troop substituted 50 camels for 50 of its horses, the camel-borne detachment approximating to mounted infantry. Its services were mostly in patrolling against bandits, including a punitive expedition in April 1871 which killed a noted bandit, Mohammed-bin-Sherwet, and included a march of 78 miles in 24 hours, over heavy sand. Also significant was an expedition in January 1890 against the Mamasin section of the Eesa Somel people, involving the Aden Troop, detachments of the 17th Bombay Infantry and Sappers and Miners, and a naval landing-party with two Gatling guns from HMS *Ranger*; it included the defeat of a nocturnal attack upon the force's *zareba* on 29 January, in which the Eesa were dispersed, despite having penetrated the *zareba* by using spears as vaulting-poles to clear the hedge. The Aden Troop also served in Somaliland from 1887 to the end of the century; the troop existed until 1929.

References

Lees, Major A. W. H. 'A Forgotten Battle: Belad Beni Bu Ali, 1821', in *Journal of the Society for Army Historical Research*, vol. XIV, 1935, pp.

166–9; note that the spelling adopted for the battle-honour was 'Beni Boo Alli'.
Moyse-Bartlett, Lieutenant-Colonel H. *The Pirates of Trucial Oman*, London, 1966

BURMA

Burma's geographical position in relation to British India (adjoining eastern Bengal and Assam) brought its inhabitants into contact with the British; but during the second half of the 18th century most of Burma's military effort was expended in internal warfare or in conflict with China and Siam. The internal struggle was between the Burmans and the Peguans (Talaings or Mons), supported by the British and French respectively (Dupleix sent two ships to support the Peguans); but they were defeated by Alaungpaya (or Alompra), a chieftain whose military skill made him master of the country. Britain established a trading post at Negraid, but it was destroyed in 1759 by Alaungpaya, who suspected the British of assisting the Peguans. The remainder of the century was occupied by wars involving Burmese attempts to conquer Siam, ultimately unsuccessful, and the successful resistance to a Chinese invasion. In 1795 the Burmese were involved in a dispute with British India over a force which entered the Chittagong district in pursuit of robbers, and further friction became inevitable: the Burmese protested about the use of British territory as bases for Arakanese rebels (1811–15), and there were Burmese forays into territory under British protection.

First Burma War

Burmese encroachments resulted in the first serious outbreak of Anglo–Burmese hostilities; in the south, on the Chittagong frontier, a party of Burmese attacked a British detachment at Shahpuri Island on 24 September 1823, and in the north in January 1824 two Burmese armies, from Manipur and Assam (which the Burmese had conquered in 1819) entered Cachar, which was under British protection. In response, war was declared on Burma on 5 March 1824.

The British planned to drive the Burmese from the territory recently taken in Assam, but otherwise to adopt a defensive posture there and on the Chittagong frontier, and to concentrate upon an attack by sea on Rangoon. The Burmese, however, assembled some 30,000 men under General Maha Bandula for operations on the Chittagong front, and overran a small sepoy force at Ramu on 17 May 1824. The British positions around Chittagong were reinforced, and an expedition, drawn principally from the Bengal Army, was sent by the coastal route into Arakan, commanded by Brigadier-General J. W. Morrison and collaborating with a naval flotilla. Burmese failure to capitalise upon their initial success prevented much action until the British advance began on 1 January 1825, which continued until the city of Myohaung was taken on 31 March.

The main British seaborne expedition, comprised mainly of Madras units, was commanded by Brigadier-General Sir Archibald Campbell, and assembled in the Andaman Islands. On 10 May 1824 it landed at Rangoon which was almost undefended. With the end of the rainy season in late October, the Burmese court at Ava recalled Maha Bandula from Arakan, and by late November the British at Rangoon were surrounded by a Burmese army perhaps 60,000 strong. Desperate attacks were made against the British positions (notably at Kemmendine, for their defence of which the 26th Madras Native Infantry were awarded the name of that place as a battle-honour), but a British counter-attack on 15 December defeated Bandula and scattered his forces. Campbell's short dispatch announcing the victory contained a telling comment: 'When it is known that thirteen hundred British

The landing at Rangoon, 11 May 1824: under cover of naval bombardment, troops are rowed ashore in ships' boats. The flag resembling a White Ensign with red horizontal stripes is the naval ensign of the East India Company, known (from the design) as 'the gridiron'.

Burmese troops wearing the distinctive, bell-shaped helmet.

infantry stormed and carried by assault the most formidable entrenched and stockaded works I ever saw, defended by upwards of twenty thousand men, I trust it is unnecessary for me to say more in praise of men performing such a prodigy; future ages will scarcely believe it.'[1] (The troops concerned were 700 men drawn from the 13th, 38th, 41st and 89th Foot and Madras Europeans, and 600 from the 9th, 12th, 18th, 28th, 30th and 34th Madras Native Infantry; Campbell classed them all as British.)

Campbell decided to advance on Prome, some hundred miles higher up the Irrawaddy, beginning on 13 February 1825; the first attack upon the Burmese position at Danubyu ('Donabew') having failed, he concentrated his force and took it unopposed on 2 April, Bandula having been killed by a rocket. On 25 April Prome was entered and Campbell remained there for the rainy season; as much as the determined Burmese resistance, the terrain, rains and unhealthy climate proved a severe test for the British forces. During the summer Morrison made progress in Arakan, and the Burmese were cleared from Assam; but in late November a determined attack was mounted against Campbell at Prome by a large Burmese army which was beaten off, and then dispersed when Campbell counter-attacked on 1 December, the Burmese commander, Maha Nemyo, being killed. The Burmese retired up the Irrawaddy to the fortified position at Malun, and on 26 December 1825 sued for peace. A treaty was negotiated, but when it appeared that the Burmese were preparing for further conflict, Campbell attacked and carried the Malun position (19 January 1826). The Burmese withdrew to the ancient city of Pagan for a final defence

before the capital, Ava; there they were defeated on 9 February, and with the British only four days' march from Ava, they accepted the terms negotiated previously. By the Treaty of Yandaboo, Burma ceded the Arakan to Britain, renounced claims upon Assam and other frontier regions, and agreed to pay an indemnity; the British expedition then withdrew.

Second Burma War

Relations between Britain and Burma remained pacific as long as the king who had signed the treaty, Ba-ggi-daw, was in power; but he was supplanted by his brother, Tharrawaddi, in 1837, who gave evidence of his dislike of the British, which was continued by the son who succeeded him in 1846, Pagan. On 15 March 1852 Lord Dalhousie issued an ultimatum concerning Burmese transgressions of the treaty and hostilities towards British ships and trade; when no reply was received, an expedition was dispatched under Lieutenant-General Henry Godwin, as before collaborating with a naval force. On 5 April this expedition took Martaban, and Rangoon on 12–14 April, when the Burmese army retired northwards; on 19 May Bassein was taken, and on 3 June Pegu, after a sharp fight around the Shwe-maw-daw pagoda. During the cessation of hostilities for the rainy season, it was decided to annex the lower Irrawaddy valley; consequently, Godwin occupied Prome on 9 October. In December 1852 Pagan was informed by Dalhousie that the province of Pegu was henceforth British, and that resistance would result in the destruction of his kingdom. The official proclamation of annexation was issued on 20 January 1853.

Third Burma War

In February 1853 King Pagan was dethroned by a revolt against his oppressive rule, and the leader of the revolt, Mindon, was crowned as his successor. While not provoking British military action, King Mindon initially refused to accept the British occupation of Pegu, but accepted a British envoy at his court in 1855. In 1862 the province of 'British Burma' was created (later Lower Burma), and in 1867 a treaty was agreed at Mandalay which established normal diplomatic relations between Britain and Burma. Upon Mindon's death in 1878, however, he was succeeded by his son, Thibaw ('Theebaw'), whose rule caused some internal unrest; the British Resident was withdrawn in 1879, but Thibaw encouraged diplomatic contacts with France and Italy. Finally, Burmese interference with British trade, and the imposition of a huge fine upon the Bombay–Burma Trading Corporation, prompted the viceroy, Lord Dufferin, to issue an ultimatum (22 October 1885), demanding protection of British subjects and interests. On 7 November Thibaw instructed his subjects to drive the British into the sea, and two days later his rejection of the ultimatum was received in Rangoon.

Consequently, the British assembled three brigades under the command of Major-General Harry Prendergast (who had won the Victoria Cross in the Indian Mutiny), intent on the removal of Thibaw. The British advanced at such speed that the Burmese had little chance to organise; using some 55 vessels (many belonging to the Irrawaddy Flotilla Company and available for use at Rangoon), they pushed up the Irrawaddy, engaging and neutralising Burmese shore-batteries, and on 17 November dispersed a Burmese force at Minha. On 26 November, as the flotilla approached Ava, Thibaw offered to surrender, and on the following day ordered his army to lay down its arms. On 28 November Mandalay was occupied, and with Thibaw in custody, the war was over in less than a fortnight.

Upper Burma was annexed formally by the British on 1 January 1886, but elements of the Burmese army, which had been permitted to disperse with their arms, became guerrillas or bands of dacoit bandits. The problems they caused were so serious that reinforcements had to be sent from India, and much arduous service was experienced amid the jungles as successive operations were mounted against the dacoits. Command of the British forces passed to General Macpherson in September 1886, and after his death a month later, to Sir Frederick Roberts. The areas of Lower Burma (that territory acquired after the First Burma War) and Upper Burma (the remainder, annexed 1886) were administered as provinces of India.

Later Operations

The task of pacifying the country proved more difficult than the overthrow of Thibaw, in part because of the nature of the terrain and the fragmented nature of the opposition, largely bands of marauders or self-appointed 'princes' whose depredations fell as much upon the civilian inhabitants of the region as upon the British. (The British tended to regard all the guerrillas as mere bandits, making no distinction between criminals and those motivated by a desire to combat the occupation of their country.) Roberts established a network of posts and deployed small, lightly equipped columns to disperse reported gatherings of bandits, but the privations of waging such operations through heavy jungle were considerable. A measure of the nature of the service is the fact that in addition to the India General Service Medal's clasp 'Burma 1885–87', awarded for service in the Third Burma War and subsequent operations, two additional clasps were authorised, 'Burma 1887–89' and 'Burma 1889–92', for service in the 'pacification' operations, the latter awarded for no less than eleven separate operations during a three-year period. Finally, order was in general restored, and the system by which individual villages were made responsible for maintaining order in their vicinity was found to be most effective.

Some operations took place in the border states between India and Burma; in addition to those noted in the section on India, others included:

Chin-Lushai expedition: the Chin Hills form a mountainous district of Upper Burma between the Lushai district of eastern Bengal and the plains of Burma. The Chins, Lushais and Kukis of Manipur, believed to be of similar Tibetan origin, caused some turbulence by raiding from their own territories. With the British occupation of Upper Burma, it was possible to penetrate their mountainous country from two sides, as in the Chin-Lushai expedition of November 1889–April 1890, in which the Burma Column of Brigadier-General W. P. Symons operated against the Chins, and the Chittagong Column of General Tregear against the Lushai.

Chin Hills expedition: further punitive operations occurred in the Chin Hills, under Brigadier-General Palmer, between October 1892 and March 1893.

Kachin Hills expeditions: the Kachin Hills form a mountainous district of Upper Burma, inhabited by the Kachin people (known as 'Singphos' on the Assam frontier). To deter their raiding, numerous small actions were necessary, and two larger expeditions. British occupation of Bhamo from December 1885 initiated trouble with the Kachins, but the main hostilities were Kachin attacks on a police column and settlements in December 1892; an expedition was put in hand immediately and the rising had been crushed by March 1893. From 1895 a definitive northern border was established, the British taking responsibility for the Kachin tribes on their side; those to the north were told they would be unmolested provided that they did not raid into British territory, but continued bad behaviour necessitated the dispatch of two small columns in December 1895 which quickly suppressed the trouble. It remained necessary to keep a strong police presence in the area as a guard against possible trouble, however.

Military Forces

Although numerous, the Burmese forces were not reckoned as very formidable in the open field, preferring to use bamboo stockades to confine an enemy, or to defend positions fortified by stockades and rifle pits. During the First Burma War their forces were largely 'tribal', only a proportion being armed with muskets, the remainder carrying traditional spears and swords (*dah*s); for example, Campbell reported the Burmese at Danubyu as consisting of 15,000 men, only 10,000 of whom were 'musketeers', and a typical collection of arms was that captured on 7 March 1825 at an advanced post at Danubyu, including four iron 6pdrs, two iron 4pdrs, 58 *jingal*s, 362 muskets and 630 spears. The artillery was mixed and not especially well-served: a typical array of ordnance was captured at Danubyu, including 28 brass guns (of nine different 'natures', including seven 1pdrs, twelve 2pdrs and one 9pdr), 110 iron guns (of fifteen 'natures', including twenty-four 3pdrs, twenty 4pdrs, two 1½pdrs and one 24pdr), one iron 12pdr carronade and 269 *jingal*s. They did, however, possess a flotilla of what were described as 'first-rate war-boats' for river navigation, an unusual form of military force. It was not uncommon for elephants to be used as artillery teams (even the British employed them), but as a form of 'fighting vehicle' they were not common; yet, as Campbell reported concerning a Burmese sortie from Danubyu, 'a scene at once novel and

interesting presented itself ... Seventeen large elephants, each carrying a complement of armed men, and supported by a column of infantry, were observed moving towards our right flank: I directed the body guard, under Captain Sneyd, to charge them, and they acquitted themselves most handsomely, mixing boldly with the elephants; they shot their riders off their backs, and finally drove the whole back into the fort.'[2] (The unit involved was the Governor-General's Bodyguard, the only cavalry in Campbell's force; it provides a rare example of the use of cavalry firearms in combat, as presumably their sabres would hardly reach men riding in a howdah!)

The proportion of firearms probably increased for the Second Burma War, but the general standard of the 'regular' army probably declined throughout the 19th century, as did the numbers; the army was estimated at 50,000 strong in 1852 but probably was only about 15–20,000 in 1885. The regulars wore coloured jackets (red seems to have been popular but apparently there was little attempt at uniformity), with striped trousers or a loincloth, and a most distinctive, spiked helmet made of lacquered bamboo, somewhat resembling British tropical helmets and similar to bell-shaped or conical head-dress worn at the time of the First Burma War (when they were said to make good targets for British musketry!). Irregulars were equipped in a more primitive fashion, with bows and spears. Contemporary accounts, for example an illustrated article in *The Graphic* of 4 October 1879, depict a force devoid of discipline and armed with guns, spears or

Karens of the Burma Military Police, c.1898. A good source of recruits, the Karen people were hill- and mountain-dwellers, divided into two groups: the Sgaw and Pwo clans, or 'White Karens', many of whom embraced Christianity, and the Bghai or 'Red Karens', the most lawless of the people. These adjectives derived from the colour of their civilian dress.

bamboo canes bearing small pennons, the cavalry mounted impracticably on small native ponies, dressed like the infantry and armed with *dahs*. Field artillery consisted of light pieces dragged by four men, and a battery of 80 elephants each with two small cannon mounted on the howdah. The whole force was described as 'raw levies', undisciplined and much prone to desertion, presumably because of the erratic issue of pay and supplies. Even the river-craft, so well-regarded by Campbell, had declined, so that in 1885 the flotilla was largely out of repair, and like the shore batteries armed with smoothbore ordnance with which the Burmese had little skill.

Probably more formidable, certainly when acting as guerrillas in their own jungle terrain, were the dacoits. They had existed before the British occupation of Burma, the previous administration having been unable to keep them in check; many were just bandits who terrorised the rural villages, but their ranks were swollen by ex-soldiers and those unwilling to accept British annexation of their country. They formed bands under the command of chiefs or leaders who styled themselves 'boh' or 'bo' ('colonel'), dressed in civilian costume and carried whatever arms they could acquire, from firearms to *dah*s. Such bandits existed well into the 20th century and necessitated considerable forces to police the country.

The British made use of some locally raised forces. For example, in the first conflict on the Arakan front during the First Burma War, the small force defeated at Ramu comprised 350 Bengal Native Infantry, with some 250 men of the Chittagong Provincial Battalion and 400 of the Magh Levy. The former of these was an example of 'local force', and the latter a newly formed corps of Arakanese refugees who had fled to Chittagong to escape Burmese oppression. (The term 'Magh' was applied at the time to describe these Arakanese refugees; its later use by the Burmese was to describe Chittagonian Buddhists, while in Bengal it described Arakanese. The origin of the name is debatable, but it may be a Bengali abbreviation for 'despicable dog', originating from Arakanese raids into eastern Bengal in the 17th century.) Both these units fled when attacked at Ramu, leaving the regular sepoys (elements of 2/20th and 1/23rd, later 40th and 45th Bengal) no option but to retire.

Other local forces were transformed into police; for example, the Arracan (*sic*) Local Battalion, which existed in 1830 and probably before, and the Pegu Light Infantry, were both converted to police in 1861, and there also existed a 1st Pegu Native Sappers from 1850. After the annexation of Upper Burma, the Upper Burma Military Police was formed, composed principally of Sikhs and Gurkhas; these were absorbed into the Madras Army between 1891 and 1893, taking over the numbers 10, 12, 33, 32, 30, 31 and 29 for the 1st–7th Burma Battalions respectively. They retained their designation 'Burma' after their Madras title, but only the 93rd still kept it after the

1903 reorganisation. The 10th Madras (1st Burma) had the name 'Rifles' added in 1892, '1st Burma Gurkha Rifles' in 1895, and in 1901 became the 10th Gurkha Rifles. Other battalions of Burma Military Police remained as auxiliary corps, including some recruited from the Karen people of Lower Burma and the Southern Shan States; they were described as 'wonderfully smart at picking up their drill and handling their arms. Born and bred on the mountains, they are famous at hill-fighting, but a little slow on the plains. The Karen makes a specially useful native soldier, as, being a demon-worshipper, he has no caste, and will eat anything!'[3]

There were also auxiliary (volunteer) units, as in India, including the Rangoon Volunteer Artillery (formed 1879), the Rangoon and Irrawaddy State Railway Volunteer Rifles (formed 1879), becoming the Burma Railways Volunteers in 1897), the Moulmein Volunteer Rifles (formed 1877), the Rangoon Volunteer Rifles (formed 1860) and the Upper Burma Volunteer Rifles (formed 1886). An interesting aspect of the Third Burma War was the organisation of the British mounted contingent. No cavalry was allocated for the expedition (the terrain being unsuitable), but at Prendergast's request a mounted infantry corps was formed, riding local Burmese ponies, and composed of some 30 men of the Royal Scots Fusiliers, 50 policemen and fourteen members of the Rangoon Volunteers, with officers from all three units.

Burma remained a province of India until 1937, Burmese units remaining part of the Indian Army until that date.

Notes
1. Campbell's dispatch, 16 December 1824; *London Gazette*, 24 April 1825.
2. Campbell's dispatch, 2 April 1825; *London Gazette*, 25 October 1825.
3. *Navy and Army Illustrated*, vol. VIII, 22 July 1899, p. 412.

References
Bruce, G. *The Burma Wars 1824–1886*, London, 1973.
Featherstone, D. *Victoria's Enemies: An A–Z of British Colonial Warfare*, London, 1989.
Knight, I. *Queen Victoria's Enemies (4): Asia, Australasia and the Americas*, London, 1990.
Laurie, Colonel W. F. B. *Our Burmese Wars ... an abstract of military and political operations 1824–26 and 1852–53*, London, 1885.
Snodgrass, Major. *Narrative of the Burmese War: detailing the operations ... from ... landing at Rangoon in May 1824 to ... peace at Yandaboo*, London, 1827.
Stewart, A. T. Q. *The Pagoda War: Lord Dufferin and the Fall of the Kingdom of Ava 1885–86*, London, 1972.

CEYLON

The first European settlement in Ceylon was established at Colombo in 1518, on the orders of the Portuguese viceroy of Goa, and for more than a century the Portuguese endeavoured to establish control over the island by conquest, frequently involving appalling brutality by all concerned, Portuguese, Sinhalese and especially the 'Caffir' troops imported by the Portuguese from Africa. The Portuguese only subjugated the coastal regions, however; the interior, generally known as Kandy after the city of that name, was not impenetrable but was ideal guerrilla country. Three Portuguese armies were destroyed while attempting to conquer the interior, in 1594, 1630 and 1638, the Kandyans not attempting static defence but retiring into the forest and mountains until their enemies had succumbed to disease, ambush and occasionally pitched battles. When the Portuguese were finally defeated it was by an alliance formed in 1638 between a new wave of Dutch colonists and the Kandyan ruler Raja Sinha II; Colombo was captured in 1656 by a Dutch and Sinhalese force (commanded by Raja Sinha in person) after a terrible siege conducted with calculated cruelty, in which the Dutch showed the Portuguese none of the common humanity which might have been expected from fellow-Christians in a foreign land. The last Portuguese stronghold was captured in 1658.

The Dutch proved little better as colonists than had the Portuguese, and were unable to extend their rule beyond their coastal provinces. A revolt against Dutch oppression in 1761 was supported by the Kandyan king, Kirti Sri, and having re-established control in the maritime provinces the Dutch determined to capture the interior. Their first attempt to penetrate to Kandy failed (1764), but with a new army (about two-thirds of which were Malays, more used to the climate and conditions than Europeans) the Dutch captured Kandy in February 1765. Harassed and ravaged by disease, they had to evacuate the interior by the end of August; and in the following year Kirti Sri concluded a peace which confirmed the Dutch in possession of the coastal provinces.

In their turn, the Dutch were dispossessed of their colony during the period of Anglo-Dutch conflict which followed the capture of Holland by the French and the creation of the French-satellite Batavian Republic. A British force from India, commanded by Colonel James Stuart of the 72nd Foot, arrived off Trincomalee on 1 August 1795, which fortress surrendered after a brief siege on 26 August. Against only limited resistance, various Dutch positions were captured, until on 15 February 1796 Colombo capitulated, completing the British capture of the island. The most effective part of the Dutch garrison, apart from the Malays who were determined troops, was the Swiss regiment of De Meuron; its 'proprietor', the Count of that name, whose brother was actually in command, was persuaded to transfer its service from Dutch to British pay from October 1795. De Meuron's Regiment served with distinction in the British Army throughout the Napoleonic Wars.

Initially Ceylon was placed under East India Company jurisdiction, but the imposition of the Madras revenue system caused unrest, and in 1798 the colony was placed directly under the control of the crown, British possession

Charles-Daniel de Meuron (1738–1806), colonel-'proprietor' of the Swiss regiment which bore his name, which transferred from Dutch to British service in October 1795 at the time of the capture of the Dutch holdings in Ceylon. The regiment served at Seringapatam but in October 1806 most of its personnel were drafted to other corps, the cadre returning to Europe to recruit, serving in the Mediterranean 1807–13 and then in Canada where it was disbanded in July 1816. Charles-Daniel de Meuron attained the rank of lieutenant-general in British service.

being confirmed by the Treaty of Amiens. British authority, however, was confined to the coast; the interior was controlled by the last Kandyan king, Sri Wickrama Raja Sinha, a somewhat obscure relative of the previous king, Rajadhi Raja Sinha, whom he had succeeded upon his death in 1798. The Kandyan royal family was more Dravidian than Sinhalese, from the practice of selecting brides from southern India, but as the Sinhalese aristocracy could never suppress their rivalries sufficiently to support a Sinhalese candidate, the basically Indian royal family continued to rule. The succession was not by direct line, the king being chosen by the previous king's ministers. The new king's chief minister or *Adigar*, Pilima Talauva, himself had designs on the throne and offered to help the British depose the king, which offer was rejected. So were British attempts to turn Kandy into the sort of client-state which existed in India; but in 1802, on the failure to obtain redress for goods stolen from native merchants under British protection, the British governor, the Hon. Frederick North, ordered an invasion of Kandy.

North's resources were entirely insufficient, comprising two British battalions (19th and 51st) and a detachment of the 80th, a Native Infantry battalion and artillery borrowed from India, and an untrustworthy battalion of Malays, which had to garrison the British possessions as well as wage war. Nevertheless, on 31 January 1803 the British commander, Major-General Hay Macdowell, sent two columns into the interior. On 21 February they entered the city of Kandy, which was entirely deserted, and attempted to place on the throne one Muttusamy, a brother of three of the late king's wives. This aroused no enthusiasm among the Sinhalese, but pretended negotiations continued while the British were almost marooned in Kandy, harassed by guerrillas and stricken by disease. Under a truce, Macdowell withdrew most of his force, leaving in Kandy only a small detachment of 19th Foot and Malays, under the command of Major Adam Davie of the Malay Regiment. With his command devastated by sickness and devoid of support, in June 1803 Davie surrendered to Pilima Talauva; whereupon his men, sick and helpless included, were massacred. One German sergeant survived the butchery of the sick, and Corporal Barnsley of the 19th, fearfully wounded, escaped to carry news of the disaster to British territory; some of the Malays and Indian troops were spared after agreeing to enter Sinhalese service, but those who remained loyal to their British oath of allegiance were murdered. 'King' Muttusamy and his entourage were beheaded, and Davie and one other officer were taken into captivity.

The Kandyans then attempted to invade British territory, but their forces were not effective in other than guerrilla operations, and were beaten off with some ease. It proved impossible for the British to make any impression upon the centre of the island, with a sickly and demoralised force and inept leadership; a blockade of Kandy proved impracticable with the numbers of troops available, and small British raids to destroy villages and crops succeeded only in arousing Sinhalese anger. Major-General David Wemyss replaced Macdowell, with no greater success; but in July 1805 Major-General Sir Thomas Maitland succeeded North as governor, and also took military command. Although no formal treaty was negotiated, the war came to an end when British raiding columns were withdrawn, and Maitland set about restoring the military and fiscal state of the colony, which had become chaotic under the previous administration. The Kandyans released their Malay and sepoy prisoners, but Davie remained a captive until his death in about 1812, not attempting to escape but sending pathetic messages to the British. The last, dated August 1811, asked that if they were unable to rescue him, at least send him a pistol to allow him to end his existence.[1]

The increasing oppression of his subjects by the king (including the beheading of Pilima Talauva in 1812) and his murder of native traders from Colombo gave the British another excuse to intervene in Kandy, and Maitland's successor, Lieutenant-General Sir Robert Brownrigg, planned an invasion in 1815. He organised his forces in eight 'divisions' (of between 230 and 700 men each), advancing by five routes; there was little resistance and Kandy was entered on 11 February without the death of a single member of the British force. There they were greeted by Sergeant Theon, the German survivor of the Davie massacre, who like Davie had been treated with indifference during his captivity, had married and settled there. Sri Wikrama was captured on 18 February, the British saving him from the vengeance of his maltreated subjects; he was taken to India and lived in comfortable exile until his death in 1832. On 2 March 1815 a convention between the British and the Kandyan chiefs officially granted sovereignty of the entire island to the British.

In late 1817 a rebellion took place, beginning in the east of the island; small British columns were sent to destroy villages, but the disturbances spread and reinforcements had to be sent from India. The revolt became so serious that it is sometimes styled the Third Kandyan War, or the Uva Rebellion (from the area in south-east Ceylon in which it began), and a pretender to the throne, one Doresamy, was crowned in May 1818 with the support of some of the Kandyan chiefs, notably Keppitipola of Uva; Doresamy adopted the name Kirti Sri in an attempt to inspire the Kandyans to emulate their ancestors. Although no major actions took place, sporadic fighting gradually gave the British the advantage, and support for the rebellion declined. An attempt by the rebels to invade another province, the Four Korales, ended in a major reverse, and with the British offering pardons in exchange for a cessation of hostilities, resistance collapsed. The rebellion never had universal support, some local leaders having taken the part of the British; and it was discovered that Doresamy was not the real person of that name, who had a claim to the Kandyan throne, but was an impostor named Vilbava. He fled into obscurity (and when apprehended in 1830 was convicted of treason but given a free pardon), but most of the leaders of the revolt were captured and sentenced to a comfortable exile in Mauritius. Two, including Keppitipola, were executed in November 1818.

Following the suppression of the revolt, a revised system of government was established in Ceylon, by which each province was administered by a government agent (similar to a Collector in India), with the indigenous chieftains exercising only the authority permitted by the government. With the integration of Kandy and the coastal provinces into a single system of government, there was no further warfare in the island.

Military Forces

Kandy. The belief that the Sinhalese were not naturally a martial people perhaps led to an under-estimation of the difficulties of waging a guerrilla-style war in very difficult

One of the great military heroes of the Victorian era was Sir Hector 'Fighting Mac' Macdonald (1853–1903), who by his own abilities rose from private to the rank of major-general, and who was especially distinguished in command of a Sudanese brigade during the reconquest of the Sudan. Appointed to command the garrison in Ceylon, he shot himself in March 1903 rather than face an investigation into allegations of indecency.

climate and terrain. The greater part of the Kandyan army were civilian levies, many armed with bows (especially those of the eastern provinces), and others with firearms acquired by trade, frequently not in good condition; some of these were kept in provincial 'armouries' rather than belonging to the levies themselves. There was also a feudal 'militia' of hereditary soldiers, residing upon land owned by the king or territorial chiefs in return for military service, or who received pay when under arms; the two principal groups, sometimes styled 'regiments' (although this term is hardly appropriate in its European sense) were the Atapattuwa and Maduwa. In the early 19th century at least some of these troops were uniformed after a fashion. The king's forces, however, relied to a considerable extent upon foreign mercenaries, including Africans (generally known as 'Caffirs', 'Caffres' or 'Kaffirs', as originally employed by the Portuguese, and who were sometimes accused of being responsible for much of the worst brutality during the Kandyan wars); Malabars, whose Indian origin reflected that of the Kandyan kings, some of whom were given land grants in return for military service, and who in the early 19th century at least were uniformed as sepoys, in red jacket and turban and blue trousers; and Malays, originally recruited by the Dutch, and who were probably the most formidable of the Kandyan forces. The recruitment of foreign mercenaries continued despite the British occupation of the coastline; Sri Wikrama, for example, enlisted some 700 Tamils before the 1815 campaign. Despite the sizeable population, the forces which could be fielded by the Kandyan kingdom were not generally as large as might have been expected, as the levies and feudal 'militia' were mobilised in sections, not all being under arms simultaneously. Although useful as guerrillas, the Kandyan forces were not effective in the open field, the British proving that a small force of determined men could hold a defensible position against large numbers of Kandyans. The Kandyans had little artillery save *gingals*, and it was a source of some surprise to the British that bows and arrows continued to form a considerable part of their armoury, being especially popular with the Veddas, descendants of the original inhabitants of Ceylon who were subjugated by the Aryan Sinhalese in distant antiquity.

British. The British and Indian forces employed in the Kandyan Wars in general suffered more from the climate and disease than from casualties in battle. Ceylon was at times extremely unhealthy, and a measure of the toll is provided by the case of the 19th Foot, which was in Ceylon from 1796 to 1820, losing some 10 per cent of its strength every year to disease and the occasional skirmish, a loss far more severe than that of some regiments that served with greater fame in the Napoleonic Wars. As a result of such ravages of climate and illness, the employment of troops more resistant than Europeans was regarded as essential.

Originally, the Malays who had formed part of the Dutch garrison transferred to the service of the East India Company; in 1799 five companies performed well when sent on campaign to Malabar. In 1801 the corps was transferred to the King's service as the Malay Regiment, and increased to ten companies by the enrolment of more ex-Dutch Malayan troops from St. Helena. In 1802 a Sinhalese battalion was formed, whereupon the 'Malay Corps' became the 1st Ceylon Regiment, and the new formation, known as the 'Sepoy Corps', became the 2nd. In 1803 the 2nd recruited more Malayans, forming a second battalion, which in the same year was made independent as the 3rd Ceylon Regiment. At the outbreak of the 'First Kandyan War', governor North proposed that West Indian troops be sent to augment the garrison, but although an existing unit was not sent, he was given permission to purchase African slaves (including their wives and children) at between £30 and £45 a head. Recruiting was always difficult, so that men had to be found as far afield as Cochin (where 400 Malays were recruited for the 2nd Regiment), and Sinhalese and Madrassis continued to be enrolled. In January 1814 the 4th Ceylon Regiment was formed, entirely African in composition. In 1814 the 1st Regiment was converted to light infantry (and possessed a rifle company), and was composed of Malays and Javanese; at this time the 2nd was a 'sepoy' corps, and the 3rd and 4th African. In 1815 the 4th Regiment was disbanded and its personnel absorbed by the 3rd, which was itself disbanded in 1817. In 1819 the slaves were freed, and the 2nd Regiment was disbanded in 1821; Africans, who throughout had been excellent soldiers, continued to serve in the 1st Regiment, but apart from the sons of serving African soldiers, enlistment was restricted largely to Malays. In 1820 the 1st Regiment became a rifle corps, changing its name to the Ceylon Rifle Regiment in 1827. After the Dutch prohibited recruiting in Java in 1847, and when the African companies had to be reduced from three to two, another 'sepoy' company had to be formed; in 1847 the strength was increased from sixteen to 22 companies (six being sent to garrison Hong Kong), declining to eighteen companies in 1851 and fourteen in 1854. It was found impossible to recruit more Malays, Sinhalese were found to be unsatisfactory, but the descendants of the original Africans continued to provide the best men. Difficulties of recruiting continued: in 1869 the regiment was reduced to nine companies, in 1871 to eight, and in 1874 it was disbanded. Originally uniformed as a line regiment in red, from 1820 it wore the dark green of a rifle corps, the 'sepoy' companies wearing turbans in deference to their religion, the others British shakos.

Troops stationed in Ceylon at the end of the century included two companies of 'Asiatic Artillery' (Indians) and a submarine mining detachment.

Notes

1. The text of his final message is reproduced in the Hon. Sir John Fortescue's *History of the British Army*, London, 1910, vol. V, p. 164.

References

Calladine, G. *The Diary of Colour-Serjeant George Calladine, 19th Foot, 1793–1837*, ed. M. L. Ferrar, London, 1922 (important account of service in Ceylon by an 'other rank').

Johnston, Major A. *Narrative of an Expedition to Candy in the Year 1804*, Dublin and London, 1810.

Mendis, G. C. *Ceylon under the British 1795–1832*, Colombo, 1952.

Mills, L. A. *Ceylon under British Rule*, Oxford, 1933.

Pieris, R. *Sinhalese Social Organization in the Kandyan Period*,

Ceylon U.P., 1956 (includes details of the Kandyan forces).

Powell, G. *The Kandyan Wars: the British Army in Ceylon 1803–1818*, London, 1973 (essential: the best modern history, including details of the Kandyan and British forces, with an extensive bibliography).

Details of the British Ceylon corps are covered in:

Cowan, H. L. 'History of the Ceylon Rifle Regiment', in *Colburn's United Services Magazine*, vol. III, 1860, pp. 323–7.

Tylden, Major G. 'The Ceylon Regiments, 1796 to 1874', in *Journal of the Society for Army Historical Research*, vols. XXX, 1952, pp. 124–8; XXXII, 1954, pp. 107–8.

PERSIA

Because of its proximity to British India, the Persian empire came into contact with the British from the early 19th century; indeed, British officers had aided the Persians in their war against Russia in 1812 (notwithstanding Anglo-Russian friendship: having arrived in an official capacity, the British advisers stayed on as private individuals). Following Persian defeats and the conclusion of the Russian war by the Treaty of Turkmanchai (February 1828), the dominance of Russia over Persian policy became evident; and this Russian influence, at a time when Russian expansionism was regarded as the principal threat to British India, led to Anglo-Persian hostilities.

More immediately, the source of Anglo-Persian conflict was the Afghan city of Herat, long claimed by the Persians. In succession to the long reign of Fath Ali Shah on the throne of Persia, his grandson Mohammed Mirza became Shah in 1834, but only with the assistance of the British envoy was the opposition to his succession negated. Nevertheless, despite attempts to persuade him to the contrary, and under persuasion from the Russians, he determined to possess Herat, then governed by Kamran Shah. A Persian army invested Herat on 23 November 1837, but the city held out, its defence aided by the presence of Lieutenant Eldred Pottinger of the Bombay Artillery; until, under threat of British intervention, Mohammed Shah lifted the siege (9 September 1838). For some time Anglo-Persian relations remained strained, the British occupying Kharak Island in the Persian Gulf as a way of demonstrating the seriousness of their intent; but this force was withdrawn after diplomatic relations were restored with the appointment of a new British mission to Teheran in October 1841. Mohammed Shah died in September 1848 and was succeeded by his son Nasru'd-Din Mirza, whose assumption of the throne was again aided by the British and Russian envoys.

Having succeeded his father in 1851, who had deposed and murdered Kamran, Herat's new ruler, Sa'id Mahommed, permitted the installation of Persian troops. British protests obtained a new agreement of Persian non-interference in Herat, but in September 1855 Mahommed Yusuf Sadozai, nephew of Kamran, seized Herat and executed Sa'id Mahommed. The Shah ordered that Herat be occupied, and it was formally annexed by Persia on 25 October 1856. As British diplomatic protests were unavailing, war was declared on Persia on 1 November 1856.

Within days of the declaration, a division from Bombay under the command of Major-General Foster Stalker mounted an amphibious operation in the Persian Gulf, disembarking unopposed some ten miles south of Bushire on 5 December 1856. The Persians held an old Dutch fortification at Reshire, which Stalker attacked on 7 December; the defenders abandoned the position after a short fight in which the British brigade-commander, Colonel

James Stopford of the 64th Foot, was killed leading the attack. The governor of Bushire surrendered the city after a bombardment by ships of the expedition. It was decided that the expedition be reinforced, so a second division was dispatched, commanded by Sir Henry Havelock, with Lieutenant-General Sir James Outram taking overall command of the expedition. He arrived at Bushire on 27 January 1857, and on 8 February his army, about 4,500 strong, was attacked at Koosh-ab by a Persian force estimated at 6,900 strong, commanded by one Shooja-ool-Moolk. The 3rd Bombay Cavalry and Poona Horse charged with artillery support and, breaking a square formed by the European-drilled Persian infantry, routed the enemy, who left some 700 of their number dead on the field. British losses were ten killed and 62 wounded (six mortally). (It was at Koosh-ab that the Poona Horse captured the standard of the Persian Kashkai Regiment of infantry, the pole topped by a silver hand bearing a date corresponding to AD 1066, and engraved with the inscription 'The Hand of God is above all things'. From 1859 this 'Hand of God' trophy was mounted on the standard-pole of the Poona Horse, and this obscure battle was commemorated to modern times by the hand device forming the centre of the regimental badge of the 17th (Poona) Horse of the army of the independent India.)

Leaving a force at Bushire, Outram made an amphibious advance up the Euphrates to the town of Mohumra (Mohamrah); he had less than 4,900 men against an estimated 13,000 Persians, commanded by Prince Khauler Mirza; but after a naval bombardment the Persians withdrew, leaving Havelock to disembark and take the town without opposition. Outram sent a force to reconnoitre up the Karun river (three gunboats and 300 troops in three river steamers), which came upon some 7,000 Persian infantry, with cavalry and artillery at Ahwaz; at the sight of the tiny flotilla, the Persians fled. This was the final act of

the war; on 5 April Outram learned that a peace had been negotiated by which the Persians agreed to quit Herat. Apart from a small force under John Jacob, which remained at Bushire for three months pending confirmation of the terms of the treaty, the army was withdrawn.

Thereafter, Anglo-Persian relations were cordial, the Shah visiting Britain in 1873 and 1889; he reigned until his assassination (1 May 1896) by a follower of the revolutionary and anarchist Kemalu'd-Din. Nasru'd-Din was succeeded by his son, Muzaffar-ud-Din, who in 1903 was invested with the Order of the Garter, the highest award that could be bestowed by Britain. Anglo-Russian rivalry over Persia continued, however.

Military Forces

As proven by the 1857 war, the Persian army was not proficient. It consisted of regular and irregular forces, the former organised and disciplined along European lines, and uniformed in quasi-European style, though with voluminous trousers and conical head-dress giving a somewhat Turkish appearance. As mentioned above, European advisers were responsible for the introduction of European methods, and a battalion of Russian mercenaries was employed for the attack on Herat in 1838, led by the Polish General Berowski, who was killed during the operation. The regulars included the Shah's guard, usually stationed at Teheran or in attendance upon the Shah, although a battalion of some 900 was present at Koosh-ab; their red jackets with blue facings and white trousers must have presented a strangely familiar appearance to the British. The other regular units were stationed in the principal towns and provinces; in the army at Koosh-ab, for example, there were nine regiments, in addition to the guards; Outram identified these as four Sabriz regiments, the Kashkai already mentioned, two Karragoozloo regiments, an Arab regiment and a Shiraz regiment, totalling

Persian troops, 1856–7; most notable here is the zamburak, camel-borne artillery of small calibre. Third from the left is an artillery officer; also shown are a drummer and fusilier (third from right) of the Shah's guard, an infantry officer (second from right), irregular cavalry and a Kurdish irregular (fourth from right).

some 4,200 men, regimental strength varying between the 900 of the Arab regiment and 800 of the Kashkai, to the 200 of the Shiraz and the 800 total of the four Sabriz. The irregulars, mobilised only in wartime, consisted primarily of cavalry, devoid of discipline but individually used to riding and weapon-handling; and there were also some irregular infantry, styled *tuffekdji*s. The regular cavalry was said to number no more than 500.

The artillery was said to be the most proficient part of the Persian army, with the gunners reasonably trained, although the variety of ordnance must have caused difficulties of ammunition supply (at Koosh-ab it was reported that ammunition was transported on mule-back, presumably because of lack of wheeled transport). The variety of guns is exemplified by those captured at Mohumra, which included five brass 12pdrs (one described as Persian, and one unserviceable Russian gun), three brass 9pdrs, two brass guns of unknown calibre (having been buried in mud) but apparently 18pdrs, an unserviceable 8in brass mortar, two iron 9pdr carronades and four iron 6pdr carronades mounted on locally made carriages. A particular feature of the Persian artillery was the *zamburak* (or '*zembourek*') corps, small cannon of 3- or 4in calibre, or large-calibre muskets like European 'wall pieces', mounted upon a pivot at the front of a camel-saddle. These could be fired from camel-back (the animal lying down) or could be detached and, with an increased charge of powder, fired from the ground, upon their pivots; presumably the entire saddle could be used as an artillery 'carriage'. They were used as mobile fire-support, the name being derived from *zembor*, a wasp, which exemplifies their capacity for movement and stinging. An ammunition-pouch on each side of the camel-saddle contained 50 ball or grape cartridges, and a red pennon flew from a short flag-staff at the rear of each saddle. In addition to the gunner for each camel, it was possible to mount an infantryman as well, for protection; when deployed in line-of-battle, the camels were spaced at intervals of five feet. In 1853 there were some 200 camels and guns in this corps. The artillery wore blue jackets with red facings, and blue trousers.

An interesting European view of the Persian military described the army in the late 1830s:

'If I am to form an opinion of the Military from what I saw here, I should pronounce the Persian soldier, whether as regards Infantry, Artillery, or Cavalry, to be anything but a man of war. The Surbases, or regular Infantry, have their heads shorn, excepting about the temples and on the peak of the cranium, where the hair hangs in ringlets. Their covering is a cap of black sheepskin ... His scarlet uniform, with a collar and broad cuffs, sits like a loose sack on his limbs and body; the lower man is enveloped in broad white shalwaris, or trousers, tightened half-way down the calf of his legs, where they meet the edge of his sandal-shaped shoes ... His whole equipments sit loose and clumsily upon him, and he cannot move a step without

India General Service Medal 1854–95; the obverse showed a portrait of Queen Victoria, the reverse Victory crowning a classical warrior. Twenty-four clasps were authorised for actions between 1852 and 1895; 'Persia', for the 1856–7 campaign, was the second to be issued.

feeling them an encumbrance. In fact, a more ludicrous or deplorable sight than a Persian soldier will not readily be met with. The British Officers who are in the Shah's service do all they can to discipline the troops in the European fashion, but it is all "kicking against the pricks"; of such impenetrable stuff are both mind and body they have to work upon.'[1] Only limited praise was bestowed upon the artillery, which '... is much better than the infantry, and therefore more efficient in comparison. The cannon are very carefully kept; and the men are fond of their profession, and capable of being made something of; but their dress is ridiculous, and ... the carriages are much like farmers' carts ... There is something very amusing in the external of a Persian officer: they dress in a frock-coat, which descends to their knee-pan; the collar is covered with embroidery; their shoulders are encumbered with large epaulettes; their trowsers stuck into close boots; and they wear the same black sheepskin cap as the common soldiers. Although they know nothing of their profession, they are fond of making a show of their skill by words of mouth, and conceive themselves superior to the English officers who have trained them.'[2]

Notes

1. Baron Korff, 'The Camp and Army at Tauris', in *United Service Journal*, 1840, vol. II, p. 106.
2. Anon, 'Foreign Miscellany: Persia', in ibid., vol. III, pp. 244–5.

References

English, B. *John Company's Last War: A Victorian Military Adventure*, London, 1971.
Featherstone, D. *Victoria's Enemies: An A–Z of British Colonial Warfare*, London, 1989.
Hunt, Captain G. H. *Outram and Havelock's Persian Campaign*, London, 1858.

III
AFRICA AND THE
MEDITERRANEAN

AFRICA AND THE MEDITERRANEAN

ABYSSINIA

The British war with Abyssinia was unusual among colonial campaigns in that it was initiated by humanitarian motives (though involving national prestige), had no colonising intent, and was conducted with total success and hardly any loss of life on the part of the expedition.

Abyssinia was a most unusual land, inaccessible, largely Christian though surrounded by Islamic states, and, as Gibbon remarked, forgotten by the world and forgetful of it for a thousand years; or at least, so far as Europeans were concerned. It was a feudal society of tribes controlled by a *ras* or prince, frequently in conflict with one another; rulers of larger areas or provinces sometimes aspired to the title *negūs* or king, although there might be more than one *negūs*, each ruling a part of the country. Of the three principal provinces, Tigré (north), Amhara (central) and Shoa (south), the most important was usually Amhara, whose ruler exacted tribute from the others and was styled *negūs negusti*, 'king of kings'. Kassa, a minor chief from western Amhara rose to prominence by virtue of defeating his opponents, proclaimed himself *negūs negusti* after his subjugation of Tigré in 1855, and adopted the name Theodore III (or 'Tewodros'). Although his title involved such phrases as 'King of Kings' and 'Chosen of God', it is as 'Emperor Theodore' that he is generally known.

Theodore was intelligent, educated (in a monastery) and militarily reasonably skilful, which enabled him to extend his rule over the remainder of Abyssinia, by the conquest of Shoa and by victories over the Islamic Wollo Galas people, whose stronghold of Magdala he took for his own. Devoutly religious, his ambition was a crusade to deliver Jerusalem from the Turks, but campaigns against Islamic neighbours were not successful, and his attempts to modernise his country met with opposition. European contacts with Abyssinia were extensive – the first British mission was sent in 1805 – and considerable numbers of Europeans had lived there from that time (Sahela Selassié, *negūs* of Shoa 1813–47, had concluded treaties with the Government of India and with France, and had even requested Pope Pius IX to send a papal legate, who arrived after Selassié's death). Theodore's attempted modernisations led to frequent minor revolts, and the pressures these engendered, together with the death of his wife and the murder by rebels in 1860 of his trusted adviser, the British consul Walter Plowden, seem to have affected Theodore's reason, his behaviour becoming increasingly irrational.

Captain Charles Cameron was sent as Plowden's replacement, and Theodore sent a message of friendship to Queen Victoria in return. By Foreign Office incompetence, it was not acknowledged, and Theodore's suspicions were inflamed further when Cameron visited Kassala in the Sudan, on instructions from London, to investigate the slave trade and the area's cotton-growing potential.

Suspecting an Anglo-Islamic plot, in January 1864 Theodore imprisoned Cameron and his suite, followed by various European missionaries, and a member of the staff of the British Political Resident in Aden, Hormuzd Rassam, who had been sent to negotiate the captives' release. All diplomatic efforts having failed, under pressure from public opinion, and more than three years after Cameron's detention, the British government finally authorised a military expedition to liberate the captives by force.

It was decided to employ the force nearest to Abyssinia, the Bombay Army, whose commander-in-chief, Sir Robert Napier, was an experienced soldier and capable organiser. He appreciated the scale of the operation and its very considerable logistic problems, and thus ensured that adequate forces were committed: 14,214 troops, 26,254 'followers' (commissariat, labourers, etc.), 2,538 horses for cavalry and staff, 19,580 transport horses or mules, 6,045 camels, 7,086 bullocks, 1,850 donkeys and 44 elephants were landed for the campaign, a prodigious and costly undertaking. (These statistics are taken from the report of the expedition's senior naval officer, Commodore Leopold Heath, 10 June 1868, *London Gazette*, 30 June 1868; they differ slightly from other statistics, for example the official history, which states that the number of troops was 4,038 Europeans and 9,050 Indians). Most of the Indian troops came from the Bombay Army (plus a few units from Bengal and a detachment of Madras Sappers and Miners), and the force included a Naval Brigade armed with rockets. The transportation of the army and its supplies required the hiring of some 280 ships (75 steamers), and so precise was the planning that it even involved arranging with the Austrian authorities for the special minting of half a million Maria Theresa thalers of 1780, these large silver coins being the only acceptable currency in Abyssinia (other than bars of rock-salt and cartridges; only in 1894 did the Abyssinian authorities introduce their own coinage, the 'Menelek dollar' or *talari*).

Because Abyssinia had no coastline, approach had to be made across Egyptian territory. The Red Sea littoral and the town of Massawa, acquired by the Turks in 1557, had passed into Egyptian control in 1865; not until 1885 was Massawa occupied by Italy, with British approval and the removal of the Egyptian garrison, the genesis of the Italian colony of Eritrea. The use of Egyptian territory as a base of operations was therefore arranged, and in October 1867 the vanguard of the expedition landed at Zula on Annesley Bay, south of Massawa, where a harbour was established, piers constructed, and a railway laid into the hinterland. Napier landed at Zula in early January 1868, but such were the logistic problems that the advance upon Magdala was slow; as was Theodore's counter-move, for he had to build a road to accommodate his artillery. As the British approached Magdala at the end of their 400-mile march from the coast, the Abyssinians attacked Napier's advance-guard at Arogee (10 April 1868), Theodore ordering his chieftain Fitaurari Gabri (named in Napier's dispatch as 'Fetararee Gabsie') to attack what appeared to be an unprotected British supply-train. The attack was repelled with the aid of the Naval Brigade's rockets, which apparently had a profound impression upon Theodore himself, and the Abyssinians suffered some 700 dead (including Fitaurari Gabri) and 1,200 wounded; British losses were twenty wounded, two fatally.

Theodore then sued for peace, although his mood swung from bellicosity to conciliation and back again; during deliberations with his chieftains he even tried to shoot himself, only for his pistol to misfire, evidence of increasing irrationality. Napier insisted on the release of the captives, to which Theodore assented; and to his surrender, which demand he refused. His position was obviously hopeless; his Abyssinian enemies were gathering, preventing his escape from Magdala (indeed, the chieftains whose land had been crossed by Napier had actively co-operated with the British), and by giving his followers permission to surrender, Theodore was left with only a few hundred men. At the expiry of the agreed armistice, Napier stormed Magdala on 13 April 1868; despite the natural strength of the place, only limited resistance was encountered, and that ended when Theodore, realising that all was hopeless, shot himself through the mouth, ironically with a pistol presented to him by Queen Victoria. British casualties in the assault were only two officers and thirteen other ranks wounded.

With the release of the captives, there was no further reason for British presence in the country, so after destroying the defences of Magdala and appropriating its artillery (some of which was given to Napier's Abyssinian allies), Napier withdrew, the last troops leaving Eritrea on 18 June 1868, even taking their railway-lines with them. To the British, the financial cost had been immense, but the human cost amazingly small: total fatalities numbered only 48. (The number is sometimes stated to be 35; but the report of S. Currie, Inspector-General of the expedition, identified eleven officers and 37 other rank fatalities, including twenty cases of dysentery, one accidental drowning and one suicide.[1]) For Abyssinia, however, it was another matter, for the decline and death of Theodore resulted in a renewed round of civil war until a new ruler was established: Dejaj Kassai of Tigré, one of Napier's allies, who used to good effect the weaponry given him by the British. He proclaimed himself *negūs negusti* under the name of King John, and was killed fighting the Sudanese in 1889. It was his successor, Menelek II, who inflicted upon Italy one of the most comprehensive defeats ever sustained by a 'colonising' power, when General Oreste Baratieri's Italian army was all but annihilated at Adowa (1 March 1896), with the loss of some 6,500 casualties and 2,500 captured (who were treated with extreme humanity by the Abyssinians, despite propaganda to the contrary). The defeat of such a 'modern' European army by the Abyssinians is an indication of what might have happened to the British in 1868, had Napier's expedition not been so skilfully organised and commanded.

Military Forces: Abyssinia

Abyssinia had no 'standing army' in the European sense, but a feudal-style force composed of the followers of various chieftains. Although there was some attempt to impose organisation, by forming units of 50, 100, 500 and 1,000 men, with specified commanders, there was no attempt to impose discipline or practise any tactic other than a charge in attack, or a defence of static positions.

The storming of Magdala, showing the precipitous tracks up which the assault-column progressed, Madras Sappers and 33rd Foot in the lead. A chaplain, Father Goffinet, accompanied the first attackers in the hope of preventing damage to Magdala's Christian church. (Engraving by 'C. R.')

The Abyssinians were noted as being extremely courageous and prepared to charge repeatedly into British musketry in an attempt to engage in hand-to-hand combat. They wore their civilian costume, white shirt and trousers and a white cotton cloak (*shamma*) around the shoulders, although chieftains and the more affluent wore more elaborate costume, often including a coloured and embroidered, or animal-skin, cope (*lembd*) draped over the shoulders, over a decorated tunic; scarlet seems to have been a favourite colour, and was the dress of chiefs who led the attack at Arogee, Napier noting that so many were dressed in red that they 'almost bore the appearance of our troops in the distance'.[2] Those who had killed a male lion wore its mane upon the shoulders of the *lembd*, and lion-hair trimming was worn upon the head-dress, clothing and equipment. Many of the ordinary soldiers carried only spears, swords and round, hide shields, often of a convex form, decorated with metal plates and tufts of lion-hair for the more distinguished. Firearms varied from the most common, primitive matchlocks to more modern double-barrelled percussion guns which were more effective than the old muskets carried by elements of the Indian Army (Napier noted that at Arogee the 23rd Pioneers' old 'smooth bore is hardly equal to the double barrelled percussion gun of the Abyssinians'.[3] The proportion of Abyssinians who carried firearms is uncertain, although of the force of some 5,000 engaged at Arogee, Napier estimated that about 3,000 were 'regular musketeers'.

Most of the Abyssinian troops were infantry; only the most affluent were mounted, and at Arogee Napier estimated that these numbered about 500, whom he thought were chieftains rather than organised cavalry. Theodore appears to have used his mounted warriors more for skirmishing and reconnaissance than as a 'shock' weapon. Proud of his artillery, he employed German craftsmen to construct his ordnance, the most notable being an immense, 70-ton mortar styled 'Theodorus'. The size and weight of his artillery imposed some constraints on the freedom of movement of his army, but he was able to deploy seven pieces on the heights at Fahla, overlooking the battlefield of Arogee. They opened fire at 3,000 yards and despite the distance reached the British positions (Napier believed by the use of 'excessive charges of powder'), but 'the fire being a plunging one, no casualties ensued'.[4] Theodore remained at Fahla to direct his ordnance in person, his (unwilling) German technicians training the pieces; but probably because of over-loading, the great 'Theodorus' burst at its first discharge. The 'natures' of Abyssinian ordnance can be seen from the list of pieces captured at Magdala: three 56pdrs, one 18pdr and eleven 6pdrs (four Turkish, one British, cast at Cossipore, and one French), all being brass smoothbores; five brass 24in howitzers (locally made and French), three brass 12in howitzers, one brass 3in gun and four iron 1in guns.

Notes

1. *London Gazette*, 30 June 1868.
2. Ibid., Napier's dispatch, 12 May 1868.
3. Ibid.
4. Ibid.

References

Bates, Sir Darrell. *The Abyssinian Difficulty: The Emperor Theodorus and the Magdala Campaign 1867–68*, Oxford, 1979.
Bond, B. (ed.). *Victorian Military Campaigns*, London, 1967 (includes 'The Expedition to Abyssinia 1867–68', by D. G. Chandler).
Featherstone, D. *Victoria's Enemies: An A–Z of British Colonial Warfare*, London, 1989.
Holland, Major T. J., and Hozier, Captain H. M. *Record of the Expedition to Abyssinia*, London, 1870 (the 'official history').
Knight, I. *Queen Victoria's Enemies (2): Northern Africa*, London, 1989.
Myatt, F. *The March to Magdala: the Abyssinian War of 1868*, London, 1970
Napier, Field Marshal Lord. *Letters of Field Marshal Lord Napier of Magdala concerning Abyssinia, etc.* (ed. Lieutenant-Colonel H. D. Napier), London, 1936.
Stanley, H. M. *Coomassie and Magdala: Two British Campaigns*, London, 1874 (Henry Morton Stanley, then correspondent for the *New York Herald*).

CENTRAL AFRICA

Despite the title, suggestive of a large territory at the centre of the continent, British Central Africa was comparatively small; originally intended to embrace all British territory north of the Zambezi, from 1893 it referred only to the protectorate which in 1907 was re-named Nyasaland.

Following David Livingstone's discovery of Lake Nyasa in 1859, British missionaries and settlers entered the territory and, as elsewhere, British interests were centred originally around a private trading company, in this case the African Lakes Trading Corporation. From about 1885 the Corporation was involved in a private war with Arabs settled at the northern end of Lake Nyasa, in which the Corporation employed such volunteers as Frederick Lugard, who in May 1888 (when on half-pay from the British Army) commanded an expedition; he was severely wounded and after his recovery transferred his attention to East Africa. In 1889 Harry (later Sir Harry) Johnston was sent out to attempt to settle the dispute, and that with the Portuguese, whose East African colony (Mozambique) surrounded the south-east and south-west of British Central Africa. The result was the establishment of the protectorate, to which Johnston returned as commissioner in 1891, but conflict continued between the British, the Arabs and the Yao people, largely with regard to the suppression of the slave trade. (For some four years, part of Northern Rhodesia was also administered as part of the Central African protectorate.)

The Yaos, or Ajawa, were a Bantu people originating in the north of Portuguese East Africa, and who had spread into the British territory south of Lake Nyasa. They were often employed by European explorers as carriers and were noted for their intelligence and strong physique, but

Officer, sergeant and private of the Central Africa Regiment, c.1899. Recruited principally from the Yao and Atonga peoples, the corps comprised two battalions, one of which was always stationed in Central Africa and the other available for service elsewhere. The latter was not always successful, as the unit had to be transferred to Somaliland after conflict with the local population of Mauritius. No footwear was worn by the rank and file, even on parade, bare feet being usual in the men's civilian life.

their practice of slaving brought them into contact with the British, to whom they were a determined and troublesome enemy. Until their final defeat by 1896, a number of expeditions were mounted against them.

In July–August 1891 an expedition to the Mlanje area was led by Captain C. M. MacGuire against the slaver Chimkumbu, and a further expedition to the same area was necessary in August–October 1893, led by Lieutenant C. A. Edwards against the chiefs Nyassera and Mkanda. In October–November 1891 Commissioner Johnston himself and MacGuire led an expedition against the slavers Makanjira and Mponda in the region of the southern end of Lake Nyasa; Makanjira was attacked again by an expedition of November 1893–January 1894, led by Captain C. E. Johnston and Edwards; and a final expedition against him in late 1895 ended the conflict in that region. Two expeditions

were mounted against the Yao chief Kawinga (November 1891, March 1895), one against the chief Zafari (led by Harry Johnston, January–February 1892), and one against Chirandzulu (led by C. E. Johnston, December 1893). Perhaps the most notable of these minor operations was that mounted on the upper Shire River against the slaver chief Liwondi, led by Harry and C. E. Johnston, in January–February 1893. The forces of the expedition under Harry Johnston ran into difficulties, and had to be rescued by volunteers and naval personnel drawn from the ships HMSs *Herald* and *Mosquito* (both paddle-driven river gunboats, built 1890, and armed with four and six 3pdrs respectively), commanded by Lieutenants George Carr (*Mosquito*) and Charles Robertson (*Herald*). This expedition provides a rare example of two different medals being issued for the same operation: the naval personnel received the East and West Africa Medal with clasp 'Liwondi 1893', but the others received the Central Africa Medal. Another example concerned the second expedition against Makanjira, beginning November 1893; the military personnel qualified for the Central Africa Medal, but the naval personnel from HMSs *Adventure* and *Pioneer* (both river gunboats, built 1891 and 1892 respectively) received the East and West Africa Medal with clasp 'Lake Nyassa'. The final expeditions were mounted against the slavers in the area of the northern end of the lake in December 1895.

The elimination of slavery and the pacification of the slaving communities did not bring an end to conflict in the region, for in 1896–8 there occurred hostilities against the Angoni people, who resided west of Lake Nyasa, and who were harassing their neighbours. The Angoni were of Zulu origin, and had spread from Matabeleland to the Nyasa area in the earlier 19th century. Expeditions to end their raiding were mounted from January 1896, including one under Edwards against chief Tambola, and another in October against chief Odeti, who was shielding the former; and against chiefs Chikusi, Serumba and Mpezeni (October 1896, August 1897 and January 1898 respectively), and finally in April 1898.

Military Forces: Central Africa

The early local forces were those formed by the African Lakes Corporation, the majority of the indigenous population being quite willing to support and enrol in such units, assisting the British in resisting slaving and aggression. In 1891, with the formation of the protectorate, the British Central Africa Rifles was formed from a nucleus of Sikhs brought from India, and indeed the Sikh element remained throughout subsequent changes of name. In December 1898 the unit was re-titled as the 1st Battalion Central Africa Regiment, to which a 2nd Battalion was added in January 1899; from 1 January 1902 these became the 1st and 2nd Battalions respectively of the King's African Rifles.

In addition to local forces, Indian Army personnel were deployed, though not in large numbers, and the Royal

Navy also played a significant part, not least in the manning of river-craft. Two of these, *Adventure* and *Pioneer*, were constructed at Yarrow shipyard, disassembled and carried overland to Lake Nyasa, and re-assembled; *Pioneer* was transferred from the Royal Navy to the control of the British Central Africa government in January 1894, and *Adventure* in 1896.

Reference
Johnston, Sir Harry H. *British Central Africa*, 2nd edn., 1898.

East Africa
The term 'East Africa' was used to cover three British territories: British East Africa, Uganda, and Zanzibar.

BRITISH EAST AFRICA

British East Africa was the territory re-named Kenya on the change from protectorate to crown colony status in July 1920. It was bounded on the north by Abyssinia, on the east by Italian Somaliland and the Indian Ocean, Uganda to the west, and German East Africa to the south; the northern part was known as Jubaland. The inhabitants included peoples of Bantu descent in the south, others of Hamitic origin (such as the Masai), Somali tribes in the north and east, while the population of the coastal regions bore evidence of the ancient Arab and Persian settlements in that area. The spread of British interests in East Africa arose from Britain's connection with the sultanate of Zanzibar, and from a desire to limit the spread of German colonisation. In 1887 the sultan of Zanzibar granted to Britain a concession for such of his mainland territory as lay outside the agreed sphere of German influence; the association to which this concession was granted was chartered in 1888 as the Imperial British East Africa Company.

Some problems were encountered over the demarcation of British and German spheres of influence, and, the company proving unprofitable, its territory (previously known as 'Ibea' from the initials of the company) was transferred to the crown on 1 July 1895, and known henceforward as the East Africa Protectorate.

Military operations in East Africa were limited, the majority of the indigenous population accepting British rule without resistance. The spread of British administration was not immediate, however, especially in the north, and indeed it was not until an Anglo-Abyssinian commission of 1908–9 that the frontier with Abyssinia was fully delineated.

In 1890 an expedition was sent to Witu, a coastal sultanate founded by Ahmed-bin-Fumu Luti, sultan of Patta (an island off the coast), after Patta had been conquered by Zanzibar. In 1885 Ahmed placed his state under German protection, and in 1887 he was succeeded by the sultan Bakari. In 1890 Germany transferred the protectorate to Britain, and after the sultan had instigated the murder of nine Germans, an expedition under Vice-Admiral Sir Edmund Fremantle was sent to Witu in October 1890, comprising naval personnel, IBEA Company police and some Zanzibari troops; two steamers belonging to the Company were also used. Unrest continued until 1894 (including an expedition of August 1893, of naval personnel led by Captain G. R. Lindley, RN), until the recognition of Omar-bin-Hamed as sultan in 1895; he ruled thereafter with the guidance of a British Resident. In 1895–6 a revolt occurred as a result of disputed succession to a chieftainship in the Mazrui, the most important Arab clan in the coastal region; it ended when the leaders of the revolt fled to German territory in April 1896. From this period the Arab domination of the East African coast effectively ended, especially after the capture of the stronghold of the Arab sheikh 'Mbaruk at Mwele (17 August 1895) by Rear-Admiral H. H. Rawson, commander-

Seamen from Admiral H. H. Rawson's expedition in the stockade at Mwele, the stronghold of the Arab sheikh 'Mbaruk, captured by the British on 17 August 1895. The sheikh escaped and finally surrendered in German territory.

in-chief Cape and East Africa station, naval personnel, Uganda Rifles and Indian Army units. A small expedition of naval personnel was sent to the Juba River (August 1893) to rescue captives taken by the Somalis of that area, but the main trouble encountered in the colony was with the Nandi people, who raided their neighbours and British outposts and railways from the late 1890s; their resistance did not end until an expedition was sent against them in September–November 1905. As the Nandi had shown most hostility to the railway and telegraph lines (the Mombasa–Victoria–Nyanza line, built 1896–1903, ran through their territory), in 1905–6 they were removed to reserves north of the railway line.

Uganda

Uganda was bounded by British East Africa on the east, the Anglo-Egyptian Sudan on the north, German East Africa on the south and the Belgian Congo on the west; its name came from a Swahili pronunciation of the name of the Bantu kingdom of Buganda, which became one of the five provinces of the protectorate. The Baganda people inhabiting this region were remarkable in having a royal dynasty which could trace its descent at least from the 15th century.

The early period of European presence in Uganda was one of confused conflict between religions and between colonial powers anxious to secure commercial and territorial interests. The king or emperor of Buganda opened relations with the British in Zanzibar following contacts with British explorers, resulting in the arrival of Anglican missionaries in 1877; they were followed by French Roman Catholics in 1879, and the presence of increasing numbers of Zanzibar Arabs created a three-sided rivalry for religious supremacy in Buganda. The conflict between the adherents of each faction resulted in much bloodshed, virtual civil war and the ousting of kings, until the Anglo-German treaty of July 1890 assigned Uganda to Britain's sphere of interest. As elsewhere, the first British involvement was commercial, via the Imperial British East Africa Company.

In October 1890 the Company sent Captain Frederick Lugard into Uganda, with some 50 Sudanese troops; an experienced British officer who had served in the Afghan War 1879–80, Sudan 1884–5 and Burma 1886–7, Lugard had recently been campaigning in Nyasaland. In January 1891 he was reinforced by another small force of Sudanese under Captain W. H. Williams, RA. The Baganda Christians had already driven the Islamic faction to take refuge under the protection of King Kabarega of Bunyoro-Kitara (or 'Unyoro', to the north of Buganda, in what became the northern province of Uganda, adjoining Lake Albert and the Belgian Congo). Lugard succeeded in uniting the Christian factions temporarily and in April 1891 led them against the Muslims, who had been raiding the Buganda frontier, and defeated them. Then, seeking to assemble a

reliable military force, he marched through Bunyoro, defeating Kabarega's forces at Muhokya and Butanuka, to Kavalli's at the southern end of Lake Albert, to enlist into his service the Sudanese left there by Emin Pasha following the Mahdist revolt in the Sudan. Lugard succeeded in bringing away some 8,000 people (men, women, children and slaves) under an Egyptian officer, Selim Bey; with these he established posts along the Bunyoro frontier. Returning to Buganda, Lugard found the 'British' and 'French' factions on the point of civil war, and when hostilities finally broke out King Mwanga of Buganda and his 'French' party were beaten; but Lugard arranged for the king's reinstatement, and by considerable diplomacy not only settled this conflict but even came to an accommodation with the Islamic party.

The Company decided that it could no longer afford to maintain its position in Uganda, and in June 1892 Lugard left for Britain to advocate its retention; a British government commission recommended the continuance of British administration of Buganda, and Sir Gerald Portal became the territory's first commissioner. In late 1893 his successor, Colonel Henry Colville, led the Baganda army (some 15,000 strong, with 400 Sudanese) against Bunyoro, which was subdued after a number of actions, although Kabarega avoided being drawn into a decisive action, and minor hostilities continued. In June 1894 Uganda was

Captain (later Colonel Sir) Frederick John Dealtry Lugard, in the uniform of the Norfolk Regiment (identified by the Britannia collar-badge).

declared a protectorate, extended to cover Bunyoro in 1896, and the remainder of what became Uganda in subsequent years, although not until 1910 was the frontier with Belgian and German territory finally agreed. The 'British' and 'French' parties in Buganda being reconciled, the country assumed a peaceful aspect (although in 1893 it had been necessary to deport Selim Bey for conspiring against the British); but in 1897 further military action became necessary.

Captain J. R. L. Macdonald (later Sir James), who had administered the territory briefly, left for an exploration in East Africa, for which 300 Sudanese troops were required from Uganda. In July 1897 Mwanga of Buganda attempted to rebel; he was defeated and fled to German territory, where he was interned. The three Sudanese companies sent to Macdonald, complaining about pay and uninterrupted active service, mutinied in the Nandi district and marched back to Uganda, pillaging as they went; Macdonald pursued with a force of Zanzibaris. The mutineers arrived at the garrisoned post of Luba's near the Ripon Falls (alternatively spelled 'Lubwa's', which is how it appears on the appropriate clasp of the East and Central Africa Medal). From 19 October, when Macdonald engaged the mutineers, to 9 January 1898, the siege of Luba's progressed, with a large force of the 'British' faction assisting Macdonald. Other Sudanese garrisons remained loyal, as did the Baganda Islamic leader Mbogo, although some Muslims did join the mutineers. In January 1898 Mwanga escaped from German territory, declared himself a Muslim and assembled a large rebel force, which Macdonald defeated with the assistance of the Baganda army. Meanwhile, the mutineers broke out of Luba's (about 600 strong, plus 200 Muslim Baganda); to prevent them infecting the Bunyoro garrisons Macdonald pursued, then returned to the capital (Kampala), leaving Captain E. G. Harrison to subdue the mutineers. He made a successful attack on their stockaded position at Kabagambi. Mwanga made his way north to join Kabarega, and on 9 April 1899 near Kangai they were apprehended by a force under Lieutenant-Colonel J. T. Evatt. Both were deported to the Seychelles; Mwanga died there in 1903, but Kabarega, who had lost an arm in consequence of wounds sustained in the fight in which he was captured, was permitted to return to Bunyoro in 1923, but died before he reached home. With the mutineers dispersed, the last of the rebels were subdued in 1900–01, and final settlement of unrest was achieved by the Treaty of Mengo (March 1900), by which Daudi Chwa, an infant son of Mwanga, was recognised as king of Buganda (under the title of 'the Kabaka'), the kingdom to be governed by a regency during his minority. Buganda had its own parliament (the Lukiko), and formed one of six (later five) provinces of the protectorate. A particularly unfortunate consequence of the introduction of the Sudanese was the spread of sleeping-sickness which, it was thought, they brought with them; it caused devastation in Uganda from 1901 and in eight years was believed to have taken as many as 250,000 lives.

Zanzibar

The geographical position of the island of Zanzibar gave it considerable significance. The Arabs who occupied it made it the centre of the East African slave trade, and from 1832 the town of Zanzibar became the capital of the dominions of Sultan (Sayyid) Säid of Muscat. In 1856 the African section passed to one of his sons, Majid, who was in turn succeeded by his brother, with the title Sultan of Zanzibar. As well as for the commercial aspect of Zanzibar's position (the centre of trade between East Africa, India and Arabia), Britain's involvement was concerned with the suppression of the slave trade, and Britain's consul at Zanzibar exerted considerable influence over these two rulers, Majid and Bargash bin Säid; a treaty for the suppression of the slave trade throughout the Sultanate was concluded in 1873. The East African lands over which Zanzibar laid claim were appropriated by various European powers, so that Bargash's successor in 1888, Sayyid Khalifa, retained only a fragment of the original territory. British influence in Zanzibar was paramount; a British naval officer, Lloyd (later Sir Lloyd) Mathews was appointed to head Bargash's military force (and later served as prime minister), and in 1890 Zanzibar was proclaimed a British protectorate, following negotiation with France and Germany, in which Britain renounced all claims to Madagascar and Heligoland respectively, and Germany withdrew its claim on Zanzibar.

In February 1890 Khalifa was succeeded by his brother Ali, who was himself succeeded by Hamed bin Thwain (or 'Hamid bin Thuwaini') in March 1893. On his death on 25 August 1896 the throne was appropriated, with German support, by his cousin, Sayyid Khalid bin Bargash; this did not meet with Britain's approval and the resulting hostilities constituted probably the shortest war on record. British seamen and marines were landed from the two warships in harbour (the 2nd class cruiser HMS *Philomel* and gunboat *Thrush*), to join the forces of the British-administered government and to protect the British consulate. The self-proclaimed sultan mustered his own forces of some 2,500 men, two 12pdrs, a Gatling gun, a 17th-century bronze cannon and the Sultan's navy, the ex-British frigate *Glasgow* which had been presented to Zanzibar in 1878. The British cruiser *St. George* arrived, bearing Rear-Admiral H. H. Rawson, C-in-C Cape and East Africa Station, with the gunboats *Sparrow* and *Raccoon*, but the new sultan refused to relinquish office, and upon the expiry of the British ultimatum at 9 a.m. on 27 August, the squadron opened fire (the European lady residents of Zanzibar having been evacuated to the *St. George* that morning). *Glasgow* was sunk, the sultan's palace destroyed and his artillery silenced; Khalid fled to the German consulate, and the 'war' ended at 9.45 a.m. when the British ceased fire after the usurper's flag had been shot down. About 500 of his supporters were killed or wounded, against one British seaman wounded. Peace was restored within a very short time by British landing-parties, and the British government representative in Zanzibar installed in Khalid's place Hamed bin Mahommed, Hamed bin Thwain's brother. The government was re-organised, the sultan's influence greatly reduced, and in 1897 the legal status of slavery was abolished. Khalid was granted asylum in German East Africa, where he was apprehended by the British in 1917; after exile in the Seychelles and at St. Helena he was eventually permitted to return to East Africa.

Military Forces: East Africa

As elsewhere, the earliest 'British' military forces in East Africa were those organised by the trading interests, hence the employment of the Sudanese by the IBEA Company. The necessity of maintaining troops was so obvious that when the Company decided to leave Uganda in 1892, the British government paid them a subsidy to finance their continued presence until the British commission could report on the practicality of holding the territory. The potential opponents of the British were formidable not only in terms of numbers: contacts with European missionaries and traders had led to the replacement of traditional weapons such as spears with firearms, although they remained undisciplined and vulnerable to European-style tactics. During Kabarega's guerrilla operations, for example, he attempted to attack Fort Hoima (in Bunyoro) on 27 August 1894, only to be defeated by Captain A. B. Thruston whose flank attack caused Kabarega's followers to retire; more than 200 were killed, against only eight in Thruston's force. The scale of the difficulties facing the British in times of unrest was such as to necessitate the employment of regular troops: in the operations in Uganda in 1897–8, for example, the 14th and 15th Sikhs and 27th Bombay Light Infantry were deployed in addition to locally raised forces.

The British local forces originated with the Company troops. Lugard's original Sudanese, augmented by the 600 combatants (and their long train of followers) enlisted from Emin's force, formed the nucleus of the Uganda Rifles of 1895, when the British government took over from the Company. (Not all the unit were Sudanese: in 1891 four companies of Sikhs and Punjabis were added.) Macdonald, at that time surveying for the Uganda railway, increased the strength of the Uganda Rifles to 900, and in 1895 the Uganda Rifles Ordinance set an establishment of seventeen Sudanese companies in addition to the Indians. Following the mutiny in Uganda, in which the Sikh companies of the Rifles were notable in the work of suppression, Major Cyril Martyr of the Duke of Cornwall's Light Infantry was sent to reorganise the unit. Having settled the

grievances (by, for example, a four-fold increase in pay and proper issue of uniform and equipment), Martyr took six companies of Sudanese (each of five native officers and 112 other ranks, with their families) in his expedition along the Nile in response to the threat of French expansionism, which came to a head at Fashoda. This expedition, which collaborated with the Belgians, demonstrated the hardiness and abilities of the Sudanese, with all thoughts of the recent mutiny dismissed. By 1901 the Uganda Rifles comprised two battalions of some 1,364 Sudanese and 387 Indians.

A similar unit existed in East Africa, the East Africa Rifles being formed in 1895 from the Company's forces in that area, and on 1 January 1902 a new formation was decreed, the King's African Rifles, covering East and Central Africa. The 1st and 2nd Battalions Central Africa Rifles became the 1st and 2nd Battalions KAR, the East Africa Rifles became the 3rd Battalion KAR, the 1st and 2nd Battalions Uganda Rifles became the 4th and 5th Battalions KAR, and the 6th Battalion KAR was formed from local forces in Somaliland. The 5th Battalion KAR was disbanded in 1904, but re-constituted in 1916. A remarkable tradition maintained in the 4th Battalion KAR was the continued use of the Turkish reveille, dating from their origin as part of the Egyptian Army under Emin.

References

Austin, Major H. H. *With Macdonald in Uganda*, London, 1903.

Colville, Colonel Sir Henry. *The Land of the Nile Springs, being chiefly an account of how we fought Kabarega*, London, 1895.

Cunningham, Major G. G. *Report on the Military Operations against Kabarega, King of Unyoro*, London, 1896.

Dunbar, A. R. *A History of Bunyoro-Kitara*, Nairobi, 1965 (includes the campaigns against Kabarega).

– *Omukama Chwa II Kabarega*, Kampala, 1965.

Knight, I. *Queen Victoria's Enemies (2): Northern Africa*, London, 1989 (includes brief material on the Nandi).

Lugard, Captain F. *The Rise of Our East African Empire*, Edinburgh and London, 1893.

Patience, K. *Zanzibar and the Shortest War in History*, Bahrein, 1994.

Vandeleur, Lieutenant S. *Campaigning on the Upper Nile and Niger*, London, 1898 (Seymour Vandeleur served under Colville in Bunyoro).

EGYPT

Britain's long military association with Egypt arose primarily from the strategic importance of that country in relation to British possessions in the east, principally India. The first British campaign in Egypt was in support of the Ottoman Empire (of which Egypt was a semiautonomous part), in opposition to Napoleon Bonaparte's invasion, the prospect of a French conquest of Egypt presenting a threat to the British in India. The French landed in Egypt in July 1798 and defeated the Ottoman forces opposing them, but following the destruction of the French fleet by Horatio Nelson's British fleet at the Battle of Aboukir Bay (1 August 1798, also styled the 'Battle of the Nile'), the French army was virtually marooned. A British expedition in support of the Ottoman force landed in Egypt on 8 March 1801, commanded by the worthy Sir Ralph Abercromby; it fought an action on 13 March, but the decisive battle took place at Alexandria on 21 March, in which the French were comprehensively defeated. Abercromby was mortally wounded in the action; he was succeeded by a commander of much inferior capability, Major-General Hely Hutchinson, but the French surrendered before further operations were necessary. A supporting expedition from India, under Sir David Baird, arrived only after the cessation of hostilities. Another small expedition, ill-planned and under-strength, was sent to Egypt in 1807 as an interference in the virtual civil war occurring in that country, and ostensibly to frustrate French intentions; it withdrew in September 1807 after having suffered considerable losses to no useful purpose.

With the decline of the mameluke beys who had ruled Egypt under nominal Ottoman suzerainty, in succeeding years power was seized by Mehemet (or Mohammed) Ali, an Albanian officer of the Ottoman army. Having eliminated dissent in Egypt (including a massacre of the leading mamelukes in March 1811), he expanded his territory into the Sudan and, as a nominal vassal of the Ottoman empire, assisted the Turks during the Greek War of Independence. In return, Mehemet Ali demanded Syria from the empire; this led to the First and Second Turko-Egyptian Wars (1832–3 and 1839–41). Faced with the possibility of a complete collapse of the Ottoman empire, the European 'great powers' became involved, and after mediation Mehemet Ali was confirmed as hereditary ruler of Egypt, and as viceroy and governor of the Sudan, nominally still part of the Ottoman empire, but effectually independent.

The strategic importance of Egypt was enhanced by the opening of the Suez Canal in 1869, providing the easiest sea-route from Britain to India. Its construction was financed by the Suez Canal Company, a private venture in which a major shareholder was the then incumbent of Mehemet Ali's throne, his grandson Ismail Pasha, who had succeeded his uncle in 1863. In 1867 Ismail received an enhanced title from the Ottoman sultan, that of *khedive*, but as his prestige improved so his finances declined, until in 1875 his spendthrift behaviour compelled him to sell his Suez Canal shares. The British prime minister Disraeli purchased them for £3,976,582, giving Britain a controlling interest in the canal, and preventing an increase in the stake already held by France. The sum received by Ismail, however, represented barely one-twentieth of Egypt's foreign debt, and by 1876 the country was effectively bankrupt. Ismail was forced to accept the intervention of an international commission to superintend his finances, and the powers most closely involved, Britain and France, each appointed an official to run Egypt's finances, the so-called system of 'Dual Control'. In September 1878 Ismail replaced this by a constitutional ministry which included a British finance minister and a French minister of public works, but within seven months Ismail dismissed it and re-assumed his previous autocratic powers. Britain and France responded by persuading the sultan to announce Ismail's deposition and his replacement as *khedive* by his son, Mohammed Tewfik (June 1879); 'Dual Control' was re-established in the following November.

Although this system of financial management was in Egypt's best interest, it was regarded by many Egyptians as unwarranted interference by both Turks (the sultan hav-

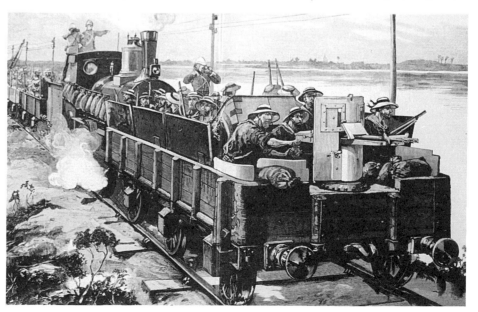

An armoured train in Egypt, 1882, with a detachment of seamen manning a 4-barrelled Nordenfelt gun in the first truck. At the rear of the train were mounted a 9pdr and a Gatling gun. (Engraving after W. H. Overend)

Tel-el-Kebir: Black Watch storm the Egyptian positions. (Print after H. Dupray)

ing deposed their *khedive*) and Europeans. Nowhere was this resentment felt more deeply than in the army, and especially among the middle-ranking officers of Egyptian background whose promotion had traditionally been blocked by the appointment of Turks to the higher positions. Resistance centred around an Egyptian-born colonel, Ahmed Arabi (or 'Urabi), who became the spokesman for the movement of those wishing to throw off foreign domination. Faced with growing Egyptian nationalism and with the *khedive* virtually powerless, Britain and France sent a joint naval force to Alexandria to demonstrate support for the *khedive* (May 1882); and demanded that Arabi be dismissed from the position of war minister, to which he had been elevated in the *khedive*'s government, which was broadly supportive of Arabi's views. The entire ministry resigned, and the *khedive* was compelled to re-instate Arabi. Encouraged by Arabi's party, popular hostility was directed towards Christians and foreigners, culminating in a riot at Alexandria on 11 June 1882 in which some fifty Europeans were killed. Although opposed to the idea of military intervention, the British government began to plan for such an eventuality, as Arabi's followers continued to improve the defences of Alexandria in the face of the threat from the Anglo-French naval force, despite demands that such fortification be suspended.

On 10 July 1882 the British naval commander, Admiral Sir Beauchamp Seymour, issued an ultimatum that unless the Alexandria forts were surrendered within 24 hours, action would be taken. The French squadron sailed away in the evening, unwilling to become involved in hostilities; and on 11 July Seymour bombarded the defences, silencing the Egyptian shore batteries by late afternoon. Arabi thereupon withdrew his forces, leaving Alexandria at the mercy of the mob until Seymour landed seamen and

marines on 14 July to restore order. He was reinforced by a small military contingent under Major-General Sir Archibald Allison, who established a defensive position around Alexandria to resist any attack from Arabi.

Further military action was now inevitable. The British had hoped that a small expedition to secure the Canal would be sufficient, but it became obvious that a major effort would be necessary to restore the authority of the *khedive*, and as neither France nor the Ottoman Empire were prepared to commit forces, the expedition had to be entirely British. Egyptian nationalist feeling was now dominant, and Arabi was appointed as commander-in-chief by a military committee.

Britain assembled a powerful force, including some 16,400 men from Britain, 7,600 from the Mediterranean garrisons and nearly 7,000 from India; the speed with which they arrived in Egypt was testimony to improved communications and modes of transport, which would have been inconceivable a generation before. The force began to disembark at Alexandria on 12 August, with their commander, Lieutenant-General Sir Garnet Wolseley, landing on 15 August. Wolseley, the Adjutant-General, not only commanded the expedition but had been instrumental in its planning, both administratively and in the formulation of its objectives, primarily the crushing of the revolt at its centre, Cairo.

The landing at Alexandria and the augmentation of the force already there was a feint to disguise Wolseley's first objective, the securing of the Suez Canal and the use of its mid-point, Ismailia, as the base for an advance on Cairo from the east, instead of the longer route from the west, from Alexandria. On 18 August part of Wolseley's force re-embarked and sailed to Port Said, on the Mediterranean end of the Canal; landing-parties secured Port Said, Suez at the southern end of the Canal, and Kantara and

Ismailia along its length, thus opening the waterway for Wolseley's force from Port Said and the Indian contingent from the south. Concentrating at Ismailia, Wolseley pushed west towards the main concentration of Arabi's forces, fighting a minor action at Magfar (24 August) and occupying Kassassin (26 August), both to secure a water-supply (via the Sweetwater Canal which supplied Ismailia, and which the Egyptians were trying to block at Magfar), and to secure the rail route from Ismailia westwards. Wolseley's position at Kassassin (commanded by Major-General Gerald Graham) was attacked by Arabi's troops on 28 August, but the attack was repelled, culminating in the celebrated, nocturnal 'moonlight charge' of the Household Cavalry and 7th Dragoon Guards, which routed the Egyptians. A further attack on Kassassin was repelled on 9 September.

With his supply-lines and railway secure, Wolseley advanced upon Arabi's main position at Tel-el-Kebir, some six miles west of Kassassin, an entrenched, 4-mile-long series of earthworks, the strongest straddling the Sweetwater Canal, behind which Arabi had gathered at least 20,000 regular troops, 2,000 tribesmen and 75 pieces of artillery (Wolseley estimated the Egyptian strength as considerably greater, and it may have been). Because of the strength of the position, Wolseley declined a daylight attack but planned a nocturnal advance; without preliminary bombardment but with artillery accompanying the assaulting brigades, to open fire as soon as the element of surprise was lost. This was an audacious plan, given the difficulty of moving silently at night, but one which worked almost perfectly. In the early dawn of 13 September Wolseley's two-pronged attack (1st Division on the right, 2nd on the left) was discovered by Egyptian sentries; but the Highland Brigade, leading the 2nd Division, was within 150 yards of the Egyptian entrenchments before the defenders were able to open fire. The 1st Division had more ground to cover under fire, but once the entrenchments were penetrated the combat, though fierce, was of short duration; by 6 a.m., barely an hour after the firing of the first shot, the Egyptians were in full retreat. Given the strength of the position, British losses were remarkably few: 57 killed, 382 wounded and 30 missing, of which the Highland Brigade lost 45 dead and 186 wounded. Egyptian losses were about 2,000 killed and an unknown number wounded, but for them it was also a moral defeat, which (as Wolseley had predicted) led to the immediate collapse of the rebellion. On 14 September Cairo was entered and Arabi surrendered, and on 25 September *Khedive* Tewfik re-entered his capital. Arabi was sentenced to death for treason, but by the influence of the British his sentence was commuted to banishment to Ceylon in December 1882; he was permitted to return to Egypt in 1901.

Even given the fact that the Egyptian forces were less well-organised than those of the British, this was a remarkably successful operation, lasting almost exactly one

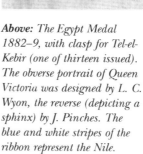

Above: The Egypt Medal 1882–9, with clasp for Tel-el-Kebir (one of thirteen issued). The obverse portrait of Queen Victoria was designed by L. C. Wyon, the reverse (depicting a sphinx) by J. Pinches. The blue and white stripes of the ribbon represent the Nile.

Above right: The Khedive's Star, issued by the Khedive in four varieties for the campaigns of 1882, 1884, 1884–6 and undated (for 1887–9), with a clasp for Tokar (1891). Manufactured in bronze in Birmingham and issued to all those (British and others) involved in the suppression of Arabi's revolt and subsequent campaigns, the reverse bore the Khedive's monogram 'MT' (Mohammed Tewfik). The lower inscription in the circlet on the obverse is 'Khedive of Egypt' in Arabic, and the date 'A.H'. The ribbon was dark blue.

month from the expedition's main landing to effective conclusion. Wolseley's appreciation of logistic necessities were to a large degree responsible, and it really was a case of 'all Sir Garnet', i.e., 'all in order' in contemporary slang.

In the aftermath of the defeat of Arabi, Tewfik ordered the creation of another army, to be raised and trained by Major-General Evelyn Wood, who was appointed its *sirdar* (commander-in-chief). Despite the original unwillingness of the British government to become enmeshed militarily in Egyptian affairs, a British garrison remained in Egypt, and henceforth, although the *khedive* was the nominal ruler of Egypt, with an Egyptian ministry, British officials were integrated into the administration, and a British commissioner was appointed, and no laws were passed without British approval. The British presence in Egypt aroused some resentment in France, the dominant power in the remainder of North Africa, but an Anglo-French understanding was concluded in April 1904, which virtually recognised the dominance of France in Morocco and of the British in Egypt. Military operations involving Egypt subsequent to 1882 were concentrated in the Sudan, and are covered in that section of this work.

Military Forces: Egypt

At the time of Arabi's revolt, the Egyptian army was equipped and organised along European lines, Ismail having employed European and American officers to train his forces, notably 48 Americans under General C. P. Stone. The army's strength fluctuated markedly, to some extent dependent upon the affluence of the government. By the early 1870s it was reported that Ismail was able to field some 100,000 equipped men, but in the period leading up to Arabi's revolt the army had been greatly diminished, so that by the time the British began to reform the army, its strength in Egypt was probably only about 18,000; in addition to the 'Army of the Delta' dispersed at Tel-el-Kebir, a further 40,000 men were distributed throughout the Sudan. Some 11,000 had been sent to Abyssinia but had met with two disasters (Gundet, 13 November 1875, and Gura, 25 March 1876), which virtually annihilated the expedition.

The rank and file were largely recruited by enforced conscription from the Egyptian *fellahin*, peasants from the Nile delta, who were generally regarded as unmilitary but who, as at Tel-el-Kebir and especially in defensive positions, were capable of considerable resolution even after being abandoned by their officers. Sudanese recruits, and those sometimes described as 'Nubians' (i.e., from the equatorial regions) were thought to possess a more martial spirit, and others were drawn from other regions of the Ottoman empire, including Albanians and Circassians. Wretched conditions, low or non-existent pay, harsh discipline and the contempt of their officers all adversely affected the morale of the conscripted and generally unwilling *fellahin*. The junior officers were mostly drawn from this population, and had little opportunity of promotion, as the higher ranks were generally the preserve of Turks or Circassians; in the period immediately preceding Arabi's revolt some 2,500 officers were dismissed as a consequence of Egypt's financial difficulties. The foreign officers were even more remote from their juniors and the rank and file, being employed mostly in administrative, technical and staff posts. Therefore unrest was rife, and Arabi's revolt held the greater appeal in that he was one of few *fellahin* to have risen to medium rank.

Although it is difficult to calculate, Arabi's force may have amounted to some 60,000 in total, distributed throughout Egypt; concentration was impossible because of the need to keep strong forces to watch the British operations outside Alexandria, and in the capital. Some of these men were in existing units, others were soldiers recalled to the army, reversing the recent reductions in strength, yet others were newly conscripted. The infantry was organised in battalions of four companies of about 200 men each, and if the Turko-Circassian higher-ranking officers had been corrupt and inefficient, the Egyptians were much better. The army was uniformed in European style, in dark blue tunic and trousers in winter and white in summer, with only the red *tarboosh* (fez) proclaiming their Middle-Eastern identity. Although the army included regular cavalry, dressed similarly to the infantry, most of Arabi's horsemen appear to have been irregular tribes-

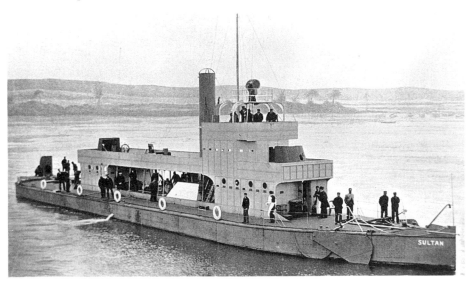

Gunboats played a significant role in campaigning on the Nile; this is the Sultan, a shallow-draught vessel (only 2 feet) built by Yarrow & Co., with a hull in eleven sections, so as to be easily transportable. She mounted two 12pdrs and eight Maxim guns.

men, wearing their everyday costume. (At Tel-el-Kebir, for example, Arabi had some eighteen infantry battalions but only one cavalry regiment, plus the irregular horse.) The standard weapon of the Egyptian army was the American 11mm (.433) Remington 'rolling-block' rifle with sword-bayonet; some 60,000 of these, manufactured in the USA, had been delivered to Egypt in 1876. It also existed as a short-barrelled cavalry carbine and artillery musketoon. There was some use of older weapons among the newly formed units, and 'traditional' weapons were carried by the irregulars. Ismail had built up a strong force of ordnance, up to 500 fieldpieces, principally 80mm and 90mm breech-loading Krupp guns, and 90mm muzzle-loading rifled howitzers.

In January 1883, after the crushing of Arabi's revolt, the new *sirdar*, Sir Evelyn Wood, was given £200,000 for the creation of a 6,000-strong *fellahin* force for the defence of Egypt; he was assisted initially by 26 officers including the future Kitchener of Khartoum.

('Said England unto Pharaoh, "I must make a man of you,
That will stand upon his feet and play the game;
That will Maxim his oppressor as a Christian ought to do",
And she sent old Pharaoh Sergeant Whatisname.')*
Egyptian officers were selected from those of Arabi's men who had been least prominent in the revolt, and NCO instructors were also drawn from the 'old' army; but the rank and file were recruited afresh, by conscripting the largest and strongest *fellahin* who had been unable to bribe officials to gain exemption. Subsequently this practice was prevented – or made official – by a regulation which permitted the purchase of exemption before a conscription-ballot was held, a proportion of the sum thus raised (styled *badalia*) being used to improve the condition of the army. Service was restricted to a five-year term with the regulars, followed by five years in the reserve, during which period men could be mobilised for manoeuvres or police service. The conditions of the ordinary soldier were improved radically, with pay and rations being distributed at the correct time, which had not been the case earlier.

Initially eight battalions were formed, in two brigades, two cavalry regiments, four artillery batteries and a camel company; the 1st Brigade had three British field officers for each battalion, but the 2nd Brigade Turks and Egyptians, and it was noted that the latter drilled their men the hardest, presumably to prove themselves the equal of the British-officered battalions. The army was competent to drill with precision some ten weeks after the first enlistments, and although words of command were given in Turkish (the ordinary language of the Egyptians was not thought suitable for curt, clearly understood commands), the *sirdar* gave his commands in German, as that language was understood by the army's British officers and by the Egyptian brigadier, who had spent time in Berlin. Drill was

based upon that of the British Army, and the disciplinary system, which in the old army was based upon the French model, was replaced by a slight modification of the 1881 British Army Act. A gendarmerie was also formed, under Colonel Valentine Baker, an ex-commanding officer of the British 10th Hussars, who had entered Turkish service after being convicted of indecently assaulting a woman in a railway carriage.

The inadequacies of the old system were demonstrated by the disasters which overtook Hicks and Baker in the Sudan (1883–4) (see that section), and to stiffen the *fellahin*, experiments were made in recruiting foreigners. A scheme to raise an Albanian battalion failed when its

Colonel Sir Francis Reginald Wingate, fourth British sirdar of the Egyptian army, in whose uniform he appears here; Evelyn Wood's ADC at the creation of the 'new' Egyptian army after Arabi's revolt, he succeeded Kitchener in supreme command in December 1899. Much of his most valuable work was as head of the Egyptian Intelligence Department; he served as sirdar and as governor-general of the Sudan 1899–1917, and was awarded a baronetcy in 1920.

members mutinied on being ordered to the Sudan, so battalions of Sudanese and inhabitants of the Equatorial provinces were formed instead. The first, the 9th (Sudanese) Battalion, was created for service at Suakin, and was found to be so efficient that four others followed, and upon them the brunt of the Egyptian army's active service fell. Some of their officers were Sudanese, some Egyptian, and the practice of employing British officers continued, even though a military school system for the education of Egyptian officers was reorganised in 1887. It was said that the Egyptians excelled at administrative duties, while the Sudanese were more martial, better marksmen and remarkably self-reliant on active service.

For the re-formed army a new uniform was designed by R. Caton Woodville, who had been present in the late campaign as a war artist. He decided that blue was the best colour to contrast with the skin-colour of the Egyptians: sky-blue with white facings for cavalry, medium blue faced cream for infantry, and dark blue faced red for artillery, all worn with the *tarboosh*; white tunic and trousers were worn in summer, although a dark blue jersey was also worn, especially by the Sudanese battalions. The British officers wore British khaki service dress.

Ultimately the army comprised eighteen infantry battalions, the 9th–14th Sudanese (by 1898, nos. 5–8 had no British officers, nos. 1–4 only four each), ten cavalry squadrons, five artillery batteries and a camel corps. Command of the Egyptian army remained in the hands of a British *sirdar*: in March 1885 Sir Evelyn Wood was succeeded by Sir Francis Grenfell, who was succeeded by Kitchener in March 1892; the fourth British *sirdar*, who had been Wood's ADC at the time of the creation of the 'new' army, was Major-General Sir Francis Wingate who succeeded Kitchener in December 1899.

Note

*Anon., 'Pharoah's Army' in *Navy and Army Illustrated*, vol. V, p. 249, 4 February 1898.

References

The following are works concerned with Egypt; others, covering operations in both Egypt and the Sudan, are listed in the section on the latter territory.

Barthorp, M. J. *War on the Nile: Britain, Egypt and the Sudan 1882–1898*, Poole, 1984.

Blaxland, G. *Objective: Egypt*, London, 1966 (overview of campaigns in Egypt from the conquest of the Persian Cambyses to Suez 1956).

Blunt, W. S. *Secret History of the English Occupation of Egypt*, London, 1907.

Bond, B. (ed.). *Victorian Military Campaigns*, London, 1967

(includes 'The Egyptian Campaign of 1882', M. J. Williams).

Featherstone, D. *Victoria's Enemies: An A–Z of British Colonial Warfare*, London, 1989.

Goodrich, Lieutenant-Commander C. F. *Report of the British Naval and Military Operations in Egypt in 1882*, Washington, 1885.

Knight, I. *Queen Victoria's Enemies (2): Northern Africa*, London, 1989.

Malet, Sir Edward. *Egypt 1879–1883*, London, 1909.

Mansfield P. *The British in Egypt*, London, 1971.

Maurice, Colonel J. F. *Military history of the Campaign of 1882 in Egypt*, London, 1887 (almost the 'official history': prepared in the Intelligence Branch of the War Office).

THE MEDITERRANEAN

Almost all British military operations in the Mediterranean region, excluding those relating to the north coast of Africa, were undertaken as a result of European conflicts, and thus cannot be regarded as 'colonial'. These included operations in or around British possessions in the Mediterranean, Malta, Gibraltar and the comparatively brief occupation of the Ionian Islands; and those involving the Ottoman Empire, for example the destruction of the Turkish fleet by an Anglo-Franco-Russian fleet under Admiral Sir Edward Codrington at Navarino (20 October 1827), which effectively ensured the independence of Greece; and the Anglo-Austrian action against the Egyptian invasion of Syria in 1840. The latter was undertaken to preserve the faltering Ottoman Empire as a buffer to the expansionist plans of others, especially Russia, and it was in pursuance of this policy that the one 'colonial' operation occurred, albeit not involving combat.

The island of Cyprus was an independent kingdom from 1192 to 1489, ruled by the dynasty of Guy de Lusignan, king of Jerusalem, until its possession passed to the Venetian Republic. Cyprus was conquered by the Turks in 1570–1, and remained part of the Ottoman Empire until 1878, when as part of the measures to guard against Russian expansionism, Britain concluded the Cyprus Convention with the Sultan of Turkey (4 June 1878). Under its terms, Britain undertook to assist the Sultan in defence of his possessions, in return for which, and for use as a base for the provision of such support, he assigned Cyprus to be occupied and administered by Britain. The British took possession on 12 June, and later in the year set out the terms of administration, by a high commissioner with the authority of a colonial governor, assisted by executive and legislative councils.

As occurred elsewhere, British military officers were employed in the colony's civil administration; the first high commissioner and governor-general, for example, was Sir Garnet Wolseley, and from March 1880 the Director of Revenue Survey was Lieutenant Herbert Kitchener, RE, later Lord Kitchener of Khartoum. A British garrison was maintained on the island, and at the height of the perceived Russian threat (1878) Indian troops were sent there (and to Malta), this being the first employment of the Indian Army in Europe. In the usual way, local forces were formed to assist the regular garrison. One of these, the Cyprus Military Police, was basically the old Turkish quasi-military force of *Zaptiehs*, although the organisation was reformed and enlarged following the British occupation. Their uniform was quite distinctive, in Turko-Cypriot style, including a white turban wrapped around a red fez, a red shirt and waistcoat with blue braid, and blue trousers and cummerbund. In 1879 the Cyprus Pioneer Corps was formed by the Cyprus Police Augmentation Ordinance, classed as a colonial regiment rather than a local force, composed of one-third Greek and two-thirds Turkish Cypriots, under British command; they wore a similar costume to that of the *Zaptiehs*, with a similar head-dress, white shirt and red waistcoat both with yellow lace, yellow or yellow-and-brown checked cummerbund, and blue trousers with yellow stripe. In March 1881 this unit was absorbed into the Military Police. In 1885 the strength of the Military Police was 650, including 629 *Zaptiehs* (216 mounted) and 21 officers, seven of whom were British. Operations conducted in Cyprus were basically of a police nature, in the suppression of banditry.

References

Donne, Colonel B. D. A. *The Life and Times of a Victorian Officer: being the journals and letters of Col. Benjamin Donisthorpe Alsop Donne C.B.*, ed. Major A. J. Harfield, Wincanton, 1986 (includes much on Donne's service with local forces in Cyprus, including many of his own paintings. The editor's paper on the Cypriot corps appeared in *Bulletin of the Military Historical Society*, vol. XXVI, 1975, pp. 1–7).

Preston, A. 'Sir Garnet Wolseley and the Cyprus Expedition 1878', in *Journal of the Society for Army Historical Research*, vol. XLV, 1967.

NORTHERN AFRICA

With the exception of Egypt (covered here separately), British involvement in the colonial warfare of northern Africa was very limited. The four 'Barbary states' (the kingdom of Morocco and the three semi-independent satellites of the Ottoman Empire, Algiers, Tripoli and Tunisia) initially came into contact with the European powers only in relation to the piratical activities of the corsairs which operated from them; this also resulted in United States' involvement, in the US–Tripoli war of 1804–5, and the US–Algerian war of 1815. Opposition to the Algerian pirates led to France's invasion of Algeria in 1830, the state being conquered by the French by 1847, despite the sterling opposition of the emir of Mascara, Abd el Kader, who resisted from 1832 until his decisive defeat at Isly (14 August 1844) and his eventual surrender in December 1847. Franco-Italian rivalry in Tunisia led to the French forcing the Bey of Tunis to accept a French protectorate (May 1881), although Italian aspirations in North Africa, as a counter-balance to French influence from Morocco to Tunis, only came to fruition in 1911–12 with their conquest of Libya.

Tangier

Britain's most notable 'colonial' actions in northern Africa resulted from the possession of Tangier, the Moroccan seaport on the Straits of Gibraltar, first acquired by Portugal in 1471 and given to Charles II as part of the dowry of Catherine of Braganza in 1662. Britain held Tangier until 1684 when, it proving too expensive, it was abandoned to the Moors.

British occupation of Tangier was disputed frequently by local chieftains and by the kingdom of Morocco, whose monarchs (of the Filāli dynasty) during the periods of British occupation were Rashid II (1664–72) and his brother Ismā'il (1672–1727), the resulting conflicts being marked by their fierce and barbarous aspect. A large garrison had to be maintained in Tangier, two regiments being created for the purpose, the 1st and 2nd Tangerines (raised 1661 and 1680 respectively), which were maintained even after the colony was abandoned, and which became the 2nd Queen's Own and 4th King's Own Regiments. The first governor and colonel of the Tangier Regiment was Henry, Lord Mordaunt, 2nd Earl of Peterborough; he was succeeded in both positions in April 1663 by Lieutenant-General Andrew Rutherford, Earl of Teviot, who was killed in one of the many actions around Tangier, on 4 May 1664. Thanks to Tangier's strong defences, combat only occurred in the outlying areas, especially when the garrison was foraging. A favourite Moorish trick was to drive cattle within sight of the walls and ambush those who came out to round them up. A sally from the garrison under Lieutenant-Colonel Fiennes was especially badly cut-up on 3 May 1662, yet two years later Teviot fell into a similar trap, leading a party to cut down a stand of timber about 1½ miles from the town, to prevent it being used as cover for an ambush. He was slain together with nineteen officers, fifteen gentlemen volunteers, a surgeon and 396 other ranks; only nine men regained the town in safety. (Captain Witham, who carried news of the disaster to London, told Samuel Pepys that the only wonder was that Teviot had not been killed earlier, because of his practice of risking his life recklessly on reconnaissance missions.)

Teviot's successor as governor was Lord John Bellasyse, who governed from April 1665 to 1666, during which period he arranged a cessation of hostilities; he was succeeded by Teviot's replacement as colonel of the Tangier Regiment, Lieutenant-General Henry Norwood. He died in 1668; both his offices were conferred upon John, Earl of Middleton, who died at Tangier in January 1675 and was succeeded in both posts by William O'Brien, Earl of Inchiquin. Hostilities had resumed during Middleton's governorship (they gave John Churchill, later 1st Duke of Marlborough, his baptism of fire: he had joined the Tangier garrison as a volunteer in 1668), and so parlous had the situation of the garrison become that the 2nd Tangier Regiment had to be formed (later the 4th Foot), and the Royal Regiment (later Royal Scots) and even five companies of Foot Guards had to be sent there (the title 'Royal Regiment' was conferred only in 1684; at the time of its Tangier service it was named after its colonel, Lord George Douglas, 1st Earl of Dumbarton). In 1680 Inchiquin was succeeded as governor and colonel of the 1st Tangerines by Colonel Sir Palmes Fairbourne, who was mortally wounded in action against the Moors in

October 1680, and was succeeded in command of the garrison by Lieutenant-Colonel Edward Sackville of the 2nd Foot Guards. He led the garrison in a ferocious attack upon the Moorish positions on 27 October, in which the 1st Tangerines lost heavily, 36 killed and 134 wounded. Sackville was succeeded as governor by Colonel Piercy Kirke, commander of the 2nd Tangerines, who removed to the colonelcy of the 1st in April 1682. Under Kirke diplomatic relations were restored with the various local chieftains and with the monarch of Morocco, but such was the expense of maintaining the garrison that it was decided to abandon it; Samuel Pepys was one of the officials sent to report and arrange the evacuation, which took place in April 1684. The garrison had consisted finally of four cavalry troops (incorporated in the Royal Dragoons), five companies of Foot Guards, sixteen companies in each of three regiments (1st and 2nd Tangier and Dumbarton's), four independent companies, and a company of miners.

Algiers

The piracy of the Barbary Coast corsairs, centred on Algiers, was a constant threat to European shipping. The European powers used a blend of threat, ransom and diplomacy to free many of those captured by the Algerines, but countless thousands were sold into slavery, and so obnoxious were the slavers that at times operations were mounted against Algiers, usually naval bombardments. Most had little or no effect: they included bombardments or coastal actions by Sir Thomas Allen's British fleet in 1669, Allen and a Dutch squadron under Admiral van Ghent in 1670 (severely damaging the port), French bombardments by the fleets of Abraham Duquesne and Marshal Jean d'Estrées in 1682 and 1688 respectively, and by a combined Spanish, Portuguese, Neapolitan and Maltese fleet in 1784. Probably the best-known action was the bombardment of Algiers by the British fleet of Admiral Lord Exmouth and the Dutch squadron of Admiral Theodore van Capellen on 27 August 1816; the British ordnance included Congreve rockets, a detachment of Royal Sappers and Miners and Rocket Troop, RHA, having accompanied the fleet. Casualties and damage on both sides were considerable, but as a result some 1,640 European slaves were released from Algerine captivity (including eighteen British and 28 Dutch); Exmouth's fleet lost some 141 killed and 742 wounded but Algerine casualties may have been as many as 5,000 troops and 5,000 civilians. Despite the damage done, the problem was not resolved; a further demonstration by an Anglo-French fleet was made (unsuccessfully) in 1819, and another (much less severe) British bombardment took place on 12 July 1824, but a renunciation of the enslavement of Christians was only made by the Algerines after a British blockade following the formal declaration of war upon Algiers earlier in the year. The problem was not fully resolved until the

French invasion of 1830, and their capture of the city of Algiers on 5 July, which at last ended the Algerine reign of terror which had lasted some three centuries.

References

Anon. *Historical Memoirs of Barbary, as Connected with the Plunder of the Seas ...*, London, 1816 (includes Exmouth's expedition).

Perkins, R., and Douglas-Morris, Captain K. J. *Gunfire in Bar-*

bary: Admiral Lord Exmouth's battle with the Corsairs of Algiers in 1816, Havant, 1982.

Poole, S. Lane. *The Barbary Corsairs*, London, 1890.

Salamé, R. *A Narrative of the Expedition to Algiers in the Year 1816*, London, 1819.

SOMALILAND

Military operations in Somaliland only just fall within the scope of this work, as most occurred after the Victorian era. Somaliland was a coastal territory along the Gulf of Aden, rounding Cape Guardafui and extending down the Indian Ocean littoral; the latter, and largest territory, was administered by Italy from 1892. The smallest of the three Somalilands was that administered from 1856 by France (*Côte française des Somalis*), at the entrance to the Red Sea; and British Somaliland was between the other two. Although British treaties with local chieftains existed from 1840, only in 1884 was British authority definitely established, succeeding the Egyptian rule imposed from 1875. British forces were established in what had been Egyptian Somaliland after the withdrawal of the khedival garrisons following the Mahdi's revolt in the Sudan, British possession of the Somali coast being desirable to secure the route east via the Suez Canal.

From 1884–6 treaties guaranteeing British protection were established with various Somali tribes, and the boundaries with French and Italian Somaliland were established in 1888 and 1894 respectively; the interior boundary with Abyssinia in 1897. Conclusion of the agreement with France involved the British relinquishing Musha Island in the Gulf of Tajura, off French Somaliland, which had been acquired by the Government of India in exchange for ten bags of rice! From 1884 to 1898 the British protectorate was administered from Bombay, and regarded as a dependency of Aden; in 1898 administration was transferred to the Foreign Office, and in 1905 to the Colonial Office.

Hostilities in Somaliland were initiated by Mahommed bin Abdullah (or 'Sayyid Muhammed Abdullah Hassan'), a *mullah* of the Habr Suleiman Ogaden tribe, who gained a wide following from his supposed supernatural powers. He preached against the infidel rulers of the region, his followers raided tribes friendly to the British, and in 1899 he declared himself the Mahdi; from the time of hostilities, he was styled 'The Mad Mullah' by the British. The allied peoples requested British protection, a 1,500-strong Somali Levy was raised by Colonel E. J. E. Swayne, and operations were commenced against the Mullah and his followers, who were called 'dervishes' by the British. The first expedition was in May–July 1901, but despite minor successes achieved against the Mullah, no decisive action was fought, and after every reverse he withdrew to organise further raids or resistance. Swayne pursued the dervishes into Italian territory (with permission) and was ambushed at Erigo (6 October 1902), suffering heavy loss but driving off the enemy. Next, a force was assembled under Brigadier-General W. H. Manning to operate from Obbia, a port in Italian Somaliland, comprising Indian and African troops and a small contingent of British and Boer mounted infantry, and collaborating with an Abyssinian force; this ended with the pursuit of the dervishes into Abyssinia and the annihilation of the British advance-guard at Gumburu (17 April 1903), while another force was stalled at Daratole (23 April). Reinforcements under Major-General Sir Charles Egerton inflicted a heavy defeat on the Mullah's forces at Jidballi in British Somaliland on 10 January 1904, the dervishes losing about 1,000 killed, against 58 British killed and wounded. These operations, including the temporary occupation by the Royal Navy of the port of Illig in Italian Somaliland (which had earlier fallen to the Mullah), brought an end to hostilities.

The Mullah began raiding the British protectorate again in 1909, and it was decided that another expedition would be futile; so British outposts were withdrawn, leaving the interior unoccupied. Raids on the coastal areas continued, despite the foundation of a camel corps constabulary in 1912, partly to keep the peace among the 'friendly' tribes to enable them to present a united front against the Mullah. (The Camel Corps was badly mauled by a dervish force at Dolmadoba in August 1913, and the unit's founder, Richard Corfield, was killed). More operations were mounted between November 1914 and February 1915, and the dervishes were defeated at their stronghold of Shimber Berris on 23 November 1914, and again on 3–4 February 1915 after they had re-occupied the place upon the British withdrawing. The destruction of this stronghold only quietened the Mullah for a time; raids continued until his forces were finally routed by aerial bombardment mounted by the Royal Air Force, beginning in January 1920 and ending with the Mullah's flight on 12 February. Bereft of support and destitute, he died a year later in the Ogaden.

The Mullah's forces were similar in composition and tactics to the Sudanese dervishes: no 'regular' army but tribal forces wearing civilian dress (commonly a white robe), armed with spears and a proportion with firearms, which increased during the campaigns until by 1920 about one-third carried rifles; initially the firearms were of old patterns but later more modern rifles were acquired. Numbers varied; at the time of Gumburu, for example, they were reported as consisting of about 4,000 cavalry and 10,000 infantry. It is a measure of the persistence of the Mullah that for operations against him, no fewer than

six clasps were authorised for the Africa General Service Medal, including one for the action at Jidballi alone.

Notable among the 'British' forces deployed in Somaliland was the Somaliland Burgher Corps, formed in January 1903 from surrendered Boers; commanded by Captain Bonham (temp. Major), 1st Battalion Essex Regiment, the unit comprised six officers and 102 other ranks (three and nine respectively of whom were British), and served in Somaliland in March–June 1903.

Reference

Jardine, D. *The Mad Mullah of Somaliland*, London, 1923.

SOUTHERN AFRICA

The first part of this section covers what became South Africa; other southern African regions, Bechuanaland, Rhodesia and Swaziland, are covered separately at the end of this section.

Early History

The first European settlement in South Africa was planted at the Cape in 1652 by the Dutch expedition of Jan van Riebeeck. The region was inhabited by the indigenous people known to the Dutch as 'Bushmen' (or *Bosjesmans*) and Hottentots. The Bushmen, who were known by other names including *Saan* (apparently the Hottentot name) or *Khuai*, were a people noted for their short stature, and whose numbers were reduced greatly by persecution in the early years of European settlement. The Hottentots were a people of mixed Bantu–Bushmen descent, called by themselves *Khoi* (or variants according to dialect); the name 'Hottentot' was a Dutch onomatopoeic word descriptive of the pronunciation and 'clicks' of their language. Both Bushmen and Hottentots were semi-nomadic, so the appropriation of land by the Europeans was not difficult; and not until 1828, after years of British rule, did an ordinance declare that Hottentots and other free, 'coloured' people were entitled to the rights enjoyed by all other British citizens.

From an early period, the Dutch settlers were styled 'Boers', meaning farmers (German *Bauer*); and as they spread from their original settlements, they encountered another 'colonising' force: Africans who had moved slowly southwards from East Africa, the Sotho and Nguni people, the former occupying the interior and the latter the eastern coastal region, until they met the Boers in the region of the Great Fish River. The first encountered by the Europeans were the Xhosa, part of the Nguni people; but they were commonly known by the name 'Kaffir' (or 'Caffer' in a common, early 19th-century spelling). This term (from Arabic *kafir*, an unbeliever) had no ethnological significance, and came to be applied to any African inhabitant of South Africa, latterly taking a pejorative meaning probably not implicit when first used to describe the Xhosa. Conflicts which occurred between the Europeans and the people they styled Kaffirs were often referred to as 'the Kaffir Wars'; the more modern practice is to describe these as the 'Cape Frontier Wars'. Some confusion may arise in the numbering of these conflicts; what is now generally known as the Fourth Cape Frontier (or Kaffir) War may be found referred to as the First, presumably because it was the first fought after the final British occupation of the Cape, and thus the Sixth War may be found described as the Third, and so on.

The earliest Cape Frontier Wars occurred in 1779–81 and 1789–93, between the settlers and the Xhosa along the eastern frontier of the European settlement. From the outset the Dutch settlement was run by a trading concern, the Dutch East India Company, which maintained a militia, but for active service on the frontier the Commando organisation was formed, mounted units of highly mobile settlers, serving at their own expense, under officers selected by themselves, and deciding upon their course of action by debate and mutual agreement. The first deployment of such troops was in 1715, to combat marauding Bushmen, and the practice lasted into the 20th century. The early conflicts resulted in the establishment of the Great Fish River as a boundary between the two expanding forces, and the second period of hostility (1789–93) included considerable persecution of the Bushmen. By this time the Hottentots had mostly become the servants and employees of the Dutch, their situation being not the most fortunate.

British Occupation, 1795

Following the French conquest of the Netherlands, the Cape passed to the jurisdiction of the French satellite Batavian Republic, which was established in Holland. The Dutch East India Company's oppressive rule had long been disliked, so that the frontier settlements were already in open revolt against the Cape authorities; and in 1795 Britain sent an expedition to appropriate the colony, its position on the route to India being of considerable significance. Major-General James Craig arrived off the Cape on 12 June 1795 with an appeal from the Prince of Orange to the Cape authorities, to allow the colony to be taken under British protection. When this was rejected, Craig sent for reinforcements from St. Helena and awaited the arrival of the remainder of his expedition under Major-General Alured Clarke. Craig landed his original force (2/78th and seamen and marines from the fleet) on 14 July, and occupied Simonstown; Clarke's reinforcement arrived on 3 September as Craig was about to be attacked. The expedition marched on Cape Town, brushed aside a Dutch force at Wynberg (14 September) and the colony surrendered to the British for a loss of some four killed and 60 wounded. An attempt to re-take it by a Dutch squadron in 1796 was defeated by its capture.

The Boer frontier colonists around Graaf Reinet remained hostile, and in February 1799 a minor rebellion was suppressed by a small British force. This contingent then had to oppose a Xhosa raiding-force of the Amagunukwebe tribe under chief Cungwa; a number of minor actions were fought against them by the British commander in the district, Lieutenant-Colonel Thomas Vandeleur of the 8th Light Dragoons (notably on 7/8 May). Reinforcements were brought by the GOC and acting governor of the Cape, Major-General Francis Dundas, and in October 1799 he fought off the Xhosa; but there was a further outbreak of revolt when a Commando attacked the magistracy at Graaf Reinet in October 1801, and some border raiding. These operations are sometimes styled the Third Cape Frontier War. By the Peace of Amiens, Britain restored the colony to the Dutch, and the British garrison was withdrawn by February 1803; the Dutch then concluded peace with the Xhosa. Perhaps the most notable event of this period was Vandeleur's action against the Amagunukwebe in May 1799, in which the disciplined fire of his small command (detachments of 8th Light Dragoons, 81st and local forces) inflicted very considerable losses; and the theory has been advanced that the merits of a disciplined force (the first ever met by Africans) were appreciated immediately by a Zulu chief who was present, and which influenced the later construction of the formidable Zulu military machine.[1]

Military Forces to 1803

The Dutch East India Company maintained a 'Burgher Militia' almost from the first settlement: Van Riebeeck organised infantry and cavalry companies in 1659, and the force was improved later in the century and modelled upon the militia in Holland. In 1789 there were seven uniformed infantry companies, and by 1795 also some 8½ companies of 'Burgher Cavallerie' or dragoons, each 100 strong. Regular troops were also deployed for the defence of the colony: upon the re-possession of the Cape after the Peace of Amiens, the 22nd Line Battalion, 5th *Jägers* (light infantry) and the 5th Battalion of the Waldeck Regiment (all units of the Batavian Republic) were sent to the Cape, and exemplifying French support for Dutch colonies at this period, in 1806 a company of the Ile-de-France Regiment was at the Cape.

On the frontiers it was usual to employ Commandos instead of the militia. Commandos were essentially irregular, un-uniformed light cavalry whose constitution was an integral part of the life of the frontier communities; service in time of danger was the legal responsibility of all able-bodied males of a certain age (usually between 16 or 18 and 60 years), who bore their own expenses. Their style of warfare changed little; the following was included in a British General Order issued at the Cape on 20 August 1795, but the tactics described were not dissimilar to those employed in the South African War of 1899–1902: 'Their mode of warfare appears by taking advantage of the Irregularity of the Country, to annoy us by a distant & Irregular Fire, which can never be formidable, altho from a Circumstance of their being all mounted, & of course their Movement being much more rapid than ours can ever be, they may at all times get round us, & direct their distant fire from every Quarter ... if this is thoroughly explained to the men they will not be alarmed or conceive the Enemy have obtained any advantage which has not been foreseen, if they should see the Galloping all around us as they probably will do.' Conversely, the 'Burgher Cavalry' (militia) were described as 'ill mounted, embarrassed with a multiplicity of Accoutrements of the use of which they are ignorant, & in general being bad horsemen & riding untrained horses'.

After the British occupation of the Cape in 1795, the Commando system was not only retained but codified, the governor of the Cape in 1797, Lord Macartney, issuing a schedule of provisions of the Commando Law. In the Third Cape Frontier War, Commandos were called out in support of the British (even in opposition to the 'rebel' Commandos) and did good service; and on the Dutch re-possession, Lieutenant-Governor Janssens issued a revised version of the old law in 1805. The basis of local government evolved from the Commando system; in 1841, for example, the rank of Commando 'troop officer', *Feld-cornet* (or *Veldcornet*) was described as 'a sort of rural police magistrate'[2] with the power of assembling the Commando for the purpose of recovering stolen cattle and similar tasks.

Other local forces were formed or taken over during the British occupation. The British merchants at Cape Town formed a volunteer corps, the Cape Association, in 1799, emulating the volunteer forces formed in Britain; but more significant was a corps formed by the Dutch East India Company of 'coloured' men, who served against the British in 1795. Its personnel were later formed into the British Cape Corps, commanded by Lieutenant J. Campbell of the 98th, and upon the re-possession entered Dutch service as the Hottentot Light Infantry. Although some Hottentots fought with the Xhosa in the Third Cape Frontier War, many supported the British, viewing British possession of the region as a way of releasing them from the servitude of having to earn their living as farm servants of the colonists. Even at this early stage, the effectiveness of mounted infantry as a mobile force was recognised: in October 1801 a company was formed of men drawn from the 8th Light Dragoons, 22nd, 34th, 65th, 81st and 91st Foot, armed with rifles.

British Occupation, 1806

With the renewal of the war against France, a second British expedition was sent to the Cape, some 6,300 men under Sir David Baird. It landed on 6–7 January 1806 and on 8 January was advancing on Cape Town when it was opposed by the Dutch commander, General J. W. Janssens, near the Blueberg. The Dutch force was scattered: the Dutch 22nd and Waldeckers gave way almost immediately, though contingents of French seamen and local forces put up better resistance. Cape Town was taken on 10 January, and on 18 January Janssens signed the capitulation which delivered the colony finally to Britain, which possession was confirmed when the Netherlands officially ceded it to Britain in 1814. Thereafter, recognising the strategic significance of the Cape on the sea-route to India, the British maintained a garrison.

Within a few years there occurred the Fourth and Fifth Cape Frontier Wars, 1811–12 and 1817–19. A 'neutral ground' had been established between the Great Fish and Sunday rivers, to separate Europeans from Xhosas; but by 1811 the latter had moved into this territory and raided the Europeans. In December 1811 an expedition was mounted to expel them, led by Colonel John Graham, then commanding the forces in the region; the site of his headquarters was named after him, Graham's Town, which became the site of the main action in the Fifth Cape Frontier War. Some trouble resulted from the colonial authorities' attempt to force restitution of stolen cattle; after some reverses the 'Kaffirs' invaded the frontier in large numbers, led by a prophet named Makana, and on 22 April 1819 attacked Graham's Town. The garrison, commanded by Lieutenant-Colonel Thomas Willshire, was only 320 strong, but held off thousands of attackers until relieved. At the conclusion of the war a band of 'neutral territory' was again established, from the Fish to Kciskamma rivers. Partly because of the perceived threat to the colony, the settlement of British immigrants was encouraged, and some 4,000 arrived in 1825; from that date ordinances were issued in English, ending the almost entirely Dutch nature of the European settlement.

Sixth Cape Frontier War

At the end of 1834 the Xhosa again swept into Cape Colony, led by a most capable chief, Maqoma of the Gaika tribe, whose resentment at being expelled from the 'neutral ground' had become unbearable. ('Gaika' is the spelling most often encountered, although 'Ngqika' is more accurate; but the former is used here as it is more familiar from other works.) Chief Maqoma (whose name often appears as 'Macomo') was not officially the leader of his people, but regent during the minority of chief Sandile, Maqoma's military reputation carrying great influence. The settlers fell back on Graham's Town and other defended posts, and urgent reports were sent to Cape Town; the governor, Sir Benjamin D'Urban (a British officer who had served with the Portuguese in the Peninsular War) gave command to Harry Smith, also a distinguished Peninsular veteran. At the age of 47, with but a single Hottentot orderly, Smith rode the 600 miles from

Cape Town to Graham's Town in six days; he arrived on 6 January 1835, and organised the defences. His forces, some regulars but with many locally raised troops, European and African (again the Hottentots mostly took the side of the British against the Xhosa), and including almost 3,000 Commandos, drove the invaders from the frontier. In late March 1835 four columns, commanded by the governor and with Smith as second in command, invaded Xhosa territory ('Kaffraria'), and swept into the land of chief Hintza, theoretically king of the whole Xhosa, who was officially neutral, but who was believed to be a driving force behind the recent raiding, to the extent that some styled the conflict 'Hintza's War'. The British gained allies in the Fingo people, dispossessed serfs of the Xhosa, and after brief hostilities Hinza accepted a peace which involved the restoration of cattle stolen by the Xhosa. Hinza was killed attempting to escape from a party which, with Harry Smith, was holding him hostage to ensure the compliance of his subjects. On 10 May 1835 D'Urban proclaimed a new territory, Queen Adelaide's Province, extending to the Kei river; but this decision was repudiated by the government in London, D'Urban was ultimately dismissed (1837) and the boundary reverted to the Fish river.

The Great Trek

The 'Great Trek' of 1835–40 was the exodus from British territory of some thousands of Boer settlers, unhappy with British administration (not least with the generally conciliatory attitude of the British government towards the 'Kaffirs'), who journeyed north and north-east to found their own states, governed by themselves. They crossed the Orange river, which formed the southern boundary of what became the Orange Free State; and, farther north, crossed the Vaal river, which separated the Orange Free State from what became the Transvaal. The leader of the first large party to occupy this region was Andries H. Potgieter who encountered opposition from the Matabele people of Chief Mzilikaza kaMashobane, who had established a small kingdom after breaking away from the Zulu state (in contemporary sources his name often appears as 'Mosilikatze'). After some hostilities on the part of the Matabele, a Boer Commando surprised and routed Mzilikaza's camp at Mosega (17 January 1837), and after further reverses the Matabele moved north over the Limpopo into what became Matabeleland.

Boer emigrants moved into Natal, initially under the leadership of Piet Retief, who attempted to negotiate with the Zulu king Dingaan, to permit the settlement without conflict. On 6 February 1838, two days after the conclusion of an agreement, Retief and his entire party were murdered on Dingaan's orders, and the Boer settlers were attacked; some 600 were killed in the following week, many where the town of Weenen was established (its name meaning wailing or weeping). For some years there had been a

small British settlement on the Natal coast, Port Natal or Durban (named after Sir Benjamin), and hearing of the Boers' plight a small party of British settlers set out to their aid, with a force of friendly Zulus, but on 17 April they were overwhelmed and hardly any returned to Durban, where the surviving inhabitants took refuge on a ship in the harbour. The surviving Boers defended themselves, despite another reverse on 11 April when a party sent to attack Dingaan was ambushed. They were reinforced, however, and on 16 December a force of some 470 Boers and 340 African servants, led by Andries Pretorius, was engaged by about 10,000 Zulus near the Ncome river. The Boers formed a defensive wagon-laager and beat off the Zulu attack with immense loss, while suffering hardly any casualties themselves, a triumph of firearms and a strong position over an enemy armed only with spears and their own courage. This total defeat of Dingaan is known by the name of the river, which ran red after the battle and was re-named Blood river, and the event passed into Boer folklore.

A British military force occupied Durban (a detachment of 72nd Highlanders was sent from the Cape) until withdrawn in December of 1839; and in the meantime the Boers declared their own state, the 'Republic of Port Natal and adjacent countries', commonly styled Natalia or Natal. They guaranteed their control of the territory by allying with Dingaan's half-brother Mpande, and supporting him in a battle with Dingaan's followers in January 1840 (Maqongqo, or 'Magango'), in which Dingaan was defeated and fled, to be murdered shortly after. Mpande became king of the Zulus and granted the Boers rights of settlement in Natal; in effect, although the Boers had hardly been engaged at Maqongqo, their assistance had been crucial, and Mpande was king by virtue of their support.

Anglo–Boer Conflict

The Natal Boers, who had established a parliament (*Volksraad*) and their capital at Pietermaritzburg, sought British recognition of their independence; Britain was prepared only to permit self-government under British control, and with a British military presence. This was so unacceptable to the Boers that when a British contingent of some 260 men under Captain Thomas Charlton Smith of the 27th Foot (who had served in the same regiment at Waterloo) marched overland and encamped near Durban in May 1842, a Commando was called out under Andries Pretorius. On the night of 23 May Smith attacked the Boer camp but was beaten off; and on the 26th the Boers occupied the port and laid siege to the British camp. A Durban resident, Dick King, rode to Graham's Town (almost 600 miles in nine days, with only one change of mount) to acquaint the British with the perilous situation of their camp; and on 26 June Smith was relieved by a force sent by sea under Colonel A. J. Cloete. The Boers were divided over their next course of action, but when the British government decided that Natal should be a British colony the *Volksraad* accepted the fact (8 August 1843), though many Boers emigrated to those areas that remained independent. In 1844 Natal was declared to be a dependency of the Cape, and when in 1845 the administration was installed under a lieutenant-governor, the power of the *Volksraad* came to an end.

The next occasion of Anglo-Boer tension occurred in the area west of Natal known as Griqualand. This had been settled earlier in the 19th century by a people of varied origin (Africans and mixed-race Europeans) originally known as Bastaards; in 1813, at the suggestion of a missionary, they adopted the name Griquas, some claiming descent from a Hottentot clan settled at Saldhana Bay, or Cape Grigriqua. Under their chief Adam Kok, some moved east in 1820 and settled in the region of Philippolis, north of the Orange river, and in 1843 the then chief, Kok's son, also named Adam, signed a treaty which placed his people under British protection. The Boer settlers were hostile and British troops were sent to support the Griquas, a skirmish occurring at Zwartkopjes on 2 May 1845. This was a very minor affair in which some 400 Boers under J. W. L. Kock, with a 3pdr gun, engaged a party of Griquas and British, ending when a troop of 7th Dragoon Guards charged and scattered the Boers, who lost two men killed. A British Resident was installed, but in later years the Griquas returned east; in subsequent conflicts they remained allies of the British, but not until October 1880 was Griqualand formally annexed to Cape Colony.

Seventh Cape Frontier War

This began in March 1846, after a minor incident gave the Xhosa a chance to express their simmering disquiet. A member of the Gaika (Ngquika) people was caught stealing an axe at Fort Beaufort – hence the alternative name, 'War of the Axe' – and was arrested. His chief, Tola, demanded his release; but the thief was manacled to a Hottentot prisoner and sent to Graham's Town for trial. The escort was ambushed and the thief freed by cutting off the arm of the man to whom he was manacled; whereupon the governor, Sir Peregrine Maitland (who had commanded a brigade of Foot Guards at Waterloo), demanded from Tola and the principal Xhosa chief, Sandile, the surrender of the murderer. When this was refused an expedition under Colonel Henry Somerset was sent to destroy Sandile's kraal in the Amatolas; it was repulsed, and the Xhosa began to raid with considerable loss of life and property. On 7 June 1846 Somerset with a mobile mounted column defeated a force of Xhosa on the Guanga (or 'Gwanga'), a few miles from Fort Peddie, an action notable for a charge by a troop of 7th Dragoon Guards with sabres, seconded by Cape Mounted Rifles and volunteers firing from the saddle, which caught the Xhosa in the open and routed them. The British were reinforced and a new commander, Sir George Berkeley, employed mobile columns to destroy Xhosa cattle and corn, but in the following May there was a renewed upsurge of unrest. The Xhosa chiefs surrendered progressively, Sandile himself in October 1847, and by the time that Harry Smith returned to the Cape as governor and commander-in-chief in December 1847, the war was all but over.

Smith's attitude is perhaps demonstrated by his treatment of Maqoma, who had been largely uninvolved in the war but had advised his kinsmen to cripple the British operations by attacking their supply-wagons. At the time Maqoma was detained at Port Elizabeth, frequently in an alcoholic stupor; at an official audience Smith made his point by addressing Maqoma, his foot on the chief's neck,

Attack on an ammunition-train, Seventh Cape Frontier War, 1846: infantry skirmish on foot around the edges of the wagon-train; Cape Mounted Rifles fire from horseback. (Unsigned engraving)

and on other occasions the surrendered Xhosa leaders (Sandile included) had to kiss Smith's foot. Under Smith's governorship Cape Colony was extended officially to the Orange and Keiskamma rivers (17 December 1847), and on 23 December the area between the Keiskamma and Kei rivers was established as a crown dependency, British Kaffraria. (It was annexed to Cape Colony in 1865, and subsequently extended by the incorporation of other regions.)

Boomplaats

On 3 February 1848 Smith endeavoured to end tension between British and Boers on the Orange river frontier by declaring British control of the territory between the Orange and Vaal rivers, to be styled the Orange River Sovereignty. This was resented by the majority of the Boers, and in July Pretorius and others compelled the British Resident, Major Henry Warden, to quit the capital, Bloemfontein, and evacuate the territory. Smith immediately concentrated his available forces on the frontier, taking personal command: about 600 British (detachments of 45th and 91st Foot and Rifle Brigade) and Cape Mounted Rifles, some loyal Boers, and about 250 Griquas under Adam Kok. On 29 August they encountered Pretorius who had deployed some 700 men at Boomplaats, including a unit of Transvaalers who took the centre of the Boer position. Smith attacked, supported by artillery, drove the Boers from their position and broke them when they tried to rally; British losses were sixteen killed or mortally wounded, and 40 wounded. Smith stated the Boer losses as 49 killed, although they reported only fourteen casualties; their artillery, a 3pdr, was knocked out by the British artillery. This action effectively ended the conflict; Pretorius and those vehemently opposed to the British retired into the Transvaal, the independence of which was confirmed by the Sand River Convention of 17 January 1852. British sovereignty in the Orange River colony was not maintained, however, a change in government policy resulting in the forcible independence of the territory in 1854, despite the objection of some of its inhabitants. The colony was declared a republic under the name of Orange Free State.

Military Forces, 1803–50

Although the British regular forces maintained in South Africa were few in number, their mode of operation was sometimes adapted to local conditions; for example, a 50-strong mounted infantry troop was formed by the 75th at the Cape, as described in 1836: 'Their horses are small, but hardy and strong ... The soldiers' equipment is but little altered. They ride in red undress jackets and forage caps; but Government has supplied them with a pair of leather trowsers. Their great-coats are folded in front; and within its folds are contained sufficient essentials for two or three weeks, namely, a second pair of trowsers, a shirt, and pair of stockings. The blankets are carried underneath the saddles. The men are armed with fusils only; and these are slung and cased in rough sheep-skin, when not near the enemy. A small waist-belt pouch contains twenty rounds of ammunition.'[3] (The 75th also maintained two 6pdrs, manned by members of the regiment.)

The regulars were supplemented by local forces, most significantly by the Cape Mounted Rifles, which although locally raised was on the establishment of the British Army. On the British re-occupation of the Cape in 1806 the Cape Regiment was re-formed (the corps originally taken into British service during the first occupation, and reverting to Dutch service in 1802), as an infantry battalion of ten companies under Major John Graham, with British officers and coloured rank and file. The unit was disbanded in September 1817, but a small force was retained for service on the eastern frontier, the Cape Cavalry and Cape Light Infantry. In November 1827 they were reconstituted as the Cape Mounted Rifles, a unit which existed until 1870 and comprised both Europeans and coloureds, although the latter ceased to be enrolled from the mid-1850s. The corps wore a rifle green uniform like that of the Rifle Brigade, and was probably the most expert military unit in the region. The Hottentot members received much praise:

'They naturally ride well and easily, if not with the correct military seat, and are quiet and orderly, but averse to restraint and the trouble of perfect neatness and smart appearance on parade. Few of them, except the non-commissioned officers, can speak English, but the officers easily pick up enough Dutch ... In a strange country, they have a natural sagacity, a quickness of sight, and perfect recollection of the principal features, that we should vainly look for in Europeans. They are well fitted for their duties of patrolling, and recovering deserters ... they are constantly accustomed to sleep in the open air; a few minutes suffice them to off saddle and secure their horses, to light a fire, and broil their ration of meat, and then lay themselves down to sleep, or sit by the fire smoking and talking.'[4] ... 'Nothing can be more efficient than the appearance of the Hottentot soldier ... in his bush-coloured jacket, clay-coloured trowsers, seated on his sturdy little steed, as though nothing had ever parted, or could ever part, the horse and his rider ... His double-barrelled percussion carbine, wrapped in sheepskin, rests its muzzle in a holster, adapted for the purpose; and across his shoulder is slung his belt, pouch containing twenty rounds of ammunition, and occasionally his canteen. When it is remembered that the average height of the Hottentot soldier is five feet one, and that he is slight in proportion, it may be imagined what a figure he cuts, when accoutred for the field; but he is the most efficient soldier for this colony for all that. He is keen-witted and intelligent, patient of hunger, thirst and fatigue ...'[5]

Although these troops performed police duties, there was also a corps of Kaffir Police, raised in 1835 and 1847–53, with white officers, based at Fort Cox near King William's Town. Most of these men mutinied in 1851.

In addition to the mobile operations at which the Cape Mounted Rifles excelled, considerable use was made of small, defended posts or forts which protected the frontier regions. Built by the army and usually named after an officer responsible for their construction, they varied from earthworks and wattle-and-daub huts to accommodate a half-company of infantry, to stone towers with accommodation for horses in the lower storey and troops in the upper, about 25 feet square and as high, either with huts nearby or as part of more extensive stone or earth defences. Swivel-guns, wall-pieces or grenade-dischargers might be mounted on the roof. Although defensive positions, the real value of such forts was as bases from which mobile parties could operate, as cover for transport and cattle, and in providing a focus against which the enemy could concentrate, giving an opportunity for mobile forces to catch and engage elusive enemy gatherings.

The Boer forces were based on the Commando system and mode of operation. They continued to be employed in British service, although when Maitland failed to introduce a new Commando Ordinance in 1846 the concept of compulsory military service virtually lapsed; nevertheless, the small British frontier garrisons relied upon Commando support in the event of trouble. The Commandos' ideal mounted infantry tactics were summarised in 1839: 'No country can produce better marksmen than the Dutch colonists of Southern Africa. Accustomed from their earliest youth to the use of their powerful gun, they have constant practice in pursuit of game ... [they] march to combat always on horseback, and only attack when the nature of the ground is in their favour: the Zulus are on foot, in masses, and have no missile weapons. The Boers approach them to within shooting distance, without risk – dismount, take their deadly aim, fire – remount quickly, and retire to load – then advance again, and continue the slaughter. They are far less brave, and infinitely less active, than the Zulus, and in a hand-to-hand fight would be quickly annihilated; but, under the circumstances above described, the barbarians have little chance. When the Boers halt for the night in their march through the enemy's country, they draw up their wagons close to each other in the form of a hollow square, lashing them together: this forms a very respectable entrenchment, and, when defended by their murderous fire, is hardly assailable by savages.'[6] Such wagon-laagers were employed on offensive operations, as bases from which Commandos operated.

The Xhosa had no central authority but were composed of related clans, in two principal groups, the Galeka (more correctly 'Gcaleka', though the former is the version used most often) and Gaika (or as noted above, more correctly 'Ngqika'); alternative terms 'amaGcaleka' and 'amaNgqika' result from the addition of the prefix 'ama', indicating 'people of'. The Gaika fought most often against the British, the Galeka (whose leader was nominally paramount chief of the whole people, like the unfortunate Hinza) being less engaged, although individual Galeka clans did support their Gaika kinsmen. Each clan and sub-clan had its own chief, making concerted action virtually impossible, and ensuring that even if the colonial powers made a treaty with one, his neighbours might well have to be dealt with individually. One contemporary account compared Xhosa clan structure with that of the clans of ancient Scotland, with numerous sub-chiefs all largely independent and acting accordingly.[7] Common to all was the regarding of cattle as currency, explaining the many raids for cattle and the hostilities which resulted; the importance of cattle was indicated by their role in Xhosa custom and tradition, for example in the sacred nature of the 'lucky' cow presented to each new wife by her father as a token of good fortune.

The Xhosa fought in their ordinary dress, which was little more than a hide cloak or *kaross*; some wore feathered head-dress with a single, upright cranc-feather representing a warrior who was especially distinguished, and leopard-skin cloaks were worn by chiefs. A practice noted during the earlier Frontier Wars was the smearing of their bodies with red clay and grease, said to be for warmth and protection from biting insects, which led to such descriptions as 'the hills were red with Kaffirs',[8] and more fanciful comparisons with the legions of Satan: 'With the exception of a mantle made of untanned bullock's hide, they are in a state of nudity. When arrayed for battle, it is usual to divest themselves even of this slight impediment to action, and grease their bodies with an admixture of red clay and some unctuous composition, which, with the addition of the wings of a blue crane, fastened one on each side of the head, in the manner of the horns worn by his infernal majesty ... complete the toilet of the warrior ... Upon [the shield] they beat their darts, producing sounds not unlike those of a gong; and ... accompany this noise with the most extraordinary antics and hideous distortions of countenance ... it requires the presence of some convincing proofs of this world to do away with a supposition in the astonished spectator that he has not already paid the debt of nature, and is being received by legions of devils in the realms below.'[9]

Latterly, traditional costume was supplemented by European jackets, blankets and hats. The traditional weapon was a light javelin with long shaft and leaf-shaped blade, the warrior carrying seven or eight to throw and reserving the last for hand-to-hand use, sometimes with a shortened shaft for close combat. Wooden clubs were also carried, and the oval leather shield was supplemented by the Zulu type, introduced by refugees from Natal. Combat was conducted on foot, although horses were used by chiefs and senior warriors; for example, Sandile's body-guard was described as 'a crowd of wild-looking horsemen. A young man was at the head of them, preceded by an advanced guard, armed and mounted. Forty others followed their chief, the young Sandeli [*sic*] ... a bright hand-kerchief formed the head-dress of each, save one, whose head was shaved in token of mourning. The corners of the handkerchiefs hanging down on the left side, gave a jaunty air to the said head-gear; the kaross concealed the form, all but the feet and right arm, the right arm carrying the war allowance of seven assegais.'[10] Sandile was seen later, riding on a sheepskin saddle, but with his bodyguard running on foot and wearing bright blue head-dress; perhaps the horse was less a symbol of rank than a necessary mode of transport, Sandile having a withered left foot.

Much admiration was accorded their skill with the spear, 'formed of a light, elastic, and very tough wood, that grows in the country, headed by a piece of iron, wrought by the Caffres themselves ... with one of these, it is said, that, in case of touching no bone, they can drive it through an ox at forty paces. When they use it against an enemy, and come nearly within spear range, they bend both knees, and, in running forward, sway their body from side to side, to make their adversary doubtful when they will deliver the blow. The spear in the mean time is held in the right hand, and has had a tremulous motion given to it, which materially assists the length of its flight and the correctness of the aim.'[11] Initially the Xhosa used a tactic similar to that of the Zulus, the younger warriors forming the centre of their line of battle and the more experienced the wings, resembling the horns of an ox, with which to outflank or encircle the enemy. As these tactics were ineffective against firearms, the Xhosa adopted a guerrilla-style of warfare, mounting rapid raids and retiring, using their mobility and knowledge of the terrain to avoid being engaged in the open field. From the 1830s they adopted firearms, but as most were outdated flintlocks with often improvised ammunition, and with no proper firearms training, Xhosa musketry was of limited effect, but their change in tactics was marked: '... many years back, they would fly from the pointing of a gun, and a handful of Europeans might rout a large body: in the last war they had become bolder, they knew the power of fire-arms [but] stood their ground more firmly, and would sometimes fight hand to hand, even breaking short their assegais, and using them not as missiles but for stabbing ... In the present war, together with greater courage, we find a new feature presented by the extensive use of fire-arms...'[12] Xhosa raiding-parties, often aimed at British supply convoys and isolated detachments, caused great consternation in the frontier districts, increased by tales of savagery and the killing of wounded enemies.

Other peoples mentioned in contemporary sources included the Tembu (or amaTembu), sometimes styled 'Tambookies', closely related to the Xhosa (supposedly descended from Tembu, brother of Xhosa who founded the tribe of that name; the Tembu were thus regarded as the senior and most royal of the clans, so that the Galeka chief, as paramount chief of the Xhosa, took his senior wife from the Tembu royal family); the related Pondo, who inhabited the Kaffrarian littoral south-west of Natal; and the Fingoes. The latter (also 'Fengu' or 'amaFengu', wanderers) were members of various tribes broken up by the Zulus, and lived for some time under Xhosa oppression; by both Xhosa and Zulu they were regarded as outcasts and serfs. In 1835 they appealed to the Cape government, and were permitted to settle in the Great Fish river region, where they adopted European dress and customs and maintained their loyalty to the British. The Zulus are covered in the appropriate section below.

Eighth Cape Frontier War

Continuing unrest among the Xhosa, and agitation by a supposed miracle-worker named Mlanjeni, led Governor Sir Harry Smith to announce the deposition of Sandile (October 1850). On 24 December Colonel George Mackinnon and a small force sent to apprehend Sandile were ambushed and suffered some loss, which was the signal for a general rising of the Gaika. The frontier districts were ravaged, and Smith was trapped in Fort Cox by a large Xhosa force. Twice Henry Somerset tried to relieve him but was beaten back, so on 31 December 1850 Smith and an escort of Cape Mounted Rifles broke out and fought their way clear, galloping to King William's Town where the governor issued a proclamation instructing the colonists to 'exterminate these barbarous savages' (words which earned him a sharp rebuke from the British government).

The situation became more serious for the British when the Hottentots of the Kat river region, previously supporters of the British and enemies of the Xhosa, joined the rebellion; the cause was ascribed to their having been rewarded inadequately for previous service, and to missionaries who persuaded them that they were oppressed. They raided the Fort Beaufort area, attacking Forts Beaufort and Hare (7 and 21 January 1851), but were driven off thanks to the support received by the British from the Fingoes; in the attack on Beaufort the Hottentot leader, Hermanus, was killed, and was succeeded by an ex-Cape Mounted Rifleman, William Uithaalder. Most alarming was the fact that not only did the Kaffir Police mutiny and join the rebellion, but some of the Cape Mounted Riflemen as well, depriving the British forces, already inadequate in numbers, of part of one of their best assets. The main Hottentot force occupied the abandoned Fort Armstrong, twenty miles up the Kat river from Fort Beaufort; there they were attacked on 22 January 1851 by Somerset (now promoted to major-general) with a force of loyal Cape Mounted Rifles, European volunteers and Fingoes. Somerset stormed the fort, killing more than 90 Hottentots and taking 160 prisoners, most of whom were enlisted by the British and served throughout the remainder of the war without trouble.

Nevertheless, many Hottentots remained in the field with the Gaika; with Maqoma now a leading commander, the war became even more bitter, with raids and ambushes on both sides. Smith harassed the enemy who were concentrated in the Amatola Mountains, a region of great natural strength, and the war spread as a punitive campaign of troops and allies (including the Pondos) raided the country of the Galeka chief Kreli, paramount chief of the Xhosa, who was believed to be in sympathy with the Gaika. After a campaign of mobile operations and raids, Smith was relieved of his duties by the British government (March 1852) and was succeeded by Major-General Sir George Cathcart. The British campaign of attrition against cattle and crops wore down the Xhosa, and hostilities ended in March 1853; shortly afterwards, British Kaffraria was made a crown colony. It was not the end of the suffering for the Xhosa, however: preparing for a renewed conflict while lamenting their recent defeat, they fell victim to a great delusion. In May 1856 a girl named Nongkwase and her father Mhlakza claimed to have been contacted by the spirits of the dead, who urged the Xhosa to destroy all their cattle and crops, which when done would be replaced by new and better cattle and corn, the dead would come to life, and their enemies would perish. Some believed this was a plan by some of the Xhosa chiefs, who would then throw the entire nation at the colonists, having thus to fight or starve; but this never occurred, and when the Xhosa had destroyed all their means of life (either from belief in the prophesy or on the orders of their chiefs), they could only beg relief from the colonists. These did what they could, but as many as 50,000 may have starved to death. Maqoma, still hostile to the colonists, supported the movement, and was deported to Robben Island off Cape Town until 1869; continuing to agitate upon his return, he was again deported and died at Robben in 1873.

Basuto Wars

Basutoland was a territory enclosed by Cape Colony on its south, Natal on the east, and the Orange Free State on the north and west. In the 1820s it was occupied by refugees from the Zulu wars in the coastal areas, and from these broken clans and fugitives a kingdom was created by the young chief Moshoeshoe (or 'Moshesh'), a people who called themselves Basotho ('the Sotho'). Initially they raised no objection to the ingress of Boer settlers, and indeed adopted much of the settlers' culture, Moshoeshoe himself even having 'a house built in the English style. So far [he] is civilised; but on my asking how many wives he had, he replied, "perhaps a hundred!"'[13] The Basuto liked to take the settlers' cattle, and the settlers were eager for Basuto land; and after some disputes a treaty was con-

cluded with Moshoeshoe which placed Basutoland under British protection, and further encroachment by settlers was prohibited. The British intervened in disputes between the Basuto and other tribes, and when the Basuto refused to accept a new boundary with the Orange River Sovereignty, the commissioner of the latter, Major H. D. Warden, took a small force into Basuto territory, mainly of the allied Baralong people but with small contingents of British troops, local settlers and Griquas. On 30 June 1851 they were defeated by the Basutos at Viervoet.

With the approaching end of the Eighth Frontier War, Cathcart was able to turn his attention to the Basuto problem, and concentrated a force at Burgersdorp, in the north of Cape Colony, composed entirely of British troops and Cape Mounted Rifles, the Viervoet débâcle having persuaded him against the employment of any local forces. In late November 1852 they marched for Moshoeshoe's stronghold at Thaba Bosiu, to repossess captured cattle, but on 20 December ran into a large Basuto force at Berea Mountain. The Basuto attacked with courage, but Cathcart's regulars held firm; yet they suffered 38 dead and fourteen wounded, against Basuto losses of 20 killed and 20 wounded (as they reported: Cathcart thought their losses probably between 500 and 600!). At this stage, with the British low in ammunition, Moshoeshoe's diplomacy ended hostilities: realising that the Basuto could not hold out indefinitely, he took advantage of Cathcart's predicament to offer peace, saying that the Basuto had been suitably chastised and that he would endeavour to keep his people in order henceforward. Cathcart accepted and withdrew, and Moshoeshoe announced his victory over the British. He may well have been correct, for no further measures were taken against the Basuto.

When Britain abandoned sovereignty beyond the Orange river, the Basuto came into further conflict with the Boers of the new Free State. Boundary disputes led to war in 1858, which was ended by the mediation of the governor of Cape Colony, but a more serious attempt to defeat the Basuto was made by the Free State in 1865. The Basuto agreed to a treaty in April 1866, but war was renewed in the following year, and Moshoeshoe appealed to Britain for assistance. In March 1868 the British announced the annexation of Basutoland, and by the Treaty of Aliwal North (12 February 1869) defined the Free State boundary, and answered Free State protests by ceding them a strip of territory. One of the most remarkable statesmen of his age, Moshoeshoe died in 1870, and in the following year Basutoland was annexed to Cape Colony.

Military Forces, 1850–70

British. British regular troops were sufficient only to provide a number of small garrisons; at the beginning of the Eighth Frontier War, for example, following reductions to make financial savings, Sir Harry Smith had only some

The 85th on the march to Grahamstown, June 1856; Ensign Stephen Wilson hitches a lift from adjutant Walker Ashe when crossing a river. The officers wear shell-jackets and forage caps, but apart from white trousers the regimental uniform is unaltered for foreign service. (Print after a sketch by Ensign Wilson)

1,700 troops, almost 1,000 of whom were occupied in a number of isolated frontier posts. This threw added responsibility on the local forces, both Smith and his successor using Commandos in relatively short-term operations, rewarding them with a share of captured cattle; Cathcart, in fact, issued a proclamation urging the mobilisation of men according to the old Commando system, which met with a moderate response, some colonists being unenthusiastic about serving under regular British officers, or with African allies. After the Eighth Frontier War attempts were made to reform the local defence system of the Cape frontier, including the 1855 Burgher Act which imposed a slight compulsion of service in an individual's home district.

In addition to the Commandos, from this period grew the practice of forming local volunteer corps, which became common in later years. A particularly effective early example was Lakeman's Volunteer Infantry, raised for the Eighth Frontier War and re-titled the Waterkloof Rangers from October 1852. They were not a typical volunteer corps of local residents, however, being formed by Captain (later Sir Stephen) Lakeman who raised his 200–250 men at Cape Town by offering a £2 bounty (to which Sir Harry Smith added a similar sum); this was a hardy and formidable corps which included ex-seamen and criminals released for the purpose. Lakeman dressed his men in leather clothing and purchased Minié rifles for them, having seen the weapons used with effect by the French in Algeria, and they served with some distinction. (In 1880 Lakeman published an account of his experiences, *What I saw in Kaffirland*). The oldest of the more conventional Cape volunteer units was the Cape Rifle Corps, formed in November 1855 (thus considerably earlier than the volunteer movement in Britain); in 1856 it became the Cape Royal Rifles and in 1860 the Duke of Edinburgh's Own Volunteer Rifles. Unlike the

British equivalent, such corps saw active service: the Duke of Edinburgh's, for example, was mobilised during the Ninth Frontier War, served as garrison troops during the Zulu War, and saw subsequent active service. As elsewhere, the local forces were not admired universally; a report from Pietermaritzburg in April 1850 noted that 'There is a yeomanry cavalry belonging to this town; but it is like most similar volunteer corps – principally child's play at soldiering.'[14]

Constabulary units were also used in a military role; indeed, their duties were often indistinguishable from those of the troops. In Cape Colony the Frontier Armed and Mounted Police was raised in 1855, and until the disbandment of the Cape Mounted Rifles in 1870 performed police duty in the Eastern Province of the Cape; after that date they were used in an increasingly military role. Their organisation on the Indian '*silladar* system' (i.e., responsible for provision and maintenance of their own horses and equipment) was found wanting during the Ninth Frontier War, and the unit was re-organised under the old title of Cape Mounted Riflemen in 1878; but unlike the original CMR they were a colonial rather than 'Imperial' (i.e., British Army) unit, and did not adopt the green 'rifle' uniform of the original formation, wearing yellow cord until 1870 and thereafter black for service, and later blue.

While the Commando system remained the basis of Boer military force, the independent states also had small regular forces. The Orange Free State had a small police corps in 1862–3 (*Rijende Diensmacht*), but more professional military expertise was required for the handling of artillery. The OFS *Staats-Artillerie* was founded in 1857 but organised formally only in 1864, under the command of an ex-Royal Artillery officer, Captain Goodman, and in the 1865–9 Basuto Wars deployed five horse artillery pieces. The corresponding unit in the Transvaal was not formed until 1874. Volunteer corps were not encouraged, reliance being placed on the Commando system, but in the Basuto Wars there existed in the OFS the Bloemfontein Rangers (1857–66), alias 'the Dirty Boys', which performed good service, and in 1864–5 apparently a separate corps of Bloemfontein Volunteers.

Basutos. Basuto methods of warfare changed markedly during the mid-19th century. Originally they fought on foot with shield and assegai, with an army organisation based on 'age regiments', a rather less formalised version of the Zulu system by which a warrior on attaining manhood would be bound to a 'regiment' of his peers, in which he would spend his military career. A weapon used by the Basuto and copied from an enemy (the Tlokwa) in the 1830s was a light, half-moon shaped hatchet (*silepe*), the blade joined to the wooden handle at right-angles by a straight stem; the weapon could be used hand-to-hand or thrown from horseback.

The horse and gun changed Basuto tactics completely. They possessed horses in sufficient numbers to produce effective mounted infantry, the classic Basuto pony being a small, hardy animal, which together with the skill and tactics of their riders led Cathcart to compare the Basuto to Cossacks. The use of firearms became the rule rather than the exception, and by 1852 the Basuto were able to field some 7,000 well-mounted men armed with muskets – mostly flintlocks. The traditional costume of breech-clout and cloak, with a war head-dress of ostrich feathers, held on by a chinstrap, gave way to an increasing use of European clothing and straw hats. Their musketry was not especially good, and it was reported that they were not comparable with the Zulu or Matabele for bravery, but they were highly effective in the guerrilla-style operations they favoured. Using natural cover they would ambush the enemy's columns, shadowing them until a weakness appeared, then dash in, and if the enemy held firm, would then wheel away and disappear as quickly. Strategically, they made good use of their mountain strongholds (Thaba Bosiu was never overcome), in which they sheltered when pressed, and were so adept at raiding that in their wars with the Boers they used the tactic to compel the Boer forces to withdraw to protect their own homes. Most of their firearms and plentiful supply of ammunition were acquired from gun-runners, as was most of the Basuto artillery; in 1865 they had six field pieces and even manufactured a 3pdr, but their use was negligible.

A typical example of Basuto tactics was demonstrated at the Berea, when Moshoeshoe's second son, Molapo, attacked a column of 12th Lancers and Cape Mounted Rifles who were attempting to drive away 4,000 cattle. Basuto infantry engaged the rearguard, and Molapo's cavalry charged out of dead ground and severely mauled the lancers. The British concentrated, so the Basuto retired; and as the British withdrew, Basuto cavalry harassed their flanks, and made off when the British cavalry reached the support of a company of 74th, which fired at long range. The same tactics were employed on the following day when Moshoeshoe led some 6,000 mounted warriors, described as in good order, most with firearms, and many in European clothing and using European saddles; again they harassed the British at longish range, approaching no closer than fifty yards, enough to force the British to expend ammunition without inflicting severe casualties. The comparison with Cossacks, the most expert at this type of warfare, was justified.

Operations to 1877
The two Boer republics almost came to blows in 1857 over attempts by some Transvaalers to bring about a union of the two states; Marthinus Pretorius (who had succeeded his father Andries) and Paul Kruger led a raid into the Free State in May, but being opposed by both Free Staters and other Transvaalers, they withdrew and the two states agreed upon the mutual recognition of their independence.

In 1873 Natal experienced unrest from some of the comparatively new arrivals in the area. In 1848 the Hlubi clan (or 'amaHlubi'), under their chief Langalibalele fled from Zululand in fear of attack by the Zulu king Mpande, and were settled by the Natal authorities at the foot of the Drakensberg range. Here they prospered, and after the discovery of the diamond fields many went to work in the mines, bringing back firearms as part of their wages. Fearful of the consequences of an armed African population, the Natal government sought to call in all unregistered guns, and in March 1873 Langalibalele was ordered to hand over his people's guns. He declined, and as tension mounted decided to move his people again, so in early November 1873 began the trek into Basutoland. A small force was sent to stop them, commanded by Major Anthony Durnford, RE; there was a brief skirmish at Bushman's Pass, in which Durnford was severely wounded and had his left arm disabled, and the Hlubi made their escape. The colonial government dispersed any Hlubi remaining in Natal, but unwilling to cause further conflict, Langalibalele surrendered to the administration in Basutoland; in August 1874 he was exiled to Cape Colony, but was permitted to return to Natal in 1886, and died in 1889. Many believed that the government's treatment of the Hlubi had been unjust, and their protests caused the British government to replace the lieutenant-governor of Natal, Sir Benjamin Pine; Sir Garnet Wolseley was sent as a temporary replacement.

Ninth Cape Frontier War
The last of the Cape Frontier Wars marked the final military effort of the Xhosa, and was notable for the conflict between the British authorities (commander-in-chief and

governor-general) and the Cape government (notably Premier Molteno and one of his ministers, J. X. Merriman), whose efforts to direct the operations of the Cape local forces severely hindered the conduct of the campaign, and resulted in the governor-general, Sir Bartle Frere, taking the unusual step of dismissing the ministry (6 February 1878).

The Fingoes, long allies of the British, had concentrated their settlement between the Kei and Bashee rivers, virtually interposing themselves between the two parts of the Xhosa, Galekas (Gcaleka) to the east and Gaikas (Ngquika) to the west. Long hostility between Galeka and Fingo resulted in violence in 1877 which became war when the colony's forces intervened and were attacked by the Galeka. Initially the Cape government employed only its own forces, the Frontier Armed and Mounted Police, local forces and African allies, and in September–October Colonel C. D. Griffith of the FAMP drove through the Galeka country, pushing the inhabitants north. The colonial government then began to stand-down its volunteers, until on 2 December 1877 a patrol of FAMP and volunteers was attacked at Umtsinzani near the Fingo border. The Galeka were driven off, but most of the clan rose in full rebellion, and were joined by the Gaika. At this point the GOC Cape, General Sir Arthur Cunynghame, realised that his British troops had to intervene, few though they were, and gathering his available force (including a naval brigade) he sent Lieutenant-Colonel Richard Glyn of the 24th Foot into Galeka territory (late December–January 1878). On 7 February one of Glyn's posts at Kentani was attacked by a Xhosa force at least 3,000 strong, mostly Galeka, though present were both chiefs Kreli of the Galeka and Sandile of the Gaika. Captain Upcher of the 1/24th had some 430 troops and 560 Fingoes, two guns and a rocket-launcher, and repelled the attack with such casualties that the Galeka were removed from the war at a stroke: the clan dispersed, many going north.

To the west the Gaika had attacked posts between the Kei river and King William's Town on 29 December 1877, and a column of 88th Foot and local forces operated in the area in January 1878, evacuating civilians. To the north, the Tembu briefly rose in support but were suppressed by the local magistrate, Major Eliot, ex-Royal Marines, with a force of Fingoes, loyal Tembu and a troop of FAMP. Before the final effort against the Gaika, reinforcements arrived (artillery and 90th Foot), and the dismissal of the Cape ministry brought forth more volunteers, as this measure guaranteed that they would be supplied properly and not left virtually to starve, as had been the case before. Cunynghame's term of duty having expired, on 4 March 1878 Lieutenant-General the Honourable Frederick Thesiger (Lord Chelmsford, from October 1878) arrived to take command, and drives into Gaika territory encountered only sporadic skirmishing. Operations went on until May 1878, Gaika resistance col-

lapsing after Sandile was mortally wounded. An amnesty was declared on 2 July 1878, by which time the power of the Xhosa had been destroyed; and the Transkei, Galeka territory, was annexed by the British. A possible consequence of the war may have been to mislead some British commanders into the belief that all African forces were akin to the variable resistance encountered, a possible under-estimation of their military capability which was to have severe consequences in the Zulu War.

Zulu War, 1879

In the strictest sense, the Zulu were more a confederation than a nation, built upon the original small Zulu clan by the conquest and assimilation of other clans into a military society. The Zulu people supposedly took the name of an early leader, but until the early 19th century were only a relatively unimportant clan resident in north-eastern Natal, alongside two more powerful neighbours, the Mthethwa (or 'Umtetwa') and Ndwandwe (or 'Undwandwe'). King Dingiswayo of the Mthethwa created the basis of a military organisation, but it was developed by one of his followers, one of the most remarkable of African military leaders. This warrior, Shaka, was a son of the Zulu chief Senzangakhona, and although not his legitimate successor, achieved the leadership of the Zulus with the support of Dingiswayo. With Mthethwa support, Shaka built a new power on the foundation of his improved military organisation, by defeating and incorporating the neighbouring peoples into the Zulu kingdom; after Shaka overcame the Ndwandwe in 1819 the Zulu state expanded with ruthless determination, leading to the subjugation or flight of all within range. The process whereby Shaka created his kingdom was styled *mfecane*: 'the crushing'.

Shaka became increasingly erratic and violent until, in September 1828 he was murdered by two of his half-brothers, one of whom, Dingaan, took Shaka's place. Events involving the Zulus and European settlers have been recounted above, notably the huge Zulu defeat at Blood river and the installation of Mpande as Dingaan's successor at the behest of the Boers. Mpande (styled 'Panda' in contemporary sources) was not as warlike as his predecessors, but maintained the military system; and in 1856 a civil war was fought between two of his sons, Cetshwayo (or 'Cetewayo') and Mbulazi (or 'Umbulazi'), in which the former's uSuthu faction defeated and massacred the latter's iziGqoza faction on the banks of the Tugela (2 December 1856). Mpande died in 1872 and Cetshwayo became king. Territorial disputes between the Zulus and the Transvaal Boers led him to be suspicious of Boer intentions, so in hope of gaining British support he requested that he be crowned king by the official who had presided over his ceremony of nomination as Mpande's heir a decade earlier, the Secretary for Native Affairs in Natal, Sir Theophilus Shepstone. The offer was accepted in the belief that it would ensure a friendly state to the north of

Natal, perhaps leading to eventual British occupation. British annexation of the Transvaal in 1877 (see below) involved the colonial authorities in the old territorial disputes, but a commission which reported on the boundary question found largely in favour of the Zulus.

Other tensions came into play, including stories of supposed brutality displayed by Cetshwayo and incursions on the Natal and Transvaal frontiers; the wish of some in Natal to open Zululand for trade and the recruitment of labour, both requiring Cetshwayo's acquiescence; and the threat posed by a powerful Zulu state to a British idea for a confederation of all southern African states, British and Boer. The new governor of Cape Colony and High Commissioner for Native Affairs in South Africa, Sir Bartle Frere, appalled at the decision of the boundary commission, believed that only the negation of the Zulu state would ensure stability. To this end, and without reference to his political masters in Britain, Frere issued an ultimatum to Cetshwayo in December 1878, so unacceptable that it was a virtual guarantee of hostilities: it demanded compensation for Boers affected by the decision of the boundary commission, fines and the surrender of those responsible for border incidents, the dismantling of the Zulu army and the imposition of a British Resident who would usurp the king's authority. Frere demanded acceptance within twenty days or military action would follow. Cetshwayo declined and on 11 January 1879 Lord Chelms-

ford's army crossed the border into Zululand to force compliance.

Chelmsford's total strength was about 16,000, although this included some 9,000 African levies of uncertain quality and little formal military experience, and garrisons to protect Natal and the Transvaal; against which the Zulus could field almost 50,000 warriors, mostly lacking modern weapons but disciplined and organised in a manner that made them the most formidable opponents the British had met in southern Africa. Rarely can an army have taken the field quite so knowledgeable about its enemy, for Chelmsford had circulated a report by a border agent, Bernard Fynney, which gave details of the Zulu organisation and tactics.

As the Natal frontier was too long to defend, Chelmsford planned to engage the main Zulu army on its own territory, dividing his main field force into three columns, to converge upon Cetshwayo's capital at Ulundi; one marched east from Helpmakaar, another operated some way to the north, and the third much farther to the southeast, marching from the coast. The operation's principal weakness lay in its division of strength, making possible defeat in detail before the columns could unite. Indeed, Cetshwayo did not commit his entire army, some troops being sent south and the older units held in reserve, the main force (more than 20,000 strong) being concentrated against Chelmsford's central column. Cetshwayo issued a

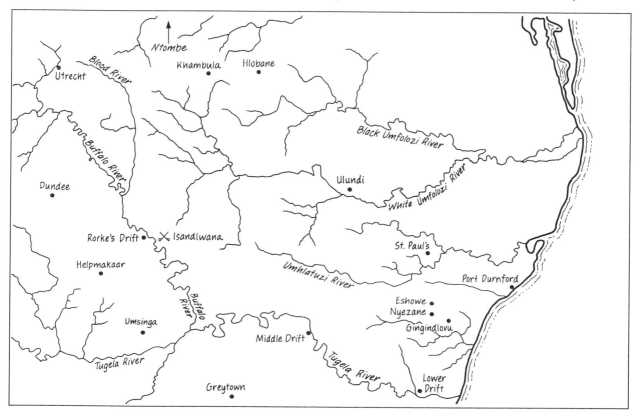

basic plan of campaign but entrusted its implementation to the old warrior chief Ntshingwayo (or 'Tshingwayo'); Cetshwayo's brother Dabulamanzi led the 'Undi corps' (or 'uNdi'), the Zulu regiments from the Ulundi area which were most closely associated with the king himself.

On 20 January Chelmsford's centre (no. 3) column established a temporary camp in the shadow of the mountain of Isandlwana, neglecting to laager their transport because their stay was intended to be brief. On the 22nd Chelmsford marched out with part of his force to oppose a reported Zulu concentration, leaving in the camp a garrison he believed adequate (822 Europeans and 431 Africans, the principal force being five companies of 1/24th and one of 2/24th); and ordered up part of no. 2 column under Lieutenant-Colonel Durnford as a reinforcement. Just after midday some 20,000 Zulus fell upon the camp; the garrison attempted to hold a firing-line some distance away, but as ammunition ran out part of the volunteer and African element of the force gave way, the regulars fell back on the camp and were overwhelmed; the official casualty return showed 858 whites and 471 Africans killed, and very few whites were among the survivors who managed to escape. It was one of the worst disasters to befall a British force during the entire period of colonial warfare.

Later in the day another Zulu force, some 4,500 strong, commanded by Dabulamanzi, attacked the post of Rorke's Drift, guarding the Buffalo river crossing on the route between Isandlwana and Helpmakaar. The defence of this post, held by one company of the 2/24th and a few others, commanded by Lieutenants John Chard, RE and Gonville Bromhead, 24th, became one of the great epics of the period, and is probably the most famous of all colonial actions. Behind improvised defences the tiny garrison held on throughout the night, until the Zulus retired with heavy losses; fifteen of the garrison were killed and two mortally wounded, and no less than eleven Victoria Crosses were awarded to the defenders. (Interestingly, Garnet Wolseley thought that they should not have been regarded as heroes, as they had no option but to fight, being unable to escape; this is somewhat harsh, although it may reflect the fact that the epic of Rorke's Drift helped palliate the catastrophe of Isandlwana.)

After Isandlwana, Chelmsford had to withdraw into Natal to begin anew. There remained, however, the other two columns. On 22 January, no. 1 column, acting on the right and commanded by Colonel Charles Pearson, beat off a Zulu attack at Nyezane (or 'Inyezana'), but learning that Chelmsford was suspending the advance, Pearson sent part of his force back to Natal and determined to hold Eshowe with the remainder. From 23 January some 1,300 troops and seamen, and 400 wagoners, were besieged there. Having received reinforcements, directed to South Africa by the government in London, where the news of Isandlwana had caused a huge stir, Chelmsford

himself marched to Pearson's relief, routing a Zulu attempt to prevent it at Gingindlovu on 2 April 1879. On the following day he reached Eshowe and evacuated its garrison on the 4th, the whole force retiring on Natal.

In the north, Colonel Evelyn Wood's no. 4 Column defeated a small Zulu force near Hlobane on 21 January, but retired on receiving news of Isandlwana. On 12 March the Zulus attacked a wagon-train, guarded by the 80th Foot, carrying supplies from Lydenburg in the Transvaal to the garrison of Luneburg, north of Wood's column; 62 of the train's 106 men were killed on the Ntombe ('Intombe') river. This minor action was chiefly remarkable for the reprehensible conduct of its surviving officer, Lieutenant Hayward (the commander, Captain Moriarty, had been killed), who abandoned his men to seek help; Colour-Sergeant Anthony Booth, who conducted the successful withdrawal of the survivors, was awarded the Victoria Cross. When ordered by Chelmsford to create a diversion to draw off Zulu resources during the relief of Eshowe, Wood ordered an attack on Hlobane on 28 March, commanded by Lieutenant-Colonel Redvers Buller, who won the Victoria Cross even though the attack failed upon the arrival of Zulu reinforcements, at a considerable cost to Wood's mounted force. Next day Wood

Rorke's Drift: fighting continues throughout the night, illuminated by the burning building in the background. (Engraving after W. B. Wollen)

In remarkably matter-of-fact language, Private Robert Jones of the 24th describes the action for which he was awarded the Victoria Cross at Rorke's Drift:

'On commencing fighting, I was one of the soldiers who were in the hospital to protect it. I and another soldier of the name of William Jones were on duty at the back of the hospital, trying to defeat and drive back the rebels, and doing our endeavours to convey the wounded and sick soldiers out through a hole in the wall, so that they might reach in safety the small band of men in the square. On retiring from one room into another ... I found a crowd in front of the hospital and coming into the doorway. I said to my companion, "They are on top of us," and sprang to one side of the doorway. There we crossed our bayonets, and as fast as they came up to the doorway we bayoneted them, until the doorway was nearly filled with dead and wounded Zulus. In the meantime I had three assegai wounds, two in the right side and one in the left of my body. We did not know of anyone being left in the hospital, only the Zulus, and then after a long time of fighting at the door, we made the enemy retire, and then we made our escape out of the building. Just as I got outside, the roof fell in – a complete mass of flames and fire ... The fighting lasted about thirteen hours, or better. As to my feelings at the time, they were that I was certain that if we did not kill them they would kill us, and after a few minutes' fighting I did not mind it more than at the present time; my thought was only to fight as an English soldier ought to for his most gracious Sovereign, Queen Victoria, and for the benefit of old England.'
(*Strand Magazine*, March 1891, p. 291. Despite the reference to 'English', Robert Jones was born in Monmouthshire. William Jones also received the Victoria Cross)

beat off a Zulu attack on his position at Khambula, convincing proof that with adequate precautions, not even Zulu courage could overcome British firepower: eighteen British soldiers were killed and eleven mortally wounded, but more than 800 Zulu dead were counted in front of the position, and hundreds more were killed in the pursuit.

Chelmsford planned a second invasion of Zululand with augmented forces, a 1st Division under Major-General H. H. Crealock to operate along the coast, and a 2nd Division under Major-General Edward Newdigate, which with Wood's 'flying column' from Khambula was to operate in the northern sector and advance upon Ulundi; Chelmsford accompanied the latter. This second advance was not without incident, notably the death on 1 June of Louis, Prince Imperial of France, who had accompanied the army as an extra ADC to Chelmsford, to gain some experience of active service; while with an unsupported patrol, he was killed in a Zulu ambush.

Chelmsford pushed on, encountering sporadic skirmishing and offers of peace from Cetshwayo; but his terms were not acceptable to Chelmsford, and a further incentive to the British commander was the knowledge that Sir Garnet Wolseley had been named as his replacement, and was hurrying to join the army. Before he could assume command, however, Chelmsford had won the decisive battle of the war: on 3 July his advance-guard of mounted infantry and local cavalry skirmished before Ulundi, and on the following day the army marched in square formation upon the Zulu king's kraal; it numbered some 4,165 whites and 1,152 Africans. The Zulu army, about 20,000 strong, fell upon the square but was driven off with huge casualties; Chelmsford's cavalry issued from the centre of the square and completed the rout. Chelmsford lost ten men killed and 87 wounded; as many as 6,000 Zulus were slain, and the Zulu kingdom was destroyed.

Cetshwayo was apprehended on 27 August by Major Richard Marter of the 1st Dragoon Guards; he was sent as a prisoner to Cape Town. Zululand was divided into thirteen chiefdoms, overseen by a British Resident, but as this was productive of disorder Cetshwayo was reinstated to a portion of his old kingdom in 1883. His second reign was short; the enemies of his uSuthu faction, led by his cousin Zibhebhu (or 'Usibebu') of the Mandlakazi, destroyed the king's kraal at Ulundi on 22 July 1883; Cetshwayo escaped but died, broken, in February 1884. His son Dinizulu sought the aid of the Transvaal Boers, and was proclaimed king at the expense of a Boer state carved out of Zululand (which was incorporated into the Transvaal in 1888); with Boer assistance, Dinizulu's uSuthu routed the Mandlakazi with considerable slaughter at Etshaneni on 5 June 1884. Continuing strife among the Zulu clans caused Britain to annex Zululand in 1887; in due course Dinizulu rebelled, and on 23 June 1888 with some 4,000 uSuthu attacked the magistracy at Nongoma which was defended by a party of Zululand Native Police and Zibhebhu with about 800 Mandlakazi. Dinizulu routed the latter, but the post held. Lieutenant-General Sir Henry Smith, commanding in South Africa, assembled a force to suppress the rebellion, including British as well as local forces and allied African levies. Although unrest was not suppressed until August, the only notable actions included that at Ceza Bush on 2 June, when a force of 2–3,000 Zulus was routed by a small British force of two troops of 6th Dragoons, a mounted infantry company, police and some 500 levies; and at Hlopekulu on 2 July, when a Zulu force under Cetshwayo's brother Shingana retired after engaging a British and African force commanded by Colonel Albert Froom of the 6th Dragoons. In September Dinizulu and other rebellious chiefs surrendered, and were exiled to St. Helena. Zululand was incorporated in Natal in 1897, and Dinizulu was permitted to return in the following year; but he was imprisoned for complicity in the last Zulu uprising, a rebellion of 1906 led by Bhambatha kaMancinza (or 'Bambaata'), arising over the imposi-

The South Africa Medal 1877–9; issued with seven clasps, including that for 1879, awarded for the Zulu War. The obverse depicted W. Wyon's portrait of Queen Victoria, the reverse L. C. Wyon's allegory of a lion (symbolising Africa) crouching in submission beside a Protea bush, with assegais and a Zulu shield in the exergue. The ribbon was orange-yellow with dark blue stripes.

tion of a poll tax. Bhambatha's rebels were joined by the Zulu clan of Sigananda (who as a youth had served in Shaka's army), but the rebellion was crushed by a colonial force commanded by Colonel Duncan McKenzie in a hopelessly one-sided action at Mhome Gorge on 10 July 1906.

Military Forces, 1870–9

British. Although their numbers were never very great, British regular forces formed the nucleus of the army which fought in the Zulu and Ninth Frontier Wars. Their weapons were the single most decisive factor: rapid-firing rifles accurate at long range, artillery, rockets and even machine-guns; when properly deployed and with ample ammunition, they were unbeatable, but in skirmishing, when attacked in small parties or with inadequate ammunition, they were still vulnerable to the suicidal bravery of the Zulus. Despite criticisms (not surprising given the devastating defeat at Isandlwana), proof that the army could adapt to local conditions is demonstrated by such tactics as

Wood's practice of laagered wagons and mounted raids copied from the Boers, and the adoption by Buller's mounted infantry of Commando practices.

The shortage of regular cavalry for reconnaissance and similar duties led to the formation of mounted infantry from the regular battalions, and increased the importance of the local forces raised in wartime, as the old Commando system no longer produced the numbers required. The response to the Commando call-out for the Ninth Frontier War was not satisfactory, and the situation was not even remedied by the Cape parliament's Burgher Force and Levies Act, passed shortly after, which retained the election of officers and absence of disciplinary power, but introduced officially the concept of payment for active service. The Cape's regular force continued to be the Cape Mounted Riflemen, about 800 strong; an artillery detachment was added in 1874, equipped originally with a 9pdr and two 7pdr mountain guns, using these plus a 12pdr and a 5½in mortar against Moorosi. A corps raised for the Ninth Frontier War was the Frontier Light Horse, formed at King William's Town by Lieutenant F. Carrington in 1877; when forming the rearguard at Hlobane it lost three officers and 26 other ranks out of 156 present, and in the skirmish before Ulundi (3 July 1879) two members, Captain Henry D'Arcy and Sergeant Edmund O'Toole, won the Victoria Cross. Another unit formed for the Ninth Frontier War was Pullein's Rangers, or Transkei Rifles, formed at King William's Town by Cunynghame from a mix of British navvies working on the railway, and coloured men; not surprisingly they were supposedly a very tough unit.

To exemplify the local mounted corps which served during the Zulu War, units present at Isandlwana included the Natal Mounted Police (formed 1874, 26 killed out of 33 present at Isandlwana), the Natal Carbineers (the senior Natal unit, formed 1855 as the Pietermaritzburg Irregular Horse, 22 killed out of 29), the Newcastle Mounted Rifles (raised 1876, seven killed out of seventeen), and the Buffalo Border Guard (formed 1873, three killed out of nine; Rorke of Rorke's Drift was a lieutenant). A further example is provided by the list of those present with Wood's 'Flying Column' in the second invasion of Zululand: the Frontier Light Horse; Raaf's Horse or the Transvaal Rangers, raised by Peter Raaf in 1879 from both whites and coloured, mainly from Kimberley; Baker's Horse, raised by Major J. F. Baker, late Ceylon Rifles in 1878, reformed for the Zulu War and again in 1880–2; the Natal Light Horse, formed 1879 from a troop of Frontier Light Horse and commanded by Captain Whalley, an ex-Papal Zouave; and the Natal Native Horse. (A full list of local corps mobilised in 1879 can be found in Appendix D of the *Narrative of Field Operations Connected with the Zulu War of 1879*.)

The Natal Native Horse was part of the African element of the British forces. Formed in 1866, this corps was regimented in 1879: three troops of amaNgwane (or 'Amang-wane') from northern Natal, old enemies of the Zulus and sometimes styled the Sikhali Horse (from the name of their chief); a troop of Basuto (Batlokwa or 'Tlokwa') under chief Hlubi Molife (who had served with Durnford in the Langalibalele rebellion); and the Edendale Contingent, Christian Zulus and Swazis from the Edendale mission. They wore European clothing with a red hat-band, and served with distinction at Isandlwana (where they shot their way clear and helped cover the flight of survivors), Hlobane, Khambula and in the pre-Ulundi reconnaissance. The unit existed until 1906 and continued to perform valuable service, being especially adept at scouting, though it was noted that they disliked dismounted duty during the 1888 rebellion.

A much inferior corps was the Natal Native Contingent, formed by Chelmsford for the Zulu War in three regiments of two battalions each (three battalions for the 1st Regiment). Although the companies of renegade Zulus were regarded as reliable troops, the remaining Natal Africans were of very limited value, often with poor officers and NCOs. These, all white, and about 10 per cent of the other ranks were armed with rifles (some outdated); the remainder carried only spears and shields, and their only 'uniform' was a red head-band. Adequate as scouts, they had limited combat value, broke at Isandlwana and were re-formed before the second invasion of Zululand, the five battalions of the 1st and 2nd Regiments being made independent and issued with a higher proportion of rifles; the 3rd Regiment, broken at Isandlwana, was disbanded, its white NCOs mostly joining Lonsdale's Horse, an irregular cavalry corps. There was also a corps of Natal Native Pioneers, one company of which accompanied each column during the first invasion, and various units of border guards, armed in traditional style and formed to help defend their own localities in case of Zulu invasion. (They should not be confused with the Border Horse, raised in the Transvaal in 1879 and commanded by Lieutenant-Colonel Weatherley; it was 53 strong at Hlobane and lost its commanding officer and 43 others killed.) A further unit, formed by Evelyn Wood in his sphere of operations and sometimes styled 'Wood's Irregulars', comprised Zulus hostile to Cetshwayo and Swazis, the latter traditional enemies of the Zulus who apparently wore their 'full dress' ceremonial costume for combat.

African units employed in later campaigns included three battalions of Zulu Levies, each 1,200 strong, which served in 1888. A much superior corps was the Zululand Native Police, also known as Nongqai, formed in April 1883, which served with distinction, especially in 1888, although its establishment was small (originally 50, later 200, and 800 during the South African War of 1899–1902); disbanded in 1904, 100 were re-enlisted during the 1906 rebellion and continued to serve with distinction.

Zulus. Shaka organised the whole of Zulu society along military lines, based on the system used by Dingiswayo. Zulu 'regiments' had no fixed establishment as in the European concept of the term, but evolved from the *amabutho* or 'guilds' into which youths were organised for ceremonial purposes. Each *ibutho* (singular) consisted of men of the same age, in which they remained for life; thus in 1879 the uSixepi 'regiment', formed by Shaka, consisted of men all 80 years of age, whereas the uVe 'regiment', formed by Cetshwayo, consisted of 23-year-olds. By forming units according to age rather than clan, the danger of cliquish, clan-inspired conflict was reduced, although there was sometimes rivalry between 'regiments' or the followers of particular commanders. Regimental strength varied from about 500 to 5–6,000, the strongest in 1879 apparently the inGobamakhosi and unQakamatye 'regiments'.

Originally each *ibutho* was quartered in a barracks-like village styled an *ikhanda*, which were distributed throughout the kingdom. Warriors were not permitted to marry until comparatively late in life, so that the king maintained a 'standing army' of bachelors; when given permission to marry, the warriors dispersed to their own homes, to be recalled when required. Most of Shaka's warriors were unmarried, but in 1879 eighteen of 33 'regiments' consisted of married men. Regiments were divided into companies (*amaviyo*), each *iviyo* (singular) about 50 strong. The 'officers' were the *izinduna*, although the rank of *induna* (singular) was not exclusively military: it might best be described as a chieftain, and the term was retained after the destruction of the military system. *Esprit de corps* was enhanced by differing 'uniforms': although when fighting the Zulus wore the absolute minimum of clothing, ceremonial regalia included a wide range of fur and feather decorations from which a warrior's *ibutho* could be identified, although the colour of the shield was the principal distinguishing mark in the field; another was the *isicoco* head-ring, a fibre circlet woven into the hair, the distinguishing mark of a married man.

'Regiments' formed part of larger formations, of which twelve existed in 1879, five of which effectively consisted of only one 'regiment', the others in these formations consisting of old men of negligible combat value. These formations are usually styled 'corps', although it is misleading to use this term in the European sense of a self-contained small army complete with its own supports and transport. The Zulu army had no such functionaries, and no cavalry (all marched and fought on foot); the only 'supports', if they can be so described, were the *udibi*, youths below military age, who acted as warriors' servants. Perhaps a more appropriate term for the higher formations (if European terminology need by applied) might be 'brigade' or 'division', but actual strength varied greatly: in 1879 the uDukuza 'corps' may have mustered as few as 500 men, whereas the Undi (or 'uNdi') 'corps', based at Ulundi, may have been about 10,000 strong. The 'corps' system was organisational more than functional, so that the component 'regiments' might not always fight together. The term used most commonly to describe a Zulu force, *impi*, did not refer to a particular organisational element but merely meant a force of armed men, so could be applied to bodies of various size. (As the Zulu army had no written records, compositions and strengths of 'regiments' and 'corps' are recorded variously; a valuable analysis of contemporary information is 'Contemporary Sources and the Composition of the Main Zulu Impi, January 1879' by J. Whybra, in *Soldiers of the Queen*, issue 53, Victorian Military Society, 1988, and a review of the Zulu army by Ian Knight appears in the same society's publication *There will be an Awful Row at Home about This*.)

Zulu forces were extremely mobile; Shaka expected his troops to cover at least 50 miles a day, barefoot (he made them discard their sandals), for days in succession, and then go into action immediately. The *udibi* boys sometimes carried grain and water, but the commissariat system usually consisted of obtaining food at local kraals or consuming captured cattle; although such was the physical hardiness of the Zulu army that it could fight even after two days without food.

Tactics and weaponry were both reformed by Shaka. Initially spears, the principal armament, were used for throwing, but as Shaka believed hand-to-hand combat to be more decisive, he replaced the throwing-spear with a shorter, broad-bladed weapon more suited for close-quarter action, styled *iklwa* (or *iXwa*; supposedly an onomatopoeic word based on the sound of the weapon being withdrawn from an enemy's body!). It was used with a large, oval, cowhide body-shield (*isihlangu*), although a smaller type (*umbhumbuluzo*) was introduced by Cetshwayo. The method of combat was to close with the enemy as rapidly as possible, use the shield to throw the opponent off-balance, and thrust with the *iklwa*; this use of shield and short thrusting-weapon by bodies of men formed with sufficient space for each man to use his weapons led to a comparison of the Zulu system with that of ancient Rome,[15] and indeed there were other similarities, not least the concept of 'military colonies' or barracks and the formidable power of marching. Some use was still made of throwing-spears, and latterly a considerable number of firearms were employed, but these were only subsidiaries to hand-to-hand combat, and Zulu musketry was not impressive. Wooden clubs with bulbous heads were also used; generally styled 'knobkerries', the Zulu name was *iwisa*.

Although the Zulus employed ambushes, their main forces' principal tactic was an attack *en masse*, to close with the enemy as rapidly as possible; guerrilla tactics were not used and the Zulus could not respond in kind to the fire-and-movement techniques of Boer Commandos and mounted infantry. Shaka's favourite tactic was

not unique to the Zulus (the Xhosa had used something similar), but was developed into a most formidable system. The classic Zulu deployment was supposedly based upon the body of a bull: the centre, representing the animal's chest, was used to occupy the enemy's attention, or was 'refused' (held back) until forces on each flank (representing the bull's horns) partially encircled the enemy; a reserve was held at the rear, representing the animal's loins, to be committed if required to complete the victory. This crescent-shaped deployment was styled *uphondo*, and although generally irresistible against an enemy with similar weapons, against formed troops with adequate ammunition, or against defended posts (Rorke's Drift, Blood river), the Zulus could not prevail; indeed, they rarely got to the close quarters achieved by the dervishes in the Sudan. Zulu successes in 1879 were achieved against small or scattered detachments which, as at Isandlwana, were deployed so as to be incapable of mutual support, or with inadequate ammunition; when these factors were not present, slaughters like Ulundi were the likely outcome. In one respect, the Zulu forces resembled European infantry of the 18th and earlier 19th centuries: once their formation was broken they were extremely vulnerable to cavalry, and at times retiring Zulu forces put up little resistance to pursuing horsemen, as in the last stages of the actions at Ulundi and Khambula. In the pursuit after the latter battle, the mounted infantry and irregular cavalry, having no sabres or lances (though some had Bowie knives to fix on their carbines), in addition to firing from the saddle at the retreating Zulus, many caught up Zulu spears for use from the saddle like lances.

(In various sources, Zulu names appear with varied spelling; useful glossaries of Zulu military terms appear in several of the sources listed, for example in Ian Knight's *Brave Men's Blood* and *The Zulus*. The reasons for the differences in spelling are summarised in the notes on Zulu orthography in Donald Morris' *The Washing of the Spears*.)

Transvaal, 1876–9

In the independent Transvaal, a confederation of some power was built up around the Pedi people (or 'Bapedi', or 'Bapeli'). Based in eastern Transvaal, the kingdom of King Sekhukhune (other spellings include 'Sekukuni', 'Sikukuni', 'Secocoeni') was regarded as a threat, and in 1876 the Transvaalers attempted to curb Pedi power. A Commando led by the Transvaal president, Thomas François Burgers, failed completely, and the Boers' Swazi allies, finding that they were expected to do most of the fighting, gave up the struggle. After this reverse, and with the state's finances on the verge of collapse, Transvaal was annexed by Britain as part of the scheme for confederation; it was resented by most Transvaalers, but there was no active opposition. (The Transvaalers were largely uninvolved in the Zulu War: a small Boer unit served under

Commandant Piet Uys, but it returned home after he was killed at Hlobane.)

In September 1878 a small British expedition was mounted against Sekhukhune, commanded by Colonel Hugh Rowlands (who had won the Victoria Cross at Inkerman), and including the 13th Foot, mounted infantry and Frontier Light Horse. A successful skirmish was fought at Tolyana Stadt on 27 October, but shortage of water and horse-sickness caused the expedition to withdraw without ever coming near Sekhukhune's main stronghold.

Only with the conclusion of the Zulu War could British forces be assembled to make a renewed attempt, but even then British attention was somewhat distracted because of reports of Boer Commandos assembling to engage the British; in the event this did not materialise during the Sekhukhune campaign. In September 1879 Sir Garnet Wolseley organised two columns against Sekhukhune, whose stronghold was known as 'Sekhukhune's Mountain' (or Tsate). Originally the Pedi army was organised in 'regiments' according to age-group, plus allied contingents; by the 1870s virtually all were armed with firearms, many very modern. Originally much stronger, by 1879 their fighting strength was probably only about 4,000, and some allied chiefs probably held back their warriors as a defence against the Swazis, who aided the British. The main Pedi defensive position was a strongly entrenched hill, 'Fighting Kopje', in advance of the capital, 'Sekhukhune Town'. Wolseley's Transvaal Field Force was about 2,000 strong, a quarter of them mounted, plus about 8,000 Swazis and other African levies. His main column approached from the north of Sekhukhune's Mountain, and a subsidiary force of four British infantry companies and the Swazis, under Major Henry Bushman of the 9th Lancers, from the south-east. Wolseley attacked on 28 November against determined Pedi resistance, but their town was overrun, and after Sekhukhune surrendered on 2 December the last defenders of the Fighting Kopje capitulated. Pedi losses were heavy (estimates ranged from 300 to 1,000); British casualties were seven killed and 37 wounded, so light because much of the fighting had been borne by the Swazis, who took most of the spoils (principally cattle). Sekhukhune was exiled, but was murdered by his brother in 1882; and as a power, the Pedi were destroyed and scattered.

The campaign again demonstrated the use of local forces, especially necessary as the only British mounted troops available were a single mounted infantry company drawn from the 2/21st and 94th. The local units included the Border Horse, Ferreira's Horse (raised at Pretoria in 1878, and having served under Buller in the Zulu War), the Lydenburg Rifles (raised 1879, 127 strong, associated with the Transvaal Rangers of the Zulu War), and the Transvaal Mounted Rifles, a coloured unit raised in 1879, 151 strong, later the Transvaal Mounted Police. The African levies included Eckersley's Contingent, raised in the Transvaal for the Zulu War, 207 strong; the Rustenburg Contingent, 639 strong, raised for the Sekhukhune campaign; and the Zoutpansberg Contingent, about 1,100 strong and including Swazis. There were also 125 of Hlubi's men of the Natal Native Horse, known at the time as 'Basuto Horse'.

Basuto Campaigns, 1879–81

Renewed unrest among the Basuto was caused by plans for their disarmament, and the first action arose over taxation of the Phuti (or 'Baphuti') clan, whose leader Moorosi (or 'Moirosi' or 'Morosi') had given his name to the stronghold of Moorosi's Mountain. An expedition was despatched in March 1879 to bring him to heel (Cape Mounted Riflemen, Cape Yeomanry and levies), but the Phuti, well-equipped with firearms, repelled the attempt (8 April). Twice in May the Phuti made counter-raids, and on 5 June a renewed assault also failed. Months of negotiation and siege having been unsuccessful, a final attack led by the Cape Mounted Riflemen on 20 November overcame resistance and killed Moorosi.

In 1880 the Cape government extended to Basutoland the Cape Peace Preservation Act of 1878, which involved disarming the African population. Some chiefs complied, but others refused to surrender their firearms, led by Moshoeshoe's son Masopha (or 'Masupha'), grandson Lerothodi, and Moletsane. Following attacks by Basuto rebels in September 1880, colonial forces were mobilised for what was styled 'the Gun War'. The Basuto launched swift attacks, assaulting or besieging Mafeteng (September 1880) and Maseru (October), but on 22 October Lerothodi's village was captured, and on 31 October that of Moletsane (by the British commander, Brigadier-General M. Clarke). Skirmishes continued even after the conclusion of an armistice in February 1881 and peace in May; Masopha only ended hostilities in September 1881. A form of self-government was introduced, but internal strife among the Basuto clans continued, and in response to appeals from the Basuto, in 1884 Basutoland ceased to be associated with Cape Colony, becoming instead a crown colony in which the authority of the chiefs was respected, and with government being conducted jointly by the paramount chief (Lerothodi from 1891) and British resident commissioner. There was little subsequent unrest, the Basuto chiefs declaring their loyalty to the crown during the South African War of 1899–1902, during which their neutrality was respected by both sides.

The Transvaal (or First Boer) War

Discontent with British administration led to renewed appeals by the Transvaal Boers for a restitution of their independence, in which they were encouraged by remarks made by W. E. Gladstone. When he became prime minister after the Liberal victory in the 1880 election, however, he made it clear that the independence of Transvaal could only be as a member of a South African Confederation.

This was clearly unacceptable, and on 13 December 1880 a meeting of some 4,000 Boers proclaimed the re-constitution of the South African Republic and appointed a provisional government consisting of Paul Kruger, Petrus (Piet) Joubert, and ex-president Marthinus Pretorius (son of Andries). Formal proclamation of the republic was made on 16 December (the anniversary of Blood river), and hostilities against the small, scattered British garrisons began with the siege of two companies of the 2/21st at Potchefstroom.

Responsibility for restoring order fell to the British commander of troops in Natal and the Transvaal, Sir George Pomeroy-Colley, who was also High Commissioner for South-East Africa; an experienced staff officer, he had never held an independent field command, and from the first seriously under-estimated the military capability of the Boers. On 20 December 1880 there occurred the first of a series of British disasters, when a party of about 200 Boers under Frans Joubert annihilated a column of the 94th Foot on their march from Lydenburg to Pretoria, at Bronkhorst Spruit; shot to pieces by the Boer marksmen, the survivors of the unprepared column were ordered to surrender by their fatally wounded commander, Lieutenant-Colonel Anstruther. Two features were especially evident in this action: the devastating Boer marksmanship which inflicted an average of five injuries upon each of the British wounded in less than fifteen minutes; and the kindly treatment accorded by the Boers to their defeated enemies once the action had ceased. Of 263 of all ranks (including 40 unarmed members of their band), 57 of the British were killed and more than 100 wounded, twenty fatally; all nine officers became casualties. Some aspects of the action seemed to belong to another age: before the shooting began, the Boers gave Anstruther the chance to surrender; immediately before the fight the 94th's band played the National Anthem; after the surrender Joubert joined the fatally stricken Anstruther in toasting Queen Victoria in champagne; and as the unwounded prisoners were marched away, the surviving bandsmen played *Rule Britannia*.

Colley gathered some 1,200 men to relieve the several besieged posts in the Transvaal, but when marching into the territory found his way barred by some 2,000 Boers at Laing's Nek. On 28 January 1881 Colley mounted a frontal attack (the last occasion in which British Colours were carried into action, by the 58th) and was duly beaten off by Piet Joubert's riflemen. Colley retired to his camp at Mount Prospect to await reinforcement, but on 7 February had to strike southwards to drive away a 300-strong Boer Commando under Commandant Nicolaas Smit which was threatening communications with Natal; in this action at Ingogo, although the Boers eventually retired, they had the best of the day. At this juncture campaigning was suspended by negotiations between Kruger and the British government; but Colley, unfavourably inclined towards the idea of negotiation, decided to do something during the hiatus of awaiting a Boer reply to the government's offer of a diplomatic solution, which included a royal commission to investigate the Transvaal's case. Having been reinforced by a column under Evelyn Wood, on the night of 26 February Colley led a force to occupy the heights of Majuba Hill, which commanded the Boer positions around Laing's Nek. This force (two companies of

A patrol of Johannesburg Volunteers leaving Barberton for the Swazi frontier, 1898; a scene which might be regarded as representative of a 'fighting patrol' in any of the South African Frontier Wars, and latterly the Boer War. This unit had a regimental medal for active service, with clasps for the Jameson Raid and for the event shown here, 'Swaziland Expeditie, 1898'.

58th, two of 3/60th and three of 92nd Highlanders – the latter newly arrived from India and wearing khaki, which contrasted markedly with the red and green respectively of the other detachments – and 64 seamen) had no artillery and could do nothing but observe the Boer positions. After detaching units for support, Colley occupied the summit of Majuba with just the 58th, two 92nd companies and the seamen. On the following morning, Boers began to ascend the hill; with accurate musketry and skill in utilising natural cover, they overwhelmed the defenders, some of whom broke and fled down the hill; of Colley's 365 men, 285 were killed or wounded for the loss of two Boers killed and four wounded. Colley was among the dead, and Evelyn Wood assumed command.

Despite the dispatch to South Africa of Sir Frederick Roberts and reinforcements, the conciliatory tone of Kruger's reply persuaded Gladstone to end hostilities, and following a truce from 6 March, terms of peace were concluded on the 21st. The besieged posts, Pretoria (defended by 1,200) and smaller British garrisons, some of less than 100 men, Marabastadt, Lydenburg, Rustenburg, Wakkerstroom and Standerton, held out; Potchefstroom was starved into surrender, but the capitulation was cancelled when it was discovered that the Boers had concealed the fact of the war's end when negotiating the surrender.

Peace was confirmed by the Pretoria Convention (3 August 1881) by which the Transvaal state (or South African Republic) was granted internal independence under British suzerainty, with a British Resident to supervise the interests of the Africans, and with British control of foreign relations; but these strictures were removed by the London Convention of 1884, by which the republic gained full independence. Paul Kruger was elected president in May 1883.

Operations, 1881–99

Conflict between the Transvaalers and various African peoples between 1882 and 1894 did not involve British forces, though some spread into Bechuanaland (covered below) and necessitated a concentration of British forces in 1884 to contain the problem. More significant was discovery of gold which increased both the Transvaal's revenue and its European population, which congregated around the goldfields; within a decade of its foundation, by 1896 the population of Johannesburg was 107,000, more than 50,000 of them being European. The new settlers, many British, were styled 'Uitlanders' by the Boers, who viewed them as a potential threat and therefore allowed them no political rights. Uitlander grievances were open to exploitation by what might be termed an imperialist faction within the British administration. Cecil Rhodes, who had made his fortune from mining in southern Africa, became prime minister of the Cape in 1890, and envisaged an expanded British holding in Africa,

'from the Cape to Cairo', with a federated South Africa. The opposition of the Transvaal to such a scheme, and that state's attempts to separate itself even from commercial access via the Cape, was the major threat to Rhodes' plans (in 1895 Kruger closed the Vaal crossings to Cape goods, intent on diverting traffic to his new railway from Pretoria to the coast at Delagoa Bay in Portuguese territory; but the Vaal was re-opened after British protests).

Rhodes and his colleague, Dr. Leander Starr Jameson, conceived a plan to force the compliance of the Transvaal: an Uitlander insurrection supported by an invasion from outside the state to compel the granting of political rights to the Uitlanders, with the resulting election of a government which would support Rhodes' plan of federation. In the event, the plan miscarried: Uitlander response was feeble, yet Jameson led his 'invasion' of some 500 volunteers from Mafeking into the Transvaal at the turn of the year 1895. On 1 January 1896 he encountered Boer resistance at Krugersdorp, and on 2 January was surrounded at Doornkop; having suffered more than a hundred casualties and missing, he surrendered to the Boer Commando. The 'Jameson Raid' had serious consequences: Jameson was tried in Britain and served a year in prison, yet was widely regarded as a hero by the British, and served as Cape premier 1904–8. Whatever the level of complicity of the British government (or at least its Colonial Secretary, Joseph Chamberlain), responsibility for the affair was pinned on Rhodes who had to resign from office; and a hardening of Boer attitudes led to even more strictures on Uitlanders in the Transvaal, and in 1897 to a treaty of mutual assistance between the South African Republic and the Orange Free State, which until then had remained aloof from Anglo–Transvaal conflict.

South African (or Boer) War, 1899–1902

The question of Uitlanders' rights remained unresolved, and Chamberlain's appointment of Sir Alfred Milner as High Commissioner ensured that British pressure would continue; Milner, a sincere believer in the concept of empire, was not averse to the exercise of military force to back the diplomatic pressure which the British government was prepared to use. Negotiations held at Bloemfontein in May 1899 between Kruger and Milner, using the good offices of president Martinus Steyn of the Free State, were inconclusive, Milner finding the proffered concessions inadequate. Believing that Kruger would yield to further pressure, on Milner's advice the British cabinet consented to a substantial reinforcement for the inadequate British forces at the Cape and in Natal. The news that 10,000 men were being dispatched from the Mediterranean and India (mid-September 1899), and that the 1st Army Corps was mobilising in England, forced Kruger's hand. Having missed the chance to capture Durban in a pre-emptive strike before the first British forces arrived, on 9 October Kruger issued an ultimatum: that British troops should withdraw from the Transvaal border; troops landed since 1 June 1899 should be removed, whereupon Boer forces would withdraw from border areas (Transvaal had mobilised on 28 September, the Orange Free State four days later); and that no British troops then at sea would be landed. Britain was given 48 hours to signal compliance, or hostilities would result. The terms were obviously unacceptable, and the war began on 11 October 1899.

The South African War of 1899–1902 – popularly known as the Boer War, perhaps more accurately as the second or great Boer War – was inevitably one-sided, as in the final analysis it involved the military strength of the British Empire against the two Boer republics. Although their fight aroused much sympathy in regions outside the empire, in Europe and the United States, and although they received some material and moral support from sympathisers (even units of foreign volunteers), the Boers were essentially playing a lone hand. Yet this obvious analysis does not represent a true assessment of the military situation, for until the arrival of British reinforcements the Boers enjoyed numerical superiority; they were well-equipped with modern magazine rifles (predominantly the German Mauser) and (unlike 1881) with trained and efficient artillery, and enjoyed the advantages of great mobility and generations of experience in the 'irregular' warfare of the region. Although the British eventually realised the importance of mobile mounted columns and in some cases developed a skill equal to that of their opponents, for most of the war the Boers enjoyed a pre-eminence in these respects.

The war can be divided into three main phases: the original Boer offensive; the British offensive against organised Boer resistance; and the long period of guerrilla warfare. Although the Boers achieved successes in all three stages, only in the first did they enjoy any real prospect of strategic success.

The combined strength of the two republics in 1899 was about 50,000 combatants, but their initial strategy negated their numerical superiority. Boer forces were sent to their western frontiers, and just across the border, to besiege British garrisons: at Mafeking, invested by the Transvaal general Piet Cronje (13 October), and at Kimberley, by Free State forces (15 October). Other Boer forces went into Cape Colony to encourage the Cape Afrikaners to join them, and to menace the strategic railjunctions at De Aar and Naauwpoort. This left some 21,000 Boers under Commandant-General Piet Joubert to oppose the Natal garrison, which even after the initial reinforcement numbered only about 13,000 regulars and 1,800 local forces, under command of General Sir George White, VC, who had been chosen to lead the initial rein-

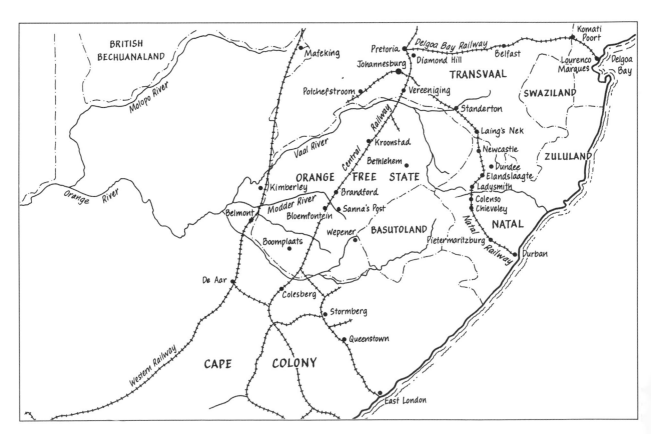

Schalk Burger, Vice-President of the Transvaal and acting President after Kruger's flight. The costume is typical Boer campaign dress, only the binoculars suggesting that the wearer was an officer.

forcement. White concentrated the Natal Field Force at Ladysmith, Natal's chief military post and an important railway junction; but the existing GOC Natal, Major-General Sir William Penn Symons, had already pushed some 45 miles north-east with 4,500 men. Isolated from immediate support, Symons was surprised on 20 October 1899 by a Boer Commando which began bombarding his camp from Talana Hill, north-east of Dundee. He attacked and captured the hill, but at heavy cost (Symons was mortally wounded while reconnoitring), and the force had to withdraw to Ladysmith to avoid being surrounded.

Meanwhile, a Commando under J. M. Kock (a veteran of Boomplaats) raided Elandslaagte, ten miles north-east of Ladysmith; they were driven away (21 October) by a force under Ian Hamilton, sent by White by rail, about

half the Commando becoming casualties and Kock receiving a mortal wound. With the approach of more Boer forces Hamilton retired on Ladysmith. Attempting to avoid an investment of the town, White devised a complicated nocturnal march to defeat the Boers to the north and east, at Nicholson's Nek; but the attack (30 October) was not properly co-ordinated and turned into a near rout, two entire battalions having to surrender (1/Gloucestershires, 1/Royal Irish Fusiliers), and only old Joubert's caution permitted the British to retire again into Ladysmith which by 2 November was besieged.

At Kimberley, surrounded by 7,000 Boers, Colonel R. G. Kekewich of the 1/Loyal North Lancashires commanded some 2,600 men (only 600 regulars, including part of his own battalion), although with Cecil Rhodes in the town he had a rival for the privilege of claiming to be in command; and in Mafeking, Colonel Robert Baden-Powell with some 1,200 police and volunteers held out against about 5,000 Boers. The position of Mafeking was the most parlous, for help from the south could only come after Kimberley and the railway were secured, although some assistance might come from a Rhodesian force being organised by Lieutenant-Colonel Herbert Plumer. The Boers did not prosecute the siege with great urgency, and although the marooning of so many men in Ladysmith was a grievous blow to the British, like the other sieges it did keep substantial numbers of Boers occupied.

With White completely isolated in Ladysmith, command of the British forces fell to Sir Redvers Buller, commander of the Army Corps sent from England, a man of South African experience but not ideally suited for independent command. The original plan had been to concentrate in Cape Colony and advance north through the Free State and on to Pretoria, capital of the Transvaal; but with Natal virtually defenceless and with Rhodes using his influence for an early relief of Kimberley, Buller found his resources impossibly stretched. Therefore, he divided his forces: part to protect the northern frontier of Cape Colony, under Lieutenant-General Sir William Gatacre (at Stormberg) and most of the cavalry division under Major-General John French (who had escaped from Ladysmith) in the Colesberg area; Lieutenant-General Lord Methuen to relieve Kimberley; and Buller himself went to relieve Ladysmith.

Methuen, a commander experienced in South African conditions but with a dearth of fast-moving mounted troops, advanced towards Kimberley, a distance of some 75 miles, against opposition which would hold a position until threatened and then retire, having inflicted more casualties than they had sustained. This happened at Belmont (23 November), when 2,000 Free State riflemen under Jacobus Prinsloo blocked Methuen's route; and at Graspan (or Enslin) two days later, when the somewhat dispirited Free Staters were reinforced by Koos De La Rey and Transvaalers from Cronje's army. On 28 November

Methuen attacked the next Boer defence-line with some 8,000 men, along the Modder river, held by 3,500 Boers and reinforced by Cronje himself. For this action, De La Rey had formulated a radical variation in Boer tactics: instead of holding high ground where they were vulnerable to British artillery, he deployed the Boer riflemen at low level, more difficult for the British to direct their fire upon, and utilising more efficiently the high power of their rifle-fire, a horizontal trajectory having the potential of inflicting more damage than one directed at a downward angle. The efficacy of this tactic was demonstrated when Methuen attacked, making little progress despite a lack of resolution among the Free Staters; and the Boers withdrew unperceived during the night. Cronje established a new position at Magersfontein a short way to the north-east, using the new deployment strengthened by entrenchments and stone breastworks. When Methuen attacked on 11 December he was beaten off with immense loss, especially among the Highland Brigade, which for much of the day lay in open ground, hardly able to reply to the Boer fire; of 948 British casualties, 747 were from the Highland Brigade, including among the killed their commander, the universally popular Major-General 'Andy' Wauchope, who had stood against Gladstone in the famous Midlothian election. Boer casualties numbered about 280. After such a reverse, Methuen had to retire on Modder river.

On the day before Magersfontein, the British suffered another defeat to the south-east, in the north of Cape Colony. Gatacre attempted to take the Stormberg position held by a Boer force which had invaded from the north; the affair was ill-managed and he withdrew, mistakenly

leaving behind 600 men who had to surrender.

On 22 November Buller left Cape Town to sail to Durban, and on his arrival concentrated at Frere, south of Colenso on the Tugela river, about 25 miles from the beleaguered Ladysmith; the presence of White's garrison had prevented Joubert from advancing any further into Natal than a raid towards Pietermaritzburg. Boer forces under Louis Botha took up a strong defensive position on the hills around Colenso, to dispute the crossing of the Tugela; Buller planned to outflank them, but on receiving news of Magersfontein decided that an immediate result was needed, so on 15 December attempted a frontal attack. Fearing the presence of spies in Ladysmith, Buller failed to inform White of his attack and this prevented the Ladysmith garrison making a concerted effort against the Boer rear. The attack miscarried: Major-General Arthur Hart, commander of the Irish Brigade, led his men into a virtual ambush on the left, and on the right the artillery commander, Colonel C. J. Long, moved two batteries so near to the Boer positions that it was impossible to remove them: two guns were brought away, ten abandoned, and Lord Roberts' son, Lieutenant the Hon. Frederick Roberts, KRRC, won a posthumous Victoria Cross in attempting to rescue them, a rare case of this decoration being awarded to father and son. Having lost 1,127 casualties and missing, Buller withdrew to Frere; Boer casualties numbered about 40. This period of three defeats was known, not surprisingly, as 'Black Week'.

Such unprecedented reverses had profound effects. Despite his earlier successes, Buller was adjudged incapable of handling so large an operation (he even advised White to surrender Ladysmith), and though retaining command in Natal, he was superseded as commander-in-chief in South Africa by the aged but vastly experienced Lord Roberts, with the recent hero of the Sudan, Lord Kitchener, as chief of staff. Also significant was the effect of these defeats on public opinion: further reinforcements were promised by Australia, Canada and New Zealand, and at Buller's suggestion a force of more than 10,000 mounted infantry was created from the existing Imperial Yeomanry and new volunteers, especially useful given the nature of the war. The volunteer battalions of regular regiments supplied companies for voluntary service with their parent corps; militia battalions relieved regulars for service in South Africa, or went there themselves for line-of-communications duty; and new units were created, such as London's City Imperial Volunteers. In South Africa locally raised units such as the Imperial Light Horse helped redress the deficiency in mounted troops.

Roberts arrived at Cape Town on 10 January 1900 to find the British situation no better; indeed, only French's cavalry in northern Cape Colony had enjoyed any success, his two brigades successfully holding in check two of the Boers' best commanders, De La Rey and Christiaan De Wet of the Free State. A minor success had been achieved

---

Dudley Kidd of the South Africa General Mission, which accompanied the army during the South African War, dispensing tea, lemonade and other comforts both spiritual and material, writes of a common experience encountered on campaign in hot climates:
'Often ... after weary hours of marching over burning and waterless plains, beside the lumbering ox wagon, I have spied a river-bed in the distance – tired and thirsty one hails with delight the prospect of some tea. On coming to the river, what do we find? Just a few large mud pools, in which an hundred oxen have been trampling. In disgust we turn to a distant side of the pool, and find some green, stagnant water with a thick, green slime on the top. Carefully brushing this back we dip our pannikin into the water and some rich bubbles of fetid gas come gurgling to the surface. But thirst overcomes all scruples, and so we fill our kettle and make our tea. On pouring it out we find it has a rich green colour, but even this is a God-send at such times.'
(Kidd, D. *Echoes from the Battlefields of South Africa*, London, 1900, pp. 32–3)

Boer artillerymen with a 75mm Schneider; note the handspike inserted in the trail for traversing the gun.

on 6–7 January, however, when the Ladysmith garrison repelled a Boer attack at Wagon Hill. While Roberts was formulating his planning, Buller made another attempt to relieve Ladysmith. He had been reinforced to about 30,000 strong by the 5th Division under Sir Charles Warren (who as Chief Commissioner of the Metropolitan Police had failed to apprehend Jack the Ripper), and planned to force the line of the Tugela by an outflanking manoeuvre by Warren, hardly the most competent of subordinates; and in a curious lapse from the responsibility of a commander, Buller acted almost as an observer, merely offering suggestions. The crucial point of Warren's attack was the prominent position of Spion Kop, which he seized on 23 January 1900; but Louis Botha's Commandos drove the British off in a sanguinary operation. Having suffered some 1,200 casualties (four times the number suffered by the Boers), Buller finally took command in full and organised the retreat. A third attempt to force the Tugela line also failed, at Vaal Krantz on 5–6 February, though mercifully with fewer casualties than the slaughter at Spion Kop.

Having reorganised the army in Cape Colony, including an improvement in commissariat and at last the provision of an adequate mounted force (supplied by local forces, newly arrived colonials and by converting regular infantry companies to mounted infantry), Roberts took the offensive against Cronje's army, which was blocking the Modder river crossing on the route to Kimberley. From 11 February Roberts sent French's cavalry on a circuitous march around Cronje's left, then making a dash for Kimberley; uncertain of French's objective, Cronje remained at Magersfontein until it was too late, and on the afternoon of 15 February Kimberley was relieved, the besiegers retiring before the British. A British diversionary attack at Jacobsdal, south of Magersfontein, on the same day, caused further confusion to Cronje. Threatened with

being trapped now that French was in his rear, Cronje had to retreat eastwards towards Bloemfontein, even though this meant crossing the British line of advance almost at a right-angle; furthermore, Cronje's 5,000-strong command was not the usual mobile Boer force, but was encumbered by some 400 wagons and many of his men's families.

Cronje retired east, approximately along the line of the Modder, his rearguard holding back elements of the British force; but to reach Bloemfontein he needed to cross the Modder from the north bank, and failed by no more than an hour to secure the crossing before French's cavalry, moving on a converging course from Kimberley, cut off his retreat near Paardeberg on 17 February. Cronje laagered on the north bank and on 18 February beat off an attack by Kitchener, temporarily in command after Roberts had fallen ill. Next day Roberts resumed command and began a siege of the position. Boer attempts to relieve Cronje came to nothing (although De Wet briefly occupied a position south of the laager, retiring on 21 February when it became obvious that he could not effect Cronje's salvation), and Cronje declined to break out with his combatants as this would have meant leaving the Boers' families behind. Without hope of relief and with supplies almost exhausted, Cronje surrendered on 27 February.

Paardeberg was a decisive action on the southern front. Having been held in check by Major-General Clements' small command around Colesberg, De La Rey was recalled to help defend the Free State after Cronje's surrender. Boer Commandos in the western Cape encouraged rebellion, but Kitchener organised mobile columns to occupy rebellious towns and drive the commandos back over the Orange river. Presidents Kruger and Steyn endeavoured to hearten the force defending Bloemfontein, but they were manoeuvred out of their chosen position at Poplar

Grove, some 20 miles east of Paardeberg (7 March), narrowly escaping a repeat of Roberts' trap which had caught Cronje; and although De La Rey fought a delaying action at Tweefontein (10 March) they were unable to prevent the capture of the Free State capital: Roberts occupied Bloemfontein on 13 March.

Roberts' achievements were finally matched by progress in Natal, from where 2,000 Boers had been withdrawn in a vain attempt to assist Cronje. Again Buller advanced in the Colenso area, using artillery bombardment and infantry attack to reduce one Boer strong point after another; he made gradual progress from 17 February, until the capture of Pieter's Hill on 27 February completed British possession of the Tugela heights. Despite Louis Botha's best efforts, British success so dispirited his men – and those of Joubert besieging Ladysmith – that many decided to go home, and on the evening of 28 February the British vanguard entered Ladysmith, to the unreserved joy of the defenders, who were almost out of supplies. Sir George White attempted to pursue the retiring Boers, but his men were too exhausted. White was invalided home; Buller remained, his reputation somewhat improved by the eventual relief of Ladysmith. (It is noteworthy that Buller never lost the trust of his rank and file; and indeed, his task had been made more difficult than necessary by White's injudicious conduct early in the campaign, which led to his being trapped in Ladysmith.)

At a council of war on 17 May the presidents of the two republics and their senior commanders determined to fight on, and although still prepared to oppose Roberts' advance, acceded to a proposal by De Wet (now Commandant-General of the Free State) that guerrilla tactics should be adopted, by using mobile Commandos (without the baggage and families which had doomed Cronje) to raid British lines of communication and isolated posts. De Wet himself began, ambushing a British force at Sannah's Post (31 March), capturing the garrison of Reddersburg, and from 9 to 25 April laying siege to Wepener, which held out until relieved. These were only minor triumphs for the Boers, however: their commandant-general, Piet Joubert, died on 28 March, and Roberts prepared to drive through the republics with about 100,000 British and colonial troops. The mobility of the Boer Commandos, however, together with the support they would receive from the civilian population, meant that much of Roberts' resources would need to be deployed as garrisons in the rear areas, considerably reducing the numbers available for offensive action.

Roberts' advance began on 3 May, co-ordinated with Buller's advance on the Natal front. The Boers realised the urgency of taking Mafeking before it could be relieved, and De La Rey was sent to assist the besiegers. On 12 May a small Boer party led by Feld-Cornet Sarel Eloff (Kruger's grandson) made a lodgement in the Mafeking defences, but they were not supported and surrendered that

Lance-Corporal George Harris of the Essex Regiment found a well-known hand to write a letter home on his behalf:

> 'Feb. 24 1900
> Hospital train going to
> Cape Town.
>
> Dear Mother,
>   Just to let you know I am getting on famous & hope to be home soon. I was hit by a bullet in the right forearm at Pardeberg where we were fighting Cronje on Sunday the 18th, and they had to take it off below the elbow. They have made a famous job of it, I have no pain and I am eating heartily. It will be quite easy to strap a hand on to the stump. We had three days in bullock-carts after we were wounded, coming in 30 miles to Modder river where the Hospital train picked us up yesterday evening. We are all very comfortable and hope to be on the way home before long. You must *not* worry about me as I am really all right. I am lying in bed smoking a cigar and dictating this letter. With much love I am your affectionate son,
>   George.
> 'Dictated. The above statements are true. Your son is coming on very well.
>   Rudyard Kipling'

evening. However, a relief column from Kimberley under Colonel Bryan Mahon united with Plumer's Rhodesians, and despite an engagement with De La Rey at Israel's Farm, some eight miles from Mafeking on 16 May, ending with the Boers' withdrawal, Mafeking was relieved that evening. The relief of Baden-Powell and his small garrison after seven months was greeted in Britain with unprecedented rejoicing, far in excess of the importance of the event; although the garrison had occupied considerable Boer resources (but surely could have been taken by a determined assault), it was less its strategic importance than the symbolism of beleaguered Britons keeping the Union Flag aloft in the face of overwhelming numbers, together with the laconic style of Baden-Powell's messages, both in the best tradition of British 'pluck', which so struck a chord in the British public consciousness.

Three days after the formal annexation of the Free State (henceforth known as Orange River Colony, 28 May) Roberts occupied Johannesburg, having taken a Boer position at Doornkop on 29 May. The Transvaal capital, Pretoria, was taken on 5 June without opposition, and Roberts rejected Kruger's offer of negotiation, being willing to accept only unconditional surrender. Any thought that the capture of the enemy capitals would end the war was premature, for the Boer leaders determined to fight on in guerrilla fashion, the Free Staters against the British rear areas and the Transvaalers initially to hold the Delagoa Bay railway, their sole conduit for outside assistance (though none came). The Boer threat to Pretoria was ended when Botha was forced to retreat after a sharp fight at Diamond Hill (11–12 June), twenty miles east of the capital. A major concentration of Boer forces under Marthinus Prinsloo was compelled to surrender at the Brandwater Basin (29 July), the largest capture (4,500 men) since Paardeberg, but marred by the escape of De Wet and others similarly determined. As Roberts pushed on through the Transvaal, it became clear that conventional warfare was ending; on 11 September Kruger entered Portuguese territory (to be followed by many Boer combatants and foreign volunteers), and a month later he sailed for Holland in an unavailing attempt to rally support. Komati Poort, the Delagoa railway post on the border of Portuguese territory, was occupied by the British on 24 September, effectively ending the independence of the Transvaal; and on 25 September 1900 the formal annexation of the state was proclaimed in Pretoria.

The Natal Field Force ceased to be an independent command in early October 1900 and Buller went home, followed in November by Roberts, Kitchener being left to supervise what was expected to be the rounding-up of fugitive Boers. The determination of the latter, however, had been grossly under-estimated, and Botha and Steyn planned to conduct a guerrilla war in the Transvaal as De Wet was doing in the Free State, and even to carry the war into Natal and the Cape. So determined were the leaders that they were not even discouraged by the British policy of farm-burning, designed to deny the guerrillas succour. Furthermore, these were not isolated bands; although no more than 25 per cent might be in the field at any one time, the Boers had a potential of some 60,000 combatants, against which about half of Kitchener's 200,000 or more troops were occupied in garrison duties and in protecting isolated outposts and railways. Faced with so mobile an enemy, Kitchener had to appeal for more mounted troops (local forces and renewed volunteering from the yeomanry), at least until the new South African Constabulary could become effective, a force being assembled by Baden-Powell and recruited in Britain and the Empire. Kitchener also re-organised his forces into mobile columns capable of making independent drives against specific areas, or in pursuing Boer commandos. For their part, the Boer commanders planned an ambitious strategy involving an invasion of Natal by Botha and a similar operation by De Wet against the Cape, where it was hoped to raise an Afrikaner rebellion; in the event neither was feasible. Kitchener arranged a conference with Botha at Middelburg (28 February 1901), but no peace resulted when the British authorities declined to approve Kitchener's plan for an amnesty for Cape and Natal rebels.

By mid-1901 Kitchener had nearly a quarter of a million troops, including 80,000 cavalry or mounted infantry, but the Boers continued to escape the British columns, concentrating for operations and separating when pursued. On 20 June the principal Boer leaders met again to confirm their determination to resist, but suffered a severe blow at Reitz on 10 July when the entire Free State government (less Steyn) was captured. Later in the year Kitchener began to extend the lines of garrisoned blockhouses originally designed to protect the railways, to limit the Boers' freedom of movement during British sweeps. Eventually some 8,000 mutually supportive blockhouses of

The service uniform of the British Army during the South African War is illustrated excellently here, worn by a group of officers of the Royal Irish Rifles posed at a railway siding, with a truck in the background. The khaki service uniform includes puttees and foreign service helmets with khaki covers; and note that some have rifles as well as the usual revolvers.

corrugated iron, turf and stone were built, with small garrisons able to patrol their immediate areas, and almost 4,000 miles of barbed-wire fencing.

Gradually, Boer resistance was ground down. The policy of impounding Boer families in 'concentration camps' was suspended; intended to deny the guerrillas succour, the policy had aroused widespread criticism (especially among the anti-war opposition in Britain), not least because of fatalities from disease in these camps; and such deportations had not only angered further the Boer belligerents, but by relieving them of their responsibilities towards their families permitted them to concentrate upon the war. Some of the previously militant Boers now supported a peace committee which endeavoured to persuade the more intransigent to give up the fight, and even formed units of National Scouts, ex-Boer combatants who had in effect changed sides. Yet still the 'bitter-enders' fought on, defying British drives against the blockhouse lines and still harassing isolated British forces; a notable success was De Wet's attack on the 11th Battalion Imperial Yeomanry at Tweefontein on Christmas Day 1901, which cost the British 348 casualties and prisoners. The scale of the British drives in the Free State was awesome: using the lines of blockhouses as perimeters, that launched by Kitchener in early February 1902 involved a cordon of men, twelve yards apart, stretching continuously for 54 miles, involving 9,000 men and moving at twenty miles per day, covering every square yard of country. De Wet twice broke through the cordon, but increasing numbers of Boers were trapped and captured.

A final Boer victory was achieved on 7 March 1902, when a small column under Lord Methuen was overwhelmed by De La Rey at Tweebosch; Methuen was wounded but De La Rey had him escorted to the nearest British hospital, and even telegraphed Lady Methuen expressing concern over his adversary's injuries. Such chivalry was not common in the later stages of the war, for there was increasing bitterness over the British impounding of non-combatants, farm-burning, and British reports of Boer brutality and abuses of flags of truce. The end was inevitable, however, and the Boer leadership was granted safe conduct to attend negotiations at Pretoria (23 March), encouraged by the suggestion of terms rather than the previous insistence upon unconditional surrender. Among those who attended were Schalk Burger, Transvaal vice-president and head of the fugitive government since Kruger's flight; the Transvaal generals Botha and De La Rey; Steyn and De Wet for the Free State; and Jan Smuts, whose forces were still diverting British resources in the western Cape. Despite the opposition of the most determined (Steyn eventually resigned the Free State presidency in disgust), the desire for peace was irresistible, and after weeks of negotiation hostilities were ended by the Treaty of Vereeniging on 31 May 1902. It was made possible by the more conciliatory attitude adopted by Kitchener and supported by the British government, motivated in part by the realisation that in the future, unified South Africa, Briton and Boer would have to cooperate; and partly, perhaps, by the respect with which many British soldiers viewed their opponents, who had fought longer and harder than could ever have been imagined. Indeed, it is likely that many British officers felt more charitable towards their Boer opponents than towards the South African industrial magnates, whose support of Britain some perceived as motivated largely by financial considerations.

By the terms of the treaty, all Boer combatants were to surrender themselves and their munitions (although rifles

The Ladysmith Town Guard
during the siege, wearing civilian clothing with the only
'uniform' being a dark red
rosette or cockade worn as a
'field sign' on coat or hat.
(Print after a drawing by Captain Clive Dixon, 16th
Lancers, Sir George White's
ADC).

The guerrilla war in South Africa, prolonging a conflict which the British believed they had already won, caused them to wonder why the Boers continued to resist in what was thought to be a hopeless cause:
'Some 40 men of our squadron went out to reconnoitre, the result of which was that a dozen of them were captured and one sergeant was killed. The Boers took their horses and saddles, ammunition and rifles and warm coats, and set them to walk into camp. The rifles and ammunition will be a great acquisition to the Boers, who were firing black powder, and using other old stuff ... Our chaps asked the Dutchmen what they were continuing the war for. "To win," they replied ...'
(Quoted in *On Active Service with the S. J. A. B., South African War 1899-1902*, W. S. Inder, Kendal, 1903, pp. 261–2)

for sporting purposes were to be permitted upon application for a licence), none who surrendered were to be deprived of liberty or property, and no reprisals were to be taken for any legitimate acts of war; the Dutch language was to be permitted in schools and law courts; military administration was to be replaced by civil at the earliest opportunity, leading to self-government; all Boers who took the oath of allegiance were to be repatriated, property was not to be taxed to pay for the war, and Britain would give £3 million to compensate for war damage; Cape rebels would only be disenfranchised, not imprisoned; and despite British concern that the African populations of the former republics should be accorded the same political rights as elsewhere, this matter was postponed until the eventual granting of self-government.

The South African or Boer War – or Second War of Independence depending upon the individual's viewpoint – was in terms of troops deployed by far the largest of all colonial campaigns. Nearly 450,000 troops had served under the British flag, 52,000 of them South Africans (not including the South African Constabulary, recruited throughout the empire), with significant contributions from Australia, Canada and New Zealand; 21,000 of these had died, 13,000 from disease, and 52,000 had been wounded or fallen ill. The Boer forces, probably numbering between 65,000 and 87,000, suffered about 4,000 fatalities in battle and as many as 20,000 (mainly non-combatants) died from disease in the 'concentration camps'.

The generosity of the agreed peace-terms led to the largely untroubled incorporation of the previous republics into British South Africa. In February 1907, after the Transvaal election, self-government was granted and Botha was appointed as prime minister; self-government for the Orange River Colony followed in November 1907, and both took part in the federation which created the Union of South Africa (31 May 1910). Louis Botha

became prime minister of the Union, and was a staunch supporter of the empire during the First World War, and Smuts became a member of the Imperial War Cabinet. Some resentments re-surfaced in 1914 with an abortive rebellion led by De Wet (in which De La Rey was killed accidentally, his sentiments at this time being uncertain); it was suppressed quickly by Botha, with purely South African forces, testimony of the rapid integration of previous foes into the British Empire.

Military Forces, 1880–1902

British. Apart from tactical changes resulting from campaigning against the Boers, two notable changes occurred in the composition of British armies. The value of artillery bombardment was appreciated fully as a mode of dislodging the enemy from prepared positions, ideally in conjunction with infantry attacks, so that the army's firepower was increased, even by the employment of naval guns. More significant was the increase in the proportion of mounted troops, cavalry and mounted infantry, so as at least to attempt to meet the Boers on their own terms. The employment of Imperial Yeomanry from Britain was a direct consequence, and an interesting factor arising from the mobilisation of yeomanry and volunteer infantry was a marked increase in the proportion of rank and file drawn from the middle and upper strata of British society, to a level perhaps never experienced before in a British army. Colonial forces provided a similar resource of mounted infantry, often experienced in fieldcraft and the 'irregular' form of warfare which developed. The war highlighted the most severe failings of the entire military system, and resulted in a complete overhaul of organisation, administration and tactical theory, though the widespread use of mounted infantry was no pointer to the future, for the true nature of 'modern' war was that demonstrated by De La Rey at Modder river: that no matter with what degree of resolution an attack was pressed home, the advantage always lay with entrenched defenders using the awesome firepower of the modern generation of weaponry.

Local troops formed a significant part of British forces. The Cape Mounted Rifles remained that colony's principal regular unit, and from 1880 to 1884 their artillery was made into a separate corps, the Cape Field Artillery, re-organised after the Basutoland campaign as a horse battery with 7pdrs. They formed a Maxim section which participated in the Langberg campaign of 1897 (Bechuanaland), and in 1899 were re-equipped with six 2½in RML mountain guns. During the South African War they also used two 15pdrs, and at the siege of Wepener used a 13pdr Hotchkiss and two naval 12pdrs. A further regular unit which existed in the colony was the Cape Infantry, formed in 1882, recruited in Britain from army reservists, given headquarters at Umtata, and disbanded in 1886.

'Long Tom': one of HMS Terrible's 4.7in guns firing at Colenso. Note the distinctive carriage of these large naval guns, and the distinctive straw hats of the Naval Brigade crew.

Others were volunteer corps formed in their localities but capable of mobilisation when required, from battalion-sized units down to small companies and local town guards. The employment of such troops varied; one of the best-known larger units, for example, the Cape Town Highlanders (formed 1885) supplied a contingent to the Langberg campaign and during the war of 1899–1902 was mobilised for lines-of-communication duty; yet volunteers from the corps formed 'A' Squadron of Kitchener's Horse, a unit raised in January 1900 and which saw much active service. Some volunteer corps existed in time of peace; others were formed for particular campaigns and were not 'volunteers' in the sense of part-timers, but voluntarily enlisted members of full-time units. A notable example of the latter was the South African Light Horse, raised at the Cape in November 1899 and commanded by Lieutenant-Colonel the Hon. Julian Byng (later Viscount Byng of Vimy, one of the most distinguished generals of the First World War). Like a number of such corps, their recruits were a mix of South Africans (officers and NCOs mostly from existing volunteer corps) including loyal Afrikaners (the Stellenbosch Mounted Infantry, part of the Western Rifles, enrolled *en masse* in November 1899, for example), and even a contingent of Texans. The unit comprised eight squadrons of about 600 men and were known as 'the Sakabulas' (from their use of the tail-feathers of the Sakabula bird upon their slouch-hats) or 'Byng's Burglars', from their somewhat careless attitude to property.[16] Winston Churchill was among the most famous members of the corps, and two further regiments formed subsequently were Kitchener's and Warren's (later Roberts') Horse.

Another of the most celebrated locally raised corps was Rimington's Guides (known as 'Rimington's Tigers', probably from the leopardskin turbans on their hats), raised in Cape Colony in 1899 by Major Rimington of the 6th Dragoons, and employed in reconnaissance and intelligence work; when Rimington was promoted in January 1901 the unit was re-named Damant's Horse after its new commander. Equally celebrated was Thorneycroft's Mounted Infantry, raised from colonial volunteers at Pietermaritzburg in October 1899 by Major Thorneycroft of the Royal Scots Fusiliers; despite 50 per cent losses at Spion Kop, it served throughout the war. Some local corps achieved regimental strength: the Commander-in-Chief's Bodyguard, for example, raised in Cape Colony in January 1900 with a strength of 100, eventually attained a strength of 1,000 men with two guns, two machine-guns and two pom-poms. The need for mounted troops even involved the integration of local forces with regulars: the Composite Regiment of Mounted Infantry which served with Buller's army in Natal, for example, consisted of squadrons drawn from the Imperial Light Horse, Natal Carbineers, Natal Police, King's Royal Rifle Corps and 2/Dublin Fusiliers. The first of these, the Imperial Light Horse, was raised in September 1899, later increased to two regiments; raised in Natal, almost half its original members were British, many Uitlander refugees from Johannesburg, the remainder from the Cape or Natal with about 10 per cent from other overseas colonies and the USA. It was distinguished especially at Elandslaagte (where its original commanding officer, Lieutenant-Colonel Scott Chisholme, 5th Lancers, was killed) and during the defence of Ladysmith; the squadron with the Composite Regiment was part of the relief-force and, with the Natal Carbineers squadron, were the first troops into the beleaguered garrison. Following this, the ILH formed part of the force which relieved Mafeking.

Other types of local force included the Cape Mounted Yeomanry, authorised as a militia force in 1878, three regiments strong (headquarters of the 1st at King William's

The creation and service of the Imperial Yeomanry was one of the most significant features of the British war effort in South Africa. This illustration shows officers of the 43rd Squadron, Imperial Yeomanry, raised in Norwich by the Loyal Suffolk Hussars in 1900; the khaki uniform and slouch hat was almost universal for such troops. Seated is the commanding officer, Captain John R. Harvey, who had previously served as a 'gentleman-ranker' in the 16th Lancers.

Town, 2nd Queenstown and 3rd Uitenhage). It was intended to provide a mobile corps for the eastern Cape frontier, of men from rural areas who could be mobilised for probably three months' active service, half the force being called out at any one time. Insufficient recruits could be found, however, and the volunteer corps were weakened by extending recruiting to urban areas; instead of the intended 3,000 men, only about 600 could be mobilised for the 1880 Basutoland rebellion, and the force was disbanded in 1881. Police units were employed in a military capacity: the Cape Police (raised 1882) served in the Langberg campaign and in the 1899–1902 war, and the Natal Police in the Zulu War and both Boer Wars. The recruitment of ex-prisoners of war prepared to fight against their erstwhile Boer comrades resulted in the for-

mation of the National Scouts in 1901, a movement in which the OFS general Andries Cronje was instrumental (he had been captured at Reitz); about 1,500 were assembled in the Transvaal, and some 480 (styled Orange River Colony Volunteers) in the ex-Free State. A similar formation, just over 100 strong, was the Somaliland Burgher Corps, formed in 1903 for service in Somaliland and probably the first South African troops to serve outside southern Africa.

'Native levies' were still employed in campaigns against African peoples; in the 1888 Zulu rebellion, for example, it was reported that the 'levies' were much more adept at bush-fighting than the white troops, although they served most effectively when closely supported by the latter: for skirmishing in Basutoland in 1880–1, for example, Cape

After escaping from Boer captivity, Captain Aylmer Haldane of the Gordon Highlanders and his fellow-escapee Le Mesurier of the Dublin Fusiliers travelled to neutral Portuguese territory in a train containing Boers:

'... soon after the train was in motion, a party of Dutchmen in another compartment burst forth into their national Volkslied. This was more than British flesh and blood could stand. We immediately rose, and speedily drowned their voices with our own. Scarcely had we got through the opening words when Uitlander after Uitlander, their faces beaming at hearing this familiar tune, crowded into our compartment and into the passage and joined us. The Dutchmen wisely ceased, and for some minutes I thought it would end in their leaving the train by an exit other than the door. After our vocal efforts had come to an end, with their usual cheers our neighbours began "La Marseillaise", and we constrained ourselves to permit them this safety-valve ...'

(Haldane, Captain A. *How We Escaped from Pretoria*, Edinburgh and London, 1900, p. 121)

Mounted Riflemen were actually intermingled with the 'levies'. It was not usual to employ Africans against a white enemy, but the concept of the 1899–1902 conflict as a 'whites only' war is not strictly accurate, because non-whites were not only used as scouts and watchmen. For example, the Namaqualand Border Scouts, who participated in the defence of Ookiep (the copper-mining town of the western Cape, attacked by Smuts in April–May 1902), was composed entirely of 'coloured' men, and they also made up the greater proportion of the Namaqualand Town Guard (formed in October 1901 by the amalgamation of the Town Guards of Ookiep, Concordia and Port Nolloth). Apart from these units, the defenders of Ookiep consisted of only 44 Warwickshire Militiamen and twelve men of the Cape Garrison Artillery, under the command of Lieutenant-Colonel Shelton of the 3/Queen's West Surrey Regiment; for their successful defence the garrison received a bronze medal (silver for officers) presented by the Cape Copper Company.

The numbers involved in the local forces were considerable; in early 1901, for example, it was estimated that including Town Guards and the 'Colonial Defence Force' raised under the old burgher system for the defence of districts, Cape Colony could field some 34,583 men.

A unique organisation created in late 1900, when it was believed that the South African War was virtually over and that only police action would be required henceforward, was the South African Constabulary. Formed by Baden-Powell, its strength expanded to more than 10,000 by the end of the war, its recruits being drawn from Britain, Cape Colony, Natal and Canada. Comprising nine divisions and

including light artillery, it served throughout the Transvaal and Free State until the end of the war, when it took on its original police duties until merged into the Transvaal and Orange River Colony police forces in 1908. The last Victoria Cross awarded in the war was won by one of its members, Surgeon-Captain Arthur Martin-Leake, at Vlakfontein on 8 February 1902; he was one of only three men to win a bar to the Cross, near Zonnebeke in 1914.

Boer Republics. The Boer forces were organised principally on the Commando system, but there were also small regular units and volunteer corps. The Transvaal (ZAR) Staatsartillerie was reorganised in 1881, still with Krupp mountain guns, members serving a 3-year enlistment and passing to the reserve at age 35. At the time of the Jameson Raid, only 70 men from the strength of 100 could be mobilised, so fifty reservists had to be called; they had only two 4pdrs and two Maxims. Consequently the corps was enlarged and re-equipped, with a strength of 400 divided into mountain, field, siege and horse batteries, with sections of telegraphers, supply, medical and veterinary personnel; and a separate 'fortress artillery' section from 1898. In 1899 ordnance included four 15cm Creusots, six 75mm Creusots, four 12cm Creusot howitzers, four 75mm Krupp howitzers, eight 75mm Krupp quick-firers, two 75mm Maxim-Nordenfelt quick-firers, and twenty-two 1pdr Vickers-Maxim pom-poms. The corps wore a Dutch-style full dress in dark blue with black facings and braid, and white helmet (busbies for the horse battery), and in undress a low shako and plain tunic; field dress included a slouch hat and pale grey-brown uniform with sky-blue facings. Strength at the beginning of the South African War was 400, with 400 reservists; in 1901, with the onset of the guerrilla war which rendered the use of artillery impossible, the unit was reorganised as mounted infantry.

As already described, the Orange Free State Staatsartillerie continued in existence. The original uniform, a low shako or kepi and blue tunic and trousers with red facings, was replaced in 1880 by a uniform like that of the Royal Artillery, including a blue cloth helmet, with orange collar and piping. In 1885, in consequence of the appointment in 1880 of a German commandant, Major Albrecht, a German-style blue uniform was adopted (of a lighter shade for officers), with black facings and a German-style *Pickelhaube*. With the 'British' uniform, field-dress was russet-coloured with black facings, replaced by grey with black piping when the 'German' uniform was used, although in the South African War khaki drill seems to have been worn. In 1880 they had twelve Armstrong guns, and in 1896 the corps was re-equipped with fourteen 75mm Krupp guns. Strength increased to 400 by the outbreak of war; they also had five 9pdr Armstrongs, a 6pdr Whitworth, three Whitworth mountain guns, a 37mm quick-firer and three machine-guns. Albrecht was captured at Paardeberg, and the unit did not exist beyond the beginning of the guerrilla war.

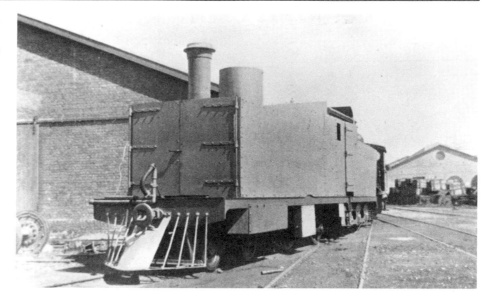

Armoured trains were used in a number of colonial campaigns, most notably in South Africa; this illustration shows a 'fortified' engine.

Other artillery pieces were captured from the British during the war, such as the ten 15pdrs taken at Colenso and the 4-gun mountain battery captured from the armoured train *Mosquito*. The Boer artillery was not manned exclusively by formal artillery units, but sometimes by members of the Commandos.

The other Boer 'regular' forces were the police units. The Transvaal police from 1881 to 1896 was part of the Staatsartillerie, when they became independent with a strength of 1,520; more than half were 'foot police' but all took the field as mounted infantry. They became known as 'Zarps' from their title 'Zuid Afrikaanische Republiek Politie'; their uniform was dark blue with black braid, cord breeches, a kepi for 'foot' and a helmet for mounted elements, although the universal slouch hat was worn on service. The Orange Free State Mounted Police (Oranje Vrystaat Rijdende Diensmacht) existed only briefly, 1862–3, and from 1889 to 1896 frontier patrolling was taken up by the Staatsartillerie, until in 1896–9 a small police force was again constituted.

There were a number of volunteer corps in the Boer republics; the Pretoria Rifles, for example, was formed in 1856, and some existed during the British annexation of the Transvaal; the Transvaal Artillery of 1877–81, for example, fielded a 6-gun battery during the Sekhukhune campaign, with a commander and NCOs seconded from the Royal Artillery. Corps which existed until the outbreak of the 1899 war (when they were incorporated into the Commandos) included the Pretoria Volunteer Cavalry (Pretoria Vrywillige Cavallerie Corps), formed 1893 as a presidential bodyguard, and served during the Swaziland expedition of 1895 and the Jameson Raid, wearing black or dark blue with green facings and shako; the Pretoria Volunteer Infantry (Vrywillige Infanterie or 'Korps Nederlanders en Oud-Nederlanders'), formed September 1899;

the Johannesburg volunteers (Vrywillige Corps), formed 1894, consisting of cavalry and infantry, wearing a light cord uniform with black braid and slouch hat; the Krugersdorp Vrywillige Cavallerie, formed 1895, dark blue uniform with white braid and shako, field dress plain blue jacket, cord breeches and slouch hat; the Carolina Vrywillige Cavallerie; and the Ermelo Vrywillige Cavallerie (dark blue with yellow braid, and shako). The Johannesburg corps illustrates the mixed nature of some of these units; the cavalry was commanded by Major B. A. Hall, a British ex-inspector of the Bechuanaland police, the infantry by Major L. E. Van Diggelen, an ex-officer of the Dutch navy. The companies were divided into 'Hollander' (Boer), German, 'Latin' (French, Italian and Spanish) and 'mixed' (Afrikaners, British, Russians and Scandinavians). The two German companies were commanded by Major Kropp, a Hanoverian who had served in the German Legion raised by Britain at the time of the Crimean War. Another officer was a survivor of Hicks Pasha's army, and the medical officer was an ex-member of the Belgian army.

The Commando system as it existed in the early period, and in the Cape, has already been noted (Commandos were mobilised from the Cape for the Langberg campaign, but not for the 1899–1902 war; the last occasion when commandos were called out was in 1922). The same applied in the two republics, though there were minor differences between states and periods. Probably about 90 per cent were mounted; the dismounted men would remain with the Commando's transport, ox-carts containing provisions and sometimes families (as so hindered Cronje in the Paardeberg campaign). The wagons also provided mobile fortifications which the Commando could use as a base: when in rectangular, circular or triangular laager, they would be chained together and

Queen's South Africa Medal for the war of 1899–1902; designed by G. W. de Saulles, the obverse depicted a portrait of Queen Victoria and the reverse Britannia, holding out a laurel-wreath to troops disembarking in South Africa. Twenty-six clasps were issued, but the duration of the war had been so under-estimated that the reverse originally included the dates '1899–1900'. When the war continued these dates were erased, but can sometimes still be seen, as here (below Britannia's wreath). The ribbon was orange with blue inner and red outer stripes.

might be fortified with a thorn-bush *zareba* or entrenchments; two or more laagers might be positioned to give mutually supportive fire, and extra wagons might be placed as 'outworks' or strongpoints projecting from the corners of the laager. A Commando was raised from the inhabitants of a particular district, and might vary in size from 200 to 1,000 men, though it was possible for much smaller units to operate, and for several Commandos to form a small army. The commander was a *Kommandant*, his deputy an *Assistent-Kommandant*; the rank between them and the troop officers was *Hoof-Veldkornet* (lit. 'chief Field-Cornet'). Each squadron or company was styled a Field-Cornetcy, after its commander, the *Veldkornet*, his deputy being the *Assistent-Veldkornet*. The latter might lead a section of about 25–35 men, although this might equally be the responsibility of the principal NCO, the *Korporaal* (hence 'corporalcy' for this sub-unit). Ordinary privates were styled *Burgher*. 'General officers' rose from *Hoof-Kommandant* to *Vecht-Generaal*, *Generaal* and *Kommandant-Generaal*, each with intermediate 'assistant' and 'vice' ranks. Officers were elected by the burghers, although in the Free State the *Kommandant-Generaal* was elected by the *Kommandants* and *Veldkornets*. Arms were originally provided by the individual, although from about the 1880s some government weapons were also available: Martini-Henrys and Sniders at the Cape, for example, and by the late 1890s the Mauser had become the most common firearm in both Boer states, with which remarkable feats of marksmanship were possible. Commandos used their own clothing, with no 'uniformity' beyond the brief use of coloured pagris, although corduroy uniforms appear to have been issued to Cape men in 1880. In the 1899–1902 war the slouch hat was by far the most common head-dress, although contemporary photographs show such diverse alternatives as sun helmets, straw 'boaters' and cloth caps. Latterly use was made of captured British equipment and uniforms, though the wearer ran the risk of being regarded as a spy if captured.

During the first part of the 1899–1902 war the Boer forces included a number of foreign volunteers, European and American, motivated by a support for Boer independence or opposition to the British. Some formed their own units, of which the most notable was probably the 'Irish Brigade'. This was composed of Irish and Irish-Americans, and was commanded by an American ex-cavalry officer, John Blake; an Irish detachment was also formed by the Irish nationalist Clan-na-Gael organisation in Chicago, and was absorbed into the Irish Brigade on arrival in South Africa in 1900. The brigade was apparently one of the few units to wear uniform, a version of US Army khaki, with a red cross arm-band and hat-badge. In late 1900 most of the foreign volunteers went home, being thought unsuitable for the guerrilla war then commencing.

The presence of Rudyard Kipling as a voluntary hospital helper in the South African War failed to impress one orderly, who found him:

'Not a bad bloke; give me two bob to drink his health fust day, just a hordinary bloke to look at. I speaks to 'im just the same as I do to you, I didn't know he was a poet nor nothink. I knowed he writ "The Absentminded Beggar", but anyone could write that. Come to speak with me every day, I hexplained the cases to 'im. First day he wanted to stay too long, so I chokes 'im off. "Beg pardon," I ses, "but it's quinine time." "What do you mean, Crich?" he ses. "Well, we generally gets a tot of beer at 12," I said, and I asked 'im to come and have a wet at the canteen, but he says, "I don't drink beer." "Oh very well," I ses, "come again tomorrow," and so he did.'

(Inder, W. S. *On Active Service with the S. J. A .B., South African War 1899-1902*, Kendal, 1903, p. 217)

Notes

1. See, for example, 'The Third Kaffir War, 1799–1802', by Major G. Tylden, *Journal of the Society for Army Historical Research*, vol. XXXVII, 1959, pp. 72–83.
2. 'The British Colonies Considered as Military Posts', by Lieutenant-Colonel Wilkie, in *United Service Journal*, vol. 1, 1841, p. 236.
3. *United Service Journal*, vol. III, 1836, p. 131.
4. 'Sketches of the Cape', by Anon., in *United Service Journal*, vol. II, 1834, pp. 350–1.
5. 'Notices from Kafirland, Written on the Spot', by Anon., in *Colburn's United Service Magazine*, vol. I, 1844, p. 505.
6. 'Notices of the Cape and Southern Africa', by Major Charters, RA, *United Service Journal*, vol. III, 1839, p. 25.
7. 'Notices from Kafirland', in ibid., p. 187.
8. 'The Kaffir War', by 'Ancient', in *United Service Journal*, vol. III, 1836, p. 231.
9. 'Wars and Administration of the Cape', by 'Fra Diavolo', in ibid., p. 397.
10. 'Notices from Kafirland', as above, III p. 187.
11. Wilkie, *op. cit.*, p.237.
12. 'The New War in Kafirland', Anon., *Colburn's United Service Magazine* 1846, II p. 564.
13. 'Notices from Kafirland', in *op. cit.*, vol. III, p. 188.
14. 'News from Natal', by Anon., *Chambers' Edinburgh Journal*, 17 August 1850, p. 111.
15. 'Some Aspects of the Zulu Wars', by Major G. Tylden, in *Journal of the Society for Army Historical Research*, vol. XVII, 1938, pp. 127–32.
16. An anecdote relating to the habits and Texan accent acquired by Byng during his service is recounted in J. Williams, *Byng of Vimy, General and Governor-General*, London, 1983, p. 47.

References

The following references are restricted primarily to military histories, but information can also be found in more general works such as G. M. Theal's *History of South Africa*, even though this is now 'dated'. Separate sections of this list are devoted to the Zulu War, and to the Transvaal and 1899–1902 wars.

Becker, P. *Hill of Destiny: the Life and Times of Moshesh, founder of the Basotho*, London, 1969.
Crealock, J. *The Frontier Journal of Major John Crealock 1878: A Narrative of the Ninth Frontier War*, ed., C. Hummel, Cape Town, 1989.
Ellenberger, D. F., and MacGregor, J. C. *History of the Basuto, Ancient and Modern*, London, 1912.
Godlonton, R. *The Irruption of the Kaffir Hordes: The Narrative and Introductory Remarks*, Cape Town, 1965 (r/p of 1835).
Lagden, Sir Godfrey. *The Basutos*, London, 1909.
Le Cordeur, V., and Saunders, C. *The War of the Axe, 1847*, Johannesburg, 1981.
Longford, Elizabeth, Countess of. *Jameson's Raid*, London, 1960.
Meintjes, J. *Sandile: the Fall of the Xhosa Nation*, London, 1971.
Milton, J. *The Edges of War*, Cape Town, 1983 (wars on the Cape frontier).
Moodie, D. C. F. *The History of the Battles and Adventures of the British, the Boers, and the Zulus, in Southern Africa, from 1495 to 1879*, 1888; see entry in Zulu War list.
Ransford, O. *The Great Trek*, London, 1972.
Rivett-Carnac, D. E. *Hawk's Eye*, Cape Town, 1966 (biography of Lieutenant-General Sir Henry Somerset).
Smithers, A. J. *The Kaffir Wars 1779–1877*, London, 1973.
Staples, I. *Narrative of the Eighth Frontier War of 1851–3*, Pretoria, 1974.
Stow, G. W. *The Native Races of South Africa*, London, 1905.
Tylden, Major G. *The Armed Forces of South Africa*, Johannesburg, 1954; corrections and additions appeared in *Africana Notes and News*, March, 1955 and subsequently. (Lists units alphabetically and contains an appendix on the Commando system; the same author's 'The Commando System in South Africa 1795–1881' is in *Journal of the Society for Army Historical Research*, vol. XXIII, 1945, pp. 34–8; both are valuable summaries of the troops and their system.)

Zulu War

Excellent critical summaries of the available printed works are given in Ian Knight's *Brave Men's Blood* and *Zulu*, and in Donald Morris' *The Washing of the Spears*.
Ashe, Major W., and Wyatt-Edgel, Captain E. V. W. *The Story of the Zulu Campaign*, London, 1880; r/p with intr. by J. P. C. Laband, Cape Town, 1989.
Bancroft, J. W. *The Terrible Night at Rorke's Drift: The Zulu War, 1879*, Tunbridge Wells, 1988.
Barthorp, M. *The Zulu War: A Pictorial History* Poole 1980.
Binns, C. T. *The Last Zulu King: The Life and Death of Cetshwayo*, London, 1989.
Bryant, A. T. *A History of the Zulu and Neighbouring Tribes*, Cape Town, 1964.
Clammer, D. G. *The Zulu War*, Newton Abbot, 1973.
Clarke, S. *The Invasion of Zululand 1879*, Johannesburg, 1979.
– *Zululand at War 1879: the Conduct of the Anglo-Zulu War*, Johannesburg, 1984.
Clements, W. *The Glamour and Tragedy of the Zulu War*, London, 1936.
Colenso, F. E., and Durnford, Lieutenant-Colonel E., *History of the Zulu War and its Origin*, London, 1880.
Coupland, Sir Reginald. *Zulu Battle Piece: Isandhlwana*, London, 1948.
Droogleever, R. W. F. *The Road to Isandhlwana: Colonel Anthony Durnford in Natal and Zululand 1873–1879*, London, 1992.
Duminy, A., and Ballard, C. *The Anglo-Zulu War: New Perspectives*, Pietermaritzburg, 1981.
Dunne, Colonel W. A. *Eyewitness in Zululand: The Campaign Reminiscences of Colonel W. A. Dunne*, ed. Lieutenant-Colonel I. H. W. Bennett, London, 1989.
Emery, F. *The Red Soldier: Letters from the Zulu War 1879*, London, 1977.
Farrer, J. A. *Zululand and the Zulus*, London, 1879.
Featherstone, D. *Captain Carey's Blunder: the Death of the Prince Imperial*, London, 1973.
French, Major G. *Lord Chelmsford and the Zulu War*, London, 1939.
Furneaux, R. *The Zulu War: Isandhlwana and Rorke's Drift*, London, 1963.
Gibson, J. Y. *The Story of the Zulus*, London, 1911.
Glover, M. *Rorke's Drift: A Victorian Epic*, London, 1975.
Gon, P. *The Road to Isandlwana*, Johannesburg, 1979.
Guy, J. *The Destruction of the Zulu Kingdom: The Civil War in Zul-*

uland 1879–1884, London, 1979.

Haggard, Sir Henry Rider. Cetywayo and his White Neighbours, London, 1882.

Harford, Colonel H. The Zulu War Journal of Colonel Henry Harford CB, ed. D. Child, Pietermaritzburg, 1978.

Jackson, F. W. D. 'Isandhlwana: The Sources Re-Examined', in Journal of the Society for Army Historical Research, vol. XLIII, 1965.

Knight, I. Brave Men's Blood: The Epic of the Zulu War 1879, London, 1990.

– British Forces in Zululand 1879, London, 1991.

– Nothing Remains but to Fight: The Defence of Rorke's Drift 1879, London, 1993.

– Queen Victoria's Enemies (I): Southern Africa, London, 1989.

– The Zulus, London, 1989.

– Zulu: Isandlwana and Rorke's Drift, 22–23 January 1879, London, 1992.

Knight, I (ed.). By The Orders of the Great White Queen: Campaigning in Zululand through the Eyes of the British Soldier, 1879, London, 1992.

Knight, I, and Langley, D. (eds.). There will be an Awful Row at Home about This, Victorian Military Society, 1979 (rev. edn. ed. Ian Knight, 1987.)

Knight, I., and Castle, I. Fearful Hard Times: The Siege and Relief of Eshowe, London, 1994.

– The Zulu War Then and Now, London, 1993.

– The Zulu War: Twilight of a Warrior Nation, London, 1992.

Laband, J. P. C. The Battle of Ulundi, Pietermaritzburg, 1988.

– Fight us in the Open: the Anglo-Zulu War through Zulu Eyes, Pietermaritzburg, 1985.

– Kingdom in Crisis: the Zulu Response to the British Invasion of 1879, Manchester, 1992.

Laband, J. P. C. (ed.). Lord Chelmsford's Zululand Campaign 1878–79, Army Records Society, 1994.

Laband, J. P. C., and Mathews, J. Isandlwana, Pietermaritzburg, 1992.

Labande, J. P. C., and Thompson, P. S. The Buffalo Border 1879: the Anglo-Zulu War in Northern Natal, 1983.

– Field Guide to the War in Zululand and the Defence of Natal, Pietermaritzburg, 1987, rev. edn.

– Kingdom and Colony at War, Pietermaritzburg and Cape Town, 1990.

Lloyd, A. The Zulu War 1879, London, 1973.

McBride, A. The Zulu War, London, 1986.

Mackinnon, J. P., and Shadbolt, S. H. The South African Campaign of 1879, London, 1880.

Moodie, D. C. F. The History of the Battles and Adventures of the British, the Boers, and the Zulus, in Southern Africa, from 1495 to 1879, 1888; the Zulu War section r/p as Moodie's Zulu War, intr. by J. P. C. Laband, Cape Town, 1988.

Morris, D. R. The Washing of the Spears, London, 1966 (important study).

Newman, C. L. Norris. In Zululand with the British throughout the War of 1879, London, 1880, r/p 1988 (author was correspondent for the London Standard).

Ritter, E. A. Shaka Zulu: the Rise of the Zulu Empire, London, 1955.

War Office. Narrative of the Field Operations Connected with the Zulu War of 1879, prepared by the Intelligence Branch, War Office (author unnamed but was in fact Captain J. S. Rothwell), London 1881 (r/p 1907, 1989) ('official' history: includes also a brief account of the Sekhukhune campaign).

Whybra, J. 'Contemporary Sources and the Composition of the Main Zulu Impi, January 1879', in Soldiers of the Queen, Issue 53 (Victorian Military Society, 1988) (important analysis).

Wilkinson-Latham, R. Uniforms and Weapons of the Zulu War, London, 1978.

Wilmot, A. History of the Zulu War, London, 1880.

Wolseley, Sir Garnet. The South African Journal 1879–1880, ed. and intr. A. Preston, Cape Town, 1973.

Young, J. They Fell Like Stones: Battles and Casualties of the Zulu War, 1879, intr. K. Griffiths, London, 1991.

Transvaal and South African (Boer) Wars

Amery, L. S. (ed.). The Times History of the War in South Africa, London, 1900–9.

Atkins, J. B. The Relief of Ladysmith, London, 1900.

Barthorp, M. The Anglo-Boer Wars: The British and the Afrikaners 1815–1902, Poole, 1987.

Belfield, E. The Boer War, London, 1975.

Bellairs, Lady B. St. J. The Transvaal War 1880–81, Edinburgh, 1885.

Burleigh, B. The Natal Campaign, London, 1900.

Carter, T. F. A Narrative of the Boer War: its Causes and Results, London, 1896 (First Boer or Transvaal War).

Chisholm, R. Ladysmith, London, 1979.

Churchill, W. L. S. (later Sir Winston). Ian Hamilton's March, London, 1900.

– London to Ladysmith, London, 1900.

Cloete, S. African Portraits, London, 1946 (includes biographies of Kruger and Rhodes).

Conan Doyle, Sir Arthur. The Great Boer War, London, 1902 ('complete edn.': orig. pub. 1900).

Danes, R. Cassell's History of the Boer War 1899–1901, London, 1901 (typical 'popular' history).

De Wet, C. Three Years War 1899–1902, London, 1902.

Duxbury, G. R. The First War of Independence 1880–81, Johannesburg, 1981.

Farwell, B. The Great Boer War, London, 1977.

Featherstone, D. Queen Victoria's Enemies: An A–Z of British Colonial Warfare, London, 1989.

Gardner, B. Mafeking: A Victorian Legend, London, 1966.

– The Lion's Cage, London, 1969 (siege of Kimberley).

Goldman, C. S. With General French and the Cavalry in South Africa, London, 1902.

Griffiths, K. Thank God we kept the Flag flying: the Siege and Relief of Ladysmith 1899–1900, London, 1974.

Grinnell-Milne, D. Baden-Powell at Mafeking, London, 1957.

Hackett, R. G. South African War Books, London, 1994 (bibli-ography of works published before 1920).

Hales, A. G. Campaign Pictures of the War in South Africa 1899–1900: Letters from the Front, London 1900 (Daily News correspondent).

Haythornthwaite, P. J. Uniforms Illustrated: the Boer War, London, 1987.

Keane, A. H. The Boer States: Land and People, London, 1900.

Knight, I. Queen Victoria's Enemies (I): Southern Africa, London, 1989.

Kruger, R. Goodbye Dolly Gray, London, 1959 (history of the 1899–1902 war).

Lehmann, J. H. The First Boer War 1881, London, 1972.

Lee, E. To the Bitter End, London, 1985 (the 1899–1902 war).

Mahan, Captain A. T. The Story of the War in South Africa 1899–1902, London, 1900.

Maurice, Major-General Sir Frederick, and Grant, M. H. History of the War in South Africa, London, 1906–10 (War Office official history).

Maydon, J. French's Cavalry Campaign, London, 1901.

Meintjes, J. Stormberg: A Lost Opportunity, Cape Town, 1969.

– The Anglo-Boer War 1899–1902: A Pictorial History, Cape Town, 1976.

Menpes, M. War Impressions, London, 1901 (account and illustrations by a war artist).

Newman, C. L. Norris. With the Boers in the Transvaal and Orange Free State in 1880–1, London, 1882.

Oosthuizen, P. Boer War Memorabilia: the Collectors' Guide, London, 1987 (comprehensive survey of the effect of a colonial war upon popular artefacts and contemporary taste).

Pakenham, T. The Boer War, London, 1979 (excellent modern history).

Pemberton, W. B. Battles of the Boer War, London, 1964.

Pretorius, F. J. The Anglo-Boer War 1899–1902, Cape Town, 1985.

Ransford, O. The Battle of Majuba Hill: the First Boer War, London, 1967.

The Battle of Spion Kop, London, 1969.

Reitz, D. *Commando: A Boer Journal of the Boer War*, London, 1933.

Sharp, G. *The Siege of Ladysmith*, London, 1976.

Smail, J. L. *Monuments and Battlefields of the Transvaal War 1881 and the South African War 1899*, Cape Town, 1967.

Steevens, G. *From Cape Town to Ladysmith: an Unfinished Record of the South African War*, Edinburgh, 1900.

Stirling, J. *The Colonials in South Africa 1899–1902*, London, 1907.

Symons, J. *Buller's Campaign*, London, 1963.

Tullibardine, Marchioness of, and Macdonald, J. C. C. A *Military History of Perthshire 1899–1902*, Perth, 1908 (the effect of the South African War upon one county).

Warwick, P. (ed.). *The South African War: the Anglo-Boer War 1899–1902*, London, 1980.

Wilson, H. W. *After Pretoria, the Guerilla War*, London, 1902.

– *With the Flag to Pretoria*, London, 1900–1.

BECHUANALAND

The vast territory of Bechuanaland extended north of Cape Colony, west of the Orange Free State and Transvaal, and was bordered by Rhodesia on the north-east and German South-West Africa on the west. The inhabitants, who had migrated from the north and mixed with the existing residents, included the Bechuana in the west and the Basuto in the east, the former divided into tribal groupings including the Batlapin, Barolong and Bakuena. The majority of the European missionaries, traders and explorers who entered the area from the early 19th century were British, providing a close connection with Cape Colony (indeed, from 1836 the jurisdiction of the Cape legal system was extended to southern Bechuanaland). However, pressure was placed upon the inhabitants by Boer settlers to the east, involving both diplomatic overtures to local chiefs and military action, neither of which achieved an extension of Boer territory (in 1868, for example, a Commando attacked the Barolong and was driven off). In response to an appeal for British protection from the Barolong and others, in 1878 southern Bechuanaland was occupied by a British force under Colonel (later Sir Charles) Warren. The reluctance of the British government to become involved, however, led to the withdrawal of even police by April 1881, and following the Transvaal War the Boers again began to expand into Bechuanaland, establishing small republics at Stellaland (capital Vryburg) and Goshen (capital Rooi Grond), against the wishes of the local people. Despite British diplomatic activity, including the conclusion of the London Convention in February 1884 which defined Transvaal's boundaries (to include part of eastern Bechuanaland), and later the dispatch of Cecil Rhodes (then opposition leader in the Cape parliament) on a mission to settle Anglo–Boer–Bechuana affairs, the Boer attacks continued, and on 10 September 1884 the territory was proclaimed to be under Transvaal protection.

Fearing the expansion of Boer territory across the continent to German South-West Africa, Britain dispatched a force under Sir Charles Warren to remove the 'illegal' Boer settlements. Almost 5,000 strong, it included British regulars (two field batteries, one with four 9pdr RML guns, one with four Gardner machine-guns, Royal Engineers, 6th Dragoons, 1/Royal Scots) and local forces (an artillery battery raised at the Cape, including recruits from existing volunteer corps, with six 7pdrs; pioneers, a corps of 'Bantu Guides', and three Mounted Rifle regiments formed for the expedition, the 1st recruited in the Cape and Britain, 2nd at the Cape and 3rd at Kimberley, each 600 strong with regular officers, and sometimes known from the names of their commanding officers as Methuen's, Carrington's and Gough's Horse respectively). In January 1885 Kruger met Warren at Modder river and attempted to prevent the expedition progressing, but Warren ignored Kruger's overtures, broke up the two 'illegal' republics without hostilities, and on 30 September 1885 Bechuanaland was taken under British protection. That part south of the Molopo river was styled 'British Bechuanaland' and made a crown colony; in 1895 it was annexed to Cape Colony. The area to the north was the Bechuanaland protectorate, which in 1895 was intended to be passed to the control of the British South Africa Company, but this was prevented by the Jameson Raid and the protectorate remained under imperial government control.

A minor military action had occurred in 1878, when a group of Bechuana in Griqualand West were involved in violence caused by cattle confiscation; they fled across the border into Bechuanaland, pursued by police and colonial volunteers. Operations continued until June/July 1878, including a sharp fight in a fortified position attacked by the colonial forces at Dithakong, before hostilities ended. More serious was a rebellion in late 1896, arising from an outbreak of the cattle disease rinderpest. The suppression of this involved the slaughtering of native cattle, which was so resented that on 24 December 1896 chief Galishwe's people attacked a detachment of Cape Mounted Police at Pokwani. This was followed by a more general rising in January 1897, and a large rebel force collected in the Langberg Mountains in the west, under chief Luka Jantje and others. Colonial forces were gathered as the Bechuanaland Field Force, and after some actions the rebels were defeated in a drive against their position at Gamasep (30 July–1 August 1897); Luka was killed in this action. (An appalling story concerns a Cape officer who requested one of his men to appropriate Luka's head as a souvenir, which was achieved by the use of a pocket-knife and chopper; the officer forfeited his commission as a result.) Bechuanaland featured in a peripheral way during the South African War of 1899–1902, as Mafeking lay just inside the border, in that part of Bechuanaland taken over by the Cape.

Military Forces

By the mid-19th century the Bechuana people were almost completely equipped with firearms, and European clothing had been adopted widely. By the time of the 1896 rebellion, many of these firearms were comparatively modern, and thus indigenous modes of warfare had been replaced by European styles.

To serve British Bechuanaland and the Protectorate, a regiment of mounted riflemen was formed from September 1885, the Bechuanaland Border Police, under Lieutenant-Colonel Frederick Carrington of the South Wales Borderers; it was also known as Carrington's Horse, although this was also the designation of quite separate corps of local horse of 1877 and 1879, both raised by Carrington (one the Frontier Light Horse), and also of a mounted infantry unit formed in 1877 from the 2/3rd, 1/13th, 1/24th and 94th Foot. Many of the BBP rank and file were from the three mounted infantry units of Warren's expedition and from the Cape Mounted Riflemen; many of the officers were British regulars. The strength was about 500, including an artillery troop. The corps' staff raised the first units of the British South Africa Police at Mafeking in 1890 (see 'Rhodesia'). Heavily engaged in the Matabele War, they were the first British troops to use the Maxim gun in action in 1893 (the artillery troop was equipped with four 7pdr RML mountain guns and four Maxims); they wore brown corduroy uniforms (later khaki twill) with blue puttees and a brown slouch hat with pagri coloured according to the troop. Upon the annexation of British Bechuanaland to the Cape in 1895, the BBP was disbanded, their duties in the Protectorate being assumed by BSAP personnel from Rhodesia, to which many BBP men transferred; more than 100 of them volunteered for Jameson's Raid.

For the Langberg campaign, in addition to the Cape police and Mounted Riflemen, the following were among the local corps which supplied the greatest numbers of men to the Field Force: Cape Town Highlanders; Diamond Fields Horse (formed 1876, part becoming the Diamond Fields Artillery in 1890; also served in Ninth Frontier and Sekhukhune campaigns; amalgamated with the Kimberley Regiment from 1899); Duke of Edinburgh's Own Volunteer Rifles (originally Cape Rifle Corps); First City Volunteers (of Grahamstown, formed 1875, also served in Ninth Frontier War and Basutoland 1880–1); Kaffrarian Rifles (formed in East London 1883); Kimberley Rifles (formed 1890); Prince Alfred's Guard (formed 1856 as Port Elizabeth Volunteer Rifles, also served in Ninth Frontier War and Basutoland); and the Queenstown Rifle Volunteers (1860–80, re-formed 1891).

Other units associated with the territory included the Bechuanaland Native Police, raised 1897 and incorporated into the Bechuanaland Protectorate Police, formed in the same year. The Bechuanaland Rifles, formed at Mafeking in January 1897, officially a Cape unit (as by then southern Bechuanaland had been annexed), formed part of the Mafeking garrison during the siege. The remainder comprised members of the Cape and BSA Police, Town Guard and Protectorate Regiment, with other associated volunteers and an African contingent enrolled by Baden-Powell as guards and known as the 'Black Watch'. The Town Guard was typical of such organisations which existed at the time, partially trained local inhabitants including Dutch, Arabs, Indians, Russians, Scandinavians, Germans and Americans, some with military experience extending back to the Crimea. The Protectorate Regiment was one of two raised by Baden-Powell in the period before the war (the other being the Rhodesia Regiment). The Protectorate Regiment was based at Ramathlabama, less than twenty miles from Mafeking (the authorities having decided that to concentrate it at Mafeking might serve to attract a Boer attack in the event of hostilities), recruited in Bechuanaland and Cape Colony with a strength of 470; a number of its men came from the Kaffrarian Rifles.

RHODESIA

The territory which became Rhodesia was bounded by the Bechuanaland Protectorate and the Transvaal in the south, Portuguese West Africa in the west, the Belgian Congo in the north-west, German East Africa in the north-east, and British Central Africa and Portuguese East Africa in the east. South and east of the Zambezi was Southern Rhodesia, Mashonaland in the north and Matabeleland in the south; north and west of the Zambezi was North-Eastern and North-Western Rhodesia (Barotseland). The campaigning of the period took place in Southern Rhodesia.

The inhabitants of this area were the Mashona, a peaceful people of various related clans whose name was apparently derived from the Matabele term *Amashuina*, describing the Mashona practice of seeking refuge in the hill-country; the name 'Shona' is more correct, but 'Mashona' is the version used in most contemporary sources. In about 1817 the chief Mzilikazi (or 'Mosilikatze') of the Khumalo clan, allied to the Zulu nation, was condemned to death by Shaka; he fled with a band of Zulus and settled in the Transvaal, until in 1837 Boer settlers drove him north of the Limpopo into Mashona territory. His people, including those subdued by his original followers in the Transvaal, were apparently given the name Matabele by the Basutos, meaning 'hidden' or 'vanishing' people, a reference to the large war-shields which concealed them; the version they adopted themselves was 'Ndabele' or 'Ndebile', although 'Matabele' is the version used in most contemporary sources. They subdued or absorbed the Mashona people, and created in their territory a class system by which the most influential were those descended from the original Zulu clan, above those who had joined in the Transvaal, while the Mashona were regarded as the lowest class, termed *Holi* by the Matabele.

Mzilikaze died in 1868, and as his recognised heir had disappeared years before, the next in line, Lobengula, succeeded to the Matabele kingdom; his power was unchallenged after his defeat in battle of a pretender who claimed to be Kuruman, the missing heir. Various colonial

Cecil Rhodes (1853–1902).

powers endeavoured to reach an accord with Lobengula, including Kruger for the Transvaal, but it was Britain that succeeded, at the instigation of Cecil Rhodes, who was interested in the mineral rights of Lobengula's territory. Having concluded an agreement, Rhodes applied to the British government for a charter for his newly formed British South Africa Company, which was granted on 29 October 1889 (thereafter it was also known as 'the Chartered Company'). As well as granting sole access to the mineral rights, the charter gave the Company almost sovereign powers and authorised its own police force; and in addition to its commercial purpose, the Company undertook to encourage colonisation and was an important part in Rhodes' vision of unbroken British territory 'from the Cape to Cairo'.

Accordingly, a 'Pioneer Column' under Lieutenant-Colonel Edward Pennefather was sent into Mashonaland in 1890 to establish the first settlements, including Salisbury; Lobengula's approval had been negotiated, the Mashona raised no objections, but some resistance was encountered from the Portuguese and Boers, both of whom intended to lay claim to part of the territory. (On 11 May there was actually a skirmish near Manica when some 500 Portuguese (Europeans and askaris) attacked about fifty Britons under Captain Melville Heyman, entrenched with a 7pdr gun. The Portuguese suffered

nineteen casualties and withdrew.) In both cases the dispute was settled in the Company's favour, but in 1893 there arose a war with the Matabele.

The Matabele continued their regular incursions into Mashona territory, including one to Fort Victoria (one of the new settlements) in July 1893, in which some 400 Mashona were killed as a reprisal for cattle-stealing. Although there was probably no hostile intent on the part of Lobengula, who was unable completely to control the more warlike elements of his people, it was used as an excuse to expand into Matabeleland by Rhodes' Company administrator, Dr. Leander Starr Jameson. Having persuaded Rhodes to approve the scheme, Jameson convinced Sir Henry Loch, High Commissioner at the Cape, of Lobengula's warlike intentions, and secured the use of 'imperial' troops for the proposed campaign. Accordingly Jameson organised two columns of Company forces, marching from Salisbury and Fort Victoria, which united on 16 October 1893, together about 700 strong and equipped with Maxim guns; the 'imperial' column, from Tuli on the border with the Bechuanaland Protectorate, commanded by Lieutenant-Colonel Goold-Adams of the Bechuanaland Border Police, comprised some 225 BBP with two 7pdrs and four Maxims, 220 volunteers and 2,000 Bechuana levies under Chief Khama.

Jameson aimed to advance upon Lobengula's capital, Bulawayo. The main column was attacked by some 3,500 Matabele on the Shangani river on 25 October; the assault was pressed with great courage but repelled with the aid of Maxim guns at a cost of about 500 casualties; the defenders lost two killed and six wounded. A much larger force assailed the column on 1 November at Bembisi (or 'Mbembisi') and was slaughtered in even greater numbers (about 1,000 casualties against four dead and seven wounded among the British). On 3 November the column and Jameson entered Bulawayo, from where Lobengula had fled, having beaten the 'imperial' column to the objective; this column from the south had been attacked at Impandene on 2 November but had dispersed their assailants with Maxim fire.

On 13 November Major P. W. Forbes of the 6th Dragoons (attached to Company forces) was dispatched to apprehend Lobengula; he had with him 90 Bechuanaland Border Police, 210 Company volunteers (ill-disciplined and including some malcontents), a 7pdr and two Maxims. After sending back his stragglers and the unenthusiastic, Forbes was left with 78 policemen, 98 volunteers and the Maxims. On 1 December Lobengula sent in a message of submission and £1,000 in gold, but his envoys were intercepted by two straggling BBP troopers who pocketed the money and concealed the message (they were sentenced subsequently to fourteen years' imprisonment). Thus, operations continued, and on the night of 3 December a detachment of 34 men under Captain Allan Wilson was sent across the Shangani to locate Lobengula; the river rose in flood, preventing their escape or rescue, and the Matabele massacred the whole party (less three couriers sent back by Wilson). This 'last stand' of the Shangani Patrol became one of the great epics of Rhodesian history; but the remainder of Forbes' column retired. A further column of 'imperial' troops was sent from Mafeking to reinforce Goold-Adams (principally BBP but with mounted infantry from several British regiments); but there was no further action, the war ending after Lobengula's death in January 1894, and with the submission of the Matabele chiefs. The radical press in particular vehemently denounced the Company for provoking the war deliberately, but the colonial secretary, Lord Ripon, absolved them of blame – hardly the fairest conclusion.

The Company prospered and expanded after the occupation of Matabeleland; notably, in June 1890 a treaty with Lewankia, king of the Barotse, placed Barotseland under Company protection, granting them mineral rights on condition that they refrain from interfering in internal administration. On 3 May 1895 the name Rhodesia was granted to the Company's territory, and in the same year it was decided that the Company should administer the Bechuanaland Protectorate. The Jameson Raid, however, caused a crisis in the Company's fortunes; the Bechuanaland transfer was never implemented, Rhodes resigned as the Company's managing director, and Jameson was removed from his post as administrator of the Company territory.

The failure of the Jameson Raid and the consequent denuding of the territory of most of its military force was a contributory cause of the Matabele uprising of 1896. Taxation and the destruction of cattle as a result of the rinderpest epidemic had been the cause of great discontent, and the weakness of the settlers was seen as an opportunity to throw off the Company yoke; and the rising was encouraged by the priests of the Mlimo cult. The rebellion was unco-ordinated but began sporadically in late March 1896, and involved the indiscriminate massacre of all white settlers and their African servants; by the end of that month the only surviving settlers were laagered in the four principal towns, Bulawayo, Bellingwe, Gwelo and Mangwe. The local volunteer forces held their own and won a number of skirmishes against their badly organised opponents, and Cecil Rhodes personally formed and accompanied the relief column of the Bulawayo Field Force from Salisbury. The Company also began to raise another contingent at the Cape, but the British government insisted that it be commanded temporarily by an 'imperial' officer, Major Herbert Plumer. This Matabeleland Relief Force assembled at Mafeking, comprising about 700 whites (including 200 of Jameson's raiders) and 200 Africans, and reached Bulawayo in late May, to find that Rhodes' 600-strong column had already arrived. Shortly afterwards more 'imperial' officers arrived, including Colonel Robert Baden-Powell, and General Sir Frederick Carrington, who

assumed overall command. Operations continued with the Matabele on the defensive, especially in the Matoppo Hills, east of Bulawayo, where some of their leaders were killed, including Chief Olimo; Plumer's force reduced the stronghold of another, Chief Secombo, and Chief Makoni was captured and shot near Umtali in September. To prevent a continuing guerrilla war, Rhodes went into the Matoppo Hills in September 1896 to negotiate with the remaining Matabele leaders; their grievances were recognised, and peace was declared on 13 October.

The departure of Rhodes and his column from Salisbury, however, was a contributory cause of a Mashona rising in June 1896, perhaps more surprising to the settlers than the Matabele rising, in that they considered themselves to have liberated the Mashona. Spirit 'mediums' helped spread the revolt by promising invulnerability to bullets, but the rebellion was not co-ordinated and devolved into separate operations against individual chieftains. The Salisbury column returned from Matabeleland, and was aided by British regulars rushed to the area and Portuguese from Beira. Four mounted infantry companies served in this Mashonaland Field Force; organised originally for service against the Matabele, they were drawn from various regiments from Britain and styled the English, Highland, Irish and Rifle companies, the latter not referring to their weapons but from being assembled from the 2/ and 4/Rifle Brigade and 3/ and 4/KRRC. Operations against individual kraals continued until hostilities ended by about September 1897, though final peace with the Mashona chiefs was not concluded until 29 October 1897.

Following the Jameson Raid and the rebellions, the government reformed the constitution of Rhodesia; it was still administered by the Company, but from October 1898 an imperial resident commissioner was appointed as a member of the executive and legislative councils, and the armed forces of the Company were placed under imperial control. The colony was not involved directly in the South African War of 1899–1902 except in the provision of forces in support of the British; nearly 1,500 men served, representing no less than 12½ per cent of the European population, the absence of so great a proportion of the able-bodied men considerably hindering the economic development of Rhodesia during those years.

Military Forces

Matabele military organisation was initially similar to that of the Zulus, with 'age-regiments', although the system was not enforced so rigidly, 'regimental' strength being considerably less than the Zulu average (with perhaps only 200–500 men per 'regiment'); and the indigenous 'lower classes' formed their own regiments, which were regarded as the least effective. Tactics were originally similar to those of the Zulus, with throwing- and stabbing-spears and axes being the principal armament, but they also possessed a considerable number of firearms, including many modern weapons: part of the original agreement by which Lobengula granted mining concessions was for a monthly payment of £100 plus 1,000 Martini-Henry rifles and 100,000 rounds of ammunition. After the slaughter incurred by charging machine-guns, such tactics gave way to a more irregular form of warfare involving guerrilla operations, ambushes and the defence of strongholds, with increased use of firearms. The Mashona had none of the military organisation of the Matabele, but operated more in clan groups led by a particular chieftain, which prevented any real attempt at concerted action.

The Company's police force was formed at Mafeking in 1890 by Carrington and the staff of the Bechuanaland Border Police, some of the BBP transferring to the new corps which was originally constituted in five troops, and styled the British South Africa Company's Police. Financial constraints led to a diminution in size and in 1892 the title was changed to Mashonaland Mounted Police; a Matabeleland Mounted Police was formed in December 1893 and the two amalgamated as the Rhodesia Mounted Police in 1895, re-titled from 1896 (officially from 1897) as the British South Africa Police. There also existed more civil police units, the Mashonaland and Matabeleland Constabularies and the Mashonaland Native Police, the latter recruited from outside Rhodesia until 1903. The 'Pioneer Column' or 'Pioneer Corps', formed in three troops, was disbanded on 1 October 1890, and thereafter the local volunteer corps were named after their place of residence (Salisbury, Gwelo, Umtali, etc.) or were units created for a particular campaign and even named after a particular purpose, e.g., the Matabeleland Relief Force Corps. In October 1899 the volunteers were reorganised in two divisions, Eastern and Western, of the Southern Rhodesia Volunteers.

During the South African War the British South Africa Police and Southern Rhodesia Volunteers served in the field; and to defend the territory, one of the two corps formed by Baden-Powell in the immediate pre-war period was the Rhodesia Regiment, based at Bulawayo and commanded by Plumer. For the defence and internal security of Rhodesia Plumer had only about 420 men of the Rhodesia Regiment, 1,000 BSAP spread across the whole territory and a fluctuating number of volunteers; the most he ever had available was about 1,760, a considerable part being taken to attempt the relief of Mafeking. He had a most capable supporter in the BSAP commandant, Colonel J. S. Nicholson, who organised resources and training; three armoured trains were constructed, to patrol into Bechuanaland. The Company was permitted to organise the Rhodesian Field Force, but reinforcements under Carrington, consisting of British and colonial troops, were permitted to enter Rhodesia via the Portuguese port of Beira. Plumer's force which marched to the relief of Mafeking consisted of the Rhodesia Regiment, a contingent of BSAP, a small contingent of Rhode-

sian volunteers and some advance elements of the imperial reinforcement, 100 Queensland Mounted Infantry, 50 New Zealanders, and four of the six guns of 'C' Battery, Royal Canadian Artillery, raised in Ontario and Winnipeg and officered by Canadian regulars and volunteers from the North-West Mounted Police; the total artillery strength was eight guns. The Rhodesia Regiment was disbanded before the end of the war, its personnel mostly joining the Protectorate Regiment or Kitchener's Fighting Scouts (a corps originally recruited at Bulawayo by Colonel Johan Colenbrander), but the BSAP remained the colony's regular military force, under the direct control of the high commissioner; and the two divisions of Southern Rhodesia Volunteers were amalgamated in 1903.

References

Alderson, Lieutenant-Colonel E. A. H. *With the Mounted Infantry and the Mashonaland Field Force 1896*, London, 1898.

Baden-Powell, Colonel R. S. S. *The Matabele Campaign 1896: being a Narrative of the Campaign in Suppressing the Native Rising in Matabeleland and Mashonaland*, London, 1897.

Cary, R. *A Time to Die*, London, 1969 (Shangani Patrol).

Cloete, S. *African Portraits*, London, 1946 (includes biography of Lobengula).

Glass, S. *The Matabele War*, London, 1968.

Knight, I. *Queen Victoria's Enemies (I): Southern Africa*, London, 1989.

Newman, C. L. Norris. *Matabeleland – And How we got it*, London, 1895.

Plumer, Lieutenant-Colonel H. *An Irregular Corps in Matabeleland*, London, 1897.

Radford, M. P. *Service Before Self:*

The History, Badges and Insignia of the Security Forces of the Rhodesia and Nyasaland 1890–1980, Wellington, 1994.

Ranger, T. O. *Revolt in Southern Rhodesia 1896–7*, London, 1967.

Selous, F. C. *Sunshine and Storm in Rhodesia: A Narrative of Events in Matabeleland before and during the recent Native Insurrection up to the date of the disbandment of the Bulawayo Field Force*, London, 1896 (Frederick Courtney Selous, who guided the Pioneer Column in 1890, was probably the most famous hunter, naturalist, explorer and scout of his generation).

Sykes, F. W. *With Plumer in Matabeleland: an Account of the Operations of the Matabeleland Relief Force during the Rebellion of 1896*, London, 1897.

Wills, W. A., and Collingridge, L. T. *The Downfall of Lobengula*, London, 1894.

SWAZILAND

Swaziland (or *Pungwane*) was a small state bordered by Transvaal on all but the east; by Portuguese territory on the north-east and by Zululand on the south-east. The inhabitants, styled Barapusa or Barabuza after a chief who unified the clan, were part of the Zulu state until 1843, until they achieved independence under a chief named Swazi, whose name they adopted. They generally maintained good relations with both British and Boers, at times serving as military allies. The independence of Swaziland was recognised by the Anglo–Transvaal conventions of 1881 and 1884, but Boer encroachment caused the Swazi chief Mbandine to request British protection; when this was declined he granted concessions to the South African

Republic, and although dual control by Britain and the SAR was agreed in 1890, following Mbandine's death in 1889, in 1894 the SAR was assigned administration of the territory, despite Swazi requests for British protection. In the South African War of 1899–1902 Mbandine's widow Naba Tsibeni, known as the 'queen regent', took the side of the British and asked that Swaziland be annexed along with the Transvaal. At the conclusion of the war a provisional administration was established under a British commissioner, and from June 1903 the governance of the territory was conferred upon the governor of the Transvaal; in December 1906 it was transferred to the high commissioner for South Africa. Nana Tsibeni remained as regent during the minority of her grandson, Sobhuza, who became paramount chief.

The Swazi forces were organised on traditional 'tribal' lines, but unlike many others, they appeared to have favoured their 'full dress' costume for campaign service. The force formed for the Sekhukhune campaign was known as the Swazi Tribal Levy, organised and commanded by Captain Macleod, late 74th; it was about 8,000 strong and lost some 600 men in the final attack on Sekhukhune's stronghold. The South African Republic's constabulary for the Swaziland border was known as the *Grenspolitie van Swaziland* (Swaziland Border Police), but after the SAR took over administration in 1894 it was styled the Swaziland Police, and was about 400 strong. From the British assumption of control, the military force used in the territory was the South African Constabulary (part of 'C' Division, HQ Heidelberg) until 1907, when a separate Swaziland Police was established.

SUDAN

Arising from their involvement in Egypt, British campaigning in the Sudan was initially an unexpected entanglement: 'Had any man dared to predict in the autumn of the year 1882, when the rebellion instigated by Arabi Pasha had been crushed ... that eighteen months afterwards British troops would be actively engaged in another part of Egyptian territory, he would have been scouted as an idle dreamer; had he ventured further, and said that two years hence the flower of the British Army would be fighting unceasingly against Time and the tremendous difficulties and varied perils incident to a river voyage along the great Nile Valley, with an objective two thousand miles distant from Cairo, the world would have pitied him as one demented. Yet how literally would the prophecy have been fulfilled!'[1]

From the 7th century Arab conquerors had entered the lands of the Nubians, the inhabitants of the Nile valley between Egypt and Abyssinia; the Arabs settled and mixed with them, imposing their customs, language and religion (although Christianity, adopted by the Nubians in the 6th

century, was still practised by some in the region as late as the 16th century). The resulting patchwork of tribes and principalities was disunited and often feuding, and lacked the cohesion effectively to resist the external pressure from Mehemet Ali of Egypt, who began his conquest of the Sudan in 1820, anxious to exploit the region's resources and to find employment for his army. The conquest of the Sudan was not accomplished without cost – during a feast given by one of the Arab princes in 1822, Mehemet Ali's son Ismail, commander of the first invasion, was burned to death – but appropriation of the territory was accomplished and expanded in subsequent years, attended by terrible atrocities perpetrated on the inhabitants. Egypt established a civil government, headed by a governor-general who wielded extreme powers, and by leasing the Red Sea ports of Suakin and Massawa from the Sultan of Turkey, Mehemet Ali monopolised the trade-routes of the eastern Sudan. Egyptian rule was oppressive and slave-raiding among the lands bordering Egyptian territory became a major industry. Later governors-general made some attempts to curb the slave trade (for which purpose a military post was stationed at Fashoda in 1865, the most southerly point held by the Egyptians), but with very limited success. Expansion continued (involving wars with Abyssinia, in which the Egyptians were usually unsuccessful), and under Ismail Pasha a new governorship was established for the Equatorial Provinces in the south.

In March 1874 Colonel Charles Gordon was installed as governor of this region, a man of devout faith and dynamic qualities whose name had been made in China. Like his

Opposite page: Captain Paul A. Kenna, 21st Lancers, who won the Victoria Cross at Omdurman during his regiment's famous charge, perhaps best-known for the participation of Winston Churchill. Kenna was decorated for rescuing Major Crole-Wyndham, whose horse had been killed, and then returning to help Lieutenant Raymond de Montmorency, who also won the VC for the action. In this photograph Kenna is wearing field equipment, as worn in the charge, including a 'Wolseley' pattern helmet which at that date was just beginning to be adopted by officers. As a brigadier-general, Kenna died at Suvla, Gallipoli, in August 1915.

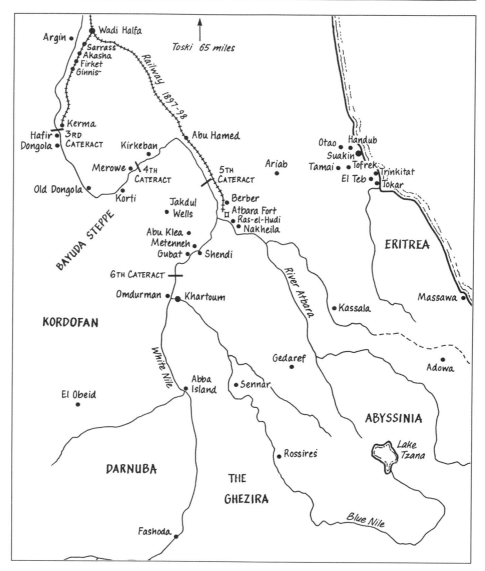

predecessor, Sir Samuel Baker, Gordon made strenuous efforts to suppress the slave trade and improve the oppressive and corrupt Egyptian administration; in October 1876 he relinquished his post, but in February 1877, under pressure from both British and Egyptian governments, accepted the governorship of the entire Egyptian territories outside Egypt, including the Sudan and the Equatorial Provinces, Darfur and the Red Sea and Somali coasts, which he governed from the Sudanese capital, Khartoum. Gordon endeavoured to institute a benevolent government and suppress slavery, and quelled unrest in Darfur in 1877 and 1878, and in Kordofan in 1878; and a revolt by the slaver Suliman Zobeir was crushed by Gordon's deputy, the Italian Romolo Gessi. (Europeans featured prominently in positions of responsibility at this time: Equatorial governor from 1878 was the German 'Emin Pasha', actually Eduard Schnitzer, originally Gordon's medical adviser;

and the Darfur governor was the Austrian Rudolph Slatin, alias 'Slatin Pasha'.) When Gordon relinquished office in August 1879, the worst aspects of Egyptian rule returned.

Such conditions made the whole area ripe for revolt, especially revolt inspired by religious fervour. This was generated by Mohammed Ahmed Ibn Seyyid Abdullah, a native of Dongola, who achieved renown as a devout religious teacher and travelled through Kordofan, denouncing Egyptian rule and predicting the coming of the Mahdi, the Islamic messiah. As his following grew, he proclaimed himself to be the Mahdi, and assumed leadership of the Baggara (or 'Baqqara' people, cattle-owning Arabs, a prominent member of whom, Abdullah (or 'Abdullahi') el-Taaishi, became one of the Mahdi's principal Khalifas or lieutenants. Gordon's successor, Raouf Pasha, sent a small force to apprehend the Mahdi and his followers, only to have it destroyed (August 1881); and on 7 June 1882 a force

Warriors of the Mahdi's ansar army, wearing the very characteristic white jibbeh (tunic) with coloured patches. These men were said to be members of the Taaishi section of the Baggara people; the weapons illustrated are typical, a spear with leaf-shaped blade and a kaskara, the straight-bladed sword with straight quillons resembling a medieval European pattern.

under Yusuf Pasha, advancing from Fashoda, was all but annihilated by the Mahdists. These successes brought the Mahdi increasing numbers of followers, whom he originally styled 'dervishes' (lit. 'poor men', i.e., religious mendicants), later '*ansar*' ('helpers'). When Egypt was occupied by Arabi's revolt, much of the Sudan was in rebellion, with the Egyptian officials in those territories having little chance of receiving support from Egypt. The Mahdists captured El Obeid (the chief town of Kordofan) on 17 January 1883, by which time almost the entire territory south of Khartoum was in a state of insurrection, except the southern Bahr-el-Ghazal and Equatorial Provinces, where temporarily their governors, Frank Lupton (Gessi's successor) and Emin respectively, were able to hold out. (The 'Gazelle river', Bahr-el-Ghazal, gave its name to the province.)

An Egyptian force about 10,000 strong (including 2,000 camp-followers) was assembled at Khartoum under the command of General William Hicks, late a colonel in the Indian Army, with the intention of recapturing El Obeid. Hicks led his somewhat disorganised army into the deserts of Kordofan; he and most of his troops were massacred at Kashgil, near El Obeid, on 3–5 November 1883. In the following month Slatin surrendered to the Mahdists in Darfur (he was imprisoned but survived); Lupton surrendered after the defection of his troops and officials in April 1884 (he died in captivity some four years later). On the Red Sea littoral, Uthmān abū Bakr Diqna (known by the contemporary spelling of 'Osman Digna'), a Suakin slave-dealer, raised the Beja people of that region in support of the Mahdi, and was appointed amir of the eastern Sudan. He invested Sinkat and Tokar, destroying Egyptian reinforcements for the former garrison on 16 October

and 4 November 1883, and on 2 December wiped out another Egyptian force near Tamanieb. In December 1883 Valentine Baker arrived at Suakin to march to the relief of the besieged garrisons; but his troops and gendarmerie were cut to pieces at El Teb on 4 February 1884. It was now obvious that a major effort was required to suppress the Mahdist revolt in the Sudan, and that it could not be accomplished by Egyptian troops; the old army (but for the Sudan garrisons) had been disbanded after Arabi's revolt, and Evelyn Wood's 'new' army was too small, too new and intended only for service in Egypt. The British government was unwilling to be drawn into a war over Egyptian possession of the Sudan, so the British agent to the Egyptian government, Sir Evelyn Baring, recommended that the Sudan be abandoned. Reluctantly, the Egyptian government concurred, but the evacuation of Egyptian garrisons was by no means easy. Charles Gordon, about to enter the service of the King of the Belgians in the Congo, was prevailed upon to return to Khartoum to superintend the evacuation; he arrived there on 18 February 1884. His instructions were not completely clear, for some contemplated the establishment of a stable government upon the withdrawal of Egyptian authority; but to facilitate the evacuation, Gordon issued proclamations announcing the independence of the Sudan, the recognition of the Mahdi as sultan of Kordofan, and revoking earlier attempts to suppress the slave trade.

Despite the unwillingness of the British government to become involved, it was clear that the port of Suakin would have to be held in order to evacuate the Sudan, but following Baker's defeat, and the fall of Sinkat four days later, Suakin itself was in danger from Uthmān Diqna.

Reluctantly the British government authorised the employment of British forces: Admiral Sir William Hewett landed a naval brigade from his fleet on 10 February 1884, which secured Suakin, and Major-General Sir Gerald Graham was sent with a small force from Egypt to Suakin, where it was joined by reinforcements *en route* home from India. On 29 February Graham's force advanced in a 'brigade square' and defeated Uthman Diqna's troops at El Teb, and on the following day evacuated some of the inhabitants of Tokar. A renewed advance from Suakin encountered the Mahdists at Tamai on 13 March 1884, and after a furious combat in which one of the two British squares was broken, the Mahdists were defeated. Graham wished to push forward to Berber, mid-way between Suakin and Khartoum, to ensure the evacuation of the latter; but this proposal was not in accord with the British government's wish to dissociate itself as soon as possible, and the force was withdrawn from Suakin, leaving only a small garrison in the port itself.

This left Gordon in Khartoum, devoid of support and soon invested by the Mahdists. The British government and its representatives in Egypt were extremely dilatory in preparing for relief despite pressure from the British public, to whom Gordon was the epitome of the Christian hero; while Gordon, unable to assist any of the other surviving garrisons, defended Khartoum and its inhabitants with great skill and resolution. Prime Minister Gladstone, who had only with the greatest reluctance sanctioned the operations in Egypt in 1882 and Graham's expedition to the Sudan, was determined to resist further military involvement, until pressure from both within and outside his government became too great to resist; even the Queen requested that some attempt be made to save Gordon. Finally Gladstone sanctioned a relief expedition, but the months of procrastination were to prove fatal.

The expedition was organised under the command of Garnet Wolseley, and it was decided to use the Nile route to Khartoum, as an advance from Suakin on the east coast would have required not only the defeat of the local Mahdist forces but also the construction of a railway and provision of water supplies through the desert. The expeditionary force comprised some 6,000 British troops from Egypt, and at Wolseley's suggestion included a flying column of volunteers from some of the army's élite units, mounted on camels. To negotiate the Nile cataracts, some 800 whalers were constructed and experienced boatmen were recruited from as far afield as Canada. These arrangements and the earlier prevarication, however, meant that the relief force did not set out until some six months after Khartoum had been virtually cut off.

As the relief-force progressed slowly along the Nile, on 17 November 1884 Wolseley received a note from Gordon, written thirteen days earlier, stating that Khartoum could only be expected to hold out with ease for a further forty days. Establishing his forward base at Korti, near the great bend in the Nile, Wolseley was faced with a choice: continue along the Nile, the course of which swung north-east and thus for a time would take the British away from Khartoum, until the river again turned south; or make a dash overland, eliminating the bend in the river, and re-joining the Nile at Metemmeh, north of Khartoum. Believing Gordon's opinion that the appearance of even a few British soldiers would so dishearten the Mahdists that the siege would be lifted, Wolseley decided to adopt both options: a 'Desert Column' principally of the Camel Corps, commanded by Major-General Herbert Stewart, would make the dash to Metemmeh (176 miles) from where a picked element would push on the final 96 miles to Khartoum; while a 'River Column' under Major-General W. Earle was to continue along the Nile, take Berber and join the Desert Column at Metemmeh.

Stewart's Desert Column, about 1,400 strong, advanced towards Metemmeh, and on 17 January 1885 was attacked furiously by some 10,000 Mahdists at Abu Klea; they briefly broke into the square but were beaten off with about 1,100 casualties; Stewart lost 74 killed and 94 wounded. On 19 January, when the column was attempting to fight its way to Metemmeh, Stewart was wounded (he died a month later) and Sir Charles Wilson assumed command. On 21 January four of Gordon's river gunboats appeared on the Nile, in accordance with the plan formulated by Wolseley, to transport the first relief-force to Khartoum; but Wilson prevaricated and not until 24 January did the first two steamers set off, reaching Khartoum on the morning of 28 January. They were, in the memorable phrase, 'two days too late': after 317 days of siege the Mahdi had ordered an assault which captured the city on 26 January amid an orgy of slaughter. Gordon was killed, apparently at his palace (though accounts of the exact circumstances of his death are at variance), despite the Mahdi's order that he must be spared. Wilson's steamers were wrecked about half a mile from Khartoum, and only with difficulty was his party evacuated by Lord Charles Beresford and a crew of naval personnel aboard another of Gordon's gunboats, *Safieh*.

In Britain the news of Gordon's death was greeted with horror; Gladstone's sobriquet 'GOM' ('Grand Old Man') was reversed to 'MOG' ('Murderer of Gordon'), and under great public pressure it was decided that Wolseley should continue to fight in the Sudan even though the purpose of the campaign was ended (i.e., relief of Gordon), and that a second expedition should be sent against Uthmān Diqna at Suakin. Wolseley therefore ordered Earle's River Column to continue its advance towards Berber; on 10 February they dispersed a Mahdist force at Kirkeban, but among the few British casualties was Earle, killed while leading an advance. Command devolved upon the more able Colonel Henry Brackenbury, who continued the advance; but the column was recalled by Wolseley, who had learned of the exhaustion of the Desert Column and realised the inability of the force to continue the campaign. By the end of March 1885 the whole force was on its way back to Egypt.

The expedition to Suakin was intended to construct a railway from there to Berber, to unite there with the Nile Army. Command was again given to Lieutenant-General Sir Gerald Graham, whose 13,000-strong force included a brigade from India and a battalion from New South Wales, contributed as a gesture of support following Gordon's death. Shortly after assembling at Suakin, Graham moved to engage the principal concentrations of Mahdists, defeating one at Hashin on 20 March 1885. A detachment under Major-General McNeill was surprised at Tofrek on 22 March, and a most furious combat ensued until the Mahdists were driven off. The campaign continued until mid-May against desultory resistance, when the entire operation was called off, Gladstone having used the 'Pend-jeh Incident' in Afghanistan as an excuse for abandoning the Sudanese venture, under the pretence that India was threatened. Many (including Wolseley) thought Gladstone guilty of deception and incompetence, but by the time Gladstone's ministry had been replaced by Salisbury's Conservative government in June 1885, the process of evacuation had gone too far to be reversed.

The Sudanese campaign ended the active career of Lord Wolseley, for although he continued to hold high office (commander-in-chief 1895–1900) his health declined and arguably he never recovered from the failure to relieve Khartoum, although the blame for that failure lay elsewhere. The end of his protagonist, however, was more definite: the Mahdi died of smallpox on 22 June, and was succeeded by Abdullah el-Taaishi, who was known as *the* Khalifa. (The Mahdi had also nominated Ali wad Helu and Mohammed esh Sherif (or 'al-Sharif') as khalifas (apostles or lieutenants), but they were deprived of their influence as Abdullah asserted his power, gradually excluding all chiefs not of Baggara origin, save Uthmān Diqna, from positions of influence). For the next thirteen years Abdullah ruled the Sudan with cruel despotism, but his attempt to extend Mahdist power into Egypt was repelled. The Khalifa's forces followed the retiring British Nile Army and skirmished with the troops holding the Egyptian frontier, but the Mahdist army was routed by General Stephenson's Anglo-Egyptian force at Ginniss on 30 December 1885, which effectively ended the First Sudan War. The entire British effort had been a failure, brought about by political vacillation and a complete misconception of the situation; and as it transpired, probably the wrong choice of route for the relief of Gordon. The only redeeming feature was the fact that despite having to face the equally intimidating forces of the Mahdi and the climate and terrain, the troops had done more than could have been expected.

The Sudan, 1885–1900

By the end of 1885 the entire Sudan was under Mahdist control, less Suakin (held by an Egyptian garrison) and a small amount of territory still held by Emin in Equatoria (to the relief of whom H. M. Stanley led an expedition in 1887, accomplishing it in 1889). The Khalifa's oppressive rule was marked by internal insurrections and external conflicts, notably against Abyssinia in 1885–9, culminating in full-scale war in the latter year during which the Abyssinian King John was killed. From April 1886 the Egyptian–Sudanese frontier was established at Wadi Halfa, all territory to the south being under the Khalifa's control, minor raids and skirmishes being contained by the new, British-trained Egyptian army, British Army support for the frontier being unnecessary from 1888. Sporadic fighting occurred around Suakin, between the garrison and Uthmān Diqna; collaborating with tribes dissatisfied with the Khalifa's rule, Colonel Herbert Kitchener, governor of Suakin, stormed Uthmān Diqna's base at Handub in January 1888 but was severely wounded in the process, and later in the year the situation had become so grave that Sir Francis Grenfell, *sirdar* of the Egyptian army, had to take command at Suakin in person. He defeated Uthmān Diqna at Gemaiza on 20 December 1888, but another blow against dervish power around Suakin had to be struck in 1891, when Colonel Charles Holled Smith defeated Uthmān Diqna at Arafit (19 February). With the conclusion of hostilities against Abyssinia, the Khalifa sent an army under his emir Wad-el-Nejumi to invade Egypt; on 3 August 1889 he was killed and his army was routed at Toski by Grenfell and an entirely Egyptian contingent (four Sudanese-Egyptian and two Egyptian battalions) before the supporting British brigade came up, conclusive proof of the quality of the Egyptian army under British discipline and command.

The return of Salisbury's Conservative government resulted in a ministry prepared to countenance the re-conquest of the Sudan, and in March 1896 Baring (now Lord Cromer, still British agent and consul-general in Egypt) was ordered to send the Egyptian army under its *sirdar*, Kitchener, to begin the recapture of Dongola province. This policy was influenced by accounts of disaffection with the Khalifa's regime which appeared in such writings as those of Slatin Pasha (who finally escaped from captivity in 1895), and by a wish to assist Italy, whose defeat by the Abyssinians at Adowa (1 March 1896) while attempting to expand their holdings in Eritrea was a potential cause of a perception of general European weakness throughout the region. (Italian forces in Eritrea had repelled a dervish attack in December 1893, and with British agreement had occupied Kassala, an advanced outpost on the Sudanese border, held by them on behalf of the Egyptians.)

Kitchener concentrated a force of five Egyptian and five Sudanese battalions, with hardly any British support save an engineer company and the machine-gun sections of the 1/North Staffords and Connaught Rangers, and on 7 June 1896 dispersed a dervish force at Firket. Aided by boats on the Nile, he advanced with a reinforced army (including more of the 1/North Staffords and additional Egyptian infantry) and fought a skirmish at Hafir (19 September), the last organised resistance before Dongola was occupied on 23 September. The province was thus recovered, and the principal sheikhs submitted to the *sirdar*. (During these operations, an Indian brigade had garrisoned Suakin to release Egyptian units for service on the Nile.) In the following year Kitchener planned a rail link across the desert between Wadi Halfa and Abu Hamed to eliminate the necessity of relying upon the looping course of the Nile. Construction by the Railway Battalion of the Egyptian army, supervised by Royal Engineers, began on 1 January 1897, the route being cleared by an Egyptian flying column under Major-General A. Hunter, who captured Abu Hamed on 7 August 1897 and occupied Berber on 5 September. In response to the threat from the Khalifa's army, Kitchener was given authority to call upon British troops, and was confirmed in overall command not only of the Egyptian army, but also of British forces in the area of operations. The first British units joined his army in January 1898.

The emir Mahmoud received the Kahlifa's permission to attack the Anglo-Egyptian advance around Berber, and to co-operate with Uthmān Diqna, whom the Khalifa had called west into the Nile region. However, on 8 April 1898 Kitchener attacked Mahmoud's entrenched camp on the Atbara River, south-east of Berber; within two hours the dervishes' *zareba* had been breached and the defenders routed, Mahmoud captured and Uthmān Diqna fled; Kitchener's casualties numbered 80 dead and 472 wounded. After reinforcement, Kitchener's almost 26,000 Anglo–Egyptian troops began their advance along the Nile towards the Khalifa's base at Omdurman (24 August).

On 1 September they came within artillery-range of Omdurman, bombarding the Khalifa's forts with field artillery and river gunboats, and the dervish army assembled on the plain before the town.

Kitchener took up a defensive position, backed by the Nile, to await the Khalifa's attack, which came on in the early morning of 2 September. It was repulsed with great slaughter; Kitchener then marched out from his *zareba* and was twice attacked, in which Hector MacDonald's Sudanese brigade and the 21st Lancers (who executed one of the last major cavalry charges in history) were greatly distinguished. Despite attacking with suicidal bravery, most of the dervishes were shot down before they came within their own weapons' range; yet despite the great disparity in the technical capabilities of the weaponry of the two armies, so determined were the dervish charges that had they been able to co-ordinate their attacks, and had not MacDonald held firm, the result could have been considerably different. As it was, some 10,000 dervishes were killed and an unknown multitude wounded; Kitchener's losses were 48 dead and 434 wounded, of whom 71 casualties had fallen among the 21st Lancers, whose 'ambush' by Uthmān Diqna had led to hand-to-hand combat. (Although styled the Battle of Omdurman, the site was not at the town; a more appropriate name might be Kerreri, the action taking place just south of the Kerreri hills, or El Egeiga, the village on the Nile around which the British defensive positions were established.)

The Khalifa having fled, the victorious army entered Omdurman on the afternoon of the battle. On 4 September a parade and service was held at the ruins of Gordon's palace at Khartoum, and the British and Egyptian flags were

First Battalion, Grenadier Guards receiving ammunition prior to the Battle of Omdurman. The men wear full field equipment minus the valise (carried with regimental baggage), with a blanket roll at the small of the back. The khaki uniform includes a helmet-cover with neck-flap and the distinctive regimental flash, a red cockade with red upper section, edged blue. Note the fabric cover around the rifles' breech-mechanism, to keep out sand and dust.

ceremonially re-raised to confirm that Gordon had been avenged. On 6 September Kitchener completed his act of vengeance by ordering that the Mahdi's tomb at Omdurman be blown up (by Gordon's nephew), and only public protest (including concern from the Queen) prevented Kitchener from sending home the Mahdi's skull as a trophy.

On 10 September 1898 Kitchener was called south, to deal with a small French expedition under Captain Jean Marchand which had arrived at Fashoda in southern Sudan, apparently with the aim of gaining a French foothold on the Nile. Reaching Fashoda on 10 July, the French had been attacked by dervishes on 25 August, and were probably saved by Kitchener's arrival on 15 September; but for a period the 'Fashoda Incident' could have had serious repercussions for Anglo–French relations, until the French withdrew in December. In the following March an agreement was reached which defined British and French interests in the Nile basin.

Operations continued to subdue remaining dervish resistance in the Sudan. From 7 September a small force under Colonel Parsons marched to occupy Gedaref, south-east of Khartoum, defeating the local leader Ahmed Fedil. Parsons occupied the town on 22 September and beat off two attacks on the 28th; Ahmed Fedil withdrew and was defeated by another column at Dakheila on 26 December, from where he escaped to join the Khalifa in Kordofan. Not until order had been restored elsewhere was an attempt made to crush the last resistance of the Khalifa, and not until 22 November 1899 was Ahmed Fedil again engaged and defeated, by a flying column under Colonel Wingate, at Abu Aadel. On 25 November the Khalifa's forces attacked Wingate near Om Debreikat (or 'Umm Diwaykarat'); they were repulsed and the counter-attack overran the dervish camp where the Khalifa, Ahmed Fedil and other leaders were killed. The Khalifa's eldest son and intended successor, Sheik-ed-din, surrendered; dervish losses in these final two actions were about 1,000, the Egyptians suffering four dead and twenty

Battle of Omdurman: 2nd Battalion, Rifle Brigade sit in reserve: the British firing-line is visible in the middle distance. The identity of this battalion is evident from the black leather equipment worn by rifle corps, as opposed to the buff-leather of line regiments. This is a rare example of a photograph taken during an engagement.

wounded. The last embers of Mahdism were extinguished with the apprehension of Uthmān Diqna in January 1900.

Britain having shared the cost of the reconquest of the Sudan, it was agreed that Britain and Egypt should share sovereignty, confirmed formally on 19 January 1899. Supreme authority was vested in a governor-general, to which post Kitchener was appointed; upon his departure for the South African War he was succeeded both in this post and as *sirdar* of the Egyptian army by Sir Francis Wingate, who had served in that army from 1883. The Sudan was placed under Anglo–Egyptian civil administration, although most of the officials were initially British Army officers, resulting in a more benevolent rule than that of the Khalifa. (Only Darfur was not ruled directly; it had revolted against the Khalifa and its sultan, Ali Dinar, was confirmed as ruler by the Sudan government on condition of his recognition of their ultimate authority by way of an annual tribute.) The immediate post-Khalifan period was not entirely peaceful; there was some unrest, and as a footnote to the Mahdist movement, it is interesting to note that a new Mahdi appeared in Kordofan in 1903, one Mohammed-el-Amin, a Tunisian. He was captured and executed in public at El Obeid; and an ex-dervish, Abd-el-Kader, who claimed to be Jesus and aroused a rebellion in the Blue Nile province in 1908, was hanged for the murder of a British official.

Military Forces
Britain. The Camel Corps formed for the Gordon relief expedition was so unusual that its composition should be detailed. It was almost a Commando-style force of selected

personnel sent from Britain or assembled from units serving in Egypt. The Guards Camel Regiment of four companies comprised detachments from the 1/, 2/ and 3/Grenadier, 1/ and 2/Coldstream, and 1/ and 2/Scots Guards, and Royal Marine Light Infantry. The second (or Heavy) Camel Corps of five companies was drawn from the 1st and 2nd Life Guards, Royal Horse Guards, 2nd, 4th and 5th Dragoon Guards, 1st and 2nd Dragoons and 5th and 16th Lancers; both these units came from England. The third regiment, the Mounted Infantry Camel Corps, was drawn from mounted infantry companies of line regiments, four companies strong: 'A' from the 1/South Staffordshire, 1/Black Watch, 1/Gordon Highlanders and 3/KRRC; 'B' from the 1/Royal West Kent, 1/Royal Sussex, 2/Essex and 2/DCLI; 'C' from 3/KRRC and 2/Rifle Brigade; and 'D' from 1/Somerset Light Infantry, 2/Royal West Kent, 1/Royal Scots and 2/Connaught Rangers; 'D' company came from England, the others from units in Egypt. Another regiment, the Light Camel Corps, was employed mainly on line-of-communication duties; it was drawn from the 3rd, 4th, 7th, 10th, 11th, 15th, 18th, 20th and 21st Hussars. The force also included detachments of the Royal Artillery with three 7pdr mountain guns, the Royal Navy with a Gardner machine-gun mounted on a 7pdr field-gun carriage, the Royal Engineers and appropriate commissariat and medical personnel; together with an unregimented detachment of 250 men of the 1/Royal Sussex, and the only horse-mounted unit, a detachment of 19th Hussars, it represented one of the most mixed and most mobile formations ever deployed by the British Army.

Sudanese. The popular conception of the Mahdist warrior is that of the 'Fuzzy-Wuzzy', a name applied indiscriminately by the British troops and popularised by Kipling's poem of the same name. While it might be a recognisable description of the Beja warriors of the eastern Sudan, it was certainly not applicable to the dervish forces in general. (The Mahdi forbade his original term 'dervish' in preference to '*ansar*', but after 1885 at least 'dervish' became the commonest British term to describe the Khalifa's followers.)

The people of the Sudan were of mixed origin (indeed, it was estimated that the land contained some 56 main tribes, a number increasing to about 600 when sub-clans were counted); the inhabitants of the northern regions were classed as Arabs (Mahdists in general were sometimes described in British sources as 'the Arabs'), but in the southern regions like the Bahr-el-Ghazal province the inhabitants were usually described as 'blacks' of various races, originating from the peoples upon whom the slavers preyed. Among the principal peoples were the Beja of the eastern Sudan, comprising the sub-clans of Hadendowa (or Hadendoa), Bisharin, Ababda, Beni-Amer, Amarar, Shukuria, Hallenga and Hamran, of which the first were the most important (the name deriving from Beja *Hada*, chief, and *endowa*, people). They were so significant (and

so formidable a part of the Mahdist forces) that the name 'Hadendowa' came to be applied more widely to describe any Mahdists in this region; the most notable member of the Hadendowa people was Uthmān Diqna. The most characteristic feature of the Beja was their hair-dressing, plastered with mutton-fat or butter and pulled upwards into a mop-like construction with separate tufts at the rear and sides, hence the term 'Fuzzy-Wuzzy'; but although the Ababda were part of the Beja, they adopted the dress and habits of the 'Arabs', and although the southern and south-eastern parts retained the Beja dialect, the remainder generally spoke Arabic.

The Baggara (or 'Baqqara') people occupied the desert country north of Kordofan; their name, meaning 'cowherds', came from their raising of cattle, and they were described as a characteristically nomadic Arab people, although darker in complexion and with a mop-style hair-dressing which like that of the Beja led to the term 'Fuzzy-Wuzzy'. They were renowned as warriors of great courage, and from them the Mahdi drew some of his most loyal followers, including the Khalifa Abdullah el-Taaishi. The Kabbabish constituted perhaps the most numerous 'Arab' people in the Sudan, their clans extending from Dongola to Darfur; their name may be derived from 'goatherds' or 'sheep-herders', which with cattle and camels formed one of their principal means of livelihood. It was believed that the ruling families preserved purer Arab blood than the remainder, but the language of all was Arabic, albeit with a distinctive pronunciation. Between the Atbara and the Blue Nile were the tribes of the Hassania, Jā'alin and Shukria, of Semitic origin. The Jā'alin had been one of the most powerful peoples of the Nile valley, and were among the chief opponents of Mehemet Ali's occupation; they were among the first in the north to join the Mahdi. They claimed to trace their descent from Abbas, uncle of the prophet. The name of the principal Shukria clan was Abu Sin, and the town of Gedaref was formerly styled 'Suk Abu Sin', marking the location of their area. The southern peoples included the most numerous of the Negro tribes, the Shilluk, whose lands west of the Nile stretched westwards to those of the Baggara, and once as far north as Khartoum; the Dinka, to the east of the Nile and in Bahr-el-Ghazal; and the Nuer, in the Bahr-el-Ghazal and south of Fashoda. Some of these, notably the Shilluk and Nuer, were in almost constant conflict with the Khalifa's authority. In addition to the indigenous inhabitants and the descendants of those unfortunates who had been taken as slaves from regions to the south, Egyptians were enrolled, voluntarily or otherwise, into the Mahdist forces; even prisoners of war, in the same way that ex-Mahdists were enrolled in the Sudanese units of the Egyptian army.

The Mahdi's earliest military organisation was based upon three divisions, each commanded by one of the Khalifas and named after the colour of its flag. The Black

Far left: The Queen's Sudan Medal: issued for service between 1896 and 1898, without clasps for individual actions. Designed by G. W. de Saulles, the obverse bore a portrait of Queen Victoria, the reverse Victory upon a tablet inscribed 'Sudan'. The ribbon was black and yellow, with a red central line.

Left: The Khedive's Sudan Medal, issued to British and Egyptian troops for actions between 1896 and 1908; with fifteen clasps lettered in English and Arabic. The obverse bore an Arabic inscription 'Abbas Hilmi the Second' and the date '1314 AH' (1897 AD); the reverse depicted a trophy of arms and the Arabic inscription 'The Reconquest of the Sudan 1314'. The ribbon was yellow with a light blue stripe, symbolising the Nile flowing through the Sudanese desert.

Flag, which became the most important from its being led by the Khalifa Abdullah, was drawn primarily from the western Sudan, including the Baggara. The Green Flag of Khalifa Ali wad Hilu was drawn from the area between the Blue and White Neles, and the Red Flag of Khalifa Mohammed esh Sherif from the northern Sudan. These were not permanent organisations in the European sense of 'divisions', as it was usual for groups to follow their own leader or emir and to attach themselves to a 'Flag' when an army gathered. There was no standard organisation of sub-units, although Flags were divided into what might equate to European battalions, styled *rubs*, each *rub* generally between 800 and 1,200 men, though numbers fluctuated. A *rub* (meaning 'quarter') was divided into four parts, one administrative and one of riflemen, one of sword- and spear-men and one of cavalry (usually Baggara). Forces were mobilised only in time of war, but from 1883 an attempt was made to create a standing army, stationed in barracks in the principal towns, principally from Africans from the south, who had formed some of the slave-raiders' private 'armies'. These were all armed with rifles and were styled *jihadiyya*, organised into 'standards' or companies about 100 strong, under an officer named a *ra's mi'a* ('leader of a hundred'), and into platoons or *muqaddamiyya* (or '*muggadamiya'*) under a platoon-leader or *muqaddam* (or '*muggadam'*). They were distributed among the other forces, sometimes forming the rifle-armed element of a *rub*.

From 1892 the *Mulazimiyya* (or '*Mulazamin'*) were formed, originally as the Khalifa's personal bodyguard, largely from *jihadiyya*, but they grew to a 'standing army' about 10–12,000 strong and eventually superseded the *jihadiyya* as the army's principal rifle-armed element; by 1898 they consisted of eighteen *rubs* of eight to ten 'standards' each. (Thereafter the Khalifa used members of his own clan, the Taaisha, as a bodyguard.) The *Mulazimiyya* and the Omdurman garrison (known as the 'Kara Army' and also originating with the *jihadiyya*) received regular pay and were mostly armed with rifles.

At first, Dervish costume was civilian dress, often a simple white cotton robe fastened around the waist and flung over one shoulder, often worn with a simple skull-cap, the wearer's head being shaven; or for the Beja loincloth or loose trousers, a cloak or scarf over the shoulders or around the waist, and the distinctive hair-style. Some of the higher-ranking personnel wore ring-mail and Turkish-style helmets, though such items may have been restricted largely to ceremonial occasions. Early in the existence of the Mahdist army, however, the Mahdi prescribed a 'uniform' for his followers, based on the *jibbeh* (tunic) worn by the Sudanese poor: a white *jibbeh* with coloured patches (representing the poverty which was regarded as virtuous), a turban with 'tail' hanging at the left side, skull-cap, trousers, plaited straw girdle, sandals and beads. Use of the *jibbeh* spread to all parts of the army, but although under the Khalifa garments were produced in 'army' clothing factories, there does not seem to have been any systematic attempt to produce 'uniforms' particular to any one unit, although the *Mulazimiyya* appear to have worn *jibbeh*s with red and blue patches and a red turban with the end pulled under the chin. Although *jibbeh*s were essentially simple garments representing poverty, many surviving examples are very finely made with most ornate patches; these may have belonged to emirs or 'officers', although some of the most senior appear to have worn plain garments deliberately, to demonstrate piety. The classic *jibbeh* with large, bold, oblong patches became common after about 1885; earlier examples often had smaller coloured decoration. Use of the *jibbeh* and similar *ansar* clothing spread to the Beja, many of whom adopted the shaven head and skullcap in place of their traditional hairstyle.

Although the dervishes relied largely on the shock action of the charge, many carried rifles, of which large numbers were acquired after each victory and by the capture of Egyptian stores. The most common were probably Remington rolling-block rifles, supplemented by 1896–8 by Martini-Henry, Italian and Belgian rifles. Some old percussion weapons were also used, including large-bore, muzzle-loading elephant guns with tripod rests, carried by a small company of the *Mulazimiyya*, the *Khashkhashan*. The weapons more commonly associated with the dervishes, however, were leaf-bladed spears, thrusting weapons and lighter javelins for throwing; and double-edged, straight-bladed swords (*kaskara*s) with quillons at right-angles to the grip reminiscent of the style used in early medieval Europe, hence the alternative term 'Crusader' pattern (indeed, some use was made of European blades). Oval shields were used by some of the peoples from the Nile area, but shields were mostly restricted to the Beja, a quite small, round or ovoid leather pattern akin to a late-medieval European buckler, with a pronounced central boss. Artillery was used mostly in a defensive role, in forts or emplacements; some modern ordnance had been captured from the Egyptians (including Krupp guns, brass mountain howitzers and even Nordenfelt machine-guns), but efficiency was reduced greatly by deficiencies in the manufacture of ammunition; the gunners were former members of the Egyptian army. A few field pieces were used at Omdurman, but positioned at too great a range to reach their intended targets, and some light guns were mounted in the three Nile gunboats captured by the dervishes, including one (*Bordein*) that had transported Wilson in his abortive attempt to reach Khartoum, been wrecked but raised and repaired by the Sudanese.

Dervish tactics were unsophisticated, but, under ideal circumstances, effective. Covered by small-arms fire, the striking-force of spear- and sword-men would approach the enemy, if possible, hidden by scrub (as at Tofrek) and rush upon them with an element of surprise, oblivious of incoming musketry until they engaged hand-to-hand. Such attacks would be conducted in silence (as reported at Abu Klea), or with the accompaniment of drumming and chanting of prayers, reaching a crescendo as the charge went in. Witnesses reported that dervish forces appeared to be well-drilled and manoeuvred with organisation, and even under fire usually advanced not at full speed but at a steady, measured jog-trot. Religious faith gave not only suicidal bravery in the charge, but the ability to remain motionless under fire, and tactics of surprise and concealment, using natural cover, led to incidents like the 'ambush' of the 21st Lancers at Omdurman, the dervishes springing up where not expected. Such was their courage that against cavalry they would dart under the level of sword-cuts and evade lance-thrusts, spearing or slashing the riders and hamstringing the horses; even the wounded, if capable of movement, would continue to hack at enemy troops within range, leading to a practice of dispatching dervish wounded as a matter of self-preservation. Not even such courage could overcome machine-gun and artillery-fire, yet even so, but for the determination and discipline of the British troops, which enabled them to resist effectively even after a square was broken, the sheer bravery of the *ansar* might well have achieved more successes than it did. Whether or not Kipling's work in general was an accurate reflection on the attitudes of the British soldier, there was much truth in his admiring lines on the Sudanese warrior: '... man for man the Fuzzy knocked us 'oller.'[2]

Notes
1. Pimblett, W. M. *Story of the Soudan War*, London 1885, p. ix.
2. 'Fuzzy-Wuzzy', from *Barrack-Room Ballads*, 1892.

References
(A number of references to the campaigning in Egypt are also concerned with the Sudan)
Alford, H. S. L., and Sword, W. Dennistoun. *The Egyptian Soudan: its Loss and Recovery*, London, 1898.
Barthorp, M. *War on the Nile: Britain, Egypt and the Sudan 1882–1898*, Poole, 1984.
Bates, D. *The Fashoda Incident 1898: Encounter on the Nile*, Oxford, 1984.
Bennett, E. N. *The Downfall of the Dervishes: being a Sketch of the Final Sudan Campaign of 1898*, London, 1898.
Bond, B. (ed.) *Victorian Military Campaigns*, London, 1967

(includes 'The Reconquest of the Sudan', C. Falls).
Brackenbury, Major-General H. *The River Column: A Narrative of the Advance of the River Column of the Nile Expeditionary Force*, London, 1885.
Brook-Shepherd, G. *Between Two Flags: the Life of Baron Sir Rudolph von Slatin Pasha*, New York, 1973.
Burleigh, B. *Desert Warfare: being the Chronicle of the Eastern Soudan Campaign*, London, 1884.
– *Khartum Campaign 1898, or the Re-Conquest of the Soudan*, London, 1899.
– *Sirdar and Khalifa: the Re-Conquest of the Sudan*, London, 1898.
Butler, Sir William. *The Campaign of the Cataracts ... the Great Nile Expedition of 1884–85*, London, 1887 (illustrated by Lady Butler).
Churchill, W. L. S. (later Sir Winston). *The River War: An*

Account of the Reconquest of the Sudan, London, 1899.

Colville, Colonel H. E. *History of the Soudan Campaign*, London, 1889.

Compton, P. *The Last Days of General Gordon*, London, 1974.

De Cosson, Major E. A. *Days and Nights of Service with Sir Gerald Graham's Field Force at Suakin*, London, 1886; the 1990 London reprint is entitled *Fighting the Fuzzy-Wuzzy*.

Featherstone, D. *Victoria's Enemies. An A–Z of British Colonial Warfare*, London, 1989.

Galloway, W. *The Battle of Tofrek fought near Suakin*, London, 1887.

Gleichen, Count. *With the Camel Corps up the Nile*, London, 1889.

Gordon, C. G. *General Gordon's Khartoum Journal*, ed. Lord Elton, London, 1961.

– *The Journals of Major-General C. G. Gordon, CB at Kartoum*, intr. A. E. Hake, London, 1885.

Jackson, H. C. *Osman Digna*, London, 1926.

Knight, E. *Letters from the Sudan*, London, 1896 (reports to *The Times*).

Knight, I. *Queen Victoria's Enemies (2): Northern Africa*, London, 1989.

– 'The Mahdist Patched Jibbeh', in *Military Illustrated Past and Present*, no.18 (1989) (important study on the most characteristic item of Mahdist equipment).

Parry, Captain E. G. *Suakin 1885*, London, 1885.

Pimblett, W. M. *The Story of the Soudan War*, London, 1885.

Power, F. *Letters from Khartoum, written during the siege*, intr. A. Power, London, 1885 (Frank Power, correspondent for *The Times*, was killed attempting to escape from Khartoum).

Robson, B. *Fuzzy Wuzzy: The Campaigns in the Eastern Sudan*, Tunbridge Wells, 1993.

Royle, C. *The Egyptian Campaigns 1882–1885, and the Events which led to them*, London, 1886 (rev. edn. London, 1900).

Slatin, R. *Fire and Sword in the Sudan: a Personal Narrative of Fighting and Serving the Dervishes 1879–1895*, trans. Major F. R. Wingate, London, 1896.

Steevens, G. W. *With Kitchener to Khartum*, Edinburgh, 1898.

Symons, J. *England's Pride: the Story of the Gordon Relief Expedition*, London, 1965.

Warner, P. *Dervish: the Rise and Fall of an African Empire*, London, 1973.

Wingate, Major F. R. *Mahdism and the Egyptian Sudan*, London, 1891.

Wolseley, Lord. *In Relief of Gordon: Lord Wolseley's Campaign Journal of the Khartoum Relief Expedition 1884–1885*, ed. A. Preston, London, 1967.

Ziegler, P. *Omdurman*, London, 1973.

WEST AFRICA

British colonies in West Africa included the Gambia, Gold Coast, Northern and Southern Nigeria, Sierra Leone, and the earlier colony of Goree; these territories are covered alphabetically, not in chronological order of military operations.

A factor common to all, which caused more loss to the garrisons than any combat, was the general unhealthiness of the area. A typical comment was that made about Sierra Leone, 'the bug-a-boo of Englishmen, the least sought after and least known of our colonies, the terror of insurance offices, the *dernier resort* to get rid of and provide for the *mauvais sujets* of large families, and the last station for which soldiers volunteer ... charitably and cheeringly designated the White Man's Grave ... fevers, plagues, a country studded with graves, the bones of Europeans whitening the surface of the land, a spot where hope itself withers, and from whence there is no return...'[1] Statistics confirm the truth of these remarks: in Sierra Leone, for example, between the years 1819 and 1836 inclusive, almost half the entire garrison died every year (in 1825, 447 out of 571). In the Gambia in 1825, of 199 men, 150 died between May and December, and almost all the rest were afflicted by chronic complaints; of a reinforcing draft of about 200 men, 98 were dead within three months.[2] So appalling was the toll from disease that it became the practice to deploy only European penal corps for whom this service was a punishment, or West Indian troops who were very much more resilient to the climate and sickness (for example, during the period quoted above, the detachment of the 2nd West India Regiment in the Gambia (40–50 strong) lost only one man, and had hardly any sick).

The Gambia

The most northerly of the British West African possessions, the Gambia's first British settlement was established in the 17th century, in pursuit of trade along the Gambia River: the 'Company of Adventurers of London trading into Africa', chartered 1618, built a fort near the mouth of the river, superseded in 1664 by Fort James on an island twenty miles from the river mouth, to protect trading interests against the Dutch. British holdings increased, and the territory was annexed to Sierra Leone in 1822, becoming an independent colony in 1843; in 1866 it became part of the 'West African Settlements' but became a separate crown colony from 1888. Military action in the territory was limited. In 1891 a slave-raider chief, Fodi Kabba, attacked members of the commission engaged in defining the boundary between British and French territory; an expedition was organised (December 1891–February 1892) involving members of the 2nd West India Regiment, Royal Navy and Gambia Police, and he was driven from British territory. In June 1900 he again caused trouble (though resident at Medina in French territory), when two officials were murdered at Suankandi; an expedition under Colonel H. E. Brake captured Suankandi, and with French collaboration Medina was taken and Fodi Kabba killed (23 March 1901). In 1894 another slaver, Fodi Silah, raided British territory; a naval brigade under Captain E. H. Gamble of the frigate HMS *Raleigh* was sent inland but was ambushed with a loss of fifteen dead and 47 wounded. The operation also involved the bombardment of Gunjur by a naval squadron; Fodi Silah fled to French territory in Senegal, where he surrendered and died. Although the slave trade had been banned in British territories in 1807, measures to eradicate the business were not decreed in the Gambia until 1906.

Gold Coast

British trading settlements on the Guinea coast were established from the early 17th century, administered ultimately by the African Company of Merchants, who used their bases for the export of slaves; this company's commercial success was crippled by the abolition of the slave trade in 1807 and it was dissolved in 1821, when the crown took over its holdings.

The dominant nation of the interior were the Asante (pronounced 'Ashanti', which was the common contemporary English spelling), a confederation of tribes organised into a powerful nation in the early 18th century by Osei Tutu, who established a capital at Kumasi. Each of the component tribes had its king, but the king of Kumasi was recognised as the paramount ruler (*Asantehene*), whose authority was represented by the 'Golden Stool', their most sacred treasure, which represented the spirit of the Ashanti people, upon which the chiefs swore fealty and which had supposedly descended from heaven upon Osei Tutu's knees. The Ashanti were governed by a monarchy and military aristocracy, the heads of the six clans into which the tribes were organised forming a national council; as a people they were noted as skilful craftsmen but with a penchant for human sacrifice. They were supposedly of the same origin as the Fanti people who occupied the coastal regions, tradition holding that they became separate during a famine, when the southern people subsisted on herbs (*fan*) and those in the north upon Indian corn (*san*). Inhabiting dense rain forest, they developed into a powerful, military society.

Although willing to trade with Europeans, especially Dutch and British, the Ashanti resented the influence of the Fanti. Pursuing a rival chief, in 1806 the Ashanti invaded and conquered Fanti territory; the British governor of the Cape Coast, Colonel G. Torrane, being unable to resist the Ashanti military force, surrendered the unfortunate individual (who had sought sanctuary with the British), and recognised the Ashanti conquest. Threats against other tribes continued, and following the crown's assumption of

power in 1821, the first British governor, Sir Charles McCarthy, organised a Fanti army to resist. His force, about 500 strong, was annihilated by the Ashanti on 21 January 1824 near the village of Bonsaso on the border of Ashanti territory. It was said that this inevitable defeat was hastened by Sir Charles's ordnance storekeeper bringing up kegs of vermicelli instead of ammunition; but whatever the case, McCarthy killed himself rather than be taken prisoner, and his skull was used for years in Ashanti ceremonies.

The governor of the Cape Coast, Hope Smith, organised the traditional enemies of the Ashanti and on 7 August 1826, at Dodowa, near Accra, in open ground which did not suit the Ashanti and with the help of Congreve rockets, he inflicted a huge defeat upon them. (This conflict of 1823–6 is sometimes styled the First Ashanti War.) Thereafter, Anglo–Ashanti relations improved, with the help of a peace-loving *Asantehene*, Kwaka Dua I, who ruled 1838–67. The Ashanti were victorious in two engagements in 1863, but the British government refused to become entangled in a war in the interior. From the time of Dodowa control of the colony passed to a committee of London merchants, but encouraged by the anti-slavery movement, the government re-assumed control in 1842. For a period the Gold Coast formed part of the West African Settlements, and as such was virtually a dependency of Sierra Leone, but in 1874 a separate crown colony of the Gold Coast and Lagos was established, the latter being separated from the Gold Coast in 1886.

Ashanti War, 1873–4

Following civil war after the death of Kwaka Dua, a more bellicose *Asantehene* came to power, Kofi Karikari. Under his less moderate rule, Ashanti grievances came to the fore (notably loss of revenue since the suppression of the slave trade, which had led to an increase in ritual sacrifice, captives no longer having the same financial value), but the

42nd Highlanders in the Ashanti War, 1873–4. This expedition was the first for which a uniform was specifically designed, of loose, Elcho-grey tweed with a belt of the same, and a light, cork and canvas helmet. The 42nd retained a little of their regimental tradition by wearing a small scarlet hackle in the helmet. (Engraving by T. Rose)

The repulse of an Ashanti attack upon Abracrampa, 5-6 November 1873; the position was held by local forces under Major Russell, and a small naval contingent under Lieutenant Wells, RN, reinforced by some 50 men of the West India Regiment. They held out until relieved by Wolseley. Among the locally raised forces deployed at this period were the Cape Coast Volunteers, 'educated men of colour' who were notably smart in appearance, wearing green with red facings. (Engraving by S. Wain)

trigger for the 1873–4 war was the Dutch decision to abandon their trading-posts in the Gold Coast. Holland ceded their port of Elmina to Britain (April 1872), but unlike the Dutch, Britain refused to pay an annual tribute to the Ashanti for its use; so Kofi Karikari marched south against tribes allied to Britain. Token support for the coastal people proving insufficient, following the initial landing of 100 marines (9 June 1873), Sir Garnet Wolseley was appointed Administrator and Commander-in-Chief on the Gold Coast.

Initially with only a few troops (primarily the 2nd West India Regiment), local irregulars and police, Wolseley drove the Ashanti from around Elmina in a minor action on 14 October 1873. His terms for peace (involving Ashanti withdrawal, compensation and their release of European captives) being rebutted, he organised a campaign, augmenting his forces by naval landing-parties and three British battalions, 1/42nd, 2/23rd and 2/Rifle Brigade. As was his practice, his carefully picked staff's organisation ensured adequate logistical preparation, even to the design of uniforms suitable for the climate. Most of the 23rd and the newly arrived 1st West India Regiment remained in reserve, the others being accompanied by huge numbers of African porters (the allied warrior auxiliaries were not enthusiastic about engaging the Ashanti, and most made off).

The Ashanti withdrew into their own territory and Kofi Karikari attempted to make peace, releasing the European captives; but Wolseley was determined to continue the advance he had begun in early January 1874 as a matter of principle, and with 2,200 men (1,500 Europeans) crossed into Ashanti territory on 20 January. The terrain was heavily forested, where the Ashanti proved a most formidable enemy and where fighting took place at close range. After some skirmishing, Wolseley fought a serious action at Amoafu (31 January) and a minor one at Odasu (or Ardahsa) on 4 February, and entered the undefended

Kumasi on the evening of the same day. Finding no *Asantehene* with whom to negotiate, or any army to fight, Wolseley burned the town and retired on the morning of 6 February. Total British losses had been eighteen killed or mortally wounded, 55 Europeans dead from disease, and 185 wounded; effectively, the expedition had been a complete success even though the Ashanti army remained in the field, though that success could be ascribed less to tactics than to Wolseley's meticulous planning and care for the health of his command; although his firepower, notably the light 7pdrs and rocket-projectors had been decisive in the bush-fighting.

Meanwhile, under the command of Captain John Glover, RN, administrator of Lagos, another column composed of local troops (principally Hausa police) approached from the east, and entered the deserted capital on 12 February. Glover's approach and fears of Wolseley's return persuaded Kofi Karikari to sue for peace, involving the renunciation of claims on neighbouring territory, an indemnity of 50,000 ounces of gold, and an attempt to suppress human sacrifice.

Ashanti Expedition, 1895–6

Following his humiliation by Wolseley, Kofi Karikari was deposed in favour of his brother Mensa, who declined to pay the indemnity. His tyrannical rule was overthrown in 1883 in favour of a new king, Kwaka Dua II, but he died in June 1884 (in the same month as ex-king Kofi Karikari), and after civil war prince Prempeh was chosen as king (March 1888); he took the name Kwaka Dua III, but is better known by his original name. His accession had been achieved with British support, and as Britain was attempting to extend control, he was requested to accept the imposition of a British protectorate and a Resident at Kumasi. Prempeh declined, and even sent personal envoys to Britain, pleading his case, as he refused to treat with the

Captain Davidson Houston, Gold Coast Hausas, wearing the zouave-style uniform of that corps, with the Ashanti Star for the 1895–6 campaign.

governor of the Gold Coast; but military action was decided upon, using the non-payment of the indemnity, and the continuation of human sacrifice, as justification. An expedition was commanded by Colonel Sir Francis Scott, comprising the 2/West Yorkshire Regiment, a 'Special Service Corps' composed of small detachments from a number of regiments, and Lagos and Sierra Leone Hausas, with the 2/West India Regiment for line-of-communication duties; it began its advance in late December 1895 and occupied Kumasi without opposition on 17 January 1896. Prempeh made his submission to the governor and was exiled to the Seychelles; a British Resident was installed at Kumasi.

Ashanti War, 1900

No king was appointed to replace Prempeh, but administration was taken over by the British Resident and supported by a small garrison. On 28 March 1900 the governor of the Gold Coast, Sir Frederick Hodgson, at a meeting of Ashanti chiefs demanded that the Golden Stool be produced; presumably he regarded it as merely the throne of the controller of the territory and did not fully appreciate its symbolic significance. The result was a rising by three Ashanti tribes (Kumasi, Asansi and Kokofu). Hodgson, his wife and other Europeans took refuge in the fort which had been built at Kumasi, and summoned assistance; this arrived in the form of 100 Gold Coast Constabulary (18 April 1900) and 250 Lagos Constabulary (29 April), the fort being attacked on the latter date. On 15 May, led by Major A. H. Morris, commissioner of the Northern Territories of the Gold Coast, a further 250 men arrived; they had marched for a month through heavy bush from the north, skirmishing *en route*. With disease having broken out and supplies low, the governor and about 600 of the garrison broke out, despite the Ashanti having erected stockades around the fort and across the tracks; with a loss of two officers and 39 Hausa dead, and double that number wounded and missing, the party reached the Cape Coast safely on 10 July.

Three Europeans and 100 Hausa were left behind to hold the fort, led by a Captain Bishop, with three weeks' rations. With no European troops available because of the South African War, the rescue had to be made by local forces, organised on the coast by Colonel James Willcocks: they included constabulary, West African Frontier Force, Central Africa, West Africa and Northern and Southern Nigeria Regiments, Sierra Leone Frontier Police and detachments of the 1st and 2nd West India Regiment. With some 1,000 men, six pieces of artillery and six Maxims, Willcocks fought his way to Kumasi on 15 July 1900, to find the beleaguered garrison largely too weak to stand. Having evacuated the sick and wounded, Willcocks took the offensive with a force augmented to some 3,500 men; many of the rebel chiefs surrendered after the Kumasi were defeated at Obassa on 30 September 1900, and the remainder were captured on 28 December. Considering the difficulties of terrain and weather (the rainy season having turned roads into mud), and the problems of providing supplies and porters, and the determined nature of the enemy, the expedition reflected great credit upon the locally raised forces, and won a knighthood for its commander. Total casualties, including deaths from disease, were 1,007 among the British forces. A leading figure in the rebellion had been the Ashanti queen Yaa Asantewa, who was captured and exiled (the queen mother traditionally exercised considerable authority, perhaps because the crown did not pass from father to son, but to the king's brother or sister's son). Following this last campaign, the territory was annexed formally on 26 September 1901, with a separate administration of a chief commissioner representing the governor of the Gold Coast.

Gold Coast: Other Operations

In addition to those against the Ashanti, other minor operations were conducted in the Gold Coast region, some regarded as sufficiently important to warrant the issue of clasps for the East and West Africa Medal. Explorations having pushed northwards, some diplomatic tension resulted over disputed territorial acquisition; but the frontiers between British holdings and those of France and Germany were defined by agreements of 14 June 1898 and 14 November 1899 respectively, delineating the extent of the Northern Territories of the Gold Coast, which was constituted as a separate district with its own commissioner in 1897, and made a distinct administration under the control of the governor of the Gold Coast in 1901. In this area a number of minor expeditions were launched between late 1896 and mid-1898, and on 28 March 1898 a detachment of Gold Coast Constabulary, commanded by the governor's ADC, Lieutenant. F. B. Henderson, RN, successfully defended the town of Dawkita when it was attacked by slavers.

Military Forces: Ashantis

Although the Ashanti had no 'regular' army in the European sense, virtually the whole male population could be mobilised in tribal and clan groups, under their own chieftains. Almost all were armed with firearms, which had been introduced into West Africa at an early date; the majority were 'trade muskets', generally long-barrelled flintlocks of dubious quality, known as 'Dane guns' (the Danish being among the earliest of the gun-traders), although many were of British manufacture. Ammunition was locally made, the powder of mediocre quality and the shot often in the form of slugs; despite a tendency to over-load (with the attendant danger of a burst barrel), quality was such that range was very limited. Unlike some African people who fired from the hip, the Ashanti understood marksmanship and impressed the British with their discipline and musket-drill, being able to fire accurately and at speed; and limited range was of less consequence in the combat of the region, protagonists firing from near-impenetrable forest at an enemy only yards away (as Wolseley observed, such bush-fighting was akin to combat in twilight, as a man was only able to see a few files to his left or right).

Swords were carried more as badges of office than as weapons, often held by their wide and impracticable blades; knives were probably used more for the removal of heads than for combat, the skulls and bones of defeated foes being treasured trophies as well as having religious or symbolic significance, used in such numbers that European witnesses were suitably appalled. Ordinary clothing was worn for battle, generally a large rectangle of cloth

Corporal and privates of the Royal Niger Hausas, a corps formed by the Royal Niger Company; it is noteworthy that their weapons, apparently Enfield or more probably Snider breech-loading rifles, were considerably outdated by the time this photograph was taken.

wrapped around the loins and thrown over the left shoulder like a plaid, or just wrapped around the waist for greater freedom of movement. Contemporary pictures also depict a tunic or smock, a tabard-like garment as worn by chieftains or more important warriors, covered with magical amulets sewn into leather or cloth pockets as was common on other items of Ashanti military equipment. Head-covering was probably not used widely, though contemporary pictures depict head-scarves, and some wore caps with shell decorations, and metal plates and plumes for senior commanders. Ammunition-pouches were carried, those armed with no more modern weapons than the old 'Dane guns' also carrying powder-horns or gourds.

Ashanti tactics, so successful in favourable terrain, involved the division of their forces into a body of scouts, an advance-guard, main body and rearguard; attacks were pressed with great courage and noise, often directed against the enemy's flanks. In addition to using the heavy bush as cover, from which to pour in musketry at close range, the Ashanti erected palisades at strategic points and across tracks as further cover and to impede the advance of an enemy. Field command was usually vested in 'generals' or experienced warriors rather than in the *Asantehene* himself.

Goree

The island of Goree off the west coast of Africa formed part of the French colony of Senegal, but was a British possession for some time. Originally a Dutch colony (hence its name, originally Goeree or Goedereede, named after an island off the Dutch coast), it was captured by the British fleet of Commodore Robert Holmes in 1663, but re-possessed by De Ruyter in 1664. France captured the island from the Dutch in 1677, but lost it to Britain in January 1759 when Commodore Augustus Keppel captured Goree and the Cape Verde district. Britain restored these territories to France in 1763, but in the Napoleonic Wars again captured Goree (1800) and the Senegal settlement of St. Louis (1809), before both were restored to France by the Treaty of Paris (although the French did not actually take possession again until 1817). During the period of British occupation, garrisons were maintained, Goree proving to be one of the least popular postings because of the unhealthiness of the climate.

Nigeria

The territory which became the British protectorates of Northern and Southern Nigeria extended north from the 'Slave Coast', the littoral on either side of the mouth of the Niger river. Taking its name from its main commercial activity, slaving, the area was first exploited by Portugal in the late 15th century, when the dominant kingdom in the coastal region was Benin, one of the most powerful states ever to exist in West Africa, and renowned for the skill of its metalworkers. British traders established contact with Benin as early as 1553, and by the end of the 18th century Britain enjoyed a virtual monopoly of trade along the entire Niger coast. Despite a number of notable explorations into the interior and along the Niger, territorial occupation was not sought beyond that necessary in the interests of trade, at least until the acquisition of Lagos.

A British trading post at Badagry, 40 miles west of Lagos, was attacked in 1851 by King Kosoko of Lagos island; a British naval force responded by seizing Lagos, deposing the king and installing in his stead his cousin Akitoye, on the understanding that he would suppress the slave trade. This was not carried out, and in 1861 his successor, King Docemo, was persuaded to exchange his territorial rights for a pension of 1,200 bags of cowries (later commuted to £1,000 per annum), and a settlement was established on Lagos island. It was a separate colony from 1863 to 1866, then a dependency of Sierra Leone to 1874, then part of the Gold Coast, and an independent crown colony from 1886 until its integration with Nigeria in 1906.

The expansion of French holdings (Dahomey to the west, Upper Senegal and Niger to the north) and German in the east (Cameroon) impelled Britain to regularise its position. British trading interests had been combined by the formation of the United African Company in 1879, and in June 1885 a British protectorate was declared, covering the coast from Lagos to the Rio del Rey, the boundary with German Cameroon; its original title of Oil Rivers Protectorate (from the palm oil which was the staple export) was changed in 1893 to the Niger Coast Protectorate. (The exact demarcation between British, French and German territory was not agreed until 1909). In 1886 the Company received a royal charter and the title of Royal Niger Company, giving control of the lower Niger area to the coast, although the territory which was to become Northern Nigeria was hardly penetrated by Europeans, and was controlled by powerful Islamic states unwilling to open their borders. Treaties were negotiated with some of these, but did little more than confirm the Company's official sphere of influence in relation to French and German possessions.

A number of minor military expeditions were undertaken in subsequent years, usually in response to hostile acts or in the suppression of slaving. Among these was the expedition against the Jebu in 1892, who had closed trade-routes to Yorubaland (the Yoruba were a group of peoples in the Lagos hinterland, originally an empire of six confederate kingdoms, which had broken down into conflict before the appearance of the British; they made no opposition to the British following a treaty of 1893 which placed the most important state, Egba, under British protection). Others included the Benin River punitive expedition (August–September 1894) against chief Nana of Brohemie, who had been raiding the surrounding area; and the Brass River expedition (February 1895), led by Rear-Admiral Sir Frederick Bedford to punish King Koko, who had attacked a Niger Company post at Akassa. Primarily naval personnel and local forces were used.

More significant was the operation against Benin in 1897. That state was much decayed from the height of its power, and although a treaty was concluded with King Overami in 1892, when the acting British consul-general, J. R. Phillips, went on a mission to the king in January 1897, his party was attacked and eight Europeans (including Phillips) were killed. A punitive expedition was organised under the command of Rear-Admiral Sir Harry Rawson (C in C Cape station), consisting of a naval brigade and some 500 Niger Coast Constabulary under Lieutenant-Colonel Bruce Hamilton. Against considerable opposition, on 17 February the expedition occupied Benin city, which was partially burned, and the expedition began to withdraw on 22 February. The king was deported and six chiefs were tried and executed; and following a further expedition in 1899 Benin was completely pacified, and was added to the protectorate. After the deposition of the king, a council of chiefs under the direction of a British Resident was established to administer the territory.

In 1897 the Royal Niger Company came into conflict with the Islamic states of Nupe and Ilorin in the north. They were associated with the caliphate of Sokoto of the Fula empire, which was founded at the beginning of the 19th century. The Fula were a powerful people extending from Senegal almost to Darfur, who subdued the Hausa states in northern Nigeria; their name had various versions, for example Fula (Mandingan), Follani (Hausa) and Fullan (Arabic). They were great slave-raiders, and the open country they inhabited produced fine cavalry. In January 1897 the Company invaded Nupe with some 500 of its own Hausa troops (Royal Niger Constabulary) and thirty British officers (some seconded from the British Army), and on 26–7 January defeated the emir of Nupe at Bida, whose force has been estimated as comprising as many as 10,000 cavalry and 20,000 infantry, but which was unable to resist the effects of artillery and Maxim fire. The expedition then moved on to Ilorin, which submitted, but the Company was unable to maintain its hold on Nupe, and the emir returned after the expedition withdrew.

As British influence spread and relations with France became strained along the western border, it was decided that a regular force should be organised for frontier defence, and that the territories of the Royal Niger Company should be placed under crown control. From 1 January 1900 the Company dropped the 'royal' from its title and reverted to being a purely commercial concern; its southern territories were amalgamated with the Niger Coast Protectorate to form the Protectorate of Southern Nigeria, and the northern territories became the Protectorate of Northern Nigeria. The legal status of slavery had been abolished in Company territory in 1897, and in 1901 slave-trading was made illegal; this, and numerous minor expeditions to suppress slaving, helped cause a decline in inter-tribal warfare, the capture of slaves having been a prime cause of such hostilities. British control was extended through the northern territories, sometimes with the co-operation of the local chieftains, at other times by military force. Kano was captured by assault in February 1903, and after another action on 17 May 1903 Sokoto capitulated, the defeat of these states completing the imposition of British rule in Northern Nigeria. (The sultan of Sokoto was replaced on 21 May 1903 by a successor chosen by a council of elders and installed by the British high commissioner, once he had agreed to British terms: that all chiefs should be appointed by Britain, that British laws should be observed, that the slave trade should cease, and that no weapons other than flintlocks should be imported.) Numerous small expeditions were necessary at times to maintain order, for example the suppression of a rebellion in Sokoto in March 1906, occasioned by a religious leader who claimed to be the Mahdi; during this revolt the local leaders remained loyal to the British, and following the defeat of a small force of the Northern Nigeria Regiment at Satiru (14 February 1906), the rebels were wiped out in an action on 10 March in which the

The confused nature of combat in the West African jungles is exemplified in this illustration of a skirmish in the 1900 Ashanti War. Locally recruited porters were essential for the transportation of supplies and, as here, the evacuation of casualties. (Engraving after H. C. Seppings-Wright)

British suffered no fatalities, but as many as 2,000 rebels may have been killed. The leader of the revolt, Dan Makafo, was convicted by the sultan of Sokoto's court and executed.

Sierra Leone

Although the first British settlement in Sierra Leone dated from the 17th century, the area was merely the haunt of slavers and pirates until the end of the 18th century, when a philanthropic scheme was launched to establish a colony for discharged Negro soldiers and sailors, and for escaped slaves, under British government protection. The colony was founded in 1787 and in 1788 Captain John Taylor, RN bought a piece of land from the local chief for its use; the first colony failed, but in 1791 the survivors were transferred to a new settlement, and the promoters of the scheme (including William Wilberforce) obtained a charter of incorporation as the Sierra Leone Company. Reverting to its original site and appropriately named Freetown, the settlement survived a French raid in 1794 and with the help of the abolitionist movement increased in size, especially after the abolition of the slave trade in 1807, in which year the Company transferred its rights to the crown. More territory was acquired by degrees, until the colony reached its full size in 1884; in 1866 Freetown was made the capital of the West African Settlements (including the Gambia, Gold Coast and Lagos), but in 1874 the two latter reverted to independent administration, and the Gambia in 1888.

Sierra Leone was an unpopular station because of the climate and disease which affected Europeans particularly (hence the employment there of the West India Regiments): '... the few dingy white faces looking despondent and languid, the listless, idle, savage natives ... present a succession and series of heart-sinking images which would soon induce the visitor to sincerely wish as I did, Would I was well out of this den of thieves and pestilence'.[3] A garrison was necessary, however, for the protection of the colony from attacks by the surrounding peoples; in November 1801, for example, the Timni or 'Timmany' tribesmen, the subjects of 'King Tom', attacked the fort of Sierra Leone and supported by a party of marksmen killed a number of European troops and civilians; they were ejected by a bayonet-charge of both troops and civilians, led by the governor. By no means were all the local people hostile, however: in this action, for example, a number of other tribes aided the settlers in opposition to King Tom.

British influence spread gradually into the hinterland, the British endeavouring to suppress the slave trade and inter-tribal conflict. A number of minor military operations were mounted, such as the punitive expedition under Colonel W. de Winton against the Yonnie tribe (November–December 1887), and to Tambi and Toniataba (March–April 1892), all involving the 1st West India Regiment as well as local forces. From November 1893 to March 1894 operations were mounted against the Sofas, Islamic raiders who were ravaging Sierra Leone and French Guinea. A French expedition was also mounted, and on 23 December 1893 it fell upon a British force encamped at Waima, mistaking the British for the Sofa followers of the chief Samory. Both sides suffered casualties before the error was realised (three British officers were killed and the French commander mortally wounded). To prevent a similar mistake, the Anglo–French frontier was agreed in January 1895, and a British protectorate was declared on 26 August 1896. More campaigning took place following protests over the introduction of a house-tax (or 'hut-tax') from 1 January 1898. An expedition was necessary against Chief Bai Bureh of the Timni, who was captured in November 1898 and deported after a difficult campaign, and a supportive revolt involved the Mendi people from April 1898. One of the main actions of the campaign centred around the siege of Panguma, whose garrison was cut off from support for two months until relieved by the second expedition to attempt it (Frontier Police, a detachment of Sierra Leone Royal Artillery and African allies), which broke through to Panguma on 23 June 1898. The most decisive action occurred at Yomundu on 6 July 1898 when this stockaded town was stormed by the Frontier Police and African allies, and a large number of rebels killed. Unrest had been suppressed by March 1899, a general amnesty having been issued by the governor on 17 January 1899.

Military Forces: West Africa

West Africa being such an unpopular posting, it was only with difficulty that troops could be found to serve there vol-untarily. Generally, only the worst men were employed there, and kept in order with the strictest discipline: in January 1802, in fact, a governor of Goree, Joseph Wall, was executed for having illegally flogged to death one of his sergeants, Benjamin Armstrong. Consequently, penal corps were employed: in August 1800 Fraser's Goree Corps was formed, absorbing an existing independent company raised in 1794, and in April 1804 was re-named the Royal African Corps. In 1805 it absorbed two black companies from Stevenson's York Rangers, in the following year was re-named the Royal York Rangers, in June 1808 reverted to the Royal African Corps, and from May 1810 began to enlist non-whites. It was disbanded in 1821 but re-formed in the following year as the Royal African Colonial Regiment, its members military criminals drafted in as a punishment, until 1826 when the recruitment of blacks was again permitted, and in June 1840 it was absorbed into the 3rd West India Regiment. Although penal corps normally served well in action, at other times they were inclined to be turbulent; for example, in 1810 a detachment in Senegal planned a mutiny because 'they did not like to be detained in Africa all their lives'.[4] When the plot was discovered, 25 were shot and 25 exiled to Sierra Leone. Their mortality-rate was not due entirely to the West African climate, but partly to the fact that so many were sent to Africa as '... banishment to a pestilential climate, which death alone could release them from ... the far greater proportion [were] delinquents steeped in crime, hardened, reckless and debauched. Aware that there was no release for them but the grave, they ... plunged into the grossest dissipation, indulging, where practicable, in an immoderate use of the worst and most deleterious spirits ...'[5]

In addition to such regular troops, local units were formed: for example, by the Sierra Leone Militia Law of October 1808, all able-bodied inhabitants of the colony aged between 15 and 60 years inclusive were enrolled for the colony's defence, including not only colonists but Kroomen and hired African labourers, and any captured slaves who had been in the colony for longer than three months. In 1810 it was recommended that Africans not settled in the colony be excluded from the militia, that men below the age of 20 should be trained as light infantry, that the artillery should be entrusted to the Negro colonists from Nova Scotia, and that bush-fighting should be left to the 'Maroon' colonists, where they could utilise their natural skills of bush-craft.

With the expansion of British holdings, quasi-military, quasi-police forces were formed in the various territories; the Royal Niger Company, for example, formed the Royal Niger Constabulary in 1887, which was the force engaged in the 1897 campaign, culminating in the victory of Bida, the first West African campaign undertaken entirely by local forces with only the secondment of British officers. Their artillery comprised one 12pdr and one 9pdr Whitworth breech-loaders, nine 7pdr mountain guns and fifteen Maxims; the three Constabulary detachments employed in the campaign (more than 1,300 rank and file in all) were accompanied by some 1,900 porters, typical of the logistical requirements of African expeditions.

Similar forces were formed in other colonies: the Sierra Leone Frontier Force (reorganised in 1891 from the Sierra Leone police), Gold Coast Constabulary and Lagos Hausas, for example. The military forces were re-organised as the West African Frontier Force, created 1898 under the control of the Colonial Office and officered by the British Army, the various colonies providing its battalions (the Gold Coast Constabulary, for example, became the Gold Coast Regiment of the WAFF in 1901). The organiser of the WAFF (from August 1897) and its commander until December 1899 was Frederick Lugard, the explorer and experienced soldier who had been instrumental in the British possession of Uganda, and who became high commissioner of Northern Nigeria; it was under his administration that the successful campaign was conducted against Sokoto. Separate police forces continued to exist after the formation of the WAFF. Freetown, Sierra Leone, was made the headquarters of the British Army in West Africa; stationed there in addition to the local WAFF battalion was a company of African Artillery and a detachment of African Engineers, both recruited from West Indians.

Many of the recruits for West African corps were Hausas (hence the use of this name in some unit-titles), a people originally inhabiting western and central Sudan who formed a powerful confederation of seven states until conquered by the Fula in the early 19th century. The Hausas were regarded as ideal recruits, being physically strong, intelligent and brave, and one of few central African peoples to possess a written language, a modified form of Arabic (about one-third of the Hausa language had Arabic roots, indicting an early influence in Hausa culture). Not all the local units were exclusively Hausa, however; for example, the Lagos Battalion of the WAFF was four-fifths Hausa and the remainder Yoruba.

In addition to the WAFF, there was also a regular unit of the British Army, the West African Regiment, formed in 1898 for duty in that region; with headquarters at Sierra Leone, most of its recruits were from the Mendi people, who had not hitherto been employed in a combatant role but who proved to be good soldiers. The regiment served in Sierra Leone, in the Ashanti campaign of 1900 and in the Cameroons in 1914–15. The West India Regiment continued to provide part of the West African garrison until disbandment in 1927, and on the disbandment of the West African Regiment in 1928, all such duties were assumed by the WAFF.

Notes

1. 'Twelve Months' Service in Western Africa', by Captain L. S. O'Connor, 1st West India Regiment, in *Colburn's United Service Magazine*, 1845, vol. II, p. 57.
2. 'Western Africa, and its Effects on the Health of Troops', in *United Service Journal*, 1840, vol. II, p. 512.
3. O'Connor, *op. cit.*, vol. II, p. 58.
4. *Edinburgh Evening Courant*, 24 November 1810.
5. O'Connor, *op. cit.*, 1846, vol. I, pp. 225–6.

References

Bacon, R. H. *Benin, the City of Blood*, London, 1898 (the author was a member of the 1897 expedition).

Baden-Powell, R. S. S. *The Downfall of Prempeh: A Diary of Life with the Native Levy in Ashanti 1895–96*, London, 1896.

Biss, Captain. H. C. J. *The Relief of Kumasi*, London, 1901.

Boisragon, A. *The Benin Massacre*, London, 1897 (Captain Alan Boisragon was one of two survivors of the attack on J. R. Phillips' party which led to the 1897 Benin

expedition).

Bond, B. (ed.). *Victorian Military Campaigns*, London, 1967 (includes 'The Ashanti Campaign 1873–74', by J. Keegan).

Brackenbury, Captain. H. *The Ashanti War: A Narrative prepared from the Official Documents*, London, 1874 (the author was Wolseley's military secretary).

Claridge, W. W. *A History of the Gold Coast and Ashanti*, London, 1915.

Crook, Major. J. J., *History of Sierra Leone*, Dublin, 1903.

Featherstone, D. *Victoria's Enemies: An A–Z of British Colonial Warfare*, London, 1989.

Fynn, J. K. *Asante and its Neighbours 1700–1807*, London, 1971.

Hall, Major W. M. *The Great Drama of Kumasi*, London, 1939 (the 1900 rebellion).

Hodgson, Lady. *The Siege of Kumassi*, London, 1901.

Home, R. *City of Blood Revisited: a new look at the Benin Expedition of 1897*, London, 1982.

Knight, I. *Queen Victoria's Enemies (2): Northern Africa*, London, 1989.

Lloyd, A. *The Drums of Kumasi:*

the Story of the Ashanti Wars, London, 1964.

McInnes, I., and Fraser, M. *Ashanti 1895–96*, Chippenham, 1987.

Martin, E. *The British West African Settlements 1750–1821*, London, 1927.

Mbaeyi, P. M. *British Military and Naval Forces in West African History 1807–1874*, New York, 1978.

Musgrave, G. C. *To Kumassi with Scott: A Description of the Journey from Liverpool to Kumassi with the Ashanti Expedition 1895–96*, London, 1896.

Myatt, Major F. *The Golden Stool: An Account of the Ashanti War of 1900*, London, 1966.

Reade, W. *The Story of the Ashantee Campaign*, London, 1874.

Stanley, H. M. *Coomassie and Magdala: Two British Campaigns*, London, 1874 (Henry Morton Stanley, then correspondent for the *New York Herald*).

Wallis, C. B. *The Advance of our West African Empire*, London, 1903 (includes the 1898 rising in Sierra Leone).

Vandeleur, Lieutenant. S. *Campaigning on the Upper Nile and*

Niger, London, 1898.

Africa

In addition to the references listed for specific regions or campaigns, the following are works of more 'general' significance:

Emery, F. *Marching over Africa: Letters from Victorian Soldiers*, London, 1986.

Featherstone, D. *Victorian Colonial Warfare: Africa*, London, 1992.

James, L. *The Savage Wars: British Campaigns in Africa 1870–1920*, London, 1985.

Lewis, D. L. *The Race to Fashoda: European Colonialism and African Resistance in the Scramble for Africa*, London, 1988.

Pakenham, T. *The Scramble for Africa*, London, 1991 (excellent account of the colonisation of the entire continent).

Wilson, Revd. J. L. *The British Squadron on the Coast of Africa*, London, 1851 (a missionary's support for the anti-slavery operations which occupied so much of the time of the Royal Navy).

IV
THE EAST

THE EAST

CHINA

Trading contacts between China and Europe had been well-established for centuries before the outbreak of Sino-European hostilities. China had always tended to regard Europeans with suspicion, and was not especially co-operative even in matters of trade, allowing only one port to be used (Canton), where commerce was conducted principally by the Portuguese, Dutch, and the British East India Company. (The Portuguese also had a settlement at Macao from 1557, but a measure of the Chinese attitude was their construction of a wall in 1573 to cut off the 'barbarians' from the rest of China, and until 1849 they insisted on maintaining their authority over the Portuguese settlement; not until 1887 was it acknowledged as a Portuguese possession. In 1802 and 1808 Macao was occupied briefly by Britain, as a precaution against seizure by France.) European merchants and Christian missionaries were allowed into China, but suffered persecution at times. Attempts to establish closer relations between Britain and China, notably diplomatic missions sent to Peking in 1793 and 1816, were unsuccessful, the Chinese seeming to have no interest in 'foreign devils' (a phrase which occurs often in contemporary and later works, becoming almost the watchword of the popular opinion concerning China's view of Europeans). The ambassador sent in 1816, Lord Amherst, who refused to *kowtow* before the emperor, was not even admitted into the imperial presence.

Nevertheless, China remained a most lucrative market for 'British' opium, grown in India and exported to China. As late as 1875 some 17 per cent of India's gross national income came from the sale of opium; and though its use had been made illegal in China as early as 1729 (to prevent its abuse by the population), in 19th century Europe opium was regarded as a legitimate medication, although its addictive properties were recognised. European demand for Chinese goods and wonderful craftsmanship, and the lack of interest expressed by China for European manufacturers, had in the past given China a most favourable trade balance in its European commerce; but as increasing quantities of opium were imported into China (despite official Chinese opposition to the trade), by the late 1830s it was imposing financial hardship, cancelling the previous trade balance, and one estimate stated that by the 1840s between 10 and 12 million Chinese were hopelessly addicted, with the consequent terrible effect upon China's economic and social framework. While the Europeans have been castigated for their lack of concern over the damage done by the opium trade, and for their lack of understanding of Chinese sensibilities, the hostile behaviour of the Chinese, who viewed all other nations as in every way inferior, did nothing to improve Sino-European relations or discourage the onset of hostilities.

First China (or 'Opium') War

Anglo-Chinese conflict first occurred during the reign of the emperor Tao-kwang (1820–50). When the monopoly of the East India Company ceased in 1834 a British minister, Lord Napier, was sent to Canton to supervise British trade; he died after a few months' residence from a fever supposedly exacerbated by the difficulties of dealing with the Chinese. In 1839 a new Chinese high commissioner was sent to Canton, Lin Tse-hsu, possessing viceregal powers and determined to suppress the opium trade. By threats and by preventing the British from entering or leaving Canton, or trading, Lin compelled the British trade commissioner at the port, Captain Charles Elliot, to surrender for destruction all opium in the possession of British merchants (Elliot had to agree to purchase the opium on behalf of the government, and then give it to the Chinese). The second Chinese demand, that no more opium be imported, was obviously unacceptable, and if trade stopped temporarily at Canton, it continued by smuggling. Elliot advised the use of military force against the Chinese, but almost a year passed before the British government decided to send troops to gain reparation for the insult to the British in Canton, financial recompense for more than 20,000 chests of opium destroyed by the Chinese, and to guarantee future security for traders (March 1840).

In effect, however, the first hostilities had occurred some months earlier, with a skirmish between British and Chinese vessels in the Kowloon estuary on 4 September 1839, and a more serious engagement on 3 November off Chuenpi, when the British ships HMSs *Volage* (6th-rate, 28 guns) and *Hyacinth* (18-gun sloop) were attacked by a force of Chinese junks when evacuating British refugees from Canton. The Chinese were beaten off with considerable loss. Not surprisingly, this was not regarded with much sorrow by the British: 'John Chinaman has come to blows with us, and suffered a loss of some five or six of his war-junks, and several hundreds of his waste population, blown up or submerged by the guns of HM ship *Volage*.';[1] but the prospect of a proper war met with considerable opposition, as articulated by a writer in the *United Service Journal*: 'the poor Chinese – with their painted pasteboard boats – must submit to be poisoned, or must be massacred by the thousand, for supporting their own laws in their own land.'[2]

A British naval force commanded by Commodore Sir J. J. Gordon Bremer arrived off Macao on 21 June 1840, then moved north to the island of Chusan, and on 5 July bombarded the port of Ting-hai, which was occupied by troops landed from the fleet, under Brigadier-General George Burrell. Negotiation began between the British and the emperor, Lord Palmerston demanding reparation for previous Chinese actions, and an island off China for use as a British trading base. The emperor refused and having exiled Lin appointed one Ch'i-shan (or 'Yi Shen') in his place. Supporting their diplomatic efforts by action, on 7 January 1841 the British captured the forts in the Canton estuary (Chuenpi or 'Chuenpee' and 'Tycocktow') with an amphibious landing commanded by Major J. L. Pratt of the 26th Foot; British casualties were no more than 38 wounded. (The forts guarding the Pearl river were sometimes styled 'the Bogue Forts', an Anglicisation of the Portuguese *Boca Tigre*, a name derived from the Chinese 'Tiger's Gate' (*Ha-mun*), the river narrows.) Of the Chinese fleet of thirteen war-junks, ten were captured and the admiral's vessel blown up by a rocket from the small British squadron commanded by Captain T. Herbert of the 6th-rate 28-gunner HMS *Calliope*. Ch'i-shan had instructions not to negotiate, but with the Chinese admiral Kuan Ti having asked for a truce, and faced with overwhelming British strength, on 18 January 1841 signed an agreement by which Hong Kong became British property. Ch'i-shan was exiled by the emperor as a result, and faced with continuing Chinese hostility the British began to advance up the estuary with a reinforced military contingent, now commanded by Major-General Sir Hugh Gough. It was an irresistible advance: Admiral Kuan was killed and on 27 May 1841 Canton was captured by Gough and the naval commander, Sir Le Fleming Senhouse. On the understanding that the Chinese would pay a reparation of £600,000 (expressed in the treaty as 6 million dollars), Elliot agreed to a British withdrawal. This was considered an insufficient sum, and Palmerston dismissed him.

Moving north again, the British force captured Amoy (26–7 August 1841) and re-possessed Chusan (previously returned to the Chinese) on 1 October. Chinhai was taken on 10 October (costing the British three dead and sixteen wounded, while the Chinese loss was 'most appalling'),[3] and Ningpo, unopposed, on 13 October; the British then suspended operations for the winter. Negotiations having proved fruitless, on 10 March 1842 the Chinese counter-attacked, and were repelled with ease. The British recommenced their northward movement, capturing Chapu (south of Shanghai) on 18 May 1842, an operation chiefly remarkable for the defence of an enclosure by 300 Chinese, the survivors only surrendering after their defences had been breached and the building set ablaze by rockets. Gough and the naval commander, Admiral Sir William Parker, moved towards Shanghai, bombarding the Chinese at the entrance of the Woosung river (16 June), and Shanghai was captured unopposed on 19 June. Progressing up the Yangtze river, the British fought the hardest action of the war at Chinkiang ('Chin-keang-foo') on 21 July; the city was captured and its military commander, Hai-lin, was burned in his own house which had been set alight on his orders. This, and the sight of women and children killed by their own people and flung into wells on the approach of the British, Gough found to be a 'frightful scene of destruction'[4] from which he deliberately removed his troops. British casualties totalled 34 dead (six-

The limitations of the flintlock musket were described graphically by an officer in the First China War, who recounted how a force of Chinese rushed upon an Indian company, one of the Chinese seizing the musket of a dead sepoy:
'The musket was picked up by one of the enemy, who, fixing his eyes on the officer ... and stepping behind a bush, deliberately rested the musket on a branch, and coolly turning over the wet powder in the pan, apparently not at all understanding the use of flint and steel, applied his own slow match to the powder, which, on exploding, lodged the ball in Mr Berkeley's right arm. At this time not a musket would go off, and little resistance could be offered against the enemy's long spears. The men, after remaining in this position for a short time, were enabled to advance to a more defensible one, where too they were soon surrounded by thousands of the enemy, who, had they possessed the slightest determination, could have at once annihilated them. The rain ceasing to fall for a time, enabled a few of the men to discharge their muskets. The enemy was not removed above fifteen yards, and every shot told as a matter of course. Many of the Sepoys, after extracting the wet cartridge, very deliberately tore their pocket handkerchiefs, or lining from their turbans (the only dry thing about them), and baling water with their hands into the barrels of their pieces, washed and dried them. They were then enabled to fire a few volleys in succession, and as each shot told with great effect in the crowd, the enemy was forced to retire ...'
('Land operations Before Canton', by 'an officer of the Force', in *United Service Magazine, 1843*, vol. I, pp. 242–3. The unit involved was presumably the 37th Madras Native Infantry, as Ensign Berkeley of that regiment was named among the injured in the operations at Canton, 25–30 May 1841)

teen from sunstroke), 107 wounded and three missing.

From this position, with the Chinese 'southern capital' of Nanking threatened, China sued for peace and hostilities were suspended on 17 August. The British Plenipotentiary in China, Sir Henry Pottinger, signed the Treaty of Nanking with the emperor's representatives aboard HMS *Cornwallis* on 29 August 1842, by which the Chinese paid further reparations, confirmed the British possession of Hong Kong, and opened four new 'treaty ports' to foreign trade, Amoy, Foochow, Ningpo and Shanghai. Opium remained illegal in China, but India's exports of the drug more than doubled in the next two decades, China being powerless to prevent it. The 'Opium War' had an even greater effect upon China, however, in proving that the much-vaunted imperial power was of little consequence when faced with modern European forces, and after such humbling the empire was fatally damaged.

Second China War

In 1850 the emperor Hien-feng succeeded to the imperial throne, and proved as little receptive to ideas of reform as had his father; this caused internal unrest, and a rival emperor established himself at Nanking in 1853, one Hung Sin-Ts'uan, who nominated himself as the T'ien Wang ('heavenly king') and announced the inauguration of the T'ai-p'ing dynasty. His appeal was partially political and partially religious, he having devised a bizarre personal view of Christianity in which he thought himself to be the brother of Christ, and the divinely appointed destroyer of those who followed false doctrine, notably the Manchu emperor and his followers. From Kwangsi province the revolt spread, marked by the utter extermination of the populations of cities against which the T'ai-p'ing rebels marched; ironically for such a genocidal process, the dynasty T'ai-p'ing t'ien-kuo meant 'heavenly kingdom of great peace'. Attempts by the legitimate emperor to deal with the usurper were interrupted by further hostilities with Europeans.

Chinese resentment at the outcome of the First China War was personified by the imperial commissioner at Canton, Yeh Ming-ch'en, an arrogant official with an obsessional hatred of foreigners, who was as obstructive as possible to the interests of European merchants. In October 1856 Chinese police seized the ship *Arrow*, anchored in the Pearl river, and took off twelve of the crew under suspicion of being pirates. *Arrow* was Chinese-built, Chinese-owned and Chinese-crewed (but for a British captain), but its Hong Kong registration gave it the right to fly the British flag, and as such China had no jurisdiction over it. The British consul at Canton, Harry Parkes, demanded an apology and release of the prisoners, and was supported by his superior, Sir John Bowring, governor of Hong Kong, who threatened military intervention. With bad grace, Yeh returned the prisoners, but as no apology was forthcoming, Bowring called up Admiral Sir Michael Seymour's fleet. On 23 October 1856 he bombarded and captured the forts which guarded the approach to Canton on the Pearl river, and bombarded Canton itself, but had insufficient forces to take and hold it. Encouraged by Yeh, the Chinese became increasingly hostile towards the foreigners, and on 15 December during a riot European commercial property was set on fire. In January 1857 Bowring appealed for military intervention to secure the British foothold at Canton.

James, 8th Earl of Elgin was sent by Britain as envoy to China, the British receiving French support as that nation had become involved to avenge the ghastly murder of a French missionary. Seymour's fleet fought actions on 27 May 1857 (when Commodore the Hon. Charles Elliot took or destroyed some 40 junks at Escape Creek) and on 1 June when Seymour burned between 70 and 80 war-junks at Fatshan Creek, but the Indian Mutiny delayed the intended deployment of military

forces until December 1857. Neither Elgin nor the French representative, Baron Gros, were enamoured of the prospect of military action, but in the face of Yeh's continuing intransigence, the bombardment of Canton began on 28 December 1857, and on the following day Seymour landed his military force (the British commanded by Major-General Charles Von Straubenzee, and a French naval brigade by Rear-Admiral Rigault de Genouilly), which captured the city by escalade. The capture was completed by 31 December for a loss of thirteen British and two French dead, 83 and 30 wounded respectively. On 5 January 1858 Yeh was apprehended by Harry Parkes, Captain A. C. Key and a party of British bluejackets; he was deported to Calcutta (where he died in April 1859) and governance of Canton was given to an allied commission of Parkes, another British representative, and a French officer.

Elgin determined to go to Peking and conclude a treaty with the emperor in person; when this proposal was rebuffed, further military action was taken. The fleet sailed to the mouth of the Peiho river (which led from the coast to Peking), and on 20 May 1858 the Taku Forts, which guarded the entrance to the river, were bombarded and surrendered. The British progressed upriver to Tientsin, and Chinese commissioners came to negotiate with Elgin and Gros; on 26 June 1858 the Treaty of Tientsin was concluded, which provided for Chinese reparations for the expenses of the recent war, the opening of ten more ports to European commerce, freedom of movement for European merchants and missionaries, the legalisation of the opium trade, and for the reception of foreign diplomatic missions in Peking.

This ended one stage of the war; indeed, what followed is sometimes termed the Third China War, but as the later operations were commemorated in British service by clasps added to the 1857 China Medal, it is possible to regard the renewed hostilities as a continuation of the same war. In accordance with the Treaty of Tietsin, Britain and France dispatched ambassadors to Peking; but these (the Hon. Frederick Bruce and M. de Bourboulon respectively) were denied entry to the Peiho river. Accordingly, Admiral Sir James Hope (Seymour's successor as naval commander) launched an attack upon the Taku Forts on 25 June 1859. Since the previous operations the forts had been greatly strengthened, and the British landing-parties had to be evacuated in the early morning of 26 June, and the fleet withdrew on 28 June with the loss of three gunboats sunk, *Cormorant*, *Lee*, and *Plover*; a fourth, *Kestrel*, was sunk on the 25th but later recovered. British casualties were considerable, 81 dead and 345 wounded, eight of whom died in the immediate aftermath; a small French detachment, commanded by Commandant Tricault, lost four dead and ten wounded.

Reaction to this defeat though not rapid was ultimately serious. In the following year an expeditionary force was

The Taku Forts: exterior of the defences after the storming, with scaling-ladders still in position.

prepared, of about 11,000 British and Indian troops commanded by Lieutenant-General Sir James Hope Grant, and 6,000 French under General Charles Montauban (better-known by the title he received in 1862 for service in China, comte de Palikao, as which he became French prime minister at the start of the Franco-Prussian War). Elgin and Gros accompanied the army. These forces (the British organised in two divisions under Major-Generals Sir John Michel and Sir Robert Napier, and a cavalry brigade) with their attendant naval forces decided first to capture the Taku Forts at the mouth of the Peiho, and on 1 August 1860 landed near Peh-tang, some eight miles

from Taku. They encountered Chinese resistance (led by General San-ko-lin-sin, whose name gave rise to the unlikely story that he was an Irishman named 'Sam Collinson'!), but the outwork fortification of Tangku was captured on 14 August (for a British loss in the period 3–14 August of one killed, 27 wounded and two missing), and on 21 August Napier led the attack on the Taku Forts, which were carried for a British loss of seventeen killed and 184 wounded.

Hope Grant and Montauban pushed upriver beyond Tientsin, the Chinese as before endeavouring to halt the advance on Peking by negotiations, until winter might

Left: Taku Forts: interior of a fort after the attack, showing a Chinese gun-position and casualties.

Opposite page: A hero of the Taku Forts: Robert Montresor Rogers, a lieutenant in the 44th Foot, was the first man upon the walls in the assault of 21 August 1860, for which he received the Victoria Cross. Later a major-general, he is shown here in the uniform of the Cameronians: he commanded the 90th (later 2/Cameronians) in the Zulu War and left the amalgamated regiment in 1882.

bring an end to the allied advance. The Prince of I, the emperor's cousin, sent a message of surrender; but the party which went to negotiate with him (including Harry Parkes) was attacked and seized near Tungchow, and in reply to this act of treachery the allies again advanced, defeating Chinese forces at Chang-chia-wan on 18 September, and at Pal-le-chiao ('Palikao') on 21 September. (In the former action, styled 'on the Chow-Ho' in the official dispatch, British casualties were one dead, seventeen wounded, one missing; in the latter, two dead and 29 wounded). On 22 September, with Peking in imminent danger, the Chinese began to negotiate in earnest, once the prisoners had been returned (some had been killed or died in captivity, the survivors – including Parkes – having been kept in the most wretched of conditions). As an act of reprisal and as an encouragement for the Chinese to negotiate seriously, the emperor's summer palace outside Peking (Yuen-ming-yuen), which had been looted by the French, was burned by the British, Elgin excusing its destruction by stating that an act of retribution was necessary following the Chinese treatment of the envoys: 'Low as is the standard of morals which now obtains in China, we should, in my opinion have still further lowered it, if we had not treated the act in question as a high crime calling for severe retribution ... the destruction of Yuen-Ming-Yuen was the least objectionable of the several courses open to me, unless I could

have reconciled it to my sense of duty to suffer the crime which had been committed to pass practically unavenged.'[5] The allies erected batteries for the bombardment of Peking, but on 13 October the city gates were opened to them. Elgin could demand what he wished, the Chinese being powerless to resist; Prince Kung, the emperor's brother, negotiated for the Chinese, and on 24 October the Treaty of Peking was concluded (and a separate treaty with France two days later), by which the terms of the Treaty of Tietsin were confirmed (and the Chinese reparations increased), Tientsin was opened to foreign trade, Kowloon was ceded to Britain, and foreign ambassadors were permitted to reside in Peking. The allied forces left Peking in November; in almost all respects, the campaign had been one of the most successfully managed of the period.

Military Forces, China 1840–60

The organisation of the Chinese military forces dated back to the invasion of China by the Manchu Tatars (or Tartars) in the 17th century, their expansion from Manchuria leading to the seizure of Peking in 1644 and the fall of the Ming dynasty, confirmed upon the death in 1662 of the last of the Mings to lead resistance against the Manchus, Prince Kuei Wang. The Manchu forces were organised in eight divisions, under different flags, hence the name 'the Eight Banners', which formed a hereditary army, each male descendant of a Manchu being entitled to rations and equipment at the emperor's expense. These 'Bannermen' remained the nucleus of the Chinese army even after they had largely become absorbed into the remainder of Chinese society. The 'native' Chinese troops who had served the empire prior to the triumph of the Manchus continued to exist under the name 'Troops of the Green Standard', employed as garrisons throughout the empire. In 1842 the Chinese forces were computed at between 800,000 and 1,800,000 in number, organised in four classes, plus irregulars. The Manchus were said to comprise 678 companies, the second class 211 companies of Mongolians, the third class 270 companies of Chinese allied to the Manchus, plus all the empire's artillerymen, all companies of 100 men each. Mainly cavalry, they were organised in the eight 'Banners', all receiving their arms, horse, rice for their family, and pay; it was these whom the British sometimes described as 'Tartars'. The fourth class, the troops of the Green Standard, were said to number 500,000, and received land-grants from which they had to cultivate their own subsistence. The irregulars included a local militia said to number about 175,000, and up to 500,000 Mongolian light horse.

Each of these classes and divisions was distinguished by its standards and uniform (a surcoat with a circular patch on front and back bearing the word '*yung*' ('brave') was common), but most of their costume was that of ordinary civilians, so as Gough remarked, 'It is so easy for a China-

The Second China War Medal, awarded for service 1857–60, with five clasps (plus a small number of clasps for 1842); designed by William Wyon, the obverse bore a portrait of Queen Victoria and the reverse a trophy of arms and the legend 'Armis Exposcere Pacem'. The ribbon was crimson with yellow edges.

man to divest himself of the appearance of a soldier, that I have no doubt many escaped by throwing off the outward uniform by which alone they are distinguished from the peasantry.'[6] A contemporary report commented upon training and tactics:

'The principal drill in which the troops, both Mandshoo (sic) and Chinese, are exercised, is shooting with the bow, both when mounted and dismounted; a portion of them are practised in discharging firearms without locks or ramrods; and a minor portion in loading and firing cannon. The dress of the troops does not differ essentially from that of the people at large, excepting in the kurma or surtout; a sort of spencer, which is of a similar colour to the standard under which the soldier serves. The feminineness of his apparel, his silk boots, and the fan with which he refreshes himself in hot weather, make him cut a very effeminate and somewhat laughable figure; and even in time of war, the addition of an iron helmet, a wadded frock, and a bamboo shield, renders his appearance still more anti-martial. The horseman is rapid in his movements, and advances to the attack with much impetuosity – at least, when no enemy is before him. But his little, slender horse, with his short, quick step, wants the qualities of

a charger. The saddle is made of very soft materials, and is raised so high, both before and behind, that it would not be too easy to throw the rider out of his seat; the stirrups, too, are so short as to bring his knee and his chin into close proximity.'[7]

The troops who engaged the allies in the open field were mostly 'Tartars'; those who defended the forts were mostly Chinese, who were capable of sterling resistance (the story of gunners having to be tied to their guns is probably no more than a misconception arising from dead gunners found with cord portfires around their wrists). Firearms were mostly obsolete matchlocks; these and the bows and arrows were used with proficiency, both being fired from horseback. The remainder carried only polearms and swords. Ordnance included a large number of jingals or 'wall pieces' and cannon which suffered from poor powder and shortages of proper shot, both arising from failings or corruption in the army's administration. The guns embraced a wide variety of 'natures'; those mounted in the defences of Chusan, for example, included nineteen iron 1–3pdrs, 24 iron 3–5pdrs, 57 iron 5–9pdrs, ten brass 9pdrs, five brass 10pdrs, five brass 12pdrs, fifteen brass 20pdrs and a brass 32pdr. The weaponry captured at Chinkiang included two 2pdrs, seven 3pdrs, four 4pdrs, two 5pdrs, two 8pdrs, one 9pdr, two 12pdrs and 'a large number of jingals, matchlocks, spears, bows and arrows'.[8] The military value of this collection may be gauged from the fact that the whole lot was destroyed!

Writing of Chinese troops encountered in 1842, Captain Granville Loch, RN remarked that 'if drilled under English officers, they would prove equal, if not superior, to the Sepoys'; he described their three-man, tripod-mounted jingals as 'very serviceable'; and 'the matchlockman carries the charges for his piece in bamboo tubes, contained in a cotton belt fastened round his waist. He loads without a ramrod, by striking the butt against the ground after inserting the ball; the consequence is, that he can charge and fire faster than one of us with a common musket ... the best marksmen are stationed in front, and supplied by people whose only duty is to load them ... At the commencement of the war many of the troops used chain-armour; latterly it was discontinued.'[9]

It was stated at the time that the proficiency and leadership of the Chinese army could be gauged from the following directive said to have been issued to the army in preparation for first contact with the British: 'You have to deal with a people that wear breeches so tight, that once the soldiers fall they cannot get up by themselves ... Paint your faces as fantastically as possible, and when you approach the enemy shout out and make the most hideous faces and grimaces possible to frighten them, and make them tumble down.'[10] If nothing else, this demonstrates one British opinion of Chinese military capability.

T'ai-p'ing Rebellion

The emperor Hien-feng died in 1861 and was succeeded by his five-year-old son, T'ung-chi; during his minority the regency was held jointly by the empress Tsz'e An (who was childless) and the new emperor's mother, Tsz'e Hsi, originally the late emperor's concubine but elevated to the position of imperial consort. The conclusion of peace with Britain and France gave the empire an opportunity to address the problem of the T'ai-p'ings.

Initially, the Europeans endeavoured to maintain friendly relations with the T'ai-p'ings in case they were victorious, but they were soon discouraged by T'ai-p'ing brutality. In June 1860 the T'ai-p'ings captured Soochow, less than fifty miles from Shanghai, and in August, at a time when the allies were engaged in the war against the Manchu dynasty, Hope Grant was informed by the British commander in Shanghai, Lieutenant-Colonel March, RM, that an imminent rebel attack was feared, to resist which March had only one company of Royal Marine Artillery, 400 marines and the Ludhiana Sikhs. Consequently, Grant detached the 44th Foot from his own army, which with units from Chusan and Hong Kong went to reinforce the Shanghai garrison, which repulsed a rebel attack on 18 August.

The Shanghai merchants financed the formation of a mercenary army for their own protection, command of which was given to Frederick Townsend Ward, an American seaman and soldier-of-fortune. This force was deployed to the west of Shanghai to prevent the advance of the rebels, and was given the name 'Ever-Victorious Army', although initially this was more a reflection upon its aspirations than its actual successes. In 1861 Ward was appointed as a general in the imperial Chinese army. Fighting continued around Shanghai for some two years, until in April 1862 the British force which had remained in northern China since the late war was moved to Shanghai as a further protection against the T'ai-p'ing rebels. This force was commanded by Brigadier-General Charles Stavely, who determined to clear the rebels from the area within a radius of 30 miles from Shanghai; in this he was assisted by Ward's force and a French contingent under Admiral Prôtet. On 20 August 1862 Ward was killed in the assault of Tseki; his successor, a Franco-American adventurer, H. A. Burgevine, was an unprincipled rogue who permitted his followers to loot and murder, and he was dismissed by the imperial provincial governor and commander in the area, Li Hung-chang. A measure of the improved relations between China and Britain was the fact that British officers were requested to be seconded to the Ever-Victorious Army, and Stavely selected as its new commander an engineer officer serving with the British forces at Shanghai, Charles George Gordon, who assumed command on 26 March 1863.

Gordon's army consisted of about 3,500 men in five or six infantry regiments, and two field and four siege batteries. They were drilled and armed in European fashion (smoothbore muskets and a smaller number of Enfield rifles), and wore a somewhat Indian Army-style costume, of brown tunic and trousers of European style, with green turban and European rank-insignia. The officers were all European or American, including a few British; handsome rates of pay for the rank and file persuaded them to serve under European officers and wear the uniform which at first attracted ridicule (as being 'Imitation Foreign Devils'), but later was regarded with pride and was in some cases held to be partially responsible for the army's success, in that the rebels were less willing to face what appeared to be European units than they were to face imperial Chinese. Gordon improved the force's discipline to the extent that it provoked mutiny and desertion; the consequent gaps in the ranks were filled by ex-T'ai-p'ing rebels.

Under Gordon's command, the Ever-Victorious Army began to live up to its name, as in collaboration with other imperial forces a drive was begun against the rebels. Gordon enhanced the mobility of his force by the employment of gunboats and river steamers, using the navigable canals and waterways, both for transportation and bombardment, the boats being armed with artillery, and commanded by American captains used to river navigation. Gordon's forces relieved the imperial garrison at Chansu (some 40 miles north-west of Shanghai); Li then ordered him to attack Taitsan, which was stormed and taken, then Quinsan, and on 5 December 1863 Soochow fell to the imperialists. This caused a rupture between Gordon and Li, over the latter's murder of rebel leaders whose safety had been guaranteed as a condition of their surrender. For some weeks Gordon withdrew the Ever-Victorious Army from imperial operations, and when he rejoined the campaign the war against the T'ai-p'ing rebellion was almost concluded. Nanking, the rebels' last stronghold, was invested; Hung, the originator of the rebellion, committed suicide by drinking a concoction of wine and gold leaf. In July 1864 Nanking was captured with the death of most of its garrison, ending the T'ai-p'ing revolt, which from its inception had cost the lives of as many as twenty million people. Gordon had disbanded his Ever-Victorious Army in May 1864, apparently disillusioned with events in China; but was rewarded by the Yellow Jacket, the highest Chinese distinction that could be given by the emperor, and until his death at Khartoum was known by the appellation 'Chinese Gordon'.

Boxer Rebellion

During the period following the T'ai-p'ing rebellion, China was beset by provincial conflicts, including the suppression of an Islamic regime established in Yunnan in 1855 and which survived until 1873, a bandit regime (Nien Fei) 1853–68, and the revolt of the Miao people (1855–81). Hostilities against the French (1883–5) over

French expansion in Tongking were ended by the Treaty of Tientsin (June 1885), the Chinese having held their own; but China was defeated in the Sino–Japanese War (1894–5) over the status of Korea, a vassal state of the empire. Japanese success resulted in the independence of Korea and the ceding of territory to Japan. The dowager empresses resigned their regency in February 1873, but the young emperor T'ung-chi died without issue in 1875; he was succeeded by Kwang-su ('Succession of Glory'), an infant nephew of the dowager empress Tsz'e Hsi (he was also nephew of emperor Hien-feng and grandson of emperor Tao-kwang). The two dowager empresses again became regents, but Tsz'e An died in 1881, leaving Tsz'e Hsi as the supreme power in the empire, aided by Li Hung-Chang.

Partly to guard against the growth of Japanese influence, the European nations began to acquire concessions in China; Russia established a base at Port Arthur, for example; Germany seized Kiaochow and Tsingtao, and Britain secured a lease on Wei-Hai-Wei. A reform movement in China, intent on modernisation, was supported by the emperor in defiance of the reactionaries, of whom Tsz'e Hsi was a conspicuous member; until in September 1898 the dowager empress executed what was virtually a *coup d'état* which restored her regency, reduced the emperor to a virtual prisoner, and suppressed the reform movement. Foreign influence, upon which were blamed all China's ills, was so resented that a clandestine society began to flourish (its origins are obscure but may date from early in the 18th century). I Ho Ch'uan or 'Fists of Righteous Harmony' was a violently xenophobic and anti-Christian society professing a determination to exterminate all foreign influence in China, and to drive out all 'foreign devils', reinforced by religious rituals and incantations which promised adherents the support of the ancient Chinese gods and invulnerability to foreign weapons. The name by which the society was known to the Europeans was 'Boxers', from the Chinese name and from their ritual shadow-boxing.

There were Boxer sympathisers at the court of the dowager empress, and Tsz'e Hsi viewed the Boxers as a force capable of preserving the dynasty against foreign influence. The degree of official encouragement to the Boxers is uncertain, but little serious attempt was made to suppress the growing power and lawlessness of the movement. Chinese Christians came under attack, and foreign property and railway lines were destroyed, and in late May 1900 two British missionaries were murdered at Yung Ching, some 40 miles from Peking. The foreign diplomats in Peking gave the Chinese government 24 hours to suppress the Boxers or they would call for European troops from the coast; when no action was taken, a force of sailors and marines was ordered to Peking to protect the Legation Quarter of the city, numbering in all some 407 men of eight nationalities, the largest contingents being some 80 men each from Britain and Russia, and about 50 from France, Germany and the USA. The senior foreign diplomat, the British minister, Sir Claude Macdonald, took charge and sent a message to Admiral Sir Edward Seymour at Taku, requesting that he advance on Peking with a supporting force. By mid-June it was obvious that the legations were under threat, for Prince Tuan (a noted reactionary and pro-Boxer) had been appointed head of the Chinese foreign ministry (Tsung-li-Yamen), and it had become evident that Boxer depredations were being assisted by imperial troops from the command of another Boxer supporter, General Tung-fu-hsiang.

The Europeans and Chinese Christians in Peking gathered in two areas of the city, the Legation Quarter and the Pei T'ang Cathedral, the latter defended by a small party of French and Italian seamen. On 11 June the chancellor of the Japanese legation, Mr Sugiyama, was murdered by Chinese soldiers; the Boxers destroyed and burned large areas of the city where were to be found foreign buildings or premises housing Chinese who had traded with foreigners; and on 19 June the foreign diplomats received an ultimatum from the Tsung-li-Yamen, requiring them to quit the city for Tientsin within 24 hours, as their safety could not be guaranteed. The diplomats agreed not to budge, but when the German minister, Baron Klemens von Ketteler, set out for the Tsung-li-Yamen on 20 June, he was murdered. At 4 p.m. on that afternoon the Chinese opened fire on the Legation Quarter.

In addition to the small military force, the defenders were reinforced by a small number of European civilians with military experience; they had small arms but only three machine-guns and an Italian 1pdr quick-firer, and an improvised cannon made from an old gun-barrel left behind in 1860, from which it was possible to fire some Russian 9pdr shells which had been brought to Peking (although the gun had been left in Tientsin). The original commander of the Legation defence, Captain von Thomann of the Austro-Hungarian cruiser SMS *Zenta*, was relieved of command almost at the beginning of the siege and replaced by the more capable Sir Claude Macdonald, who had retired from the army in 1896 at the age of 44; first commissioned into the 74th in 1872, he had served in Egypt in 1882 and as a volunteer with the Black Watch at Suakin, 1884–5.

Admiral Sir Edward Seymour, commander-in-chief of the British China Station, organised a reinforcement as soon as he received Macdonald's request, and on 10 June left Tientsin with a force of 2,100 men (of eight nationalities, including 915 British, 512 Germans and 312 Russians). Using the railway, he intended to reach Peking the same day, but the Boxers had damaged the tracks, and instead of finding the Chinese army of General Nieh Shih-ch'eng ready to assist the Europeans against the Boxers, the Chinese troops were found to be co-operating with them. Having progressed to within about thirty miles of Peking, Seymour was unable to go farther against stiff opposition, and on 17 June began to retire towards Tientsin, marching the last stage as the railway lines had been destroyed, and using junks on the Pei-Ho river to transport his casualties, numbering about 280. On 22 June Seymour occupied the Chinese arsenal at Hsiku, near Tientsin, where he waited for reinforcement.

During Seymour's absence inland, the allied naval commanders lying off Taku determined to act following the capture by the Boxers of the Chinese part of Tientsin, which put the foreign quarter at risk. To secure the route inland, on 17 June the allied admirals captured the Taku Forts by amphibious assault, after an ultimatum to the Chinese garrison to allow allied occupation had been answered by gunfire. Seamen and marines of seven nations participated, landing from eight gunboats and two destroyers; the Americans remained uncommitted following a directive from Washington which forbade them from becoming involved in hostilities against the Chinese. This capture of the Taku Forts must have been the final act which decided the Chinese government to support the Boxers: Nieh Shih-ch'eng's troops began to oppose Seymour, and the ultimatum to the Peking legations and the Chinese declaration of war on the allies on 21 June were the consequences.

Even before news of the landing had spread, however, a furious assault had been launched upon the 'International Settlement' (i.e., the foreign quarter) of Tientsin, by both Boxers and Chinese imperial troops (17 June).

Opposite page: A most unusual uniform for a British unit was that of the Hong Kong Company of Engineers (Submarine Miners), which included a Chinese-style hat and jacket, the latter with the abbreviated shoulder-title 'HK/SMRS'.

Right: Chinese warriors at the time of the Boxer Rebellion: probably the personal retinue of a person of distinction, the clothing being too uniform for typical Boxers; but the traditional weapons are like those used during the rebellion.

The 2,400 defenders were greatly outnumbered and had an over-long perimeter to defend, but with excellent positions of defence planned by the American engineer Herbert Hoover (US President 1929–33), they held out. As the telegraph to Taku was cut, a plea for assistance was taken by courier to the allied forces, by James Watts (a British member of the Tientsin Volunteers) and three Cossacks (20 June). A relief-column reached the beleaguered garrison on 23 June; on the 26th Seymour rejoined the allied forces at Tientsin, and on 13–14 July the allies captured the 'native' (i.e., Chinese) city. Nieh Shih-ch'eng was killed (or committed suicide).

Believing that the foreigners in Peking had been massacred, the allied powers decided to assemble a force sufficiently large to protect their communications before advancing; for which the German General Albrecht, Graf von Waldersee was appointed to command. Before his arrival in China, however, a message was received from the legations that they were still holding out, and were conducting an aggressive defence by making sallies against the besiegers. A relief-force was organised and command given to the British General Sir Alfred Gaselee, comprising some 20,000 men, assembled chiefly from those nations with troops nearest to the scene of the campaign: two Japanese divisions some 10,000 strong, 4,000 Russians, an Indian brigade which brought the British contingent to about 3,000 with 2,000 Americans, 800 French and smaller contingents from Germany, Austria and Italy. Following the line of the Pei-Ho, a British naval brigade left for Peking on 3 August and the main force next day; actions were fought against both Boxers and Chinese troops at Pei Tsang on 5 August, Yang Tsun on 6 August, and Tungchow on 12

Ingenuity in the field: improvised artillery with a team of Chinese ponies devised by the 'despatch vessel' HMS Alacrity *for land operations during the Boxer Rebellion.*

August. The final push towards Peking, carefully planned by Gaselee, was a chaotic scramble for prestige between Russians and Japanese; Gaselee had to order a general advance on the early morning of 14 August, with each contingent entering the city as best it could, and had Chinese resistance been better organised, the refusal of some of the allied contingents to obey the agreed plan could have proved disastrous. In the early afternoon, the 7th Rajputs and Gaselee in person reached the beleaguered legations, marking the end of the siege. Other contingents forced their own way into Peking, some after stiff resistance. The dowager empress and the emperor fled, on 15 August the allies penetrated the imperial 'Forbidden City', and on 16 August Pei T'ang was relieved. The defenders of the legations and Pei T'ang had suffered some 64 dead and 156 wounded, and twelve civilians killed and 23 wounded, plus some hundreds of Chinese Christians.

In September Waldersee and his German 'East Asia Brigade' arrived, and as peace negotiations began the Boxers were dispersed, the most notable action being the capture by the allies of the Boxer stronghold of Pao Ting Fu (20 October), after which the town was burned as a reprisal, upon Waldersee's orders. Crushing penalties were imposed upon China, including the exile or execution of many pro-Boxer sympathisers, a huge financial indemnity, the destruction of fortifications (including the Taku Forts) and a guarantee of security to foreign interests in China, backed by the presence of allied military forces. Anti-foreign societies like the Boxers and the 'Big Sword Society' were proscribed, and anti-foreign activity made punishable by death; the Tsung-li-Yamen was abolished and replaced by a more modern foreign ministry. On 7 September 1901 the Peace Protocol of Peking was concluded between China and the allied powers, and the foreign troops still remaining in Peking were withdrawn on 17 September; except for the legation guards. Foreign contingents remained at specified posts along the line of communication between the capital and the coast. On 7 January 1902 Tsz'e Hsi and the court returned to Peking, without the previous array of Boxer sympathisers, some of whom had been executed to placate the allies, and others (like Prince Tuan) exiled; Li Hung-Chang had died on 7 November 1901.

The Boxer Rebellion effectively signalled the end of the Manchu dynasty, the revolution of 1911 resulting in the establishment of the Republic of China in 1912, and confirming that China could no longer be immune from the modernisation which had been resisted for so long. The triumph of the allies over the disorganised Chinese regime brought them many commercial concessions, and for Russia their occupation of Manchuria, which in all but name became a Russian protectorate. The alliance of eight powers which, despite the internal rivalries, had suppressed the Boxer Rebellion, was of short duration: the Russo–Japanese rivalry evident during the advance on Peking proved to be only a precursor of the Russo–Japanese War, much of which was fought on Chinese territory.

Military Forces

China to 1900. The Chinese military establishment began to be reformed after the T'ai-p'ing rebellion, though some of the previous structure remained. The Manchu forces were still organised in the Eight Banners, supplemented by a territorial militia styled the Defence Army. From 1865 foreign military advisers were introduced to modernise some parts of the army, and selected units were formed from Green Standard personnel, styled *Lien chün* ('New Formations' or 'Disciplined Forces'); although superior to ordinary Green Standard units, their arming and training was not impressive by European standards. Green Standard forces were organised in brigades of infantry battalions (nominally 500 strong), cavalry (250) and garrison and support units. There were also units styled '*Yung*' ('Brave Ones'), volunteers organised in independent detachments, as formed by a number of Chinese generals and warlords; and militia from Mongolia and Tibet, poorly equipped and organised and used mainly on line-of-communications duty. From 1885 there were training establishments to improve the military education of the officer corps, but they appear to have had limited effect.

Following defeat in the Sino–Japanese War, in which the western organisation and equipment of the Japanese

Bluejackets from the cruiser HMS Orlando *with a Nordenfelt machine-gun, landed at Tientsin during the Boxer Rebellion. Their 'landing rig' includes blue uniforms with bell-bottomed trousers tucked into gaiters, and straw 'sennet' hats; the metal object atop the ammunition-boxes at right is the 'hopper' of the Nordenfelt gun, into which cartridges were fed.*

proved decisive, further attempts were made to modernise the Chinese forces and introduce more European-style organisation, weaponry and tactics. This resulted in the formation of semi-independent 'armies', though this term is somewhat misleading as the strength of most probably only equated with that of one or two European divisions, and they were generally regarded as being the personal command of a particular leader rather than an integral part of a unified army structure. Principal among these was Chang Chih-tung's Self-Strengthening Army, which in 1897 comprised ten infantry battalions, each of five 50-man companies, two cavalry units of three 60-man squadrons, two artillery battalions of four batteries each, and two engineer units; trained by Germans, their arms included Mauser and Mannlicher rifles. Another was Yuan Shih-K'ai's Pacification Army, formed in 1894 and re-organised in 1895, about 7,000 strong and including five infantry battalions, four cavalry troops, artillery and engineers. Shortly before the Boxer Rebellion General Nieh Shih-ch'eng's Tenacious Army, and General Sung Ch'iang's Resolute Army were created; both possessed modern weapons but training and discipline were poor.

Such was also the case with much of the 'Guards Army' formed in late 1898 in northern China, composed of five divisions. The Resolute, Tenacious and Pacification Armies each formed one division; another comprised the 'Kansu Braves', a disorderly Islamic force recruited in that province, mostly from *Yung* units, and the fifth was composed of Bannermen. The best of the Chinese troops (the Self-Strengthening Army and Yuan Shih-K'ai's army) were not committed in the Boxer war, their commanders taking care to preserve their forces. The greater part of the imperial troops around Peking at the time of the rebellion were the Kansu Braves. European opinions were somewhat dismissive: 'The Chinese Army is a factor that scarcely bears very seriously on the conditions in the Far East ... only a very small proportion of this force is worth anything, as but a meagre percentage is armed with European weapons, has had European drilling and discipline, or has, in fact, received any military education. The territorial troops, or "Green Flags", as they are termed, number over half a million, but they are a mere undisciplined rabble, whose main *raison d'être* is to give the handling of their pay to the provincial authorities.'[11]

Costume and equipment was extremely varied. Units with the best organisation and modern weapons tended to wear quasi-European uniform; often with a lettered panel on the breast identifying rank and unit. The less well-equipped wore civilian dress, often with a smock or tabard with identification-panels on breast and sometimes back; others wore civilian dress with no distinguishing marks. The latter was the dress worn by the Boxers, their allegiance generally identified by a red head-scarf, sash, apron, tabard or ribbons. Like the best of the various generals' armies, the 'New Formations' had some training in

European tactics and with European weapons, but the remainder (including Green Standard and Eight Banner forces, and the Boxers) used traditional Chinese weapons and tactics. The Bannermen used some primitive firearms, but also comprised archers, swordsmen and 'pikemen' who wielded a variety of polearms, including spears, tridents, and weapons sometimes described as 'halberds' but with blades more akin to a medieval European glaive than to a pole-axe. Among the Bannermen were skirmishers styled 'Tigermen', lightly-armed troops who preceded the rest, armed with swords and shields and clothed in yellow-and-black striped garments resembling tiger skin, and even having caps with 'ears' representing a tiger's head. Once the Boxer movement had received official support, attempts were made to form a type of militia units from Boxers, but it is unlikely that many received any kind of uniform before the rebellion was suppressed.

Westerners, Boxer Rebellion. The largest of the allied contingents were the two Japanese divisions, and the Russian force drawn largely from the nearest garrisons, Vladivostok and Port Arthur. The German East Asia Brigade (two infantry brigades, an *Uhlan* regiment, artillery and technical units) arrived only at the end of the rebellion; prior to that the German forces in theatre comprised only the 3rd Marine Battalion (*Seebataillon*), supporting troops and a naval brigade drawn from German ships in the East Asia Squadron. Naval personnel represented the entire contribution from Austria-Hungary (some 400 men) and the initial Italian contingent, although an *ad hoc* formation of *Bersaglieri*, infantry and *Alpini* was sent to China later, with artillery provided by the fleet. French forces included the naval brigade and units sent from Indo-China: regular Marine Infantry, Algerian *Turcos*, *Chasseurs d'Afrique*, elements of the Indo–China Artillery and locally raised units (Annamites and Tonkinese). The initial US forces were marines and seamen from the Far Eastern Squadron, but considerable reinforcements were sent, of regular infantry, cavalry, marines, artillery and supports. From Britain, the 1st Chinese Regiment and 2/Royal Welch Fusiliers were already in northern China (the latter the only British battalion to serve in the war, although detached personnel from other units were present); in addition to the usual naval brigade, the subsequent expeditionary force was drawn from the Indian Army (initially two brigades and supports, including Royal Artillery), and reinforced by more Indian units, including Imperial Service troops, notably the Jodhpur Lancers.

A number of 'local forces' were formed in the European settlements in China. The principal British colony, Hong Kong, formed a European volunteer corps in 1854, under threat of pirate and Russian operations; most members of this ephemeral unit were British. Other locally raised forces included 'Coolie Corps' of porters formed for various expeditions (the Canton Coolie Corps for North China in 1860, for example), but the Hong Kong

Allied forces in action against the Boxers in Tientsin; this engraving after H. M. Paget emphasises the international co-operation which occurred during the Boxer Rebellion: depicted are British seamen and marines (nearest the enemy), Americans (in slouch hats), Russians (left mid-ground, in white with peaked caps), Japanese (dark uniforms, front left) and French (the white-clad seaman in the foreground).

Regiment, formed 1892, was not Chinese in composition but Indian. Recruited in India, it comprised five companies of Punjabis (one transferred directly from the 7th Bengal Infantry), two of Pathans and one of Hindustanis; officers were British, seconded from British or Indian regiments. Both officers and men were engaged on a 5-year enlistment. The unit first saw action in 1899, when some Chinese opposition was encountered when taking over the New Territories; and it served in the reliefs of Tientsin and the Peking legations during the Boxer Rebellion. It was disbanded in October 1902. Also at Hong Kong were stationed four companies of 'Asiatic Artillery' (Indians with British officers) and a detachment of submarine miners.

Following the British acquisition of a lease on Wei-Hai-Wei (in Shantung province) in 1898, formation of the 1st Chinese or Wei-Hai-Wei Regiment was authorised. Commanded by Major Hamilton Bower of the Indian Staff Corps and recruited locally, its men were enrolled for a 3-year enlistment, for service anywhere in the world; officers and senior NCOs were British. It was distinguished by a somewhat unusual uniform, ordinary dress including a naval-style straw hat, white or khaki shirt and trousers, puttees and red cummerbund, with a 'dress' or winter uniform of a long, dark blue shirt of Indian Army style and a small, dark blue turban. The regiment served at Tientsin and at the relief of Peking, gaining a battle-honour for the

Heroes of colonial wars could be exploited for commercial advertising: these photographs of Sir Claude Macdonald (left), who led the defence of the legations at Peking, and Sir Edward Seymour (right), who led the relief forces, were given as cards in packs of Ogden's 'Guinea Gold' cigarettes.

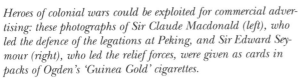

former (which featured on the badge adopted subsequently, a representation of the gate of Tientsin). Having been administered initially by the Admiralty, the colony was transferred to the Colonial Office in January 1901, and the regiment was disbanded in June 1906.

A volunteer corps was formed in Shanghai in 1853, in the face of attacks upon Europeans, which culminated in a small punitive action against a camp of imperial Chinese troops on 3 April 1854, following an assault upon some Europeans. The force engaged in this skirmish (the 'Battle of Muddy Flat', in which the Chinese were routed quickly) comprised British and American landing-parties and some volunteers, 300–400 strong in all. The original volunteer corps was augmented by a unit of Mounted Rifles, later styled Light Horse, and in 1892 by an engineer corps. The unit was mobilised during the T'ai-p'ing rebellion, the Sino–Japanese War and the Boxer Rebellion, and during various periods of civil unrest including the 'Ningpo Joss

House Riots' of 1874, and riots in 1891, 1896, 1897 and 1898, and on a number of occasions in the 20th century. A similar volunteer corps was formed by the British residents of Tientsin in 1898, which by 1900 had reached a strength of almost 100. It participated in the defence of Tientsin during the Boxer Rebellion, some of its members serving as interpreters for the Peking relief-force; but probably its most significant service was the ride made by one of its members, James Watts, who with three Cossacks carried the plea for help from the beleaguered Westerners to the allied forces at Taku, the relief of the city being the direct consequence of this notable minor epic.[12]

Notes

1. *United Service Journal*, 1840, vol. I, p. 414.
2. 'An Observer' in ibid., vol. II, p. 111.
3. Gough's dispatch, 18 October 1841; *London Gazette*, 11 February 1842.
4. Gough's dispatch, 25 July 1842; *London Gazette*, 11 November 1842.
5. Elgin's dispatch, 25 October 1860; *London Gazette*, 28 December 1860.
6. Gough's dispatch on Chapu, 20 May 1842; *London Gazette*, 18 October 1842.
7. *United Service Magazine*, 1842, vol. II, pp. 415–16.
8. Return rendered by Lieutenant-Colonel P. Montgomerie, CRA, 26 July 1842; *London Gazette*, 11 November 1842.
9. 'Closing Events of the Campaign in China', by Captain G. Loch, *Colburn's United Service Magazine*, 1843, vol. II,

pp. 447–8.

10. Ibid., vol. III, p. 468.

11. *Navy and Army Illustrated*, vol. IV, 30 April 1898, p. 137.

12. The story is summarised in 'James Watts' Ride from Tientsin to Taku, 1900', by Major A. McK. Annand, in *Journal of the Society for Army Historical Research*, 1977, vol. LV, pp. 201–9.

References

Allen, Revd. R. *The Siege of the Peking Legations*, London, 1901.

Beeching, J. *The Chinese Opium Wars*, London, 1975.

Bernard, W. D. *The Nemesis in China, comprising a History of the Late War in that Country*, London, 1846 (rev. edn.).

Bodin, L. E. *The Boxer Rebellion*, London, 1979.

Bond, B. (ed.). *Victorian Military Campaigns*, London, 1967 (includes 'The Third China War, 1860', by J. Selby).

Collis, M. *Foreign Mud: being an Account of the Opium Imbroglio at Canton in the 1830s and the Anglo-Chinese War that followed*, London, 1946.

Featherstone, D. *Victoria's Enemies: An A–Z of British Colonial Warfare*, London, 1989.

Fleming, P. *The Siege at Peking*, London, 1959.

Grant, General Sir J. Hope. *Incidents in the China War of 1860*, ed. Captain H. Knollys, Edinburgh, 1875.

Harfield, Major A. J. *British and Indian Armies on the China Coast 1785–1985*, Farnham, 1990.

Holt, E. *The Opium Wars in China*, London, 1962.

Hurd, D. *The Arrow War: an Anglo-Chinese Confusion 1856–60*, London, 1967.

Inglis, B. *The Opium War*, London, 1976.

Knight, I. *Queen Victoria's Enemies (4): Asia, Australasia and the Americas*, London, 1990.

Mann, M. *China 1860*, Salisbury, 1989.

Martin, C. *The Boxer Rebellion*, London, 1968.

Narbeth, C. *Admiral Seymour's Expedition & Taku Forts 1900*, Chippenham, 1980 (naval medal-rolls and concise history of the expedition).

Nicholls, B. *Bluejackets and Boxers: Australia's Naval Expedition to the Boxer Uprising*, Sydney, 1986.

O'Connor, R. *The Boxer Rebellion*, London, 1974.

Rasmussen, O. D. *Tientsin*, Tientsin, 1925 (includes the siege during the Boxer Rebellion).

Savage-Landor, R. *China and the Allies*, London, 1901 (Boxer Rebellion).

Selby, J. *The Paper Dragon: an Account of the China Wars 1840–1900*, London, 1968.

Smith, R. *Mercenaries and Mandarins: the Ever-Victorious Army of Nineteenth-Century China*, New York, 1978.

Swinhoe, R. *Narrative of the North China Campaign of 1860*, London, 1861.

Wilson, A. *The Ever-Victorious Army*, 1868 (r/p London. 1991).

Wolseley, Lieutenant-Colonel G. J. *Narrative of the War with China in 1860*, London, 1862.

EAST INDIES

In its widest sense the term 'East Indies' was used to include the subcontinent of India, but is used here to cover those colonies in which there was military activity, other than in mainland India or Ceylon.

Malay Peninsula

By the beginning of the 20th century the Malay Peninsula could be divided into five sections: the Straits Settlements; Federated Malay States; the non-federated Malay states under British protection; the independent state of Johor (within the sphere of British influence); and states to the north, within the sphere of influence of Siam.

Defences of Peking: the An-Ting Gate of the Tartar City, 1900.

Federated Malay States

The Federated States were independent states under British protection, each ruled by its own sultan, but these rulers were bound by treaty to accept the guidance of a British Resident, whose immediate superior was a resident-general responsible to the governor of the Straits Settlements. The states comprised Perak, Selangor and the confederation of Negri Sembilan ('Nine States') on the west coast, and Pahang on the east coast. The actual federation was effected on 1 July 1896 following the increase of British influence in the region.

A British Resident was sent to Negri Sembilan in 1887 to restore the ancient federal system; initially the states involved were Gemencheh, Gunong Pasir, Inas, Jempol, Johol, Rembau, Tampin, Terachi and Ulu Muar. In 1896 two more were added: Jelebu, taken under British protection in 1886, and Sungei Ujong, in which a civil war had been resolved in 1873 when a military force was sent in, to place the territory under British protection.

Following a period of dynastic conflict, the sultan of Pahang concluded a treaty with the governor of the Straits Settlements, and accepted a British Resident in 1888. A rebellion by some local chieftains over taxation, perhaps with the sympathy of the sultan, occurred in 1891–2, and having once taken flight the rebels returned in June 1894, raiding Pahang from Kelantan, where they had been permitted to shelter. The Resident at Pahang, Hugh Clifford, led an expedition into Kelantan and Trengganu in 1895 which ended the trouble, the rebellious chieftains being exiled to Siam.

The first European settlement in Perak was established by the Dutch in 1650, from which they were ejected by the British in 1795. In 1818 the state was conquered by Siam, but restored to independence by Anglo–Siamese treaty in 1824. A dispute over the succession to the sultanate of Perak, and threats to the safety of Chinese workers in the tin mines (who were British subjects) led Britain to intervene, and in 1874 the major contender for the throne, Abdullah, was installed as sultan with British support, in return for the appointment of a British Resident. This individual, James Birch, was somewhat insensitive to local customs, and was murdered on 2 November 1875. A punitive expedition was mounted from India under the command of General Colbourn, comprising British and Gurkha troops, a detachment of Madras Sappers and Miners, and a strong naval brigade. The murderers were apprehended and hanged, Sultan Abdullah banished to the Seychelles, and a regent appointed in his place. This was the most serious operation mounted in the region, and a clasp to the India General Service Medal was authorised for those involved in Perak between November 1875 and March 1876.

Britain's first contact with Selangor was a trade treaty with the governor of Penang in 1818. A civil war over the rulership of Selangor (1867–73) was resolved when a force from Pahang was sent (with the encouragement of the

governor of the Straits Settlements) to confirm the rule of the sultan. Following some piracy in 1874 the sultan accepted the imposition of a British Resident.

Straits Settlements

Formed in 1826 and administered by the government of India until 1867 when crown colony status was granted, the Straits Settlements comprised Singapore, Malacca, the islands of the Dindings, Penang (or Prince of Wales Island) and Province Wellesley. The governor of the Straits Settlements was also high commissioner for the Federated Malay States, British North Borneo and Sarawak, and latterly governor of Labuan.

Singapore, the most important British colony in the region, was owned originally by the sultan of Johor, until in 1819 Thomas Stamford Raffles negotiated with the Temenggong of Johor (governor) and its sultan, for the almost uninhabited island to be taken over by the East India Company as a trading station in competition against the Dutch. Initially Singapore was a subordinate post to Bencoolen, the Company's main base in Sumatra, but in 1823 it was transferred to the administration of Bengal, and to the Straits Settlements when that colony was founded in 1826. From 1889 Singapore was an independent military command; its first head was Sir Charles Warren.

Malacca fell to the Portuguese in 1511, and was taken from them by the Dutch in 1641. In 1795 the colony was captured by Britain and not restored until 1818, but in 1824 was exchanged for the East India Company settlement at Bencoolen in Sumatra, and remained in British possession thereafter.

The island of Penang was ceded to the East India Company by the sultan of Kedah in 1785 in return for an annuity. The island was virtually uninhabited, and the colony was founded in July 1786; in 1796 it became a penal settlement into which 700 convicts were transferred from the Andaman Islands. In 1805 it was made into a presidency under the East India Company, and continued as the seat of government from the formation of the Straits Settlements until Singapore was made the capital in 1837.

Province Wellesley, on the mainland opposite Penang, was ceded to the East India Company by the sultan of Kedah in 1798 in return for an increased annuity. The Dindings, islands in the Perak river and a small tract of the adjoining mainland were ceded to the British government by the treaty of Pangkor with the sultan of Perak in 1874.

Non-federated Malay States

The non-federated states were not taken under British protection until 1909, following a treaty between Britain and Siam; these were Kedah, Kelantan, Perlis and Trengganu. Kedah had maintained political relations with the East India Company from the 18th century, leasing the island of Penang to the Company; but after a period of independence, Siam re-asserted control by force in 1821.

Johor

The independent state of Johor (or Johore) maintained friendly relations with the British, ceding Singapore to the East India Company in 1819. Upon the deposition of the sultan in 1855, Britain recognised the rule of his chief minister, the Temenggong; his son, Abubakar, visited Britain and was given the title of maharajah (1879) and in 1885 was recognised as sultan. It is notable that when the 5th Light Infantry at Singapore mutinied in 1915, the sultan personally led a contingent of his troops on the Penang mail train to support the British in their suppression of the revolt.

Dutch Colonies

British involvement in Sumatra was very limited. The first trading posts were established there by the Portuguese in the 16th century, but they were driven out by the Dutch, who extended their control over the region. Britain established a post at Bencoolen (Benkulen) in 1685, but after much rivalry with the Dutch it was exchanged for Malacca in 1824, and in May 1825 Bencoolen was taken over by the Dutch. The most powerful state in Sumatra was Achin, the Achinese being a people of Malayan background, and diplomatic relations were maintained with the ruler of Achin by both Elizabeth I and James I. Although the power of the Achinese declined (especially after a chief of Arab origin ascended the throne in 1699), it was considered important by Britain to maintain good relations, and in 1819 a treaty was concluded with the government of India which excluded other Europeans from residence in Achin. When Britain left Sumatra an understanding was reached which prevented the Dutch from making war upon Achin, but in the latter half of the 19th century the Dutch consolidated their hold on Sumatra by a series of campaigns against the indigenous rulers. Britain abandoned protection of Achin by a convention agreed with the Dutch in November 1871; in 1873 the Dutch declared war and captured Achin in January 1874, but guerrilla warfare continued into the 20th century.

The Dutch began to establish themselves in Java during the 16th century, but their expansion from the original trading settlements was slow, and resistance to them continued into the second half of the 19th century. British involvement in Java occurred during a period of Anglo–Dutch hostility during the Napoleonic Wars. On orders from the governor-general of India, Lord Minto, an expedition under Lieutenant-General Sir Samuel Auchmuty was sent to Java; it landed on 4 August 1811, captured the capital, Batavia (now Djakarta), on 8 August, and engaged General Janssens' Dutch force at Weltevreede on 10 August. This drove the Dutch into a strong fortification at Cornelis, which Auchmuty assaulted and

captured on 26 August, effectively deciding the campaign. (Auchmuty's dispatch reported the killing of some 2,000 of the enemy, the capture of 5,000 troops including three generals, and the dispersal of the remainder; he reported British and Company military and naval losses to the end of the month as 129 Europeans killed, 665 wounded and three missing, and 27 Indians killed, 123 wounded and thirteen missing). Janssens made off and assembled another force; Auchmuty pursued him with a small contingent and after a short fight routed the Dutch at Jattoo (or 'Jatee Allee') on 16 September, for the British loss of two killed and ten wounded. On 17 September Janssens concluded the Capitulation of Samarang, by which Java, Macassar, Palembang and Timor were ceded to Britain. Two expeditions against recalcitrant tribesmen had to be made in 1812, both led by Sir Rollo Gillespie; against Palembang in Sumatra and a sterner test involving the storming of a large, fortified enclosure at Dyodyocarta in Java. The Dutch possessions, Java included, were restored after the end of the Napoleonic Wars.

Borneo

At the end of the 19th century the island of Borneo was composed of four political divisions: British North Borneo, administered by the British North Borneo Company; Brunei and Sarawak, under British protection; and the greater part of the island, Dutch Borneo.

Dutch trading posts were established in Borneo in 1604, British some five years later. In 1759 the British obtained possession of Balambangan island and the northeast tip of Borneo from the sultan of Sulu, and negotiated a treaty with the sultan of Brunei in 1774, but in 1775 the British military post was destroyed by local chieftains who resented the sultan of Sulu's cessation of their territory. Despite some British diplomatic contacts with local rulers during their occupation of Java, this left the Dutch with a virtual monopoly on Borneo, but Dutch colonisation was slow and they were unable to enforce a check upon the huge fleets of native pirates which operated from Borneo, menacing the trade-routes to Singapore.

In 1838 the remarkable James Brooke appeared in the region; the son of an East India Company civil servant, he was a gentleman-adventurer and sailed his schooner *Royalist* to Sarawak, a province of Brunei, whose sultan, Omar Ali, was an ineffective ruler whose territory was beset by civil war. Brooke allied himself to Muda Hasim, the sultan's heir and regent in Sarawak, suppressed the insurrection and was rewarded with the position of Rajah of Sarawak. In 1843–4 Brooke and Captain Henry Keppel of the Royal Navy (acting in the interests of British trade) broke up the pirate fleets; and in July 1846, with the assistance of a small British naval force, prevented a perceived attempt to re-possess his 'kingdom' by sailing into Brunei bay and extracting from the sultan confirmation of his title and sovereign rights to Sarawak, mining rights in his dominions, and the annexation by Britain of the island of Labuan, where coal deposits had been found. A final defeat of the pirates was achieved in 1848 by a combination of the Royal Navy and Brooke's forces. In 1857 there was an insurrection in Sarawak, involving the Chinese who had worked as gold miners in the region for generations; but Brooke's nephew, Charles Johnson Brooke, raised a force of Malays and Dyaks and expelled the rebels. Charles succeeded as Rajah on James Brooke's death in 1868, and in 1888 Sarawak became a British protectorate.

In northern Borneo (or Sabah) in 1878 the sultan of Sulu transferred his rights to a commercial company (in which was involved Admiral Sir Henry Keppel, Brooke's collaborator), and in 1882 a royal charter was granted to the British North Borneo Company. Its territory was increased progressively, and in 1888 it was made a British protectorate, but government control extended only to external relations, administration remaining with the Company. Labuan, a crown colony from 1848, was placed under Company administration in 1890, after which the governor of North Borneo received a royal commission as governor of Labuan in addition to his commission from the Company; this remained the case until Labuan was attached to the Straits Settlements in 1905. Expansion of Company territory (by agreement with the sultan of Brunei) was resented by some of the indigenous population and led to some violence and raiding. The most troublesome of the local leaders was Mat (or Mahomet) Saleh, against whom a number of punitive expeditions were organised, including one in 1897 led by the Resident of Labuan, Mr. Hewett, with a small force of police and Sikhs, which fought a minor action in December; and another under Captain C. H. Harrington in January 1898. An agreement was reached with Mat Saleh in 1898, but he caused further trouble and in 1899 Harrington led an expedition into Saleh's Tambunan territory, during which Mat Saleh was killed (31 January 1900). His followers caused some unrest for a time. For these operations the British North Borneo Company issued two campaign medals, one with clasps for the 1897–98 expeditions (and a later clasp for an expedition to Rundum in 1915–16), and one specifically for the Tambunan expedition of 1899–1900.

French Colonies

The French colonies of Ile de France and Bourbon – the islands of Mauritius and Réunion respectively – provided bases for French commerce-raiders during the Napoleonic Wars, and thus were targets for British occupation.

Mauritius was first claimed by Portugal, but from 1598 was colonised by the Dutch, its name a tribute to their *stadtholder*, Maurice of Nassau. They abandoned the island in 1710; from 1715 to 1767 it belonged to the French East India Company (which changed the name to Ile de

France), and thereafter to the French government. As a base for French raiders it presented a threat to the British East India trade, so after the loss of four frigates in an action at Grand Port in August 1810 the British sent an expedition under the command of Major-General the Hon. John Abercromby (son of Ralph, the 'hero of Egypt'). Abercromby's force of British and Company troops, some 10,000 strong, landed on 29 November 1810; and although the smaller French garrison of General Decaen made a sturdy resistance, the island was surrendered on 3 December. British casualties were 29 dead, 99 wounded and 45 missing, of whom three were 'supposed to be dead'.[1] British possession of Mauritius was confirmed by the Treaty of Paris in 1814.

Réunion island was originally named Mascarenhas after its Portuguese discoverer, but after it had been possessed by France (1638) its name was changed to Bourbon; this royalist term being unacceptable to the French republican government, it was changed to Réunion in 1793 (also known as Ile de Bonaparte during the Napoleonic empire), reverting to Bourbon upon the restoration of that dynasty, and finally to Réunion in 1848. It was a possession of the French East India Company until 1767, then of the French government. To prohibit the use of the island as a base for French ships, a British expedition was sent in 1809, under Lieutenant-Colonel Henry Keating of the 56th, which captured the island of Roderigues, raided Bourbon in September and captured the port of St. Paul. Using Roderigues as a base, an expedition for the occupation of the whole island was prepared, of British and Madras troops, led by Keating; these landed on 7 July 1810, and after some resistance by Colonel St. Susanne's French garrison, the governor surrendered on 8 July and the town of St. Paul on 10 July. The island remained in British hands until restored to France in April 1815.

Military Forces, East Indies

The only truly organised military forces encountered by the British in the East Indies were those which garrisoned the Dutch and French colonies. Governor-General Janssens' force in 1811 comprised an artillery regiment of three battalions, nine infantry and two *Jäger* battalions, a cavalry regiment and six garrison battalions (with garrison battalions detached at Macassar, Palembang and Timor). These were part of a virtually newly created colonial army, formed by Marshal Daendels from his arrival as governor-general in January 1808, using the existing European garrison and some sailors as a cadre, and conscripting local natives to fill the ranks; of almost 18,000 under arms in 1811, less than 2,500 were Europeans, and all regiments were partly European and partly native. On 3 August 1811, for example, the day before the British landing in Java, the Dutch force at Batavia comprised 185 staff, 1,801 Europeans, 1,397 Amboynese and 9,981 'natives', with 213 Europeans, 184 Amboynese and 774 'natives' non-effective from sickness. The statistics of individual units exemplify this unusual practice of integrating European and 'native' troops within the same corps: the 3rd Line Regiment, for example, comprised 140 Europeans, 405 Amboynese and 1,405 'natives', plus 33 staff and 26 Europeans and 224 'natives' sick. Evidently some élite companies were entirely European (a European *voltigeur* company is listed at Batavia and a grenadier company at Surabaya), and some auxiliary forces were all 'native', as the Samarang Legion is noted as having two staff (presumably Europeans) and 65 'natives', and the Surabaya Legion one European and 1,836 'natives'. The force of ordnance was considerable: at Batavia, Weltevreede and Cornelis the British captured 504 iron guns, 209 brass guns, 35 brass mortars and nineteen brass howitzers. The fact that some of the Dutch levies were not formidable seems proven by an incident at Jattoo, when a large body of cavalry, armed with spears and wearing cocked hats, turned and fled when attacked by a single British officer (Auchmuty's ADC) and were pursued for some miles by this officer and one other member of the general's staff, without attempting resistance!

The French forces were fewer in number. On Mauritius, the Ile de France Regiment was some 800 strong (including more than 200 foreigners, mostly Irish, conscripted from prisoners of war), plus a sepoy battalion, a naval battalion, an artillery contingent and a mounted bodyguard troop, together about 2,000 strong; with a National Guard perhaps 2,500 in number, including two battalions of African slaves (*Chasseurs de la Réserve*) officered by their white owners or plantation overseers, considerably fewer than the 10,000 National Guardsmen quoted in some British sources. The French troops in Réunion included a small unit of *Chasseurs de la Réunion* raised from the white inhabitants, with a few 'free Negroes', some three companies of *Cipahis* (sepoys) formed from prisoners of war, and three National Guard companies.

British forces in the East Indies were drawn from the British and Indian armies and navy, and some locally raised corps were employed. As in other climes, many locations were found unhealthy for Europeans, so as early as about 1686 the East India Company authorised the enlistment of 'Topasses' at Bencoolen, local inhabitants of Portuguese descent who were adjudged more likely to survive the climate and local cuisine than the British, whose high mortality was at that time ascribed to bad housing and a diet of buffalo and rice. The recruitment of Malays was an important resource in the late 18th and early 19th centuries (see the section on Ceylon), and use of local recruits continued, the roles of military and police often merging: at Labuan, for example, the military garrison was withdrawn in 1871 because of ill-health, after which peace was maintained by a small police force of Punjabis and Malays. Brooke's force that defeated the pirates in 1843 was a mixture of British seamen from Keppel's HMS *Dido*, Brooke's sloop *Jolly Bachelor*, and a force of Dyaks aboard native boats (*prahus*); for the final drive against the pirates in 1848 Brooke's native 'army' was about 3,000 strong. Latterly Sarawak's military force consisted of some 250 Sikhs and Dyaks under a British commandant, a small police force and a 'navy' consisting of some small steam-vessels.

A more 'regular' force was the Java Hussars (or Java Volunteers), two cavalry troops formed in 1812 under Captain L. H. O'Brien of the Madras Cavalry, which was disbanded when Java was restored to the Dutch; and the Bourbon Regiment, a 'native' corps formed there in April 1811, taken on to the regular establishment in January 1812, which served there and in Mauritius until sent to the West Indies in 1815, being disbanded in April 1816 and the men transferred to the 1st West India Regiment. Because of riots and internal unrest, a Singapore Volunteer Rifle Corps was formed in 1854 and existed until December 1887 when it was disbanded; a new Singapore Volunteer Artillery was formed in February 1888. In 1901 corps of European engineers and rifles were created in addition to the artillery, and two infantry companies, one Eurasian and one Chinese. A company of 'Asiatic Artillery' (recruited from Indians) and a submarine mining detachment were stationed at Singapore, and at Mauritius two companies of 'Asiatic Artillery', with officers and NCOs seconded from the Royal Artillery.

Note
[1] Return of casualties by Deputy-Adjutant-General W. Nicholson, in Abercromby's dispatch of 7 December 1810; *London Gazette*, 13 February 1811.

References
Chartrand, A. *Napoleon's Overseas Army*, London, 1989 (includes the Dutch and French forces in the East Indies).
Harfield, Major A. *British and Indian Armies in the East Indies 1685–1935*, Chippenham, 1984.
Thorn, Major W. *Memoir of the Conquest of Java*, London, 1815.
(Excellent modern studies are Harfield, Major A. 'Richard Cannon and the Conquest of Mauritius', in *Journal of the Society for Army Historical Research*, vol. LXVIII, 1990, pp. 232–42; and Chartrand, R. 'The French Version of the Capture of Mauritius in 1810', in ibid., vol. LXIX, 1991, pp. 130–3.

JAPAN

Although no 'colonial war' was fought against Japan, some military and naval activity was necessary in defence of British interests at the time of the first major ingress of western influence into Japan, which as in China was met with considerable resentment from the more traditional elements in Japanese society. At the head of that society was the emperor, but the central temporal authority was the *shōgun*, a 'generalissimo' bearing a title which dated from the 12th century and was derived from its original function of commander-in-chief of the Japanese forces (from *sho*, to hold, and *gun*, army). The holder of the office of *shōgun* from 1857 was Keiki, known as Yoshinobu, inheritor of some two and a half centuries of the *shōgunate* being held by the Tokugawa clan. (In contemporary dispatches the *shōgun* is referred to as 'the Tycoon', a name used at this period). Although theoretically the chief temporal power in Japan (the *mikado* being the spiritual power), the authority of the *shōgun* was not sufficient to curb the anti-foreign propensities of the territorial rulers, the *diamyōs*.

Under a policy directed towards the expulsion of foreigners from Japan, introduced by reactionary members of the ruling authorities, a number of murderous attacks were made upon westerners resident in Japan, and in 1863 the local chief at Shimonoseki had his shore-batteries open fire on western ships. As the *shōgun* had insufficient power to exact reparation, a punitive expedition, of mostly British ships was sent to demolish the forts, destroy the chief's ships and disperse his military followers. Some three months later action had to be taken against another chieftain, the *daimyō* of Satsuma, after an attack on a party of Britons in which one traveller was killed and two injured. This was not part of a deliberate anti-foreigner policy but was the consequence of a breach of etiquette by the travellers, who were attacked as they forced their way through the cortege of the Satsuma *daimyō* on the road from Yokohama to Yedo (now Tokyo); any Japanese attempting the same would have met with similar retribution. Consequently, the *daimyō* refused to surrender the perpetrators, and as the *shōgun*'s influence was again insufficient to force compliance, Vice-Admiral Augustus Kuper was sent with a naval force to exact revenge, accompanied by Colonel Edward St John Neale, the British *chargé d'affaires*. The latter's diplomatic efforts proving unavailing, on 15–16 August 1863 Kuper's squadron bombarded the shore-batteries at Kagoshima, captured three steamers belonging to 'the Satsuma', sank five of his junks, and opened fire on his palace; Kuper reported that 'there is every reason to suppose that the palace has been destroyed, as many shell were seen to burst in it, and the fire, which is still raging, affords reasonable ground for believing that the entire town of Kagosima [*sic*] is now a mass of ruins'.[1] The squadron involved (which suffered thirteen dead and fifty injured in the operation) consisted of HMSs *Euryalus* (flagship, a frigate), the paddle-sloop *Argus*, gun-vessels *Coquette* and *Racehorse*, corvette *Pearl* and sloop *Perseus*. The Japanese artillery in the shore-batteries included 58 'siege guns', eleven field-guns and twelve mortars.

Continuing hostilities against foreigners culminated in an attack on the British legation at Yedo, in which the British minister, Sir Rutherford Alcock, narrowly escaped with his life. When the *shōgun* declared his inability to prevent further attacks or to guarantee the safety of the legation, Alcock applied for a British force to protect it; the vanguard, two companies of 2/20th Foot, landed at Yokohama on 23 January 1864. It was increased to include the whole of the 2/20th, detachments of the 67th and 2nd Baluch Regiments, and a half-battery of Royal Artillery; a second half-battery of two 9pdrs and a 24pdr howitzer was formed in March 1865 and crewed by members of the 2/20th. On 20 October 1864 this British force held a review at Yokohama, which members of the Japanese government attended, to demonstrate British power and to support those *diamyōs* favourably disposed towards the westerners. In this it succeeded completely, as Alcock reported: 'Of all the triumphs a soldier can win, none can be more satisfactory, or so entirely without alloy, as a moral victory such as has now been gained [by] the men, who have thus peacefully, but most efficiently, upheld the interests and dignity of our country, at a time when both were in danger, and any evidence of weakness must have seriously compromised them.'[2]

Further demonstrations of western power were made, notably by a British, French and Dutch fleet in 1865, before agreements were concluded and the modernisers in Japan began to take their country, at great speed, into the modern world; perhaps the most notable mark of modernisation was the voluntary resignation of the *shōgunate* by Keiki, in October 1867; he was the last holder of this office. Before the 20th were withdrawn from Japan in April–May 1866, they suffered an atrocious crime committed as an anti-foreign protest: on the road to Yokohama on 21 November 1864, Major George Baldwin and Lieutenant Nicholas Bird were ambushed and murdered by two samurai. Four Japanese were executed by the Japanese authorities as a result, the chief murderer, Shimiduz Seiji, in public and in the presence of the 2/20th in December 1864. (Baldwin must be counted as exceptionally unfortunate, having only a short time before joined the 20th from the 31st, in which he had survived the Crimean and Chinese campaigns, including the storming of the Redan at Sevastopol. His father, who had served at Waterloo with the 3/14th, had been killed at Chillianwalla.)

Notes

1. Kuper's dispatch, 17 August 1863; *London Gazette*, 30 October 1863.
2. Alcock to Lieutenant-Colonel

H. R. Browne, 20th, quoted in Smyth, Lieutenant B. *History of the XX Regiment 1688–1888*, London and Manchester, 1889, p. 303.

V
THE AMERICAS AND
THE ATLANTIC

THE AMERICAS AND THE ATLANTIC

BERMUDA

An important trading post and naval harbour, Bermuda was first colonised by Britain in 1612 as an offshoot of the Virginia Company. In 1614 the Bermuda Company became responsible for the colony, until the revocation of its charter in November 1684, when the crown assumed direct control, through a governor.

Because of its strategic position, Bermuda was defended from the earliest period: eight or nine small forts were built by the early settlers, and in 1614 one of these drove away two Spanish ships. Progressively, a formidable array of defences was established; as early as 1624 no fewer than six forts protected each of the principal anchorages, Saint George's Harbour and Saint Catherine's Harbour, and by about 1700 the entire vulnerable coastline of the Bermudan islands was protected by a string of fortifications. At times of danger this defensive system was upgraded, with modern ordnance being installed during the Victorian period.

Bermuda's strategic position as an Atlantic outpost resulted in its becoming one of the most important naval bases, garrisoned by British troops; but there was in addition an organisation of local forces. From 1687 a militia was organised, including troops of horse formed from the most prominent inhabitants, and from 1690–1 militia service was demanded of every male settler aged between 15 and 60 years, who were ordered to bring with them to muster any male slaves over 15 years of age, armed as their master and the local militia commander thought fit. In 1702 a troop of horse grenadiers was formed, and although interest in the militia declined in peacetime, every bout of hostilities caused a re-organisation. The 1758 Militia Act, for example, organised the local forces into an infantry regiment and a troop of cavalry. The militia served not only to protect against foreign incursion, but to guard against slave insurrection, as in 1761 when a planned uprising was foiled just in time, and the militia was mobilised as a precaution. The guns of the many fortifications were manned by a mix of regular troops (although a permanent garrison of Royal Artillery was not established until 1829) and militiamen trained to use the ordnance. The last Militia Act was that of 1813, which provided for two infantry battalions and a cavalry troop, with an obligation of service on all men aged 17–55, and even after the Napoleonic Wars the militia remained in being, albeit with declining enthusiasm. A British military presence remained in Bermuda until 1957, and the local forces were re-established with the creation of the Bermuda Militia Artillery and Bermuda Volunteer Rifles, authorised in 1892 although recruiting began only in 1895. The Bermuda Regiment was formed in 1965 by the amalgamation of the successors of these corps.

References

An excellent study of the local forces is 'Notes on Bermuda Military Forces 1687–1815', by R. Chartrand, in *Military Collector and Historian*, vol. XXII, Washington, DC, 1970, later reprinted in *Bermuda Historical Quarterly*. The various fortifications and military events are chronicled in the latter journal, and in the *Bermuda Journal of Archaeology and Maritime History* (Bermuda, from 1989).

CANADA

Much of the early military activity involving the British in North America arose not out of conflict with the indigenous peoples, but from hostilities between the principal colonising powers. The native American people were drawn into these conflicts; but when compared with the 'Indian Wars' of the 19th century which occurred in the United States, there was remarkably little friction between the equivalent communities in the British sphere of North America.

The two principal colonising powers in Canada were Britain and France, whose North American colonies had been established in the 17th century. Anglo–French hostility in Europe inevitably extended to North America, although to a degree these conflicts were independent

Garrison artillery: an 11in rifled muzzle-loader on its traversing carriage, Fort George, Bermuda. (Photograph courtesy of Thomas and Gayle DeVoe)

wars, given the distance between North America and the respective European capitals. The 'New World' version of the War of the Austrian Succession, for example, is more commonly styled 'King George's War' (1740–8); its main operation was the British capture of the French fortress of Louisbourg (16 June 1745), which was returned to France by the Treaty of Aix-la-Chapelle (1748). At this period France held the important territory on the shores of the St. Lawrence, and sought to extend into the interior; British possessions were concentrated in what is now the north-eastern United States, and those parts of Canada now represented by Newfoundland, Nova Scotia and Hudson Bay.

The decisive stage in the struggle for Canada occurred in what is often styled 'the French and Indian War' (1754–63), Anglo–French hostilities, which had begun before the Seven Years War embroiled both nations in Europe. Among the main military actions was the catastrophic defeat of Major-General Edward Braddock's British expedition against the French Fort Duquesne, which occurred in a Franco–Indian ambush on the Monongahela (9 July 1755); a British attempt to capture Louisbourg failed in mid-1757, and on 9 August of that year the British garrison of Fort William Henry, which had surrendered after a siege and been guaranteed safe exit, was massacred by the Indian contingent of the French army of the Marquis de Montcalm. Renewed British operations resulted in the capture of the French strong points of Louisbourg (27 July 1758) and Fort Ticonderoga (26 July 1759); and, the most decisive action of the war, the Battle of Quebec (or Battle of the Plains of Abraham). In this action of 13 September 1759, Montcalm's French army was defeated by James Wolfe's British expedition, both commanders receiving mortal wounds; and a renewed British offensive in the following year led to the surrender of the French in Canada (8 September 1760). The whole of northern North America was ceded officially to Britain by the Treaty of Paris (10 February 1760) which ended the Seven Years War, but the French settlers remained in the ex-French territory, giving that region its uniquely French character.

The British hold on Canada was threatened briefly in the early part of the American War of Independence, when American expeditions captured Ticonderoga (10 May 1775) and Montreal (13 November); but their attack on Quebec was repelled (31 December 1775), and in 1776 the Americans withdrew from Canada, having failed to inspire revolt as had occurred in the southern colonies. The effect on Canada of the American War was felt most strongly by the settlement, principally in New Brunswick and Ontario, of thousands of loyalists from the southern colonies, who sought refuge in Canada in preference to residing in the newly independent United States, a valuable asset to Canada and a population with an abiding hostility towards Americans, the United States having declined to compensate the emigrant loyalists for the great financial losses they had suffered by their exodus.

Government of Canada had been controlled by the terms of the 'Quebec Act' (22 June 1774), which granted the French inhabitants the liberty to pursue the Roman Catholic religion and confirmed the French civil law, while introducing the English code of criminal law; government was by a governor and council. A new system of administration was introduced by the 1791 Constitutional Act, which divided the region along the Ottawa river into Upper and Lower Canada, each with its own government. Lower Canada, chiefly French, retained its old system, to which a representative assembly was added; Upper Canada, mainly British, adopted British civil and criminal law and a legislative assembly or, as stated by the first governor, John Graves Simcoe, it received the British constitution and everything that secured and maintained it.

The War of 1812 against the United States provided another opportunity for the latter to annex part of Canada, but again without success. There was considerable action along the frontier, notably in the Niagara region, including the Battle of Queenston (13 October 1812) when Sir Isaac Brock (who was killed in the action) repelled an American advance under Stephen Van Rensselaer. The Americans burned York (now Toronto) in April 1813, but the defenders of Canada (a small number of British troops and locally raised forces) prevented any lasting territorial gains. The willingness of the emigrant loyalists to defend Canada is understandable; but the French population also showed little enthusiasm for the prospect of American invasion. Reporting the formation of the French corps of Canadian Voltigeurs, the *Quebec Gazette* noted that 'The Canadians are awaking from the repose of an age secured to them by good government and virtuous habits. Their anger is fresh, the object of their preparation simple and distinct. They are to defend their King, known to them only by acts of kindness, and a native country long since made sacred by the exploits of their forefathers.' (There were a few disloyal voices which actively supported the Americans, perhaps most notably Captain Andrew Westbrook, Ebenezer Allan (who had held a British commission during the War of Independence), and Simon Zelotes Watson, a surveyor from Montreal who became a major in the US Army, whom Isaac Brock reported as leading a troop of cavalry, a man 'of a desperate character who has been allowed to parade with about 20 men of the same description ... vowing as they went along the most bitter vengeance ...')[1]

The 1837–8 Rebellions

Despite the successful national effort in the War of 1812, earlier political dissent was not extinguished, and rebellions occurred in 1837–8. The first of these, in Lower Canada, is sometimes styled 'Papineau's Rebellion' from the name of one of its leaders, Louis Joseph Papineau (1786–1871), a prominent French-Canadian politician and lawyer. When attempts to gain constitutional and financial reforms for the French-Canadians of Lower Canada were unsuccessful, resistance by force was decided upon. The rebels, styled *Patriotes* or *les Fils de la Liberté*, were comparatively few in number and badly led; nevertheless, some sharp actions were fought between them and the small number of British troops led by Sir John Colborne, the Waterloo hero, who commanded the British forces in Upper and Lower Canada.

In November 1837 warrants were issued for the arrest of Papineau and others, and two forces were dispatched 'in aid of civil power' to the settlements of St. Denis and St. Charles, on the east bank of the Richelieu river, northeast of Montreal. Colonel Charles Gore led the force which marched on St. Denis, the flank companies of the 24th, the light company of the 32nd, a detachment of Montreal Cavalry and a 12pdr howitzer. On 23 November he encountered a determined rebel force at St. Denis and was forced to retire with a loss of six dead, ten wounded and six missing, and lost his howitzer when the freezing cold and bad roads caused the horse-team to give out. The second column, under Colonel G. W. Wetherall, consisted of four companies of his own 2/1st, two of the 66th, a detachment of Montreal Cavalry and two 6pdrs. At St. Charles it found the rebels in a stockaded position, commanded by Thomas Brown, one of the few British *Patriotes*. Wetherall drew up his troops 'hoping that a display of my force would induce some defection among these infatuated people';[2] instead, they fired on him, Wetherall charged, overran and burned the position for a loss of three dead and eighteen wounded; sixteen prisoners were taken, 56 dead rebels were counted within the stockade and more were consumed in the burning buildings. On his return march Wetherall dispersed another rebel force at St. Oliviere, where he overran an abbatis and 'two contemptible guns mounted on carts',[3] and two more rebels were killed before the rest made off.

Papineau had fled before the fighting, finding sanctuary in the United States; on 1 December he was declared a rebel and a price was put on his head. Gore returned to St. Denis on 1 December; the rebels fled and his howitzer was recaptured. A few skirmishes occurred elsewhere (Colborne, for example, particularly commended the Missisquoi Militia for routing a party which had returned to the attack after re-organising in the United States), but the main rebel force gathered at St. Eustache, west of Montreal, against which Colborne moved. The rebels were about 250 strong, led by Amury Girod (a Swiss) and Dr. John Chénier; Colborne's force of some 2,000 regulars and volunteers engaged them at St. Eustache on 14 December 1837. Girod fled, but Chénier and his followers put up a stiffer resistance until driven away from the buildings they had occupied by

The Canadian climate resulted in many adaptations of uniform from the time of the earliest military service in that country; typical is this fur-trimmed winter dress of an officer of the 60th, 1846, including a rifle-green frock-coat with black trimming and belts, and a fur cap. (Print by P. W. Reynolds, after Henry Martens)

artillery and the advance parties of 1st, 32nd and Montreal Volunteer Rifles; Chénier was killed together with about 70 other rebels, Colborne losing one man killed and eight wounded. On the point of capture, Girod shot himself. Among the 'trophies' taken by the victors were a cap of liberty upon a pole, and a white standard bearing a black eagle and the motto 'Free as Air'. (Not surprisingly, the leaders of the rebellion were castigated in Britain; Papineau, it was said, 'never through life possessed one generous feeling of moral or physical courage', while 'General' Brown was described as 'a miserable squalid-looking person, of short stature and contemptible appearance; his countenance being stamped with an expression of discontent, meanness and indecision of character in mind – in fact, by his own country-men he would be termed a "crooked cretur". Not long before the rebellion he became a bankrupt ironmonger, and thus having nothing to lose, but everything to gain, he placed himself at the head of the factious army. In this capacity, however, he proved himself unworthy of the confidence of the poor deluded victims whom he and his leader Papineau had seduced into their service.'[4] Such invective was not uncommon for the period!)

Another disturbance occurred in December 1837, 'Mackenzie's Rebellion', named after William Lyon Mackenzie, an Upper Canada politician of extreme republican views, who gathered supporters with the intention of seizing Toronto. These were soon dispersed but he fled to the United States, collected another band and seized Navy Island in the Niagara river, whence a few incursions were made, but the rebels fled when loyal forces approached. Like Papineau, Mackenzie remained in exile until the 1849 Amnesty Act; both re-entered politics but had little effect in their subsequent careers.

Further unrest occurred in the Richelieu river region in October 1838. In early November about 4,000 insurgents assembled at Napierville, about fifteen miles from the US border, where on 4 November Dr. Robert Nelson was proclaimed president of the Canadian Republic. (Nelson, whose brother had defeated Gore at St. Denis, was a kinsman of Horatio Nelson, Britain's greatest naval hero; ironically, the son of her greatest military hero was on the other side: Lord Charles Wellesley, the Duke of Wellington's second son, commanded the 15th Foot.) On 8 November Nelson and a large body of insurgents attacked a small garrison of local volunteers (mobilised in view of the rebel threat) in the Methodist church at Odelltown; the post was defended successfully. Colborne assembled a strong column (1st Dragoon Guards, 7th Hussars, Grenadier Guards, 15th, 24th, 71st, 73rd and two artillery batteries, commanded by Major-General Sir James Macdonell) and rebel forces were dispersed, including gatherings at Boucherville (which fled before the 66th) and Beauharnois, where on 10 November Colonel L. Carmichael with 23 engineers, 131 men of the 71st and more than 1,000 Glengarry Militiamen defeated another force. A sterner fight was put up by what Colborne described as 'United States pirates' near Prescott, who were engaged by a detachment of Royal Marines, 44 men of the 83rd, one company each of the Glengarry and Stormont Militia and two companies of 2nd Grenville Militia, commanded by Colonel Plomer Young. The first attack had to withdraw because of the 'particularly true and steady'[5] rifle fire of the 'pirates', but when reinforcements arrived on 15 November (four companies 83rd, two 18pdrs, a howitzer and two gunboats armed with 18pdrs) the rebels surrendered. Local forces had been used to considerable effect in the War of 1812, and in 1837–8 the militia again proved its value: Colborne had great confi-

dence in the Glengarry men in particular, Scottish settlers who were regarded as a most valuable resource of loyal individuals who already possessed some antipathy towards the French population which formed a large part of the rebel forces. Indeed, Colborne reported that his main concern was that 'if these disgraceful proceedings on the American frontier cannot be guarded against by the American Government, it will soon become impossible to prevent acts of retaliation on the part of the population of Upper Canada'[6] such was the general dislike of the Americans.

Following the insurrections the government was reformed by the unification of Upper and Lower Canada by the Act of Union in 1840. This did not end the fears of the French-speaking community, and when the Canadian legislature passed the Rebellion Losses Bill in 1849, compensating citizens of Lower Canada for damage inflicted by the loyalists during the unrest, the latter protested vehemently at this 'reward for rebellion', even stoning the governor, the Earl of Elgin, and burning the parliament buildings in Montreal. As the unified state did not work as envisaged, the British North America Act of 1 July 1867 created the Dominion of Canada, combining the

As with most colonial forces, the uniform of Canadian units resembled closely those of the British Army, The 2nd Queen's Own Rifles of Canada illustrated here wore a rifle-green uniform with red facings and black braid, akin to that of the British King's Royal Rifle Corps, but with a white helmet. (Print after H. Bunnett, c.1890)

Canadian winter uniform: a trooper of the Royal Canadian Dragoons, c.1897.

provinces of New Brunswick, Nova Scotia, Ontario and Quebec, with its own administration, legislature and prime minister, with a lieutenant-governor for each province and a governor-general overall.

The Fenian Campaigns

The presence of the United States to the south did not always make for good relations, and there was some tension along the border areas. In 1859, for example, there was a danger of conflict over the exact demarcation of the frontier between British and US territory in the Pacific north-west, and both sides began to assemble forces before the matter was resolved amicably; the dispute was not finally settled until 1872 when international mediation (by Wilhelm I of Germany) awarded the disputed San Juan Islands to the USA. More serious was the 'war scare' of 1861 when the US Navy seized the commissioners from the Confederate States to Britain and France, from the British mail-packet *Trent*, but the prospect of British intervention in the American Civil War was averted. There was minor border skirmishing during the Civil War, but real hostilities occurred in the post-war period, arising from

the formation in the USA in 1858 of the Fenian Brotherhood, which derived its name from an Anglicisation of *fianne*, the legendary war-band of the Irish hero Find Mac-Cummaill ('Finn MacCool'), and was dedicated to achieving the independence of Ireland. The Irish immigrants in the United States, many with experience of military service in the Civil War, proved a source of recruits, and the presence of Fenian organisations in the northern United States made Canada an obvious target for an attack on Britain. The Fenian forces were not the haphazard collections of insurgents who had fought the 1837–8 campaigns, but organised battalions of the 'Irish Republican Army'; most of their equipment was American, and some were even uniformed in bright green shell-jackets, worn with US-style blue kepis (with a green band, sometimes bearing a brass harp-badge and regimental number), and light blue trousers, some with green stripe; these were probably ex-US Army garments, and some Fenians probably wore their old Civil War uniforms.[7]

The Canadian authorities mobilised against the Fenian threat: by early June 1866 some 20,000 Canadian volunteers were under arms. On the night of 31 May/1 June 1866 Colonel (or 'General') John O'Neill, a Civil War veteran, crossed the Canadian border with about 800 Fenians. On 2 June they met a Canadian force, 850 strong, commanded by Lieutenant-Colonel Alfred Booker, at Ridgeway; the Canadians comprised the 2nd Battalion, Queen's Own Rifles, some companies of the 13th Battalion and York and Caledonian Rifle Companies. Initially the Fenians began to waver, but the Canadians were thrown into disarray by fears of an attack by cavalry (which the Fenians did not possess) and retired in confusion, having suffered 49 casualties, including ten dead. There was a further skirmish at Fort Erie, but before more Canadian forces could arrive, O'Neill re-embarked his command to return across the Niagara; but he was apprehended by the gunboat USS *Michigan*, the American authorities having decided to act against those using the USA as a springboard for invasion. There was minor skirmishing later in the month, but the Fenian trouble subsided for some years.

On 25 May 1870 O'Neill led some 350–400 Fenians to the border near Franklin, Vermont; but alerted to the possibility of an incursion, a Canadian militia force was waiting, and engaged before all the Fenians had crossed the frontier; the Fenian main body returned fire from within the United States. As Canadian reinforcements came up the Fenians broke, and it was only with difficulty that the Canadian commander, Lieutenant-Colonel Osborne Smith, prevented his men from pursuing across the border. No casualties were suffered by the Canadians, and about twenty by the Fenians. Another minor incursion was repelled two days later near Huntingdon, Quebec, by a combined Canadian/British detachment (the British, a company of the 69th), again without casualties; and apart from a minor foray in Manitoba in the following year, Fenian operations were at an end. O'Neill had been arrested by the US authorities after the Franklin raid, and was apprehended on the US side of the border before he could participate in the Manitoba incursion.

The Red River Expedition, 1870

On 19 November 1869, more than a year of negotiation resulted in the transfer of the Hudson Bay Company territories to the crown, uniting Rupert's Land and the North-West Territories with Canada, as the province of Manitoba. This aroused anxiety among the inhabitants of this sparsely populated region, largely of mixed French-Indian ancestry, known as Métis. The residents of the Red River region consequently turned back the new lieutenant-governor at the frontier, and established their own provisional government under the leadership of Louis Riel (1844–85) to negotiate their own terms of entry of the Red River Colony into the Dominion. The affair might have ended peacefully, had not Riel, with some brutality, executed one of his opponents, Thomas Scott, on 4 March 1870. Scott was an Orangeman from Ontario, and consequently demands increased for a forcible suppression of the 'Riel rebellion'.

Command of the Red River expedition was given to the Deputy Quartermaster-General in Canada, Colonel Garnet Wolseley, whose force consisted principally of seven companies of 1/60th and two 7-company militia battalions formed especially for the expedition, named the 1st Ontario and 2nd Quebec Rifles; plus supporting services, 1,200 strong in total. This force marched from Toronto on 14 May 1870 and arrived at Fort Garry on 24 August, having covered 1,118 miles. Fort Garry, the Hudson Bay post taken over by Riel's government, was approached in battle array, but the 'rebels' had fled and no action was necessary. The expedition's march, under arduous conditions, was a logistical triumph, and laid the foundation of Wolseley's reputation. The 60th began the return journey five days later; apart from a small contingent at Halifax, they were the last British troops to garrison Canada, all future military effort being in Canadian hands.

The North-Western Rebellion, 1885

By 1878 all British possessions in North America had been incorporated into the Dominion of Canada, with the exception of Newfoundland (which remained independent until 1949). Despite the collapse of the 1870 'rebellion', unrest among the Métis had not been extinguished; those who had moved west to Saskatchewan found that civilisation followed them, and economic hardship among some of the Canadian Indian people was a further cause of turbulence. Not having been arrested after the 1870 'rebellion', after an unsuccessful foray into Canadian politics (1873–5) Louis Riel had retired from public life, living in Montana from 1879; but in 1884, in response to an appeal

from the Métis in Saskatchewan, he returned to lead them.

After some months of agitation, hostilities began at Duck Lake on 26 March 1885, when a detachment of fewer than 100 North-West Mounted Police and volunteers were put to flight by a large body of rebels led by a buffalo-hunter, Gabriel Dumont; twelve of the government side were killed (nine of them Prince Albert Volunteers) and 26 wounded. Shortly after this nine whites were murdered by Cree Indians at Frog Lake, suggesting that the Métis rebellion might be the signal for a wider uprising and causing the despatch of an expedition. Until it arrived the settlers in the vicinity of Battleford congregated with the police in the protection of the fortified post.

Commanded by General Frederick D. Middleton, with the exception of seventeen British officers employed on staff duties, the expedition was entirely Canadian, formed by mobilising militia. Middleton organised his force into three columns, construction of the Canadian Pacific Railway enabling the expediting of more than 5,000 men, with artillery and machine-guns, to cover in days the distance that had taken Wolseley months; the speed of government reaction and the efficiency of organisation and transport is demonstrated by the fact that the first action against the rebels occurred less than a month after the fight at Duck Creek. On 24 April a rebel position at Fish Creek was stormed successfully, and on 1 May the column commanded by Colonel Otter of the Infantry School at Toronto engaged the Indian allies of the Métis at Cut Knife Hill. This was basically a reconnaissance by 325 men with two 7pdrs and a Gatling gun; the Indians of Chief Poundmaker held their position and the government force withdrew. On 12 May Middleton attacked Riel's headquarters at Batoche; deducting men needed to protect his camp, sick and baggage-guards, Middleton had only 495 men in the firing-line, opposed by about 600 rebels; but the latter were routed and the rebellion was crushed virtually at a stroke. Some minor skirmishing occurred on succeeding days, but by the end of May the campaign was concluded, and the Crees who had perpetrated the Frog Lake murders were captured on 2 July. Treatment of the rebels was lenient (one of the leaders, for example, the chief Big Bear, was sentenced to life imprisonment but was pardoned); but Riel, who had surrendered on 15 May, was convicted of treason and hanged at Regina on 16 November 1885.

Overseas Expeditions

The North-West Rebellion was the last campaign fought in Canada; thereafter, the nation's military effort was directed overseas. The first Canadian regiment to serve abroad – if it can be regarded as a true Canadian unit – was the 100th Foot, the sixth British regiment to bear that number, which was raised in Canada in 1858. It originated from an offer by Canadian militia officers to form a regular line regiment, as a gesture of support to the crown at the time of the

Indian Mutiny; fourteen of its first officers were ex-Canadian militiamen; its lieutenant-colonel was George de Rottenburg, previously Assistant Quartermaster-General in Canada and Adjutant-General of Canadian Militia; its major, Alexander Roberts Dunn, born at Dunstable, York (now Toronto), was the first Canadian-born winner of the Victoria Cross (as a lieutenant in the 11th Hussars, at the charge of the Light Brigade at Balaclava). The regiment was recruited in Canada in April–May 1858 and sailed for England in the same year; as a British line regiment it received the title of Prince of Wales's Royal Canadian Regiment, and in 1881 was amalgamated with the 109th Bombay Infantry to form The Prince of Wales's Leinster Regiment (Royal Canadians). Its first return to its country of origin was in 1898, when it went to Halifax, Nova Scotia.

For the Gordon relief expedition, a unit of 386 Canadian boatmen was formed to handle the whalers on the Nile, Wolseley having requested a contingent of *voyageurs*, doubtless remembering the value of such men in the Red River expedition. The Canadian government decided that they should be civilians, hired under contract and not wearing uniform, although they were commanded by a Canadian militia Red River veteran, Lieutenant-Colonel Fred C. Denison, a lawyer and member of a Toronto family very distinguished in Canadian military affairs. The men recruited were not all as proficient as those remembered by Wolseley, for in addition to those used to an outdoor life, loggers and rivermen, some were urban dwellers with no knowledge of boats. Many, however, proved invaluable to the expedition, and the contingent lost sixteen men from accidents and disease; and their paymaster, Lieutenant-Colonel W. N. Kennedy, another militia officer, died in England on the way home.

Although Canadian public opinion was initially not unanimous in supporting Britain in the South African War, some 7,368 Canadians went to South Africa. The first Canadian unit in the field was the 2nd (Special Service) Battalion, Royal Canadian Regiment (the infantry of the 'Permanent Force'), which arrived virtually untrained in South Africa yet performed most creditably at Paardeberg, where they suffered considerable losses, only a couple of weeks after embarking on their first campaign. All were volunteers who had served with the militia, like those who followed; those, apart from a field brigade of artillery and medical and support units, were cavalry or mounted rifles: the Royal Canadian Dragoons, Lord Strathcona's Horse and 1st–6th Canadian Mounted Rifles, many of whom did not see campaign service. During the war the first Victoria Crosses were won by members of Canadian units: the first by Sergeant Arthur Richardson of Lord Strathcona's Horse, at Wolve Spruit, Standerton, 5 July 1900, and the other three at Komati river, 7 November 1900, by Lieutenants Hampden Cockburn and Richard Turner, and Sergeant Edward Holland, all of the Royal Canadian Dragoons. Of these, only Richardson (a native of Stockport) was not Canadian-born.

Military Forces

Virtually the whole of Canada's military force was composed of militia or volunteers; only latterly was there a small 'Permanent Force' of 'regular' troops.

With the union of Upper and Lower Canada, there were some 426 battalions of militia, based on universal liability for service; but as they mustered for only one day per year, effectiveness was low, and this led to the formation of some rather more enthusiastic volunteer corps. The 1846 Militia Act divided the population into two classes, those of 18–40 years of age who were the first liable for service, and those aged 40–60 as a reserve; for emergencies 30,000 men could be enrolled by voluntary enlistment, or by ballot in the event of there being insufficient volunteers. There was also a regular unit, the Royal Canadian Rifle Regiment, which was raised in 1840 and existed until 1870; it was composed of British veterans initially of 15 years' service (finally reduced to 10 when recruits became scarce), and was intended to garrison the Canadian border and prevent desertion to the USA (a constant problem for the British forces in Canada). The age of the members of the corps (nicknamed 'the Bullfrogs') made the unit unfit for frontier service in the worst of the Canadian climate.

The 1855 Militia Act created, in addition to the Sedentary Militia, an Active Militia of up to 5,000 volunteers who were paid for ten days' training per annum (twenty days for artillery); so popular was this service that a second category was created in 1856 for those in excess of the original quota, who were unpaid. Originally formed in independent companies, battalion-sized units were created from 1859. One of the most unusual units was the Victoria Pioneer Rifle Corps, formed at Vancouver in 1860 from American Negroes settled in that area, armed and equipped by the Hudson Bay Company. Although sanctioned by the governor the corps had no official financial support and was not on the official establishment (perhaps because of prejudice on the part of the other inhabitants of the area), and it faded away in 1866. In 1863 new Militia Acts put the Active Militia on an equal footing, all to serve without pay; and the Volunteer Militia was permitted to be increased to 35,000. In case of emergency, although militia units might be mobilised for service in their own area (as during the Fenian incursions), for service elsewhere units were created for specific duties, though recruited from militiamen, as in the case quoted above of the two rifle battalions created for the Red River expedition. The small 'regular' or Permanent Force comprised the Regiment of Canadian Artillery, a company of mounted infantry, and the personnel of the cavalry and infantry schools, which acted as training cadres. A Royal Military College was established at Kingston in 1875.

The assembly of forces for active service is exemplified by the creation of the expedition to the North-West in 1885. In addition to the mobilisation of the 2nd, 10th, 32nd, 35th and 90th Battalions of militia, a provisional infantry battalion was formed from two companies of the 46th Battalion and one each from the 15th, 40th, 45th, 47th, 49th and 57th, generally known as the 'Midland Battalion' or 'Midlanders', from the component battalions originating from the Midland district. Another battalion, the Simcoe Rangers, was formed from four companies of the 35th Simcoe Battalion and four of the 12th York Rangers; two new battalions, one styled light infantry, were raised in Winnipeg, and among others to be called out were the 7th, 9th and 65th, a provisional battalion from the 63rd, 66th and Halifax Garrison Artillery, and a sharpshooter company was selected from the Governor-General's Foot Guards. Mounted units were formed (Boulton's and French's Scouts) and new local companies were called out, including such exotically named units as the Rocky Mountain Rangers and the Moose Mountain Scouts. Not all the mobilised corps formed part of the main expedition, being stationed at different locations; Middleton's force was composed as follows:

1st Column (Middleton): 'A' Battery artillery (Quebec), 10th Battalion (Royal Grenadiers), 90th Battalion (Winnipeg), Midland Battalion, part Winnipeg field battery, part Infantry School Corps; Boulton's, Dennis' and French's Scouts.

2nd Column: 'B' Battery artillery (Kingston), 2nd Battalion (Queen's Own Rifles), 35th Battalion, Todd's Sharpshooters (from Foot Guards, as above), part Infantry School Corps, part Winnipeg field battery.

3rd Column: 32nd and 65th Battalions, Strange's Rangers, North-West Mounted Police.

Local forces co-operated with these units; at Fish Creek, for example, the government force included 45 members of the Battleford Rifles.

By the beginning of the last decade of the 19th century, the military establishment was divided into twelve Military Districts: four for Ontario, three for Quebec, and one each for British Columbia, New Brunswick, Nova Scotia, Manitoba and Prince Edward Island. The 'Permanent Force' included two cavalry troops (Royal Canadian Dragoons), three artillery batteries and four infantry companies (Royal Canadian Regiment), composed of men enlisted for three years' permanent service and officered from the Royal Military College. The non-'regular' forces included the following:

Cavalry: Governor General's Horse Guard (location Ontario); 1st Cavalry (Hussars) (London); 2nd Cavalry (Dragoons) (Oak Ridges); 3rd Provisional Cavalry (Prince of Wales's Canadian Dragoons) (Coburg); 4th Cavalry (Hussars) (Kingston); 5th Cavalry (Dragoons) (Montreal); 6th Cavalry (Hussars) (Montreal); 8th Princess Louise's New Brunswick Cavalry (Hussars), and Queen's Own Canadian Hussars (Quebec). Four independent troops were the King's Troop (Hussars), Prescott Troop (Dragoons), Princess Louise's Dragoon Guards and Win-

nipeg Troop (Dragoons); the latter was the only cavalry unit to participate in the 1885 campaign.

Artillery: sixteen field, eighteen garrison and one half mountain batteries; three engineer companies.

Infantry battalions (with titles where they existed): Governor-General's Foot Guards, 1st Battalion Prince of Wales's Regiment, 2nd Queen's Own Rifles of Canada, 3rd Victoria Rifles of Canada, 4th vacant (ex-Canadian Chasseurs of Montreal), 5th Royal Scots of Canada, 6th Fusiliers, 7th Fusiliers (originally London Light Infantry), 8th Royal Rifles, 9th Voltigeurs de Quebec, 10th Royal Grenadiers, 11th Argenteuil Rangers, 12th York Rangers, 13th, 14th Princess of Wales's Own Rifles, 15th Argyle Light Infantry, 16th Prince Edward, 17th Levis, 18th Prescott, 19th Lincoln, 20th Hallon (Lorne Rifles), 21st Essex Fusiliers, 22nd Oxford Rifles, 23rd Beauce, 24th Kent, 25th Elgin, 26th Middlesex Light Infantry, 27th Lambton (St. Clair Borderers), 28th Perth, 29th Waterloo, 30th Wellington Rifles, 31st Grey, 32nd Bruce, 33rd Huron, 34th Ontario, 35th Simcoe Foresters, 36th Peel, 37th Haldemand Rifles, 38th Dufferin Rifles, 39th Norfolk Rifles, 40th Northumberland, 41st Brockville Rifles, 42nd Brockville, 43rd Ottawa and Carleton Rifles, 44th Welland, 45th West Durham, 46th East Durham, 47th Frontenac, 49th Hastings Rifles, 50th Huntingdon Borderers, 51st Hemmingford Rangers, 52nd Brome Light Infantry, 53rd Sherbrooke, 54th Richmond, 55th Megantic Light Infantry, 56th Grenville (Lisgar Rifles), 57th Peterborough Rangers, 58th Compton, 59th Stormont and Glengarry, 60th Missisquoi, 61st Montmagny and L'Islet, 62nd St. John Fusiliers, 63rd Halifax Rifles, 64th Rifles (Voltigeurs de Beauharnais), 65th Mount Royal Rifles (sic: a Montreal corps), 66th Princess Louise Fusiliers, 67th Carleton Light Infantry, 68th King's County, 69th 1st Annapolis, 70th Champlain, 71st York, 72nd 2nd Annapolis, 73rd Northumberland, 74th, 75th Lunenburg, 76th Rifles (Voltigeurs de Chateauguay), 77th Wentworth, 78th Colchester, Hants and Pictou Highlanders, 79th Shefford Highlanders, 80th Nicolet, 81st Portneuf, 82nd Queen's County, 83rd Joliette, 84th St. Hyacinthe, 85th, 86th Three Rivers, 87th Quebec, 88th Kamouraska and Charlevoix, 89th Temiscouata and Rimouski, 90th Winnipeg Rifles, 91st Manitoba Light Infantry, 92nd Dorchester, 93rd Cumberland, 94th Victoria (Argyle Highlanders), 95th Manitoba Grenadiers, 96th Algonia Rifles. There were also three independent companies: the New Westminster, St. John, and St. Jean Baptiste Rifles.

The Canadian Navy had a military origin, and the use of vessels on the lakes, especially during the War of 1812 is well-known. A marine militia was authorised in 1863 and some were mobilised during the Fenian unrest in 1866 their service including the conversion and manning of the steamer *Rescue* as a gunboat. This was later supplemented

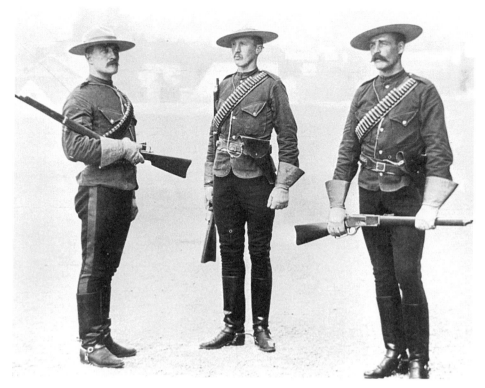

Members of the North-West Mounted Police, 1897, armed with the eight-shot Winchester repeating carbine, Model 1876, some 846 of which were issued to the corps and carried from 1878 to 1914. Other weapons issued to the 'Mounties' included some 200 Lee-Metford carbines in 1895.

by the *Prince Alfred*, a gunboat equipped with two Armstrong guns and four brass howitzers; by 1870 it had been fitted with iron shutters to protect the crew from small-arms fire. The 1868 Militia Act provided for a 'marine militia', but the only unit formed was the naval brigade at Halifax. In 1880 the Admiralty lent Canada the 1859 wooden corvette *Charybdis* (armed with twenty 8in guns and a 68pdr) as a training vessel, commanded by a Royal Navy officer on loan, but the trip across the Atlantic finished off her ancient boilers; she had to be towed to Halifax, was officially returned to the Royal Navy in August 1882, and was sold in Halifax in 1884. Not until 1910 was a Canadian navy created by the acquisition of the British cruisers *Niobe* and *Rainbow*.

In addition to the military forces, there was also the North-West Mounted Police, a quasi-military constabulary, created after the ceding of the North-West Territories to Canada by the Hudson Bay Company. For three years there was complete lawlessness in these vast territories, until on 23 May 1873 the prime minister, Sir John A. Macdonald, signed an Act establishing the North-West Mounted Police; this name was perhaps chosen in preference to 'mounted rifles' to obviate any objections from the US government to the presence of a military force in the region. Recruits from varied backgrounds assembled at Fort Dufferin, Manitoba, including not only backwoodsmen but ex-soldiers, adventurers and many men from good families, both British and Canadian; the unit's first commissioner (police ranks were

used) was Lieutenant-Colonel George A. French, a British officer attached to the Canadian militia. On 8 July 1874 six troops set out from Fort Dufferin on 'the Long March' to the North-West, 300 men with a train of wagons, drivers, equipment and two 9pdrs. This march took them almost 2,000 miles to distant outposts across the breadth of the continent. From that time, the NWMP became responsible for keeping the peace throughout this vast region, often operating in small parties of two or three constables, and performed their task so well that they won the respect of both whites and Indians alike. Originally uniformed in British dragoon style, although the force's costume evolved as a result of the experience of service in the frontier districts, the red tunic was retained for most duties; although not the most practical colour, it was instantly recognisable, especially to the Indians who ranged across the US/Canada border and who often had hostile intent towards the blue-coated US soldiers but who respected the red-coats as representatives of a perhaps less threatening power. In the modified active service uniform, the original helmet was replaced by a fur busby or a flat-brimmed hat, giving the appearance, according to one contemporary witness, of a cross between a Montana desperado and a Sardinian *chasseur*!

In time of emergency, the Mounted Police acted in a military capacity, in which they performed with distinction; in the North-West Rebellion they were employed not only as a reconnaissance force but as a major combat element: in the action at Cut Knife Creek, for example, the government force comprised 75 Mounted Police (50 of them mounted, with two 7pdrs and a Gatling gun), 80 artillerymen, 60 of the Queen's Own Rifles, 45 each from the Infantry School Corps and Battleford Rifles, and 20 of the Governor-General's Foot Guards. It was appropriate that this remarkable force received the title 'Royal' in 1904; and in 1920 they adopted their modern title, Royal Canadian Mounted Police.

Notes

1. Brock to Sir George Prevost, 26 July 1812; quoted in *Documents Relating to the Invasion of Canada and the Surrender of Detroit*, ed. Lieutenant-Colonel. E. A. Cruikshank, Ottawa, 1912, p. 92.
2. Dispatch, 27 November 1837; *London Gazette*, 26 December 1837.
3. Dispatch, 28 November 1837; *London Gazette*, ibid.
4. Anon. 'Sketches of some of the Principal Leaders of the Canadian Revolt in Lower Canada', in *United Service Journal*, 1838, vol. I, pp. 520–1.
5. Young's dispatch, 14 November 1838; *London Gazette*, 7 December 1838.
6. Colborne's dispatch, 17 November 1838; *London Gazette*, ibid.
7. See 'Irish Republican Army (Fenian Brotherhood)', by F. Back and W. Colwell, in *Military Collector and Historian*, vol. XL, no. 1, spring, 1988.

References

Chappell, M. *The Canadian Army at War*, London, 1985 (mostly post-1901).

Chartrand, R. *Canadian Military Heritage*, Montreal, 1993.

Dent, J. C. *The Story of the Upper Canadian Rebellion*, Toronto, 1885.

Dornbusch, C. E. *The Lineages of the Canadian Army 1855-1961*, Cornwallville, N.Y., 1961.

Evans, W. S. *The Canadian Contingents and Canadian Imperialism*, London, 1901.

Featherstone, D. *Victoria's Enemies: an A-Z of British Colonial Warfare*, London, 1989.

Goodspeed, Lieutenant-Colonel D. J. *The Armed Forces of Canada 1867-1967*, Ottawa, 1967.

Knight, I. *Queen Victoria's Enemies (4): Asia, Australasia and the Americas*, London, 1990.

Lindsey, C. *Life and Times of William Lyon Mackenzie*, Toronto, 1862.

Macdonald, Captain J. A. *Troublous Times in Canada: A History of the Fenian Raids of 1866 and 1870*, r/p London, 1985.

Maclaren, R. *Canadians on the Nile 1882-1898*, Vancouver, 1978.

Mann, M. *A Particular Duty: The Canadian Rebellions 1837-38*, Salisbury, 1986.

Moore Smith, G. C. *The Life of John Colborne, Field-Marshal Lord Seaton*, London, 1903 (contains much pertaining to the 1837–8 unrest).

Ross, D. *Military Uniforms from the Collection of the New Brunswick Museum*, Saint John, N.B., 1980 (excellent study of Canadian military dress, including some British items).

Ross, D. and Tyler, C. *Candian Campaigns 1860-70*, London, 1992.

Senior, E. K. *British Regulars in Montreal: an Imperial Garrison 1832–54*, Montreal, 1981.

– *Roots of the Canadian Army: Montreal District 1846-1870*, Quebec, 1981.

Stacey, C. P. *Records of the Nile Voyageurs 1884-1885: the Canadian Voyageur Contingent in the Gordon Relief Expedition*, Toronto, 1959.

Stanley, G. F. G. *Canada's Soldiers: The Military History of an Unmilitary People*, Toronto, 1960.

Summers, Brigadier-General J. L., and Chartrand, R. *Military Uniforms in Canada 1665-1970*, Ottawa, 1981.

Taylor, F. *Louis Joseph Papineau*, Montreal, 1865.

Upper Canada Historical Arms Society, *The Military Arms of Canada*, West Hill, Ontario, 1963.

SAINT HELENA

The South Atlantic island of Saint Helena is remembered principally as the final exile of Napoleon; yet it was an important safe anchorage and source of fresh water and provisions for shipping, a significance which only declined with the introduction of effective food preservation, which made the call at St. Helena to avoid scurvy no longer necessary.

The island was discovered in May 1502 by the Portuguese navigator João de Nova, who found it uninhabited. The Portuguese made no permanent settlement and by the mid-17th century it was being used by the Dutch, but this ceased after their colony was established at the Cape. Saint Helena was then appropriated by the British East India Company as a staging-post between Britain and India; in May 1659 an expedition under John Dutton landed and established a fort, but in January 1673 it was captured by Dutch forces from the Cape. The governor fled to Brazil, whence he dispatched a sloop to warn British shipping of the fate of the island; this vessel encountered a squadron under Captain Richard Munden, who had been sent to reinforce the island. Determined to re-capture it, Munden landed some of his troops at Prosperous Bay, on learning that a Saint Helena slave aboard the governor's sloop could show them a path up the cliffs. This the slave, Black Oliver, duly did; and an audacious soldier, known to history only as Tom, scaled the most difficult part of the cliff and pulled up his fellows on a rope, they urging him to 'Hold fast, Tom!'; hence the name given to that place, Holdfast Tom. With troops taking the fort in the rear, and Munden's fleet engaging it from the sea, the Dutch defenders capitulated (5 May 1673). By a royal charter of December 1673 the East India Company was recognised as 'absolute lords and proprietors' of the island, giving it complete power over the inhabitants; its plantations were worked by slaves, the importation of whom was prohibited from 1792, and all were freed between 1826 and 1836. Authority was vested in the governor, holders of which office included (1741–2) Robert Jenkins of 'the War of Jenkins's Ear'.

No enemy action was ever launched against Saint Helena (although a French raid in 1706 captured two ships anchored off Jamestown), but the Company maintained a garrison throughout its occupation. This was supplemented by a militia, service in which was required of all settlers as part of their condition of tenure (later capable of commutation by payment of a fee; although with increased threat, service again became compulsory in 1804, a measure so unpopular that it was discontinued). The 'regular' garrison consisted of artillery and infantry, recruited in a similar manner to the Company's European regiments in India, but while the artillery was a good corps, some trouble was experienced with the infantry, the irksome routine of garrison duty leading to indiscipline and even mutiny. Two companies of Malays, ex-prisoners of the Dutch, were formed in 1795 to man the garrison and field artillery. When Napoleon was exiled to Saint Helena under the governorship of Sir Hudson Lowe, it was thought necessary to maintain a strong garrison of regular troops for the duration of his captivity.

In 1795 governor Brooke contributed infantry and artillery to the expedition to the Cape; but whereas he was commended for his action, governor Robert Patton was dismissed for sending nine officers and 174 men to participate in the South American operations in 1806–7.

Company forces remained in existence until Saint Helena was transferred from the East India Company to the Crown on 23 April 1834; but the Company continued to administer the island until the arrival of the British garrison in 1836, initially detachments of the 91st Foot and Royal Artillery (although an RA detachment had been stationed there since 1815). Upon the arrival of the new garrison the Company troops were dismissed and left to make their own way to Britain or the Cape. From January 1842 a new Saint Helena Regiment was formed as part of the British Army, for garrison duty; it existed until June 1863 when it was disbanded, the officers being transferred to the 5th West India Regiment. In 1879 the governor (H. R. Janisch, son of Hudson Lowe's clerk), on receipt of the news of Isandlwana, dispatched the garrison's infantry to South Africa in HMS *Shah*, the third time that part of the garrison had been sent for operations overseas. In subsequent years Saint Helena was used as accommodation for prisoners of war, including Dinizulu and many Boers during the South African War of 1899–1902. The military garrison was finally withdrawn in 1906.

SOUTH AND CENTRAL AMERICA

There was only limited British military involvement in South America, most notably the disastrous foray of 1806–7, undertaken initially without government sanction and culminating in an ill-managed attack on the Spanish colonists of Buenos Aires (5 July 1807), a comprehensive reverse which forced the British to evacuate the region, with the court-martial and dismissal of the British commander, Lieutenant-General John Whitelocke.

The only British colony in South America was that which became British Guiana, one of three non-Spanish colonies on the Guiana coast, the others being Dutch Guiana (Surinam), and French Guiana (Cayenne). The first Dutch colonists were established on the coast of Demerara and Essequibo in the early 17th century; British interest in Surinam was ceded to the Dutch by the Peace of Breda (1667). The region which became British Guiana comprised the Dutch colonies of Berbice, Demerara and Essequibo, which were captured by the British in 1781 and placed under the authority of the governor of Barbados;

but in 1782 France (then an ally of the Dutch) took the colonies, and they were restored to the Netherlands by the peace of 1783. In 1796 they were again captured by Britain, restored by the Peace of Amiens, captured again in 1803, ceded to Britain in 1814–15, and consolidated into the single colony of British Guiana in 1831. Boundary disputes with other colonies were not immune from military action during this period: Surinam, for example, was captured by a British expedition in 1804, and Cayenne by an Anglo–Portuguese invasion in 1809, and although officially restored in 1814, not until 1817 was it really surrendered by the Portuguese to France.

The British colonies required military support, for which reason HMS *Peacock* was sent to the region in 1813, at the time of Anglo–American hostilities; and it was while cruising off Demerara that *Peacock* was destroyed by the American *Hornet* (23 February 1813), but the colony suffered from no further American action. Internal unrest, however, sometimes necessitated the deployment of the troops that were maintained in garrison. The most severe outbreak was on the east coast of Demerara in 1823, by slaves demanding their freedom; one of those capitally convicted of encouraging the revolt was the Revd. John Smith of the London Missionary Society. This became something of a *cause célèbre* in Britain and Smith's sentence was commuted to expulsion from the colony and the West Indies, but he died in gaol in Georgetown, the capital, before the decision reached the colony. Local forces deployed during the period of martial law which obtained from August 1823 to January 1824 included the Demerara Militia (infantry), artillery and cavalry; the former remained in existence, but the cavalry disappeared in 1861. Detachments of the West India Regiments were frequently in garrison; for example, in 1842 part of the 1st Regiment was sent from Demerara to the Brazilian frontier in the Pirara expedition to expel Brazilian raiders from British Guiana territory. Riots against the Portuguese inhabitants of the colony in 1847 necessitated the use of the military, and further unrest occurred in 1862 and 1889. About 1884–5 boundary disputes with Venezuela presented a threat of aggression, and as late as 1905 riots in Georgetown (arising from serious economic hardship) were so serious that not until the arrival of HMSs *Sappho* and *Diamond* was the situation restored completely.

The British colony in Central America, British Honduras, was established in 1638 by wood-cutters; although they and their successors followed that occupation, many were ex-buccaneers and frequently made themselves objectionable to the adjacent Spanish settlements, leading to a number of attempts to expel the British. The first British troops sent there were a detachment of Gooch's American Regiment in 1742, to supervise the formation of a corps of Indians to serve against the Spanish. A Spanish attack in 1754 was routed, and by the treaty of 1763 Britain extracted a guarantee that the wood-cutters would not be

During the mid- to late 19th century, the services of the Royal Navy were not restricted to 'colonial' campaigns: this depicts Captain James Hope of the paddle-frigate HMS Firebrand *with three boat-loads of seamen cutting the boom across the River Paraña at Obligado on 20 November 1845, to open navigation to Paraguay. This had been blocked by the Argentinian dictator Juan Manuel Rosas, necessitating combined British and French naval action; when the boom was cut, British and French naval brigades landed and captured the overlooking forts. Ironically, upon his deposition in 1852, Rosas escaped in the paddle-gunboat HMS* Locust, *and spent the remainder of his life in exile in Southampton. (Print after T. S. S. Crowther)*

molested, while agreeing to demolish the fortifications they had erected. The British continued to probe into Spanish territory, however, and in September 1779 the Spaniards attacked and destroyed Belize. The settlers returned in 1783, and although their rights were confirmed by treaties of that year and 1786, they continued to harass the Spaniards. Upon renewed conflict between Britain and Spain, the settlers fortified an island in Belize harbour (Saint George's Cay) and with the assistance of the sloop HMS *Merlin* beat off a Spanish attack. This ended the military threat to the colony, but not for some time did Britain claim it as anything more than a concession from the king of Spain, its position as British territory being established by a series of treaties beginning with that with Mexico in 1826; British sovereignty was confirmed finally with the settlement of boundary disputes with Guatemala in 1859.

A military presence in British Honduras was necessary because of occasional Indian raids from Yucatan; the West India Regiments were employed there, for example during the 1848–9 hostilities in Yucatan. The last serious incursion was in 1872, when a detachment of the 1st West India Regiment made a gallant defence of Orange Walk against an attack by Santa Cruz Indians. From 1887, when the West India Regiments were withdrawn, Honduras maintained its own military force, the British Honduras Constabulary (Frontier Force), mounted infantry and artillery quite separate from the civil police, whose authority was limited to Belize. The BHC personnel were West Indian with British officers (the corps' Inspector-General was a member of the Executive Committee which assisted the governor), and at the end of the 19th century it was maintaining a 4-gun howitzer battery and one Maxim gun. It garrisoned four forts (the headquarters at Barlee, Cairns, Corosal and Orange Walk) and a blockhouse and seven outposts along the frontier river, Rio Hondo.

Probably the most notorious personality associated with British presence in Honduras was Edward Marcus Despard, who participated in the British capture of the Spanish Black River Settlements (on the coast between Honduras and Nicaragua) in October 1782, and who became governor of the Bay of Honduras and in 1784 took over administration of Yucatan. He was recalled to answer specious charges and though acquitted received no compensation; this rankled so much that he devised a plan to assassinate the king and seize the Tower and Bank of England. He was executed for treason in 1803 for this so-called 'Despard conspiracy'.

Another, and totally unsuccessful, foray into Central America was the San Juan expedition to the Spanish colony of Nicaragua in 1780, which was destroyed by sickness. Despard was the expedition's engineer but it was most remarkable for the participation of the naval commander, Horatio Nelson, who himself only just survived the fevers of the area.

WEST INDIES

The main campaigning in the West Indies occurred during the French Revolutionary and Napoleonic Wars, principally an extension of the hostilities being waged in Europe. Possession of a number of West Indian islands varied between Britain, France and Spain, either by conquest or treaty, until Britain became the dominant power in the Caribbean. Ultimately, British holdings included Jamaica, Barbados, Trinidad and Tobago, the Bahamas, the Leeward Islands (including Saint Kitts, Nevis, Antigua, Montserrat and Dominica); and the Windward Islands (Saint Lucia, Saint Vincent and Grenada); France retained Guadeloupe and Martinique, and shared Saint Martin with the Netherlands, whose other possessions included Curaçao, Aruba and other small territories; Denmark possessed Sainte Croix, Saint Thomas and Saint John. Haiti remained independent, despite European attempts to possess it, and was frequently in a state of hopeless anarchy.

Vast resources were expended in the possession of the West Indian territories, economic and mercantile considerations taking precedence over the lives of the military and naval personnel expended in attempts to capture or hold the islands, and over any moral qualms arising from the odious institution of slavery, which until its abolition by Britain provided the workforce for the agricultural economy of the islands. (Although the slave trade was abolished in 1807, the institution of slavery was not ended in British possessions until partial abolition in 1833, and total abolition in 1838). Despite considerable combat between the colonising powers, principally Britain and France, it was not the casualties of battle that were so costly, but the climate and its associated diseases, against which contemporary medicine had virtually no defence.

It would be difficult to over-state the effects of West Indian service on regiments sent there; service of even a few months could destroy a battalion more completely than any battle, and at least until the mid-19th century statistics are scarcely credible. For example, in the Leeward and Windward Islands alone, between the years 1796 and 1805, 24,916 troops *died*, not including those whose health was so broken as to cause them to be discharged. Even this was not the worst posting: taken together, Jamaica and Honduras were even more fatal, when between 1808 and 1828 the average death-rate was 15.5 per cent of the garrison annually.[1] So fatal was the climate and sickness that some could only explain it as divine retribution for the abhorrent practice of slavery: one writer described the West Indies as 'the theatre of the crimes of Europeans, committed against avowed principles of their religion; and they are at the same time the theatre of their punishment. The yellow fever avenges the cause of the injured African. This destroying angel, while it mows down squadrons of Europeans as it were at one stroke, passes his hut and does him no injury ...'[2]

This was one reason for the formation of corps of Africans, or of those born in the West Indies, who suffered far less from the effects of climate and disease than did Europeans. For example, in 1839 it was recorded that the annual mortality of European troops in Saint Lucia, Dominica, Tobago and Jamaica was between 12.3 and 15.3

per cent; for 'coloured' troops it was between 3 and 4 per cent. A more detailed example was provided by the mortality in Jamaica from April to September inclusive, 1841: the three British battalions in garrison (2/60th, 68th and 82nd) and the Royal Artillery lost ten officers and 268 men, almost all dead of fever, representing more than 22 per cent of the white garrison; in the same period, the 2nd and 3rd West India Regiments lost one (white) officer and sixteen men.

Military Forces
The first 'coloured' units were small, independent corps like Malcolm's Royal Rangers (formed in Martinique in 1794 under Lieutenant Malcolm of the 41st, an early expo-

Private of the 5th West India Regiment, c.1814; their version of the British infantry uniform of the period included a red jacket with facing-coloured half-lapels (in this case green) and one-piece 'gaiter-trousers' or 'mosquito trousers', here in blue. The 5th at this period was largely African in origin, and served at New Orleans. (Aquatint by I. C. Stadler after Charles Hamilton Smith, published 1815)

nent of light infantry tactics), but in 1795 some were reorganised as infantry regiments upon the British establishment. Although some recruits were West Indian-born, until 1807–8 the government reserved the right to have first pick of slave-ships arriving in the West Indies; between 1795 and 1808 some 13,400 men were purchased in this way, at a cost approaching a million pounds. Despite occasional problems such as the mutiny of the 8th West India Regiment at Dominica in 1802, the West India Regiments proved to be very good troops. The force reached a peak of twelve regiments by the end of the French Revolutionary Wars; all but the first two regiments had been disbanded by 1819, but the 3rd was re-raised in 1840 and disbanded in 1870, and a 3rd Battalion was formed again in 1897 and disbanded in 1904. A 4th Regiment was re-formed in 1862 and disbanded in 1865, and a 5th existed 1862–3. In the later period, the 1st Regiment recruited mainly Jamaicans and the 2nd Barbadians.

The West India Regiments' resistance to disease led to their employment in West Africa, a location even more unhealthy for Europeans. A recruiting depot was established at Sierra Leone in 1812, and in 1818 the headquarters and eight companies of the 2nd West India Regiment moved to that country and fought in the Ashanti War of 1824. From then until the end of the First World War there was always a detachment or more of the West India Regiments in the region, where they performed most valuable service. Two Victoria Crosses were awarded to the West India Regiments for service in Gambia: to the Virgin Islander Private Samuel Hodge of the 4th, for service at Tubabecelong, 30 June 1866, and to the Jamaican Lance-Corporal William Gordon of the 1st, for service at Toni-ataba, 13 March 1892. West Africa was not their only sphere of operations: the 1st Regiment ranged from Brazil in 1842 to Honduras in 1848–9 and 1872, for example. Initially they wore a uniform similar to that of British infantry, but from 1858 they became the only British troops to wear Zouave uniform (although the style was used by some colonial troops, for example the Gold Coast Hausas). Officers continued to wear British-style uniform, but the others retained elements of Zouave dress (for example tasselled caps or *chéchias*) even on campaign, for example in the Ashanti War of 1873–4, when the West Indians wore white tunics or smock-shirts and white trousers or their baggy, blue Zouave trousers. All officers, some senior NCOs and even some musicians were Europeans.

Forces also existing at the end of the 19th century included the African Artillery, three companies recruited from West Indians with British commanders, one company in Sierra Leone and the others in Jamaica and Saint Lucia, with officers and NCOs from the Royal Artillery; and the African Engineers, a company of fortress engineers in Jamaica, with detachments at Saint Lucia and Sierra Leone, and a submarine mining company in Jamaica.

In addition to the regular regiments and British garrisons, the West Indian colonies had their own militias from the earliest days of colonisation, including not only the European settlers and their servants but in the early period even their slaves. By the beginning of the 19th century these forces were generally restricted to freemen, but continued to embrace virtually the entire male population: in Jamaica, for example, the 1802 Militia Act established four battalions formed of 'every male person of free condition, save only the members of his majesty's council, the speaker of the assembly, and the chief justice of the island ... and persons who have borne commissions and have not been degraded by sentence of a court-martial,'[3] the latter presumably to avoid the indignity of ex-officers being compelled to serve in the ranks.

Sergeant (left) and corporal bugler, 2nd West India Regiment, c.1898, wearing the distinctive zouave costume of these regiments: white waistcoat and turban, scarlet zouave jacket with yellow braid, blue trousers with yellow piping, and white French-style gaiters. Both wear the Ashanti Star, awarded for the campaign of 1895–6.

Some such organisations were not especially efficient; one critic stated that 'Our colonists are inordinately fond of "playing at soldiers"; and the truth is, where the mode life is as monotonous as in the colonies, it is not very surprising that such devotion should be paid to that which, if it does nothing more, creates a little stir and excitement ... The men having been baked in the sun for three or four hours ... they are dismissed [and now] comes the reward of the young officer for all the arduous toil he had undergone, and the uncomfortable position in which he has been placed. 'Tis then that, with span new coat, golden epaulettes, shining sword, stately step, and warlike glance, he struts on foot, or careers on horseback, though the town, acknowledging the encouraging smiles of fair friends, or, as he goes, exciting the admiration of the multitude ... No one who hopes for promotion must offend the colonel, and consequently the influence which he exercises in every department, whether military, civil, or mercantile, is overpoweringly great. And it may readily be believed that this influence is not always exercised in a fair, judicious, or disinterested spirit; and that, in the days of oppression, it was very often used as an engine to check the rising ambition, if not to crush the daring and independent spirit, of the coloured or black man. At the same time neither the public nor private character of many who held the rank of colonel would bear scrutiny on the point of honesty, sobriety, intelligence, or wealth.'[4]

Even worse opinions were held of some militia formations. Sir William Stuart of the 86th, sent as part of the small British garrison to Tortola (one of the Virgin Islands) following the discovery of a conspiracy of rebellion among the slaves, described how 'to guard against any such peril in the future, a coloured militia was established, the officers being composed in a great measure of the white and Creole gentlemen, with a few whose complexions were of a deeper dye ... of all the unmitigated villains, the coloured men were the worse I ever met with ... The coloured Militia were a most insolent, overbearing, insulting set of fellows, looking like pirates and murderers, and no doubt some of them, if not all, would with opportunity have been both.'[5] Antagonism between the military and the civilian population, including a duel between the British commander and one of the island's magistrates, in which the latter was shot in the thigh, culminated in fights, and only the withholding of ammunition from the militia prevented a battle. Even so, encouraged by some of their officers, the coloured militia assembled to oppose the small force of 86th, and bloodshed might have resulted had not the 86th received reinforcements, as Stuart recalled: 'About four miles from the town, nearly five hundred free Africans were located. These men were Government pensioners, and formed an armed Militia of their own, with white officers. During the time of the excitement they marched in, as if for parade ... When the

coloured scoundrels saw them approaching, they cheered loudly, expecting to be joined by them, but were rather disappointed when Massa Blackee, marching through and past them, called out, "We King Billy's sodgers – we fight under buccra sodger!" and ranged themselves under my command. If resort to arms had been necessary, this was certainly a great acquisition to my strength.'[6] No further conflict occurred and the affair subsided with apologies from the militia's senior officers, and the cashiering of some of the troublemakers.

The threatened revolt in Tortola exemplified the co-operation sometimes found between colonising powers, in the face of a common threat: in addition to the British company, the Danish authorities of Saint Thomas (about twenty miles from Tortola) sent 200 of their troops to help protect the colonists on Tortola. This was a welcome reinforcement despite the character of the Danes: 'The Danish soldiers were dressed like our men, in red, but they had a slounging lubberly appearance, very different from the smart military carriage of British soldiers. They, however, seemed in one respect not unlike them, and that was in their partiality for liquor ... They were composed of almost every nation under the sun, except British, the great majority being Germans. Two Scotchmen and an Englishman had a short time before formed part of their number, but had died of delirium tremens from drink ...'[7]

Later in the 19th century the calibre of the local forces was improved greatly, and included cavalry (usually styled light horse, yeomanry, and later mounted infantry), formed from those possessing their own mounts, planters and their dependants, considered to be among the most convenient and reliable ways of suppressing insurrection.

Jamaica

Second in area to the Bahamas at some 4,207 square miles, Jamaica was by far the most populous of the West Indian colonies (in 1881 the population was just over 584,000, more than three and one-third times as many as the next most populous). Originally a Spanish colony, it passed by force of arms into British possession in 1655; from 1661 it was administered by a governor and executive council, with a constitution based on that of England, and British possession was recognised by the Treaty of Madrid, 1670. Apart from a threatened invasion by France and Spain in 1782 (prevented by the victory of Rodney and Hood at the Battle of the Saints, 12 April 1782), all Jamaica's military activity was directed towards the suppression of internal unrest. Slave insurrections were not uncommon (one account treated such revolts in so matter-of-fact a manner as to state that the 1782 revolt was only remarkable for the appearance of the person called Three-Fingered Jack!), but more significant was the 1795 Maroon War.

The Maroons were descendants of the slaves of the Spaniards, who had fled to the mountains upon the

British conquest of 1655, and for generations had raided the white settlements and had attracted fugitive slaves from the plantations. They became especially formidable in the 1730s under the leadership of a chief named Cudjoe, and after a number of abortive attempts to chastise them, the government of Jamaica concluded a treaty in 1738 which granted an amnesty to the Maroons, who in return undertook to surrender runaway slaves and act as allies to the settlers. This they did, for example assisting in the suppression of the 1760 slave revolt; they were reported to have eaten the heart of one of the leaders of the insurrection, a slave named Tacky. The 1795 Maroon War arose from the diminution of the power of the chiefs, and the replacement of one of the white Residents among them; seeking to punish them for driving away the new Resident, the British attempted to draw a cordon around Maroon territory. The first British attempts were notably unsuccessful, until two troops of 17th Light Dragoons were trained in bush warfare, operating as dismounted skirmishers and fighting the Maroons on their own terms. Faced with a formidable enemy, the Maroons surrendered; and against the promise of the officer responsible, Colonel Walpole of the 13th Light Dragoons, that they should not be sent out of the island, they were exiled to Nova Scotia.

The most serious slave insurrection occurred at the end of 1831 and beginning of 1832, caused partly, it was said, by the belief that emancipation had already been granted; nonconformist preaching was also blamed, so that the revolt was sometimes styled 'the Baptist Insurrection'. The troops in garrison included the 22nd, 56th, 77th and 84th, who were joined by naval landing parties; but no major battle occurred, the insurgents abandoning their stockaded position at Greenwich Hill when the government forces advanced. The rebellion faded away after an amnesty was offered on 3 February 1832 to all who returned to their estates within ten days; but a number of outrages were committed, and the cost of the suppression of unrest was calculated at £161,596.

Among the actions of the 1831–2 rebellion was an attack by three columns of rebels on the Western Interior regiment of militia on 29 December 1831. Interestingly, this included an early example of adopting a tactic against an undisciplined enemy which under more conventional conditions was restricted to repelling cavalry: '... the main body of the WI regiment ... had been formed into solid square, and kept up a considerable firing of musketry ... reserved their fire until the rebels had advanced within thirty or forty yards, when they commenced a very rapid fire, which continued for about twenty minutes, when the enemy disappeared in all directions ... we had one man killed and four wounded, and Major King's and Serjeant Sewell's hats were shot through, but they received no injury ... the rebels ... admitted they had lost ten men killed and twenty-five wounded ...'[8]

By a decree of 1837, the following were the numbers of rank and file to be provided by each district of the island, which illustrates the considerable size of the force: Kingston 1,500; Saint Elizabeth 800; Saint Thomas in the East, Westmoreland, Saint James and Trelawny 600 each; Saint Andrews, Hanover, Saint Catherine, Clarendon and Saint Mary 500 each; Saint Georges 400; Manchester 350; Port Royal, Portland, Saint John and Saint Dorothy, Saint Thomas in the Vale, Saint Ann Eastern and Saint Ann Western 300 each; and Vere 200. The local forces included cavalry from the 17th century, such as the Jamaica Light Horse of the mid-19th century.

Further violence occurred in October 1865 when a mob stormed the court house at Morant Bay to rescue a prisoner, beginning what was described as 'a most serious and alarming insurrection of the Negro population'.[9] The imposition of new taxes, following the installation of a new governor, Edward J. Eyre in 1865, had caused much discontent, inflamed (in Eyre's opinion) by remarks to the colonial secretary in London by Dr. Underhill, secretary of a Baptist organisation, which were made public in the island. Revolts occurred in surrounding districts, and although white civilians were evacuated under military escort, some murders were committed with a brutality which 'could only be paralleled by the atrocities of the Indian mutiny'. Almost the entire force of militia of the district at the centre of the outbreak, 22 strong, were massacred. The only British regiment in Jamaica was the 2/6th, but the 1st West India Regiment had personnel available, and also employed were naval landing-parties and Maroons, the latter 'unbounded in their devotion and loyalty'. The revolt was suppressed with vehemence, and the severity of retribution (hanging or flogging of those convicted by court-martial) was excused by Eyre in terms of discouraging the spread of rebellion: 'Disaffection and disloyalty still exist in nearly all the parishes of the island, and had there been the least hesitation or delay in dealing with them in the parishes where they became developed in rebellion, I confidently believe that the insurrection would have been universal throughout the entire island, and that either the colony would have been lost to the mother country, or an almost interminable war and an unknown expense would have had to be incurred in suppressing it.' Eyre attributed the outbreak not to the undoubted economic hardships experienced by much of the population, but to seditious literature and demagogues 'endeavouring to bring into contempt the representative of the Sovereign, and all constituted authority'; and George William Gordon, a coloured member of the House of Assembly and a Baptist preacher, who was held to be among the most culpable, was tried by court-martial and sentenced to be hanged. Eyre also claimed that 'the rebels are not the poor or the starving, but persons who are well off and well to do in the world, and better educated than the lower class of Negroes in general usually are'. Despite his protestations, however, the extreme force used in the suppression of the revolt provoked much controversy in Britain; Eyre was recalled and a prosecution instituted against him, but the jury threw out the indictment.

The men of the 1st West India Regiment were especially praised for their loyalty, even though the insurgents they arrested, or whose property they were ordered to burn, were not only their fellow-islanders but in many cases their kinsmen. The Jamaica House of Assembly voted £100 for the purchase of plate for the regimental mess as a tribute to the unit's loyalty during this melancholy period. It was the last serious insurrection in Jamaica; with the installation of a new administration and the crown colony system of government, the economic situation began to improve, and a new constitution was granted to the island in 1884.

British regiments were garrisoned in Jamaica throughout, and some troops were raised specifically for service there: the 99th (or Jamaica) Regiment of Foot was formed in Britain in 1779 by the West India merchants, and embarked for Jamaica in 1780. The alligator badge of Jamaica (normally associated with locally raised Jamaican forces and worn, for example, on their belt-plates) was borne on buttons, grenadier and light company caps, and Colours; it was disbanded in 1784. The 20th Light Dragoons was raised in 1791 for service on the island, and from that date until 1802 was titled 'Jamaica Light Dragoons'; its helmets also carried the alligator device. As reorganised in 1885, the Jamaica Militia comprised an infantry battalion and two garrison artillery companies; every member of the infantry volunteered for service in South Africa in 1899.

Barbados
One of the smaller West Indian territories (166 square miles, with a population in 1881 of almost 172,000), Barbados was first settled by the British in 1625. Acquired without conquest or opposition from other colonising powers, the island was never out of British possession, and threatened only briefly by the French in 1805. The wars against America caused economic hardship, but the abolition of slavery in 1834 had no bad consequences; the only serious unrest being riots in 1875–6, provoked by proposed confederation of the Windward Islands (of which Barbados is geographically part), but the island retained its independence. In addition to local forces, British units were deployed in garrison in the island, and one of the emigrant corps, which existed from 1803 to 1817, the York Light Infantry Volunteers, was originally titled (1803–4) the Barbados Volunteer Emigrants. Local forces included cavalry from at least the beginning of the 18th century, and in the mid-19th century included the Barbados Yeomanry.

Trinidad and Tobago
Second in size to Jamaica (1,754 square miles, plus 114 square miles of Tobago), but with a population in 1881 less then Barbados (just over 171,000), Trinidad was discovered by Columbus in 1496 and remained a Spanish possession until captured by a British expedition from Martinique in 1797, British possession being confirmed by the Treaty of Amiens (1802). Although no campaigning took place within the island, a militia was formed in the early years of British administration, involving all male residents aged between 15 and 55 years (provided that they were freemen), and including cavalry (the Royal Trinidad Light Dragoons existed in the first half of the 19th century) and artillery as well as the usual infantry. The force dwindled in the 1830s, and in 1879 the Trinidad Volunteer Force was formed, including light horse, garrison artillery and infantry (as part of the Trinidad Light Horse a troop existed for a time in Tobago, and one at Tacarigua was known from 1889 as the Burnley Carabiniers, named after the Hon. H. W. Burnley); there was also the Trinidad Constabulary, a semi-military body.

The associated small island of Tobago was ceded to Britain by France in 1814; until 1889 it was part of the Windward Islands, but in that year was joined to Trinidad, originally retaining a degree of independence, but ten years later its administration and laws were merged with those of Trinidad.

Windward Islands
Named from the fact that they were the most exposed to the prevailing wind of all the West Indies, the Windward Islands comprise the following (with areas and approximate population in 1881): Saint Lucia (233 square miles, 38,500), Saint Vincent (140 square miles, 40,500), and Grenada (133 square miles, 42,500). Although geographically part of the Windwards, Barbados retained its independence; Tobago was administered as part of the Windwards until 1889. The islands were a confederation with a common governor-general (resident in Grenada) but separate administrations.

First settled by France, possession of Grenada passed from the French West India Company to the French crown in 1674. The island was surrendered to the British in 1762 and ceded formally by the Treaty of Paris (1763); it was recaptured by France in 1779 but restored to Britain by the Treaty of Versailles (1783). The principal military activity in Grenada took place during the French Revolutionary Wars, when in March 1795, supported by the French, a mulatto named Julien Fédon led a revolt of the Negro inhabitants, native Caribs and many of the French residents. A small British force was sent from Saint Lucia to support the existing small garrison and local volunteers, joined by naval landing-parties and the crews of three armed vessels sent by the Spanish governor of Trinidad from his own small garrison. Further reinforcements were received from Barbados (including the 25th and 29th), but by the beginning of 1796 the British were still able only to hold the town of Saint George's. Sir Ralph Abercromby's expedition, organised to redress setbacks in the West Indies, arrived in March 1796 and after a desperate fight carried the insurgents' main position overlooking Saint Andrew's Bay (then known as Marquis Bay or Port Royal) on 25 March, showing little mercy to the rebels, whose brutal treatment of British captives was well-known. In June 1796 Brigadier Nicolls landed a force on the west of the island to attack Fédon's main camp, and another column marched from the east coast. Most of the rebels surrendered (fourteen out of eighty renegade whites were hanged) but Fédon and 300 followers fled to the mountains. His post was overrun on 18 June, and in July Fédon himself was surprised; he disappeared over a precipice and was not heard of again. With the extinction of this rebellion, Grenada remained secure in British hands, although the losses incurred in the revolt were enormous, including the economic ruination of much of the island by the destruction of plantations, and in loss of life; about a quarter of the island's slaves were killed or lost by their owners. The local forces had included from 1795 a battalion of Royal Black Rangers (composed of trustworthy slaves) and a corps of light dragoons; they were re-organised in July 1801 into five infantry regiments (and another in the adjacent island of Carriocou), the Grenada Light Dragoons and two artillery companies attached to the Saint George's Regiment.

English settlers in Saint Lucia were driven away by the indigenous Caribs in 1641; French settlers were sent from Martinique in 1660, and were defeated by the British in 1663, but the island was restored to France by the Peace of Breda (1667). Britain still maintained settlers there until they were expelled in 1723; Saint Lucia surrendered to the British in 1762, but was restored to France by the Treaty of Paris (1763). Again captured by the British in 1778, it was again restored to France by the Treaty of Versailles (1783). In April 1794 it was surrendered to Sir Charles Grey's expedition, but the energetic French Commissioner of the Convention at Guadeloupe, Victor Hugues, encouraged insurgency, and Britain was compelled to evacuate the island in June 1795. The following April Abercromby landed a strong expedition, and after hard fighting the rebels surrendered on 25 May 1796. The island was returned to France by the Treaty of Amiens, but again capitulated to the British in June 1803, and British possession was made official in 1814. No further military action took place in Saint Lucia, but a British garrison was maintained until the withdrawal of imperial troops in 1905.

Despite early British claims to Saint Vincent, the island was regarded as 'neutral' in terms of Anglo-French Caribbean rivalry, and confirmed by the Treaty of Aix-la-Chapelle (1748). Britain took possession in 1762, con-

firmed by the Treaty of Paris (1763), but some conflict with the Caribs ensued until a treaty of 1773 granted them a reserve in the north of the island. Saint Vincent was surrendered to France in 1779, but restored to Britain by the Treaty of Versailles (1783). Urged by Hugues, the Caribs rose in 1795, and despite the death of the Carib king Chateaugai in a defeat by a detachment of 46th and a naval landing-party from HMS *Zebra*, when he was threatening the capital, Kingston, in March 1795, the British garrison was so small that initially they could do no more than hold the capital, which was roughly the position after a year of effort, despite reinforcements for both sides (the French aided the Caribs). On 9 June 1796 Abercromby's army stormed the rebel stronghold at Vigie, however, which virtually ended hostilities with the capitulation of most of the rebels and the capture of seventeen pieces of ordnance. The suppression of the insurrection ended campaigning in Saint Vincent.

Leeward Islands

Their name deriving from their being less exposed to the prevailing winds than the Windward Islands, the Leewards included the following British possessions and their dependencies (with area and approximate population in 1881): Antigua (108 square miles, 35,000), Dominica (291 square miles, 28,000), Saint Kitts (63 square miles) and Nevis (50 square miles, together 41,000), Montserrat (32½ square miles, 10,000), and the Virgin Islands (58 square miles, 5,000). They also included the tiny Dutch islands of Saint Eustatius and Saba, the French colonies of Guadeloupe and Martinique, and Saint Martin, partly French and partly Dutch. The principal British possessions formed a colony under one governor, divided into five 'presidencies': Antigua (with its dependencies Barbuda and Redonda), Saint Kitts (with Nevis and Anguilla), Dominica, Montserrat, and the Virgin Islands.

Antigua was colonised by the British in the 17th century; it was attacked by France in 1666 but quickly re-possessed, and was confirmed as British by the Treaty of Breda. Thereafter, although garrisoned and used as a harbour, it saw no more warfare. Although not regarded as among the most unhealthy of West Indian postings, it is noteworthy that after a career including the Peninsular and Waterloo campaigns, the final sentence of the account of his military career written by Lieutenant-Colonel Jonathan Leach of the 95th was devoted to that part of his service which had made the most painful impression upon him: 'All the friends of my early life are entombed in Antigua',[10] typical of the effect on morale caused by the sicknesses which decimated so many regiments.

Dominica was first settled by the French, but after some Anglo–French rivalry it was agreed in 1748 that it should be left to the Caribs; yet the French settlement increased, resulting in its capture by Britain in 1761.

Right: Officer of the Trinidad Yeomanry, c.1896: the uniform was khaki, with a khaki slouch hat edged green, bearing the star of Trinidad and a cock-feather plume. Other ranks wore similar uniform but with white canvas gaiters, and bandoliers. Martini-Henry carbines were carried until 1903.

Below: The unusual cut of the zouave costume of the West India Regiments gave scope for caricature, as in this print after Major Thomas S. Secombe.

India Regiment and local militia with which to defend the island, but put up a most creditable fight, and although the capital (Roseau) was taken by the French, Prevost withdrew to a fortified position; unwilling to commence an all-out siege, the French left. Among the local forces, as late as 1831 there was organised a corps of Colonial Rangers intended to suppress insurrection and apprehend runaway slaves.

Saint Kitts, or Saint Christopher, was settled by the British in 1623; five years later it was divided between Britain and France, but from the Treaty of Utrecht (1713) it was wholly British. Nevis was first colonised by British from Saint Kitts in 1628. Montserrat was colonised by the British in 1632 but captured by France in 1664; restored in 1668, it was taken again by the French in 1782, and restored in 1784. The Virgin Islands include the Danish possessions of Saint Thomas, Sainte Croix and Saint John; the principal British possession was Tortola, colonised in 1666. Saint Thomas and Saint John were captured by Britain during periods of Anglo–Danish hostility (1801–2, 1807–15) but were restored. The American part of the Virgin Islands were originally dependencies of Puerto Rico, ceded by Spain in 1898.

Bahamas

The Bahamas archipelago consists of 29 islands and innumerable separate rocks and cays, with a total area of 5,540

Ceded to Britain by the Treaty of Paris (1763), Dominica was seized by the French in 1778, but restored in 1783. A French attempt from Guadeloupe to capture the island in 1795 was unsuccessful, but in 1805 the French General Lagrange landed. The British commander, General Prevost, had only about 300 of the 46th, 400 of the 1st West square miles (4,424 for the main islands); population in 1881 was about 43,500. The most important island, New Providence of 85 square miles, contains the capital, Nassau. The first settlement was British, in 1646; in 1680 there was a Spanish attack, and in 1703 another blew up the New Providence fort. For some years it was left as a haunt of buccaneers (the most famous probably Edward Teach, alias Blackbeard), but the first royal governor, Woodes Rogers, was installed in 1718, and a better class of settler was introduced, agriculture replacing piracy as the principal occupation. Briefly in 1776 New Providence fell into American hands, and the Spanish held it from 1781 until its recapture by the British in 1783. No further military events of note occurred, although Nassau became a centre for blockade-running during the American Civil War.

French Colonies

The principal French colonies were Guadeloupe (688 square miles) and Martinique (380 square miles). Martinique was first colonised from 1635, passing from private ownership to the French crown in 1674; the indigenous Caribs were largely exterminated and the island re-populated by slaves (unlike the British colonies, slavery was abolished only in 1860). Britain attempted to capture the island in 1666, 1667 and 1693, and the Dutch in 1674, but Britain only succeeded in 1762. Martinique was restored to France in the following year, but was taken again in 1793 and held until the conclusion of the French Revolutionary Wars; Britain captured it again in 1809, but its final restoration to France occurred in 1815. Probably its most famous citizen was Napoleon's empress Josephine, her father, M. de la Pagerie, being one of the French colonists.

Guadeloupe was also first colonised by the French from 1635, and also passed from private ownership to the crown in 1674; originally a dependency of Martinique, it was separated from that island only in 1775. Britain attempted its capture in 1666, 1691 and 1703, and succeeded in 1759, but Guadeloupe was restored to France in 1763. In April 1794 Britain again gained possession, but a revolt by Victor Hugues, aided by the Negro population whom he had given their freedom, made the British position untenable, and they evacuated the island in December. In 1802 Napoleon sent an expedition to re-establish slavery (it was finally abolished only in 1848), and Britain again held the island from 1810 to 1816.

The island of Haiti enjoyed perhaps the most sanguinary history of any in the region. Originally a Spanish colony (Hispaniola), its original inhabitants were exterminated and replaced by African slaves who were shipped in from 1512. French colonists occupied part of the island and were confirmed in possession by the Treaty of Ryswick (1697), their part being styled Saint-Dominique or 'San Domingo'. The French Revolution saw the beginning of hostilities between the three resident groups (whites, mulattos and slaves), noted for appalling brutalities on all sides. France gained possession of the whole island in 1795, and from 1793 to 1798 Britain waged a hopeless and appallingly costly campaign which achieved nothing, and was initiated by French royalists who in 1792 offered Britain sovereignty over the island in return for British protection against the French republicans or slave revolt. By 1801 the remarkable Toussaint l'Ouverture had restored order and established a form of constitutional government, with himself as governor for life, but holding allegiance to France. Napoleon was suspicious and determined to restore slavery; he sent an expedition under General Leclerc, who encountered stern resistance. Toussaint accepted peace-terms but found French guarantees worthless; he was seized and sent to France, where he died in prison in 1803. Outraged at this treachery, the San Domingans renewed the fight, under Jean Jacques Dessalines, and compelled the French to withdraw in November 1803. From then the island sank into anarchy, beginning with the assassination of Dessalines in 1806; the eastern part was re-taken by Spain but threw off Spanish control in 1821, was briefly re-united, but in 1844 split into the republics of Santo Domingo and Haiti. Civil war and revolution continued throughout the 19th century.

Notes

1. 'Contributions to Statistics of the British Army', by H. Marshall, originally in *Edinburgh Medical & Surgical Journal*, July 1835, and republished separately.
2. Letter signed 'A White Man', *Gentleman's Magazine*, February, 1803 p. 136.
3. *An Act Concerning the Militia*, 9 December 1802.
4. 'Short Notes on the West Indies, by a Late Resident', in *Chambers' Edinburgh Journal*, 11 January 1845, pp. 20–1.
5. Stuart, Colonel W. K. *Reminiscences of a Soldier*, London, 1874, pp. 199–200, 202–3.
6. Ibid., p. 215
7. Ibid., pp. 199, 221–2.
8. Dispatch by Colonel W. S. Crignon, 2 January 1832; *London Gazette*, 22 February 1832.
9. Dispatch by Governor E. J. Eyre, 20 October 1865; *London Gazette*, 17 November 1865. Succeeding quotations in this section are from the same.
10. Leach, Lieutenant-Colonel J. *Rough Sketches of the Life of an Old Soldier*, London, 1831, p. 411.

References

Ashby, T. 'Fédon's Rebellion', in *Journal of the Society for Army Historical Research*, vols. LXII, LXIII, 1984–5 (excellent modern account of the operations in Grenada, exemplifying many of the problems encountered in the region).

Buckley, R. N. *Slaves in Red Coats: The British West India Regiments 1795-1815*, New Haven and London 1979 (most important study).

Caulfield, J. E. *One Hundred Years' History of the Second Battalion, West India Regiment, 1795-1895*, London, 1899.

Duffy, M. *Soldiers, Sugar and Seapower: the British Expeditions to the West Indies and the War against Revolutionary France*, London, 1987.

Ellis, Colonel A. B. *History of the First West India Regiment*, London 1885.

Fortescue, Hon. Sir John. *History of the British Army*, vol. IV, London, 1906 (useful study of military activity in the West Indies 1795-1801).

VI
AUSTRALASIA AND
THE PACIFIC

AUSTRALASIA AND THE PACIFIC

AUSTRALIA

The nation of Australia came into existence on 1 January 1901 by the federation of the six states which had hitherto been independent. The oldest was New South Wales: a penal settlement had been founded at Port Jackson in 1788, to which British criminals were sent for the next half century. Van Dieman's Land, later Tasmania, was occupied as early as 1803 as an auxiliary penal colony under New South Wales, achieving separate government in 1825; South Australia was created in 1836; the colony of Victoria achieved its independence from New South Wales in 1851, Queensland in 1859, and Western Australia became a self-governing colony in 1890. Each colony had its own administration and governor, the first being installed at Sydney in 1788, the earlier incumbents ruling with almost total power in their own hands.

Although there was no Australian 'colonial war' in the accepted sense, conflict did occur between the settlers and the indigenous Aborigines. Their society having no concept of territorial ownership, organised hierarchy or hereditary or elected leaders, there was no possibility of organised resistance to the settlers, conflict being limited to isolated skirmishes which occurred as the colonists

The 'Southern Cross' insignia of the New South Wales forces: a helmet-plate in gilded brass.

spread into the hinterland. Although limited, such conflicts were often sanguinary in the extreme and marked by massacre and retribution; but as the Aborigines had basically only stone-age weapons the contest was entirely unequal and could have terrible consequences. Probably the most extreme example concerned the inhabitants of Tasmania, who, after 'a petty and harassing warfare ... attended on both sides by acts of great oppression and inhumanity', it was decided, should be transported to Flinders Island in the Bass Strait, where 'the conquered savages were taken from the almost boundless hills and forests of their native land, to linger out an indolent and miserable existence on a few circumscribed and cheerless acres on a desert island'. In the words of his account of 1844, the dwindling band (of which only 57 were then still alive) were fed daily by the government storekeeper, 'and it is amusing to hear him crying out such names as Hannibal, Pompey, Bonaparte, Cleopatra, Venus, Desdemona, &c. when the sable representatives of these *great folks* come running forward with their little wooden platters, and receive their allowance for the day'. Prophetically, the observer noted that 'cruel necessity required that these rude and ignorant savages should be placed under some control; but their lot is now so degraded and humiliating, so totally opposed to, and destructive of, their natural feelings and habits, that I am sure no reflecting mind that considers their past and present state, but must admit that the oppressor's yoke has fallen heavily upon them, and that they are a doomed and unhappy race, and fated soon to be numbered with those tribes who have lived and passed away'.[1] The last of the indigenous Tasmanians died in 1876.

Ironically, the only organised military action that occurred in Australia was fought between whites, and arose from objections to the imposition of licence-fees and commissions on the gold-miners of Victoria. A Ballarat Reform League was established to represent the miners' case; there were outbreaks of unrest and in November 1854 detachments of the 12th and 40th Foot were sent to the goldfields to support the local constabulary. On 28 November there was a conflict between troops and 'diggers', and the latter determined to erect a stockade to defend the mine-workings, on Eureka Plateau. A rudimentary military organisation was attempted by the miners, whose civilian firearms were supplemented by a few home-made pikes, and two units of Americans even aspired to military titles, the American First Rifle Brigade and the Independent California Rangers Revolver Brigade. On 3 December, after some of the best-armed miners had marched out to meet troops rumoured to be approaching from Melbourne, the Eureka Stockade was stormed by a small force of troops and police. A few of the attackers were killed, but the stockade proved no obstacle, and after some 'diggers' had been killed the remainder were captured, together with their 'Southern Cross' flag. Minor though the action was, it had considerable effect as a number of reforms followed, and the arrested men were acquitted when brought to trial. Their leader, Peter Lalor, was even elected to the state legislature as member for Ballarat.

Military Forces

Until the garrison was withdrawn in 1870, British troops were stationed in Australia, to protect the settlements and as security against internal unrest, regarded as an essential duty given the convict nature of many of the settlers. In 1789 a regiment was formed specifically for service in Australia, the New South Wales Corps; but its discipline was not good (it was nicknamed 'the Rum Puncheon Corps' from its officers' participation in the rum trade, and was involved in the arrest of the governor, William Bligh!), and in 1808 it was taken into the line as the 102nd Foot, returning home in 1810. Its place was filled by a succession of British regiments, beginning with the 1/73rd in 1810; often more than one regiment was represented in the Australian garrison: for example, the 11th, 51st, 58th, 65th, 96th and 99th all served in Australia in 1846. The last British troops to leave were the 2/14th, 2/18th and elements of the Royal Artillery, the final garrison withdrawing in 1870.

Locally raised forces existed from the formation in 1800 of two volunteer corps in New South Wales, the Sydney and Parramatta companies, raised from free men to combat a perceived threat of rebellion by Irish convicts. They were disbanded in 1801 but 'Local Associations' were re-formed in 1803 and existed until 1809. When the 102nd returned to England in 1810, men who wished to remain in Australia were formed into veteran companies, which existed until 1823; and three Royal Veteran Battalion companies were raised in England in 1826–33 for service in New South Wales and Tasmania, members receiving a land-grant in those colonies after two years' service.

In 1851 a proposal was made to permit the formation of volunteer corps in New South Wales, which was acted upon when a threat of Russian invasion occurred during the Crimean War. The 1st New South Wales Rifle Volunteers were formed, together with mounted rifles and artillery; and interest was stimulated by the demands on the regular forces to go to New Zealand in 1860. In all, three artillery batteries, a troop of mounted rifles, fourteen rifle companies in Sydney and its suburbs and six in the country areas were formed. In 1867 an attempt was made to stimulate recruiting by the passing of the Volunteer Land Act, by which five years' effected service was rewarded by a fifty-acre land-grant, but abuse led to its repeal in 1878. The colony re-organised its forces on the withdrawal of the British garrison in 1870, and in 1871 a 'regular' battery of Permanent Artillery was formed; by 1874 there were eleven artillery batteries, an engineer corps, two rifle regiments in Sydney and one each in the northern, southern and western districts. In 1878 a system of partial payment of volunteers was introduced, and the infantry were re-organised as

the 1st Regiment New South Wales Infantry. Ultimately there were four partially paid numbered regiments, four of unpaid reserves (the 5th Scottish Rifles, formed 1885; 6th Australian and 7th St. George's English Rifles, 1897, and 8th Irish Rifles, 1899), and other unpaid local corps. A troop of Sydney Light Horse was raised in 1884, later joined by troops at Illawarra, West Camden, Hunter River, Ulmarra, Upper Clarence and Grafton; all were part of the unpaid reserve. Forming the 1st New South Wales Cavalry, they were converted to lancers (traditionally as a result of the New South Wales Contingent's meeting with the 5th Lancers during the Sudan campaign), and as the New South Wales Lancers won universal admiration by their participation in the 1897 Diamond Jubilee celebrations in England, and the training of a squadron in Britain in 1899. Another fine regiment of mounted infantry, the 1st Australian Horse, was raised in 1897.

The first Australians to see campaign service were the 2,368 men who went to New Zealand during the 1863–4

The sergeant-major of the Victorian Mounted Rifles (his crown rank-badge just visible above the right cuff) with Daisy, the regimental mascot, c. 1898. The elaborately pleated khaki pagri was a notable regimental distinction.

war, but these served in New Zealand units. In 1885, however, an offer was accepted for a volunteer contingent to be sent from New South Wales to the war in the Sudan, and by the end of March the New South Wales Contingent had arrived at Suakin. It comprised a headquarters (five officers, two chaplains, three NCOs), an artillery battery (six officers, 184 other ranks), an infantry battalion (seventeen officers, 514 other ranks) and an ambulance corps (three officers, 32 other ranks); all were volunteers, enrolled for the purpose, because it was not feasible to send an existing unit *en masse*, though it included many members of the existing NSW forces (the 1st Regiment, for example, supplied 76 members). The Contingent was welcomed enthusiastically – their fine appearance and physique was especially remarked upon, in contrast to the thin, pale men often seen in British ranks – and the infantry arrived wearing red tunics, only changing into khaki on their arrival. Their presence was equally a demonstration of loyalty, as expressed in characteristic language: 'To be allowed to share in the perils and glories of the battlefield as part of a British Army, was regarded at once as a distinction of which Australia might be proud, and as a guarantee of their future position of British subjects. The help which they were now giving might be slight, but Australia in a few years would number ten millions of men, and this small body was an earnest of what they might do hereafter. If ever England herself was threatened ... they would risk life, fortune – all they had – as willingly as they were sending their present contingent. It was a practical demonstration in favour of Imperial unity.'[2]

Tasmania's military forces originated with the formation of volunteer units in 1859–60, the first being the Hobart Town Artillery, but enthusiasm waned and in 1867 the survivors were reconstituted in two artillery units, one in the north and one in the south, the latter ceasing to exist and leaving only the Launceston Artillery. In 1878 a renewed attempt to create a volunteer force led to the expansion of the artillery and the formation of the Tasmanian Volunteer Rifle Regiment, and in 1883 an engineer corps. Initially styled 'Local Forces', in 1885 the name 'Defence Forces' was adopted, and the 1886 Defence Act made all male inhabitants aged 18 to 55 years liable to serve (although it was not enacted). In 1885 a small Permanent Force of artillery was enrolled, and a large reserve was formed from the members of the rifle clubs authorised by Act of Parliament in 1889.

South Australia's military force dated from 1840–1, but the militia unit formed then was of brief duration. A Militia Act was passed at the time of the Crimean War which authorised the compulsory formation of 2,000 men, selected by ballot if insufficient volunteers were forthcoming, but it was unnecessary to enact this legislation. Numerous rifle corps existed – thirteen were amalgamated in 1860 to form the Adelaide Rifles – and in 1877 the military forces were re-organised, to include mounted units which had originated with the Reedbeds Mounted Volunteers of 1860. A small Permanent Force of artillery was created, and after a further re-organisation in 1886 the state's forces comprised the Permanent Force (an artillery battery), the Militia (the Adelaide Lancers, Adelaide Rifles and two artillery batteries) and the Volunteer Force (eleven mounted infantry companies and four infantry battalions).

Victoria formed its first military units in 1854, the Melbourne Volunteer Rifles (which became the Victorian Volunteer Artillery), the Geelong Rifles and the Victorian Yeomanry. The force was expanded in 1859 and re-organised in 1872, but in 1883–4 the Volunteers were replaced by a Militia which included partial payment for military service. Ultimately the state maintained a Permanent Force of artillery (formed 1870) and engineers, and the Militia which included the Prince of Wales's Light Horse (the original yeomanry, reduced to one troop in 1885 when most joined the new Victorian Mounted Rifles, which was increased to two battalions in 1891), three field and eight garrison artillery batteries, four rifle battalions, and various cadet units (the latter a feature of the reserve forces of the Australian colonies). The Militia included a Nordenfelt battery with three machine-guns, formed in 1885 and converted to the Victorian Horse Artillery in 1889, and re-equipped with 12pdrs. When by 1899 the artillery in Australia had become integrated, the Victorian horse, field and garrison artillery all formed part of the Victorian Regiment of Royal Australian Artillery.

The Queensland military forces originated with the formation of volunteer mounted rifle, artillery and infantry companies in 1860, but they were never numerous until the Queensland government passed the 1884 Defence Force Act, which made military service a liability for all males aged between 16 and 60 years. The resulting organisation included a Permanent Force of two artillery batteries, the Defence Force of men paid when on duty (mounted infantry, garrison artillery, three infantry regiments and some companies), and a Volunteer Force of unpaid men; with six cadet corps and a reserve of rifle clubs which received arms and ammunition from the government at less than cost price.

Although an ephemeral corps of Swan River Volunteers had existed as early as 1829, the Western Australian forces were generally created in 1862; three small units were formed, followed by mounted rifles and artillery in 1872, and in 1874 the 1st Battalion West Australian Volunteers was formed from three of the existing rifle corps. The 1894 Defence Act created the Western Australian Defence Force, an entirely voluntary body with no 'Permanent Force', including artillery and infantry.

The Australian colonies all responded to the call-to-arms arising from the South African War of 1899–1902. Among the first in the field was the troop of New South

A classic 'mounted infantry' uniform as worn by the Victorian Mounted Rifles, formed in December 1885 and expanded to two battalions in 1891. (Print after H. Bunnett, c. 1890)

An example of colonial uniforms based closely on those of the British Army: the Victorian Artillery's costume was copied from that of the Royal Artillery (blue with red facings and gold lace). (Print after H. Bunnett, c.1890)

Wales Lancers which had been training in England, and other Australians were already in South Africa when the war began, many working in the gold-fields; the Imperial Light Horse, for example, was raised by Walter Karri-Davies, a man from Broken Hill who recruited among the Australians mining near Johannesburg. Even before the outbreak of hostilities, Queensland had offered 250 mounted rifles to the British government in the event of war, followed by New South Wales and Victoria; and in September 1899 a joint offer of 2,500 men was made by the combined state administrations. Some 16,632 Australians served in the war, all volunteers, in some 57 units, almost all formed specifically for the campaign. Each unit maintained a 'state' identity, although some were part of a numbered sequence of units encompassing more than one state. The majority of units were Mounted Rifles, Mounted Infantry or 'Bushmen' (often entitled 'Imperial Bushmen'), but the New South Wales contingents included artillery and medical personnel.

The federation of the previously -independent states in 1901 created a single Australian army, a fact exemplified by the formation of the eight battalions of Australian Commonwealth Horse which arrived in South Africa only at the very end of the war, in March 1902. Although three of its battalions were raised from only one state (5th New South Wales, 6th Victoria, 7th Queensland), the remain-

der for the first time combined men from more than one state in the same unit.

It is likely that the Australian units in South Africa exerted an influence greater than their numbers; as many were experienced horsemen, used to an outdoor life, they were expert mounted infantry able to meet the Boer Commandos on their own terms. Some importance was also placed on what might be termed their national spirit, perhaps born of the more independent, necessarily self-reliant lifestyle of the non-urban colonies; as Kitchener remarked of the defence of Elands River in August 1900, when elements of the 3rd Queensland Mounted Infantry, New South Wales Citizen Bushmen, 3rd Victorian and 3rd West Australian Bushmen held out against a severe Boer attack, only 'colonials' could have survived under such circumstances. Perhaps the Australians' skill at mounted rifle tactics helped to keep their casualties reasonably low, suffering some 1,400 during the war, including 508 fatalities (251 killed in action, the remainder from disease). The first Victoria Cross to be won by an Australian was awarded to Captain Neville Howse of the New South Wales Army Medical Corps, for an action near Vredefort on 24 July 1900; but he was not the first Australian-born winner, being a Somerset man. That distinction is held jointly by Lieutenant Guy Wylly and Private John Bisdee of the 3rd Tasmanian Imperial Bushmen, both Tasmanian-born, who both won the VC at Warmbad on 1 September 1900.

Naval Forces

The possibility of Royal Naval ships being diverted from Australian waters during the Crimean War led to the formation of the first Australian navy: the ketch *Spitfire* armed with a 32pdr, built at Port Jackson for the New South Wales local forces, and the 580-ton steam sloop *Victoria*, for that colony's navy, which by 1861 was supplemented by two companies of the Victorian Naval Brigade. A similar formation was created in New South Wales in 1863, of shore-based seamen intended for harbour defence. The Victorian ship is chiefly of note from its landing of a detachment of seamen in New Zealand in December 1860, the first Australian forces to serve overseas.

The New South Wales Lancers became to the British public perhaps the most popular and best-known of all colonial corps, from visits to Britain by contingents in 1893 and 1897, and a full squadron's visit in 1899 for the purpose of training; the latter went directly to South Africa on the outbreak of war and were thus the first Australian troops in the field. The popularity of the corps can be gauged by its depiction on the cover of a children's picture book.

The Colonial Naval Defence Act having authorised colonies to provide their own maritime defence, by the mid-1880s Victoria had a small flotilla, headed by the 1868 Jarrow-built turret-ship *Cerberus*, armed with four 10in muzzle-loaders, and including two gunboats and several torpedo-boats and armed steamers. In 1881 New South Wales purchased the 1863 Woolwich-built corvette HMS *Wolverine* (sixteen 8in guns, one 7in, four 40pdrs) as a training ship.

In 1887 the colonies agreed to form a Royal Navy Auxiliary Squadron, based in Australian waters to supplement the colonies' defences, and to pay a subsidy to Britain for their upkeep; they could not be sent from Australian waters without the consent of the colonial governments, and were quite separate from vessels maintained by individual states. In 1900 New South Wales authorised the dispatch of HMS *Wallaroo* to the China coast at the time of the Boxer Rebellion (this was originally the 2nd class cruiser *Persian* of 2,575 tons, armed with eight 4.7in and eight 3pdr guns). She was accompanied by the entire South Australian navy, the 920-ton 1884 cruiser *Protector* (one 8in, five 6in guns). Both New South Wales and Victoria contributed a naval brigade for land service in China, which together formed the Australian Naval Contingent, comprising 260 N.S.W. and 200 Victorian seamen, with field guns. They had been waiting to go to South Africa, when the Chinese emergency arose; and with them was a draft of 25 soldiers, also bound for South Africa, but who volunteered to go to China provided that they were not forced to join the navy. A compromise was reached and these 25 were designated the New South Wales Marine Light Infantry. At Hong Kong the Naval Contingent was re-equipped (the Victorians had Martini-Enfields), and their Nordenfelt machine-guns and 9pdr muzzle-loaders were replaced by 12pdr breech-loaders. The Victorians served at Tientsin and the New South Welshmen at Peking, where they formed a mounted infantry unit, riding small Chinese ponies; the Contingent left China in March 1901.

Notes
1. Anon. 'An Unexpected Visit to Flinders' Island in Bass's Straits', in *Chambers' Edinburgh Journal*, 20 September 1845, p. 189.
2. Quoted in Richards, W. *Her Majesty's Army, Indian and Colonial Forces*, London, n.d., p. 349.

References
Abbott, J. H. M. *Tommy Cornstalk: being some account of the less notable features of the South African War from the point of view of the Australian ranks*, London, 1902.

Austin, Brigadier M. *The Army in Australia 1840-50: Prelude to the Golden Years*, Canberra, 1979.

Barton, L. C. *Australians in the Waikato War 1863-64*, Sydney, 1979.

Denton, K. *For Queen and Commonwealth*, Sydney, 1987.

Festberg, A. N., and Videon, B. J. *Uniforms of the Australian Colonies*, Melbourne, 1971.

Field, L. M. *The Forgotten War: Australian Involvement in the South African Conflict of 1899-1902*, Melbourne, 1979.

Hutchinson, F., and Myers, F. *The Australian Contingent: A*

History of the Patriotic Movement in New South Wales, and an Account of the Despatch of Troops to the Assistance of the Imperial Forces in the Soudan, Sydney, 1885.

Knight, I. *Queen Victoria's Enemies (4): Asia, Australasia and the Americas*, London, 1990.

Laffin, J. *The Australian Army at War 1899-1975*, London, 1982.

Montague, R. *Dress and Insignia of the British Army in Australia and New Zealand 1770-1870*, Sydney, 1981.

Murray, P. L. *Official Records of the Australian Military Contingents to the War in South Africa*, Melbourne, 1911.

Nicholls, B. *Bluejackets and Boxers: Australia's Naval Expedition to the Boxer Uprising*, Sydney, 1986.

Stanley, P. *But Little Glory: The New South Wales Contingent to the Sudan, 1885*, Canberra, 1985.

Sutton, R. *Soldiers of the Queen: War in the Soudan*, Sydney, 1985.

Wallace, R. L. *The Australians at the Boer War*, Canberra, 1976.

Wedd, M. *Australian Military Uniforms 1800-1982*, Kenthurst, 1982.

FIJI

Although there was no British campaigning in the Fijian archipelago, it provides an example of a colony at the end of the 'far-flung battle-line' which maintained its own military force.

By the mid-19th century the system of tribal or clan chieftainships in Fiji had evolved into a kingship recognised by the majority. King Thakombau, indebted to King George of Tonga for assistance in crushing an attempted usurper, also faced a large financial claim from the USA for an alleged insult to their consul; to extricate himself, he offered sovereignty to Britain in 1859, on condition that the American claim be resolved. Despite increasing European settlement in Fiji, this was declined more than once, until in 1871 a constitutional government was formed by British settlers under Thakombau. This proved so ineffectual that in 1874 Britain finally accepted sovereignty of Fiji, to act as a station on the route between Australia and Panama, from where greater control could be maintained over the Polynesian labour traffic. The governor of Fiji was also 'high commissioner for the Western Pacific'. The Fiji Armed Constabulary was formed upon the British taking control, and its commander, Colonel Claude Francis (ex-British Guiana Police) in 1898–9 organised the Fiji Volunteer Corps, four companies strong, which (unlike the Constabulary which was composed of Fijians) was exclusively European in composition, and had a cadet corps attached. A singular feature of the uniform of the Constabulary's Fijian personnel was the lack of shoes and head-dress (which could not be accommodated over the traditional hairstyle), and the use of the Fijian kilt (*sulu*) in place of trousers.

NEW ZEALAND

The colonisation of New Zealand involved some of the most bitter conflict encountered by British or colonial forces, the result of the calibre of the Maori warriors against whom they fought, 'the grandest native enemy' according to Sir John Fortescue. In the indigenous inhabitants of New Zealand, the early European explorers discovered what might be described as a warrior society, whose first encounter with the *paheka* (white man) involved the killing of four of Abel Tasman's men at the place he named Murderers' Bay. The warfare existing in Maori society did not arise from conflict between 'states' or dynasties, but from motives present at tribal, clan or individual level. Chief among these was the concept of *mana*, a term perhaps best described as a mixture of prestige, authority and power, the individual's *mana* increasing or decreasing according to his actions. A second motive for conflict was *utu*, revenge or retribution for an insult and could turn individual disagreement into tribal bloodfeud, carried on for many years. A subsidiary cause of hostilities was the practice of *muru*, plunder. All this resulted in a warrior society accustomed to warfare, so that the Europeans faced a much more formidable enemy than might otherwise have been the case.

Although the wars in New Zealand are sometimes styled 'the Maori Wars', they never involved a wholesale 'national' war; instead, the conflicts were fought by individual tribes, and involved 'loyal' Maoris (*kupapas*) who took the part of the British against the 'rebels' (as hostile Maoris were sometimes styled). The 'loyalists' probably had the same basic aim of survival as had the 'rebels', but chose to accomplish it by not opposing the settlers; and old animosities probably had much significance also, the colonial powers making use of such enmities in a policy of 'divide and rule'. Indeed, it was remarked that in some cases members of one Maori tribe might support another in its conflict with the settlers not out of any fellow-feeling or antagonism towards the whites, but simply because 'From childhood have the deeds of bravery of a past generation been instilled into the Maori mind, and thus fitted it to think and speak of war not only as a means of revenge and punishment towards an aggressive enemy, but as an ennobling practice, worthy to be followed by the great on earth. It was not until after many of the Waikatos had been slain that a general ill-feeling against Europeans began to evince itself ... "blood for blood" being the Maoris' idea of justice.'[1]

New Zealand Colonial Wars

Colonisation of New Zealand was comparatively slow, even following Cook's rediscovery in 1769. The first contacts between British and Maoris occurred in the late 18th and early 19th centuries, one of the first evidences of the ingress of European civilisation being the trade in firearms: the first battle between Maori tribes involving them probably took place in 1807. In succeeding years the trade in muskets had a considerable effect on inter-tribal warfare, and even some of the first British missionaries

Maori warriors performing a war dance, modern firearms and cartridge-boxes appearing somewhat incongruous with tattooed faces! (Unsigned engraving)

used firearms as trade goods. The first British troops in New Zealand, in the widest sense of the term, were members of the 57th aboard a convict ship which put in at a whaling station; but the first deliberate deployment was in 1834, when after a number of minor skirmishes between Maoris and European traders, a detachment of 50th Foot from New South Wales was sent with HMS *Alligator* to secure the release of nine prisoners from the brig *Harriet*, which had been wrecked; some of the crew had been killed and the remainder captured.

Skirmishes between the local inhabitants and whalers, who often ill used the Maoris, led to calls from missionaries for an official British administration instead of just the British Resident, installed in 1833. Accordingly, Captain William Hobson arrived in HMS *Herald* in January 1840, raised the British flag and by the Treaty of Waitangi (6 February 1840) reached an accord with many Maori chiefs. The first British garrison – detachments of the 80th and 96th Foot – arrived shortly after. The possession of territory was a major cause of unrest; the concept of land-ownership was interpreted differently by Europeans and Maoris, and even caused dispute between Europeans: the New Zealand Company, which had begun to settle without official approval, found that its purchases were not recognised by the new British administration. The European concepts of the rights of purchase and personal possession of land were largely alien to the Maoris, and their own ideas were not understood by the majority of the settlers, one of whom articulated a common view of the people he described as 'savages' who could not 'be considered in any shape as connected with true civilisation. If a race cannot comprehend the increased value of property by interchange, they are unfit occupants as independent rulers of so important a

country.'[2] Failure to understand each other's viewpoints inevitably led to conflict. The first serious clash arose in the area of one of the New Zealand Company settlements, the 'Wairau affair' in which some colonists were killed by the chief Te Rauparaha in June 1843. No action was taken against him.

First New Zealand War
The first of the New Zealand Colonial Wars, sometimes styled the First Maori or Flagstaff War, occurred not in the south of North Island, where the recent incident had occurred, but in the very north. The transfer of the capital to Auckland, farther south, had caused some economic depression in the area around the Bay of Islands, the territory of the chief Hone Heke Pokai, one of the supporters of the Treaty of Waitangi. Having become disenchanted with the settlers (now represented by Robert Fitzroy, commander of HMS *Beagle* on Darwin's voyage and Hobson's successor as governor), Hone Heke protested by cutting down the flagpole he had erected at Maiki Hill for the display of the British flag (July 1844). Fitzroy, helped by the pro-British chief Tamati Waka Nene, quietened the unrest; but on 9 January 1845 Hone Heke cut down the re-erected flagpole, and again for a third time after it had been put back. On 11 March, and in the face of defences constructed by the small garrison and the settlers of Kororareka, Hone Heke and his ally Kawiti attacked and drove the settlers away. Fitzroy appealed for assistance to New South Wales and received the 58th Foot, which reached the Bay of Islands in late March 1845, to be welcomed by Tamati Waka Nene and his anti-Hone Heke faction. Lieutenant-Colonel William Hulme of the 96th attacked Hone Heke's *pa* (stockaded fortification) at Puketutu on 8 May with a detachment of his own regi-

ment, the 58th light company and a landing-party of sea-men and marines, with a Congreve rocket detachment, but this first action against a *pa* demonstrated the strength of this unique Maori style of fortification and the deter-mination of the defenders; the attackers withdrew.

Hone Heke had no success when he attacked Tamati Waka Nene's *pa* at Pukenui on 12 June 1845; nor had Colonel Henry Despard, newly arrived from Sydney with two companies of the 99th, when he attacked Kawiti's *pa* at Ohaeawai on 1 July with elements of the 58th, 99th and naval personnel: he lost 40 men, but the *pa* was aban-doned during the night, having served its purpose, and Despard destroyed it. Fitzroy was replaced as governor by Captain George Grey, who attempted to make peace; when no response was received, he accompanied Despard to attack Hone Heke and Kawiti at Ruapekapeka *pa*. Hav-ing breached it with artillery (the heaviest being three 32pdrs), the *pa* was stormed on 11 January. It was almost deserted: being a Sunday, Hone Heke had withdrawn with most of his followers to hold divine service, never imagin-ing that the British would fight on the Sabbath! Unable to recapture the *pa*, the Maori forces dispersed and the war effectively ended. Grey exerted no reprisals and the area became peaceful again.

Lack of retaliation for the Wairau troubles caused Te Rauparaha and his nephew Te Rangihaeata to continue hostilities at the southern tip of North Island, where set-tlers began to be driven off their land. The British garri-son was increased and posts established, one of which was attacked on 16 May 1846, at Boulcott's Farm. In retalia-tion, Te Rauparaha was arrested by a naval landing-party, and Te Rangihaeata's *pa* at Horokiri was bombarded (6 August 1846) until he made off; once his raiding ended he was permitted to live in peace, and his uncle was allowed to return home.

Second New Zealand War

New Zealand was granted self-government in 1852, and a ministry was established from 1856; and the discovery of gold, especially after 1861, brought a renewed wave of set-tlers, although peace between them and the Maoris was broken only by isolated incidents. Within the Maori nation there originated the 'King movement', an attempt at unity in the face of colonisation, and to prevent fratricidal inter-nal warfare: in 1858 a Maori king was elected, Potatau te Wherowhero. Tension, however, increased, and the set-tlers no longer relied entirely on British troops for their security: to provide a more immediate form of self-defence, local militia and volunteer corps were raised in the white settlements.

The Second New Zealand Colonial War, also styled the Waitara or First Taranaki War (or to the Maoris *Te riri paheka*, 'the white man's anger'), broke out in the Waitara area on the west of North Island in 1860, inevitably over land ownership. A local chief, Te Rangitake (usually known as Wiremu Kingi), objected to the sale of a tract of land by another Maori magnate, Te Teira. The governor of New Zealand, Colonel Thomas Gore Browne, tried to mediate, but without success, and a number of minor actions occurred. On 17 March 1860 Colonel C. E. Gold with the 65th and some artillery attacked a *pa* at Te Kohia, which was abandoned in the usual way; reinforcements were received by both sides (the local Maori forces sup-plemented by sympathisers from other areas), and after an injudicious attack on Wiremu Kingi's *pa* at Pukatakauere on 27 June 1860, further reinforcements were sent to New Zealand, commanded by the GOC Australia himself, Major-General Thomas Pratt.

Learning from previous experiences of frontal attacks against defended *pas*, Pratt adopted a new tactic, of digging saps towards the palisades to permit an

A Maori tattooist at work; the facial and body-decoration borne by Maori warriors increased their intimidating appearance. (Unsigned engraving)

*The difficulties of storming a
defended* pa *are exemplified in
this engraving after R. Caton
Woodville.*

approach under cover. This proved successful, but a less cautious attack was made at Mahoetahi *pa* on 6 November 1860, against Maori reinforcements from Waikato, who were driven away. Pratt returned to conventional siege tactics against Wiremu Kingi, the Maoris abandoning two *pas* before the main engagement at Te Arei *pa*. Finding that the British would no longer make frontal attacks against their defences, and having no answer to the sapping save attempting to rush the besiegers (who were themselves entrenched), the Maoris sued for peace, the government agreeing to an inquiry into the Waitara land acquisition.

Third New Zealand War

This was the most protracted, although it is possible to divide hostilities into four phases or campaigns. Again, ownership of land was the cause of conflict, initially in the Waikato region. Sir George Grey was re-installed as governor in 1861, but despite his abilities and the respect in which he was held by the majority of the Maoris, he encountered strong opposition from the King movement in the Waikato region, where the extension of a road toward Maori land was regarded as a threat. The first serious hostilities, however, occurred once again in Taranaki, when a party of 57th Foot was ambushed and wiped out (with only one survivor), but although sporadic fighting continued in the Taranaki region, most of the trouble was caused by roving Waikato Maoris. It was against the Waikato region that the first campaign was directed, local forces being left to defend the Taranaki settlements. Unlike earlier conflicts, this involved considerable numbers of British troops; in addition to the Royal Artillery, the following regiments were present during the war: 65th (1846–65), 12th, 40th and 57th (1860–6), 2/14th (1860–7), 43rd, 50th and 70th (1863–6), 2/18th (1863–70) and 68th (1864–6).

Commanded by General Sir Duncan Cameron, an expedition was mounted by the British against the Waikato Maoris, supported by river gunboats to provide logistical assistance and to bombard Maori positions. On 12 July 1863 the Waikato campaign began in earnest when Cameron crossed the Magatawhiri river, and five days later successfully stormed a Maori position at Koheroa. During this period, as a counter to Maori guerrilla tactics, the government created the Forest Rangers, local forces intended to fight the Maoris on their own terms; the most famous of their members was the German Gustavus Von Tempsky, who had wide experience of exploring in Australia and the Americas. Despite the skill of such troops, and the evidence of Pratt's successes, Cameron reverted to older methods, choosing all-out attack instead of siege. On 20 November he attacked Rangiriri *pa* with about 1,300 men (including elements of the 12th, 14th, 40th, 65th and naval personnel); the outworks were overrun but three attempts to penetrate the main defences failed, and after suffering considerable losses Cameron halted the assault. Having expended their ammunition, those Maoris unable to escape surrendered next day.

Cameron pressed on, capturing without opposition the capital of the Maori king Tawhiao te Wherowhero (who had succeeded his father Potatau) at Ngaruawahia on 8 December 1863. On 20 February 1864 the village of Rangiaowhia was captured, and on the following day an entrenchment near Hairini Hill. The final major engagement of the Waikato campaign occurred at Orakau, at the *pa* of the Maori leader Rewi Manga Maniapoto. Cameron besieged him and his 300 followers, but, anxious to prevent casualties on both sides (like the rest of the British troops he had come to respect the Maoris), asked Rewi to surrender. Someone, perhaps Rewi himself, called back, 'Friend, we shall fight you for ever and ever!' The Maoris also refused to send out their women and children; but as their supplies were exhausted (the principal weakness of the *pa* was that it was rarely supplied with water), Rewi broke through the siege-lines and escaped into the bush with all his people (2 April 1864). This was effectively the end of the Waikato campaign, and much Maori land was confiscated by way of reparation.

The next campaign occurred in the Bay of Plenty area, where the tribes in the Tauranga region took up arms in support of the Waikato people. When reinforcements to the local troops could be spared by Cameron, an assault was made on perhaps the most famous of the Maori fortifications, the Gate *pa* on 29 April 1864 (its name derived from its position near a gate in the boundary between Maori and settlers' land). The attack by the 43rd, 68th and a naval brigade was repulsed, and the Maori defenders retired during the night. Given the disparity in numbers – the Maoris were about 300 strong, the attackers 1,700 – it

was a considerable reverse; but Cameron left for affairs father south, leaving Lieutenant-Colonel H. H. Greer in command, and it was under his direction that the final action of the Bay of Plenty campaign was fought, the successful storm of Te Ranga *pa* on 21 June 1864 by the 43rd, 68th and 1st Waikato Regiments. Although there were other outbreaks in the Tauranga region until 1869, the main hostilities moved elsewhere. In contrast to the barbarity often expected when fighting a 'savage' enemy, and on occasion experienced against the Maoris, it is noteworthy that in March 1864 the British were sent a list of 'binding laws' for the district of Tauranga, signed by five Maori chiefs, informing the British of the chivalry which would be observed in the coming campaign: any man, wounded or unhurt, who turned his musket-butt or sword-hilt towards the Maoris would be saved; no unarmed men, women or children would be touched; and any man could seek sanctuary in a church and would not be molested, even if armed. Similar chivalry was observed in the Maoris' treatment of British wounded in the action at the Gate *pa*. The concept of announcing and abiding by such rules before a battle was unknown among the nations involved in 'civilised' European warfare!

The third phase of the war might be styled the Hauhau campaign, from the name of the quasi-religious movement which inspired it. Its creator was Te Ua Haumene, who founded a sect styled Pai Marire ('good and peaceful') with a mixture of Christian and Maori theology and Maori nationalism, the movement reinstating earlier, barbarous practices such as the decapitation of the enemy and with an enhanced role for *utu*, revenge. He also

The attack on the Gate Pa, 29 April 1864: members of the Naval Brigade attempt to penetrate the defences. The leader of the naval contingent, Commander Edward Hay, of the sloop HMS Harrier, was mortally wounded; his coxswain, captain-of-the-foretop Samuel Mitchell, was awarded the Victoria Cross for bringing him away, even though Hay ordered him to save himself. Captain J. F. C. Hamilton of the corvette HMS Esk was also killed in the action, shot through the head while cheering on the storming-party. A second VC won in the action was awarded to Assistant-Surgeon William Manley of the Royal Artillery, for assisting Hay and others. (Print after W. H. Overend)

instructed his followers to cry 'Hau! Hau!' to protect them from bullets. The movement began in the Taranaki region but spread to the centre of North Island; there was no defined course of campaign, but numerous minor engagements over the succeeding months, from the first serious outbreak as early as April 1864. The Hauhau campaign involved a marked change in British tactics: most of the British units were withdrawn, operations devolving upon local forces which, like the Forest Rangers, were able to meet the Maoris in the bush on terms of near parity. At first the British campaign merely limped along, Cameron being at odds with his political masters; he eventually resigning his command. The governor, Sir George Grey, even took the field in person, commanding a force entirely of local volunteers and allied Maoris, and captured the *pa* at Wereroa, after barely a skirmish, but against which Cameron had declined to act. The tactics of irregular bush-fighting by the British were continued under Cameron's successor, Sir Trevor Chute, although the war was still little more than a series of guerrilla actions: on 14 January 1866, for example, Chute with the 10th and 14th Foot stormed and captured Otapawa *pa* .

The operations in the last stage of the war devolved upon two Maori leaders, Titokawaru and Te Kooti. The former departed somewhat from the Hauhau line by introducing ritual cannibalism to strike terror into the *paheka*, and the Maoris struck a telling blow in a fierce fight at Te Ngutu-o-te-Manu on 7 September 1868, where Von Tempsky, then commanding a unit of Armed Constabulary, was killed. Titokawaru won another action against local forces at Moturoa on 7 November 1868, but on 2 February 1869 his *pa* at Tauranga-ika was besieged; the Maoris slipped away without waiting for an assault. Despite a price on his head, Titokawaru was never apprehended and survived to play a peaceful role in Maori–settler politics.

Te Kooti Rikirangi Te Turuki was originally a 'friendly' Maori, imprisoned for suspected complicity in Hauhau hostilities; but he escaped and became a capable guerrilla leader. He was also the founder of the Ringatu Church, a near-Christian movement, and unusually was not a chief but a 'commoner' raised to prominence by his own ability. On 10 November 1868 one of his typical guerrilla raids murdered some 70 people, whites and Maoris, at Poverty Bay; but he abandoned his guerrilla tactics to raise a *pa* at Ngatapa, which was stormed on 2 February 1869. He continued to wage a hit-and-run war, which finally fizzled out with a number of minor raids and running fights. After the final skirmishes in 1872 he remained a fugitive until he received a pardon under the Amnesty Act, and the government even gave him a grant of land. Although the problem of land ownership was not solved by the conflict, future disagreements were conducted peacefully, such as the civil disobedience movement in Taranaki a decade after the final hostilities in the New Zealand Wars.

Military Forces

Maoris. Having no institution of kingship or dynasties, the Maori people fought the Europeans in the same 'organisation' as before, hostilities being based on, and usually initiated by, the individual tribe (*iwi*) or clan (*hapu*, a subtribe). These were led by a chief (*ariki*), often the eldest male of the leading family, but to some extent leadership depended on the *mana* of the individual; although it was only in the latter stages of the Colonial Wars that 'commoners' came to be regarded as potential leaders, any member of the leading family whose personal *mana* was sufficiently impressive might become the *ariki*, and as there was no formalised hereditary or elective leadership, there might be several *arikis* in one clan. With no organised hierarchy of rank or discipline, an *ariki* led by personal example, and as hand-to-hand combat was traditionally favoured, the chief was thus often in a position of considerable hazard; and if defeated or killed, all his followers might retire, irrespective of the current state of the battle.

While maintaining many aspects of traditional warfare, the Maoris readily adopted firearms, and in some cases were considerably more effective with them than were the Europeans. Traditional weaponry included spears and rocks to be thrown at the enemy, but more popular were hand-to-hand weapons, wooden, stone or whalebone clubs, many sharpened to produce bladed 'axes' or 'swords'; more conventional axes, on long or short hafts like European hatchets or felling-axes, were adopted after metal axe-heads were introduced as trade-goods by the settlers. More significantly, the introduction of firearms caused a shift from the traditionally favoured hand-to-hand combat. By the 1840s many Maori warriors had acquired flintlock muskets, and by the 1860s the more effective, double-barrelled percussion shotguns were in common use, especially deadly in the short-range fire-fights which occurred in the close confines of the bush. Although European clothing was introduced progressively, especially in the earlier campaigns the Maoris fought in their traditional costume of flax 'kilt' and cloak, though to give maximum freedom of movement many fought almost naked. European belts, cartridge boxes and the equipment necessary for the use of firearms were worn together with traditional items of dress, though even these were sometimes decorated; wooden gun-stocks were often magnificently carved with traditional Maori patterns. Ammunition was always in short supply, especially percussion caps, which the Maoris sometimes attempted to improvise; in this regard the settlers always had a distinct advantage over their Maori opponents.

Another important feature of indigenous warfare was the fortification styled a *pa* (or *pah*). (The name attracted some humorous comment: writing of the training of officers, one commentator noted how a subaltern could be confounded by finding his enemy '... ensconced behind a stockade. Now, as his *Ma* had never taught him how to take a *pah*, and no one else has shown him the way, he is perfectly at fault ...'[3]) The *pa* was a combination of earth-work and palisade, constructed with skill at strategic points and virtually inviting the enemy to attack. Often the size was not great: Maori forces, being based upon the individual tribe, were sometimes less than 100 strong, and the average *pa* probably measured something less than 100 by 50 yards in size. They consisted of a network of inter-connected trenches, parapets and rifle-pits, with earth banks and subterranean chambers (proof even against artillery fire), flanking works and usually a double palisade 15 feet high, the fencing often having flax mats affixed with gaps along the bottom, providing firing-slits through which the defenders, ensconced in trenches behind the palisade, could fire at the attackers. Formidable to an enemy intent on hand-to-hand combat, *pas* were vulnerable to artillery, and by the 1860s there was a fashion of replacing the double palisade by a single fence, intended less as a defence then an obstacle to slow the attackers' rate of advance, and to render them vulnerable as they attempted to clamber over. This was the essence of the *pa* as a fortification: rarely was it ever intended to hold a *pa* to the proverbial last ditch, as in some European warfare. Instead, it existed as a challenge to the enemy and as a way of inflicting the maximum casualties upon the attackers; once penetrated, the defenders would quite happily abandon the position and slip away to await another day. In the Colonial Wars, the *pa* was useful in this way and enabled the Maoris to take a considerable toll of their attackers; and while the Maoris were also effective in guerrilla-style actions, they were never a match for the British in the open field because of their total lack of discipline and the fact that in battle each man acted for himself.

Those who encountered the Maoris in the Colonial Wars observed unusual contradictions. Although the mutilation of enemy bodies and cannibalism had largely died out before the wars, they were re-introduced at a later date, probably to frighten the enemy; yet among the Maoris Christianity had made very considerable advances, so that often the British were fighting co-religionists. At times ruthless, the Maoris could equally exhibit remarkable chivalry in action, and among other European military practices they adopted was the use of flags: believing the British flags to have powerful *mana*, they designed and flew their own, sometimes even incorporating the cross symbol associated with European and Christian armies. The Maoris remained a most intimidating foe, not least because of their extensive tattooing, including elaborate and incised facial tattoos (*moko*), allied to the belief that a warrior's head was the most sacred part of his body, hence the practice of collecting and preserving the heads of enemies. Equally intimidat-

Captain R. Snow (right) and Lieutenant Neave, Canterbury Mounted Rifles, c.1898, wearing braided patrol-jack

ing were war-chants and dances (a flavour of which may be gleaned from the *haka* still performed by New Zealand rugby teams); a contemporary witness described how a Maori chief

'suddenly rose from the ground and leaped high into the air with a tremendous yell. He was instantly imitated by his party, who ... joined in a measured guttural song recited by their chief, keeping exact time by leaping high at each louder intonation, brandishing their weapons with the right hand, and slapping the thigh with the left as they came heavily upon the ground. The war-song warmed as it proceeded. Though still in perfect unison, they yelled louder and louder, leaped higher and higher, brandished their weapons more fiercely, and dropped with the smack on the thigh more heavily as they proceeded, still the final spring was accompanied by a concluding whoop which seemed to penetrate one's marrow.'[4] This impression is accurate: the Maoris were among the bravest and most formidable enemies ever encountered.

Settlers. Unlike many local forces formed in European colonies, those in New Zealand were created as a direct response to a threat of hostilities, and saw much hard service; indeed, they undertook almost the whole of the military effort in the later stages of the New Zealand wars.

The first military forces in New Zealand were British troops, usually small detachments sent from Australia and only increased in numbers in the event of a threat of hostilities. After the First New Zealand War, Sir George Grey petitioned for a permanent military force, and in November 1846 the Royal New Zealand Fencibles were created, recruited in Britain from army pensioners of good character, at least 15 years' service and below the age of 48. They arrived in New Zealand from 1847 to 1853, each man being given a house and an acre of land (officers 50 acres) and, although liable for active service at any time, were allowed to follow a civilian occupation, with only one parade per week. They were established in a cordon of four settlements around Auckland, to protect the town from any threat from the Waikato Maoris to the south. A fifth settlement was established at Mangere in June 1849 for a company formed from 80 Ngati Mahuta tribesmen, 'friendly' Maoris commanded by their own NCOs and British officers, the first true Maori military unit as distinct from the allied tribes who fought alongside the British. The Fencibles were mobilised only in April 1851, when three companies stood-to in the face of an attempted invasion of Auckland by the Ngati Paoa tribe, which was discouraged without conflict.[5]

Most subsequent local forces were raised from among the existing settlers, and to their existence has been attributed much of the suppression of hostilities ('The willingness of the settlers to take up arms for the defence of their country and their homes, and the readiness with which they offered their services, was an object lesson to the Maoris, and proved to them the determination of the settlers to defend their homes against any further outbreak. This attitude of the settlers proved a salutary lesson to the Maoris, and created a lasting peace.'[6])

The 1845 Militia Act made service compulsory for all able-bodied males aged between 18 and 65 years, with service restricted to a distance of 25 miles from the local police office; mandatory personal service was removed in 1858 when 'substitution' was permitted, by which a man selected for militia service could pay for another to take his place. Militiaman volunteered to serve as pioneers in the war in the north in 1845–6, and the Wellington Militia was involved in the actions in their area in 1846. The volunteer forces were different, in that service was as voluntary as the name implied, and membership of a volunteer corps gave exemption from the liability of militia service. Each company (officially 60 rank and file and three officers) was self-financed, supplemented later by a government allowance, eventually three pounds per capita, to defray uniform and incidental expenses, although weapons were issued by the government. Companies were trained as independent units and permitted to elect their own officers; service consisted of weekly drills until called out for active service, when they were usually mobilised for a three-month period, when they received pay. Most units were rifle corps, though cavalry and artillery also existed. Training and discipline was not always of the highest standard, however, some units at

the time being described as largely a waste of public money.

Another form of 'local force' were the Military Settlers, an extension of the Fencible concept; in 1863 more than 2,500 men were recruited in Australia and Otago to settle in the Waikato area, who after three years' service received land-grants according to rank (50 acres for a private, 400 for a major, for example). These formed the 1st–4th Regiments of Waikato Militia, and served in the 'Waikato War', including the operations around the Gate *pa*. A further ten companies of Military Settlers were established in other areas, including Taranaki and Hawke's Bay.

An example of the constitution and disposition of the local forces is provided by a list of those existing in November 1864:

Auckland: Auckland Regiment of Militia; 1st–4th Regiments Waikato Militia; Auckland Cavalry Volunteers; Auckland, Remuera, North Head, Onehunga, Mauku, Papakura Valley, and Wairoa corps of Rifle Volunteers; Auckland and Onehunga Naval Volunteers.

Wellington: 1st, 2nd (Hutt) and Wairarapa Battalions of Wellington Militia; Castle Point Militia; Wairarapa Cavalry Volunteers; Wellington, Taita and Castle Point corps of Rifle Volunteers.

Rangitikei: Rangitikei Cavalry and Rifle Volunteers.

Wanganui: Wanganui Militia; Wanganui Cavalry and Rifle Volunteers.

Napier: Napier Militia; Napier Cavalry and Rifle Volunteers.

Taranaki: Taranaki Militia; Military Settlers; Taranaki Mounted and Rifle Volunteers.

Nelson: Nelson Militia; Nelson Rifle Volunteers.

Marlborough: Marlborough Militia; Marlborough Rangers Volunteers.

Canterbury: Canterbury Militia; Canterbury Yeomanry Cavalry and Rifle Volunteers.

Otago: Otago Militia; Dunedin Artillery Volunteers, Otago Rifle Volunteers; Dunedin Volunteer Naval Brigade.

Southland: Invercargill Militia; Invercargill Volunteers.

In addition to the militia and volunteers, the need for a more permanent military force was recognised, especially after the withdrawal of British troops by 1870 (the 2/18th was the only regular battalion in New Zealand after 1867). Consequently, the New Zealand Armed Constabulary was created by Act of Parliament in 1867 and embodied in 1868, in effect a permanent military force, although officers had police titles of rank. Many of the earlier volunteers enrolled in the Armed Constabulary, perhaps most notably Von Tempsky, who became an inspector. The Constabulary's Field Force acted as a regular army and was engaged in much hard service. At its peak the Armed Constabulary comprised nine divisions, each of between 60 and 100 men (i.e., the equivalent of a volunteer company), two divisions being composed of Maoris. In the later stages of the war, it was the Maori element (the Arawa

Sergeant-major of the Canterbury Mounted Rifles, c.1898, wearing the single-breasted tunic of the corps' rank and file, and displaying its initials on the shabraque. The unit was formed in 1885.

Flying Column) which served in the field against the Te Kooti guerrillas, the 'white' companies being deployed on garrison duty and protecting the settlements. In 1881 the Field Force officers were transferred to the Militia list, and the force re-titled as 'Constabulary', but its military role continued with the formation of artillery, engineer and torpedo branches, until under the 1886 Defence Act the military and police branches were separated, the former becoming the Permanent Militia. The Armed Constabulary wore a blue, military-style uniform, but somewhat ironically, at a time when the Maoris were adopting items of European clothing and equipment, the Armed Constabulary developed a campaign dress based on the Maori kilt (*rapaki*). This 'shawl dress' replaced trousers with a kilt-like shawl or blanket belted around the waist, worn with bare legs and stockings or puttee-style gaiters, which was found to be the most serviceable dress for fighting in the bush.

Throughout the New Zealand Wars, the settlers relied heavily on co-operation of allied Maoris (*Kupapas*), some in tribal bands under their own chiefs, but others integrated into European-style units. In addition to their adoption of British military equipment and discipline, even European names were adopted; perhaps the most famous, 'Major Kemp', who served from 1864 and against Titokowaru and Te Kooti, was actually named Kepa Te Rangihiwinui. As 'Major Kemp' he received a full military funeral some three decades after his active service.

The creation of the Permanent Militia in July 1886 established a 'regular' army, but it was extremely small: the original proposal called for 120 Garrison and 50 Field Artillery, 20 engineers, 110 riflemen and a 50-strong Torpedo Corps. Even this was economically insupportable, so the field artillery and engineers disappeared, followed by the rifles; those remaining (less than 200 by 1889) were trained to act as auxiliary police and prison warders. In 1897 the force was re-named the 'New Zealand Permanent Force' and re-organised into two companies, no. 1 artillery and no. 2 submarine miners and engineers. In 1898 a column of 120 men with two Nordenfelt and two Maxim guns was dispatched to the Hokianga district in the face of potential Maori hostility, but there was no conflict. From the 1880s most of New Zealand's military activity was directed towards the construction of coastal defences, in the erroneous perception of a Russian threat, although the fortification programme was quite slow in progressing because of financial constraints.

Volunteer forces were also maintained, ultimately embracing cavalry, mounted rifles, artillery, engineers, rifle and cadet corps. By 1879, for example, the country was divided into twenty Volunteer Districts, which included eleven mounted corps, 34 rifle corps and six of naval volunteers. The first naval volunteers were formed at Auckland in 1860 as a shore- and coastal-operating force. The first New Zealand naval vessels were a rowing boat and a specially commissioned gunboat (the first warship built in New Zealand), both armed with a brass 3pdr gun. During the South African War of 1899–1902, New Zealand provided ten contingents, in all numbering 6,343 men, the first New Zealanders to serve overseas on active service. The New Zealand Mounted Rifles rendered useful service in the war; the units which served in South Africa were recruited from volunteers specifically for the purpose, as the existing volunteer corps were only liable for home-defence service. A tribute to the loyalty of the colony is the fact that the first New Zealand Contingent set sail for Cape Town only ten days after the declaration of war.

Although fifteen Victoria Crosses were awarded for the New Zealand Colonial Wars, members of the local forces were ineligible for the decoration. To compensate, the New Zealand Cross was instituted for the members of these forces by Sir George Bowen, governor of New Zealand, on 10 March 1869; it ranked next to the Victoria Cross. The decoration was introduced without official sanction, but as five had been awarded before Bowen informed the authorities in London, his order in council was ratified, although he received a rebuke. Only 23 awards were made, nine to the Armed Constabulary and three to Maoris, including one to 'Major Kemp'; its limited issue makes the New Zealand Cross one of the rarest decorations for gallantry. The first New Zealander to win the Victoria Cross was Captain Charles Heaphy of the Auckland Militia, at Waiari on 11 February 1864; his case was unusual in that although local forces were not eligible for the VC, the rule was relaxed because at the time he was commanding British troops. Although he had been in New Zealand since 1840, he was London-born; the first New Zealand-born VC winner was Farrier-Sergeant-Major William Hardham of the 4th NZ Contingent, at Naauwpoort, South Africa, on 28 January 1901.

Notes

1. Grayling, W. I. *The War in Taranaki during the Years 1860-61*, New Plymouth, 1862, pp. 30–1.
2. Ibid., p. 31.
3. 'Instruction of Officers', by Colonel Firebrace, in *Colborne's United Service Magazine*, 1847, vol. II, p. 484.
4. Chambers' *Edinburgh Journal*, 9 August 1845, p. 86.
5. An interesting history of this force is 'The Royal New Zealand Fencibles', by J. Bryant Haigh, in *Bulletin of the Military Historical Society*, vol. XVIII, 1967.
6. Hughes, Lieutenant-Colonel R. *Historical Sketch of the 7th (Wellington West Coast) Infantry Regiment from 1865 to 1915*, Feilding, NZ., 1916, p. 6.

References

Alexander, Major-General Sir James. *Bush fighting, illustrated by remarkable actions and incidents of the Maori War in New Zealand*, London, 1873.
– *Incidents in the Maori War 1860-61*, London, 1863.
Barthorp, M. J. *To Face the Daring Maoris: Soldiers' impressions of the First Maori War 1845-47*, London, 1979.
Belich, J. *The New Zealand Wars and the Victorian Interpretation of Racial Conflict*, London, 1986.
Buick, T. L. *New Zealand's First War*, Wellington, 1926.
Carey, Lieutenant-Colonel R. *Narrative of the Late War in New Zealand*, London, 1863.
Cowan, J. *The New Zealand Wars: a history of the Maori Campaigns and the pioneering period*, Wellington, 1922–3.
Dalton, B. J. *War and Politics in New Zealand 1855-70*, Sydney, 1967.

Dornbusch, C. E. *The New Zealand Army: A Bibliography*, Cornwallville, New York, 1960.
Featherstone, D. *Victoria's Enemies: An A-Z of British Colonial Warfare*, London, 1989.
Featon, J. *The Waikato War, together with some account of Te Kooti Rikirangi*, Auckland 1879; rev. edn. ed. Captain G. Mair, Auckland, 1923.
Gibson, T. *The Maori Wars: the British Army in New Zealand, 1840-1872*, London, 1974.
Grace, M. S. *A Sketch of the New Zealand War*, London, 1899.
Gratling, W. I. *The War in Taranaki during the Years 1860-61*, New Plymouth, 1862.
Gudgeon, T. W. *Defenders of New Zealand*, Auckland, 1887.
– *Reminiscences of the War in New Zealand*, London, 1879.
Hall, D. O. W. *The New Zealanders in South Africa 1899-1902*, Wellington, 1949.
Harrop, A. J. *England and the Maori Wars*, London, 1937.
Holt, E. *The Strangest War: the Story of the Maori Wars 1860-1872*, London, 1962.
Knight, I. *Queen Victoria's enemies (4): Asia, Australasia and the Americas*, London, 1990.
Knox, R. (ed.). *The Maori-European Wars*, Wellington, 1973.
Montague, R. *Dress and Insignia of the British Army in Australia and New Zealand 1770-1870*, Sydney, 1981.
Parham, W. T. *Von Tempsky: Adventurer*, Auckland, 1969.
Ryan, T., and Parham, W. T. *The Colonial New Zealand Wars*, Wellington, 1986 (excellent comprehensive modern study).
Wickstead, Major M. *The New Zealand Army: A History from the 1840s to the 1980s*, Wellington, 1982.

SAMOA

The geographical position of the Samoan archipelago attracted European and American traders and settlements, but as the indigenous inhabitants had an established kingship there was initially no attempt at annexation. In 1877–9 the USA, Germany and Britain secured harbours and trading concessions, and it was agreed between them that no single power should

Officers of 'Gaunt's Redcaps' with two of their Samoan 'other ranks': seated, rear, Lieutenant Gaunt (lieutenant-colonel) (left), Lieutenant Lewis (HMS Tauranga, adjutant); front, left to right: Lieutenants Hickman (HMS Royalist), Heathcote (HMS Torch, major) and Shuter (HMS Porpoise); also present is the unit's vivandière, Tulia, wearing a red cloth head-scarf as a 'field-sign'. This lady not only accompanied the corps in action but on one occasion captured a German flag.

appropriate the islands. In 1887–8 a civil war was fought over the succession to the throne, Germany supporting one of the claimants, Tamasese, and the American and British Residents the other, Malietoa Laupepa. Following Malietoa's deportation by the Germans, the Americans and British transferred their support to his successor, Mataafa. He defeated Tamasese, but a conference held by the three powers in Berlin restored Malietoa Laupepa, and by a treaty of 14 June 1889 they guaranteed the autonomy of Samoa, virtually established a protectorate, and set up a president and chief justice for the town of Apia, one of the chief ports (on Upolu island). Mataafa refused to accept this arrangement, was declared a rebel, but after some fighting surrendered in 1893. Malietoa Laupepa died in August 1898 and a relative of his, Malietoa Tanu, was accepted as king by USA and Britain, and his succession was confirmed by Chief Justice Chambers, the American administrator; but the Germans supported Mataafa, whom they had been cultivating since the end of the rebellion, and who thus favoured German interests. A landing-party of seamen and marines from the cruiser HMS *Porpoise* went ashore to protect the Residencies of Chambers and the British consul, and in January 1899 hostilities commenced, the king-elect and his retinue having to take refuge aboard the British warship.

With Mataafa's faction, supported by the Germans, in the ascendant, a meeting was held in March 1899 between the Malietoans and the Anglo–US naval forces (commanded by the American Admiral Kautz, the senior officer present), which decided to attempt to reinstate

Malietoa. Mataafa's supporters were ordered to return to their homes; they responded by attacking the Malietoans, which caused the allied ships (the US flagship *Philadelphia*, *Porpoise* and the corvette HMS *Royalist*) to bombard the rebel positions. To oppose the Mataafian forces (known as 'White Caps') a Samoan corps was formed and drilled by Royal Navy personnel. This force, known as 'Gaunt's Brigade' or 'Gaunt's Redcaps', with officers from HMSs *Porpoise, Royalist*, the cruiser *Tauranga* and the sloop *Torch*, undertook much of the fighting, leaving the bluejackets and marines as a reserve and to protect Apia, which the Mataafians attempted to raid. A number of amphibious operations were made against Mataafian positions, using the Samoans with support from the Anglo-American naval forces, such as the capture of the Mataafian stronghold of Vailima in April 1899, in which 'Gaunt's Redcaps' were in the forefront of the action.

The situation being difficult to resolve militarily, fighting subsided when Mataafa agreed to withdraw behind a line fixed by Kautz and the senior British officer present, Captain Stuart of the *Tauranga*; and the three powers decided to settle affairs between themselves. Early in 1900 the Berlin treaty was abrogated; Britain withdrew all claims to Samoa, and the remainder was divided between Germany and the USA, the region to the east going to the United States and the greater area, to the west, to Germany (including the two largest islands, Savaii and Upolu). Appointed as arbitrator, in 1902 the King of Sweden decided that Britain and the USA were liable for injuries resulting from their military actions in 1899.

VII
BIOGRAPHIES

BIOGRAPHIES

Baden-Powell, Robert Stephenson Smyth, Baron Baden-Powell of Gilwell (1857–1941)

Robinson's *Celebrities of the Army* noted on page 3 that 'The war in South Africa has made and consolidated several notable reputations, but, perhaps, no single officer will have come out of it with a greater accession of both popularity and professional esteem than the gallant cavalryman who is commonly known as, *tout court*, "B. P."' Indeed, before the war Robert Baden-Powell was little-known; after it, he was a national hero.

The seventh son of the Revd. Baden-Powell, vicar of Plumstead and an Oxford professor, Robert Baden-Powell was raised among famous literary figures and was a considerable polymath, a talented writer, artist, musician, horseman, polo-player and prize-winning pigsticker, with a pleasant demeanour and a reputation as a humorist. Commissioned from Charterhouse into the 13th Hussars, he served in Zululand and India, but made his name as a commander of irregulars in the Ashanti and Matabele campaigns. As one of the foremost enthusiasts for, and exponents of 'scouting' (reconnaissance and irregular warfare), his skill was reflected in the publication of his book *Aids to Scouting*, a growing reputation and the nickname said to have been given him by Africans, 'He-who-sees-by-night'. In 1897 he was given command of the 5th Dragoon Guards, and in July 1899 was sent to South Africa to raise two irregular corps from the settlers of Bechuanaland and Rhodesia; thus he came to command the garrison of Mafeking, the siege of which made his fame.

Militarily, the defence of Mafeking was not of crucial importance, although its investment did occupy considerable numbers of Boer troops. More significant was the manner of its defence, Baden-Powell's laconic messages appealing to the public as exemplifying British sang-froid or 'pluck' in adversity. While conducting an active defence, with raids and deceptions upon the besiegers, Baden-Powell devoted much of his time to the maintenance of morale, arranging entertainment (personally acting, singing and entertaining in garrison concerts), publishing his own siege newspaper (*The Mafeking Mail*, printed on whatever scraps of paper were available, even ledger-sheets), and issuing his own banknotes for use during the siege. The superscription on the menu of the Mafeking Hotel's Christmas Dinner epitomises the spirit created by Baden-Powell: 'May Xmas find you glad and well/In spite of Kruger's Shot and Shell'.

After the relief of Mafeking, which provoked more joy at home than almost any other event, 'B. P. was a national hero, though his subsequent military career never matched the high days of Mafeking. Promoted to major-general, he led the new South African Constabulary until 1903, and after holding the position of Inspector-General of Cavalry (1903–7) he retired as a lieutenant-general in 1910 to concentrate on his scouting movement for youth, which followed his ideas on military scouting and field-

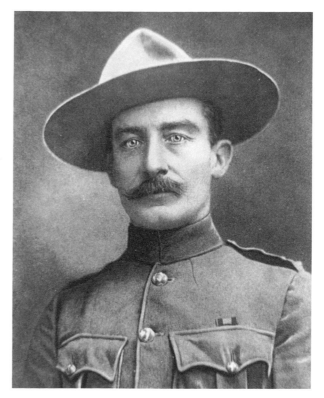

Robert Baden-Powell, in his familiar uniform of colonial irregulars.

craft. The uniform of his 'Boy Scouts' was based on his own favoured campaign dress and that of the South African Constabulary, whose motto 'Be Prepared' (which used his initials) Baden-Powell took for the Scouting movement. He spent the remainder of his life working tirelessly for the Scouting ideal, though his later fame should not conceal the fact that for a time in 1900 he was probably the most popular living Englishman.

References

The following are among many works concerning the career of 'B. P.':

Aitken, W. F. *Baden-Powell, the Hero of Mafeking*, London, 1900.

Baden-Powell, Lady O., and Hillcourt, W. *Baden-Powell: The Two Lives of a Hero*, London, 1964.

Baden-Powell, R. S. S. *African Adventures*, London, 1937.

– *Adventures and Accidents*, London, 1934.

– *Indian Memories: Recollections of Soldiering, Sport, etc., by Lieutenant-General Sir Robert Baden-Powell KCB*, London, 1915.

– *Sketches in Mafeking and East Africa*, London, 1907.

– *The Downfall of Prempeh: A Diary of Life with the Native Levy in Ashanti 1895-96*, London, 1896.

– *The Matabele Campaign 1896: being a Narrative of the Campaign in Suppressing the Native Rising in Matabeleland and Mashonaland*, London, 1897.

Begbie, H. *The Wolf that Never Sleeps*, London, 1900.

Fletcher, J. S. *Baden-Powell of Mafeking*, London, 1900.

Jeal, T. *Baden-Powell*, London, 1989.

Kiernan, R. H. *Baden-Powell*, London, 1939.

Reynolds, E. E. *Baden-Powell*, London, 1942.

Botha, Louis (1862–1919)

Of all the generals of the Boer forces in the South African War, Louis Botha rose to the greatest prominence (Jan Christian Smuts, who is probably even better-known, did not hold such high rank during the war). Botha was born a British citizen (at Greytown, Natal), but settled in the Vyrheid district, which he represented in the *Volksraad* in 1897. A highly prosperous farmer and political moderate, he abstained from voting on the question of war, but when it came took the field under Lucas Meyer and soon distinguished himself. His victory at Colenso and his major participation in that at Spion Kop led to his appointment to command the Transvaal forces after the death of Joubert.

Louis Botha, wearing a 'uniform' for service in the South African War.

After the fall of Pretoria he helped organise and sustain the guerrilla war, but was sufficiently realistic to accept the inevitable, and was among the Boer leaders who advocated an armistice to prevent further damage being sustained; he was a chief representative in the negotiations which led to peace.

After the war Botha took a leading political role, working to achieve reconciliation and a return to prosperity. He was invited to form a ministry upon the granting of self-government to the Transvaal in 1907, and declared his support for the British Empire. Upon the inauguration of the Union of South Africa (in the construction of which he played a leading part), Botha become the state's first prime minister. In this office he was faced in 1914 with undertaking a military campaign against German South-West Africa, and a rebellion by some of his old colleagues, notably Christiaan De Wet. Approval of Botha's support of the British connection was not universal (two years earlier General Herzog had led a split in Botha's own cabinet), but under Botha's guidance the majority of Afrikaners followed his direction, and the 1914 rebellion was suppressed without much difficulty, Botha ensuring that the troops used were of Afrikaner origin, so as not to inflame relations between Boer and British South Africans. In these operations, and those which subsequently captured German South-West Africa, Botha took the field himself, again demonstrating his military capabilities. Re-elected in 1915, he sent Smuts to Britain as South African representative to the Imperial War Cabinet, but attended the Paris peace conference in person; but the amount of work affected his health, and he died shortly after his return. Louis Botha's career was remarkable: having been a courageous and skilled enemy of the British, he became one of their most loyal supporters, winning the trust of both British and Afrikaners. A modest man without personal ambition, his sense of compromise and understanding of all parties served his country well.

References

Engelenburg, F. V. *General Louis Botha*, Pretoria, 1929.

Meintjes, J. *General Louis Botha*, London, 1970.

Spender, H. *General Botha: the Career and the Man*, London, 1916.

Buller, Sir Redvers Henry (1839–1908)

Redvers Buller occupies an unusual place in the ranks of British generals of the Victorian era, professionally discredited and savaged by the press, yet who never lost the support of, and popularity with, both the public and his own men.

Scion of an old and distinguished family (his mother was niece to the Duke of Norfolk), Redvers Buller entered the army in 1858 and served with the 60th in China in 1860. He encountered Wolseley in the Red River campaign of 1870 and became one of the foremost members of the so-called 'ring', serving with Wolseley as head of intelligence in the Ashanti expedition and in Egypt in

Redvers Buller in the uniform of the King's Royal Rifle Corps, of whose 1st Battalion he was colonel 1895–1908, and 2nd Battalion 1895–8.

1882, and as chief of staff in the Sudan in 1884–5. In South Africa he gained considerable distinction in command of irregular light horse, winning a Victoria Cross for saving the life of Captain D'Arcy of the Frontier Light Horse at Hlobane, and for rescuing two other men on the same day (28 March 1879). In the Transvaal War he served as Evelyn Wood's chief of staff and commanded a brigade in the Sudan under Graham, winning promotion to major-general. In the Sudan under Wolseley he took command of Stewart's column after the latter was wounded, and received a KCB after his victory at Abu Klea.

From 1887 Buller served as Quartermaster-General, and from 1890 as Adjutant-General, rising to the rank of lieutenant-general in 1891 and general in 1896; many thought that he, not Wolseley, should have been commander-in-chief. After this important, reforming period, he took command at Aldershot in 1898 and was chosen to lead the South African Field Force in 1899. Sadly, he was discredited by his failures in South Africa; replaced by Roberts as commander-in-chief in the theatre, he reverted to the subordinate command of GOC Natal, where his failures continued, notably the disaster at Spion Kop; not even the eventual relief of Ladysmith could rehabilitate

his reputation. He remained in command in Natal until November 1900, when he returned to his duties at Aldershot. In October 1901 he made a speech in his own defence, in reply to severe public criticism; it was taken as a breach of discipline and Buller was removed from his command, and this ended his military career.

Throughout his tribulations, Buller never lost the popularity he enjoyed with the public and the army; although never regarded as a brilliant general, this popularity was presumably founded upon the dogged determination he displayed, even in the worst circumstances, perhaps reflecting the traditional temperament of the British Army. His appearance probably helped: avuncular, heavily-built, with a ruddy complexion and a heavy moustache, an impression articulated at the time: 'There is no stronger character in the British Army than the resolute, almost grimly resolute, absolutely independent, utterly fearless, steadfast, and always vigorous commander ... this big-boned, square-jawed, strong-minded and strong-headed man was born a soldier ... of the very best English type, needless to say the best type of all, since, short of Oriental cunning, it combines the qualifications most admired in every other war-like nation ...'* Indeed, there is some justification for the view that Buller somewhat unfairly shouldered the blame for some of the army's more general failings.

References

Butler, L. *Redvers Buller*, London, 1909.

Melville, C. H. *The Life of General Rt. Hon, Sir Redvers Buller*, London, 1923.

Powell, G. *Buller, a Scapegoat? A Life of General Sir Redvers Buller VC*, London, 1994 (important rehabilitation of Buller's military reputation).

Campbell, Sir Colin, Baron Clyde (1792–1863)

If any commander of the period might be described as 'the soldiers' general' it was probably Colin Campbell, a tough, quick-tempered Scot, proud of his nationality. The son of a Glasgow carpenter named Macliver, he called himself Campbell after an uncle of that name put him through school and procured a commission for him. Despite a heroic career in the Napoleonic Wars (he was wounded severely at San Sebastian and at the crossing of the Bidassoa) his promotion was slow and it was 1832 before he became lieutenant-colonel of the 98th. He led them with distinction in China in 1842 and was highly praised for his conduct in the Second Sikh War, for which he was awarded the KCB. The Crimean War propelled him to the forefront of public attention, as commander of the Highland Brigade, in part because Highlanders loomed large in popular esteem from their exotic appearance and fine combat record, and thus their commander attracted attention, especially as Campbell was both fiercely proud and fiercely devoted to his Highland troops.

* Robinson, Commander C. N. (ed.). *Celebrities of the Army*, London, 1900, p. 2.

Colin Campbell, Baron Clyde.

those under his command was due in part to his wonderful memory; at the Secunderabagh, for example, he recognised Sergeant Joe Lee of the 53rd whom he had encountered in the Punjab years before, and addressed him not merely by name but even remembered his regimental nickname, 'Sergeant Dobbin'.

His task completed, Campbell left India in 1859; he returned home with a peerage, as Baron Clyde, the thanks of parliament, and a handsome pension; but his exertions had taken a toll of his health, and he did not long survive his retirement.

References
Burne, Sir Owen. *Clyde and Strathnairn*, London, 1895.
Forbes, A. *Colin Campbell, Lord Clyde*, London, 1895.
Shadwell, Lieutenant-General L. *The Life of Colin Campbell, Lord Clyde*, Edinburgh, 1881.

Cetshwayo kaMpande (c.1827–84)

The Zulu king Cetshwayo kaMpande was probably the best-known opponent of the British in Africa; many alternative spellings of his name include 'Cetywayo' and 'Cetewayo'. He had most distinguished forebears, the son of the Zulu king Mpande and nephew of the previous kings, Dingaan and the great Shaka; but although he was Mpande's first-born son he had no automatic right of succession, as the seniority of wife, rather than the age of the child, determined the heir. Consequently, Cetshwayo had to assert his right of succession against one of his many half-

Campbell was an obvious choice as the experienced, hard campaigner needed in India at the time of the Mutiny, and on being offered the command by Palmerston, his reaction was typical: when, he was asked, would he be able to set out?; within twenty-four hours was the reply, and he was as good as his word. As commander-in-chief, however, his reputation and fiery temper were not matched by his speed of action, because he took pains to organise before engaging the enemy. Despite criticism (he was nicknamed 'Sir Crawling Camel'), his prudence was justified by the success of his operations, though they lacked the dash often regarded as the key to success in India. However, there was nothing timid about his conduct in battle, and personal bravery, prudence and care were the hallmarks of his command rather than tactical or strategical genius. Campbell's rapport with the common soldiers was considerable, despite accusations of favouritism for his Highlanders; his personal preference was demonstrated at the storming of the Secunderabagh when, after the first attack had failed, he called to Colonel Ewart of the 93rd, 'bring on the tartan – let my own lads at them.'* The veneration with which he was regarded by

King Cetshwayo kaMpande.

*Forbes-Mitchell, W. *Reminiscences of the Great Mutiny 1857-59*, London, 1897, p. 47.

brothers, Mbulazi. Each gathered a faction, Cetshwayo the uSuthu and Mbulazi the iziGqoza, and in late 1856 Mbulazi took his followers to Natal to seek support from the white settlers. Cetshwayo and the uSuthu followed and annihilated the iziGqoza on 2 December at 'Ndondakusuka on the Tugela river, with the deaths of perhaps 30,000 iziGqoza and their dependants; the battlefield was marked by piles of remains for decades and became known as Mathambo, 'the place of bones'.

Consequently, Cetshwayo was crowned king and acknowledged as such by the British, upon Mpande's death in 1872. The British made it obvious that their support depended upon his good conduct, but while not wishing to antagonise them, Cetshwayo determined to assert his authority by maintaining a strong army. After a series of minor incidents the British governor of Cape Colony and the High Commissioner for Native Affairs in South Africa, Sir Bartle Frere, imposed on him a series of demands that amounted to the virtual dismantling of his authority and the disbanding of his power-base, the army. Cetshwayo could never accept such terms and war was inevitable. The king's own military participation in the war was minor, apart from issuing general directions for the opposition to the British invasion forces. His attempts to avert conflict were unsuccessful, and probably nothing short of total defeat of the Zulu army would have satisfied the British after their defeat at Isandlwana. Cetshwayo became a fugitive after the Battle of Ulundi, but on 27 August 1879 he was apprehended by Major Richard Marter of the 1st Dragoon Guards. Deprived of his kingdom, Cetshwayo was taken to Cape Town and visited London in 1882, during which time the Gladstone government announced his restoration as king – but in fact over only a portion of his realm. He was re-installed as king in January 1883, but was soon attacked by his enemies, headed by his cousin Zibhebhu kaMaphita of the Mandlakazi, a powerful clan of northern Zululand. Cetshwayo was defeated and fled; he died in February 1884. With him died any hope of an independent Zululand; his only surviving son, Dinizulu, attempted to become king, but even his succession was disputed, as Cetshwayo's senior wife gave birth to a son after Cetshwayo's death. In 1889 Dinizulu was exiled to St. Helena, allowed to return home in 1898, but was prosecuted for complicity in the 1906 Zulu rebellion and sentenced to four years' imprisonment. He was ultimately paroled with a pension and died in 1913.

References

Binns, C. T. *The Last Zulu King: The Life and Death of Cetshwayo*, London, 1963.

Haggard, H. Rider. *Cetywayo and his White Neighbours*, London, 1882.

Laband, J. P. C., and Wright, J. *King Cetshwayo kaMpande*, Pietermaritzburg, 1980. (See also more general works on the Zulu nation listed under South Africa)

Chelmsford, Frederick Augustus Thesiger, 2nd Baron (1827–1905)

Lord Chelmsford enjoys the unfortunate reputation of a general who won the final battle in a war, yet that victory never cancelled the defeat for which he is sometimes blamed.

Frederick Thesiger was the eldest son of the Rt. Hon. Sir Frederick Thesiger, 1st Baron Chelmsford, a distinguished Lord Chancellor and Attorney-General. Two of his sons followed him into legal and parliamentary life, but Frederick entered the army in 1844. He gained considerable experience of regimental duty in the Crimea and Indian Mutiny (where he commanded the 95th), and of staff duty in India and Abyssinia; after serving at home as ADC to the Queen, he became Adjutant-General in India, then took command at Aldershot and in 1877 was promoted to major-general. In March 1878 he assumed command of the imperial forces in South Africa, and succeeded to the barony on the death of his father in October of that year.

Chelmsford acquitted himself well in the Ninth Cape Frontier War, but was faced with a much more formidable enemy when the Zulu War began. The degree to which Chelmsford was culpable for the defeat at Isandlwana is a matter of debate; one view (as taken by Sir Reginald Coupland in *Zulu Battle Piece*) is that if he can be blamed for under-estimating the enemy he faced, equally guilty were

Frederic Thesiger, Baron Chelmsford.

the more distinguished generals who made the same mistake against the Boers, with even less excuse. Whatever the case, it was decided that Wolseley should be sent to South Africa to take command, while retaining Chelmsford, despite Wolseley's own assessment: that Chelmsford was a very nice fellow and a gentleman, but God forbid he should ever command an army in the field. However, Chelmsford won the Battle of Ulundi before Wolseley arrived; then, having virtually ended the war, he resigned his command, having taken Wolseley's appointment, and the latter's issue of orders to units nominally under Chelmsford's command, as an unpardonable slight. Although rewarded – the Queen's support never diminished and he received the KCB – he never again went on active service. Having been appointed lieutenant-general in a local capacity in South Africa, reverting to major-general upon Wolseley's arrival, he received the rank permanently in 1882, and that of general in 1888. Chelmsford died on 9 April 1905 during a billiards match at the United Service Club; despite the royal support (Edward VII retained him as Gold Stick) and subsequent honours, the shadow of Isandlwana never left him.

References

French, Major G. *Lord Chelmsford and the Zulu War*, London, 1939.

Laband, J. P. C. (ed.). *Lord Chelmsford's Zululand Cam-*

paign 1878–1879, Army Records Society, 1994. (See also more general works on the Zulu War listed under South Africa.)

Piet Cronje.

Cronje, Piet Arnoldus (1835–1911)

Piet Cronje was among the most talented of the Boer generals, and unlike the majority had made a study of modern warfare. Although best-known for his command in the South African War of 1899–1902, he also distinguished himself considerably in the Transvaal War of 1881, and was one of three Boer commandants (with Malan and Potgieter) who accepted Jameson's surrender at Doornkop. In the 1881 war the Transvaal-born Cronje was a noted firebrand, and was one of the first to be confronted with a British allegation of the use of explosive bullets, against the tenets of 'civilised' warfare, to which allegation he did not deign to reply. He commanded the contingent which forced the surrender of the British detachment at Potchefstroom, where he was accused of fooling the British by concealing from them his knowledge of the armistice (Joubert apologised for his behaviour); but although unremitting in his determination during hostilities, once the surrender was concluded he revealed the generous side of his nature, allowing entertainments to be arranged for the British and making a farewell speech when the garrison marched away.

This attitude was not reciprocated in the later war until after Cronje's own surrender, for he was regarded as something of a villain by the British; but despite his continuing courage and energy, he was unable to repeat his earlier successes. In 1899 he commanded in the western theatre, inflicted a major reverse upon Methuen at Magersfontein, but was finally caught and forced to surrender at Paardeburg on 27 February 1900. When Roberts met him to arrange the surrender, he complimented Cronje warmly on a gallant defence; Cronje merely scowled. Accompanied by his wife, he was sent to St. Helena as a prisoner until the conclusion of the war.

Forever a stern opponent of the British, Cronje looked the part, Mortimer Menpes articulating the British perception of him: 'The great Boer General was not prepossessing. In fact, one did not like to look at him at all – so coarse were his manners, so unpicturesque his appearance. He wore a loose, ill-fitting overcoat, a felt hat drawn so far over the ears that it almost rested on his shoulders; the head was pushed forward, with a brutal, cruel expression. General Cronje is a heavy man, cunning and vulgar, with a long, unkempt beard, and rude manners ...*

(Piet Cronje should not be confused with General A. P. Cronje who supported the creation of the National Scouts and Orange River Colony Volunteers, formed from ex-Boer soldiers in support of the British at the end of the conflict.)

*Menpes, M. *War Impressions*, London, 1901, p. 200.

De La Rey, Jacobus Hercules (1847–1914)

Jacobus De La Rey is not the best-known of the Boer Generals, but was among the most talented. Born and resident in the Lichtenburg district, he had almost no formal education but rose to prominence by his strength of character, and was suitably patriarchal in appearance: *The Times* History described his hooked nose and huge beard as giving him the appearance of an Old Testament warrior-prophet! A member of the *Volksraad* of the South African Republic from 1893, he was not a militant and voted against war, but supported it when it came.

De La Rey had no training in military affairs, but had a natural skill. His plan for defence at Magersfontein, involving camouflaged trenches in front of the high ground which would otherwise have been regarded as the obvious defensive position, was quite innovative, as was the narrow design of the trenches (to maximise cover from shrapnel) and the use of barbed wire. A very different tactic which he also employed was that of firing from the saddle, on the move, instead of dismounting to shoot as was the usual practice. His most notable successes probably came during the guerrilla stage of the war, especially his capture of Methuen at Tweebosch, near Klerksdorp, on 7 March 1902; but it was perhaps for his manner of waging war that De La Rey was most known. Without compromis-

Jacobus De La Rey (right), dressed for active service in the South African War.

ing effectiveness, he conducted his operations with an old style of chivalry which quite belies the contemporary British criticisms of Boer 'atrocities'; it was his humanity and courtesy, even more than his military skill, which earned him the respect, even admiration, of his enemies. His treatment of the British prisoners at Tweebosch is typical: after rendering what assistance he could, De La Rey issued rations to the 600-odd prisoners and directed them to the nearest British post, and despite the importance of the injured Methuen, he would not contemplate keeping him a hostage but sent him to the nearest British hospital. Even this generosity was not enough: De La Rey arranged for a telegram to be sent to Lady Methuen, expressing his concern for the wounds suffered by her husband.

He played a prominent part in the peace negotiations, and after the conclusion of hostilities went to India to persuade the Boer prisoners of war there to accept the peace and take the oath of allegiance. In 1907 he was returned unopposed to the first Transvaal parliament, but in the brief rebellion of 1914 his sentiments are unclear; it is conceivable that he may have favoured the rebel cause. On 14 September he was driving to Potchefstroom with Christian Beyers, commandant-general of the South African Defence Force, who was one of the leaders of the rebellion, when they were fired on by a police patrol attempting to catch car-thieves. De La Rey was killed, a sad end to a gallant general. A hospital named after him was founded at Lichtenburg; among other British officers to contribute to the cost of its foundation was Methuen.

Reference

Meintjes, J. *De La Rey, Lion of the West*, Johannesburg, 1966.

De Wet, Christiaan (1854–1922)

Christiaan (or 'Christian') De Wet was the most elusive, and one of the most skilled, of the Boer guerrilla commanders, who constantly frustrated British attempts to capture him, at the same time striking against isolated British posts. A veteran of the Transvaal War (in which he served as field-cornet), he was born at Leeuwkop of a prominent Orange Free State family. He was a fierce supporter of his cause, a determination perhaps concealed by the appearance of good humour and by an undemonstrative nature. De Wet distinguished himself in the action at the Tchrengula Hills near Ladysmith in 1899, where he was wounded and where two British battalions were forced to surrender. As a general, he transferred from Natal to the west and won further laurels by his victories at Sannah's Post and Reddersburg. In later operations he consistently eluded British attempts to corner him, yet struck with devastating effect against unsupported posts. He remained among the most intractable of the Boer commanders, resisting all persuasion to support the moves for peace. (His brother Piet, a Boer leader in the earlier stages of the war, surrendered and joined the National Scouts

Christiaan De Wet. (Print after a portrait by Lance Calkin)

organisation of Boers who changed their allegiance; Christiaan remarked that if he again encountered his brother he would shoot him!)

Having frustrated British efforts to trap him, De Wet succeeded Martinus Steyn as president of the Free State, and advocated continued resistance; until, finally, more realistic counsels prevailed and he joined the ranks of those in favour of peace. He published an account of his campaigns (*Three Years' War*) and in 1907 was elected to the Orange River Colony parliament, becoming minister of agriculture. He never fully accepted the extinction of independence, however, and in 1914 took the field with other Boer leaders to exploit the British pre-occupation with the European war, and re-establish an independent state. Most South Africans remained loyal to prime minister Botha, however, who assumed personal command of the pro-British forces and defeated De Wet's 2,000-strong commando at Mushroom Valley, near Winburg on 12 November. His horses unable to outrun Botha's motorised columns, De Wet was captured on 1 December; he was sentenced to six years' imprisonment for treason, but, in the lenient manner in which most of the 1914 rebels were treated, was released after six months.

Reference
De Wet, C. *Three Years' War*, London, 1902.

Rosenthal, E. *General De Wet: A Biography*, Cape Town, 1946.

Gordon, Charles George (1833–85)

'Gordon of Khartoum' occupied a unique place in the pantheon of Victorian heroes, a combination in the public view of military hero and Christian martyr.

The fourth son of General H. W. Gordon, Charles Gordon was commissioned into the Royal Engineers in 1852. He served in the Crimea, with the Commission set up to define the boundaries between Russia and the Ottoman Empire, and in the war in China in 1860; he then went with the British force sent to Shanghai to protect the European community from the T'ai-p'ing rebels. Gordon was nominated by the British commander to take command of the 'Ever-Victorious Army' (March 1863), and from the outset demonstrated his ability to engender loyalty, even adoration, among unenthusiastic and even untrained followers, and his affinity with non-European troops. For his successes with the 'Ever-Victorious Army' he gained a British lieutenant-colonelcy, the highest Chinese honours, and the nickname 'Chinese Gordon' by which he was known for the remainder of his career.

Charles Gordon, in Egyptian uniform.

In early 1874 Gordon went to Egypt, at the request of the Khedive, as governor of the equatorial regions, and subsequently of the whole Sudan. Here he accomplished much, including in his own agenda for the suppression of the slave trade, as well as in his more official duties of exploration, reformation of the administration and in maintaining the rule of the Khedive in a turbulent area. He resigned in 1879, and the next three years saw him undertake a wide array of tasks. He agreed to take charge of the Congo Free State, in succession to Stanley, at the behest of King Leopold II of the Belgians; served briefly as secretary to the Marquess of Ripon, governor-general of India; went to China at the request of the inspector-general of customs, to persuade the government against hostilities with Russia; served as commandant of Royal Engineers in Mauritius until promoted to major-general; was appointed commandant of colonial forces at the Cape, resigning over what he perceived as the duplicity of the Cape government in its dealings with the Basuto; and finally, having temporarily run out of official appointments, went to Palestine to study the antiquities of Biblical history.

After a year of pursuing his own interests, he returned home to prepare for his agreed position in the Congo; but was requested by the British government to return to the Sudan to organise the Egyptian evacuation in the face of the Mahdi's revolt. With his instructions perhaps ambiguous, Gordon attempted also to make arrangements for the future government of the country, causing a delay which led to his being besieged in Khartoum. His plight became a *cause célèbre* in Britain, and the subject of intense criticism of the government for its perceived lack of effort to save him. It was entirely due to Gordon's efforts that Khartoum held as long as it did, and on his death on 26 January 1885, when the city at last fell to the Mahdi's assault, he was immediately perceived as a true Christian martyr, with as much public mourning as the government attracted criticism. That the relief-force arrived only two days later was at once a tragedy and an irony.

Charles Gordon's military reputation has, perhaps, suffered from the near canonisation accorded him after his death. Even his contemporaries were not universal in their praise, but for all the criticisms of impulsive behaviour and temperament, he was a soldier of considerable skill, most especially in his ability to inspire loyalty and to transform mediocre material into effective forces; it was remarked that as a leader of non-Europeans, his power of command was probably unique. Although not outwardly religious, he was a devout Christian who practised his beliefs, making everything of secondary importance behind his concept of God and duty.

References
Perhaps because of the public perception of Gordon as a hero unnecessarily martyred, he has been the subject of probably more biographies than any other military personality of the period. Among these are:
Elton, Lord, *General Gordon,*
London, 1954.
Forbes, A. *Chinese Gordon,* London, 1884.
Garrett, R. *General Gordon,* London, 1974.
Gordon, C. G. *The Journals of Major-General C. G. Gordon CB at Kartoum,* intr. A. E. Hake, London, 1885.
– *General Gordon's Khartoum Journal,* ed. Lord Elton, London, 1961.
Gordon, Sir Henry W. *Events in the Life of Charles George Gordon,* London, 1886 (by Gordon's brother).
Hope, E. *General Gordon: The Christian Hero,* n.d. (c.1887).
Johnson, P. *Gordon of Khartoum,* London, 1985.
Marlowe, J. *Mission to Khartum: the Apotheosis of General Gordon,* London, 1969.
Nutting, A. *Gordon: Martyr and Misfit,* London, 1966.
Pollock, J. *Gordon, the Man behind the Legend,* London, 1993.
Trench, C. Chenevix. *The Road to Khartoum: A Life of General Gordon,* New York, 1978.

Gough, Hugh, 1st Viscount (1779–1869)

One of the bravest and most determined generals to campaign in India, Hugh Gough was born in county Limerick, his family no stranger to military affairs: his father was colonel of the Limerick City Militia, two brothers had distinguished careers in the Napoleonic Wars, and a brother-in-law was killed at Bayonne. Hugh entered the army in 1794, and after service at the Cape and in the West Indies led his 87th Foot with great distinction during the Peninsular War, perhaps most notably at Barrosa; he was wounded at both Talavera and Nivelle. After spending some time as a magistrate in Ireland, he was promoted to major-general in 1830, was given a divisional command in India in 1837, and went to China as commander-in-chief, for which service he received a baronetcy. In August 1843 he was appointed commander-in-chief India, and won his great victory at Maharajpore.

In the First Sikh War, Gough again commanded the army in person, most unusually having as his second in command his political master, the governor-general, Sir Henry Hardinge, whose influence was important in curbing Gough's permanently offensive spirit – it was said that his idea of tactics was simply to batter away with an oak stick! Indecisive actions at Mudki and Ferozeshah were followed by victory at Sobraon, and Sir Hugh was rewarded with a barony. In 1848 he again exhibited less tactical genius than aggression, so that following the heavy losses at Chillianwalla, it was thought advisable to replace him by Sir Charles Napier. Even in the army, where he was most popular, his style of command was criticised; one participant at Chillianwalla (which he described as 'a devil of a battle ... the Sikhs fought with greatest gallantry, and ... our men ... were quite heroes') wrote that 'I hear on all sides that it would be a wise and prudent measure on the part of the Governor-General to recall Lord Gough from the Punjab and restrain his ill-judged valour within our peaceful provinces. His Lordship fancied himself at Donnybrook Fair, and was in the thick of it, in the mêlée, and lost to sight!'* However, before Gough could receive news

*Letter dated 15 January 1849, in *Illustrated London News,* 10 March 1849.

Sir Hugh, later Viscount Gough; apart from the breast-star of the Order of the Bath, the most important decoration seen here is the Army Gold Cross at the neck, awarded for the Peninsular War actions of Talavera, Barrosa, Vittoria and Nivelle. (Engraving by G. Stodart)

of his supersession, he had won the decisive victory of Gujerat, which ended the war. He received a viscountcy and other honours, but did not again see active service, although he was sent to the Crimea to invest Pélissier and others with the Order of the Bath. Gough attained the rank of field marshal in 1862.

It is perhaps unfair to criticise Gough too severely for the casualties sustained in his tactics against the Sikhs, if only because the Sikh army was the best-disciplined and most formidable force encountered by the British in India. Nevertheless, a distinctive figure in his characteristic, long white coat matching his white hair and moustache, Hugh Gough was the epitome of the 'fighting general'.

Reference

Rait, R. S. *Life and Campaigns of Hugh, 1st Viscount Gough,* London, 1903.

Grant, Sir James Hope (1808–75)

Few general officers were as admired or so popular as Sir James Hope Grant. Born into a talented family of Scottish gentry (his brother was Sir Francis Grant, the celebrated portraitist and president of the Royal Academy), James entered the 9th Lancers in 1826. A brigade-major in China in 1842, he fought in the First Sikh War (including Sobraon) and commanded the 9th at Chillianwalla and Gujerat, rising to the rank of brevet-colonel by 1854. Initially commanding the cavalry division in the Indian Mutiny, he was promoted to brigadier-general by Campbell who gave him command of the column which marched to the relief of Lucknow. Promoted to major-general, he played an important role in the eventual suppression of the rebellion, and with the local rank of lieutenant-general was given command of the British contingent in the Anglo-French expedition to China in 1860. In reward for his most competent execution of this campaign, he was appointed a GCB; in 1861 his lieutenant-generalship was made permanent, and he became CinC of the Madras Army. On his return home in 1865 he was appointed quartermaster-general, in 1870 took command at Aldershot and in 1872 reached the rank of general; he made a considerable contribution towards the reform of army training.

Sir James Hope Grant.

Apart from his military skill and personal bravery, Hope Grant was most admired for his kindly demeanour (he was deeply religious) and, perhaps, his slight eccentricities, which included a very quick way of speaking and his being accompanied on campaign by a huge violoncello (he was a gifted musician), carried on a camel, which both perplexed and terrified the natives. Lord Roberts wrote of him with a warmth typical of those who served under his command, and recounted an anecdote characteristic of his kindly ways: after a particularly dangerous exploit, 'we succeeded in making our way to the main body of the force, where we found Hope Grant in great anxiety about us ... The dear old fellow evinced his satisfaction at our safe return by shaking each of us heartily by the hand, repeating over and over again in his quick, quaint way, "Well, my boys, well, my boys, very glad to have you back! Never thought to see you again."'*

References

Grant, Sir James Hope. *Incidents in the Sepoy War 1857-58, compiled from the Private Journal of General Sir Hope Grant*, ed. Captain H. Knollys, Edinburgh, 1873.

– *Incidents in the China War of 1860*, ed. Captain H. Knollys, pubd. posth., 1875.
Knollys, Sir Henry. *Life of General Sir Hope Grant*, London, 1894.

Hardinge, Henry, 1st Viscount Hardinge of Lahore and King's Newton (1785–1856)

Henry Hardinge, son of the Revd. Henry Hardinge, entered the army in 1799 as an officer in the Queen's Rangers. Three of the five Hardinge brothers had distinguished military careers, one becoming a major-general, and George Hardinge was killed in circumstances of great distinction when in command of HMS *St. Fiorenzo*, in capturing the French frigate *La Piedmontaise* in 1808. Henry had a notable career in the Peninsular War, was at Moore's side when the general received his mortal wound, and as DQMG of the Portuguese army instigated the advance of Lowry Cole's division which turned Albuera from likely defeat to victory. Serving as liaison officer with the Prussian headquarters, he lost his left hand at Ligny. Hardinge became a firm friend of Wellington's (he was the Duke's second in the famous duel with the Earl of Winchilsea), was secretary at war in the ministries of Wellington and Peel, and in 1830 and 1834–5 was chief secretary for Ireland.

In 1844 Hardinge succeeded Ellenborough as governor-general of India, and on the outbreak of the First Sikh War generously offered to serve as second-in-command to Sir Hugh Gough. This was a curious arrangement and prone to cause confusion, and indeed Hardinge briefly asserted his authority as governor-general at Ferozeshah, insisting that Gough not engage until he had been reinforced, which probably saved the day. Throughout the campaign, Hardinge's cool head probably did much to temper

Sir Henry, later Viscount Hardinge, wearing the sword supposedly carried by Napoleon at Waterloo, and given to him by the Duke of Wellington. (Engraving by G. Stodart)

Gough's fiery aggression, and at the conclusion of the war Hardinge was rewarded with a viscountcy and a pension of £3,000 p.a. for his life and those of his next two successors. It was notable that during the war he wore a costume perhaps consciously modelled upon that of his friend and mentor, Wellington: a plain cocked hat and blue civilian frock-coat decorated only with the GCB, with the sword reputedly worn by Napoleon at Waterloo, a gift from Wellington in 1816. Hardinge returned home in 1848, succeeding Wellington as commander-in-chief in 1852, rising to field marshal in 1855; his management of the Crimean War, on Wellingtonian principles, was perhaps not the most felicitous. He resigned in July 1856 from ill-health, and died in September of the same year. His career had proved that Wellington's assessment was correct: 'A plain, straightforward, just and excellent man of business.'*

Hardinge married the daughter of the Marquess of Londonderry, sister of Viscount Castlereagh and of another of Wellington's subordinates, Charles Stewart, the

*Roberts, Lord. *Forty-One Years in India*, London, 1900, p. 165.

*Quoted in Griffiths, A. J. *The Wellington Memorial*, London, 1897, p. 304.

3rd Marquess; Hardinge's younger son became CinC of the Bombay Army, one grandson served with the Camel Corps in the Nile expedition, and another, unusually, also became governor-general (viceroy) of India (1910–16), and was awarded the title of Baron Hardinge of Penshurst.

Reference
Hardinge, C. *Viscount Hardinge and the Advance of the British Dominions in the Punjab*, London. 1900.

Havelock, Sir Henry (1795–1857)

Henry Havelock was another of those who occupied the place of 'Christian hero' in the Victorian pantheon. Originally destined for a legal career, his military progress was slow: lacking influence and the finance to purchase promotion (his father, a Sunderland ship owner, had suffered a business failure), he served 23 years before he rose beyond the rank of lieutenant. To offset these disadvantages Havelock made an earnest study of his profession, and his experience became considerable in both regimental and staff appointments (DAAG in Burma, he published a history of *Campaigns in Ava* (1828); and served in Afghanistan and against the Sikhs. Possessed of a deep and overt religious belief, Havelock became a Baptist in India, preferred the company of missionaries to that of his fellow-soldiers, and made earnest attempts to superintend the spiritual welfare of his men (for a time, the 13th Light

Sir Henry Havelock. (Engraving by C. Holl)

Infantry was nicknamed 'Havelock's Saints'!). Having reached the rank of colonel, Havelock became adjutant-general of the troops in India, and in 1857 was given command of the 2nd Division for the Persian campaign.

At the outbreak of the Indian Mutiny Havelock was aged 62, white-haired and not possessed of the appearance of a dynamic commander; a very small man who always dined wearing his sword and a vast array of medals, he could have been taken for a caricature of a general; but, as Lady Canning remarked, although he might be fussy and tiresome, he gave the impression of being made of steel. As brigadier-general he was given an independent command for the first time, to take a column in support of Lucknow and Cawnpore and destroy any enemy he encountered. He set off from Allahabad on 7 July 1857 and routed a large enemy force at Fatehpur on 12 July, a remarkable action in which not one fatality was suffered by Havelock's force. Accordingly, he remarked that the success was due to 'the blessing of Almighty God on a most righteous cause, the cause of justice, humanity, truth and good government' (Field Force Order, 13 July 1857); but took care to add that in addition to divine approval, the British artillery, the Enfield rifle and British 'pluck' had also played a part. Havelock broke through to reinforce the Lucknow garrison, but the fatigues of the march had proved too great, and he died of dysentery at Lucknow on 24 November 1857, universally mourned as a true Christian hero: 'Reader, Havelock yet speaks, and will live in the hearts of thousands, as long as our language endures.'[*] His last words to his son (his aide), 'See how a Christian can die', were entirely in character. Although he lived to receive news of his KCB for the first three actions of the campaign, he never knew of his promotion to major-general or of his baronetcy.

(Havelock's three brothers also followed military careers: his eldest brother William was wounded at Waterloo and killed at Ramnuggur; Thomas died of fever in Spain serving with De Lacy Evans in 1836, and Charles became a general in Ottoman service.)

References
Brock, Revd. W. *A Biographical Sketch of Sir Henry Havelock KCB*, London, 1958.
Cooper, L. *Havelock 1795-1857*, London, 1957.
Forbes, A. *Havelock*, London, 1890.
Marshman, J. C. *Memoir of Major-General Sir Henry Havelock KCB*, London, 1860.
Pollock, J. C. *Way to Glory: the Life of Havelock of Lucknow*, London, 1957.

Hodson, William Stephen Raikes (1821–58)

One of the great heroes of the Indian Army, 'Hodson of Hodson's Horse' enjoyed a military reputation sharply at odds with the criticisms of his detractors. William Hodson was the son of a clergyman, educated at Rugby and Cam-

[*]Gowing, T. *A Soldier's Experiences; or, a Voice from the Ranks*, Nottingham, 1907, p. 464.

bridge, and at a comparatively late age was commissioned into the army of the East India Company. Through the influence of Sir Henry Lawrence, in 1847 he was appointed as adjutant of the Corps of Guides, and later commanded the corps, with civil authority over Yusafzai. The appointment ended in controversy, with two inquiries over alleged financial mismanagement (one found him guilty, the other discovered only irregular accounting), and maltreatment of his own men and those over whom he had jurisdiction; and more than one superior expressed their lack of trust as to Hodson's integrity with money.

Although still only a lieutenant in 1857, the Indian Mutiny resurrected Hodson's career. As commander of his corps of irregular cavalry, Hodson's Horse, and as head of the Intelligence Department, he proved to be invaluable. Sir Robert Montgomery, Judicial Commissioner of the Punjab during the Mutiny, wrote that 'Many men are as brave, many possess as much talent, many are cool and accurate in judgement, but not one combines all these qualifications as he did.'[1] Equally valuable were his constant good spirits ('Affairs at times looked very queer ... Hodson's face was then like sunshine breaking through the dark clouds of despondency and gloom',[2] and his skill at intelligence matters so great that 'He used to know what the rebels had for dinner in Delhi.'[3] Idolised by his own Indian troopers, Hodson possessed near-legendary skill with sabre and hog-spear: 'In a fight he was glorious. If there was only a good hard skrimmage he was as happy as a king. A beautiful swordsman, he never failed to kill his man ... smiling, laughing, parrying most fearful blows, as calmly as if he were brushing off flies, calling out all the time ... "What's that? Do you call yourself a swordsman?"'[4] His reputation was dented, however, by renewed accusations of looting and similar financial irregularities, and most notably by his exploit involving the three sons of the king of Delhi, whom he took into custody, supposedly under a guarantee of safe conduct. When taking them to British lines Hodson's small escort was surrounded by a crowd, and fearing an attempt to liberate the princes, in his own words, 'seizing a carbine from one of my men, I deliberately shot them one after another ... I am not cruel, but I confess I did rejoice at the opportunity of ridding the earth of these wretches.'[5] Hodson's Sikh troopers shouted with delight, but posterity has been less forgiving.

Hodson was mortally wounded on 11 March 1858 attempting to storm a building at Lucknow, refusing to await the arrival of powder-bags for use as grenades. William Forbes-Mitchell of the 93rd attempted to pull him back, but he stepped into the doorway and was shot through the liver; Forbes-Mitchell's account disposes of the rumour that Hodson was killed while looting. He died next morning. For all his courage and military talents, Hodson's reputation remained tainted by suspicions of financial irregularity and the cold-blooded killing of the 'Delhi princes'. J. W. Sherer, who had been Hodson's fag at Rugby, met him shortly before his death and has left a reasoned judgement. Hodson, he said, had 'convinced himself that a stern political necessity existed at the moment' that he shot the princes, and that after his death, Hodson 'was injudiciously held up as a notable specimen of a type of soldier he could not, and did not, pretend to emulate. But there are grades between Philip Sidney and Trenck, and if he bore an indistinct likeness to the first, I must say I think he should not have been compared to the second.'[6]

William Hodson.

Notes
1. Mackenzie, Colonel R. H. 'Hodson of Hodson's Horse', in *Cavalry Journal*, 1911, vol. VI, p. 181.
2. Hodson, Revd. G. H. (ed.). *Twelve Years of a Soldier's Life in India*, London, 1859, p. 181.
3. Ibid., p. 318.
4. Ibid.
5. Ibid., p. 302.
6. Sherer, J. W. *Havelock's March on Cawnpore*, 1857, London, n.d., pp. 288–9. The reference is to Colonel Franz Trenck, leader of an Austro-Hungarian Pandour corps in the mid-18th century, infamous for its brutality and pillaging.

References
Early biographies broadly in Hodson's favour include:
Hodson, Revd. G. H. (ed.). *Twelve Years of a Soldier's Life in India, being Extracts from the Letters of the Late Major W. S. R. Hodson*, London, 1859 (the editor was Hodson's brother).
Hodson, Revd. G. H. *Hodson of Hodson's Horse*, London, 1889.
Trotter, Captain L. J. *A Leader of Light Horse: a Life of Hodson of Hodson's Horse*, Edinburgh, 1901.
The opposing view is presented by:
Chamberlain, General Sir Craw-

ford. *Remarks on Captain Trotter's Biography of Major W. S. R. Hodson*, 1901.

Holmes, T. R. E. *Four Famous Soldiers*, Londonm 1889.

A more modern biography is:

Cork, B. J. *Rider on a Grey Horse: a Life of Hodson of Hodson's Horse*, London 1958.

Jhansi, Lakshmi Bai, Rani of (c.1828–58)

Of all 19th-century military commanders, Lakshmi Bai was surely the most unusual. That she was literate, articulate and politically skilled is singular enough, given the usual role of women in 19th-century India; that she was expert with the sword, and a commander of troops, is even more unusual.

Born Manakarnike, daughter of an official at the court of the exiled Peshwa at Bithur (where she may have learned her skill with arms), she changed her name to Lakshmi Bai on her wedding in 1842 to Gangadhar Rao, Rajah of Jhansi, a widower much older than she and without an heir to his important and pro-British central Indian state. The only son of Lakshmi Bai died aged three months, so the Rajah adopted a five-year-old relative as his heir before his death in November 1853. By an agreement reached with Jhansi's British political agent, the Rani was authorised to rule the state during her lifetime, with the heir Damodar presumably succeeding her; but despite her obvious capability, the governor-general, Lord Dalhousie, decided to annex Jhansi, depriving the ruling family of their control in return for a handsome pension. Nevertheless, the Rani remained a loyal supporter of the British even in the early stages of the Mutiny. In June 1857 the British inhabitants of Jhansi were massacred by the rebels, but it is unlikely that the Rani was implicated; indeed, she had to pay a ransom before the mutineers would leave Jhansi. When she reported the event to the British, she was suspected of complicity. With the British presence temporarily removed, the Rani raised an army and personally led it to victory over the Dewan of Orchha, who had taken the opportunity to repay old grievances by invading the state.

Sir Hugh Rose arrived before Jhansi with his army in March 1858, determined to avenge the massacre; and only when her final protestations of loyalty were rejected did Lakshmi Bai decide to fight. Tantia Topi's rebel army was routed by Rose in its attempt to relieve the Rani's beleaguered garrison, and on 3 April the city was stormed with the death of some 5,000 inhabitants. Rose reported that scarcely a house in Jhansi did not contain some item of British plunder, which convinced him that the Rani and all her subjects were 'more or less concerned in the murder and plunder of the English', and attributed the Rani's stern defence to the fact that 'the rebel confederacy knew well, that if Jhansi, the richest Hindoo city and most important fortress in central India fell, the cause of the insurgents in this part of India fell also'.* Rose also noted that the Rani's father was apprehended in a breakout from the city, and was promptly hanged.

Lakshmi Bai herself escaped with a small bodyguard, and to continue the fight joined the Rao Sahib, but they were defeated at Kalpi on 22 May; she then joined Tantia Topi, with whom she looted Gwalior after the Maharaja Sindhia refused to forsake his British alliance. On 17 June 1858 Rose surprised the rebels at Kotah-ki-Serai; the Rani attempted to stay the flight of her troops, reputedly charging with a sword in each hand, her reins in her teeth, but was shot by a member of the 8th Hussars; she rode away but lived for only a few minutes. Her cremation ceremonies were unfinished when the 8th Hussars drove away the mourners.

Apparently it was not just Victorian sentiment which led British witnesses to portray the Rani in a heroic light; not only does she appear to have been the most resolute member of her army and personally brave in combat, but seems to have possessed military and administrative skills the equal or superior to those of any other Indian leader of the war. Whether she was involved in the Jhansi massacre, and whether she would have joined the rebels had it not been for Rose's intractable attitude, is uncertain. Sir Owen Burne, in *Clyde and Strathnairn* (1895) described her as the 'Indian Joan of Arc', which is probably an appropriate title for this most remarkable princess.

References

Smyth, Rt. Hon. Sir John, Bt. *The Rebellious Rani*, London, 1966.

Tahmankar, D. V. *The Rani of Jhansi*, London, 1958.

Joubert, Petrus Jacobus (1831–1900)

Born in Cape Colony of Huguenot descent, Petrus Joubert was orphaned in early life and migrated first to Natal and later to the Transvaal, settling in the Wakkerstroom district. A successful farmer, he studied law, was elected to the *Volksraad*, served as attorney-general and in 1875 deputised as president during Thomas Burgers' absence in Europe. Although he later gained the reputation of a moderate, during the British annexation he refused to accept any official post, instead assisting with the agitation which led to the Transvaal War. From 1880 he was commandant-general of the Boer forces, a member of the triumvirate which ran the provisional government at Heidelberg, and commanded at Laing's Nek and Majuba. Having assisted in the peace negotiations, he stood as Kruger's opponent in the 1883 election, and was defeated heavily. In 1893 his platform was that of the progressive faction which sought to redress some of the grievances felt by the Uitlanders; he was again defeated by Kruger, but protested at the latter's alleged vote-rigging. He stood again in 1898 against his old adversary, but the Jameson Raid had occurred in the meantime, and Joubert was massively defeated, polling only about one-sixth as many votes as Kruger.

*Rose's dispatch, 30 April 1858; *London Gazette*, 16 July 1858.

Petrus Joubert.

Joubert took little part in the events which led to the South African War of 1899, but on its outbreak took command of the Boer forces. He was somewhat criticised for his perceived sympathy for the Uitlander position, and did not, or could not, impose a firm hand upon the direction of the war; his defensive strategy was said to be in character with his cautious nature. He was, however, noted for the chivalrous manner in which he conducted operations; for example, when General Penn Symons died of the injury he received at Talana, Joubert sent a message of sympathy to his widow. As the war progressed, his health deteriorated, further decreasing his active participation; and despite his moderation, which had discouraged offensive action, he was genuinely mourned when he died of peritonitis at Pretoria on 28 March 1900; he received a state funeral. If a commander's worth can be gauged from the words of his enemies, Joubert's was undoubted: Sir George White described him as a soldier, gentleman, and a brave and honourable opponent, and Roberts' message of condolence to Kruger remarked that his gallantry was exceeded only by the humanity and chivalry which marked his command.

Reference

Meintjes, J. *The Commandant-General: Petrus Jacob Joubert*, Cape Town, 1971.

Kitchener, Horatio Herbert, 1st Earl Kitchener of Khartoum (1850–1916)

'K of K' is probably the most recognisable of all British generals of the period, although this fame is perhaps as much due now to Alfred Leete's First World War recruiting-poster than it is to Kitchener's colonial campaigns.

Son of a lieutenant-colonel, Horatio Kitchener was commissioned into the Royal Engineers in January 1871, at which time he was serving as a volunteer with a French field ambulance in the Franco–Prussian War, where he experienced his baptism of fire. After employment on survey work in Cyprus and Palestine, in 1883 he was promoted to captain and attached to the Egyptian army. In the Nile expedition of 1884–5 he served as DAA&QMG, was commandant at Suakin 1886–8, and in an action at Handub on 17 January 1888 was wounded severely by a bullet which broke his jaw. In 1888 he commanded a brigade (including the actions of Gemaiza and Toski), from 1889 to 1892 served as adjutant-general, and in 1892 succeeded Grenfell as Sirdar of the Egyptian army, completing the work of reform begun by his predecessor. In 1896 he won the action of Firket, and being appointed a British major-general in the same year, commanded the joint Anglo–Egyptian forces which re-possessed the Sudan and destroyed the Mahdist power at Omdurman. Rewarded with a peerage, in 1900 Kitchener was promoted to lieutenant-general and sent to South Africa as Roberts' chief of staff, where his organisational skills and indefatigable energy proved crucial; succeeding Roberts as commander-in-chief, he remained in South Africa until the war was finally extinguished. He then went to India as commander-in-chief, where he reorganised the three presidency armies into a unified force (and caused the resignation of the viceroy, Lord Curzon, against whom he had come into conflict). On leaving India in 1909 he was promoted to field marshal, and in 1910–11 used his organisational skill to reform the colonial and dominion forces.

In 1911 Kitchener was appointed British agent and consul-general in Egypt, a position of almost complete authority, in which he instituted reforms to improve the condition of the country and its inhabitants; and shortly after being advanced in the peerage to an earldom was in England on leave when the First World War began. Two days after the declaration of war he was appointed Secretary of State for War, and for the next year and a half virtually ran the British war effort, being one of those who realised that a protracted struggle was inevitable, and who planned accordingly. Never an easy associate, he found it difficult to delegate or work as part of a team, and his influence declined following the Dardanelles disaster, some of the blame for which may be accorded to him. When leading a mission to Russia he was lost at sea on 5 June 1916 when the cruiser HMS *Hampshire* struck a mine; his death was regarded by the public as an appalling

Horatio Kitchener, later Earl Kitchener of Khartoum.

calamity, but some members of the government perhaps did not much mourn his loss.

Kitchener's role in the World War has, perhaps, tended to obscure his very considerable successes in the colonial sphere; and his stern, cold demeanour did nothing to advance his popularity with those who knew him. Watch-ing him conduct a battle, 'viciously chewing the ends of unlighted cigarettes', Mortimer Menpes thought him hard, inscrutable and devoid of imagination, and noted how everyone fell silent when he appeared: 'No officer in the British army ... is held in such mortal fear'.[1] Kitch-ener's ambition and tireless energy admitted of no friendships and no patience with those of lesser enthusiasm; even a contemporary paean of praise admitted that 'it would be ridiculous to suggest that Lord Kitchener has exactly what one would call a loveable character. It is possible that he has found it necessary deliberately to suppress many human emotions as likely to interfere inconveniently with the attainment of his objects. But the result is not altogether pleasing. No harder taskmaster ever lived ...'[2]

Notes

1. Menpes, M. *War Impressions*, London, 1901, pp. 75, 84.
2. Robinson, Commander C. N. *Celebrities of the Army*, London, 1900, p. 27.

References

Arthur, Sir George. *Life of Earl Kitchener*, London, 1920.
Cassar, G. H. *Kitchener: Architect of Victory*, London, 1920.
Esher, Reginald, Viscount. *The Tragedy of Lord Kitchener*, London, 1921.
Kellett, R. *The King's Shilling: the Life and Times of Lord Kitchener of Khartoum*, London, 1984.
Magnus, Sir Philip, *Kitchener: Portrait of an Imperialist*, London, 1958.
Warner, P. *Kitchener: the Man behind the Legend*, London, 1985.

'Oom Paul': President Paul Kruger.

Kruger, Stephanus Johannes Paulus (1825–1904)

Reviled by the British, Paul Kruger (as he was generally known) was the leading Boer personality during the South African War, and was known almost universally by the homely nickname '*Oom Paul*' ('Uncle Paul'). He was born in Cape Colony, apparently of distant German ancestry (Jacob Kruger had been sent to the Cape by the Dutch East India Company in 1713), and as a child participated in the Great Trek. Although his education was rudimentary, his experiences of outdoor adventure were prodigious, and at the age of fourteen, after he had already participated in actions against the Matabele and Zulu nations, he settled with his family north of the Vaal. At seventeen Kruger was an assistant field-cornet, and participated in several campaigns and expeditions; in 1856–7 he joined Pretorius in the attempt to compel a union between the Transvaal and Orange Free State. Throughout his life, Kruger was extremely devout, having been raised in the Dopper Sect of the Dutch Reformed Church, the most extreme form of Calvinism; this helped to guide his actions in his political career, and perhaps imposed a degree of inflexibility.

During Pretorius' tenure as president, Kruger was elected commandant-general of the Transvaal forces, and participated in the faction which opposed the succeeding president, Thomas Burgers. Kruger campaigned against British annexation, and opposed them during the Transvaal War, being one of those who ultimately negotiated peace terms. In 1883 he was elected president of the Transvaal, and despite an undistinguished record of economic management, was re-elected in 1888, 1893 (although accused by his opponent, Joubert, of tampering with the returns) and 1898. His unwillingness to compromise, leading to what were perceived as discriminations against the Uitlanders (principally British settlers) exacerbated the strained relations between Britain and the Transvaal, leading to the outbreak of war in 1899. It was his leadership of the Transvaal – effectively of all Boer resistance in the earlier part of the war – for which Kruger is most remembered, but his personal appearance also contributed to his fame: his stern expression, frock-coat, top hat and patriarchal beard became instantly recognisable far beyond Britain and South Africa, and provided inspiration for cartoonists both pro- and anti-Boer. With the fall of Pretoria, and too old to take to the open country on commando, Kruger went to Europe in an unavailing attempt to gain European support for the Boer cause; and from his departure in September 1900 ceased to exercise any political influence. While resident at Utrecht he dictated his memoirs, which were published in 1902, and he died at Clarens, on Lake Geneva, in July 1904. He was buried at Pretoria on the following 16 December, appropriately, perhaps, on the anniversary of the Battle of Blood River, at which he had been present as a boy.

References

Cloete, S. *African Portraits*, London, 1948.
Kruger, S. J. P. *The Memoirs of Paul Kruger*, London, 1902.
Nathan, M. *Paul Kruger: His Life and times*, Durban, 1944.
Fisher, J. *Paul Kruger, his Life and Times*, London, 1975.
Meintjes, J. *President Paul Kruger*, London, 1974.

Lawrence, Sir Henry Montgomery (1806–57), and Lawrence, John Laird Mair, 1st Baron Lawrence (1811–70)

The Lawrence brothers were among the most influential British personalities in mid-19th century India, the sons of Colonel Alexander Lawrence, who had volunteered for the forlorn hope at the storming of Seringapatam.

Born in Ceylon of an Irish Protestant family, with a mother descended from John Knox, it is perhaps not surprising that Henry Lawrence grew into a somewhat stern and puritanical figure. Joining the Bengal Artillery in 1823, he gathered wide experience of campaigning and of non-military duties, as Resident in Nepal in 1843, and Resident at Lahore in 1846. Attaining the rank of general officer, his long experience of the Sikhs (in 1842 he had managed their contingent, and in the First Sikh War had been aide to Hardinge) made him an ideal choice as chief commissioner for the Punjab following its annexation in 1849, but conflict with Lord Dalhousie led to his replacement by his brother John in 1853, Henry becoming the governor-general's agent in Rajputana. His time was not devoted exclusively to matters military and political; he was an influential writer and military reformer, and estab-

lished the most famous philanthropic institutions in India, the Lawrence Asylums, expending most of his resources during the last thirteen years of his life on these and other charities. The most able and far-sighted of administrators, he had warned of the potential of discontent before the Mutiny, and in March 1857 accepted the command at Lucknow, as Chief Commissioner of Oudh, just in time to put the Residency into a defensible state. During the siege, a shell burst in his room (2 July 1857) and inflicted a mortal wound; he died two days later. His preferred epitaph was 'Here lies Henry Lawrence, who tried to do his duty', but those aware of his character were rightly most effusive in their lamentations. Sir Herbert Edwardes, announcing news of his death, wrote that 'We have all lost a friend, a master, an example – a second father. The Punjab, India, England has lost the noblest of public servants. Anything so distressing as this I have not yet heard, though Heaven knows there has been no lack of bloodshed. Thousands, black and white, will mourn him. For *him* indeed we cannot grieve, for he was a humble and sincere Christian, prepared to die at any time, and he has died at last for his country. But, for ourselves, we must lament all our lives, for never shall we see his like again. Now and then only,

Sir Henry Lawrence, at the period of the siege of Lucknow.

John Lawrence, later Baron Lawrence.

like meteors, such men are born, and those who happen to see and know them are most fortunate. It is a standard of public and private worth, which elevates our own while thinking of it ... There is no getting over it; it remains a lifelong regret ...'*

John Lawrence was born in England, and made his career in India in a civil rather than military capacity. The distinction between military and civil duties, though defined clearly, was often blurred in practice, and he showed military capability in organising Sikh levies after the First Sikh War. Having been Henry's aide, he replaced his brother as chief commissioner in the Punjab, and during the early stages of the Mutiny again exercised his military talents, disarming untrustworthy units in the Punjab and forming an army, principally of Sikhs, to assist in the suppression of the rebellion. Hailed as 'the saviour of India', he was rewarded with a baronetcy, and having returned home in 1859 was sent to India again in 1864 for a five-year term as viceroy and governor-general. His rule was marked by financial prudence, a deep concern for all those under his jurisdiction, and a great interest in Christian education. Upon his final return to Britain in 1869 he became Baron Lawrence of the Punjab and of Grately (Hampshire), and took as the supporters of his arms a Pathan of the Guides Cavalry and an officer of Sikh irregular cavalry.

Other brothers of the two most famous Lawrences included Alexander William (1803–68), a major-general and colonel of the 2nd Madras Light Cavalry, and Sir George St Patrick (1804–84), a lieutenant-general.

Paul, Baron Methuen.

References
Aitchison, Sir Charles. *Lord Lawrence*, Oxford, 1892.
Bosworth Smith, R. *Life of Lord Lawrence*, London, 1883.
Edwardes, Sir Herbert, and Merivale, H. *Life of Sir Henry Lawrence*, London, 1873.
Edwardes, M. *The Necessary Hell: John and Henry Lawrence and the Indian Empire*, London, 1958.
Innes, Lieutenant-General J. *Sir Henry Lawrence*, Oxford, 1898.
Lawrence, H. *The Journals of Honoria Lawrence: India Observed 1837–1854*, ed. Lawrence, J. and Woodiwiss, A., London, 1980. (wife of Henry Lawrence).
Lawrence, J. *Lawrence of Lucknow*, ed. A. Woodiwiss, London, 1990.
Morison, J. L. *Lawrence of Lucknow*, London, 1934.
(Sir George Lawrence's memoirs are *Forty Years' Service in India*, London, 1874)

Methuen, Paul Sanford, 3rd Baron (1845–1932)

Lord Methuen was one of the most unfortunate generals of the period, but despite his reverses and the appointment of his juniors over him, he remained undaunted and doggedly continued to perform the duties asked of him. The reason, in a contemporary view, was because 'Lord Methuen is a Peer, and a Guardsman, and ... a genuine flesh-and-blood Briton, in whom sporting and athletic tastes are strongly developed ...'*

Although his peerage dated only to 1834, Methuen came from an ancient family; one of his ancestors had negotiated the 'Methuen Treaty' with Portugal (1703), which resulted in the popularity of port-wine in Britain. Commissioned into the Scots Fusilier Guards in 1864, Paul Methuen served in the Ashanti expedition, was military attaché to the embassy at Berlin (1878–81), HQ commandant in Egypt (1882), and in 1884–5 led Methuen's Horse in Bechuanaland. Succeeding to the barony in 1891, he served as major-general commanding Home District (1892–7), on the North-West Frontier (1897–8), and as lieutenant-general was given command of the 1st Division in South Africa at the beginning of the 1899 war. Despite his earlier wide experiences, he lacked the touch of luck or genius required by a successful commander; checked at

*To Harry Lumsden, 8 August 1857; quoted in Lumsden, General Sir Peter, and Elsmie, G. R. *Lumsden of The Guides*, London, 1899, p. 205.

*Robinson, Commander C. N. *Celebrities of the Army*, London, 1900, p. 10.

Modder River, he was defeated heavily at Magersfontein, where the reputation of the British forces took a heavy beating, especially as they included units regarded as among the army's élite. Methuen had little more success in subsequent appointments, and after almost a year in pursuit of De Wet, it was Methuen himself who was captured, severely wounded, by De La Rey at Tweebosch. He was immediately set free by his chivalrous opponent, that he might receive proper medical treatment. Methuen enjoyed no further active field command; he served as GOC Eastern Command 1904–8, CinC South Africa 1908–12, and CinC Malta 1915–19, having attained the rank of field marshal in 1911. From 1920 he was Constable of the Tower of London. As was remarked at the time, his sense of duty led him to continue to do his best despite all circumstances, thus giving reason to praise even so unfortunate a commander.

Mohammed Ahmed Ibn Seyyid Abdullah (1848–85), known as The Mahdi

The title *Mahdi* (Arabic, 'he who is guided truly') was assumed by a number of Islamic leaders, and based upon a declaration by Mohammed that one of his descendants would rule with justice, and be called *al-Mahdi*. The most famous of those who assumed the title included the third Abbasid caliph, Mohammed al-Mahdi in the late eighth century; 'Obaid-Allah al-Mahdi, first caliph of the Fatimite dynasty in the tenth century; and Mohammed ibn Abdullah ibn Tumart, founder of the Muwāhadis or Almohades in the twelfth century; the town of Mahdia, Tunisia, was named after the second of these.

Mohammed Ahmed ibn Seyyid Abdullah was born in Dongola province. His study of religion induced him to gather a group of followers and he developed a reputation for sanctity. He travelled through Kordofan, denouncing the oppression of the Egyptian rulers of the Sudan, predicting the coming of the Mahdi to free the people, and urging all true believers to act against their oppressors. His increasing influence compelled the authorities to take action, but Mohammed Ahmed not only repelled their attempts to apprehend him, but announced himself as the Mahdi and gathered a large force. An Egyptian expedition under Yusef Pasha was almost annihilated in June 1882; by January 1883 almost all Sudan south of Khartoum was in revolt, and the capital of Kordofan, El Obeid, was captured. In the following November the Mahdists destroyed Hicks Pasha's force at Kashgil, and the Mahdi's follower, Uthmān Diqna ('Osman Digna'), having raised the tribes in the eastern Sudan, crushed Valentine Baker's force at El Teb in February 1884. It was in the face of this revolt that Gordon was sent to evacuate Khartoum, only to be besieged there and killed when the city fell to the Mahdists on 26 January 1885. This marked the peak of the Mahdi's career; he outlived Gordon by barely six months, dying of smallpox at Omdurman on 22 June 1885.

Although he began the Mahdist movement, it is difficult to be precise about his degree of control, as almost from the beginning he was aided greatly by Abdullah el-Taaishi, who succeeded him as the Khalifa and who was defeated by the Anglo–Egyptian forces at Omdurman in 1898. A final indignity occurred after the Battle of Omdurman, when in revenge for the death of Gordon, Kitchener ordered the Mahdi's tomb to be razed (it was done by Gordon's nephew) and his bones thrown into the Nile. The skull was retrieved and given to Kitchener with suggestions that it be made into an ornament or inkstand; Kitchener considered donating it to the Royal College of Surgeons in London, but such was the public outcry against this desecration (even by the Queen) that the skull was buried secretly in an Islamic cemetery at Wadi Halfa.

References

Wingate, F. R. *Mahdism and the Egyptian Sudan*, London, 1891.
Works by captives of the Mahdi include:
Ohrwalder, Father J. *Ten Years' Captivity in the Mahdi's Camp*, trans. F. R. Wingate, 1892.
Slatin, R. *Fire and Sword in the Sudan: a Personal Narrative of Fighting and Serving the Dervishes 1879–1895*, trans. F. R. Wingate, London, 1896.
(See also sources listed for the section on the Sudan.)

Nana Sahib (Dhondu Pant), (1825–59?)

The Nana Sahib occupied a singular place in the 19th-century British catalogue of villainy, universally despised by all who knew of him: 'the extraordinary individual who ... has achieved for himself a reputation stained with infamy, and overwhelmed with execration'.[1]

Dhondu Pant was the adopted son of Baji Rao II, the peshwa, who had been granted an East India Company pension in return for his dethronement in 1818. Despite the loss of power, the pension was handsome, but it did not continue after Baji Rao's death. Having no male child, he nominated Dhondu Pant, the Nana Sahib, as his heir; who, believing that he should be entitled to an extension of the pension after Baji Rao's death (1851), pursued his case as far as the Court of Directors of the Company in London. The rejection of his appeal rankled, and the Mutiny provided an opportunity for revenge. British observers were not generally critical of Nana Sahib before the Mutiny; one, who met him in 1853, described him as 'about twenty-eight years of age; he looked, however, at least forty. His figure is very fat ... his face is round, his eyes very wild, brilliant, and restless; his complexion, as is the case with most native gentlemen, is scarcely darker than a dark Spaniard; and his expression is, on the whole, of a jovial, indeed somewhat rollicking, character'.[2] He was a generous host who delighted to show off his collection of fine weapons, and was a good billiards player; but did not display the pornographic pictures which supposedly he collected, and it was noted that in addition to his gentlemanly manners he added 'passions of the strongest and most vindictive nature; a monomaniac on the subject of what he believed to be his wrongs'.[3]

Nana Sahib agreed to lead the Cawnpore mutineers. He dissuaded them from marching on Delhi in favour of attacking the Europeans in Cawnpore, and planned a career for himself as the new peshwa, to which title he had not been permitted to accede. Responsibility for the massacres at Cawnpore was blamed on him, including the slaughter of the women and children hostages, who Nana Sahib's sepoys refused to harm; so the appalling deed was done by five wretches not concerned with the sense of honour felt by most Indian warriors. Nana Sahib was not an inspired military leader (indeed, the extent of his personal influence as a commander is unclear), and he was defeated, notably at Fatehpur. He fled with the remnant of the rebels to Nepal in 1859 and is supposed to have died there, of a fever, in September of that year. His exact fate remains uncertain, for there were several reports of his being seen alive subsequently, and even one report of his capture in 1895, by which time the British administration had no further interest in him; much different from the situation of 37 years earlier, when his death was surely a high priority for every British soldier in India.

Notes

1. Anon. *History of the Indian Mutiny, giving a detailed account of the Sepoy Insurrection in India*, London, n.d. (*c.*1858–9), p. 301.

2. Ibid., p. 305.

3. 'Nana Sahib', in *Chambers' Journal of Popular Literature*, 3 April 1858, p. 224.

Reference

Gupta, P. C. *Nana Sahib and the Rising at Cawnpore*, Oxford, 1963

(See also the histories of the Mutiny listed in the section on India.)

Sir Charles Napier, in the uniform worn during the campaigning in Sind.

Napier, Sir Charles James (1782–1853)

Sir Charles Napier was perhaps the most distinguished member of a distinguished family. Of the four sons of Colonel George Napier, one (Sir William) became the author of the classic history of the Peninsular War; one (General Sir George) lost an arm in the Peninsula; one (Captain Henry) served in the Royal Navy and wrote a learned *Florentine History*; and the eldest was Charles James. Commissioned at the age of 12 (subsequently going on half-pay to allow him to return to school!), he was greatly distinguished in the Peninsular War (at Corunna he was wounded, captured, and treated so well by Marshals Soult and Ney that ever after he held them – and Napoleon – in the highest regard), and was wounded severely in the jaw at Busaco. He served against the United States in 1813, was appointed Inspecting Field Officer at Corfu in 1819, and from 1822 to 1830 was governor of Cephalonia, where his rule was of great benefit to the inhabitants, until he resigned after conflicts with Sir Frederick Adam, high commissioner of the Ionian Islands.

Napier spent the next several years in literary pursuits (ranging from a translation of de Vigny to treaties on colonisation to historical romance – *William the Conqueror* was published posthumously) until in 1839 he was appointed to command the Northern District, then in ferment with Chartist agitation. Always a great humanitarian of very liberal views, this post must have caused him anguish; but by showing sympathy towards the social conditions which had led to the unrest, he was able to maintain the peace without political repression, a considerable achievement. At an age when most men would have been seeking retirement, Napier accepted a command in India in the hope of earning enough to provide for his daughters. His victory in Sind in 1843, which stabilised India's western frontier, he probably regarded more in terms of releasing the inhabitants from the perceived tyranny of the Baluchis, whose rule had been akin to that exercised by the Mamelukes in Egypt. Napier reputedly announced his success to the governor-general by the one-word message '*Peccavi*' ('I have sinned'); though in fact *Punch* was probably responsible for the pun. As governor of the subjugated province, Napier exerted a benevolent rule (for example he suppressed slavery and *suttee* or widow-burning), but he was so ruthless against rebellious hill tribes that he was nicknamed 'Satan's brother'.

Napier's difficult temperament caused conflict with every authority from the governor-general downwards, and in 1847 he returned home. Despite subsequent quarrels with the directors of the East India Company, they appointed him to succeed Gough after the sanguinary battle of Chillianwalla; but Gough ended the war before Napier could assume command. His last spell of Indian service ended, not surprisingly, in a quarrel with the governor-general, and he resigned. He did not long enjoy his retirement in England: his health having suffered in his Indian service, he died in 1853. Hardinge remarked that 'Sir Charles Napier, above sixty, achieved feats which would have broken down many a younger man; and in his whole conduct there was displayed every quality which could adorn public and private life; bravery, humanity, and Christian feeling; nor could the honour of the British Army be in better hands.'* Napier was an unmistakable figure, favouring on campaign an Indian poshteen over his frock-coat, immense side-whiskers, moustache and beard, which with a large, hooked nose, thick spectacles and apparent lack of care for smartness created a singular appearance. Although his quarrels with those in authority have overshadowed his abilities as a general, his reputation as a great humanitarian has never been questioned, exemplified by his care for those under his jurisdiction, irrespective of nationality or station. When a bronze statue by G. G. Adams was erected in his honour in Trafalgar Square, the majority of subscribers were private soldiers; he could have received no finer tribute.

References

Bruce, W. N. *Life of General Sir Charles Napier*, London, 1855.
Holmes, T. R. E. *Four Famous Soldiers*, London, 1889.
– *Sir Charles Napier*, Cambridge, 1925.
Lambrick, H. T. *Sir Charles Napier and Sind*, Oxford, 1952.
Lawrence, Lady Rosamond. *Charles Napier, Friend and Fighter*, London, 1952.
Napier, P. *I Have Sind: Charles Napier in India 1841-1844*, London, 1990.
– *Raven Castle: Charles Napier in India 1844-1851*, London, 1991.
Napier, Sir William. *Life and Opinions of General Sir Charles James Napier*, London, 1857 (important early biography by Charles' brother).

Napier, Robert Cornelis, 1st Baron Napier of Magdala and Carynton (1810–90)

Robert Napier was the son of Major Charles F. Napier, who had fought at the storming of Cornelis in Java (26 August 1811: hence Robert's second name) and died in March 1812. Born at Colombo and educated at Addiscombe, Robert joined the Bengal Engineers in 1828. For some years he was employed on construction projects, both civil and military (he designed the 'Napier system' of cantonments), but saw campaign service against the Sikhs, at Mudki, Ferozeshah (where he joined the 31st in the storming of the Sikh entrenchments, and was wounded) and Sobraon. He received a brevet majority for the campaign, and in the renewed hostilities served at Multan and

Robert, Baron Napier of Magdala.

Gujerat and was made a brevet lieutenant-colonel. Appointed chief civil engineer in the Punjab, he spent several years on public works and commanded a column in frontier actions in 1852–3. Napier was appointed military secretary and adjutant-general to Outram's force for the relief of Lucknow, directed its defence after the first relief, and was wounded at the second. As brigadier-general commanding the engineers he formulated the plan for the recapture of Lucknow; was second in command to Sir Hugh Rose in the march on Gwalior, and commanded the division in the operations which ended with the capture of Tantia Topi.

In 1860 Napier commanded the 2nd Division in the expedition to China, and was promoted to major-general for his services there. As military representative on the council of the governor-general he acted briefly in that role after the sudden death of Lord Elgin, and in 1865 took command of the Bombay Army. Promoted to lieutenant-general in 1867, in the same year he was given command of the expedition to Abyssinia, which campaign he conducted with great skill and complete success; for which he was showered with rewards, including a barony (named after Magdala, his greatest triumph) and a pension. Commander-in-Chief in India 1870–6, he was promoted to general in 1874, from 1876 to 1883 governed and commanded at Gibraltar, and was nominated to command the expedition which it was proposed to send to Constantinople in 1877. In 1883 he reached the rank of field marshal. Twice married, he had no less than nine sons (of whom four served in the India Army, and two in the British), and six daughters.

Reference
Napier, Lieutenant-Colonel H. D. *Field-Marshal Lord Napier of Magdala: A Memoir*, London, 1927.

Nicholson, John (1822–57)

John Nicholson was one of few British military personalities for whom the adjective 'charismatic' would be appropriate. Losing his physician father when a child, he was raised in somewhat impecunious circumstances in Ulster, and was given an East India Company cadetship by an uncle as an act of charity. After serving in the First Afghan War he received civil appointments in Kashmir and the Punjab, following his acquaintance with Henry Lawrence.

John Nicholson.

In the Second Sikh War he was political officer with Gough's army and performed valuable intelligence services. His subsequent administration of Bannu province, the most turbulent of areas, became legendary with both British and Indians; not only did he bring peace but established a reputation for justice and fairness, combined with severity towards wrongdoers and immense courage, probably unmatched by any other British military or civil official in the history of India. Such was his commanding presence (he was immensely imposing, huge and powerful and with an immense black beard) that he was worshipped as a god, by a sect which called themselves 'Nicholseyns', surely a unique honour for any British general.

On the outbreak of the Mutiny he did more than any other to ensure the loyalty of the Punjab and to capture Delhi. Commanding a mobile column, he destroyed a force of mutineers from Sialkot near Gurdaspur; and was sent by John Lawrence to put fire into the force at Delhi. He defeated another rebel force at Najafgarh and did, indeed, put heart into the army and its commanders at Delhi, in a way which probably would have been impossible for any other. Having forced General Wilson to take action, Brigadier-General Nicholson personally led a column in the assault on Delhi; shot in the back as he turned to exhort those following him, he died nine days later.

Sir John Lawrence stated that Nicholson's brief but memorable career seemed to have been made for that moment, and that without him, Delhi could not have fallen. Even if that is an exaggeration, his significance was enormous, though his reputation as a 'Christian hero' does not sit comfortably with some of his statements: he was ruthless in his treatment of wrongdoers, and especially of mutinous sepoys, whom he suggested might be burned, flayed or impaled instead of just being hanged, the latter he suggested being too humane a punishment. (Those rebels he did capture *were* hanged, apparently without even the pretence of a court-martial). Despite this, and an imperious manner which grated on some of his superiors, his bearing and attitude left an unforgettable mark on those who knew him. Even Lord Roberts, with his wide experience, wrote: 'Nicholson impressed me more profoundly than any man I had ever met before, or have ever met since. I have never seen anyone like him. He was the beau-ideal of a soldier and a gentleman. His appearance was distinguished and commanding, with a sense of power about him which was to my mind the result of his having passed so much of his life among the wild and lawless tribesmen.' Consequently, his loss was felt the more severely; as Roberts remarked, recalling how he found the mortally wounded Nicholson abandoned by his *doolie*-bearers who had gone off plundering: 'Other men had daily died around me, friends and comrades had been killed beside me, but I never felt as I felt then – to lose

Nicholson seemed to me at that moment to lose everything.'*

References

Pearson, H. *The Hero of Delhi*, London, 1939.

Trotter, Captain L. J. *The Life of John Nicholson, Soldier and Administrator*, London, 1897.

Outram, Sir James, Bt. (1803–63)

The son of a distinguished Derbyshire civil engineer, James Outram was educated at Aberdeen (his mother's home, his father having died when James was two years old), and in 1819 secured an East India cadetship. His energy attracted notice, and his fearless hunting escapades became almost legendary; they helped him establish excellent relations with the Company's Indian troops, especially the light infantry corps of Bhils which he trained. An ADC in the First Afghan War (where he captured a standard), he was promoted to major in 1839; as political agent in Sind he opposed the policy of Sir Charles Napier, but after his defence of the Residency at Hyderabad Napier described him as 'The Bayard of India'. Outram served in a number of political appointments, making himself unpopular with the Bombay government over his campaign against corruption, and in 1854 was appointed Resident at Lucknow. Two years later he carried out the annexation of Oudh, and became chief commissioner of the province, but was sent as lieutenant-general to command the Persian expedition, where he won his major victory at Koosh-ab.

Outram was recalled from Persia at the time of the Mutiny, and was given command of two divisions and the commissionership of Oudh. He joined Havelock's force with his own and unselfishly conceded command to Havelock, stating that he wished only to serve as a volunteer; but was unable to refrain from issuing orders and even countermanding some of Havelock's, the latter being too gentle a man to resist. Eventually they were able to co-operate, with Havelock in command, and together they effected the first relief of Lucknow. Outram took command at Lucknow, and led its garrison until the second relief; and having organised the evacuation of the Residency, led its re-possession when Campbell returned to capture the city. Created a baronet on 10 November 1858, Outram remained as commissioner of Oudh, advocating more leniency than the governor-general was prepared to grant, though Outram was able to extract concessions. His health having suffered from hard campaigning, Outram returned to Europe in 1860, and died at Pau in March 1863; he is buried in Westminster Abbey under the inscription 'The Bayard of India'.

James Outram was not an impressive figure; having been a sickly child, he was small and had a hesitant manner, but was universally liked and admired by his subordi-

Sir James Outram.

nates (except, perhaps, by Havelock's son, who threatened to resign over what he perceived as Outram's interference in his father's plan of campaign). During the Mutiny Outram seemed to smoke cigars continually; of which he must have had a liberal supply, for he was noted as being very generous with them.

References

Goldsmid, Major-General Sir F. J. *James Outram: a Biography*, London, 1881.

Outram, Sir James. *The Campaign in India 1857-58*, London, 1860.

Trotter, Captain L. J. *The Bayard of India: A Life of General Sir James Outram*, Edinburgh, 1903.

Roberts, Frederick Sleigh, Earl Roberts of Kandahar (1832–1914)

'Bobs' was among the most revered of British generals, by both the public and the men he led, a veneration probably increased by his small stature and elderly appearance in his last campaign. Born at Cawnpore and educated at Eton, Sandhurst and Addiscombe, Frederick Roberts was commissioned into the Bengal Artillery in 1851. Joining a

---

*Roberts, Lord. *Forty-One Years in India*, London, 1900, pp. 33, 130.

Frederick, Earl Roberts of Kandahar; the Victoria Cross is prominent as the first of his row of medals.

battery at Peshawar in the following year, he became aide to his father, General Sir Abraham Roberts, to whom he was virtually a stranger, having met him only briefly, at the age of twelve, when Sir Abraham was on leave in England. Frederick's military career was spent almost entirely in staff appointments, but he contrived to remain in the thick of the action. In the Indian Mutiny he participated in the storming of Delhi and the relief of Lucknow, and was awarded the Victoria Cross for two separate acts of heroism at Khudaganj. He served in the Ambela campaign, was assistant quartermaster-general in Abyssinia, and in 1871 commanded a column in the Lushai expedition; but in addition to his battlefield talents he was also a skilled organiser, and thus was chosen to superintend the visit to India of the Prince of Wales in 1876 and the Delhi durbar on New Year's Day 1877, when the Queen was proclaimed Empress of India.

Roberts assured his reputation in the campaign in Afghanistan (1878–80), first in command of the Kurram Field Force as a major-general, and as lieutenant-general in command of the Kabul Field Force. Although superseded in overall command by the arrival of Sir Donald Stewart, Roberts undertook the relief of the besieged Kandahar, involving his legendary 'Kabul to Kandahar' march, culminating in victory at Kandahar. Rewarded with a baronetcy and command of the Madras Army, Roberts was appointed commander-in-chief in South Africa, but hostilities had ended by the time he arrived; declining the post of quartermaster-general, he returned to India and in 1885 became commander-in-chief in that country. In this post his organisational skill was of great value (he had recommended the merger of the three presidency armies as early as 1878), and in 1892 he was raised to the peerage as Baron Roberts of Kandahar and Waterford. In the following year he left India and in 1895 was promoted to field marshal.

Following the reverses of the South African War (including Colenso, where his only son was mortally wounded in an action for which he was awarded a posthumous Victoria Cross), Roberts was appointed commander-in-chief, arriving in January 1900. Although much of the subsequent success may be attributed to his chief of staff, Kitchener, their partnership was effective, and Roberts handed over command to Kitchener when the war entered its guerrilla phase. Roberts returned to Britain to occupy the post of commander-in-chief (the last incumbent, the office being abolished in 1904), stopping at Osborne to receive the insignia of the Order of the Garter from the Queen. Twelve days later he received an earldom in the last audience given by the Queen before her death; and when attending her funeral, Wilhelm II of Germany bestowed upon Roberts the Order of the Black Eagle, so far had his fame spread beyond the British Empire. Roberts devoted his final years to campaigning for a system of universal military training in preparation for any

wider hostilities, and died as he had lived, among a British army, when visiting the B.E.F. in France. He may not have been a military genius of the highest rank, but was a most skilled and far-sighted organiser with an intimate knowledge of the characteristics and requirements of the Indian Army, and was consistently successful in difficult and arduous campaigns. The most kindly, unassuming and courteous of men, he was justifiably popular, and even his homely nickname, 'Bobs', was evidence of the warmth in which he was regarded universally.

References

Farwell, B. *Eminent Victorian Soldiers*, London, 1986.

Forrest, G. W. (later Sir George). *Sepoy Generals: Wellington to Roberts*, Edinburgh, 1901.

Forrest, Sir George. *Life of Lord Roberts*, London, 1914.

Hannah, W. H. *Bobs: Kipling's General; the Life of Field Marshal Lord Roberts of Kandahar*, London, 1972.

James, D. *Lord Roberts*, London, 1954

Jerrold, W. L. *Lord Roberts of Kandahar*, London, 1901; updated as *Field Marshal Lord Roberts VC*, London, 1914.

Roberts, Lord. *Forty-One Years in India*, London, 1897 (Roberts' autobiography).

Roberts, Lord., B. *Roberts in India: The Military Papers of Field Marshal Lord Roberts 1876–1893*, Army Records Society, 1993.

Rose, Hugh Henry, 1st Baron Strathnairn of Strathnairn and Jhansi (1801–85)

Hugh Rose was born in Berlin, son of the British minister at the Prussian court, and perhaps appropriately, given this background, much of his earlier career was more distinguished diplomatically than militarily. Educated in Berlin, and at the Prussian military cadet school, he entered the British Army in 1820, reaching the rank of major within six years. After service in Ireland, Gibraltar and Malta, in 1840 he was sent on special service by the foreign office to assist the Ottoman Empire expel Mehemet Ali's army from Syria, in which he distinguished himself considerably. From 1841 to 1848 Rose was British consul-general for Syria, doing much good work in protecting the local Christians and mediating in hostilities with the Druses; in 1851 he was appointed to the British embassy in Constantinople, and as *chargé d'affaires* deputised for Sir Stratford Canning during the latter's absence. Having played a role in the events leading to the Crimean War, during that war he served as British commissioner with the French army, with local rank of brigadier-general; wounded on the day after the Alma, he so impressed the Allied commanders that he was promoted to major-general and received both the KCB and the *Légion d'honneur*.

At the beginning of the Indian Mutiny, Rose took command in central India and extinguished the rebellion there, defying the rigours of the climate and campaign despite being described as having a weakly and even effeminate appearance. His campaign began unimpressively with a slow advance, but he pressed on with greater

Sir Hugh Rose, later Baron Strathnairn.

der-in-chief of the Bombay army, succeeding Campbell as CinC India in 1861. He commanded in Ireland from 1865 to 1870, received a peerage in 1866, and was promoted to general in 1867 and to field marshal ten years later. Upon relinquishing the Irish command he retired from military life.

Reference
Burne, Sir Owen T. *Clyde and Strathnairn*, London, 1895.

Selous, Frederick Courteney (1851–1917)

Colonial exploration and campaigning involved or produced a number of remarkable characters, chief among whom was Frederick Selous, soldier, explorer, hunter and naturalist, whose exploits became almost legendary. Educated at Rugby and in Germany, his explorations in Africa arose from his interest in natural history, and as early as 1872 he was granted permission by Lobengula to hunt anywhere in his territory. Ranging over central Africa, he explored and studied the indigenous peoples and wildlife for almost two decades, and in 1890 guided the British South Africa Company's 'pioneer column' into what became Rhodesia. In 1892 Selous was awarded a medal by the Royal Geographical Society as a testimony to the value of his explorations and the valuable scientific work they involved, but he returned to Africa in time to participate in the Matabele War of 1893, during which he was wounded. Settling on an estate in Matabeleland, Selous featured prominently in the suppression of the 1896 rebellion, and then returned to England, but not to retire; he continued to undertake hunting expeditions, such as that which he organised for Roosevelt in East Africa in 1909. Upon the outbreak of the First World War he immediately offered his services to the British government, but was rejected on grounds of age; but he persisted and was commissioned into the 25th Battalion of the Royal Fusiliers in February 1915; this 'Service Battalion' had been raised in London by the Legion of Frontiersmen in that month, and embarked in April for East Africa, arriving at Mombasa in May 1915. Selous participated in numerous engagements in East Africa, being promoted to captain and being awarded the DSO. Four days after his 65th birthday he was killed in action at Beho Beho (4 January 1917), a year after the death of his eldest son on the Western Front. Such was the reputation of this most remarkable of explorers, hunters and scholars that his name was taken as the title of the Rhodesian army's élite anti-terrorist unit, the Selous Scouts, formed in 1973 and existing until 1980.

References
The best-known of Selous' numerous important writings is his account of the 1896 rebellion, *Sunshine and Storm in Rhodesia*, 1896; an early biography is J. G. Millar's *Frederick Courteney Selous*, London, 1918.

audacity, besieging Jhansi and defeating Tantia Topi's relief-force against odds of about twelve to one; and then captured Jhansi itself. Despite temperatures of 115° F in the shade, which ravaged his army with sunstroke, Rose pursued the rebels and again defeated Tantia Topi, insisting on playing an active role, even though he twice fell from his horse during the action; from the effects of the heat. Ill-health persuaded him to take sick leave, but he abandoned this on news of the defection to the rebels of the Gwalior forces; Rose pressed on, defeated the rebel forces at Kotah-ki-Serai (where the Rani of Jhansi was killed), and went on to take Gwalior (19 June 1858). Only then, with the rebellion effectively crushed, did Rose finally retire. It has been said that his contribution to the suppression of the Mutiny was not fully recognised; certainly, the Central India force received no prize-money despite a lengthy legal case. In 1860 Rose was promoted to lieutenant-general and in the same year became comman-

Smith, Sir Henry George Wakelyn, Bt., of Aliwal (1787–1860)

'Harry' Smith (the name he used throughout his life) is perhaps remembered as much for his adventures during the Napoleonic Wars than for his participation in a number of colonial campaigns, although the latter were of greater significance. The son of a Cambridgeshire surgeon, Smith was commissioned into the 95th Rifles in 1805; he served in Whitelocke's disastrous South American expedition, and throughout the Peninsular War. One of the best-known characters in the army, he found fame by the rescue of two Spanish ladies from the sack of Badajoz, one of whom, Juana Maria de los Dolores de Leon, he married. She became idolised throughout the army for her courage, beauty and pleasant character, and followed her husband during his subsequent military service; the town of Ladysmith was named for her.

Harry Smith served briefly in the War of 1812 against the United States, and at Waterloo; then a period of gar-

Sir Harry Smith, wearing an undress frock-coat.

rison duty followed until in 1828 he was ordered to South Africa. He commanded a division in the Sixth Frontier War (1834–6), and accomplished his legendary ride from Cape Town to Grahamstown, more than 600 miles, in less than six days. He was appointed governor of Queen Adelaide province, but his governorship ended in acrimony when his policies were not supported by the government. Instead, Smith was appointed deputy adjutant-general to the army in India; he had a miraculous escape at Maharajpore, when a roundshot bruised his leg, and when awarded the KCB after the battle insisted that he be called 'Sir Harry', not 'Henry'. In the First Sikh War he commanded a division at Moodkee and Ferozeshah, and, given an independent command, won the battle of Aliwal, which brought him a baronetcy. Under Gough's command he led a division at Sobraon, and in 1847 returned to South Africa as governor of Cape Colony. In the following year he crushed the Orange River rebellion at Boomplaats, and in December 1850 was faced with the Eighth Frontier War, in which he was weakened by having acceded to the suggestion that his military strength be reduced. Consequently, although his operations received approval in military circles, Earl Grey recalled him in 1852, before the conclusion of the campaign. Although relieved of campaign duty, he was found employment (perhaps as a tacit acknowledgement that his treatment might not have been entirely fair), and having declined command of the Madras Army on health grounds, Smith was given home commands, of the Western, and then Northern and Midlands districts. He was considered, briefly, as Raglan's successor to the Crimean command, but was retired in 1859. Denied a peerage, he lived on modest means until his death in 1860; his wife, the faithful Juana, lived until 1872.

Although not the greatest of commanders, Harry Smith probably would have had some justification for believing himself badly used. Nevertheless, his name and the events of his career lived after him in the placenames of Aliwal North, Harrismith, and, most famously, Ladysmith in Natal, the site of a siege even better known than that which had brought Harry and Juana together. Whatever his disappointments, however, he must have treasured more than any tangible reward the tribute paid him in the House of Lords by his hero and friend, the Duke of Wellington, who when speaking of Aliwal remarked that never had he read of a battle in which more ability, energy and experience had been shown, or one in which a commander better displayed his abilities.

References

Harington, A. L. *Sir Harry Smith, Bungling Hero*, Cape Town, 1980.

Lehmann, J. H. *Remember you are an Englishman: A Biography of Sir Harry Smith*, London, 1977.

Moore Smith, G. C. (ed.). *The Autobiography of Sir Harry Smith*, London, 1902.

Tantia Topi (or Tatya Tope) (*c*.1819–59)

'Tantia Topi' was a *nom-de-guerre* adopted during the Indian Mutiny by a Maratha subordinate of Nana Sahib, who for a short period held a high command in the rebel forces. His true identity was somewhat obscure; apparently he was really Ramchandra Panduranga, but the British at the time suggested alternatives, including his being the son of the peshwa Baji Rao's officer 'Ramchunder Punt', elder brother of Pandurang Rao, alias the Rao Sahib (cousin of Nana Sahib), or even Bhow Tambakar, ex-minister of Baroda. The name he adopted was apparently a Dekhani military title, the second word meaning 'leader' or 'captain'. Originally an aide of Nana Sahib, sometimes accused of instigating the massacres at Cawnpore, he later commanded in person and proved to be perhaps the most talented of the Indian leaders. He arranged the defence of Bithur, which posed a severe trial to Havelock's force, and repelled Windham at Cawnpore; but was beaten by Campbell on 6 December 1857, and by Rose in his unavailing attempt to relieve the siege of Jhansi, in June 1858. He was pursued and fled into Rajputana as his followers dispersed, and was arrested by the Rajah of Nawar who, having been opposed to the British, had been persuaded to rehabilitate his reputation by betraying Tantia, who was hanged as a consequence, on 18 April 1859.

Almost uniquely among the leaders of the Mutiny, Tantia received generous recognition from his enemies, as a uniquely capable opponent: 'The marvellous activity, fertility of resource, and swiftness of action of the blood-stained instrument of the massacre of Cawnpore, made him a foeman worthy even of Englishmen's steel ... Ubiquity was in the man. He had a wonderful genius for wild warfare, and extraordinary skill in the employment of his knowledge of the locality, and he swept with strange facility across vast tracts of country to the surprise of his enemies ... As is well known, he paid the forfeit of his life for his sanguinary deeds; but we cannot withhold our tribute of admiration from a man who showed such military genius in guerrilla warfare, and eluded us so resolutely and so long.'*

Wolseley, Garnet Joseph, Viscount (1833–1913)

If the popularity of a military leader is a gauge of his abilities, then the expression 'all Sir Garnet', meaning 'all in order', is ample testimony to the general who lent his name to it, Garnet Wolseley, one of most able commanders of the Victorian era.

Coming from a comparatively humble background (the son of a County Dublin shopkeeper), Garnet Wolseley made his way in the army by his own abilities. Commissioned in 1852, he served in Burma (wounded and mentioned in dispatches), the Crimea (twice wounded,

promoted to captain after less than three years' service, mentioned in dispatches and awarded the *Légion d'honneur*), and in the Indian Mutiny, where in addition to being present in many actions was appointed deputy assistant quarter-master for Hope Grant's division. After only seven years' service, and at the age of 25, he was promoted to lieutenant-colonel, a remarkable achievement for a man with so little influence from birth or social position. He accompanied Grant to China as DAQMG, and published a history of the war upon its conclusion. In late 1861 he went to Canada and remained there until 1870, performing staff duties as well as commanding the Red River expedition in which his organisational talents proved their worth. In 1871 Wolseley was appointed assistant adjutant-general at the War Office, collaborating most valuably with Cardwell in the reform of the army, but it was his command of the Ashanti expedition which made him a household name. For this campaign he gathered a group of the best young staff officers in the army, the foundation of what became known as 'the Ring', whose members accompanied him in succeeding campaigns, to the considerable resentment of older officers and of those not included in his circle.

Promoted to major-general after the Ashanti expedition, Wolseley went to Natal as governor and commanding general in 1875, then to a seat on the Indian Council, to Cyprus as lieutenant-general and high commissioner in 1878, and in 1879 to South Africa again as governor of Natal and Transvaal and to succeed Chelmsford in command of the forces in the Zulu War. He returned home as quartermaster-general in 1880, becoming adjutant-general in 1882, and later in that year was given command of the British forces in Egypt. After his victory at Tel-el-Kebir he was promoted to general and given a peerage as Baron Wolseley of Cairo and Wolseley. He served as adjutant-general until 1890, being called away to Egypt again in 1884 in the unavailing attempt to save Gordon, from which he emerged with a viscountcy despite the frustration of his task by political prevarication. In 1890 Wolseley was given command in Ireland, in 1894 was promoted to field marshal, and in the following year became the penultimate commander-in-chief of the British Army, in which office he was replaced by Roberts in 1901.

Despite Wolseley's campaign successes, it was perhaps his later periods of home service which were the most significant, for the reforms he supported in the face of heavy opposition from reactionary elements led by the Duke of Cambridge, his predecessor as commander-in-chief. Even if 'the Ring' were not the most perfect of organisations, especially when campaigns increased in scale beyond the personal supervision of the commander (it was criticised for stifling the opportunities of those outside it, and including some whose failings later

*'The 17th Lancers in the Embers of the Mutiny', in *Navy and Army Illustrated*, vol. I, pp. 107–8, 21 February 1896.

became obvious when left unsupervised), the reforms carried out under Wolseley did much necessary modernisation of the army, to prepare it for the more major undertakings. It was in such matters that Wolseley's true contribution was marked.

References

Arthur, Sir George. (ed.). *The Letters of Lord and Lady Wolseley, 1870–1911*, London, 1922.

Beckett, I. F. W. 'Wolseley and the Ring', in *Soldiers of the Queen* 69, Victorian Military Society, June 1992 (a most valuable analysis).

Farwell, B. *Eminent Victorian Soldiers*, London, 1986

Lehmann, J. *All Sir Garnet: A Life of Field Marshal Lord Wolseley*

1833–1913, London, 1964 (US edn. entitled *The Model Major-General*).

Low, C. R. *A Memoir of Lieutenant-General Sir Garnet Wolseley*, London, 1878.

Maurice, Major-General Sir Frederick, and Arthur, Sir George. *The Life of Lord Wolseley*, London, 1924.

Maxwell, L. *The Ashanti Ring: Sir Garnet Wolseley's Campaigns 1870–1882*, London, 1985.

Preston A. (ed.). *In Relief of Gor-*

don: Lord Wolseley's Campaign Journal of the Khartoum Relief Expedition 1884–1885, London, 1967.

– *Sir Garnet Wolseley's South Africa Diaries 1875*, Cape Town, 1971.

– *The South African Journal 1879-1880*, Cape Town, 1973.

Wolseley, Viscount. *The Story of a Soldier's Life*, London, 1903 (autobiography to the end of the Ashanti campaign).

'All Sir Garnet': Viscount Wolseley.

VIII
SOURCES

SOURCES

CONTEMPORARY AND MODERN HISTORY

Journalism

The period generally associated with colonial campaigning, approximating to the reign of Queen Victoria, occurred at a time of increasing public literacy, and with it a demand for accounts of campaigns probably greater than that for any previous period of warfare. Despite an often dismissive attitude towards the individual soldier, public interest in, and support of, British military campaigns was widespread, and encouraged by the patriotic aura which surrounded the events and personalities of the time.

The most immediate transmission of this information was by the medium of newspapers, the circulation of which increased markedly after the reduction in tax to one penny in 1836, and its abolition in 1855. Initially much of their information concerning military operations was transmitted in the form of official dispatches, and at the other end of the scale by the publication of 'letters from the front'. The latter are still of use to the historian provided that Wellington's *caveat* be remembered, to the effect that: 'As soon as an accident happens, every man who can write, and who has a friend who can read, sits down to write his account of what he does not know, and his comments on what he does not understand';[1] while the official dispatches understandably present a particular view. Regarding colonial operations, such reports were not a 19th-century innovation; for example, *The London Gazette* of 5–9 January 1681 carried a long account of the ceremonies which welcomed the King of Fez to Tangier. The specialist war correspondent, however, was a new feature, the first journalist who accompanied an expedition apparently being C. L. Grüneisen, who reported for the *Morning Post* on the Carlist War, in which De Lacy Evans' British Legion was involved.

The most famous and influential of the war correspondents was William Howard Russell (1821–1907, knighted in 1895) of *The Times*, whose reports from the Crimea were not only classics of their genre but had a profound effect on the public opinion of the conduct of the war. Although Russell's Crimean dispatches were the most famous, he also reported on a number of other campaigns, including the Indian Mutiny (on which he also wrote *My Diary in India 1858–59*), the American Civil War, Königgrätz, the Franco–Prussian War, and accompanied Wolseley to Zululand and Egypt. Although Russell was the greatest of the early war correspondents, he was not alone in enjoying international fame, and some of the later correspondents are worthy of especial note.

Among these was Archibald Forbes (1838–1900), the son of a Presbyterian minister, who at an early age became interested in military history, an interest presumably stimulated by meeting, when a youth, Lord Saltoun, the

Archibald Forbes, doyen of war-correspondents.

defender of Hougoumont. Although initially disappointed with the hero, 'a very queer-looking old person, short of figure, round as a ball, his head sunk between very high and rounded shoulders, and with short stumpy legs [and] a droll-shaped jacket the great collar of which reached far up the back of his head',[2] Saltoun fired his imagination with stories of Waterloo and, further encouraged by hearing Russell lecture on the Crimea (and influenced by the squandering of his inheritance), Forbes enlisted in the Royal Dragoons. On being invalided from the army he became a journalist, and as a war correspondent worked for the *Morning Advertiser* during the Franco–Prussian War, transferring to the *Daily News*, whose special correspondent he remained until his retirement. He was present in the Carlist War in Spain, in Serbia in 1876, the Russo–Turkish War, at the British occupation of Cyprus, in Afghanistan in 1878, and most notably in the Zulu War, making a famous ride (ultimately of 295 miles in 55 hours, partially through bush still infested with Zulus) to convey the news of the victory of Ulundi. Subsequently his health broke down, but he continued to write and lecture as a military expert, never afraid to criticise the high command (latterly especially Wolseley, whose friendship he had claimed earlier), perhaps his personal experience as a 'ranker' leading him to regard the army in a different light from many correspondents.

A correspondent whose career covered the later colonial wars was Bennet Burleigh (*c.*1840–1914), a Glasgow-born adventurer who supposedly had fought with the Confederate army during the American Civil War (which presumably has led to his being described as an American). In 1882 Burleigh reported from Egypt for the Central News Agency, and was recruited there by the *Daily Telegraph* whose chief correspondent he remained until the end of the century. He reported from the campaigns at Suakin, the Gordon relief expedition, the Ashanti war, Sudan in 1898 and the South African War, and from a number of non-British campaigns; and in the 20th century from Somaliland, the Russo–Japanese War, the Italian campaign in North Africa and the first Balkan War, until his health finally gave out. A big, imposing man with a large moustache and larger voice, Burleigh was not universally popular with his contemporaries, but won a great reputation by virtue of his courage under fire as well as by his style of reporting. Mortimer Menpes recalled first meeting Burleigh on top of a *kopje* in South Africa, when 'he handed me his card in the middle of a battle' and was such an institution that he 'never hesitated to look through Lord Roberts' telescope!'[3] In the style of these early correspondents, Burleigh was not an unbiased reporter, but was very much on the British side, and at times behaved as if he were one of the army instead of an officially non-combatant observer. In the crisis at Tamai he was heard to shout 'Give it them! Hurrah! Three cheers!'; he was officially mentioned in dispatches for helping to steady the line at Abu Klea, and after a cartridge jammed in the Martini-Henry he had picked up (forcing him to use his revolver), his remarks on faulty equipment were followed by an official inquiry. By a lone ride which emulated Forbes' exploit in South Africa, Burleigh ensured that the *Daily Telegraph* published the news of Gordon's death 36 hours before its confirmation by the official dispatch.

Other correspondents also made a major contribution to the public knowledge and perception of colonial campaigning. George Warrington Steevens (1869–1900) of the *Daily Mail* was a classical scholar whose literary talent and wit elevated the standard of writing; he reported from Egypt in 1898, but his career was sadly curtailed when he died of enteric fever during the siege of Ladysmith. Some correspondents achieved fame by covering one campaign: Norris Newman of *The Standard*, for example, wrote memorably on the Zulu War, and only by accompanying Chelmsford did he escape death at Isandlwana; he later discovered the wreck of his own tent, with his belongings scattered around the decaying bodies of his servants. Others became more famous for their deeds than for their dispatches; Henry Morton Stanley, for example, was a correspondent for the *New York Herald*, who was present in the Abyssinian and Ashanti campaigns, but who is better-known for his African exploration; and best-known of all

An example of the contemporary artwork as published in illustrated periodicals, relying upon second-hand reports and the artist's imagination rather than personal observation: a detail of a scene showing the repulse of an attack on the siege-lines at Delhi, not markedly authentic despite being produced by one of the leading artists of the period, Gustave Doré (1832–83).

was Winston Churchill, who combined his literary and journalistic work with the duties of a serving officer.

Important though the contemporary correspondents' work still is, there were a number of constraints upon them, not least the physical danger. The more audacious never let this interfere with their work (when Burleigh was hit by a spent bullet at Abu Klea he told Melton Prior, *The Illustrated London News*' artist, to pick it out of the hole in his neck and then resumed firing at the Dervishes!), but the job of correspondent could be hazardous in the extreme. Even Russell almost met an untimely end during the Indian Mutiny when, ill with sunstroke, he attempted to flee from rebel cavalry and was only saved when William Forbes-Mitchell of the 93rd, commanding an ammunition-carrying party, shot a *sowar* who was about to cut down the correspondent. Others were not so fortunate; for example, when Harry Parkes was seized near Tungchow while attempting to negotiate with the Chinese in September 1860, among the party so treacherously kidnapped was *The Times*' correspondent Bowlby, who died in the seventh day of his captivity, reportedly of having been bound so tightly that mortification ensued.

Two correspondents with Hicks' army disappeared in the Sudan, their fate uncertain but probably killed at El Obeid; they were Edmund O'Donovan and Frank Vizetelly (younger brother of the well-known publisher Henry). At Abu Kru John Cameron of *The Standard* was shot dead (as he was about to partake of a tin of sardines), and later St. Leger Herbert of the *Morning Post* was also shot dead, perhaps because his red coat had attracted enemy fire. Frank Power, formerly O'Donovan's secretary but raised to the status of *The Times*' correspondent, was one of only three Britons in Khartoum during the siege, the others being Gordon and his aide, Lieutenant-Colonel J. D. Hamill Stewart; Power accompanied Stewart in his attempt to carry a plea for help to the telegraph at Dongola, and both were murdered *en route*. The Hon. Hubert Howard of *The Times* and the *New York Herald*, a noted adventurer who had been wounded in Matabelcland, was especially unfortunate, being killed by a stray shell from a British gunboat at Omdurman; and a further casualty of this campaign was the *Manchester Guardian*'s Henry Cross, who died shortly after the battle from enteric fever.

With such hazards, it is not difficult to appreciate the motivation of those correspondents upon whom Mortimer Menpes cast a jaundiced eye during the South African War: '... the correspondents to whom the British Public owes so great a debt, and to whose powerful imaginations are due the brilliant descriptions of battles which were never fought, of guns which were never fired, and of shells which never burst. Far be it from me to cast doubt upon these gentlemen; but I must say that I have seen a correspondent surrounded by bursting shells ... More than one, indeed, was not too proud to accept the shelter of an underground cave, whence – to his power of imagination be all the credit –he would send remarkably thrilling sketches of the great battles he had not witnessed ... I learnt to love these dear men for the recitals of the hardships which they had never undergone ...'[4]

A further constraint upon the objectivity of war-reporting were the personal sentiments of the individuals concerned. Even when critical of methods of operation or of particular commanders, many were understandably pro-British and not especially inclined to present an 'enemy' perspective. Those who did attracted some criticism; Ernest Bennett, for example, who reported on the Sudan in 1898 for the *Westminster Gazette*, was publicly attacked by Burleigh for being unpatriotic and deliberately untruthful, and another with whom Burleigh was at some odds was Henry Nevinson of the *Daily Chronicle*, whose sympathies were too pro-Boer for some tastes. The American correspondent Richard Harding Davis was another regarded as reprehensibly pro-Boer, whose comments would have offended many British readers.

A limit on correspondents' activities was the disapproval they encountered from some commanders; Wolseley, for example, considered journalists a 'race of drones', the curse of armies, who ate the rations of fighting men and did no work (an opinion on which *Navy and Army Illustrated* commented, 'Although these words were written five-and-twenty years ago, it is unlikely that Lord Wolseley will ever be allowed to forget that he wrote them'![5]) Nevertheless, Wolseley cultivated those like Forbes who initially portrayed him in a favourable light, and formed a high opinion of Stanley after seeing him coolly firing at the Ashanti; while Evelyn Wood publicly acknowledged Burleigh's patriotism and integrity. Menpes found many commanders unusually obliging, notably Roberts, and when interviewing and sketching John French he found that noted cavalry commander so nervous and shy that he never noticed that the newspaper he was reading (for the pose in the portrait) was upside-down! In other quarters, correspondents met great hostility. Kitchener lamented Steevens' death (for Steevens' dispatches had been very complimentary), but in general his attitude resembled that of Wolseley, and is exemplified by a story concerning the operations before Omdurman, when he was informed that a party of journalists was waiting for a statement. After keeping them waiting until he was ready, he left his tent and pushed them aside with, 'Get out of my way, you drunken swabs!'[6] Following the publication of his criticisms of the conduct of North-West Frontier operations, Winston Churchill of the 4th Hussars had annoyed so many in the army's hierarchy that it was only by the efforts of his influential mother that he was allowed to accompany the army in the Omdurman campaign, against Kitchener's wishes, in the dual role of serving officer attached to the 21st Lancers and correspondent of the *Morning Post*.

Censorship also affected the correspondents' ability to report accurately, especially during the South African War; yet their complaints had to be moderated lest they be stripped of accreditation and refused permission to accompany the army. Sensible though some of this censorship was, if only for operational reasons, it made the correspondents' task more difficult (for example, when trying to report the action at Spion Kop, Burleigh was limited to 150 words to be sent by telegraph). A noted example of how the system might be beaten was employed by Edgar Wallace (the future novelist) during that war, who employed a friend to set up a rudimentary semaphore at the peace conference, which allowed him to send news of its conclusion before any of the other correspondents. It was not unknown for a correspondent to be removed for expressing criticism of the conduct of a particular operation; for example, *The Standard*'s correspondent Macpherson so annoyed Roberts with his reporting of the operations in the Khost region (January 1879) that

Roberts arranged for his removal, cultivating instead those who would present him in a more favourable light, notably Howard Hensman, the only journalist to accompany him to Kabul, and author of *The Afghan War 1879-80* (London 1881). Indeed, one officer remarked that there were no 'independent Special Correspondents' in this campaign to reveal what had actually happened![7]

Books

The next stage after the reports of correspondents in the press was the production of histories and eye-witness accounts of campaigns, many of which were received eagerly by a public wishing to know more extensive details of recent events. Many of these, often published only a short time after the events they described, were written by the war correspondents; for example, Burleigh, Churchill, Steevens and Bennett all published works on the Sudan campaign of 1898. From the beginning of the 19th century it had been common for officers to write accounts of their own service (as the number of memoirs on the Napoleonic campaigns bear witness), but these were usually more autobiographical than attempts to describe the history of a campaign. There was an increase in the number of soldier-authors who published histories or personal accounts while still in the service, some of whom were quite distinguished. For example, Henry Brackenbury, who wrote for *The Times* and published *The Ashanti War: A Narrative*, was Wolseley's military secretary in that war, in Natal in 1875 and during the Zulu War, and served on his staff in Cyprus and the Sudan; while Baden-Powell's considerable output included works on the Ashanti War of 1895–6 and the Matabele rising of 1896. Additional commercial appeal would accrue to any work written by a famous participant of recent events, for example *The Benin Massacre* written by Alan Boisragon, one of two survivors of the party whose ambush led to the 1897 Benin expedition; *The Military Operations at Kabul* (1843) by Lieutenant Vincent Eyre, who had survived Afghan captivity; and *My Three Years in Manipur, and Escape from the Recent Mutiny* (1891) by Ethel Grimwood, the heroine of the Manipur revolt. *Fire and Sword in the Sudan* (1896) by 'Slatin Pasha' – who had endured years of Dervish captivity, wrote a bestseller and consequently was lionised by British society – was not only a commercial success, but, by its revelations concerning the Khalifa's regime, paved the way for the following British intervention in the Sudan.

A feature of some of the work of soldier-authors, perhaps not so prevalent earlier, and conceivably influenced by the style of some war correspondents, was a preparedness to express criticism of their superiors, even including

An example of the 'heroic' style of illustration prevalent during the period: the Grenadier Guards at Biddulphsberg, a typical South African scene by Richard Caton Woodville.

the government policy which had initiated certain campaigns; for example, Emilius De Cosson remarked that the Sudan campaign of 1885 was a strange case of 'a Conservative army making a political demonstration to keep a Liberal government in power ... British soldiers ... turned into party agents for political purposes ...'[8]

As with the same style of work concerning earlier wars, the 'eye-witness' presentation invariably gives a view of events seen from only one point, and in those produced many years after the events they describe there exists the possibility of recollections becoming blurred by time. In many cases, however, thrilling or terrifying incidents made such an impression upon witnesses that their memoirs remained vivid, so that such personal accounts form an important historical source. In some cases, accounts were committed to paper shortly after the event, often in letters, sometimes in short articles which, although insufficiently significant for publication in book form, provided material for valuable articles in such publications as the *United Service Journal*. Furthermore, many who wrote 'personal' accounts based them on diaries or notes taken at the time, often with meticulous care; as Lady Sale wrote at the very beginning of her *Journal of the Disasters in Affghanistan, 1841–2* (London, 1843): 'I have not only daily noted down events as they occurred, but have often done so hourly.' Even those which do not contribute very materially to a more general understanding of the campaigns in question, are of value in recording the minutiae of military life on campaign, or reflect the attitudes of the period (the latter perhaps exemplified by the somewhat unusual title of Lieutenant V. Majendie's *Up Among the Pandies; or, a Year's Service in India*, London, 1859).

To complement the work of eye-witnesses or 'journalistic' productions, the popular interest in military events led to the publication of histories written by those who were not present, especially on subjects of current interest, and biographies or uncritical eulogies of personalities, for example the large number of publications on Charles Gordon and the like. These varied from the worthy – many are still of value, especially those which (for example) contain extracts from letters of other contemporary material unavailable elsewhere in published form – to paper-backed 'penny-dreadfuls' of only curio value, representative of a genre but unreliable in content.

Although official dispatches were published in the press, and used in the compilation of later histories, what might be termed 'official histories' were few. Some works are almost like official histories, for example Colonel J. F. Maurice's *History of the Campaign of 1882 in Egypt*, while others made use of official documents with official approval; Brackenbury's *The Ashanti War*, for example, used such documents with Wolseley's permission. In general, governments of the Victorian era were less secretive than later in the matter of official communications, publishing material which to later generations might have

appeared too sensitive for immediate release; but this was not invariably the case. This is exemplified by the treatment accorded to Captain Joseph Davey Cunningham, son of the Scottish poet Allan Cunningham. After service against the Sikhs, Joseph Cunningham was appointed political agent at Bhopal, during which duty he wrote his *History of the Sikhs*. This work proved to be the ruin of his career, for in July 1849 he was publicly dismissed from his office for having made unauthorised use of official documents which he had encountered in his official duties. Sent back to his unit, he returned to engineering tasks and died in camp in 1851 at the age of only 38. (Cunningham's family demonstrates the links between military service and literary ability, which were not uncommon at this time; two of Joseph Cunningham's brothers served in the Indian Army, Sir Alexander Cunningham, who rose to the rank of major-general, was director-general of the Indian Archaeological Survey and wrote an *Ancient Geography of India* (1871) and *Coins of Medieval India* (1894); and Francis Cunningham, whose work on early dramatists included the publication of editions of Ben Jonson, Christopher Marlowe and Philip Massinger.)

The first of the genuine official histories was *Record of the Expedition to Abyssinia*, by Major T. J. Holland and Captain H. M. Hozier, 'compiled by order of the Secretary of State for War' and published by H. M. Stationery Office in 1870. This was followed by *Narrative of the Field Operations Connected with the Zulu War of 1879*, 'prepared in the Intelligence Branch of the Quartermaster-General's Department', HMSO, 1881, apparently produced in something of a haste as one of the maps had not been printed by the time of publication. Its issue was very limited and a reprint was undertaken only in 1907, and then only in a comparatively small edition. (At this stage it is perhaps convenient to note the important modern practice of reprinting early works, allowing ready access to sources otherwise difficult to obtain. The Zulu War *Narrative*, for example, was re-issued in 1989 by Greenhill Books of London.) The next official history was that for the Second Afghan War, compiled under the aegis of Major-General Sir Charles MacGregor, though apparently much of the compilation was actually performed by Captain Pasfield Oliver, ex-Royal Artillery. Although six volumes were completed, it was suppressed immediately, as was an abridged 2-volume version printed in 1897. Not until 22 years later did a single-volume *Abridged Official History* appear, greatly reduced in historic value; the reason for the suppression of the original version is still unclear, but perhaps it was done so as not to offend Afghan sensibilities at a delicate moment.[9]

Obviously some of the contemporary productions should be viewed with an element of circumspection, as many (not unnaturally) present a one-sided view of events, and those produced shortly after the events they describe are of course devoid of the analysis which is often only possible from subsequent research. Although errors of fact or

Left: The Naval Brigade occupying Alexandria, 1882: a drawing by Melton Prior showing typical MS notations to enable his eye-witness sketches to be transformed into engravings for publication, e.g., 'white blankets', 'donkey', 'Gatling Guns', 'Midshipman dark blue', etc.

Below: An example of the souvenirs of colonial wars and heroes popular in the later 19th century: a woven silk portrait of Charles Gordon.

interpretation might be expected in some of the 'popular' histories written shortly after the event, some contemporary material was more contentious at the time. An example of a personal memoir which was heavily criticised was R. G. Wilberforce's *An Unrecorded Chapter of the Indian Mutiny*, published in retirement in 1895 and savaged by his fellow ex-officers of the 52nd over matters of accuracy. Especial vitriol was reserved for Wilberforce's assertion that a popular marching song at the time had contained uncomplimentary sentiments about the regiment's officers. While it is perfectly feasible that such a song did exist – most officers would not have objected had the song been vaguely comic in character – an ex-bugler who claimed to have written all the regiment's marching songs decried Wilberforce's assertion as being completely false.

Questions regarding the veracity of sources were not restricted to works published long after the events they described; William Napier's history of his brother's conquest of Sind, for example (a campaign which attracted perhaps more opprobrium than any other) was denounced by one John Sullivan at India House in 1846 as one of the most disgraceful books ever printed in Britain, a criticism probably arising more from political considerations than from inaccuracies of military fact. Another unusual case concerned the autobiography of Sita Ram, a unique personal account by an Indian Army NCO of the mid-19th century; difficulties in matching the information it contains with known events and personalities have caused doubts to be expressed concerning its veracity, or whether its English 'translator' in some way embroidered or even fabricated the story.[10]

As with most other campaigns, colonial warfare produced its legends and distortions of the truth, of which a typical and long-lived example was the tale of 'Highland Jessie' at Lucknow, wife of one of the besieged garrison, who some time before the relief claimed that she could hear bagpipes, the signal that their salvation was at hand. Of uncertain origin, the story became more elaborate with the re-telling, the heroine's name being established as Jessie Brown, and evolving into popular songs, poetry and even a stage play. The story, and even the existence of Jessie herself, was dismissed totally by a number of writers, and the tale does not appear in survivors' memoirs; yet William Forbes-Mitchell of the 93rd was so convinced of its truth that he wrote about it at length, devoting to it six pages of his autobiographical account of the Indian Mutiny, contributing a long letter on the subject to *The Calcutta Statesman* newspaper in 1891, and claiming that he had often heard an eye-witness account of the incident told by a Mrs. Gaffney who had shared the same room at Lucknow with Jessie. Where, then, does the truth lie, between complete fiction and an elaboration of a (just) feasible, factual incident? The case for the latter is perhaps strengthened by one of the criticisms of the story, to the effect that the 78th Highlanders had not played, or indeed had not carried, their pipes at Lucknow. This in itself is unlikely, given the affection with which pipes were regarded in Highland regiments, and was refuted by no less an authority than the regiment's surgeon, Joseph Jee (who won the Victoria Cross at Lucknow), although the pipe-major claimed that they were too busy to play, which may seem unlikely. That the 78th *did* have their pipes with them was confirmed by Forbes-Mitchell, who recalled hearing them playing '*On wi' the Tartan*' inside the Residency, as the 93rd of the second relief-force were playing outside. Whatever the truth, the incident produced the song '*Dinna Ye Hear It?*' by Alexander Maclagan, with its perhaps less than imaginative refrain:

'O dinna ye hear it? dinna ye hear it? dinna ye hear it?
High o'er the battle's din, dinna ye hear it?
High o'er the battle's din, hail it and cheer it!
'Tis the Highlander's slogan! O dinna ye hear it?'

A further complication with contemporary sources is that the meaning of some comments can be mistaken. As a minor example, *Celebrities of the Army* (ed. Commander C. N. Robinson, London, 1900) remarked of Redvers Buller, 'Bravery – well, a Victoria Cross is fair evidence of that, especially if it is won twice over, as it was in Buller's case.' (p.2). This was not meant to imply that Buller had been awarded the VC on two occasions, but merely that he had performed two deeds on the same day, either of which would have merited the decoration. However, an important modern history, which quotes other parts of the *Celebrities* text (without indicating the source) proceeds to state (not in quotation-marks) that Buller *had* actually won the VC twice.

Modern Sources

Such *caveats* apart, the results of modern scholarship have considerably transformed the study of colonial warfare, both in the breadth of material which has now been examined, and the style of treatment accorded to the subject. Whereas many of the earlier volumes were written to provide the public with entertainment or an account of what might almost be termed 'current affairs', and in a minority of cases for use as an instructional aid for officers, modern productions are of course now regarded exclusively as history. Whereas some 19th-century productions took the provision of an entertaining story as the primary criterion, the more substantial modern works place scholarship as the principal attribute (although the work of the leading and most prolific modern authors on the subject, such as Ian Knight and Michael Barthorp, to name just two, proves that it is possible to combine research and scholarship with a readable style quite as accessible as that of the 'popular' authors of the 19th century).

The development of modern scholarship has led to the elimination of the bias which can be found in some earlier works, although the definition of bias perhaps varies according to the viewpoint of the individual. Some 'revisionist' history has led to the use of terms unfamiliar to previous generations, as (for example) when describing the Indian Mutiny as the 'War for Indian Independence'. As an example of the effects of the re-assessment of some colonial campaigns, it is interesting to note that in the Indian Army, an organisation in which the perpetuation of tradition has continued from the importance it was accorded when under British command, certain battle-honours are now no longer celebrated or even regarded as being acceptable. It might be thought unusual that an army in which the badge of the 17th (Poona) Horse features the 'hand of God' standard captured at Koosh-ab (1857) and carried atop its own standard-lance from 1859, should at the same time regard as tainted hard-won honours gained under British command during the Mutiny of 1857–8; yet it should be recalled that no British regiments ever claimed, or were awarded, battle-honours for Sedgemoor or Culloden, where an army similarly fought its fellow-countrymen, perhaps a precedent for the Indian Army's judicious selection of those honours to be commemorated. On the matter of terminology, which modern standards have in some cases caused to change (for example the substitution of 'Cape Frontier Wars' for the earlier name 'Kaffir Wars'), perhaps an acceptable compromise would be that suggested by an important Indian study of the Indian Army of the later 19th century: that in the case of the 1857 conflict, for example, the terms 'Mutiny' or 'Revolt' might be used equally without any special preference (*The Military System of India 1850–1900*, K. M. L. Saxena, New Delhi, 1974).

A development in the content of modern works is the greater interest in the nature and composition of the 'enemy' forces, and in general a more sympathetic view of Britain's opponents than that adopted in earlier years. The earlier lack of concern in appreciating the 'enemy' viewpoint (understandable in the circumstances of continuing hostility in which many of the earlier works were produced) is perhaps typical of a more general lack of interest in the enemy, which was not restricted to colonial campaigns; as an officer observed of the French he had fought at Waterloo: 'We regret, exceedingly, that we are not informed ... as to the name or quality of our opponents. They might have been the Old Guard – Young Guard – or no Guard at all; but certain it is, that they were looking fierce enough and ugly enough to be anything.'[11] It is likely that much of the army regarded its opponents in the same way as expressed in the regimental song of the 57th Foot, alias the 'Die-Hards' of Albuera:

> 'Be they Russians or Prussians or Spanish or French,
> At scaling a rampart or guarding a trench,
> Neither bayonet nor bullet our progress retards,
> For it's just all the same to the gallant Die-Hards.'[12]

There was, of course, interest in 'native' customs and armed forces, and a number of works were published which described them; but with a few exceptions these were not as sympathetic or balanced as has been the coverage of such topics in modern works, which have tended to redress the balance between the viewpoint which divided combatants into 'ours' and (to use Kipling's term) the 'pore benighted 'eathen', as evident in some works, into a more equal and fairer analysis of the opposing forces. It is hardly surprising if some earlier histories present a view more one-sided than had they concerned a European campaign, as in many cases the 'enemy' had no precise organisation, which when compared with the mass of material available to illuminate the British perspective made it inevitable that the coverage of both sides could not be treated equally. Even today, when it is often possible to establish exactly how many British troops were present in a particular engagement, and exactly who among them was killed or injured, the opposing forces often can only be estimated to within several thousands.

Another change evident in the more modern study is a broadening of interest, to embrace campaigns which in the 19th and early 20th centuries tended to be of interest only as 'current affairs', to be supplanted in popularity by whichever was the latest colonial campaign. Initially, works on Indian campaigns were the most numerous, presumably due in part to the frequency of conflict in the subcontinent, with other regions taking very much a secondary place. (For example, it is interesting to note that James Grant's *British Battles on Land and Sea* devoted exactly half its coverage of colonial warfare to India; African affairs occupied less than one-quarter of this space, and only managed so much by the inclusion of

extensive coverage of the recent Abyssinian and Ashanti campaigns.) In terms of popular appeal, there has been a remarkable increase of interest in the Zulu War, a campaign of comparatively brief duration and limited political and strategic significance when considered alongside larger undertakings, and including only two events which made it markedly different from other campaigns: the defeat of a sizeable British force and the heroic and successful defence of an isolated post by a tiny British contingent. Neither of these events was unique, yet they have seized the public imagination more than, for example, a similar catastrophe at Maiwand, or the equally epic, if more prolonged, siege of the Residency at Lucknow.

Inevitably, to some degree levels of interest reflect publications, and vice versa, and the increased interest in the Zulu War may be gauged from the number of modern studies which have appeared, its wider appeal evident by the number of these works which originated outside the continent in which the war occurred. A noted precursor was Sir Reginald Coupland's *Zulu Battle Piece: Isandhlwana* (London, 1948); a good survey of the earlier published material appears in *The Washing of the Spears* by Donald R. Morris (London, 1966), itself a modern 'classic' on the subject which also has been the stimulus for much popular interest. Perhaps the most effective influence towards the growth of fascination with the war, however, was the 1963 film *Zulu*, a superb rendition of the defence of Rorke's Drift in which historical inaccuracies may be forgiven in the light of its spectacle, ambience and powerful narrative. Reflecting the growth of interest, recent years have seen unprecedented research and publication of the most important studies concerning every aspect of the Zulu War, including Zulu culture and the 'Zulu perspective' of the conflict. The modern published scholarship on this war is probably greater and more prolific than on any other colonial campaign, to the effect that the many publications of such authorities as Professor John Laband and Ian Knight are as absolutely essential for the study of the subject as are the contemporary eye-witness and official accounts; and probably of even greater value, in that they represent not only the product of extensive research but also the balanced analysis which takes into account the experiences and viewpoint of both sides. Despite the difficulties of researching a military force which possessed no bureaucracy and no tradition of written accounts, the presentation of the 'Zulu perspective' found in such works permits the most complete appreciation of both sides involved in the war.

Complementing the material published in book form is that which has appeared in periodicals. Much valuable information can be found in contemporary works, for example the *United Service Journal* (later titled *Colburn's United Service Magazine*), the illustrated papers and magazines (as noted below), and journals such as *Navy and Army Illustrated*. Periodicals containing modern research include society publications such as *Journal of the Society for Army Historical Research*, and commercial publications such as *Military Illustrated Past and Present*. None of the above has a content concerned exclusively with colonial campaigns, but it is a measure of the recent interest in all aspects of the subject, from modelling and wargaming to uniform-study and the most learned of dissertations, that some publications have been devoted exclusively to the colonial period. Among these are *Savage and Soldier* magazine, and perhaps most importantly *Soldiers of the Queen*, the journal of the Victorian Military Society, which has published the research of some of the most prominent specialists in the subject, and is an essential source of those interested in any aspect of colonial warfare.

Manuals and Regimental Histories

Two other species of publication worthy of note are regimental histories and instructional manuals. Despite early examples which might be considered as types of regimental or corps history, such as Captain J. Williams' *Bengal Native Infantry: an Historical Account... 1757–1796* (London, 1817), the first serious attempt to produce a concise series of regimental histories was that undertaken by Richard Cannon of the Adjutant-General's office; but these were criticised devastatingly by a leading professional journal: 'After several years of patient expectation, this project is at length felt to be a failure; the few specimens doled out at long intervals, being meagre and

A 'patriotic' bonbon dish produced by the popular magazine Ally Sloper's Half-Holiday. Typical of its genre, it depicts Roberts and Kitchener 'Wiping something off a slate', a quotation from Kipling's 'Absent-Minded Beggar'. The word Roberts is erasing is 'Majuba'.

monotonous, and, as they proceed, utterly deficient in that individuality and spirit which should distinguish the annals of corps varying, like the individuals composing them, in distinctive services and characteristics.'[13]

Despite criticisms of Cannon's histories, they are of note as early examples of their type; but fuller and more valuable regimental histories were produced in subsequent years. With few exceptions, these are not listed here in any part of the bibliography, as only a limited number are concerned with colonial campaigns, and those primarily concern colonial units. For comprehensive listings, the reader is referred to A. S. White's *A Bibliography of Regimental Histories of the British Army*, London 1965, enlarged edn. London, 1988; and to R. Perkins' *Regiments of the Empire: A Bibliography of their Published Histories*, privately published, 1989, revised and enlarged as *Regiments and Corps of the British Empire and Commonwealth 1758–1993: a Critical Bibliography of their Published Histories*, 1994.

Official tactical and instructional manuals were published throughout the 19th century, the first authorised version being *Rules and Regulations for the Movements of His Majesty's Infantry*, published in 1792, being an amended re-issue of Sir David Dundas' *Principles of Military Movements* of 1788. In addition to the manuals issued with official sanction, there were many private publications intended to simplify or elucidate the often complex official issues. Some of the official productions were restricted to particular parts of the army (e.g., *Infantry Drill; Regulations for the Royal Engineer Services*), others were very specialised (e.g., *Drum and Flute Duty for the Infantry Branch of the Army; Instructions and Regulations for the Service and Management of Heavy Ordnance for the Royal Regiment of Artillery*). In addition to the very detailed official issues, others sought to combine everything needed by the officer into one pocket-sized volume, such as Captain F. A. Griffiths' *The Artillerist's Manual and British Soldier's Compendium, of Infantry Exercise, Sword Exercise, Artillery Exercise, Equipment, Fireworks, Fortification, Mathematics, Gunnery, &c &c &c.* (Woolwich, 3rd edn., 1843). Eventually even more material was made available to the officer who wished to broaden his knowledge of military affairs, with the publication of works prepared by the Intelligence Branch of the Quartermaster-General's Department, including such exotic titles as the Duc d'Audiffret-Pasquier's speech on the re-organisation of the French Army; the work of Captain W. S. Cooke of the 22nd Foot on the *Armed Strength of Sweden and Norway*, and Lieutenant J. J. Leverson's translation of General Skobeleff's report on the *Siege and Assault of Denghil-Tépé*. If the relevance of such publications is doubtful in the context of colonial warfare, it was perhaps no more than the traditional reception of official manuals in some quarters. A story was told of the redoubtable Colonel Francis Skelly Tidy, who had commanded the 3/14th at Waterloo and later served in Burma, when discussing the latter war and the *Field Exercise and Evolutions of*

Surgeon Jee dressing the wounded under fire at Lucknow.

Exemplifying the popularity of heroes of colonial wars with the Victorian public is this embossed tin depicting 'Victoria Cross Episodes' which contained McVitie & Price oatcakes. This illustration shows Joseph Jee of the 78th at Lucknow, who won the Victoria Cross on 25 September 1857, although the tin probably dates from the early 1880s; it also showed the exploit in Afghanistan for which James Collis won the VC, which was gazetted in May 1881 but which he forfeited in November 1895.

the Army, *Revised by Major-General Sir Henry Torrens, Adjutant-General to the Forces* (London, 1824): 'One of the party remarked, that the learned work of Sir. H. Torrens had been translated into Burmese, and might do mischief, as giving them an insight into European tactics. "Oh!", said Tidy, "there is no fear of that. We cannot understand it in English, still less will the Burmese be able to make anything of it."'[14]

While some of the privately produced manuals are simply elucidations of the complex official materials, others made more general remarks concerning the military life. Some of the advice imparted appears somewhat unusual: 'I feel sure it is a mistake for a man accustomed to take his few glasses of sherry or claret, or glass of bitter beer at dinner, suddenly to abstain from these, under the impression that by so doing he will improve his shooting ... during the Wimbledon meeting of 1862, I was most careful to avoid all forbidden fruits, as I imagined them, such as pastry, wine, ale, &c; and the consequence was, that I was in a perfect state of misery ... Last year I lived like a sensible man, and not only had better health, but was much more fortunate ...';[15] 'The habitual use of alcoholic drinks does a great deal to bring families into that low and feeble condition of body alluded to as a prolific cause of idiocy ... by pretty careful enquiry, with an especial view of ascertaining the number of idiots of the lowest class, whose parents were known to be *temperate* persons, it is found that *not one quarter* can be so considered ... What evils and what virtues have not been imputed to tobacco! ... we wish to direct the attention of the reader to its great power as an *anti*-aphrodisiac ...'[16]

However, there were available latterly manuals of greater relevance to the practicalities of warfare as might be experienced in colonial campaigns. Wolseley's *Soldier's Pocket Book* was regarded highly (though not above criticism), but the best distillation of experience and intelligence in the context of colonial warfare was Charles Callwell's *Small Wars: Their Principles and Practice*, London, 1896 (revised 1899 and 1906), the definitive work on the subject. (It has been reprinted again under the title *Small Wars: a Tactical Textbook for Imperial Soldiers*, intro. Colonel P. S. Walton, London, 1990). Callwell's text has the stamp of authority as befitted a practical soldier with experience of what he wrote, having served as a gunner in the Second Afghan and Transvaal Wars, and as a staff officer in the South African War of 1899–1902. The benefits of similar practical experience are evident in other works such as Captain G. J. Younghusband's *Indian Frontier Warfare*, London, 1898, and Harry Lumsden's *Frontier Thoughts and Frontier Requirements*, written in 1861 and reprinted as an appendix in *Lumsden of the Guides*, by General Sir Peter Lumsden and G. R. Elsmie, London, 1899.

LITERATURE

A considerable body of fiction was produced in the era of, and about, colonial warfare, although comparatively little of what might be termed 'classic' status, as few of the great novelists took colonial campaigns as the background to their subjects, despite the dramatic or didactic potential provided by the clash of cultures involved in may colonial wars. (Jules Verne's *The End of Nana Sahib*, for example, is hardly that author's most successful or best-known work.)

Much of the contemporary popular fiction might now be termed 'juvenile', not so much for its style as for its principal intended audience, teenaged boys, although the actual readership was probably far wider and more adult (and, as 'Search-Light' observed in 1899, 'Girls in these days do not seem generally to demand literature differing essentially from that enjoyed by their brothers. They can revel in the breathless happenings of pirate company, and feel the zest of strange adventures by flood and field just as much as any eager boy'![17] The format of much of this genre was reasonably standard, involving a hero who upholds every honourable trait expected of an English gentleman, and events (and often historic characters) featured in recent or current campaigns. The obvious intention, apart from the need to entertain, was to provide the reader with examples of behaviour to be emulated and to present a 'patriotic' view of the events described; however, sympathetic treatment of the enemy was not unknown.[18]

Some Victorian writing, including much of the popular literature, involves a style burdened by what according to some modern standards would be regarded as sentimentality, and dialogue which might now be taken as being somewhat unrealistic:

'The doctor's sharp ear had caught the sound of the first shot. He knew the report as well as he knew the colonel's voice, and rushed back to see by what extraordinary means his faithful and beloved piece had been discharged. As he entered the room he saw Margaret putting back the gun where she had found it. "Why!" he gasped, "you don't mean to say that it was you who were potting the rissaldar-major?" "I couldn't resist the temptation to try to get the business over," she replied. "I'm sorry I didn't do better. I'm afraid I've wasted some of your precious cartridges."'[19]

However, the style of expression which might now be regarded as Victorian sentimentality was not seen as such at the time; for example, at Laing's Nek, Lieutenant Elwes of the Staff, attempting to lead a hopeless charge, actually did shout 'Floreat Etona!' to another ex-Eton boy, Adjutant Monck of the 58th (which formed the subject of a painting by Lady Butler); and Quintin Battye of the Guides, when mortally wounded during the siege of Delhi, really did quote Horace: appropriately, '*Dulce et decorum est pro patria mori*', undoubtedly without the later irony accorded it by Wilfred Owen.

Among the most notable writers of fiction were those who had considerable knowledge of military affairs. The doyen of them all was George Alfred Henty (1832–1902), who wrote about eighty of the most superior type of 'juvenile' novel, and who by the 1890s had become something of an institution, immensely popular and prolific (for the Christmas trade of 1899, for example, he had no less than five new books published). He was, however, more than just an author of 'patriotic' stories; he served with the Purveyor's Department in the Crimea and, tiring of peacetime duty, had become a journalist and war-correspondent, reporting on the Austro–Italian War of 1866, Garibaldi, Abyssinia, the Ashanti campaign, the Franco–Prussian War, the Carlist War of 1873–6, Russia at the time of the conquest of Khiva, and the Turko–Serbian War which led to the Russo–Turkish War of 1877–8. Such experience must have been invaluable in his later career as a novelist, which began when he became editor of a boys' magazine, the appropriately named *Union Jack*, to which he contributed stories. Within the confines of the genre, Henty's books are of a high standard, and many are instructional: descriptions of real battles and even tactical maps are included; as *The Standard* remarked when reviewing Henty's *With Frederick the Great*, 'the boy who reads it will know as much about the Seven Years War as many an adult student of Carlyle's masterpiece.' Sometimes this element was criticised mildly: 'Mr. Henty is an astonishing man. For more years than I care to remember he has been pouring forth stories of adventure which have won him world-wide repute ... There is something of the prig in his heroes, perhaps, and behind his glowing pages the schoolmaster lies hid; but he is such a skilful contriver that these points are rarely discerned by his readers ...'[20]

As with much of the genre, Henty's work was also instructional in a different sense, in contrasting the concept of British chivalry (to be emulated by readers) with the behaviour of others:

'"I know he wasn't killed on the spot, for he shouted after I left him ... I know that I ought to have paused a moment and given him another stab, but I could not bring myself to do it. It is one thing to stab a man who is trying to take one's life, but it is quite another when he has fallen and is helpless." Zaki made no reply. He could scarcely understand his master's repugnance to making matters safe when another blow would have done so, but it was not for him to blame ...'[21]

The effect of this was expressed succinctly in the *Christian Leader*'s review of Henty's *By Sheer Pluck: A Tale of the Ashanti War*. 'Morally, the book is everything that could be desired, setting before the boys a bright and bracing ideal of the English gentleman.' Henty's own sentiments are clear from his preface to his tale of the 1898 campaign in the Sudan: 'Thus a land that had been turned into a desert by the terrible tyranny of the Mahdi and his successor was wrested from barbarism and restored to civilization, and the stain upon British honour caused by the desertion of Gordon by the British ministry of the day was wiped out. It was a marvellous campaign – marvellous in the perfection of its organisation, marvellous in the completeness of its success.'[22]

Henty was not the only novelist with military experience; another prolific author was Lieutenant-Colonel F. S. Brereton, who was first commissioned into the 60th Rifles in 1855. The work of such novelists ranged through the entire scope of British (and to a lesser extent world) history, and such was their popularity that their youthful readers must have absorbed many basic historical facts (albeit from one perspective), which has probably not been the case with succeeding generations as Henty and his like declined in popularity. Indeed, the titles of many novels are such that without knowledge of the author they might easily be presumed to be works of genuine history: Henty's productions included *The Dash for Khartoum*; *The Tiger of Mysore*, *With Clive in India, or the Beginnings of an Empire*; *Through the Sikh War, a Tale of the Conquest of the Punjab*; *On the Irrawaddy: A Story of the First Burmese War*; *Maori and Settler: A Story of the New Zealand War*; *For Name and Fame, or Through Afghan Passes*; *With Buller in Natal*; and *With Roberts to Pretoria*. Henty's work was by no means alone in possessing such ambiguous titles: for example, Brereton wrote *One of the Fighting Scouts*, and J. Percy-Groves *The War of the Axe, or Adventures in South Africa*. (The need to differentiate fact from fiction still exists; see 'Zabange – Pure Fiction' by Julian Whybra, in *Soldiers of the Queen 61* (Victorian Military Society 1990), which proves that a Zulu account of Isandlwana, elsewhere accepted as genuine, is relatively modern fiction).

Another novelist of great popularity, who set a number of his stories in colonial campaigns, was James Grant (1822–87). The son of an officer of the 92nd who had fought in the Peninsular War, James Grant had personal military experience as an officer of the 62nd Foot (1840–2), and from 1859 as an officer in the 1st City of Edinburgh Rifle Volunteers. From an early age he made literature his career, his first novel, *The Romance of War; or the Highlanders in Spain* (1846), being arguably his most famous, and based on his father's experiences. His subsequent prodigious output included stories set in India, South Africa, Afghanistan, Burma and the Sudan, and included among the most successful *Frank Hilton, or The Queen's Own*; *Shall I Win Her?* (set in the Cape Frontier Wars), and the perhaps oddly-named *Fairer than a Fairy*, together with a host of novels concerning earlier campaigns. Given his background (he was raised in barracks in Newfoundland, where his father was in garrison), it was probably inevitable that Scottish military life formed the basis of many of his stories, his national feeling being so strong that he was a founder and leading member of the National Association for the Vindication of Scottish Rights. Grant's novels are not as authentic in matters of fact and background as some others, but he must have referred to published histories, to the extent that Captain W. R. King suggested that Grant had used passages from his own *Cam-*

Below: Virtually no medium was immune from the display or adaptation of patriotic or topical symbols. One of the most unusual forms of illustration was upon sweet confectionery: blocks of mint- or other flavoured sugar-cake were sold with designs impressed or printed in 'French-cream-pink' vegetable dye. No subject was too outrageous for such decoration (even a series depicting the Tay Bridge Disaster, including a scene of 'Viewing the Dead'), but less bizarre are these portraits of contemporary personalities, taken from the carved wooden blocks used to impress or print the design upon sugar-tablets.

Largely as a result of colonial campaigning, the army became a popular symbol in commercial advertising as in this trademark adopted by the confectionery manufacturer Fryer & Co., of Nelson, Lancashire; this version of the company's symbol depicts an artilleryman wearing the busby of 1855–78, but the design was modernised progressively until at the time of the South African War one version showed a gunner of the naval brigades.

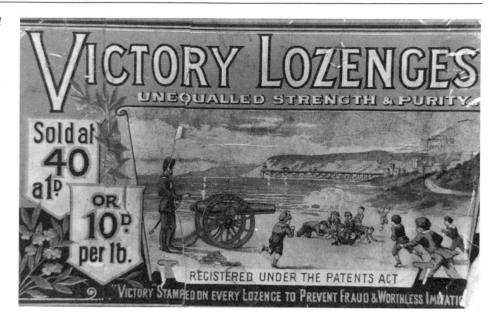

paigning in Kaffirland: Scenes and Adventures in the Kaffir War of 1851–52* for *Shall I Win Her?* Whatever the inaccuracies in his novels, Grant was regarded as an authority on military affairs (it was said to be partly due to him that yellow facings were adopted by Scottish non-'Royal' regiments from 1881, yellow being the ancient royal colour of that country); and he published a number of non-fiction works, including *Old and New Edinburgh* (an enormously successful best-seller), *British Heroes of Foreign Wars*, and his notable three-volume *British Battles on Land and Sea*, much of which was concerned with colonial warfare.

Despite the belief that Hentyesque stories were intended for a youthful audience, many published for adults were of a very similar style, even the fiction which appeared in *Navy and Army Illustrated*, for example. Younger children were also catered for in the field of colonial wars or 'patriotic' literature, some of which doubtless also appealed to a much older audience. There was, for example, Mrs. Ames' *ABC for Baby Patriots* and the companion *Pictures for Little Englanders* by Frank Green and A. S. Forrest, and at the time of the South African War another illustrated by Forrest, *Ten Little Boer Boys* which included the verse:

> 'Seven little Boer boys,
> Full of naughty tricks,
> One abused the white flag,
> And then there were six'

which presumably was intended to caution the readership that this was a practice of which to beware when dealing with Boers!

The prevalent social and national attitudes can be exemplified by the following verse from *Army and Navy*

Drolleries by Major T. S. Seccombe (London, n.d. but originally published *c.*1874), a book of children's verses with plates of superb quality printed by Kronheim; it concerns trophies appropriated during the Ashanti War:

> 'Where King Coffee Calcali came off second best,
> And lost his state gingham, which now, by the way,
> Can be seen at South Kensington any fine day,
> Where the Great Unwashed stare at it just as they please,
> Or sit 'neath its shadow and eat bread and cheese;
> Which shows us how vain is the glory of kings,
> And the pomp of umbrellas and similar things.'

Colonial campaigns have not been in the forefront of subjects of modern popular fiction, perhaps the dislike of 'colonialism' in some quarters having had an effect. Certainly, colonial campaigns have produced few works suitable for comparison with the several series of novels on the Royal Navy of the Napoleonic Wars, or the many on conflicts of the 20th century, for example. Notable exceptions include M. M. Kaye's *Far Pavilions* (1978), while George Macdonald Fraser's anti-hero *Flashman* is perhaps the best-known series of adventures with a Victorian setting. Some similar works of fiction are based entirely upon historical events, for example Alexander Fullerton's *The White Men Sang* (1958), a dramatisation of the last stand of the Shangani Patrol.

A considerable amount of poetry and verse relates to colonial campaigns or to the society which waged them. Much of this was topical if not especially distinguished, for example *Lines on the Rescuing of the Colours of the 24th* by 'L. G. F. G.', printed in 1879:

'The tidings come alas too true,
Sad tidings these for English ears,
The Zulus who were so despised
Have crushed the gallant 24th,
Their colours ta'en, the savage hands
Of Cetewayo with the rest
Of that most numerous Zulu host,
Had snatched them from the dying men.'

(Written in March 1879, the final lines, 'Let's not abuse an absent man / If one of us were in his place, / He would not p'r'aps excel Chelmsford' do not take into account that general's ultimate victory.)

Much of the contemporary poetry is overtly patriotic and celebratory, reflecting the belief that British conquest was an unqualified, civilising influence, as in Duncan Tovey's *Khartoum*:

'We have fashioned a mighty Empire, but not with the sword alone,
For mercy has followed the victors' feet in the lands we have made our own ...
That the swords may be turned to ploughshares, that strife and oppression cease,
And ever the English tongue shall be prosperity, light and peace.'[23]

Comparatively little poetry of note seems to have been produced on active service, and the Victorian army does not seem to have produced figures of the status of the great soldier-poets like Ewald von Kleist (1715–59, mortally wounded at Kunersdorf) or the generation of poets of the First World War. Much of what did appear was light-hearted, such as the first verse of *B. P.*, a paean of praise to Baden-Powell 'by a Lady' which appeared in *The Mafeking Mail* (No. 111, 6 April 1900) during the siege:

'Our Colonel's a jolly good fellow,
An out and out stunner is he,
And this you may bet, that we'll never forget
Our gallant Commander B-P.'

or this extract from *How I Was 'Run In'* by 'Turpentino Gallipot', in which an officer recounts a nocturnal march in an attempt to find his unit's camp, accompanied by two idiot 'rankers' who claimed to know the way but were more lost than he was:

'With main and with might, I trudged thro' the night,
But my legs were beginning to tremble;
And, ye gods! my delight when I first saw a light
'Mid the tents, I could scarcely dissemble.
Down the hill – we are there! to my tent I'll repair,
For my feet felt as though they'd no toes on,

As for that idiot pair not a thought would I spare,
But I'd quickly turn in, with my clothes on.'[24]

Altogether more serious were the works of more established poets. Sir Henry Newbolt (1862–1938) enjoyed a literary and legal career (although during the First World War he worked for the Admiralty's records department, and wrote *A Naval History of the War 1914-1918*, London 1920, before completing Sir Julian Corbett's official history on the same subject), but much of his poetry was concerned with colonial and other warfare, throughout which ran the theme of duty, honour and patriotism. Much of Newbolt's work might now be regarded as over-sentimental but at the time expressed beliefs which were honestly held. Probably only *Drake's Drum* and his most famous poem, *Vitaï Lampada*, are now known, but his 'patriotic' work also covered late Victorian colonial campaigns, including a number on the Boer War, and *The Gay Gordons* with its suggestion that a mitigating factor to the death of the Highlanders killed storming the heights of Dargai was that '... they passed in the hour of the Gordons' pride/To the skirl of the pipers' playing'. *Vitaï Lampada*, which presented the virtue of the public-school ideal of 'playing the game' (though never for personal glory), contrasted the ordeal of the tail-end batsman making a stand on a broken wicket, with that of a subaltern attempting to rally a broken square in a desert campaign; with the Gatling jammed and the colonel dead, the regiment blinded by dust and smoke, 'when the voice of a schoolboy rallies the ranks: "Play up! Play up! and play the game!"' Impossibly idealistic though it might be, the virtues which Newbolt celebrated found a receptive audience in at least certain sections of Victorian and Edwardian society.

Sir Francis Doyle, Bt. (1810–88) also lacked personal military experience, although his father was Major-General Sir Francis Hastings Doyle, Bt.; despite a civilian career, including the Customs Service and from 1867 to 1877 the post of professor of poetry at an Oxford college, Sir Francis produced a number of military poems, including one concerning the heroic behaviour of the troops aboard the sinking troopship *Birkenhead*, but he is perhaps best remembered for his *The Private of the Buffs*. This exemplary narrative was based on an actual incident, in which Private John Moyes of the 3rd Foot, captured at Peh-Tang in China in August 1860, was murdered for refusing to kow-tow before a mandarin. The poem was considerably in error – Moyes was not a 'Kentish lad' but apparently a Scottish veteran of fifteen years' service, including the Crimea and two reductions from the rank of sergeant – but it was accurate in that, like all British troops on campaign,

'To-day, beneath the foeman's frown,
He stands in Elgin's place,
Ambassador from Britain's crown
And type of all her race.'

and finally, with a touch which would have appealed to a Victorian audience with its reference to Leonidas and Thermopylae:

'So, let his name through Europe ring –
A man of mean estate,
Who died, as firm as Sparta's King,
Because his soul was great.'[25]

Probably the foremost exponent of what has been termed 'literary Imperialism' was Rudyard Kipling (1865–1936), who although not a soldier was born in Bombay, and worked in India and South Africa, and was thus entirely familiar with the subjects about which he wrote. Kipling was perhaps even more distinguished as a storyteller than as a poet, but his military writing is probably best-known for his poems published in book form in 1892 as *Barrack-Room Ballads*, including such immortals as *Tommy, Gunga Din, Mandalay, Fuzzy-Wuzzy* and *Screw-Guns*. Although some of this work might now be regarded as perhaps patronising, in its attempt to reproduce the diction of the ordinary soldier, and too 'imperialist' for some modern tastes, it was written with affection and in an attempt to portray the soldier more accurately than in some contemporary literature; and at least in *Fuzzy-Wuzzy* the 'enemy' is accorded the respect due to a brave fellow-warrior. Kipling's military verse may not be the genuine voice of 'Tommy', but approaches it nearer than most, and not all was entirely the product of the author's imagination but was rooted more in fact or in a reflection of contemporary opinions. The narrator's regard for Gunga Din, for example, was shared widely by troops who had witnessed the bravery of *bhistis* under fire, and others bear an even closer connection to fact. Most notable is the poem *Snarleyow*, its title being the name of an artillery team-horse. Although the poem elaborates on reality, the essence of the story is an anecdote of Ferozeshah, recounted by N. W. Bancroft in *From Recruit to Staff Sergeant*, first published in Calcutta in 1885. The singular name of the horse – Bancroft calls it 'Snarley Yow' – must surely establish it firmly as the inspiration for Kipling's poem.[26] Similarly, a line in *Loot* (an' now I'll bid good-bye, for I'm gettin' rather dry/An' I see another tunin' up to toot) would seem to have originated with the song 'Bang Upon the Big Drum' which was popular during the Second Afghan War. In addition to poetry, Kipling also used military settings for some of his stories, of which *Soldiers Three* is perhaps the best-known.

The popularity of Kipling among the army which he celebrated is not certain; it was noted that his *Absent-Minded Beggar* was not especially popular with some, despite its great reception at home; yet his *Recessional* was sung in Pretoria by the army which had captured the place (perhaps they were attracted by the mention of 'our far-flung battle-line', for in one sense they represented one end of it). The lyrics of popular songs represent another form of contemporary poetry, although most of these were written at home rather than on campaign, and only a minority of those popular with the army concerned colonial campaigns, for example the Abu Klea song 'Colonel Burnaby' (an example of one written in the army, rather than a civilian song adopted by it). While it might be thought that most 'patriotic' songs emanated from civilian sources, some were genuinely popular with the army, notably 'Soldiers of the Queen'. Many songs popular on campaign were no more than the staple fare of the music-hall, and others of no military connotation whatever (for example 'The Whitechapel Polka', sung in Egypt and the Sudan, which concerned the exploits of Jack the Ripper), but more 'patriotic' lyrics were to be found in some regimental songs, such as 'Bravo, Dublin Fusiliers'. The tone of such songs is exemplified by lines from the latter:

'Boers have derided men of our race, insulted Britain's dear old flag,
Boasted Majuba – said we were curs, called our flag "the old white rag."'[27]

Lest it be thought that such sentiments were entirely the product of home-based idealists with no conception of the realities of active service, there is evidence of the popularity of such beliefs among the troops themselves, and towards the end of the century at least 'God Save the Queen' was taken up spontaneously as an expression of genuine emotion; if, as was reported, the doomed Shangani Patrol sang it shortly before they were overrun, their motivation would have been appreciated by many soldiers as a demonstration of emotion genuinely expressed

For example, it is a remarkable (though perhaps typical) fact that when advancing into a heavy fire of grapeshot at Cawnpore in December 1857, the whole of the British force joined in singing 'The Battle of the Alma', accompanied by the band of the 93rd, a wildly-patriotic composition to the tune 'The British Grenadiers':

'Come, all you gallant British hearts
Who love the Red and Blue,*
Come drink a health to those brave lads
Who made the Russians rue ...'[28]

Typical of the sentiments expressed by such songs, perhaps, were the verses of 'Comrades, hark! The Call has Sounded', used for years at the parades of the Gloucester Volunteer Artillery, and sung to Haydn's composition best-known as the hymn 'Glorious things of Thee are spoken', or as the German anthem 'Deutschland über Alles':

*Red and Blue = Army and Navy.

'Comrades, in these days of terror,
What are England's sons to do?
Law despised and God forgotten –
What if God forgets us too?
Trust in Him and keep your order;
Comrades, let them scoff who will;
God is still the God of England,
England's sons are loyal still.

God of Battles! God of England!
Be as Thou hast been before!
Guard us as we form and muster,
Lead us as we march to war.
Thus believing, thus achieving,
This our watchword still shall be;
"England's sons are faithful soldiers,
True to England, true to Thee."'[29]

The popularity of military affairs at home is exemplified by the publication of large numbers of musical compositions and songs with a military theme, often with decorative covers depicting scenes described in the songs. Examples of the many based on colonial campaigning were such compositions as 'The Abyssinian Gallop', 'The Ashantee Expedition March', 'The Lancers' Aliwal Polka', 'The Ali Musjid Gallop', 'The Candahar March', 'How Cavagnari Fell', 'Chinese Gordon's March', 'Havelock's Indian March', 'Gordon's Safety! England's Honour!', 'The Khyber Pass', 'The Kassassin Gallop', 'Magdala Waltzes', 'The Siege of Mooltan', 'The Noble 24th, or Vanquished Not Disgraced', 'The Battle of Sobraon', 'The Soudan Expedition', 'The Transvaal War March', 'The Garnet Wolseley March', 'The Triumphal Entry into Delhi', 'On the Veldt', 'The Zulu Expedition Grand Military Fantasia', and even compositions named after particular units, such as 'The Tenth Bengal Irregular Cavalry Polka'.

ART

The art of the period of the colonial wars was exceptionally varied, but with some exceptions can be divided into the categories of uniform-illustration, campaign scenes in prints or journalistic form, and history painting; although in many cases these divisions overlap.

Especially from the 1830s there was a steady market for prints depicting military uniforms or military scenes although, as with most uniform-illustrations, the majority depicted full dress or uniform worn at home; only a minority showed the uniforms worn in the colonies, although all are of value in that overseas dress was based on that worn at home during this period. Among the best and most numerous series of prints were those published by Ackermann of London, with notable artists including Henry Martens and Michael Angelo Hayes (1820–77), the latter the son of Edward Hayes, RA, and who in 1842 was appointed Military Painter in Ordinary to the Lord Lieutenant of Ireland. The work of such artists, like that of many of the foremost print-producers of this period, was mostly the result of careful personal observation and is thus of the greatest historical value. Less common were similar works concerning colonial forces, although William Hunsley's *Costumes of the Madras Army* (published

A typical use of colonial warfare in an advertising medium; the circular structure behind the soldier represents a South African War corrugated iron blockhouse.

in Madras 1840–1) and *Ceylon Rifle Corps* are notable series, as are the same artist's pictures of the Madras Camel Howitzer Battery and an elephant battery. The most valuable examples of illustrations of colonial units, or of British troops serving in colonial campaigns, but drawn by artists resident in Britain, are those which note the original source, for example the Martens plates in Ackermann's series *Costumes of the Indian Army* (1844–9) which bear the notation 'from a sketch by Capt. Fredc. Ainslie, 21st Fusiliers', which elevates such works to the level of authenticity implicit in 'eye-witness' drawings.

During the later Victorian period, uniform-illustrations tended to be intermixed with more scenic views of army life, so that the principal uniform-illustrators are also known for campaign scenes and the depiction of historical incidents; though in many cases the latter are more decorative than necessarily accurate from a historical viewpoint.

Of the many illustrators of this type of work, the doyen was Richard Simkin (*c.*1851–1926), whose extraordinary output included literally thousands of watercolours produced from the mid-1870s until after the First World War. Most famous was his series of 177 chromolithographs produced for the *Army and Navy Gazette* between 1888 and 1902, depicting figures or groups generally in dress uniform, but including some in other orders of dress and even on campaign. The accuracy of these and similar illustrations is generally good; Simkin lived in Aldershot until about 1890 and thus had many regiments to observe close at hand, but so popular did his work become that he found it impossible to fulfil all the commissions he received, and for a time employed a staff of young ladies at his studio in Catford to hand-colour some of his drawings. After moving to Herne Bay, Simkin became more divorced from his subject-matter and made greater use of other references and photographs; although much of his work is accurate and of high artistic merit, some errors are present even in illustrations of troops of his own era, and although some of the 'historic' work is recognisably based on contemporary sources, some is inaccurate and some 'action' scenes of previous battles are stilted or somewhat 'wooden' in appearance. Nevertheless, Simkin remained hugely popular – he executed commissions for many regiments – and he remains the most important of the later Victorian uniform-illustrators, and at his best was the equal of any in terms of artistic merit and period ambience.

Harry Payne is best-known for his work in the less-exalted end of the military-illustration market, notably for scores of well-executed popular postcards depicting military uniforms (principally of his own era) and, with less authenticity, scenes from British military exploits of the past. Like Simkin, Payne's work concentrated upon dress uniforms worn at home, with little of 'colonial' content, but he had the advantage of familiarity with military life

and military equipment: he served in the West Kent Yeomanry from 1883 to 1906, revelled in his part-time soldiering, looked extremely impressive in uniform and retired with the exalted rank of sergeant. His artistic career began about 1881 and lasted until the end of the First World War, encompassing such varied subjects as cigarette cards, advertisements and non-military studies in addition to the main body of book, periodical and postcard work. Some of Harry Payne's earliest work was executed in conjunction with his brother Arthur, notably a picture-book *On and Off Duty: Episodes of Military Life* by Captain Percy Groves (London, n.d., but *c.*1890), which included some Indian Mutiny scenes and a plate of Indian Army subjects; and from 1893 (without Arthur) a series of *Illustrated Histories of Scottish Regiments*, also by Groves, which included illustrations of colonial campaign uniforms as well as modern full dress. The acceptance of the accuracy of Payne's work (at least in the depiction of the uniforms of his time) may perhaps be surmised from his continuing work in *Navy and Army Illustrated* and *The Cavalry Journal*, both periodicals aimed mainly (the latter exclusively) at a military audience.

Many other artists produced uniform-illustrations during the later 19th century, including some of colonial troops (notably the plates in Walter Richards' *Her Majesty's Army*, for example, *c.*1890), many of which are very accurate. Special mention should be accorded to Major Alfred Crowdy Lovett, whose watercolours of Indian Army subjects (dating from the late 1890s) are not only among the most distinguished artistically, but are faultless in depiction of uniform-details; the majority were reproduced in Major C. F. MacMunn's *The Armies of India* (London, 1911). Many are portraits of named individuals, and it is possible to appreciate the accuracy of the uniform-details by comparison with photographs of the same men.[30]

The public demand for images of campaigning was traditionally satisfied by the publication of prints, a practice which continued throughout the 19th century. Many of those concerning colonial wars were from, or based on, illustrations by officers who were present; these included, for example, a series of Burmese scenes after sketches by Captain Frederick Marryat (the author, who was senior naval officer at Rangoon May–September 1824); prints of Bhurtpore after Captain G. B. P. Field and Major John Luard; and series on Canada (1837) by Captain Lord Charles Beauclerk of the Royal Regiment; First Afghan War by Lieutenant J. Wingate; China (1847) by Lieutenant Martin of the 42nd Madras; Multan by Assistant Surgeon John Dunlop of the 32nd; China 1859–60 by Major W. G. R. Masters, RMLI; views of campaigning in China, India and South Africa by Lieutenant-Colonel Sir Harry Darell, Bt., 7th Dragoon Guards; and of the Indian Mutiny by Captain D. Sarsfield Greene, Royal Artillery, Captain George F. Atkinson, Bengal Engineers, and of Lucknow by Lieutenant-Colonel D. S. Dodson.

The demand for campaign scenes increased markedly with the advent of the popular illustrated paper, notably *The Illustrated London News* (first published 1842) and *The Graphic* (founded 1869). From the former's coverage of the 1848 revolution in France, when the French artist Constantin Guys was commissioned to supply pictures of the fighting, the status of the war-artist or artist-correspondent was established. Even after the development of technology which permitted the reproduction of photographs, the illustrated journals relied on 'eye-witness' sketches from campaigns to attract their readership, which produced a most valuable body of work depicting scenes on active service.

Although some pictures which appeared in periodicals (as in many 'popular' books and prints) were entirely the product of home-based artists' imagination, and thus of no historic significance, publishers were always keen to announce that their illustrations were based on eye-witness sketches submitted by their own correspondents in the field, or by officers present on campaign; but as illustrations could not be reproduced photographically in the earlier years, the original sketches were transformed into engravings by craftsmen employed by the newspapers. In many cases this was done with meticulous accuracy, but there always remained a tendency to 'improve' on the original sketch, sometimes at the expense of authenticity. This rarely affected the main points of the composition, but more often called into question the minutiae of the illustrations; if, for example, a home-based artist perfectly familiar with a soldier's equipment were asked to 'tidy' or reproduce a campaign sketch which intended to show (say) a pattern of pouch or canteen used overseas, he might be tempted to draw instead the pattern which he knew from personal experience, not realising that troops abroad might be using a different pattern. Thus, even illustrations based on 'eye-witness' sketches should be regarded with a degree of circumspection, if it is suspected that this process may have occurred during the transfer from original sketch to published engraving. (An interesting comment on this process was made by Lieutenant Francis Cornish of the 17th Bengal Cavalry concerning an action in which he was involved in the Tirah in 1897: 'I hope you have seen the picture of the Barki (or Barkai) patrol drawn by John Charlton in the *Graphic* ... I can't imagine how one Lionel James, who sent the sketch, got hold of the details, but though of course utterly unlike what happened, it is not half a bad picture for conveying the idea of the thing.'[31]

Many of the original sketches included manuscript notations, highlighting salient features of the illustrations, either as a guide to the engraver or for use in captioning the final engraving, such notations being omitted from the published version. Technological improvements from the early 1880s, however, permitted the reproduction of the original sketches (even if more conventional, 'worked-up' versions were published subsequently), presenting the reader with an even more immediate image, complete with the artist's manuscript comments. This process was not without hazard: considerable trouble resulted from the publication of a Melton Prior sketch in *The Illustrated London News* in March 1884, 'The 42nd Highlanders taking the Enemy's strong position at the Battle of El Teb', which included among other notations a statement that the picture showed British troops 'shooting wounded Rebels in the trenches'. The influence of such illustrations is shown by the fact that this caused questions to be asked in parliament, and provided evidence for those critical of the British methods of waging war (actually, as wounded Dervishes were almost as dangerous and just as hostile as the unwounded, shooting those who still posed a threat was an understandable action).[32]

The aforementioned Melton Prior of *The Illustrated London News* was one of the leading artist-correspondents, who covered numerous campaigns including the Zulu War, the Ashanti campaign, South Africa, Egypt, the Sudan, the Balkan conflicts, India and the Russo–Turkish and Russo–Japanese Wars. Sharing the dangers with the troops, Prior became something of a national institution by producing accurate drawings depicting the realities of war, rather than the somewhat sanitised versions of some of the earlier type of 'battle-painting'. He was among the first to find the body of the Prince Imperial, riding out with Archibald Forbes in the search-party; at Abu Kru Prior was twice grazed by bullets, saw Cameron of the *Standard* killed, and performed the funeral ceremonies for him and later for Steevens at Ladysmith; and survived a number of other hair-breadth escapes. As he was principally an artist, Prior was able to work in collaboration with the correspondents of other newspapers (notably Forbes), as they were not prime competitors.

Prior's opposite number for the main competitor, *The Graphic*, was at first Charles Fripp, a mercurial character who objected to official constraints on his activities (during the Zulu War Prior and Forbes had on one occasion to restrain him physically from attacking those – Buller included – who had ordered him from a position of danger). He continued as a correspondent-artist and produced some of the best illustrations of the South African War. Another outstanding artist-correspondent for *The Graphic* was Frederic Villiers, who covered the Franco–Prussian War, Egypt and the Sudan, worked as a more conventional correspondent in the Balkans for *The Standard*, and in the Sudan in 1898 represented both *The Illustrated London News* and *The Globe*. He experimented with a cine camera in the Balkans, and attempted to capture the Battle of Omdurman on cine film, from the deck of a gunboat, but when the vessel opened fire the concussion blew down his camera and exposed his film. Following this débâcle Villiers returned to his sketch-pad, and endured two years of service on the Western Front during the First World War before he finally retired at the age of 65. (He was among those artists whose work benefited artistically from re-working by home-based artists, because his talent for figure-drawing was limited).

As drawing was regarded as an important part of an officer's education (essential for military engineers and surveyors), many talented individuals produced sketches or more finished compositions on campaign. As had occurred with the production of prints, many of these officers sent sketches to the illustrated periodicals, which were often published either with the name of the original artist ('from a sketch by ...') or with a caption which stated simply, 'by a military officer'. This source of illustrations was invaluable in those cases when an illustrated paper initially had no artist of its own in the field, as was the case, for example, in the early Indian Mutiny with both *The Illustrated London News* and *The Illustrated Times*. Included among the most talented were Henry Hope Crealock, who retired as a major-general in 1879,[33] and Colonel Cornelius Francis (Frank) James of the Bombay Grenadiers, who contributed sketches to illustrated periodicals and who exhibited his paintings with success; he produced many significant illustrations of the Abyssinian campaign.[34]

Despite any alterations to the images originally produced by artist-correspondents or other eye-witnesses, the published pictures were usually reasonably accurate, at least in feeling if not always in the minutiae, and projected a fairly accurate image of events on campaign. Even the best of the illustrated periodicals, however, were not always reliable, of which the following are extreme examples. William Forbes-Mitchell told how *The Illustrated London News* published a picture of an Indian banker and commissariat contractor, Ajoodia Pershad, and claimed it depicted Nana Sahib; this arose from the illustrator's search for a portrait of the latter, but having only one Indian picture at hand, used that. When told that everyone in India would realise that it did not depict Nana Sahib, 'The artist declared he did not care for people in India; he required the picture for the people of England.'[35] A similar case was reported concerning an illustrated paper published at the seat of the South African War, which used the same engraved portrait for a series of interviews with different personalities; when questioned, the editors admitted that, being unable to reproduce their artist's sketches, they had used the only block they had available, an advertisement for hair-restorer. Even the genuine artist-correspondent might be criticised on grounds of accuracy: for example, it was claimed that a plan of Abu Klea, used as a reference for subsequent pictures, was in fact only drawn a week after the action by an artist who at the time of the battle was some two miles away, safe from the scene of the combat.[36]

The final classification of art lies in the realm of history-painting, a form of artistic expression which increased markedly during the era of colonial conflict. From the end of the Napoleonic Wars until the Sikh Wars the genre had gone into a decline, but it revived thereafter. Although there was always the need for a picture to be effective artistically, even at the expense of accuracy, a number of prominent artists had personal knowledge of their subject: Godfrey D. Giles, for example, who painted a number of excellent canvases, had served in the Indian Army in Afghanistan, with the Egyptian gendarmerie at El-Teb, and was present at Tamai, the subject of perhaps his most famous paintings. (He also provided some of the uniform plates for Walter Richards' *Her Majesty's Army*, and represented *The Graphic* in the Kimberley relief column during the South African War.)

Some of the history-painters overlapped into the field of newspaper-illustration, of whom the most important was undoubtedly Richard Caton Woodville (1856–1927). The son of an American father and Russo–German mother, he became an ardent imperialist and supporter of British colonial operations, although his own military service was spent at home in the Berkshire and North Devon Yeomanry. He did, however, travel in hazardous regions such as the Balkans and North Africa, and went to Egypt in late 1882 to gather material for subsequent pictures. Through his style and prolific contributions to periodicals (notably *The Illustrated London News*), much of the public perception of later colonial warfare originated with his work, and although he presented essentially a 'heroic', even melodramatic version of events, paintings like his 'Maiwand: Saving the Guns' and the memorable vignette 'The Absent-Minded Beggar' tend to support his claim to be 'the English Meissonier'. He continued to illustrate battle-scenes during the First World War, in the same style which had appealed to popular sentiment during the Victorian era, and his later work, though still as competent artistically and reasonably accurate in terms of uniform and equipment, bore only limited relation to the appalling conditions which actually prevailed. Perhaps recognising that his era had passed, he shot himself in 1927.

A number of the most famous battle-painters of the Victorian era produced memorable canvases of colonial actions, although much history-painting was directed towards earlier wars. This was the case with the first rank of battle-painters, among whom may be included Lady Butler (Elizabeth Thomson), Robert Hillingford, Ernest Crofts, Vereker Hamilton and William Barnes Wollen. Elizabeth Thomson (1846–1933), wife of Sir William Butler, a distinguished soldier, is probably the most famous of the Victorian battle-painters, although her fame was probably founded more upon her Napoleonic scenes (most notably, perhaps, 'Scotland for Ever!' and 'Quatre Bras', the latter heralded by Ruskin as the first pre-Raphaelite battle-painting) and those of the Crimea (notably 'The Roll Call') than those of colonial campaigns, although

'Remnants of an Army', depicting Dr. Brydon's arrival at Jalalabad in 1842, was also one of her most celebrated. Robert Hillingford (1825–1904) concentrated more on earlier wars, but did produce some 'colonial' material in scenes of troops departing from Britain, and a canvas commemorating the end of the South African War of 1899–1902. Ernest Crofts (1847–1911) similarly concentrated on earlier campaigns, although his work had the added authenticity of one who had witnessed troops on campaign, he having followed the German army in Schleswig-Holstein and in the Franco–Prussian War, and even if he rarely saw actual combat, the experience must have been of value. Vereker Monteith Hamilton (1856–1931) was an artist whose principal battle-paintings concentrated on the colonial wars; the brother of the future general Sir Ian Hamilton, he had gone to India in 1886 and presumably gained a sense of the ambience of the country for the canvases he produced subsequently, including, for example, his 1895 'Storming of the Cashmere Gate', based on sketches taken at the site of the action and under Lord Roberts' supervision. William Barnes Wollen (1857–1936) was another whose work ranged widely over various historic periods, but included some memorable 'colonial' subjects, for example 'The Last Stand of the 44th Regiment at Gundamuck, 1842', through to the South African War; his 'Imperial Light Horse at Waggon Hill, January 6, 1900', is almost as far removed from conventional battle-painting as could be, showing khaki-clad figures crouching behind rocks, only half-visible in the twilight, and altogether more realistic than the conventional approach.

Other notable painters of this genre included the artist-correspondent Charles Fripp (1854–1906), whose 'The Last Stand at Isandhula' (*sic*: Isandlwana) is among the most famous images of the Zulu War, and was based on the artist's experiences covering the war for *The Graphic*; his 'The Attack on General Sir John McNeill's force near Suakim', depicting a battle at which he had been present, is one of the most spirited and authentic scenes of the horror and confusion of such a close-quarter fight. Another artist-correspondence, Frederick Villiers, also exhibited pictures in addition to his 'journalistic' work. Others included James Princip Beadle (1863–1947), whose best-known work showed earlier wars; and John Charlton (1849–1917), whose most spirited and probably best-known 'colonial' work was 'British Artillery entering the enemy's lines at Tel-el-Kebir', though his later painting 'Charge of the Light Brigade' is probably equally famous. (Evidence of how an artist might exploit one theme is provided by Charlton's artillery picture; its genesis was an illustration he executed for *The Graphic*, and it was strongly echoed in a later painting, 'Placing the Guns', set in the Sudan.) Louis Desanges (1822–87) produced a number of pictures in a series depicting Victoria Cross incidents (1859–61, including Indian Mutiny scenes), and probably

the only major painting of the Ashanti campaign, using Melton Prior's first-hand sketches. Orlando Norie (1832–1901) was a prolific watercolourist who specialised in military subjects, many of his pictures showing scenes at home but including some campaign studies, and work in oil was not unknown. David Cunliffe, an artist based in Portsmouth and perhaps best-known for uniform-studies and scenes of troops at home, also produced two noted 'campaign' subjects, both involving the 13th Light Infantry, 'The Heights of Truckee' and 'The Sortie from Jellalabad 1842', the latter remarkable for its depiction of early campaign uniform, about which he was presumably advised by participants in the action. Thomas Baines (1820–75) was one of these artists whose work was restricted to one region or campaign; he produced a series of pictures based on his own observations, or upon accounts of participants, showing the Cape Frontier Wars (1846–7 and 1851–2), including some work for *The Illustrated London News* and some published in print form.

Not all the artists who produced images of colonial warfare were British; Louis Desanges, for example, was French, and the Swiss Frank Feller was the painter of the well-known 'The Last Eleven at Maiwand', showing the last stand of the 66th. The great French battle-painter Alphonse de Neuville (1835–85) produced memorable depictions of Rorke's Drift and the attack of the Black Watch at Tel-el-Kebir, the latter painted with such close co-operation of those actually present that named individuals, from commander to private soldiers, are identified. His two other well-known Zulu War scenes, showing the escape of Melvill and Coghill from Isandlwana, and the discovery of their bodies, are not devoid of inaccuracies and are perhaps somewhat too sentimental and contrived to be as effective as his other works. Even the title of the latter, 'The Last Sleep of the Brave', is somewhat melodramatic and perhaps not as effective as its apparent French title, 'Morts pour le Drapeau'.[37]

For historians the question of accuracy looms larger than for art critics, and on the subject of 'realism' it is interesting to reflect upon some contemporary remarks: '... the English are less a military than a warlike nation. Realistic battle-pictures are not acceptable to the ordinary gallery visitor. Unmitigated accuracy in horror painting is repellent to our people. So far from revelling in blood, like the French – if the average Salon may be called to witness – the public shrinks from the sight of real sanguinary warfare. We are not a blood-loving people; and we do not care to have the horrors of the battlefield thrust upon us in the peaceful name of Art ... we like to have our battle-pictures prepared, so to say, for delicate stomachs – on the clear principle that nothing is permissible in art which revolts.' A further restriction, it was stated, was a lack of interest in 'battles in which blacks are the foe – where the fight is between civilisation and savagery – where the enemy is to be shot down at long range than fought at close quarters;

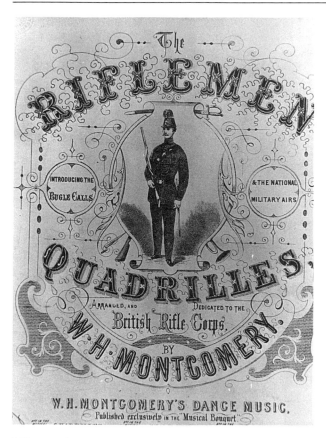

Military subjects were popular in the field of sheet-music and songs. This is a typical example of c.1860.

and where the chivalry of war is totally absent on the other side.' A criticism made of Caton Woodville was that while the details in his pictures might be carefully observed, his pictures were less like pictures than 'illustrations painted huge', suggestive of a critic more concerned with artistic composition than the historical accuracy of the scenes depicted.[38] (In the field of art criticism, there is sometimes a tendency to overlook errors of fact and to evaluate only the 'artistic' element of a work or art, in the case of critics not equally concerned with historical accuracy; for the most expert form of military and artistic study, the reader is recommended to Peter Harrington's *British Artists and War: The Face of Battle in Paintings and Prints 1700–1914*, London, 1993, a most important work.)

It was natural that in the field of popular art, British reverses were portrayed in the most heroic light; indeed, some of the most popular paintings were those which depicted British 'pluck' in adversity. Presumably this accounts for the popularity of scenes of 'last stands' and images such as George Joy's 'Death of General Gordon', which emphasise the nobility of sacrifice in defeat. Occasionally, however, paintings were criticised for being too dismal, which (for example) caused Joseph Paton to alter

his 'In Memoriam'; originally intended to show a group of women and children awaiting a perhaps grisly fate during the Indian Mutiny, it was amended by the addition of a group of Highlanders in the background, so that it presented the moment of salvation.[39]

Many of the history painters went to considerable lengths to ensure the accuracy of their subject-matter, and some were enthusiastic students of arms and armour; for example, Seymour Lucas (1849–1923) was a leading figure in the Kernoozers' Club, an association of arms and armour collectors and enthusiasts, of which Crofts and Hillingford were among other distinguished members. Just as the great French battle-painters like de Neuville surrounded themselves with references and pieces of arms, armour, uniforms and military accoutrements, so did some of the British artists, and otherwise took great care to study the subject so as to portray their work as accurately as possible. In some cases this included sketching soldiers from life, and when Lady Butler was painting her 'Roll Call' she employed ex-soldiers (including at least one Crimea veteran) to stand as models, dressed in uniforms and equipment of the period acquired from second-hand shops. Her 'Quatre Bras' was painted after she had arranged for 300 Royal Engineers to march and drill especially for her benefit, to observe exactly how a square was formed; and for her 'Balaclava' she used as the model for the central figure an actual survivor from the charge of the Light Brigade. For 'The Defence of Rorke's Drift', commissioned by the Queen, Lady Butler was able to include actual portraits of all the VC winners, most of the individuals in question being ordered to sit for her, re-enacting the action and wearing the costumes worn at the time. Lady Butler went to Egypt with her husband, and although she was not actually in the theatre of campaign, made many sketches of the region, had Wolseley sit for her picture 'After the Battle' (of Tel-el-Kebir), and when preparing the illustrations for her husband's book *The Campaign of the Cataracts, being a Personal Narrative of the Great Nile Expedition of 1884–85* (London, 1887), she obviously used his knowledge to achieve maximum authenticity.

Similar efforts seem to have been made by many of the battle-painters, if for no other reason than the knowledge that their work would be scrutinised by many of the participants of the scenes they portrayed. So convincing were some paintings that participants imagined that the artist had actually been present; others are far less accurate. As in the realm of newspaper illustration, one difficulty which may be encountered is the fact that an artist painted what was believed to be accurate, often from personal observation of troops, but which failed to take into account modifications made on active service without the artist's knowledge. Thus, Lady Butler's 'Rescue of Wounded, Afghanistan', which probably represents Maiwand, shows gunners of the Royal Artillery wearing dark blue 'frocks', whereas in fact they wore khaki during this

A typical 'patriotic' cover for a book of sheet-music, in this case the pianoforte score of John Pridham's 'The Triumphant Entry into Delhi'. (Print after G. Brandard)

campaign; Lady Butler's portrayal was presumably based on her own observations of gunners in Egypt and the Sudan, where blue frocks *had* been worn.[40] This hazard of portraying a correct uniform but in the wrong circumstances was recognised by the best of the artist-correspondents, hence the frequent manuscript notations present on their original sketches, intended as guidance for the engraver; for example, when Melton Prior sent sketches of the Royal Navy in Egypt in 1882 he included such notations as 'white Caps – Dark Blue Coats & Trousers'; 'Naval officer – white covering to Cap, Blue Jacket'; 'white blankets', etc.[41] Although many contemporary illustrations are irreplaceable sources for information on the appearance of troops on campaign, such factors should always be borne in mind when illustrations are evaluated.

PHOTOGRAPHY

From the middle of the 19th century the technological development of photography permitted the most accurate record to be made of the appearance of troops and loca-

tions on campaign. Initially, however, the process was ponderous, and not until the 1890s were cameras sufficiently portable, and exposure-time sufficiently short, for real 'action' images to be recorded.

Military subjects were recorded almost from the birth of conventional photography, and within a comparatively short time photographs of great sophistication were possible; the work of Roger Fenton in the Crimean War, for example, is regarded rightly as among the early classics of the photographer's art. Military subjects, however, had been recorded for some years before the Crimean War, despite the fact that because of the technical processes involved, only certain subjects were suitable. The earliest 'war' photographs so far discovered apparently date from the US–Mexican War, produced by the daguerreotype process, by which images were recorded directly upon chemically-coated metal plates. This and similar techniques were somewhat impracticable for most 'campaign' use, but the calotype process, invented by Fox Talbot and patented in 1841, utilised a paper negative which was easier and cheaper to use, although it produced a more 'grainy' image than the daguerreotype. This process was used by the first British-colonial military photographer, John MacCosh (1805–85), a surgeon of the 31st Bengal Native Infantry and 2nd Bengal Europeans in the Second Sikh War, and who served with the Bengal Artillery in Burma in 1852–3. In both these campaigns he produced remarkable images, both portraits and views, achieving high standards considering the limitations of calotype, the problems of climate and tribulations of campaign. He recommended all assistant-surgeons to take up photography (presumably thinking that their knowledge of chemicals would facilitate the hobby) and produce images of people, wildlife and landscapes as an academic study; and advised the use of sturdy, brass-bound cameras made of seasoned wood, not the more portable cameras popular in Europe, which would admit light though the cracks caused by the shrinkage induced by the climate.

The early enthusiasm for photography led to a number of major developments in mid-century, which not only improved the quality and ease with which photographs could be taken, but more importantly opened the subject to a much wider field. Notable developments were the glass-plate negative of Frederick Scott Archer (1851), which permitted more than one print to be produced from each exposure, and the use of improved processes, especially collodion, which were simpler to use in the emulsion and dry form. Gelatin emulsion, originating with Dr. R. L. Maddox as early as 1871, and in wide use by the end of the decade, reduced the difficulties of photography even further, and the development of the 'box' camera in the 1890s produced an apparatus for everyman. Instead of ponderous mechanisms with glass-plate negatives, which necessitated a careful selection of subject because of the difficulty and expense involved in the preparation of every image, portable roll-film cameras such as those first produced by the Eastman Company of Rochester (USA) in 1888 enabled officers to make personal records of their travels, and thus it was possible for any soldier to become a front-line photographer.

Studio and portrait photography remained the preserve of the professional, so that most garrison towns, even in comparatively isolated colonial stations, included a photographer's studio. Many genuine 'campaign' photographs were taken by professionals employed by the illustrated periodicals, but just as the earliest photographers were all enthusiastic amateurs, so many of the important military photographs in the later 19th century were taken by amateurs, officers who packed a camera as part of their campaign kit. Such was the popularity of the new medium that within a year of its foundation in 1854 the Bombay Photographic Society had almost 200 members, and from 1855 cadets at the Company's training-college at Addiscombe were trained in photography, presumably as an aid to military duty and to record the process of military and civilian construction-work supervised by the army. Later it became commonplace to take cameras on campaign; indeed, engineers were specially trained as photographers for the Tirah campaign, for example, while on other occasions civilian professional photographers accompanied the army in a semi-official capacity. One of the most important of the early campaign photographers was Felice Beato, an Italian, who took some memorable landscape views of Indian Mutiny scenes, and was also present in China in 1860. Professional photography spread throughout the sphere of British influence and produced such outstanding 'local' photographers as Lala Deen Dayal, the official photographer to the Nizam of Hyderabad, whose company Dayal & Sons was responsible for some extremely good images of Indian manoeuvres in the 1880s and 1890s.

Although group photographs and landscapes were always popular, probably the most prolific form of photographic record was the portrait, notably of the small *carte-de-visite* style; and in addition to such photographs being specially commissioned by the sitter, their relations or friends, commercial photographers and their agents also sold images to the general public, sometimes of famous individuals, scenes and even photographic reproductions of paintings, so that a contemporary photograph-album which contains (for example) original photographs of European crowned heads does not necessarily imply that the owner of the album had any personal acquaintance with the famous individuals included in the collection. An innovation which attained great popularity from the 1860s was the stereoscopic photograph, a system whereby dual images recorded from slightly different angles could be seen through a hand-held viewer to produce a three-dimensional picture. Numerous military subjects were

available in this form; the American company of Underwood & Underwood was the leader in the field, producing both individual cards and boxed sets of up to 150 cards (on the South African War, for example) in immense quantities, up to 25,000 per day by the turn of the century.

Technical restrictions must be remembered when evaluating contemporary photographs for their historic or artistic content. The earliest processes, which did not use a negative – daguerreotype (which recorded the image on silver-coated copper), ambrotype (on glass) and tintype (on sheet iron) – produced 'reversed' images, a mirror-image of reality, which must be remembered when using such photographs as references for the appearance of uniform and equipment. (It was not unknown for sitters to attempt to compensate for this by deliberately altering the appearance of their equipment; if a sword-belt were worn upside-down, for example, so that the slings hung on the right side, it would appear in the photograph the they were (correctly) on the left side, even though the belt-clasp would be upside-down!) Until the later technological developments, exposure-times were so long that only posed photographs were possible, initially precluding any spontaneous images, although on rare occasions it was possible for photographs to be taken under fire (for example, Surgeon-Major P. G. Fitzgerald, temporarily attached to the 1st Madras Fusiliers, took a group photograph of fellow-officers on the roof of the Alumbagh house outside Lucknow in February 1858, roundshot actually passing over their heads during the exposure. Hardly surprisingly, he bemoaned the fact that his subjects were 'very unsteady' and so produced a less than perfect picture![42] A further restriction on the immediacy of photography lay in the ponderous nature of the equipment required with early cameras, which meant that early 'battle' photographs were limited to scenes of the aftermath. That Roger Fenton (and later James Robertson, who photographed Sevastopol after its capture) recorded no images of the carnage of war was probably because no opportunity was available, rather than from reasons of taste and decency, for contemporary mores included ideas which to modern eyes seen distinctly odd. 'Formal' portraits of the dead were quite common in the mid-19th century, and Beato was observed at a Taku fort in 1860 eagerly photographing a group of dead Chinese sprawled around a gun, a scene which he described as 'beautiful,[43] an adjective which to modern eyes appears quite inexplicable, even in terms of artistic composition! (Similar 'taste' is evident in two of Beato's Indian Mutiny scenes, one showing two Indians suspended from a gallows, the other of skeletons scattered outside the Secunderabagh at Lucknow.) None of the contemporary photographers, however, dwelt upon the terrible realities of war, although a few such images emanated from the South African War, for example. The majority of 'campaign' photographs presented to the public exhibit what might be termed the 'acceptable' face of warfare, not its consequences, a standard which has been applied equally at times during the twentieth century.

Apart from such matters of taste, another factor must be considered in regard to the evaluation of photographs. The demand for 'action' images being greater than the capacity of photographers to supply them, many 'posed' or 'staged' photographs may be encountered, some arranged in so amateurish or melodramatic a fashion that their 'staging' is obvious. Included among these are scenes showing troops in foreign service uniform but photographed in Britain, one of which purports to depict the storming of a kopje in South Africa but was probably actually staged at Hampstead. Less obvious faking could be achieved by removing the background from a photograph and substituting a new one, turning what was obviously a peacetime scene into one which supposedly depicts active service.

Despite the later innovations which permitted photographs to be reproduced in newspapers, this development did not immediately signal the end of the artist-correspondent, for there remained a large demand for 'action' scenes, and artistic rather than photographic images continued to flourish even in the illustrated papers current during the First World War.

Cover for the sheet-music of the song 'Dinna' ye Hear It?' by Alexander Maclagen and J. P. Knight, taken from Frederick Goodall's painting 'The Campbells are Coming!', referring to the story of 'Jessie' at Lucknow.

Notes

1. Wellington to Robert Craufurd, 23 July 1810; *Dispatches of Field Marshal the Duke of Wellington*, ed. J. Gurwood, London 1834–8, vol. VI, p. 287.
2. Forbes, A. *Camps, Quarters, and Casual Places*, London, 1896, p. 155.
3. Menpes, M. *War Impressions*, London, 1901, pp. 149–50.
4. Ibid., pp. 138–9.
5. *Navy and Army Illustrated*, vol. III, p. 29, 8 January 1897.
6. Magnus, P. *Kitchener: Portrait of an Imperialist*, London, 1968, p. 166.
7. Boyce Combe of the 9th Lancers, in *Letters from B. A. C. (Afghanistan 1878-80)*, privately-printed, London 1880 (in which the names of officers were deliberately omitted for publication, where possible).
8. De Cosson, E. A. *Days and Nights of Service with Sir Gerald Graham's Field Force at Suakin*, London, 1886, p. 7.
9. The best and very plausible account of the suppression is 'The Strange Case of the Missing Official History' by Brian Robson (author of a major history of the Second Afghan War), in *Soldiers of the Queen 76*, Victorian Military Society, 1994.
10. The case for its authenticity is given, for example, in 'The Autobiography of an Indian Soldier', by Colonel Sir Patrick Cadell, in *Journal of the Society for Army Historical Research*, vol. XXXVII, 1959, and some of the questions it poses in ibid., vol. XXXVIII, 1960, pp. 88–9.
11. 'G. H.' in *United Service Journal* 1834, vol. I, p. 399; presumably either Lieutenant George Harrison, 79th, or Captain George Holmes, 92nd.
12. Winstock, L. *Songs and Music of the Redcoats*, London, 1970, p. 230.
13. *United Service Magazine*, 1842, vol. I, p. 564.
14. *United Service Journal*, 1836, vol. III, p. 144.
15. Heaton, Captain. *Notes on Rifle-Shooting*, London, 1864, pp. 15–16.
16. Smith, H. *The Volunteers' Manual of Health and Vigour*, London, 1860, pp. 55, 80, 81.
17. *Navy and Army Illustrated*, vol. IX, p. 319, 16 December 1899.
18. This theme is explored, for example, in 'Boer War Fiction', by R. W. F. Droogleever, in *Soldiers of the Queen 52*, Victorian Military Society, 1988.
19. 'An Empire Saved: The Story of a Second Mutiny', by W. Wood, in *Navy and Army Illustrated*, vol. VIII, p. 43, 1 April 1899.
20. 'Search-Light' in *Navy and Army Illustrated*, vol. IX, p. 319, 16 December 1899.
21. Henty, G. A. *With Kitchener in the Soudan*, London, n.d., p. 127.
22. Ibid., p. vi.
23. Quoted in *Navy and Army Illustrated*, vol. VII, p. 281, 10 December 1898.
24. Hart, Colonel C. J. *The History of the 1st Volunteer Battalion The Royal Warwickshire Regiment*, Birmingham, 1906, p. 160.
25. The true story of Moyes is recounted in 'A Postscript to "The Private of the Buffs"', by J. P. Entract, in *Journal of the Society for Army Historical Research*, vol. XLI, 1963, pp. 42–5.
26. This unusual name was presumably derived from the title of Captain Marryat's story *Snarley-Yow, or the Dog Fiend* (1837).
27. Composed by G. D. Wheeler; quoted in *Songs and Music of the Redcoats*, L. Winstock, London, 1970, p. 359; the text of *The Whitechapel Polka* can be found in ibid., p. 195, and this excellent work should be consulted for a detailed account of the songs popular with the army.
28. Forbes-Mitchell, W. *Reminiscences of the Great Mutiny*, London, 1897, p. 141.
29. *Navy and Army Illustrated*, vol. VII, p. 161, 5 November 1898.
30. See 'Major A C. Lovett: Soldier-Artist', by R. G. Harris, in *Journal of the Society for Army Historical Research*, vol. LXVII, 1989, pp. 1–15.
31. *Letters and Sketches of Francis R. Warre Cornish, late Captain 17th Bengal Lancers*, Eton, 1902, pp. 277–8.
32. This illustration is reproduced in P. Johnson's *Front Line*

Artists, London, 1978, p. 126.

33. Some of his sketches are reproduced in *Military Drawings and Paintings in the Royal Collection*, by A. E. Haswell Miller and N. P. Dawnay, London, 1966, vol. I.

34. See *An Artist on the March: Paintings of India, Abyssinia and Kashmir*, by Colonel Cornelius Francis James, St. Peter Port, Guernsey, 1989.

35. Forbes-Mitchell, *op. cit.*, pp. 158–9.

36. See Harrington, P. *British Artists and War: The Face of Battle in Paintings and Prints 1700-1914*, London, 1993, p. 221.

37. See Chabert, P. *Alphonse de Neuville: l'épopée de la défaite*, Paris, 1979, p. 73.

38. 'Battle-Painting and Mr. Ernest Crofts, R A.', by M. H. Spielmann, in *Cassell's Magazine*, 1902, pp. 421–3.

39. The full story of this painting can be found in Harrington, *op. cit.*, pp. 165–6.

40. See Boris Mollo's appendix, 'The Depiction of Uniform', in *Lady Butler: Battle Artist 1846-1933*, by P. Usherwood and J. Spencer-Smith, Gloucester and London, 1987, p. 179; and a reconstruction of the uniform actually worn in *The British Army on Campaign (3) 1856-1881*, by M. J. Barthorp, London, 1988.

41. *Illustrated London News*, 5 August 1882.

42. 'Roof of Alumbagh House: Officers of the Picket, February 1858', by M. A. Cane, in *Journal of the Society for Army Historical Research*, vol. LV, 1977, pp. 135–7.

43. Rennie, D. F. *British Arms in North China and Japan*, London, 1864, p. 112.

References: Source-material
The following works relate to matters raised in the foregoing section; bibliographies are not included below, nor are articles, although some are important sources for informed criticisms, for example 'Military Historians and the South African War: A Review of Recent Literature', by I. F. W. Beckett, in *Soldiers of the Queen 54*, Victorian Military Society, 1988.

Anon. *The Army in India 1850-1914: A Photographic Record*, London, 1968 (an important study including material relating to early photographers).

Army Museums Ogilby Trust. *Index to British Military Costume Prints 1500-1914*, London, 1972.

Atkins, J. B. *The Life of Sir William Howard Russell, the First Special Correspondent*, London, 1911.

Barnes, J. *Filming the Boer War: The Beginnings of the Cinema in England 1894-1901*, vol. IV, London, 1992

Bowie, J. *The Empire at War*, London, 1989 (photographs, 1848-1908).

Bullard, F. *Famous War Correspondents*, London, 1914 (includes Russell, Forbes, Villiers, etc.).

Butler, Lady Elizabeth. *An Autobiography*, London, 1922 (Elizabeth Thompson, Lady Butler, the artist).

Cane, M. *Harry Payne, Military Artist 1858-1927*, Kingston, 1977.

Carman, W. Y. *Richard Simkin's Uniforms of the British Army*, Exeter, 1982–5 (includes a biography of the artist which notes his methods of working, and evaluates the degree of reliability of his uniform studies).

Carter, A. C. R. *The Work of the War Artists in South Africa*, London, 1900.

Churchill, W. L. S. *Young Winston's Wars: the Original Despatches of Winston S. Churchill, War Correspondent 1897-1900*, ed. F. Woods, London, 1972.

Crookshank, Lieutenant-Colonel C. de W. *Prints of British Military Operations: A Catalogue raisonné with Historical Descriptions covering the Period from the Norman Conquest to the Campaign in Abyssinia*, London, 1921.

Desmond, R. *Victorian India in Focus*, London, 1982 (early photography in India).

Forbes, A. *Memories and Studies of War and Peace*, London, 1895 (on being a war correspondent).

Furneaux, R. *News of War: Stories and Adventures of the Great War Correspondents*, London, 1964.

– *The First War Correspondent: William Howard Russell of 'The Times'*, London, 1944.

Greenwall, R. *Artists and Illustrators of the Anglo-Boer War*, Cape Town, 1992.

Hankinson, A. *Man of Wars: William Howard Russell of The Times, 1820-1907*, London, 1982.

Harrington, P. *British Artists and War: The Face of Battle in Paintings and prints, 1700-1914*, London, 1993 (the outstanding work on the subject, which appreciates both the military and artistic aspects, unlike some criticisms which concentrate only on the latter).

Hichberger, J. W. M. *Images of the Army: the Military in British Art 1815-1914*, Manchester, 1988.

Hodgson, P. *Early War Photographs*, Boston, 1974.

– *The War Illustrators*, London, 1977.

James, Colonel L. *High Pressure: being some Record of Activities in the Service of The Times Newspaper*, London, 1929 (includes India, Sudan, South Africa).

Johnson, P. *Front Line Artists*, London, 1978 (the artist-correspondents).

Menpes, M. *War Impressions*, London, 1901 (account and illustrations by a war artist during the South African War).

Oosthuizen, P. *Boer War Memorabilia: the Collectors' Guide*, London, 1987 (excludes medals and militaria: concentrates on memorabilia, commemoratives, etc., and the influence of a colonial war upon popular decoration and culture).

Prior, M. *Campaigns of a War Correspondent*, ed. S. L. Bensusan, London, 1912 (memoirs of Melton Prior).

Usherwood, P., and Spencer-Smith, J. *Lady Butler, Battle Artist 1946-1933*, Gloucester and London, 1987.

Villiers, F. *His Five Decades of Adventure: Frederic Villiers, War Artist and Correspondent*, London, 1921.

– *Pictures of Many Wars*, London, 1979.

Wilkinson-Latham, R. *From our Special Correspondent: Vietnam War Correspondents and their Campaigns*, London, 1979.

Worsick, C., and Embree, A. *The Last Empire: Photography in British India, 1855-1911*, London, 1976

References: Colonial Wars
In addition to the references listed under individual sections, the following cover more than one theatre of war or are of more 'general' content.

Barthorp, M. *The British Army on Campaign 1816-1902*, London, 1987–8: four-part series covering (1) 1816–53, (2) The Crimea 1854–56, (3) 1856–81, (4) 1882–1902.

Bond, B. (ed.). *Victorian Military Campaigns*, London, 1967 (includes accounts of Sikh Wars, Third China War, Abyssinia, Ashanti 1873–4, Transvaal, Egypt 1882 and Sudan 1896–9 campaigns).

Bowie, J. *The Empire at War*, London, 1989 (collection of photographs relating to numerous campaigns).

Duncan, J., and Walton, J. *Heroes for Victoria*, Tunbridge Wells, 1991 (includes a number of campaigns and the British forces involved).

Farwell, B. *Eminent Victorian Soldiers: Seekers of Glory*, London, 1986 (includes Gordon, Gough, Kitchener, Macdonald, Napier, Roberts, Wolseley and Wood).

– *Queen Victoria's Little Wars*, London, 1973.

Featherstone, D. *Colonial Small Wars 1837-1901*, Newton Abbot, 1973.

– *Victoria's Enemies: An A-Z of British Colonial Warfare*, London, 1989.

Forrest, G. W. *Sepoy Generals: Wellington to Roberts*, Edinburgh, 1901.

Haythornthwaite, P. J. *Uniforms Illustrated: Victorian Colonial Wars*, London, 1988.

Joslin, E. C., Litherland, A. R., and Simpkin, B. T. *British Battles and Medals*, London, 1988 (originally published under this title but with Major L. L. Gordon as the author, in succeeding editions from 1947 to 1979. Covers not only all the campaign medals and clasps awarded for colonial operations, but includes brief histories and lists the units involved in each particular operation).

Knight, I. *Queen Victoria's Enemies*, London, 1989–90: four-part series covering (1) Southern Africa, (2) Northern Africa, (3) India, (4) Asia, Australasia and the Americas.

Smith, P. C. *Victoria's Victories: Seven Classic Battles of the British Army 1849-1884*, Tunbridge Wells, 1987 (includes Gujerat, Taku Forts, Magdala, Ulundi, Tel-el-Kebir and Tamai).

Encyclopedia Britannica: the 11th edition (1910–11, i.e., that published after the era of colonial warfare) is useful for statistics, brief histories and details of institutions of the various territories, and for the background to the campaigns.

References: biography and personal reminiscences
The following includes biographies of significant individuals not listed in the biographical section, and a short selection of the very many published works of autobiography, memoirs and reminiscences.

Adye, General Sir John. *Recollections of a Military Life*, London, 1895 (includes Indian Mutiny, Egypt).

Anderson, Captain R. P. *A Personal Journal of the Siege of Lucknow*, ed. T. C. Anderson, London, 1858.

Anon. *Camp and Barrack-Room, or, the British Army as it is*, London 1846 ('by a late Staff-Sergeant of the 13th Light Infantry'; actually Staff-Sergeant Perceval).

Baden-Powell, Sir Robert. *Indian Memories*, London, 1915 (regimental duty in India).

Bancroft, N. W. *From Recruit to Staff Sergeant*, Simla, 1900 (orig. pubd. Calcutta, 1885, r/p with intro. by Major-General B. P. Hughes, Hornchurch, 1979) (Bengal Horse Artillery).

Blood, Sir Bindon. *Four Score Years and Ten: The Reminiscences of Sir Binden Blood*, London, 1933 (India, Zulu War, Egypt, South African War).

Bodell, J. *A Soldier's View of Empire: The Reminiscences of James Bodell, 1831–92*, ed. K. Sinclair, London, 1982 (China, Australia, New Zealand).

Brook-Shepherd, G. *Between Two Flags: the Life of Baron Sir Rudolph von Slatin Pasha*, New York, 1973.

Butler, Lieutenant-General Sir William. *Sir William Butler: An Autobiography*, London, 1911 (Egypt, Sudan, Ashanti, Red River campaigns).

Calladine, G. *The Diary of Colour-Sergeant George Calladine, 19th Foot 1793-1837*, ed. Major M. L. Ferrar, London, 1922 (includes Ceylon).

Coates, T. F. G. *Sir George White, VC: The Hero of Ladysmith*, London, 1900.

Colborne, Colonel the Hon. J. *With Hicks Pasha in the Soudan*, London, 1884.

Cree, E. H. *The Cree Journals: The Voyages of Edward H. Cree, Surgeon, RN 1837–1856*, ed. and intro. by M. Levien, Exeter, 1981 (includes service in China; illustrated by Cree).

De Cosson, Major E. A. *Days and Nights of Service with Sir Gerald Graham's Field Force at Suakin*, London, 1886; the 1990 London reprint is entitled *Fighting the Fuzzy-Wuzzy*.

Donne, Colonel B. D. A. *The Life and Times of a Victorian officer: being the journals and letters of Colonel Benjamin Donisthorpe Alsop Donne, CB*, ed. Major A. Harfield, Wincanton, 1986 (illustrated by Donne; includes Egypt, Sudan, Cyprus, West Indies).

Dundonald, Lieutenant-General Earl of. *My Army Life*, London, 1926 (includes Gordon relief expedition, South African War).

Edwardes, E. *Memorials of the Life and Letters of Major-General Sir Herbert Edwardes*, London, 1886.

Forbes-Mitchell, W. *Reminiscences of the Great Mutiny 1857-59*, London, 1897 (1st edn., 1893) (93rd Highlanders).

Forrest, G. W. *Life of Field Marshall Sir Neville Chamberlain*, Edinburgh, 1909.

Gordon, J. *My Six Years with the Black Watch 1881-1887*, Boston, 1929 (includes Egypt, Sudan).

Gowing, T. *A Soldier's Experience, or, A Voice from the Ranks*, Nottingham, 1907 (sergeant-major, 7th Fusiliers; includes Indian service).

Granville, T. *With the Cape Mounted Rifles: Four Years' Service in South Africa*, London, 1881 (campaigns 1877–81).

Hamilton, I. B. M. *The Happy Warrior: A Life of General Sir Ian Hamilton*, London, 1966 (includes Second Afghan War, Gordon relief expedition, North-West Frontier, South African War).

Harford, Colonel H. *The Zulu War Journal of Col. Henry Harford CB*, ed. D. Child, Pietermaritzburg, 1978.

Hervey, Captain A. *A Soldier of the Company: Life of an Indian Ensign, 1833-43*, ed. C. Allen, London, 1988.

Holmes, T. R. E. *Four Famous Soldiers*, London, 1889 (biographies of Sir Charles and Sir William Napier, Hodson and Sir Herbert Edwardes).

Jones, Captain O. J. *Recollections of a Winter Campaign in India in 1857-58*, London, 1859.

Keates, C. *A Soldier's India*, intro. by Revd. M. J. Fisher, Chapel-en-le-Frith, 1986 (Royal Artillery, 1887–95).

Lambrick, H. T. *John Jacob of Jacobabad*, London, 1960 (commander of the Scinde Horse).

Lumsden, General Sir Peter, and Elsmie, G. R. *Lumsden of The Guides: A Sketch of the Life of Lieut. Gen. Sir Harry Burnett Lumsden*, London, 1899.

Martin, D. *Duelling with Long Toms*, Ilford, 1988 (heavy artillery, South African War).

Munro, Surgeon-General William. *Reminiscences of Military Service with the 93rd Sutherland Highlanders*, London, 1883 (includes Indian Mutiny).

Pearman, J. *Sergeant Pearman's Memoirs*, ed. Marquess of Anglesey, London, 1968 (3rd Light Dragoons, including Sikh Wars).

Richards, F. *Old Soldier Sahib*, London, 1936; r/p, intro. by R. Graves, London, 1983 (classic account of rank-and-file in India).

Robertson, Field Marshal Sir William. *From Private to Field Marshal*, London, 1921.

Royle, T. *Death before Dishonour: the True Story of Fighting Mac*, Edinburgh, 1982 (biography of Major-General Sir Hector Macdonald).

Sale, Lady. *A Journal of the Disasters in Affghanistan 1841-2*, London, 1843; r/p as *Lady Sale: the First Afghan War*, ed. P. Macrory, London, 1969.

Shand, A. I. *General John Jacob: Commandant of the Sind Irregular Horse and Founder of Jacobabad*, London, 1900.

Slatin, R. *Fire and Sword in the Sudan: A Personal Record of Fighting and Serving the Dervishes 1879-1895*, trans. Major F. R. Wingate, London, 1896.

Smith, G. L. *A Victorian RSM: from India to the Crimea*, Winchester, 1987 (mainly Crimea, but includes Indian service 1836–8).

Smith-Dorrien, Sir Horace. *Memoirs of Forty-Eight Years' Service*, London, 1925 (includes Zulu and South African Wars).

Smithers, A. J. *The Man Who Disobeyed: Sir Horace Smith-Dorrien and his Enemies*, London, 1970 (much on First World War, but includes Zulu and South African Wars).

Stuart, Colonel W. K. *Reminiscences of a Soldier*, London, 1874 (86th Foot, West Indies, India).

Sylvester, J. H. *Cavalry Surgeon: the Recollections of John Henry Sylvester*, ed. A. McK. Annand, London, 1971 (India 1848–67, including Indian Mutiny, with 14th Light Dragoons and Beatson's Horse).

Tucker, F. *Private Tucker's Boer War Diary*, ed. P. Todd and D. Fordham, London, 1980 (Rifle Brigade).

Tytler, H. *An Englishwoman in India: The Memoirs of Harriet Tytler 1828-1858*, ed. A. Sattin, intro. by P. Mason, Oxford, 1988 (the only English woman with the army on 'the Ridge' at Delhi).

Waterfield, R. *The Memoirs of Private Waterfield*, ed. A. Swinson and D. Scott, London, 1968 (32nd Foot, India 1842–57).

Williams, C. *The Life of Lieut.-General Sir Evelyn Wood, VC*, London, 1892.

Wilson, Captain T. F. *Defence of Lucknow: A Diary recording the Daily Events during the Siege of the European Residency*, London, 1858 (published as being by 'a Staff Officer').

Wood, Lieutenant-General Sir Evelyn. *From Midshipman to Field Marshal*, London, 1906.

IX
GLOSSARY

Military service in the colonies introduced a new vocabulary into British military argot, and from the service of British troops and their dependants in such regions many words were absorbed into the English language in general (e.g., bungalow, chutney, loot, pyjamas). Such words are now so familiar as to require no explanation; but others may be found in contemporary sources without an immediate translation, for example:

'... when I then ferreted out the remnant of my ration rootie, I found the sun had made it hard and dry as a sapless twig ... suddenly a loud cry of "bout hatcha rootie gurhum rootie" rang through the camp. This was the cry of the lug wollah, and going to the tent door I shouted "Hedherow lug wollah", until the fellow appeared and supplied me with a two pice lug. The dhoud and muckin wollahs next coming round, a pice worth from each enabled me to fare sumptuously.' (*Camp and Barrack-Room, or, The British Army as it is, by a late Staff Sergeant of the 13th Light Infantry*, London, 1846, p. 125.)

Many Indian words which came into common use in the army were of Hindustani origin (Urdu), although not exclusively; Pushtu, for example, was the source of many words originating from the North-West Frontier. The cry 'Ya Hasan! Ya Hosain!' heard during the Islamic Moharram ceremonies (i.e., the first month of the year) was corrupted by the British to 'Hobson-Jobson', originally meaning excitement, but also came to be used as descriptive of Anglo-Indian argot, probably popularised by its use as a subtitle for Colonel Henry Yule and A. C. Burnell's *Glossary of Anglo-Indian Colloquial Words and Phrases* (London 1886). The extent to which words of Indian (and other overseas) origin entered the vocabulary of the British Army can be gauged from the glossary in *The Long Trail: What the British Soldier Sang and Said in the Great War of 1914-1918*, J. Brophy and E. Partridge, rev. edn. London, 1965. (By the same process, some English words infiltrated other languages; for example, the colloquialism 'manwar' used in the Arabian peninsula to describe a warship obviously originates with the archaic British term 'man-o'-war').

A very common feature encountered in contemporary sources is the different spelling of foreign words, where they were rendered phonetically from languages which in written form did not use the Roman alphabet. These spellings could be considerably divergent (Lady Sale, for example, uses the spelling 'pyjania' for 'pyjama'), and apart from the most common variation in the use of different vowels, words are sometimes even given different initials (e.g., *qizilbash, khizilbash*). In some cases in the following glossary two or more common spellings are given, although these do not represent all the varieties which may be encountered. Similarly, archaic military terms and colloquialisms are listed, as some might not be identified by modern dictionaries. Contemporary military dictionaries are a useful reference (e.g., *A Military Dictionary comprising Terms, Scientific and Otherwise, connected with the*

Science of War, Major-General G. E. Voyle and Captain G. de Saint-Clair-Stevenson, 3rd rev. edn., London, 1876); and for the terminology of non-British weaponry, G. C. Stone's *A Glossary of the Construction, Decoration and Use of Arms and Armor in all Countries and in all Times* (New York 1934, r/p 1961) is of use.

abbasi: Rajput straight-bladed sword; *abbasi tulwar* = a Punjabi slightly curved sabre.

abdar: Indian butler, or more literally a water-cooler.

acquittance roll: document showing the monthly settlement of accounts of a company, troop or battery.

adigar: Kandyan minister or officer of state; the senior of these was sometimes styled the *mahadigar*, by the addition of the prefix 'maha' = great.

adjutant: in addition to the military appointment, 'adjutants' was a nickname given to scavenging birds of prey in India, presumably reflecting the common opinion of the holders of the military office.

adjutant onderofficier: senior NCO or warrant officer in the forces of the South African Republic.

aeen: a heavy, hard wood (*Terminalia glabra*) from Madras, used especially by the Bombay gun-carriage construction organisation.

Afghan stock: the exaggeratedly curved musket-butt used by the inhabitants of Sind.

African pepper: soldiers' argot for sand, from the amount of it which found its way into their food.

agterryer: African servant who attended a Boer commando; lit. 'after-rider'.

ahir: Maratha curved sword.

ajat: an Indian expelled from his caste.

akali: Sikh religious zealot.

ak dum: 'instantly' (from Hindustani)

alkhalak, alkalak, alkaluk: long-skirted Indian cavalry tunic.

amabutho: Zulu organisation of 'guilds' according to the age of the members, and by extension, Zulu 'regiments'; plural of *ibutho*.

amakhanda: Zulu military barracks-village (plural of *ikhanda*).

amaviyo: Zulu 'company' within a 'regiment' (plural of *iviyo*).

amir, ameer: Indian or Afghan commander or chief; from Arabic amīr.

angarep: Egyptian bedstead.

angarka: loose robe as worn by the inhabitants of the North-West Frontier.

anna: one-sixteenth of an Indian rupee; by extension, a term for a sixteenth part of anything.

ansar: name given by the Mahdi to his followers, lit. 'helpers'.

ardeb: Egyptian measure equal to five bushels; from Arabic *irdab*.

ariki: Maori chief or leading warrior.

arrack: Indian alcoholic spirit, distilled from rice or palm sap, from Arabic *araq* = juice.

arsty: colloquialism for 'slow down' from Hindustani *ahisti*.

ASC: Army Service Corps (British Army, 1869–81 and post-1888).

asil: Maratha sword.

aspi: Sikh horse artillery.

assami: Indian office or appointment, applied particularly to an appointment in irregular cavalry.

assegai, assagai, hassegai: Southern African spear; the term is not of African origin but a French or Portuguese version of Arabic *azzaghāyah*.

ATA: Army Temperance Association.

atapattuwa: a class of Kandyan feudal 'militia'.

atishkana: Indian artillery park (from Persian *atish* = fire).

atta: Indian flour or ground corn (Hindustani).

ayah: Indian native nurse or maidservant.

ayda katti: the large knife-sword of the Coorgs.

ayenee: a tree from Southern India and Burma (*Artocarpus hirsuta*), providing wood suitable for gun-carriage construction.

babu, baboo: Indian clerk, originally a title of respect but later used derogatively of one who wrote unnecessarily complicated English, hence 'Babu-English'.

badmash, budmash: Indian bad character or scoundrel; *badmashi* = villainy.

bagdadder: Indian Army nickname for a soldier who drew his rum ration but sold it to his follows; the 'bag-dadding-rate' was the price at which such illicit rum-sales were made.

bagh: Indian garden, usually surrounded by a wall.

baghi: Indian mutineer or rebel.

bagh nakh: lit. 'tiger's claws'; an Indian knuckle-duster with four or five curved blades affixed; latterly used mainly by assassins, it was not considered to be an honourable weapon.

bahadur: Indian title for a brave warrior, added to the individual's name; also a boaster, hence verb 'to bahadur' = to brag (from Hindustani *bahadur* = brave).

ball: generic term for all kinds of bullet, not just musket-balls but the later type of projectiles as well; ball-cartridge = ammunition.

bandy: Indian covered cart, usually of Madras origin.

bank: Maratha knife with exaggeratedly curved blade.

Bangalore Gallopers: nickname of the 13th Light Dragoons, from their reckless style of riding.

bannermen: members of the Chinese Manchu forces, the army of 'the Eight Banners'.

banyan, banian: Indian loose jacket; also an Indian merchant, and a tree of the fig family. 'Banyan days' was a nautical expression for days when no meat-ration was issued, from the vegetarian diet of banyan traders.

barghir: Indian cavalryman, the follower of a native officer who maintained for him his horse and equipment.

barrow: Indian colloquial adjective for 'big', the opposite of the similar term *chota/choter*.

barutdan: Indo-Persian powder flask.

bassoolah: Indian adze, smaller and with a shorter handle than the European type.

bat: in addition to the ordinary English military usage (as in 'batman'), *bat* in Hindustani was an affair or matter, and was used to signify language, e.g., 'crab-bat' (q.v.); to 'sling the bat' was to be conversant with a particular foreign language

batta: Hindustani term for 'donation'; living-allowance paid to a soldier in India in addition to his pay. This varied according to location, hence 'single-*batta* station', 'double-*batta* station', etc.

bazu band: armoured arm-guard used in India and Persia, protecting the forearm from wrist to elbow.

BBP: Bechuanaland Border Police.

beegah: Indian measure of land equal to 20 *cottah*s or 14,400 square feet.

beiruk: standard of black, white and yellow, issued to each unit of 1,000 men in Hyder Ali's Mysore army.

bendie: a wood from the Bombay region (*Thespesia populnea*), used for the manufacture of spokes for artillery wheels.

Bengal light: blue illumination-flare composed of saltpetre, sulphuret of lead and sulphur in proportions 6:1:2; despite the name it was used in European warfare, not just in India.

bhala: Maratha cavalry lance or spear.

bhang: Indian narcotic, hashish or Indian hemp.

bhanghys: baggage; in India, boxes suspended from each end of a pole, carried over the shoulder.

bhisti, bheestie: Indian water-carrier, as attached to British units in India; probably derived from Persian *behisht* = heaven or delight, reflecting the relief provided by a water-carrier to a thirsty man.

bildar: Indian excavator or sapper.

Billait: see 'Blighty'.

Billy Stink: British Army colloquialism for rough Indian alcohol.

biltong: preserved, sun-dried salted meat, used as an 'iron ration' in South Africa.

BL: artillery classification: 'breech-loader'; BLR, 'breech-loading, rifled'.

black hole: common term for a military guardhouse or cell, not invariably referring to the infamous imprisonment of Europeans at Calcutta.

black pot: colloquialism for an Indian medical orderly (presumably from their dispensing of medicines from black bottles or jars).

blackwood: a tree of southern India (*Dalbergia latifolia*), the wood used in the manufacture of artillery carriages at Bombay.

Blighty: 'billait', 'blayut', 'wallyte', Indian term for Europe (Hindustani *bilaik*), perhaps from Arabic *walayat* = a kingdom or province; Anglicised as 'Blighty', meaning Britain.

blokes: colloquialism for a fellow or man, used as the nickname for the Punjab Garrison Battery, which took this title in 1889 and became the Frontier Garrison Artillery in 1901.

Blue Caps: (or 'Neill's Blue Caps'): nickname of 1st Madras Fusiliers in the Indian Mutiny, from the name of their commander (Lieutenant-Colonel James Neill) and their blue forage-caps.

bo, boh: Burmese title for a leader of a war-band or of dacoits, approximating to 'colonel' or 'leader'.

bobagee: Indian cook.

bobbery: colloquialism for a noisy quarrel or disturbance (from Hindustani *bāp re!* = 'O father!').

bosh, bash: colloquialism in India for nothing, humbug; probably from Turkish *bosh* = worthless.

bouilli: stewed beef, a term used for canned, preserved meat; hence 'bully beef'.

Brahmin: member of the Hindu priestly class, the highest caste.

Brummagen: derogatory adjective for cheaply produced arms made in Birmingham; used especially in New Zealand.

Buckmaster's Light Infantry: nickname (1840–56) of 3rd West India Regiment, from the tailor of that name putting light infantry wings on the uniforms of the battalion-company officers; the name even appeared in the *Army List*.

buckra, buccra: West Indian expression for a white man, said to mean 'demon' in the dialect of the Calabar coast; by extension, anything belonging to the whites, e.g., '*buckra* soldiers'.

buckshee, bukshee: colloquialism for surplus, a gift, something free, and by extension anything acquired without payment; from Hindustani, a development of Persian *baksheesh* = a gratuity.

budgerow: keel-less barge as used on the Ganges.

Bullfrogs: nickname of the Royal Canadian Rifle Regiment (1840–71).

bundok, bandak: Indian term for a gun, adopted as a British Army colloquialism for a rifle. Orig. Hindustani *banduk*, Arabic *bunduk*, said to be derived from *banadik*, Arabic for filberts, because they came from Venice (Arabic *banadik*), a term used at first for pellets and later applied to firearms. In Indian usage the term apparently came to describe a flintlock, though ultimately its use was much wider.

bun-puncher: derogatory colloquialism for a teetotaller.

burgher: in South Africa, a Boer settler, used also as the rank of private in a Commando; in Ceylon, a person of European ancestry.

burgue, burgoo: old army colloquialism for porridge, orig. from Arabic *burghal* = wheat-porridge.

burj, boorja: Indian tower or bastion.

burkandaz: Indian matchlockman (from Arabic and Persian *burk* = lightning, and *andaz* = throwing).

Button-stick: brass plate with a notch cut down the centre, used to protect the cloth when cleaning tunic-buttons.

bye-and-bye: Zulu nickname for a piece of artillery, said to date from their first contact with the British: when Lieutenant Farwell mounted guns around his house at Port Natal, he answered African questions about what they were by saying 'you shall see bye and bye'.

bywoner: South African squatter or white farm worker.

C & TC: Commissariat and Transport Corps, British Army 1881–8.

cacolet: folding chair carried one each side of a mule, for casualty evacuation.

cantonment: that part of an Indian town occupied by the garrison.

Cape Guards: nickname of the 72nd Foot, current in the late 1830s, from their long service in that colony.

carbonatjee: South African meat preserved by toasting or broiling in ashes.

carte de visite: lit. 'visiting card'; a small portrait photograph.

cash: Indian or Chinese coin of low value.

Catch-em-alive-ohs: nickname of the North-West Frontier levies such as the Khyber Rifles.

chagul: Indian water-bottle.

chakram, charka: Sikh throwing-quoit.

chalo!: Indian call for 'come on!'.

chamra: Hindustani for 'leather'; used to refer to a soldier's set of equipment.

chandmaree: Indian term for target- or range-practice.

chaony: Indian encampment or cantonment.

chapkan: Indian coat.

chapli, chappli: Indian leather or woven grass sandal.

char, cha: Indian term for tea (Hindustani); *char-wallah*, a teetotaller.

charjama: Indian saddlecloth.

charpoy: Indian litter or bed.

chatty: Indian metal water-bowl, usually brass.

chee-chee, chichi: derogatory description of the speech of Eurasians.

cheri: Indian term for a village, as in Pondicherry.

chilanum: Maratha doubly curved, double-edged dagger.

chillum: that part of an Indian hookah containing tobacco, and by extension any kind of tobacco-pipe.

chillumchee: Indian bowl for washing hands.

chit, chitti, chutti: an order or pass, or a short note, from Hindustani *chitti*; also used to describe a short leave.

chittack: Indian weight, just under two ounces; see '*chuttack*'.

choga: Indian long-sleeved coat or gown, sometimes with a hood.

chokey: a gaol or police station; from Hindustani *chowki* = a shed.

chokidar: Indian watchman or caretaker.

chokra: an officer's page in India, generally a young recruit.

choora, chura: large, straight-bladed knife, North-West Frontier and Afghanistan.

chota, choter: Indian adjective for 'small'.

chota hazri: Hindustani 'little breakfast'; used in India for a refreshment-break on the march, resembling 'afternoon tea'.

chubarrow, 'chub': colloquial expression for 'be quiet!', from Hindustani *chuprao*.

chuckler: Indian cobbler or leatherworker.

chudder, chadar: Indian garment, a wrap worn around the body; also used to describe a loincloth.

chupao: Indian night attack, surprise or foray; verb, to attack at night or surprise.

chupatty, chapati, chow-patty: Indian cake of unleavened bread.

chupkun: Indian quilted coat providing protection against sword-cuts, as worn by the Sikhs.

chuprassie, chuprassy, chaprassie: a responsible servant or messenger in India; from the wearing of a *chuprass* or *chaprass* = a badge of office.

chuttack: Indian unit of measurement: of land, one-sixteenth of a *cottah* or 45 square feet; of weight, one-sixteenth of a *seer* or one-eighth of a pound; see '*chittack*'.

circar, sarkar: 'government', term used in India commonly applied to officialdom.

CIV: City Imperial Volunteers, South African War; not to be confused, as happened at the time, with 'ICV', the First City Volunteers of Grahamstown.

civvies: army term for civilian clothes.

clink: colloquialism for prison, at least 18th-century in origin if not earlier.

CMR: Cape Mounted Rifles.

colonial allowance: allowance granted to British regiments to meet the extra expenses of foreign service; in 1878 this applied to Africa, Ceylon, China, Mauritius, the Straits Settlements and the West Indies; in India regiments received a separate India pay, and troops in the Mediterranean received extra rations instead.

commandant: commanding officer of a unit; see also '*Kommandant*'.

Commando: Boer military force formed by a version of *levée en masse*; less precisely, one who served in such a force.

compoo: a formation of Indian troops organised along European lines; equivalent to a brigade.

compound: enclosed ground surrounding a British building in India; from Portuguese *campenha* = a yard, or Malay *kampong* = an enclosure.

congee: Indian term for rice, or water in which rice had been boiled; *congee*-house, a colloquialism for prison (where presumably it was the principal diet).

connae: Indian term for food.

coolie: Indian term for a labourer, generally Indian or Chinese; from Hindustani *kuli*, or Tamil *kūli* = hire.

Coorg knife: a knife (see '*ayda katti*') characteristic of the Coorgs, a broad-bladed chopper-like weapon. A small version used more as a tool than a weapon was the *pichangatti*, a Tamil name signifying 'hand knife'.

corps troops: an army's supporting services (commissariat, transport, etc.) not attached at brigade or divisional level.

coss: an Indian measure of distance, usually taken as about 1¾–2 miles.

Cossack post: a cavalry outpost, usually of four men.

cottah: an Indian measurement; of land, 720 square feet; also a Madras weight = 16 *chuttack*s.

CRA: commandant (or commander), Royal Artillery; a title used by the senior artillery officer of an expedition, or of a division, or in a colony; CRE, the same for Royal Engineers.

crab-bat: colloquialism for pidgin Hindustani, consisting largely of oaths, used by British troops in India.

crackers: thorn-proof leather trousers worn in South Africa.

cranchee: a rudimentary Indian carriage, drawn by ponies.

cranny: an Indian clerk who could write English.

crop: an army haircut; the basic varieties were 'regimental crop' (in which the hair was uniformly cut all over to a length of about ½ an inch), and a 'respectable crop', undertaken with more care and leaving more hair at the sides.

crore: ten *lakhs* of rupees, or £1 million.

cuddy: the public cabin of an East Indiaman.

cushoon: Indian infantry formation, regiment or brigade, as used by the Mysore army.

cutcha: Indian term for soft or unripe, colloquially used as the opposite of *pukka*.

cutchery: an Indian court-house; the same term was used in the Mysore army for a brigade.

cutwal: Indian police officer.

dacoit: Indian or Burmese bandit; dacoity, the practice of banditry; from Hindustani *dakait* = a robber.

dah: Burmese sword.

dak, dawk: originally '*dak*' was the Indian mail-post, travelling by relays (from Hindustani *dak* = a relay of men); '*dak* bungalows' were government buildings erected every ten to twenty miles along roads in India, where travellers could rest for the night.

dalwel, dalwey: Burmese sword.

dammer: resinous exudation from a number of species of Indian trees, used by arsenals to waterproof packages of ammunition.

damper: Australian term for unleavened bread baked in the ashes of a camp-fire.

dandi: Indian sedan-chair type of litter, carried upon bearers' shoulders.

Dane gun: trade guns supplied to West Africa, generally flintlocks of inferior quality; in the Gold Coast the term originated from 18th century Danish muskets.

dastar bungga: the conical Sikh turban around which

throwing-quoits could be placed; unlike the ordinary Sikh turban, it had an internal cane framework.

daur, dour: Indian foray or raid.

DCLI: Duke of Cornwall's Light Infantry.

deen! deen!: Indian (Islamic) war-cry, meaning 'Religion! Religion!'.

dekko: to look, to watch, or used as a noun ('a *dekko*'); from Hindustani *dekhna*.

derah: Sikh 'brigade'; lit. a camp which accommodated a 'brigade group'.

dervish: the name given originally by the Mahdi to his followers, lit. 'poor men' or religious mendicants, later replaced by *ansar*, but in British accounts the Sudanese Mahdists in general where known as dervishes. (From Persian *darvish* = a poor man).

dhal: an Indian small, round shield; also an Indian pulse or split-pea.

dhall bush: Indian wood (*Cytisus cajan*) used to make charcoal for gunpowder.

dharmsala: Sikh temple.

dhobie, dhobie-wallah: Indian laundry-man.

dhoolie, doolie, duli: covered Indian palanquin, often used to carry the sick; from Hindustani *doli*.

dhoora: cereal resembling Indian corn.

dhoti: Indian loin-cloth.

dhoudh: Indian term for milk; *dhoudh-wallah*, a milk-seller.

dhurree: Indian coarse cotton carpet, also styled a *satringee*, used as a flooring for tents; issued to European soldiers in India, in which to fold bedding during a march.

dil: Indian term for spirit or 'heart' (e.g., to lose one's *dil* was to become discouraged).

Dirty-shirts: nickname for the Royal Munster Fusiliers; from the Indian Mutiny appearance of the Bengal Europeans.

dissawa: governor of a Kandyan province (*dissawane*).

disselboom: Afrikaans for 'pole'; generally the shaft of a horse-drawn vehicle.

diwan, dewan: Indian royal court or principal officer of state; Indian financial minister or steward; *dewani* or *dewanny* = the office of *dewan*.

dixie: military cooking-pot (from Hindustani *degshai* or *degchi*).

doab: in India, a tract of land between two rivers (from Persian *dōāb*, 'two waters'.

Dogra: term originally applied to the Rajput clans north of the Ravi, later extended to the 'hill Rajputs' south of the Ravi, and used in a military sense for all such Rajputs enlisted in the Indian Army.

donga: river-bed, often dry.

doolally, doolally-tap: colloquialism for insane, or a sufferer from sunstroke, from the hospital at Deolali in India; or from boredom at this station among men waiting to go home, being kept at Deolali until their time was expired. '*Tap*' is Hindustani for fever.

dop: colloquialism for Cape brandy.

dorp: South African town or village.

drift: South African ford through a river.

dubash, dobash: Indian interpreter (Hindustani *do-bash* = 'two-languaged'); by extension, an officer's head-servant. It was stated in 1844 that *dobash* or *dobashee* was a term peculiar to Madras.

dubber: Indian vessel of untanned hide, used for holding oil; also known as a *koopah*.

Ducks: nickname of the Bombay Army (from Bombay Duck, a fish of the Scopelidae family).

duffadar, daffadar: Indian cavalry sergeant; *kot-daffadar* = troop sergeant-major.

Duff-eater: nickname given by Irish troops in East India Company service to English members of the European Company regiments, from the traditional consumption of plum-duff (pudding) by the English; to duff, to do incompetently.

Dumpies: nickname for the Bengal European Light Cavalry, from the under-sized recruits whom they were permitted to enrol.

dun: a tract of terrain at the foot of hills, or valley.

dunga-wallah: Indian colloquialism for a mutineer (from *dunga* = argument or row).

dungee, dungaree: Indian coarse cotton cloth.

durbar: a meeting of dignitaries or conference of ministers in the presence of the ruler of a state; in military terms, an assembly of officers for the issuance of orders. From Persian *dar-bār* = a prince's court (lit. 'door of admittance').

duty man: not necessarily a soldier whose turn it was for a particular duty, but used colloquially for a man assiduous towards his occupation, who did not attempt to escape his duties or seek appointments with lighter responsibilities.

ek dum!: 'instantly!' (from Hindustani).

elephants' lugs: nickname given to large ration cakes in India, made from coarse flour, bran and chopped straw; from their resemblance to elephants' ears.

factory: a European trading-settlement in India.

fakir: Indian holy man, religious mendicant or penitent (from Arabic *fakr* = poverty).

fanam: small Indian coin; in Ceylon it equalled one-twelfth of a rix-dollar, i.e., British two-pence.

fanti: mad (from Hindustani).

Fauj-i-Ain: Sikh 'regular army'.

fellah, plural *fellahin*: term for the agricultural or labouring population of Egypt, applied contemptuously by the Turks, and used to describe the population from which the greater part of the Egyptian army was drawn. (From Arabic = 'tiller of the soil').

feringi, feringee, feringhee, faringee: Indian term for a European or foreigner, a corruption of 'Frank'.

FG: abbreviation for (i) 'field gun', (ii) 'fine grain' (of gunpowder).

field-cornet: see *Veldkornet*.

firangi: Indian straight-bladed sword as used by the Marathas, sometimes with European blade; derived from the same source as '*feringi*'. *Feringiha* was an early Indian term for a cannon, evidently regarded as a foreign invention.

Flamingoes: Indian Mutiny-period nickname for Hodson's Horse, from their scarlet shoulder-sash and turban worn with a khaki uniform.

Fogs: 'Old Fogs' was the nickname of the East India Company's Foot Artillery.

fontein: South African spring or rivulet.

frock: undress tunic, usually devoid of the ornamentation found on the dress tunic.

FS: 'field service', as in 'f.s. cap'.

funk-hole: an earthwork shelter, a term dating from the South African War, but not implying criticism of its occupants despite the civilian colloquialism 'funk' = cowardice.

furlough: leave; in India this was often of considerable duration, both for British officers returning home for a period of months, or for Indian enlisted men travelling to their homes for a similar period.

fuzzy-wuzzy: British Army nickname for the Sudanese or dervish warriors in general, although it originated from the 'fuzzy' hairstyle of the Beja people of eastern Sudan.

gagra-wallah: Indian nickname for a Highland soldier, lit. 'petticoat-man', from the wearing of the kilt.

galloper: light fieldpiece attached to a cavalry regiment.

Garvies: nickname of the 94th Foot, at one time composed of small men; 'garvie' is a colloquialism for herring.

gasht: Indian term for a military patrol.

gentleman-ranker: colloquialism for a man of good family or education who was serving in the ranks.

ghari, gharry: Indian cart (Hindustani); *gharrywan, ghareewan* = a gharry-driver.

ghat: landing-place on an Indian river-bank; a mountain pass, or chain of mountains (Hindustani).

ghazi: Indian religious fanatic; *ghaza* was a murder committed for religious reasons by an Islamic warrior against a Christian or Hindu.

ghee: Indian clarified butter (Hindustani *ghī*).

ghorchurra: Sikh irregular cavalry.

ghubara: Persian term for a bomb or shell.

ghurrah: Indian clay water-pot.

ghurrie: circular gunmetal plate issued to regiments in India for the purpose of striking the hours.

gingal: see '*jingal*'.

Gippy: slang for Egyptian.

gobrowed: Indian term to indicate 'dumbfounded'.

GOC: 'general officer commanding'.

godown: Indian storehouse or granary.

golees: Indian balls or bullets.

golundauze: Indian Army 'native' artillery; lit. a thrower of balls, from Persian *gol* = a ball, and *andakhtun* = to throw.

gomashta: Indian clerk or assistant storekeeper, as in 'commissariat gomashta'.

goojers, gujars: Hindu bandits; later applied to any Indian bandit.

Granth: the holy book of the Sikh religion.

grasshopper-gun: nickname for a *jingal*.

greyback: British Army flannel shirt, from the colour.

gridiron: common nickname of the East India Company's horizontally-striped naval ensign.

griffin, griff: colloquialism for a British newcomer to India; it was stated in 1838 that a newcomer remained a 'griffin' until he had served a year and a day in India ('Burmah and the Burmese during the Late War', Major Bennett, 2/Royal Scots, in *United Service Journal* 1838, vol. III p. 77); 'griffin' was used during the First World War as a colloquialism for information.

guddeelah: protective, padded saddlecloth for a draught-elephant in India, to prevent harness from chafing.

gudgee: Indian cloth used to line military tents.

gunfire: in India, daybreak dusk or/as signalled in cantonments by the firing of a cannon; in British Army slang, tea (as consumed at these times of day, especially dawn).

gunny: coarse cloth or canvas manufactured mainly in Bengal from the fibres of the plants *Corchorus olitarius* and *Corchorus capsularis*; used for manufacturing sacks, bags, sandbags, etc., for military use. *Gunny*-bag, colloquialism for a bag of such material used for containing bedding, equipment, artillery, or engineering materials.

gup: news or rumour (e.g., 'camp *gup*'); from Hindustani.

gurdwara: Sikh temple.

gurrah: coarse Indian muslin.

guttery: quilted bed-cover used in India.

hackery: Indian two-wheeled cart, usually drawn by bullocks; mostly used in Bengal.

Hadendowa: a sub-clan of the Beja people of eastern Sudan, sometimes usd to describe the whole of the Beja, known to the British soldiers as 'Fuzzy-Wuzzies'.

haji, hadji, hajji: title of respect for one who had performed a *haj, hadj* or *hajj* = an Islamic pilgrimage to Mecca.

hani: Maori staff with a long, flattened end and a carved head, used as a wand of office by important persons, and as a weapon.

Hapu: Maori sub-tribe or clan.

havelock: sun-curtain or rectangle of cloth suspended from the rear of a head-dress to shield the neck from the rays of the sun; named after Sir Henry Havelock.

havildar: Indian infantry sergeant; *havildar-major* = sergeant-major.

hazirbash: member of the Afghan ruler's bodyguard, lit. 'ever-ready'.

heliograph: signalling-device invented by H. C. Mance which used a mirror to flash reflected sunlight over large distances, using Morse Code; in India messages could always be read in ordinary weather over a distance of 50 miles with the naked eye, and it was possible to read signals up to 80 or 100 miles without the aid of a telescope.

highlow: a low boot or high shoe.

hoeroa: Maori long, whalebone club.

hookum: colloquialism for a regulation or rule, from Hindustani.

hopper: Indian thin rice-flour cake.

hun: large water-skin carried on camel-back.

ibutho: Zulu organisation or 'guild' formed according to age of its members; singular of *amabutho*; by extension, a Zulu 'regiment'.

ikhanda: Zulu military barracks-village; singular of *amakhanda*.

iklwa, iXwa: Zulu stabbing-spear.

ILH: Imperial Light Horse.

imma: Sudanese turban, part of the *ansar* 'uniform' decreed by the Mahdi.

impi: large formation of Zulu warriors; term used indiscriminately to describe anything from an army to a smaller contingent. Its original Zulu meaning was either a body of armed men, or war.

imshi: expletive meaning 'go away'; from Arabic.

indaba: South African term for a conference, originally involving native people but used more loosely for any meeting or discussion.

Indian: in the late 18th and early 19th centuries the term 'Indian' was used by the British who served or lived there to describe themselves, i.e., a British resident of India.

induku: Southern African, especially Xhosa, throwing-club.

induna: senior Zulu civil or military leader; singular of *izinduna*.

inspan: South African term: to harness-up a draught-team (opposite of 'outspan').

isicoco: Zulu warrior's head-ring, the symbol of a married man.

isihlangu, ishilunga: Zulu large-sized war-shield.

iviyo: Zulu 'company' within a 'regiment' (singular of *amaviyo*).

Iwi: Maori tribal grouping.

iwisa: Zulu name for a knobkerrie.

IY: Imperial Yeomanry.

izinduna: Zulu senior civil or military leaders (plural of *induna*).

izzat: the concept of honour among the inhabitants of the North-West Frontier of India.

Jack: usually the nickname of a British seaman ('Jack Tar'), but in India 'Jack Sepoy' described the Indian soldiers of the Company forces; 'Jack Morbus' was a nickname for cholera in India.

jagdir-i-fauj: Sikh feudal levy.

jaggery: coarse sugar made in India and the East Indies from the sap of the coconut palm (from Hindustani *shakkar*).

jagir, jaghir, jaghire: feudal land-grant in India, in which the grantee kept the revenue from the land and paid no rent; *jagirdari* = this system; *jagirdar* = one who held a *jagir*. See also *jagdir-i-fauj*, from the feudal responsibilities of *jagirdars*.

jai khalsa jee!: Sikh war-cry, 'victory to the *khalsa*'.

jamaat: Indian mosque.

jambiya: Arab and Indian curved-bladed dagger.

jampan, jompon: an Indian open sedan-chair type of *dhoolie*, carried by four men; *jampanee, jomponny* = a bearer of such.

janbazees: Afghan cavalry, literally 'triflers with life', translated by the British in 1842 as 'dreadnoughts'.

janghirs, janghees, janghers, jangirs: Indian shorts.

jawan: Indian term for a young man or warrior.

jehad, jihad: Islamic holy war.

Jellalabad Heroes: nickname of the 13th Foot after their defence of Jalalabad.

jemadar, jemedar: Indian second-lieutenant.

jezail: Indian long-barrelled musket.

jhool: Indian coarse blanket for covering animals.

jibbeh, jibba: tunic or smock with coloured patches, worn as part of the costume of the Sudanese *ansar*; orig. the smock of the Sudanese poor and adopted deliberately to associate with them.

jihadiyya: part of the Mahdist *ansar* forces, generally rifle-armed 'regular' troops.

jingal, gingal: an Indian small-bore cannon or swivel-mounted large musket, also used in China; it was also the nickname of the vegetable aubergine, from its Tamil name *brinjal* or *bringall*.

jinsi: Sikh field artillery.

jirga: council of Indian tribal elders, or a deputation.

jodhpurs: riding-breeches, loose on the upper leg but tight on the lower.

John Company: nickname for the East India Company.

jorawallah: Indian grass-cutter employed to cut the forage for two horses; received the pay of two men but from it had to maintain a pony to transport the cut fodder.

joridar: Hindustani for 'pair'; used in the *silladar* system (q.v.) to denote two troopers who shared a *syce* and a mule.

jowar: Indian corn.

juldee, jildi: Hindustani exhortation to 'be quick', 'hurry'.

jumper: undress jacket or frock, *not* a sweater as in the modern usage of the term.

juq: Indian infantry company, as in the Mysore army; *juq-dar* = commander of the same.

jyntee, jointee: wood of a small tree, *Oeschynomine sesban*, used in India to produce charcoal for gunpowder, principally at Calcutta.

kaffir, kafir, caffer, caffre: in South Africa, a generic term for 'native', later derogatory; in India, an infidel.

kahar: Indian hospital assistant.

kajawah: pannier carried by a camel, to transport supplies or casualties.

kakauroa: Maori long-handled battle-axe.

kala pani: Indian term for the sea, lit. 'black water'.

kaman: Indian composite bow.

kanat: Indian tent-wall.

kaross: Xhosa cloak.

kaskara: Sudanese straight-bladed sword with simple cross-hilt.

kastane: distinctive national pattern of sword used in Ceylon, with a slightly curved, single-edged blade often of European manufacture, and often with ornate quillons and a single knuckle-bow.

katar: Indian dagger with a broad, straight, double-edged blade and a handle made of two parallel bars connected by two or more cross-pieces. Blade-length could occasionally extend to two or three feet, and rare examples had curved or multiple blades.

kedeesh: low-quality horse used as pack-transport in Egypt.

khaki: dust-coloured uniform-cloth, from Hindustani '*dust*'. 'Khakis' was the nickname for the Corps of Guides, from their early use of this colour; 'khaki patch', army slang for a slice of the day's beef ration, eaten for breakfast.

khalassie, khalasie: orig. an Indian sailor, chiefly from the Chittagong district, also employed in arsenals and to supervise camp-equipment on the march; Indian servants whose job it was to pitch tents.

khalifa: title associated with 'caliph' lit. 'successor', a name assumed by the successors of Mohammed; in the Sudan, one of three lieutenants of the Mahdi, but '*the* Khalifa' was applied to the chief of these, Abdullah el-Taaishi.

khalsa: Sikh army.

khanda: Indian sword with a broad, straight blade, generally widening towards a blunt point, sometimes double-edged, with a broad guard and a spike on the pommel.

khanjar: double-edged, curved-bladed dagger used in India, the Middle East and the Balkans; the name is Arabic for knife or dagger, without an indication of a particular pattern.

khansama: Indian butler; the 'mess-*khansama*' was the servant who supervised a mess.

Khedive: title of the viceroy of Egypt; Khedeviate, Khedevate, his office or territory (from Persian *khadiw* = a prince).

khitmagar, khitmugar, khidmutgar: Indian head-servant or table-servant (from Persian *khidmat* = service).

khud: precipitous hillside in India; *khud*-stick, a pointed staff used as an alpenstock when climbing a *khud*.

Khyber knife: European term for the single-edged, straight-bladed knife without a guard, characteristic of the region around the Khyber Pass.

kila: Indian fort; *kiladar* = fort-commandant.

kilij, qilij: Turkish or Persian curved sabre, generally with a 'mameluke' hilt and quillons at right-angles to the blade.

Kingite: supporter of the Maori 'King movement', i.e., one hostile to the British colonists.

klewang: Malayan sword with straight blade widening towards the tip, often with a hatchet point.

kloof: South African valley.

knobkerrie: African bulbous-headed wooden club; the Zulu name was *iwisa*.

KOB: King's Own Borderers (1881–7).

kodallie: Indian tool used in construction of earthworks, with a head like a hoe positioned almost parallel to a short handle, and used in a sitting or kneeling position.

Kommandant (commandant): leader of a Boer Commando, equating to colonel; *Assistent-Kommandant* was the rank lower, i.e., lieutenant-colonel; *Kommandant-Generaal* was the highest rank, *Vice-* and *Assistent-Kommandant-Generaal* the lower ranks of general officer.

koopah: see '*dubber*'.

kopje: South African hillock.

kora: national sword-pattern of Nepal, with a curved, single-edged blade widening very much towards the point.

KOSB: King's Own Scottish Borderers (after 1887).

kotal: summit of a pass crossing an Indian mountain range.

kot-daffadar: Indian cavalry troop sergeant-major.

kotiate: Maori wood or whalebone club with two lobes on each side of the handle, the shape resembling that of a violin.

kotwal: Indian civil official; '*bazaar kotwal*' was the official who superintended a bazaar, 'city *kotwal*' was the magistrate.

kowtow, kotow: servile gesture accorded to the Chinese emperor and similar dignitaries, a triple kneeling or prostration with the head bowed to the ground.

KOYLI: King's Own Yorkshire Light Infantry (after 1887).

kraal: South African native village or corral for stock.

krantz: South African pass between two hills.

kris: Malayan dagger, often with a flamboyant (wavy or undulating) blade.

kroomen, krumen: inhabitants of the African coast, used usually of Liberia, who were noted as being skilled seamen.

KRRC: King's Royal Rifle Corps.

kshetriya: member of the Hindu military caste.

KSLI: King's Shropshire Light Infantry (after 1882).

kukri: Gurkha knife.

kulah khud: Persian iron helmet generally with a spike on top, mail neck-guard and nasal-bar, as worn in India.

kullah, khulla: pointed cap around which a *pagri* or *lungi* was wrapped, to produce a turban.

kullum: a Bombay light wood (*Nauclea parviflora*) used for artillery-fuzes.

kunkur: Indian limestone used for the metalling of roads, and in the preparation of lime (*ghooting*).

kupapa: Maori name for those Maoris who fought alongside the British.

kurta: long-skirted tunic worn by Indian cavalry; not to be confused with *kurtka*, the Polish-style lancer-tunic.

kurwar, khurwah: Indian measurement equal to about 700lbs.

kutchery: Indian court-house or administrative office; *kuzzilbash, kizzilbash*: see '*qizilbash*'.

laager: South African encampment; usually used to describe a fortified perimeter formed from wagons, but more loosely for any encampment.

lakh, lac: Indian measure of 100,000, usually applied to rupees, representing £10,000.

Lal kurti paltan: lit. 'red-coated regiment': nickname of the 1st Gurkhas, which until 1888 was the only Gurkha corps to wear red coats (the 2nd Battalion wore green from its formation in 1886).

lance-*daffadar*: Indian cavalry corporal (lance-corporal was 'acting lance-*daffadar*').

lance-*naik*: Indian infantry lance-corporal.

landdrost: South African magistrate.

lantaka: Malayan-manufactured brass cannon, generally of small bore, from two to seven feet long, generally swivel-mounted and used ashore and afloat; they were highly prized and even served as a form of currency.

lascar: Indian labourer or inferior type of workman; usually used in relation to a deck-hand aboard ship, but could be used in a military sense, e.g., 'gun-lascar'; from Persian *lashkari* = a soldier.

lashkar: Indian war-band or tribal 'army', sometimes referring to a group about 100 strong, but could be applied to an armed force irrespective of size.

lathi, latee: thick cane or stick used as a bludgeon; in India *lathial, lattial* = a bodyguard or watchman, or anyone armed with a *lathi*.

LG: 'large grain' (of gunpowder).

Limitford: Indian argot on the North-West Frontier, for a modern rifle; from 'Lee-Metford'.

linseed lancer: army slang for a military doctor.

lobster: very old colloquialism (civilian and naval) for a soldier, still in use in the early 20th century; presumably orig. from the red coat, although the 17th-century use was a reference to an armoured soldier's iron 'shell'.

local rank: temporary promotion given to a British officer on campaign, orig. to enable him to have parity with an officer of similar seniority but higher rank who belonged to a non-British Army unit, as in the East India Company or Indian armies.

log, logue: Indian term for 'people'; used as a suffix, e.g., *babalog* = children; *Sikhlog* = the Sikhs; *Sahiblog* = the gentry.

loll-bazaar: that part of an Indian town where brothels were situated; '*loll-bazaar* woman' implied a prostitute rather than simply a dweller in the *loll-bazaar*.

Long Tom: South African War nickname for the 155mm Creusot gun, but also used for any long-barrelled artillery piece.

loosewallah: colloquialism for a thief in India, especially a rifle-thief; from Hindustani *lus*.

lota: Indian small metal pot.

LS: 'land service' (e.g., of artillery, 'LS carriage').

lug: an Indian cake; *lug-wallah* = vendor of same.

lunghi, lungi: Indian term for a strip of cloth, usually applied to the turban, generally of the decorated type used by cavalry.

machufat: camel-saddle.

Maconochie: canned stew of meat and vegetables, best known from its use during the First World War, but also issued in South Africa during the 1899–1902 War.

madu: Indian parrying weapon comprising a pair of buck horns joined horizontally, with a small hand-guard (usually resembling a circular shield) protecting the hand-grip in the centre; the horns were often metal-pointed for delivering a thrust, but the weapon was usually held by a swordsman in the left hand, for parrying the opponent's blows. It was popular with the Bhils.

maduwa: Kandyan feudal militia.

maffick: colloquial verb, to celebrate with abandon; from the riotous celebrations in Britain which followed the news of the relief of Mafeking.

mahdi: title assumed by a number of Islamic leaders, lit. 'he who is guided truly' (Arabic), a successor of the prophet Mohammed. In the 19th century the title was claimed most famously by Mohammed Ibn Seyyid Abdullah.

mahout: Indian elephant-driver.

maidan: Indian open space or parade-ground.

malik: Indian tribal headman.

malum: to understand (Hindustani).

mamootie: Indian large hoe used for digging, carried with the siege-train.

mana: Maori concept of power, reputation or influence.

march: in India the term 'march' was used for any journey, military or civilian, so prevalent was the use of the military terminology in the earlier 19th century.

maro: apron worn by Maori warriors.

Maroon: fugitive slave living in West Indian mountains, usually describing those in Jamaica descended from slaves who escaped in the 17th century; apparently derived from *cimarron*, from Spanish *cima* = a mountain-top.

marrow: noun and verb, colloquialism to hit or strike.

masjid, masji, musji: Islamic mosque or place of prayer.

maulvi: Indian Islamic learned man, or scholar or teacher, usually of religion.

maund: Indian weight, usually reckoned as equal to 80 pounds; actually it was equal to 100 pounds troy or $82\frac{2}{7}$ pounds avoirdupois, which was termed the '*bazaar maund*'; a '*factory maund*' was equal to 74 pounds $10\frac{2}{3}$ ounces avoirdupois. A *maund* was equal to 40 seers or 3,200 *tolah*s *mehter, mehtar*: Indian sweep or scavenger; one of the lowest caste.

memsahib: Indian term for a European married lady, from 'madam-sahib'; sometimes abbreviated to 'the mem'.

merai, mere: Maori jade war-club.

Métis: Canadian mixed-race people of French and Indian descent.

MI: Mounted Infantry.

ML: artillery classification, 'muzzle-loading'; MLR = 'muzzle-loading, rifled'.

mohur: Indian gold coin (orig. 'Mogul'); in the mid-19th century reckoned as 30 shillings sterling.

moke battery: colloquialism for a mule-borne battery of mountain artillery, from 'moke' = donkey.

moko: Maori ritual facial tattoos.

mokum: Indian cavalry regiment, as in the Mysore army; *mokumdar* = commander of same.

mom-raughun: mixture of beeswax, mutton-fat or oil, turpentine and camphor, used for preserving harness in India.

Moors, Moormen: in the early period of colonisation in India, the British followed Portuguese practice and referred to Muslims as 'Moors'; also used as a generic term for all Indians, pre-Mutiny. 'Moors' could even be used instead of 'Moorish' to describe an Indian language.

Moplah knife: a distinctive chopper-like knife-sword used by the Moplahs of Malabar, with a wide, double-edged blade curving towards the tip, akin to a medieval European falchion, with no hand-guard.

MT: Mountain Train.

muckin, muckim: Indian term for butter; *muckin-wallah* = vendor of same.

mufti: 'plain clothes', i.e., out of uniform.

mujahideen: Islamic warrior engaged in war for religious reasons.

mulatto: a person of mixed race, the term originally Spanish; in 1838 it was stated that in Tobago it had the precise definition of the offspring of a black woman and a white man.

mulazimiyya: Sudanese *ansar* 'regular' force which superseded the *jihadiyya*, originally the khalifa's bodyguard.

Mull: nickname for a member of the Madras Army, or a civilian official of Madras.

mullah, mulla: Islamic priest.

mulligatawny: Indian peppery or curried soup, from Tamil *milagu tannir* = 'pepper water'.

munshi, moonshi: Indian secretary, interpreter or language-teacher.

muncheel: a litter used in the Madras and Bombay regions: virtually a hammock suspended on a pole and carried by two men.

muqaddamiyya, muggadamiya: platoon of Sudanese *ansar jihadiyya*; *muqaddam* = officer of same.

mussack, mussick, mussuk: Indian skin water-bag.

mustee: a person of mixed race; in 1838 it was stated that in Tobago it had the precise definition of the offspring of a quadroon woman and a white man.

nabob: orig. a territorial governor of the Mogul empire (Hindustani *nawab, nawwab*); in English, used to describe a European who had enriched himself in the east, or a man of very great wealth.

naik, naick, naique, naigue: Indian infantry corporal.

nanukshee (or '*nanukshee rupee*'): Sikh coin worth slightly more than a Company rupee.

nappy: Indian barber employed by a regiment to shave the men.

narnal: Indian small cannon, sufficiently light to be carried by a man.

nautch: exhibition of professional dancing by Indian *nautch*-girls.

nawab: orig. a territorial governor of the Mogul empire (see '*nabob*'); Indian prince or landowner.

negūs: Abyssinian title for a tribal 'king'; *negūs negusti* = 'king of kings', the country's principal ruler.

nek: South African mountain-pass or passage between hills.

ngutu-parera: Maori nickname for a flintlock musket; lit, 'duckbill', from the shape of the hammer.

nigara: Indian war-drum.

nimcha: Arab sword, straight-bladed or slightly curved, with a knuckle-bow and drooping quillons; also used by the Marathas.

nizam: title of the sovereign of Hyderabad, used from 1713; contraction of Hindustani *nizam-ul-mulk* = 'regulator of the state'.

Nongqai: alternative designation for the Zululand Native Police.

noozle: colloquialism for a commissariat store.

nullah, nala: Indian dry ravine or dry water-course; sometimes used for the arm of a river of a small stream.

numdah: felt pad used as a saddle-cloth in India; also spelled '*numnah*', although '*numdah*' was recorded as being the universal pronunciation in India; from Persian *numad* = a coarse cloth.

NWMP: North-West Mounted Police.

OFS: Orange Free State (see 'OVS').

oke: Turkish weight as used in Egypt, 3½ pounds troy, 2¾ pounds avoirdupois.

oont: camel (Hindustani).

Opperwachtmeester: senior NCO of South African Republic mounted forces.

outspan: South African term, orig. the unyoking of draught-animals; by extension and in common parlance, to encamp.

OVS: abbreviation for Orange Free State (*Oranje Vrystaat*).

pa, pah: Maori fortification of palisades and trenches; sometimes used to describe a Maori village.

pagoda: Southern Indian gold coin (orig. from the device borne upon it); 'pagoda tree' was a colloquialism for a source of great wealth, as if gold coins grew on trees.

pagri, pugri, puggaree, puggree: the cloth of a turban, or a cloth worn around a tropical helmet.

paheka: Maori name for the white race.

pal: Indian tent; *palkee* = a small tent; *palanquin* also used for this definition.

palanquin, palankeen: a light litter for a single person, carried on the shoulders of two bearers; also used to describe a small tent; or a light, two-wheeled carriage (from Hindustani *palang* = bed).

paltan, pultun, pulton: Indian regiment, orig. from French *peloton* = 'platoon'; a term often used unofficially by Indian Army regiments to describe themselves, e.g., *Noka-ka-Pulton,* as used by the 35th Bengal Native Infantry.

panchayat: Indian meeting of village elders, or more generally a negotiation; lit. 'a fivesome'.

pandy: nickname for rebellious sepoys during the Indian Mutiny, orig. from the name of Mangal Pande, a mutineer of the 34th Bengal Native Infantry; by extension, a nickname of any Indian. 'Pandy hornpipe', colloquialism for execution by hanging.

pani, pawnee: Indian term for water.

panji, punji: sharpened stakes used to impede the progress of an enemy by being placed in the ground; used in Assam, Burma and Malaya.

parang: Malayan machete or wide-bladed, chopper-like jungle knife.

pata: Indian gauntlet-sword evolved from the *katar,* a long, straight-bladed weapon with a hand-guard in the form of a gauntlet and forearm-protector; as this armour precluded movement of the wrist, it was probably generally restricted to cavalry use, as 'fencing' would have been severely impaired.

patisthanaya: Sinhalese pole-arm with a bladed head very similar to and presumably copied from a European partizan.

patiti: Maori short-handled tomahawk.

pattisa: Southern Indian sword with a long straight double-edged blade widening towards the point. The same name is sometimes used for the Indian two-handed battle-axe.

patu: Maori club made of stone, wood or bone, of a spatulate shape with sharp edges. Variations included *patu paraoa,* of whalebone; *patu onewa,* of basalt; and *pato pounamou* (or *merai*) of jade.

peddowk: a tree (*Pterocarpus dolbergiodies*) growing in Burma and the Andaman Islands, the wood used for the manufacture of gun-carriages in Burma and Madras.

peemah: a tree (*Lagerstonemia reginae*) growing in India and Burma, producing a light, tough wood used for the manufacture of gun-carriages in Madras.

pegu jar: large, glazed pottery vessel used in Indian arsenals for holding oil, etc.

peon: a footman or messenger, used in southern India instead of *chuprassie,* orig. used to describe a foot-soldier; from Spanish.

pesh kabz: North Indian and Persian dagger with T-section straight or slightly upcurving long blade, and a plain grip without quillons; evidently designed originally for forcing through the defences of a coat of mail.

peshwa: the chief minister of the Maratha Confederacy, a hereditary office resident at Poona.

phowra: Indian hoe (see *mamootie*).

phukni: Hindustani term for a firelock (musket).

phunsee: a tree of the Bombay region (*Carallia integrifolia*) used by the Bombay arsenal for the manufacture of artillery sponge-staves.

pice: Indian copper coin, ¼ *anna*; from Marathi *paisa.*

pie: Indian coin, one-twelfth of an *anna.*

Piffer: member of the Punjab Irregular Force, later Punjab Frontier Force (acronym).

pindari: Indian light horse, bandits who accompanied the Maratha armies; term of uncertain origin, also rendered as *pindaree* and (in a 1788 vocabulary) *bindarra.*

pipe-clay sergeant: colloquialism for a man appointed temporarily as an NCO to supervise a draft of recruits during their march to join their regiment, and reverting to his original rank upon arrival.

plain clothes: civilian dress, *mufti* (q.v.).

Polish-*wallah:* an Indian servant hired to clean a soldier's kit; not a vendor of polish.

pom-pom: 1pdr or 37mm Vickers-Maxim quick-firing gun; named from the sound it made.

poorbeah: high-caste Hindu of Oudh, as recruited by the Bengal army.

posho: East African flour.

poshteen, posteen, pustin: heavy Indian overcoat of goat- or sheepskin, with the fleece worn inside.

pouwhenua: Maori club with spiked end.

pozzy: British Army argot for jam; the term apparently originated in South Africa in the last quarter of the 19th century, when it was used to describe any kind of sweetmeat.

pukhal, pakhal, puckauly: Indian large leather water-bag, commonly carried on a mule or bullock; from Sanskrit *pai* = water, and *khāl* = hide.

pukka, pucca, pakkha: Hindustanti adjective for genuine, strong or good, widely adopted in English.

pulouar: Indian *tulwar* with a curved blade and quillons downturned towards the blade.

punkah: fan-like device for circulating air in a room in India, operated by a cord pulled by a *punkah-wallah* or *punkah-coolie;* from Hindustani *pankha* = fan.

purge: army colloquialism for beer; later used as a verb for 'grumble'.

puska: Indian building-material made of chopped straw and dried mud, so strong as to make good fortifications.

putrid fever: common early colloquialism for typhus.

puttee: long strip of cloth wound around the lower leg in

place of gaiters; also described a bandage. From Hindustani *patti*.

puttoo: goat-hair cloth made in Kashmir.

pyjamas: loose trousers worn by Indian cavalry; from Hindustani *pāejāma*, lit. 'leg-clothing'.

qizilbash, khizilbash: a descendant of the Persian garrison of Afghanistan, resident around Kabul; orig. the name signified 'red-top', from the colour of their head-dress.

quadroon: a person of mixed race; in 1838 it was stated that in Tobago it had the precise meaning of the offspring of a Mulatto woman and a white man. From Spanish 'quarter-blooded'.

quaker: dummy gun made from wood.

quarter-guard: a guard mounted about 80 yards in front of the centre of a camp

Queenite: a Maori supporter of the British, i.e., one who supported Queen Victoria, as opposed to a 'Kingite'.

Queen's: definition of British regiments in India, to differentiate them from Company forces, e.g., a unit might be referred to as the '29th Queen's' even when that word was not part of the official regimental title.

Queen's Allowance: allowance made towards the expenses of the officers' mess of a British regiment, half to help with purchase of wine and half to help defray daily mess expenses.

QF: artillery classification 'Quick-Firer' (referring not to the speed with which a gun could be handled, but to the recoil-absorption mechanism which obviated re-aiming after every shot).

Qui Hai: nickname for a member of the Bengal Army, or a civil official of the Bengal Presidency.

RA: Royal Artillery.

rag: colloquialism for an Indian brothel.

rag-fair: army colloquialism for kit-inspection (18th-century in origin).

raj: Indian term (from Sanskrit *rājan* = king), lit. 'rule' or 'kingdom'; 'the *Raj*' can be used for British rule in India, or for the period in which it occurred.

Rajput: Indian member of a tribe descended from the old royal races of Hindus, or of a warrior caste; from Sanskrit *rājan* = a king, and *putra* = son.

ranker: colloquialism for a member of the rank-and-file, a private soldier.

rangar: term applied by Hindus to any Rajput who had, or whose ancestors had, converted to Islam.

rani: wife of a *rajah* (from Sanskrit *rajñi* = queen).

rapaki: Maori waist-shawl.

ra's mi'a: Sudanese *ansar* officer, a company commander of *jihadiyya*, lit. 'leader of a hundred'.

ratan, rattan: a species of palm (*Calmus*), the best from Malacca, which produced canes used in basketwork, and for strong fences or hurdles when woven between stakes; when burned it yielded black pigment for paint.

RBL: artillery classification, 'rifled breech-loader'.

RE: Royal Engineers.

Red Men: nickname for the Bengal Horse Artillery, from the red helmet-mane worn in the mid-19th century.

ressairdar: Indian officer of Native Cavalry who commanded the left troop of a squadron (this was different from *ressaldar*, see 'risala').

RFG: 'rifle fine grain' (of gunpowder).

rhebab: Indian stringed instrument akin to a guitar, popular on the North-West Frontier.

rifle pit: a one-man entrenchment generally in the shape of an inverted cone, with sandbags or parapet made from the spoil of the excavation; generally 4 feet deep, about 4½ feet in diameter across the top and 2½ feet in diameter across the bottom.

risala, ressalah: Indian cavalry regiment or squadron; *risaldar*, an Indian lieutenant of an Indian cavalry regiment; *risaldar-major*, the senior Indian officer of such a regiment. In the Mysore forces a *risala* was an infantry battalion, and a *risaldar* its commander.

RLG: 'rifle large grain' (of gunpowder).

RM: *rissaldar*-major; see '*risala*'.

RMA: Royal Marine Artillery; Royal Military Academy.

RML: artillery classification, 'rifled muzzle-loader'.

RMLI: Royal Marine Light Infantry.

road-sergeant: subordinate rank in the Indian Department of Public Works.

Rohilla: member of a tribe of Afghan origin, generally resident in Rohilkand province.

room guard: duty taken in turn by soldiers living in barracks, being responsible for distribution of rations, washing-up and cleaning.

rootie, roti: Hindustani for bread; by extension, sometimes used for a meal; 'rooty-gong', the long service and good conduct medal, so called because its award was said to be almost as regular as the issue of rations.

RSF: Royal Scots Fusiliers.

rub: battalion-sized group of *ansar* warriors; lit. 'quarter', from its four component parts.

rukh: tract of land in India, overgrown with thorn-bushes and grass.

rungu: alternative name for knobkerrie.

runn: an area of boggy land in India, such as that over which a tide flowed (from Hindustani *rān*).

rupee: Indian coin weighing 180 grains troy; standard composition was eleven-twelfths silver and one-twelfth alloy, and generally was equivalent to 2 shillings sterling. The 'imperial *rupee*' or *tolah* (q.v.) was the standard weight in India, and the diameter (one-tenth of a foot) made it a standard of length. From Sanskrit *rūpya* = silver.

ryot: Indian agricultural worker or peasant; from Hindustani *rayat* = a subject.

SA: Small Arms.

SAA: Small Arms Ammunition.

SAC: South African Constabulary.

sahib: Indian term approximating to 'Sir' used by Indian troops and civilians to imply a European officer or dignitary, or Europeans in general. *Sahib-log* (or *sahib-logue*), European people (see '*log*').

saintie: Indian and Chinese weapon used in conjunction with a sword for parrying a blow: a steel bar with a hand-grip in the middle and a spear-point at one end.

saji muttee: Indian term for carbonate of soda, used for cleaning paint from gun carriages and for removing grease.

Sakabulas: nickname for the Imperial Light Horse in the South African War, from their use of sakabula-bird feathers in their hats. Their later nickname, 'Cocky-olly-birds' was derived similarly, although this name was shared with the King's Own Borderers (later King's Own Scottish Borderers), from the initial 'KOB'.

saleetah: Indian term for the *gunny*-cloth bag containing a soldier's bedding on the march, or the bag in which tents were packed.

SALH: South African Light Horse.

Sam Browne: officer's belt, generally with a single, diagonal shoulder-brace; named after General Sir Samuel Browne, VC (1824–1901).

Sammy: British Army argot for a Hindu religious image (presumably from *swami* = lord, the term addressed to a deity); 'sammying' = religious ceremonies, 'sammy-house', Hindu temple.

sandcrack: complaint common to horses in dry country, especially in India, lack of moisture on the ground causing the hoof to become brittle; cured by linseed meal poultices and by covering the sole with cow-dung.

sand-rat: army colloquialism for a cheap and often unhealthy prostitute in India.

sangar: defensive stone breastwork, orig. in India, but applied to other regions; not to be confused with *sanger*, a Southern Indian and Sinhalese ceremonial weapon with glaive-like blade; nor with *sangu*, a central Indian all-steel spear with triangular or quadrangular sectioned point.

santel: barge as used on the Nile.

sarnai: Indian flute or pipe.

satringee: see '*dhurree*'.

saul: a tree (*Vatica robusta*) common in the north-west provinces of India, Assam and Burma, yielding a strong wood used in the construction of gun carriages.

SB: artillery classification, 'smooth-bore'.

SC: post-nominal abbreviation for a Sub-Conductor of the Ordnance Commissariat Department in India.

Scarlet Lancers: nickname of 16th Lancers, from being the only light cavalry regiment to wear scarlet tunics.

schan de grach: a drink made of ginger beer and sweet ale, popular in the army in the mid-19th century.

scran: army colloquialism for food, probably dating from mid-19th century, although its civilian use (meaning rubbish) is much older; scran-bag, a haversack.

seedie: native crewman aboard ship, especially used in Africa.

seer: Indian weight of about 2 pounds, or about 2¼ pints; one-fortieth of a *maund*.

sepoy: Indian private soldier (of infantry), commonly used as an adjective (e.g., 'sepoy regiment') or in the plural to describe Indian soldiers in general; from Hindustani *sipahi* = a soldier.

serai: enclosed yard with buildings or rooms around, usually for the accommodation of travellers in India.

shahghasses, shah guzees: Afghan household troops or court officers.

shamiana: Indian, very large tent with removable sides, used for receptions, etc.

shamshir: Persian or Indian sabre with long, very curved blade.

shave: a rumour; presumably from the origin of many stories being the barber's shop (in civilian life).

shikar: in India, hunting or sport: *shikari, shikaree* = a hunter.

shoka: East African long-handled battle-axe, generally with a triangular blade.

shotel: Abyssinian sabre with exaggeratedly-curved, double-edged, diamond-sectioned blade.

shubkoon: surprise attack at night in India.

Siah Posh: lit. 'black-coats': nickname of the Punjab Rifles, from their use of rifle-green uniforms.

sickleghar: Indian employed to clean metal-work in an arsenal.

silepe: Basuto axe with wide-edged, narrow blade, attached to the haft by a tang at right-angles to both haft and blade.

silladar system: arrangement by which an Indian cavalryman was responsible for providing everything except his arms and ammunition and upkeep; primarily used to refer to the system by which each man owned the horse he rode. From Hindustani *silah* = a weapon, and *dar* = bearer or owner of.

sipahdar: brigade-commander in the Mysore army.

sirdar, sardar: Indian term for a leader, chief or nobleman; sometimes used in place of 'commander-in-chief'. *Sirdar-i-sirdan* = chief general or generalissimo. From Hindustani *sardār*, Persian *sar* = head, and *dār* = holding.

sirkar, sircar, sarkar: Indian term for government or authority, or the holder or such an office; from Hindustani *sarkār*, and Persian *sar* = head, and *kār* = agent or representative.

sissoo: Indian hard wood (*Dalbergia sissoo*) used in the construction of gun-carriages.

sjambok, jambok: leather whip used in South Africa.

skilly: army nickname for gruel or thin stew.

slingers: 'to be on slingers' was army argot for the state of penury which precluded the purchase of extra food to supplement the ration.

sloop-of-war: colloquialism (perhaps originally civilian) for a prostitute (rhyming slang for 'whore').

smart money: a sum paid by a recruit to release himself

from his enlistment, permitted before he was legally attested.

smasher: slang term for felt hat with a brim.

sola: plant of the genus *Aeschynomene* used in the manufacture of tropical helmets; hence 'sola topee' (alternatively 'solar', implying protection from the sun).

soldiering: army argot for the cleaning of kit.

soondree: Indian flexible wood (*Heriteria minor*) used for shafts and wheel-spokes of gun-carriages and other vehicles.

soorkey: pounded brick-dust, mixed with lime to make mortar, stucco, etc., used in India in place of European *pozzuolana* and hydraulic cements.

sowar: Indian cavalry trooper (from Hindustani *sawar* = a horseman); *sowari* = a train of attendants or retinue.

spruit: South African stream or small river.

squad bag: canvas bag provided for troops on the march (one per 25 men) to relieve them from carrying complete kit; in India a small squad bag was issued to each soldier.

SS: 'sea service', e.g., 'SS musket'.

STAA: Soldiers' Total Abstinence Association.

Star of the Line: nickname of the 29th Foot, from their unique, star-shaped pouch-badges.

stellenbosch: verb, to be cashiered; from the camp at that place in the South African War; slang term for vicious bombardment used during First World War.

subedar, subadar, subahdar: Indian captain of infantry; *subedar*-major, the senior 'native' officer of an infantry regiment. From the Indian term for the governor of a province (*subah*) of the Mogul empire.

sudder bazaar, suddar: Indian cantonment bazaar; *sudder, suddar* = adjective for chief or supreme, from *sadr* = a chief.

sultani: heavy-bladed, slightly curved sword (southern India).

sulu: Fijian 'kilt'.

sun: to be 'in the sun' was a colloquialism for being drunk; the symptoms of intoxication and sunstroke being not dissimilar.

sun-curtain: protective flap hung from the rear of a head-dress to shield the neck from the heat of the sun; see 'havelock'.

swaddy, squaddie: colloquialism for an ordinary soldier, orig. from dialect swad or swaddy, a country bumpkin; later associated with 'squaddie', a squad-member.

syce, sice, saice: Indian groom or mounted attendant (from Hindustani *sāis*).

syrang: early Indian rank, a *subedar* of artillery.

tabar: Indian battle-axe.

tact, tack: to be 'on the tact' or 'tack' was army argot for abstinence from alcohol.

taggia: Sudanese skull-cap, part of the *ansar* 'uniform' decreed by the Mahdi.

tagra: Indian term signifying strong, fit or powerful.

taiaha: Maori hardwood club, generally with an axe-shaped 'blade'; also called *tewha-tewha*.

taluqdar, talukdar: landed gentry of Oudh; one who presided over a *taluk* = a subdivision or a district.

tamasha: a display or entertainment in India, and by extension an exciting event.

tangan: Tibetan pony.

tangi: Indian defile.

tank: Indian pond surrounded by a low, earthen embankment.

tao: Maori spear.

tap, tapped: fever, to be stricken with; from Hindustani *tap* = fever.

taps: the military punishment of 'taps' was one in which the offender had to answer his name to the sergeant of the guard every hour or half-hour throughout the day.

tarboosh: a fez (head-dress) (from Arabic *tarbūsh*).

Tartars: British term describing Chinese Manchu forces.

tat: East Indian *gunny*-cloth or matting.

tattoo, tattoe, tat: Indian pony.

tatty, tatti: panel or screen of woven grass or straw, blocking a window or doorway, used in the hot season in India to keep a room cool; a *tatty-wallah* sat outside, sprinkling water on the *tatty*.

tewha-tewha: see '*taisha*'.

thakoor: Indian term meaning 'lord', used as a title and term of respect; also to describe a Rajput chief or noble.

thana, thannah: Indian police-post; *thanadar, thannadar*, a police official in command of a *thana* or ward; to march '*thana* by *thana*' was to go from one police-post to the next, ensuring a safe lodging at each, as when (for example) transporting a prisoner from one district to another.

tiffin: term used in India to describe a lunch; verb 'to tiff', to take luncheon. From old English *tiff* = a draught of beer.

time-expired men: soldiers whose term of enlistment was completed; those on foreign service were sent home to the regimental depot for discharge, rather than being discharged on the due date in the country where they were currently serving.

tindal: head lascar or labourer; early Indian army rank for NCO of artillery.

toa: Maori warrior.

tobrah: Indian term for horse's nose-bag.

toddy: in addition to the common definition, the word was used to describe palm wine in India (from Hindustani *tār* = palm-tree).

toki: Maori axe; the type used for combat usually had a European head and a wood or bone haft. *Toki poto* = a short-handled hatchet; *toki kakauroa* = a long-handled battle-axe.

tolah: Indian weight: 3,200 *tolah*s = 1 *maund*, 80 *tolah*s = 1 *seer*, 32 *tolah*s = 1 pound troy or 0.823 pounds avoirdupois; also known as an 'imperial rupee', that coin weighing one *tolah*.

tommy: British Army nickname for ration bread.

Tommy Atkins (more commonly, just 'Tommy'): nickname for the British soldier.

tonga: an Indian light, two-wheeled cart, with accommodation for four.

tope: Indian grove or shady copse.

topee, topi: Indian term for a sun-helmet (from Hindustani *topi* = hat, perhaps after Portuguese *topo* = top); *topee-wallah*, a European (i.e., one who wore a topee).

torador: Indian matchlock musket.

traps: possessions, equipment.

trek: colloquially used for a march, adopted after service in South Africa; from Dutch *trekken* = to draw.

trooper: (i) a cavalry private; (ii) a troopship.

trooping season: annual period (October to March) when troops routinely arrived at and departed from India.

tuffekdjis: Persian irregular infantry.

tuhseeldar, tahsildar: Indian sub-collector of revenue; an official in charge of a *tahsil* or district.

tullub: Indian term signifying a demand, but used colloquially by Indian troops to describe their monthly pay.

tulwar: Indian curved sabre.

tummee: Burmese term for food.

tuparu: Maori name for double-barrelled shotgun.

tycoon: title by which the Japanese *shōgun* was known to foreigners, from 1854 until the resignation of the last holder of the office in 1867; from Japanese *taikun* = 'great prince'; hence '*tycoonate*'.

tyre: Southern Indian term for curdled milk; from Tamil *tahir*.

udibi: Zulu youth who acted as a warrior's servant.

uitlander: Boer term for all non-Boers living in the Boer republics; lit. 'foreigner'.

umbhumbuluzo: smaller variety of Zulu shield.

umkhonto, um-konto: Southern African (Xhosa) throwing-spear.

uphondo: Zulu crescent-shaped troop deployment.

usutu, uSuthu: the name of Cetshwayo's own Zulu faction, used as the Zulu war-cry in the 1879 war.

utu: Maori concept of vengeance or repayment of slights or old scores.

vakil, vakeel: Indian agent, attorney or businessman.

valise: army knapsack.

Veldkornet: lit. 'field-cornet'; company officer, equivalent to captain, in a Boer Commando; *Assistent-Veldkornet* was the rank lower, or subaltern, and *Hoof-Veldkornet* the rank higher, equating to major.

veldskoenen: South African 'field-shoes'.

vesuvian: a safety-match.

Vierkleur: lit. 'four-colour', the flag of the Transvaal republic.

watchtmeester: sergeant of South African Republic mounted forces.

WAFF: West African Frontier Force.

wahaika: Maori club, usually wood, sometimes bone, often highly decorated.

waler: best-known as the name for a sturdy breed of horse from New South Wales, but applied also to members of the NSW Contingent in the Sudan.

wali: Indian governor or ruler.

wallah, walla, wollah: Indian term for a man or fellow; usually used in conjunction with another word to describe an occupation or a characteristic, e.g., *muckin-wallah, loose-wallah*, etc.; competition-*wallah*, a member of the Indian Civil Service who secured an appointment by the competitive system introduced in 1856.

WAR: West African Regiment.

waster: South African term for an idle fellow.

Waterloo Day: old army term for pay-day, i.e., a day of celebration.

wazir: Indian chief minister.

Westies: nickname of West India Regiments.

wideawake: soft felt hat, so called from the material having no nap.

wing officer: European field officer or captain who commanded one of the two 'wings' of an Indian infantry regiment, post-Indian Mutiny.

wordi-major, woordie-major: adjutant of Indian irregular cavalry.

writer: junior East India Company civil servant.

yaboo: Afghan pony.

yaghi: a rebellion in India, or descriptive of a state of independence.

yataghan: a sabre with a blade which curved in two directions, originally from Turkey and North Africa, but this shape of blade was not uncommon in India. It was also used for British bayonets, notably the 1856 sword-bayonet.

Yellow Horse, Yellow Boys: nickname of Skinner's Horse, from their yellow uniform.

Yeos: nickname of the East India Company's European infantry; from the pronunciation of 'Europeans'.

zaghnal: Indian axe with a broad, curved, knife-like blade.

zamburak, zembourek: Indian swivel-gun carried on the back of a camel; said to be from Hindustani *zembor* = a wasp, exemplifying the rapid movement and 'stinging' of such mobile artillery.

ZAR: initials of the Transvaal (South African) Republic: Zuid Afrikaansche Republiek.

zareba: defensive hedge constructed from thorn or other bushes.

Zarps: English name for the Transvaal (South African) Republic police, Zuid Afrikaansche Republiek Politie.

zemindar, zamindar, zemindhar: Indian landowner; a term applied variously: to the landlord class in Bengal, Oudh and the North-West provinces, but to the yeoman class in the Punjab. From Hindustani *zamin* = land.

zillah: Indian administrative district; from *zila*, rib, hence a 'side' or district.

zubberdust: Indian term for overbearing, lit. 'with the strong arm'.

INDEX

Figures in *italics* indicate captions for illustrations